ISBN 978-1-5279-3973-8
PIBN 10914045

English
Français
Deutsche
Italiano
Español
Português

www.forgottenbooks.com

Mythology Photography **Fiction**
Fishing Christianity **Art** Cooking
Essays Buddhism Freemasonry
Medicine **Biology** Music **Ancient
Egypt** Evolution Carpentry Physics
Dance Geology **Mathematics** Fitness
Shakespeare **Folklore** Yoga Marketing
Confidence Immortality Biographies
Poetry **Psychology** Witchcraft
Electronics Chemistry History **Law**
Accounting **Philosophy** Anthropology
Alchemy Drama Quantum Mechanics
Atheism Sexual Health **Ancient History**
Entrepreneurship Languages Sport
Paleontology Needlework Islam
Metaphysics Investment Archaeology
Parenting Statistics Criminology
Motivational

F

The N

WAS

PROCEEDINGS

AT THE ANNUAL MEETING OF

THE NATIONAL CIVIL-SERVICE REFORM LEAGUE

HELD AT

WASHINGTON, D. C., DEC. 12 AND 13, 1895.

WITH THE ADDRESS OF THE PRESIDENT,

HON. CARL SCHURZ,

AND OTHER MATTERS.

———

NEW YORK:

PUBLISHED FOR THE

NATIONAL CIVIL-SERVICE REFORM LEAGUE.

1895.

Publications of the National Civil-Service Reform League

Proceedings at the Annual Meeting of the National Civil-Service Reform League, 1882, with address of the President, George William Curtis. Per copy, 8 cts.

The same, with address of the President, for '84, '85, '86, '87, '89, '90, '91, '92, '93, '94 and '95. Per copy, 8 cts.

Civil-Service Reform under the present National Administration. By George William Curtis. (Address of 1885.)

The Situation. By George William Curtis. (Address of 1886.)

Party and Patronage. By George William Curtis. (Address of 1892.)

Civil-Service Reform and Democracy. By Carl Schurz. (Address of 1893.)

The Necessity and Progress of Civil-Service Reform. By Carl Schurz. (Address of 1894.)

The Influence of the Spoils Idea upon the Government of American Cities. By Herbert Welsh. (1894.)

The Reform of the Consular Service. By Oscar S. Straus. (1894.)

The Interest of the Workingman in Civil-Service Reform. By Herbert Welsh. (1895.)

The Appointment and Tenure of Postmasters. By R. H. Dana. (1895.)

Civil-Service Reform as a Moral Question. By Chas. J. Bonaparte.

Constitution of the National Civil-Service Reform League.

Good Government: Official Journal of the National Civil-Service Reform League. Published monthly at 54 William St., New York. One dollar per year. Ten cents per single copy.

    It is the aim of the management to make GOOD GOVERNMENT not only an aggressive and fearless advocate of the principles of Civil-Service Reform in the broadest sense, but a perfectly trustworthy record of the current history of the reform movement in political affairs generally. It numbers among its staff of editorial contributors many of the conspicuous authors and orators engaged in the movement, and some of their most important papers and addresses appear first in complete form in its columns. As GOOD GOVERNMENT publishes yearly an exhaustive table of titles and topics of its own, and as it is one of the group of periodicals to which reference is made in the annual supplement to Poole's Index, it is a necessity to every well-stocked reference library.

For other publications, see third page.

PROCEEDINGS

AT THE ANNUAL MEETING OF

The National Civil-Service Reform League

HELD AT

WASHINGTON, D. C., DEC. 12 AND 13, 1895.

WITH THE ADDRESS OF THE PRESIDENT,

HON. CARL SCHURZ,

AND OTHER MATTERS.

———

NEW YORK:

PUBLISHED FOR THE

NATIONAL CIVIL-SERVICE REFORM LEAGUE.

1895.

PRESS OF GOOD GOVERNMENT.

ANNUAL MEETING

OF THE

NATIONAL CIVIL SERVICE REFORM LEAGUE,

DECEMBER 12 AND 13, 1895.

Pursuant to call duly issued, the fifteenth annual meeting of the National Civil Service Reform League was held at Washington, D. C., on the 12th and 13th of December, 1895. Among the delegates in attendance during the several sessions were the following:

BALTIMORE: Charles J. Bonaparte, M. E. Lyle, Cleveland P. Manning, Edgar G. Miller, William Reynolds, L. P. Hennighausen, G. W. Sattler, A. P. Shanklin and C. A. E. Spamer.

BOSTON: Samuel B Capen, Arthur Hobart, Jonathan A. Lane, Samuel Y. Nash and J. G. Thorp, Jr.

BROOKLINE: Dana Estes.

BROOKLYN: William G. Low, Truman J. Backus and Edward Cary.

BUFFALO: Sherman S. Rogers and Charles B. Wheeler.

CAMBRIDGE: Richard Henry Dana, W. W. Vaughan and Morrill Wyman, Jr.

CINCINNATI: N. H. Davis.

CORNELL UNIVERSITY: C. L. McGovern.

DISTRICT OF COLUMBIA: John W. Douglass, John Joy Edson, Harry English, Charles C. Glover, H. H. Glassie, Geo. Wm. Hill, Rev. Teunis S. Hamlin, Dr. Frank S. Howe, Francis E. Leupp, Tallmadge A. Lambert, Charles Lyman, Rev. Dr. Alex. Mackay-Smith, Henry B. F. MacFarland, Theodore W. Noyes, Charles W. Stetson, Frederick L. Siddons, A. L. Sturtevant, Gen. Ellis Spear, C. C. Snow, Rufus H. Thayer and Adolph G. Wolf.

HARVARD UNIVERSITY. A. S. Ingalls.

HOPKINSVILLE, KY.: James Roaman.

INDIANA: Wm. Dudley Foulke.

NASHVILLE, TENN.: Herman Justi.

NEW YORK: Carl Schurz, Silas W. Burt, Charles Collins, Alfred Bishop Mason, George McAneny, George Haven Putnam, W. J. Schieffelin, Oscar S. Straus, Henry Villard, C. W. Watson and Everett P. Wheeler.

PHILADELPHIA: Herbert Welsh, Charles Chauncey, W. W. Montgomery, Charles Richardson, Edward S. Sayres and R. Francis Wood.

PRINCETON COLLEGE: H. B. Armes, A. G. Lybyer, W. E. Lampe and W. J. Wright.

ROCHESTER: Elbridge L. Adams.

ST. PAUL, MINN.: Charles P. Noyes and A. R. Kiefer.

YALE UNIVERSITY: Lanier McKee.

In response to invitations extended by the League to affiliated societies, delegates were also present from a number of such organizations, as follows:

BOSTON:—*Massachusetts Reform Clnb:* Andrew Fiske and Samuel Y. Nash.

Municipal League: Samuel B. Capen, J. G. Thorp, Jr. and Arthur Hobart.

CAMBRIDGE.—*Library Hall Association:* R. H. Dana, J. G. Thorp, Jr. and Morrill Wyman, Jr.

MARIETTA, O.—*Citizens' Association:* Prof. John C. Shedd.

NEW YORK.—*Council of Confederated Good Government Clubs:* Wm J. Schieffelin and M. D. Rothschild.

Board of Trade and Transportation: Oscar S. Straus.

PHILADELPHIA.—*Municipal League:* Charles Richardson and Herbert Welsh.

TROY, N. Y.—*City Club:* Mont G. Curtis.

Citizens' Association: Rev. T. P. Sawin.

WASHINGTON.—*Civic Centre:* John M Gregory Rev. Alex. Kent, Charles Lyman, Mrs. Ellen S. Mussey, Miss Josephine Clark, Rev. Dr. S. M. Newman, Edwin Willetts and W. F. Willoughby.

Board of Trade: Henry F. Blount, Gardiner G. Hubbard, Myron M. Parker, Simon Wolf, John B. Wright and S. W. Woodward.

The morning session of the 12th, commencing at 10.30 o'clock, was occupied by a joint meeting of the General and Executive Committees, held in the rooms of the Cosmos Club.

At 2.30 o'clock in the afternoon, an open meeting of the League was held at the Cosmos Club, the president in the chair. An address of welcome was made by Hon. Charles R. Ross, president of the Board of District Commissioners, who was introduced by Mr. John Joy Edson, president of the Civil Service Reform Association, of the District of Columbia.*

* Page 48.

The president then withdrew, calling Mr. Sherman S. Rogers to the chair, and the following papers were read:

"The Appointment and Tenure of Postmasters." Richard Henry Dana.*

"The Important Function of Civil Service Reform." F. L. Siddons.†

"Results of Recent Agitation of Consular Service Reform." Jonathan A. Lane.‡

"Superannuation in the Civil Service." Wm. Dudley Foulke.§

The annual address of the president, "Congress and the Spoils System," was delivered at Metzerott's Hall at 8 o'clock on the evening of the 12th. It is as follows:

---

* Page 51.   † Page 60.   ‡ Page 63.   § Page 76.

CONGRESS AND THE SPOILS SYSTEM.

An Address delivered at the Annual Meeting of the National Civil Service Reform League at Washington, D. C., December 12, 1895.

By Hon. Carl Schurz.

It is with a feeling of peculiar satisfaction that I greet the fifteenth annual meeting of the national Civil Service Reform League at the seat of the National Government—the place where the necessity of the Reform we advocate has been most conspicuously demonstrated, and where also its most conspicuous and fruitful successes have been achieved.

No intelligent observer who visits Washington from time to time can fail to be struck with the evidences of the constant growth of the national Government in the magnitude and scope of its functions, corresponding to the multiplication of the public and private interests that come into contact with it. From a thin string of agricultural settlements on the Atlantic coast, here and there dotted with small trading towns, this Republic has in a century expanded into a vast empire spanning a continent, excelling in wealth and material power every other nation on the globe. With its growth it has changed its character. Its bucolic stage has long been passed. Its agricultural interests, however great, have lost their former predominance. That great store of rich virgin lands which formerly offered homes and sustenance to the advancing population, has shrunk to petty proportions, and will soon altogether cease to play

an important part in our social development. The expansion of our industrial activities and of our facilities
of communication has attracted large masses of humanity to our cities, several of which are already far beyond
the million line, while others are pressing hard upon it.
According to present appearances the time is not very
distant when a majority of the American people will be
congregated in towns. Altogether, we cannot close our
eyes to the fact that in some important respects we are
approaching the social conditions of the old world. It
is true, we still observe striking and essential differences,
but they are gradually growing less.

Under these circumstances the municipal governments
of our large cities are confronted by problems of unac-
customed and constantly increasing magnitude and complexity; and the State and national governments, too,
find themselves burdened with new duties and responsibilities which force an enlargement of their functions
and their machinery, and more exactingly tax their
working capacity as well as their wisdom. I do not
mean to inquire here whether this expansion of the province of government is desirable or undesirable, but
merely to point it out as a fact and to invite attention
to some of its consequences.

There are certain propositions so self-evident and so
easily understood that it would appear like discourtesy
to argue them before persons of intelligence. Such a one
it is, that as the functions of government grow in extent,
importance and complexity, the necessity grows of their
being administered not only with honesty, but also with
trained ability and knowledge ; and that in the same
measure as this necessity is disregarded in a democratic
government, the success and the stability of democratic
institutions will be impaired. But while every sane
man accepts this proposition as self-evident in theory,
it may be said that every opponent of Civil Service
Reform denies it in practice—and, I regret to add, a
good many men deny it in practice who would object
to being called opponents of Civil Service Reform.

When I speak of the success and stability of democratic institutions being imperiled, I do not mean the danger of a sudden, grand and startling collapse, but I mean the danger of a gradual decay of those elements which are essential to their vitality. I have always been a firm believer in the excellence of democratic government—the government, as Abraham Lincoln defined it, of the people, by the people and for the people. It is a government of the people, inasmuch as in the people all sovereignty resides. It is a government by the people, inasmuch as the people make the laws and direct the conduct of public affairs through their servants chosen by them for those objects. It is a government for the people, inasmuch as public offices are instituted and charged with certain functions and endowed with certain powers to be administered solely for the service and benefit of the people, and for no other purpose. These are the vital requirements of democratic government. In the same measure as these requirements fail to be fullfilled—as any element of sovereignty passes away from the people, or as the making of the laws and the conduct of public affairs cease to be controlled by the people's will, or as the administration of the public offices is diverted from the purposes for which they have been instituted—that is to say, as the offices are used to serve ends other than the public benefit, or are entrusted to persons not apt to give to the people the best attainable service—in that measure democratic government fails.

It is said that democratic government is practically government through political parties. This can be true only in a limited sense. If political parties are what they ought to be—organizations of citizens caused by different currents of opinion as to principles of government or certain questions of public policy, and set on foot and put to the work of persuasion for the purpose of making this or that set of opinions prevail in the conduct of public affairs—they serve a legitimate end. But whenever they seek to divert the public offices, instituted solely for the service and benefit of the people, from their true purpose in order to use them for their own service and benefit, to this extent turning the government *through* political parties into a government *for* political parties, they strike at one of the vital principles of democratic government. And in the same measure as they succeed in this, democratic government fails to be government for the people.

The appearance among us of American men and women who have fallen in love with the splendor of monarchical courts, and who also please themselves by imaginative imitations of aristocratic society, has from time to time called forth ingenious speculation as to whether the great democracy of the American Republic will not eventually be turned into a monarchy. I am convinced that, if there be any such danger at all in store for us, it will not come from such coteries of weak minds and impotent ambitions; but it might arise either from a failure of democratic government to afford the necessary protection to individual rights, to property, to public order and safety, so that society would turn for that protection to a strong man, or from democratic government becoming an instrument of private cupidity and falling into the hands of the chief of an organization looking for plunder.

There has actually been such a monarchy on a small scale in existence among us. I have seen it in operation, and so have many of my hearers. We have witnessed in the greatest city of the United States one man wielding the powers of municipal government like a monarch, in some respects like an absolute monarch, too. Standing at the head of a pretended political organization ruled by him with autocratic power, he made appointments and dismissals in the public service of the city by merely issuing his orders. He determined what candidates for office should within his dominion be submitted to the popular vote, and his followers with prompt obedience enforced his pleasure. He gave audience to citizens having business with the municipal government, and either granted or refused their petitions like a sovereign. He ordered his agents in the Legislature of the State to pass this bill or to defeat the other bill, and it was done. Citizens became accustomed to approach him as supplicants approach a king. Aside from the public taxes for his municipal government he levied a separate revenue, the payment of which could not be refused without danger—a sort of civil list, partly under the euphonious title of "campaign funds," partly without any euphony—for the use of which he never thought of accounting. He grew rich in a marvelously short time, and when a popular uprising against his rule broke out which threatened to become too formidable to resist, he abdicated and withdrew to his estates.

This was monarchy—not, indeed, a monarchy surrounded by the pomp of a court of nobles with ancient names, escutcheons and gold lace, and ribbons and stars and crosses—rather a very vulgar sort of monarchy whose vassals and high dignitaries were a Mayor and police commissioners and heads of municipal departments and district leaders and ward politicians with names and antecedents and manners and social standing anything but aristocratic—but a monarchy for all that, with most of the essential attributes. To be sure the title of this monarch was not that of king, but that of "Boss" —but a boss clad with regal power which he exercised with arbitrary authority until, like some French kings, he had to yield to a popular upheaval amounting to a revolution. Such things happened, as everyone acquainted with the history of Tammany Hall knows, in this very Republic; and if we speculate upon the manner in which monarchy—not in name but in fact—may rise up among us, here is the living example.

The development of political bossism into something like actual monarchy is, to be sure, an extreme case. But all political bossism has a tendency in that direction. When in a political party the selfish element obtains controlling influence it will, for mutual benefit, naturally seek to organize itself into what we call a machine; and machine rule will usually, for the more certain attainment of its selfish ends through united and well regulated action, drift into more or less irresponsible one-man rule—the one man to rule the machine for its and his benefit, to rule through the machine the party organization, and to rule through the party organization, as the case may be, the municipality or the State. And this rule he does not exercise by bringing his fellow-citizens, through persuasion, to his own way of thinking, if indeed he have any, with regard to principles or politics, or measures touching the public interest, but by distributing among the selfish politicians composing his organized corps of mercenaries, in the true feudal fashion, as rewards for services rendered, or as inducements for services to be rendered, things of value, such as public offices with their emoluments and opportunities, which things of value do not belong to him but to the public—he doling them out among his henchmen, not for the benefit of the public but for his and their own.

How far the aspirations of bossism, thus established, are already reaching, found recently a curious illustration in the newspaper report that some of the State bosses, not content with their local autocracy, met together in conference to agree upon certain persons to be put forward as candidates for the Presidency of the United States—just as in the old times of the German Empire the princes wearing the high dignity and power of "Electors" met together to agree upon a selection for the imperial crown. Equally striking was another piece of news going through the press, that when the boss of one State was hard pressed in an election by an uprising of citizens impudently wishing to govern themselves, the boss of another State, although not of the same party, but inspired by a feeling of common interest and of comradeship, sent a strong troop of his own experienced and fearless repeaters to aid the struggling brother boss at the polls—just as the Czar of Russia in 1849, when the Emperor of Austria was in danger from the Hungarian revolutionists, sent his hard pressed brother-Emperor a Russian army to help him subdue the insurgent subjects and save the monarchical authority. Even if these stories had been wholly invented by newspaper reporters, it would be a significant sign of the times that they were generally believed as entirely natural occurrences. And as to their naturalness, given the premises, there can be no doubt.

Do you ask how such utterly undemocratic developments can become possible in a Republic like ours? Simply by the existence of the spoils system, which allows that which belongs to the public, especially the public offices, to be diverted from public to private use. Without that system, political bossism, in the form at least in which we know it, would not be possible. With that system and all its demoralizing influences kept alive in our politics, bossism will not only continue to exist in spite of occasional reverses, but it will propagate itself from State to State and bring forth results which, if predicted now, would severely tax popular credulity. Fortunately, with an intelligent and vigorous people like ours, the growth and recognition of such an evil usually bring with them the recognition of the remedy. As the spoils system evolved its most characteristic and most undemocratic products, the machine and the boss, to more and more conspicuous power, and the corrupt, rapacious and debasing tyranny of that power was more and more widely felt, the people in constantly widening circles turned with a just instinct to the true corrective. It is a remarkable fact that Civil Service Reform, which twenty years ago struggled, apparently in vain, to win the favorable attention of the great mass of citizens, has of late years marvelously risen in popular interest. The reason is that the popular intellect, stimulated by disgust with existing abuses and by apprehension of worse things to come, began to see in Civil Service Reform the only effective method to destroy the spoils system which was robbing, oppressing and degrading them—that is, the only effective method to restore the public offices to the service of the public ends for which they were originally instituted, and make the government in this sense once more what it was designed to be, a government, not for the benefit of the politicians, or of machines, or of political parties, but a government for the people.

Then the popular mind also readily appreciated the practical benefit conferred upon every branch of the public service in which the merit system, the essential feature of Civil Service Reform, has been introduced and faithfully enforced. And every day the popular demand grows more general and more energetic for its extension over wider fields. The merit system has stood the test of practical experience so triumphantly that the vociferous objections and revilings of it, in which the spoils politicians used to delight, have sunk to a mournful mutter. That awful spectre of an overbearing, office-holding aristocracy consisting of Department clerks, revenue collectors and custom-house weighers has ceased to haunt our nights. The dire prediction that only college-bred men could, under the competitive examination system, become Government scribes, has withered in the frost of statistical showings. And the harrowing fable that candidates for letter-carriers' places are examined on the exact distance between the moon and the planet Mars has gone to sleep forever. All these and similar fictions are drowned by the declarations of one Department chief after another that they cannot understand how without the merit system the business of their offices could ever have been carried on; by the contentment of public servants working under Civil Service Rules, that at last they have escaped the debasing dependence on political favor and may be proudly conscious of standing on their merits; by the popular call for further extension of the system, such as the emphatic demand of the merchants that the consular service be put under Civil Service Rules; by the grateful satisfaction of the inhabitants of our large cities as the Reform gradually takes root in the different branches of municipal administration; by the sentiment rapidly spreading among all classes of our people that our political contests must cease to be scrambles for spoils and plunder.

Thus Civil Service Reform has no longer to struggle for its right of existence. So much is triumphantly established. The problem remains how to secure, by further conquest, what we have won ; for the results the Reform movement has achieved will not be entirely safe until its success is complete—until the spoils system is *totally* abolished, and the new order of things has supplanted it in the ordinary ways of thinking and the political habits of the people.

We all know that, as we owe to our legislative bodies the enactment of the existing Civil Service Laws, so it is in the legislative bodies that the most dangerous attempts are made to circumvent or subvert them. At the same time, whatever the Executive power may do in the way of extending the Reform, the aid of legislation is required to give it endurance and security. Now I must confess that of all those who are charged with public duties, the legislator, especially the member of Congress, seems to me by far the most interested in the total abolition of the patronage system. He should desire that abolition all the more ardently, as the growth of our Government and the swelling magnitude and complexity of the problems before the legislator demand the devotion of all his mental and moral faculties with constantly increasing severity for his real duties, and more and more sternly forbid any dissipation of them in unworthy employments. Permit me to discuss this branch of my subject somewhat elaborately. I shall not argue the constitutional aspect of the interference of members of Congress with the appointing power, but unfold the possibilities developed by existing custom ; and in doing so, I speak to some extent from the personal experience gathered during six years' service in Congress and four years in an executive position which kept me in constant official and personal contact with Senators and Representatives.

Let us picture to ourselves a candidate for Congress in a large district and follow him in his career—a man of good character, fine abilities, and with an honorable ambition to serve his country. It is the year of a Presidential election, with a new deal of patronage in prospect. First, he has to get the nomination from his party convention. He enjoys the good will and respect of his neighbors, but he finds that this is not enough. The primaries which elect delegates to the Congressional district convention are in many cases controlled by the most adroit and pushing politicians, who want office and are especially keen when a change of administration is impending. Our candidate finds that to beat his rivals for the nomination he will need the aid of some of those alert politicians, and, in turn, they let him know what places he is to procure for them if elected. The candidate being once started, and, of course, anxious to succeed, tries to persuade himself that such things are always done, and that there is really no harm in opening a prospective reward to persons willing to render the country the valuable service of making him a member of Congress. Still he recoils from the thought of making a downright bargain for his nomination. Morally he cannot afford to purchase his nomination with a promise of office. Neither can he afford, he thinks, to lose his nomination by bluntly refusing the promise. He begins to compromise with his conscience and honor, and calls up his diplomatic adroitness, answering the demand for office in ambiguous phrase : he will "take the matter into favorable consideration"; he will "do the fair thing"; he smiles, he winks, he nods, having not yet learned by experience that all these things are taken by the place-hunter as positive promise, no matter what his own mental reservations may be. And thus he is, without knowing it, soon deeply mortgaged, having, perhaps, in this vague way promised the same office to several people ; and such promises are sure to be presented for redemption.

Well, he is nominated, and now the campaign begins. The district threatens to be close, and he looks for help. That help is freely offered. Some men take a sincere interest in the cause the candidate stands for, and give him their aid unselfishly. Others, who are effective local stump speakers, or whose influence can reach some particular class of people, or who can disarm certain opposition by personal work, or who are just the men to get out the vote, or who can do great good by the wise expenditure of some money, and so on, are of opinion that they should not be expected to "hustle about" for nothing. He accepts their services, and this gives them "claims" upon him—claims to be satisfied, of course, with offices. Carried away by the heat of the struggle he not merely continues to open prospects by vague speech and to smile and wink and nod, but he makes positive pledges, perhaps not a few of them. The mortgages rise to a formidable amount.

The election comes and he triumphs. His bosom swells with the proud consciousness of honors won and of distinction to be achieved in the service of his country. Being a man of honorable purpose he thinks of going to work at once to prepare himself for his legislative duties, the importance of which he earnestly appreciates. To these duties he wishes wholly to devote himself. But no; he has not yet time for that. Other more pressing business intervenes. His mail is heavy with petitions and recommendations for office, bearing long strings of names in favor of men of whom he may never have heard—covering all the federal appointments in his district many times over. Estimable men whom he cannot afford to offend seek places for their friends and dependents. But by the men who have "claims" upon him he is most strongly reminded that first of all his time and labor belong to his "friends." There will be a change of administration and, of course, vacant places without limit. In the first place it is to be taken for granted that, according to custom, he will have all the postoffices in his district at his disposal. Then it is suggested that he should consider it a duty of honor to fill some consulships from his district, if not even a foreign mission. And indeed there are gentlemen among his constituents who, having done valiant battle for him, now think that foreign air would do good to them and their wives, and that their daughters should have first-class music lessons abroad. Then there are others who maintain that they have fairly earned Indian agencies, or revenue positions, or places as chiefs of bureaus or at least of divisions in some Department at Washington. They and their friends all insist that the new member of Congress is in honor bound to procure them these things, that he certainly can do it if he will, that it will cost him only a word, and that if he fails to do it, his party in the district will suffer grievously, and he himself in particular.

About the time the new President goes into power our new Congressman, loaded with petitions and recommendations, rushes on to Washington to plunge into that fearful spoils-carnival called a change of administration. He travels in lively company, not a few of his constituents who hold, or believe they hold, his promises go with him to keep him to his work, each expecting him to make *his* case a special one. The poor man's first night in Washington is troubled with disquieting visions. Has he not seen among his traveling company Smith, to whom he during the campaign opened a prospect for the postmastership at Blankville, while he had positively promised that postmastership to Jones? And here they are both in bodily presence, each anxious to close the final mortgage each holds on the same piece of property.

Our new member of Congress has always considered himself a man of integrity and honor. He now instinctively feels that he is in a situation in which a gentleman ought not to be. Has he not do' e a thing which a gentleman ought not to do? It is often the case that we become for the first time clearly conscious of the true nature of an offence when we have to confront its consequences. But our friend has hardly time for self-reproach. How can he get rid of the conflict of claims between Smith and Jones? Both are influential constituents whom it would be dangerous to offend. Smith is perhaps the better man for that postoffice, but Jones holds the clearer promise. Our friend concludes that the clearer promise must be kept; that he will explain his embarrassment to Smith, ask Smith to give way to Jones, and tell Smith that he shall have "something equally as good," as the current phrase is. Ah, poor man, he has to learn yet what a terrible scourge he has prepared for his back by that promise of "something equally as good," for Smith will faithfully stay by his side until he gets it.

And a good many other expectant constituents will stay likewise. Wherever our unfortunate statesman is, they are. They are there when he goes to bed late at night, they are there before he gets up in the morning. There are the Joneses calling for their postoffices, the Smiths demanding "something equally as good," and many others "claiming" many other things—and all these things without delay. Our friend, his political creditors at his heels, rushes first to the general Post Office Department to satisfy his Joneses. There he finds the rooms and corridors thronged with other statesmen and their friends, crowds of Joneses and Smiths. The same anxious faces, the same eager eyes, the same nervously twitching lips, the same pictures of misery. After hours of restless waiting he succeeds in being listened to about the postoffice in Blankville, the papers covering that place are sent for, and our friend is blandly informed that there is no vacancy in that postoffice. "What?" exclaims our Congressman. "No vacancy? Why, of course, you will make one. Remove the incumbent. I must have that place. I have promised it to Mr. Jones, this meritorious friend of mine." The answer comes, calm and cruel: "The present postmaster has been in about two years. His record as an officer is excellent. There have never been any charges against him. There is absolutely no cause for removing him."

This is to our friend a thunderclap from a clear sky. Is he to confess himself powerless to get Jones the post-office he has promised? It would ruin his prestige in his district, and Jones would become his enemy. What is to be done? Appeals to the Postmaster General and even to the President avail nothing. But was not something said about there being no charges against the present Blankville postmaster? Might not that defect be remedied? Why not get up some charges against that postmaster, be he ever so good an officer and blameless a man? This is the way out. Now to work!

When our member of Congress is again alone with

himself the recollection that he once was a gentleman painfully struggles up in his mind. What! Is he to instigate or even to countenance the trumping up of charges affecting the official and perhaps even the personal character of an honorable man to effect the removal of that man from an office efficiently filled, and this merely to enable him, the member of Congress, to redeem a promise which he never ought to have made? He would not look into a mirror at that moment for fear of seeing his own face. He does not dare to listen to a warning voice speaking within him. With cowardly haste he seeks refuge in the thought that politics is politics; that this is the custom of the country, and that so long as that custom permits and even obliges members of Congress to use the offices of the Government as rewards for their henchmen—why, such things will be done, whatever their character and effect. And thus the shameful game of trumped-up charges is played. And our friend has more Joneses to provide with more postoffices, which causes more conferences at the Department, in some cases the trumping up of more charges, the disappointment of more men who had promises, the making of more pledges to "furnish something equally as good," and more sacrifices of honor and self-respect.

But now comes the task of getting for his friends places which are not, like the postoffices, regarded as "belonging" to the member of Congress, but for which he must compete with other members, and even with the more formidable Senators—places in the Departments, or consulships, or foreign missions, or revenue offices, or Indian agencies, and what-not. He visits the Departments, one after another, and humbly seeks in each the favor of that awful potentate, the appointment clerk, who can keep him informed of existing vacancies and who also may see to it that his papers are opportunely brought to the attention of the Secretary whenever a good chance for catching an office occurs. And, oh! those hours of desolate standing around, and of anxious waiting for a propitious moment when he can pour his supplications into the ear of the President or of Cabinet ministers, painfully aware that the more impressively he speaks the more he is in danger of being set down by them as an intolerable bore.

That, however, is not the worst of it. Presently he discovers that he cannot possibly secure all the places he asks for, that he cannot gratify all the hopes he has excited—perhaps only very few of them—and that he must concentrate his efforts upon those few and drop the rest, lest he lose all. As to the few to be favored he is sorely tempted to select those whom he may expect to be the most useful to him, with scant regard for their fitness as to the places desired. But how drop the rest? Can he tell them that he is unable to press their claims to a successful issue, while they see him press the claims of others? This would be the way to make enemies. It cannot be thought of. But what else can he do? Make them believe that he is pressing their claims, but that after heroic efforts he is defeated by superior influence; throw the responsibility upon the President or the Cabinet ministers. And then comes the distressing spectacle of a member of Congress with a confiding constituent by his side appearing before a Department chief and making a glowing speech on the virtues of that constituent, and on his own ardent desire to see this excellent man placed in office according to his merits, assuring the Department chief, and charging him so to inform the President, that this is the Congressman's special request—while the Department chief thus addressed has been before advised by the same member of Congress that he cares nothing about this man but really wishes another to be provided for. And then the member of Congress accepts the warm thanks of the confiding constituent for this spendid effort of friendship.

In this manner weeks and weeks pass after the incoming of the new administration, and still our friend has on his hands a formidable number of pursuers to whom he has promised "something equally as good," and others, too, to whom he has promised nothing, but whom he thinks he cannot afford to offend by blunt refusals.

Some have left Washington but flood him with letters. Others have stayed and indomitably dog his steps. Some owe boarding bills in Washington, and have no money left for the home journey. In his despair he pays their bills, and buys them their railroad tickets to deliver himself of the insufferable infliction, promising to move heaven and earth for them in their absence. But there are a few who still have funds and will not go, and from them the wretched statesman, jaded and disgusted, at last runs away himself and hurries home. But there he finds no rest. Incessantly he is pestered by the reproaches of the disappointed, and by the impatience of those who are still expectants. He begins to doubt whether the patronage business has not made him more enemies than friends. Fortunate he is if he does not find himself forced to run away once more, without leaving his address behind, into some solitude far from the madding crowd. And yet he may have to fear that quiet solitude more than the distracting bustle he has escaped; for it will bring to him moments of self-contemplation when memories will rise up before him of promises made to be broken, of confidence invited to be betrayed, and of honor and self-respect lost, never to be retrieved. And yet, of the political debts which the spoils system seduced him to contract, only the most pressing have been paid.

So far he has gone only through the experience of the first months after the incoming of the new administration while Congress was not in session. The time arrives for Congress to meet, and now he thinks he will atone for it all by giving his whole soul to that duty for the performance of which he really was elected. But, alas! the old torment will not let him go. The men with claims who have not been provided for are still dogging his heels or mercilessly pelting him with letters, and like an errand boy they keep him running from Department to Department. Every new chance opening revives the pressure. The work is never, never done; and although it abates somewhat, it continues to trench most severely on the time, working power and

good humor which should wholly belong to the legislator's real duty.

Well, our friend tries hard to do the best he can under
the circumstances, and flatters himself with the belief
that he has at least his political home machine tolerably
well arranged, but new complications arise. One of
the office-holders appointed upon his recommendation
so grossly misconducts himself as to make his removal
imperative. There is no doubt as to the facts. But the
delinquent public servant calls upon his Congressional
patron for protection. Has he not a right to do so?
Has he not been appointed simply by way of reward
for services rendered to the member of Congress? Has
he ever been expected by his patron to earn his salary
by downright hard work for the public? Was he not
rather to have "a good time" while in office, and to
make out of it what he could? And now because he
did so he is to lose the reward he had earned, and to
be disgraced by removal to boot. Will the Congressional patron leave his client in the lurch? Our friend
is a little puzzled at first. In spite of the many rebuffs
it has suffered the old conscience speaks once more.
Does his sense of duty permit him to endeavor to keep
in office, to the evident detriment of the service and of
the public interest, a man he knows to have proved
himself unworthy? But there is also another voice
speaking to him. Has not this unworthy public servant
friends or relatives who exercise influence in his district? True, he ought never to have recommended this
man for office, but can he now afford to make enemies
of him and his clan? True, the integrity of the service and the public interest are entitled to consideration ; but can he afford that consideration when one of
his appointees is concerned and he himself has so much
at stake? Well, he seeks to have the removal recalled.
He does not find a willing ear. He begs, he protests,
he blusters, he threatens, he entreats, he implores the
Administration to do a thing which he knows it cannot
do without being false to its public duty.

But still other complications come to plague him.

The Administration follows some policy which he feels himself in conscience bound to oppose ; or vicious practices are discovered in some Government Department which his sense of duty commands him to denounce. His first impulse is to obey that command. But—has he not appeared before the President and before the Department chiefs as a petitioner for favors in the shape of offices for his friends? Will he not have to solicit similar favors again, and if he criticizes and opposes the Administration, will it not have the power not only to refuse further favors needed by him, but even to remove the persons appointed upon his recommendation? Nay, may not those very persons, his political retainers, the members of his home machine, if he opposes the Administration, turn against him and denounce him as a mug-wump and a renegade, for the purpose of winning the favor of the Administration and of thus saving their own necks? He keenly feels that here his moral independence as a legislator is at stake—that moral independence which, if he is to do his duty to his country, can never be surrendered. But can he afford to maintain it at the risk of losing all the dearly-bought results of the management of the patronage in his district, and even of turning his own handiwork against himself? No; unless there be in him some of the stuff of which martyrs are made, the moral independence of the legislator will die as a sacrifice at the shrine of that patronage. And to many legislators making that sacrifice, it will hardly occur that it bears all the features of a bargain essentially corrupt.

Here I will stop, although the catalogue of perplexities, embarrassments, reductions, debasements and abandonments of their true duty, which the spoils system imposes upon members of Congress, is by no means exhausted. But it is enough. Will you say that the picture I have drawn is, after all, only a creation of fancy? I call it a picture of the possibilities brought forth by the spoils system ; but only too much of it is a picture of reality. Indeed, I have known Senators and members of the House of Representatives who with good conscience and just pride could affirm that they never made a direct or indirect promise of office to bring about their nomination or election; that they never recommended any person for appointment whom they did not honestly believe well qualified for the place to be filled, and that they never depended upon the manipulation of the patronage to advance their political fortunes. Such men, however, while resisting its temptations and debasing influences, have by no means been exempt from the harassing and distracting effects of the spoils system, and, I am sure, they are among the foremost to condemn it and to favor its abolition. Neither do I ignore the fact that there are members of Congress who, moved by the impulse of gratitude or by generous sympathy, take hearty pleasure in doing a good turn to a friend, or in trying to aid a struggling ambition, by securing to them a comfortable living or an opportunity to rise, and who to this end submit to work and trouble without selfish motive.

But on the whole, the effect of the patronage system is certainly such as I have described it. In a number of instances, by no means small, the picture I have drawn is true in every touch, and in many more it is true in very great part. I speak of this with assurance, for I know it from my own personal observation. During the years of my official life I was not only myself exposed to the office-seeking pressure, but I have many a time heard the confessions of national legislators speaking of their experiences and doings just as I have portrayed them, some with the brazen indifference born of debasing habit, others with the accents of deeply mortified self-respect, of humiliation and shame. More than once I have listened to men of originally noble impulses and high-minded ambition, as they told the story of their miseries—how, seduced by what they accepted as the custom of active politics, they had entangled themselves in the meshes of questionable engagements almost without knowing it; how they had sometimes been forced to recommend for office men whom they knew to be unfit; how the misconduct of such men,

demanding protection at their hands, subjected them
to abominable perplexity and self-abasement; how their
pride was humbled by their attitude as beggars for
favors not only before members of the Government but
even before Department clerks; how, not seldom, their
sense of honor and duty revolted when they had to urge
the removal of a worthy officer simply to make room for
one of their own henchmen; how they felt themselves
like bondmen in their relations to those in power, on
account of the persons to be put or to be kept in office;
how the patronage business robbed them of their time,
spoiled their working capacity, enervated their spirits,
and hampered and clogged in every possible way their
one time supreme ambition to devote themselves heart
and soul to their legislative duties for the common good,
and how they now cursed the galling, debasing, disgusting servitude to which the patronage had subjected
them.

And more than that. Many a time when, as Secretary of the Interior, I had to remove public servants for
peremptory cause which absolutely left me no choice, I
received the visits of members of Congress who had recommended the appointment of the men in question, and
who now, although they had to admit the reasons compelling the dismissal, yet assailed me with remonstrances, threats, supplications, and even tears, to move
me to a violation of my obvious duty. And I do not
remember an instance of such appeal when, on the part
of the supplicant, the matter of the public interest was in
the least drawn into consideration. But I do remember
more than one case in which the member of Congress
demanding the revocation of such a removal, went as
far as to threaten that unless I complied the appropriation for my Department would have a hard time in passing the House.

It was in a magazine article written by Gen. Jacob D.
Cox, ex-Secretary of the Interior, that I first found a
description of Senators and members of the House of
Representatives personally introducing to a Cabinet
minister constituents of theirs as candidates for certain

places, extolling the merits of those constituents in the warmest language, and with apparently earnest eloquence urging their appointment, while the Cabinet minister had in his desk notes from the same statesmen cautioning him not to pay any regard to their recommendations. I must confess that this startled me. Being at that time a member of the Senate myself, I inquired of two Cabinet ministers then in office whether any instances of such duplicity had ever come to their own personal notice. The answer was that indeed they had, and they were by no means infrequent. But I have not to depend upon other men's testimony; for a few years later I, myself, sitting behind my desk as Secretary of the Interior, looked into the eyes of Senators and Representatives who played before me the same ignoble trick, and into the eyes of their confiding victims, and I did not know whom to pity most, the deceiver or the deceived. If there is anything I have to be sorry for it is that I contented myself by disregarding their recommendations altogether instead of uncovering the dastardly fraud on the spot.

There can be no serious doubt, therefore, as to the facts. No man of experience in our political life can honestly question them. Nor do I state these facts now for the first time. I discussed them in the Senate of the United States many years ago without meeting a denial. Can there be any doubt as to their significance? It means that the use of patronage by members of Congress is essentially corrupt and corrupting. It is not that gross form of corruption which consists in passing bribe money from hand to hand. But it is that more dangerous and demoralizing, because more insinuating, corruption which wraps itself in the garb of party zeal, of gratitude, of generous sympathy, and in this disguise is received and countenanced among respectable people. Never has there been a more elaborate combination of self-deception and deception of others. Look at the elementary facts. A public place instituted solely for the service of the people, and, according to legal intent, to be filled with a person fitted for that service, is promised by the legislator to a person as a reward or inducement for service rendered or to be rendered to *him*, with slight, if any, regard for the fitness of that person for public duty. The performance of that promise the legislator calls an "honorable obligation," while in fact the honor was lost when the obligation was incurred. The legislator seeks to obtain that office for his retainer from the executive, representing it as an appointment to be made in the public interest, while in fact it is the carrying out of a private bargain. The legislator calls the obtaining of this office an exercise of his legitimate influence, while in fact he has accepted a favor which undermines his moral independence by putting him under the influence of the executive. Having bribed a useful politician with the promise, he is himself bribed by the executive by the fulfillment. This manipulation of the patronage the legislator calls taking care of his constituents, while in fact he is seeking to take care of himself. He calls it doing his duty, while in fact by meddling with the executive function he is doing something which the Constitution never intended that he should do ; and he does this at the expense of the time, working power and moral force he should devote to the great duty which the Constitution really imposes upon him.

If, as we must assume, government to be honest and beneficial must be based upon truth, then the manipula- tion of the patronage by members of Congress is in the highest degree repugnant to good government, for it is the very hotbed of multiplied falsehood.

If, to make democratic government truly a govern- ment for the people, it is essentially required that public offices should not be diverted from the public purpose for which they are intended, then the manipulation of the patronage by members of Congress insidiously un- dermines democratic government, for of all the perver- sions known the most colossal in dimensions and the most demoralizing in effect is that which turns the legislator into an office-broker and a spoils-monger.

If it is true, which nobody will deny, that as our Government grows greater in the magnitude and variety

of its functions, it requires, in the legislative no less
than in the executive sphere, greater ability, knowledge,
application and moral courage to deal with the vast and
complex problems confronting it, then there can be no
bitterer satire upon the growth of the Republic than the
legislator to whom that growth is of especial importance
on account of the increasing number of postoffices and
revenue places he has to look out for; and no sadder
spectacle than the legislator who, although possessing the
ability as well as the ambition to serve the Republic
according to the needs of the time, permits himself to be
dragged away from his real duty, and to be crippled in
power and wrecked in morals by the tyranny of so vicious
an abuse.

I risk nothing in saying that there are very few members of Congress who have not often at heart secretly
cursed this abominable practice, and wished it had never
existed—aye, very few who in their inmost hearts will not
to-day admit every word I have used as literally true. I
have indeed heard some proclaim with an assumption of
superior manliness that they are gentlemen who think it
a matter of honor never to forget their friends, and who
believe in rewarding them for every service accepted
from them. They may be told that there is no objection
to their remembering their friends, but that they would
be better gentlemen and also better legislators if they
rewarded those who have done them a good turn at their
own expense and not at the expense of the public.

I have heard others say: "Yes, the spoils system is a
curse, a greater curse to members of Congress than to
anyone else. We heartily wish it did not exist. But it
has come upon us by tradition; it is part of the political customs of the country. We are its victims, its
slaves. What can we do but submit and make the best
of it?" This is the voice of despondent weakness.
The answer is simple: "If you wish it did not exist,
why do you not make it cease to exist? If you gave
half the energy and labor you fritter away in manipulating the patronage, to the task of abolishing the detestable evil, it would soon completely disappear, and you

would be free to give yourselves altogether to your duties to the country." Then, why not go to work with a clear purpose and resolute determination until the task is finished?

There are in fact only two classes of members of Congress who have a real interest in preserving the patronage. One of them consists of those who are so weak in intellectual ability and acquirements that they must despair of maintaining themselves in public life unless by bribing men with places and salaries they build up for themselves a mercenary following. And the other class consists of abler men, who by attracting to themselves through the distribution of spoils the selfish and unscrupulous element in politics, seek to organize for their own use and purposes a power strong enough to maintain itself by sinister means in defiance of public opinion, and thus to subjugate to their own will their party organizations, and through them their districts or States. And in a democracy so abhorrent and dangerous a power should never be permitted to exist. But these two classes of members of Congress, the hopelessly incapable and the aspirants to boss-ship, form together only a small majority. They are vastly outnumbered by those whose interests lie in the opposite direction, and who, it is to be hoped, will recognize that they have infinitely more to gain than to lose by the complete abolition of the patronage system.

Every member of Congress who cherishes the glory and well-being of his country, the safety of its democratic institutions, and the efficiency of its government, and who values his own honor and dignity as a man and his usefulness and moral independence as a legislator, will, therefore, heartily rejoice that the merit system has gained so large and so firm a lodgment in our administrative machinery. He will, with a sense of relief, contemplate the deliverance of the clerical force in our great Government Departments at Washington, and in the larger Government establishments throughout the country, from the baneful touch of spoils politics. He will, whatever his party relations may be, give ungrudg-

ing credit to former Administrations for having established the reformatory system, and to this Administration
for what it has done to advance it—for having put under
Civil Service Rules the whole Department of Agriculture
up to the very top, the Government Printing Office, and
important parts of the Indian service, of the Customs
service, of the Internal Revenue service, of the Postal
service, and the Geological Survey, making, down to the
first of November, an addition to the competitive list
of more than 12,500 places. He will thank the Secretary of the Navy for the great improvements in the regulations governing his laboring force. He will watch
with jealous care the enforcement of the Civil Service
Law and of the Rules made under it, and never fail to
expose and censure any neglect or violation of them,
no matter by members of what party they be committed.
He will go farther. He will understand that the vicious
influences of the patronage system will continue to poison
our political life and to vex and harass him especially,
so long as there is subject to appointment by favor a
number of places sufficient to keep alive the office-seeking mania, and to give a chance to the spoils-mongering
politician. He will therefore welcome with gladness
every possibility to extend the operation of the merit
principle, not only to every place within the limits
originally contemplated by the Civil Service Law, but
also outside of them.

Thus he will heed with eager satisfaction the universal and emphatic demand of the mercantile community
that the consular service shall cease to be the football
of political machination.

He will, therefore, applaud the recent order of the
President instituting thorough examinations for aspirants
to consular places, not, indeed, as a final measure, but
merely as a "step in the right direction," as the report
of the Secretary of State called it, an advance toward
a more thorough and permanent reform to be embodied
in appropriate legislation of which, it may be hoped, a
provision for *competitive* examinations will form a dis-
tinctive feature.

He will earnestly endeavor to promote the practical
adoption of that wise recommendation recently made by
the Postmaster-General that the Assistant Postmasters-
General, for obvious reasons, be withdrawn from the
reach of political changes, and be put upon the footing
of merit.

He will seriously consider whether there are not other
Assistant Secretaries in other Departments who, with
great advantage to the public interest, might for the same
reasons be put upon the same footing, thus introducing
in our Government the non-partisan under-secretary,
the expert Departmental business manager, who exists
in almost every well regulated government, and is
looked upon as indispensable. Even in our own Government this system is not without precedent, as all
know who remember the late Assistant Secretary Hunter
of the State Department.

Our conscientious member of Congress will earnestly
favor the recommendation recently made in the annual
report of the Secretary of the Interior that the whole
Indian service be rescued from the dangerous touch of
party politics—especially dangerous in this instance—
by giving it a non-partisan head and organization; and
it will readily occur to him that there is not the slightest reason of a public nature why the rule of the merit
tenure should not be applied to the various Commissioners in the Interior and Treasury Departments, and
to the auditors, comptrollers, registers and so on, whose
duties have nothing to do with the so-called "political
policy" of the Administration.

But with especially keen interest will he remember
the forcible plea made last year by the late Postmaster
General, Mr. Bissell, and repeated by his successor, Mr.
Wilson, demonstrating the absolute necessity, for reasons
of the public interest, of taking the whole Postal service, the postmasters included, altogether out of politics; and he will therefore hail with especial joy the
recent order of the President, authorizing the Postmaster-General to consolidate with the principal postoffices
the smaller ones surrounding them, so as to make them

mere branch offices, and to place all persons employed therein under the Civil Service Rules. This order, if acted upon with courage and energy, will bring forth inestimable benefit. It will give the people better service by localizing its direction according to local wants. It will immensely simplify the system of accounting which now has to deal with over 70,000 individual postmasters, a great many of whom, as they are at present selected, will never learn how to make a correct report —and thus lead to better business methods, prompter returns and greater economy. It will draw many thousands of postoffices, from top to bottom, under the protection and control of the Civil Service Law. And this involves to our member of Congress a blessing of incalculable value.

The postoffices scattered by thousands all over the land have done more than anything else to keep alive the spoils idea among our people. More than anything else they have been the prizes fought for in national contests by local politicians. More than anything else they have served to demoralize the popular mind with the notion that a change of party in power must mean a partisan change in all the offices, and thus to turn our party contests into scrambles for plunder. It is no exaggeration to say that the postoffice used as party spoil has been the bane of American politics. It has especially been the curse of the member of Congress, hounding, tormenting and degrading him every day of his official life. To be rid of that curse will be to him a true deliverance. Every postoffice, the disposal of which he loses, will be so much gain to his working power, to his freedom and moral independence, to his usefulness and dignity as a legislator. He will, therefore, not only do the utmost in his power to aid the Postmaster-General in the work of reörganizing the postal service according to the President's order, but he will zealously promote the passage of a law bringing under effective Civil Service Rules those postoffices which the President's order cannot reach. He will contribute to this result all the more gladly, as, with the postal service taken out of party politics, the greatest citadel of the spoils system will have fallen.

He will go still farther. Candid reflection will con·vince him that the four-years-term law must be repealed. That vicious law was a fraud in its inception. Being passed under the pretence of utility, while it was only in fact to serve the wire-pulling machinations of a candidate for the Presidency, and signed by a well-meaning President without consideration, it has proved ever since one of the most prolific sources of demoralization and mischief to the service, to the public interest and to our whole political life. The foremost statesmen—Jefferson, Madison, John Quincy Adams, Clay, Calhoun, Webster, Benton and many more—have condemned it and demanded its repeal. What they did not accomplish should be accomplished now; for it must be clear to the plainest understanding that the merit appointment must logically be accompanied by the merit tenure. Indeed, *merit appointment with merit tenure* comprehends the whole program of Civil Service Reform.

Need I say what this means to the member of Congress? Not the surrender of any privilege or power of value. It means the emancipation of Congress from the scandalous and debasing slavery of the patronage. It means the restoration of the legislator to his true functions. It means the removal from party spirit, from party contests and from party government of the demoralizing element of the meanest selfishness.

It may seem extravagant to hope so much. Why should we consider it so? There are some among us who stood at the cradle of the Civil Service Reform movement. They remember the time when the practical politician looked upon the Civil Service Reformer as a visionary dreamer of singularly hopeless conceit—as little better than a harmless idiot who might be tolerated at large without the slightest danger to the existing order of things. When we remember that time, which does not lie very far behind us, and then contemplate the marvelous change that has since taken place, will the hope for the complete triumph of the cause we advocate still appear extravagantly sanguine? Indeed, who would but a few years ago have ventured to predict that the entire ministerial part of the national service would be under the merit system by this time? There is but very little of it outside now. And I trust my imagination does not delude me when I believe President Cleveland to be determined, as to the extension of classification, to leave to his successor little or nothing to do that can be done by executive action alone. Is it unreasonable to expect that Congress will also do that which the enlightened public opinion of the country and the development of the Republic so clearly and forcibly demand?

At our last annual meeting I spoke of the remarkable strength the Civil Service Reform movement had gained in public sentiment. I am happy to add now that the growth of that strength has continued. It was strikingly manifested by the overwhelming popular majority by which the merit system was adopted for the municipal government of Chicago, and by its successful introduction. Efforts are being made in various other places to follow this great example. We have indeed to deplore two occurrences which show that the spoils politicians have by no means given up the battle, but still strive to recover what they have lost. One of these occurrences is the passage by the legislature of Massachusetts, in spite of the Governor's spirited resistance, of a law striking a vicious blow at the integrity of the merit system in the public service in that State, and at the same time at the honor and the true interests of the war veterans. And the other is the utterly lawless conduct of the Mayor of Indianapolis, who has simply declared himself not bound by the provisions of the city charter prescribing the introduction of the merit system in the municipal service. Such things admonish us that militant watchfulness must still be the order of the day in the Reform camp. I am glad to say that in Massachusetts the constitutionality of the obnoxious law is ably contested in the courts; and we all know that the champions of Civil Service Reform in Indiana are of too belligerent a spirit to let the refractory Mayor sleep on his spoils laurels in comfort.

On the other hand, in the State of New York and in its great cities the Reform system has made most cheering progress. The embodiment in the State Constitution of the Civil Service Reform clause, and its faithful observance by the Governor, the Mayors of the great municipalities and the respective Civil Service boards, have caused a very large extension of Civil Service Rules and a vigorous enforcement of them. One of the most important features of that progress consists in the adoption and the successful operation in the large cities of the labor-registration system, which rescues the laboring men doing public work from the tyrannical control and the rapacity of political bosses and machines. And now in • Maryland, too, the day of Reform has dawned with unexpected brilliancy, and I trust that old State will step into the front rank of its champions. There are several others that promise to follow her.

Nothing could be more encouraging than this steady growth of the Civil Service Reform movement in popular favor. Most of its former opponents in the press have become converts to its side. That without the introduction of the merit system no permanent overthrow of corrupt machine rule and no thorough reform of our large municipal governments can be expected, is now a truth generally accepted by the popular understanding. Such convictions bring to the movement the aid of organizations bearing different names but having ends in view of which Civil Service Reform is a prerequisite. The Civil Service Reform associations proper, which not many years ago led a somewhat lonesome life in the field of public endeavor, are constantly reënforced by additions to their number. It is one of the most cheering signs of the time that such associations are being established at our universities and colleges, enlisting in our work the rising generation that will speak the word of the future. We may especially congratulate ourselves upon the recent organization of a Women's Auxiliary Civil Service Reform Association in New York, several of whose members have already achieved enviable renown for important public enter-

prises successfully conducted, and all of whom will, no
doubt, bring powerful aid and encouragement to this.

With such successes and such moral forces behind us
we may indeed hope to see the day when our party warfare will be contests of opinion free from the demoralizing and repulsive interference of the plunder-chase ;
when a change of party in the national Administration
will no longer present the barbarous spectacle of a spoils
debauch, torturing the nostrils of our own people and
disgracing the Republic in the eyes of civilized mankind; when our Presidents and heads of the executive
Departments will no longer be the almoners of party
government, in danger of their lives from the furious
onset of the begging throng, but will be respected as
officers of state having high duties to fulfill which demand all their strength and ability; when the public
offices, national, State and municipal, will cease to be
the feudal fiefs distributed by bosses, or the merchandise of spoils-jobbers, and again serve the true purpose
for which they have been instituted, thus becoming once
more an integral element of government for the people;
and when our legislators, escaped from the shackles of
the spoils bondage, no longer beset by the snares and
pitfalls which have threatened to wreck their morals and
their self-respect, no longer supplicating for executive
favor, will be able and proud to devote all their energies to the great tasks which at a time so full of difficult
problems the country imposes upon them. And thus,
while in years gone by we found an incentive to strenuous effort in the greatness of the obstacles to be overcome, we may now work on inspired by the hope of complete achievement.

MEETING OF THE LEAGUE.

COSMOS CLUB, December 13, 1895—10.30 A. M.

The President took the chair.

The Secretary called the roll of delegates.

The first business in order being the election of a president and vice-presidents for the ensuing year, Mr. Bonaparte, of Baltimore, moved that the Secretary be directed to cast one ballot for the re-election of Hon. Carl Schurz as president, and for the re-election of the present vice-presidents. The motion was put by Mr. Bonaparte and carried unanimously. The Secretary cast the ballot and the nominees were declared duly elected.

Mr. Estes, for the Auditing Committee, appointed by the General Committee, reported that the Committee had examined the accounts and vouchers of the Treasurer, as submitted in his report to the General Committee, and that they had been found to be correct. On motion the report was accepted.*

Mr. Schieffelin, for the Finance Committee, submitted a budget of estimated expenses for the ensuing year, amounting to $4,500. On motion of Mr. Welsh the various items of the budget were approved, and the expenditures involved duly authorized. At the suggestion of Mr. Schieffelin, the Chairman appointed Mr. C. W. Watson, of New York, a member of the Finance Committee, with authority to countersign vouchers.

Mr. Bonaparte, for the special committee appointed to report on additions to the Classified Service, and on the recent Executive order concerning the Consular Service, submitted a written report, which, on motion, was adopted and ordered filed.†

Mr. Straus reported verbally for the Committee on Consular Reform, stating the action taken by the committee in promoting the bills to re-organize the Consular Service, introduced in the last Congress by Senators Morgan and Lodge. The

---

* Page 47.   † Page 132.

committee had had a hearing before the Senate Committee on Foreign Relations, which subsequently reported favorably the Morgan bill, modified in several respects. The bill, however, had not reached a vote before the adjournment of Congress. The committee had not as yet considered the practical relation of the recent executive order to the matter of legislation, nor determined whether or not the Morgan bill, if re-introduced, should be changed to embrace any feature of the new plan. On motion the report was accepted.

The Secretary reported the efforts made by the League during the pendency of the Morgan and Lodge bills to secure favorable action from Chambers of Commerce, Boards of Trade and other similar organizations. The most important of these, representing every large city of the country, had responded, and copies of the resolutions and memorials adopted had been forwarded to Messrs. Morgan and Lodge and presented in the Senate. The Secretary added that he had been informed by Senator Lodge at the close of the last session that the bill then pending, or a similar measure, would be re-introduced shortly after the assembling of the fifty-fourth Congress.

Mr. Dana stated that Senator Lodge had informed him that the bill would be re-introduced during the present month.

Mr. Siddons asked Mr. Straus whether he would favor the enactment of a law based on the recent executive order. Mr. Straus replied that he probably would, but with something more; the plan if made permanent should be changed in various respects, and competitive examinations should be substituted for the "pass" examinations now proposed.

The president called for a report from the Committee on Legislation, appointed in pursuance of action taken at the September meeting of the Executive Committee. The secretary stated that the committee had not organized, a permanent chairman not having as yet been secured. He had submitted to the individual members of the committee, however, the following proposed measures of legislation:

(1) A bill to exclude political influence in the appointment of postmasters and to assure to postmasters tenure during good behavior.

(2) A bill to provide for the re-organization of the Consular Service.

(3) A bill to prohibit the solicitation of political assessments or contributions, in any manner, from officers or employees of the United States.

(4) A bill to provide for the selection of all laborers employed by the Government, through a system similar to that in operation in the Navy Yard.

(5) A bill to provide for classification under Civil Service rules, of the employees of the District of Columbia.

(6) A bill to give the Civil Service Commission power to investigate all cases of dismissal and, in the course of any inquiry they may make, to administer oaths and examine witnesses.

When the Committee is organized these suggestions would be at once considered, and the work of preparing bills taken up. The bill to re-organize the Consular Service would continue to be the especial charge of the Committee on Consular Reform; that relating to the District of Columbia would be prepared and promoted by the local Association. With both these bodies the committee would confer. The president announced subsequently that he had appointed to the Committee on Legislation Messrs. Sherman S. Rogers, of Buffalo; Dorman B. Eaton, of New York; R. H. Dana, of Cambridge; John C. Rose, of Baltimore, and F. L. Siddons, of Washington, and that Mr. Rogers had consented to serve as chairman.

Mr. Charles W. Stetson, of Washington, read a report of the efforts made by the local association to secure the adoption of civil service rules in the District government.*

Mr. Estes read a letter from a correspondent stating that Hon. J. T. Kilbreth, Collector of the Port of New York, had suggested that action be taken by the League toward securing the transfer of all deputy collectors from the excepted to the competitive list, such a step being, in the opinion of the collector, highly important to continued improvement in the efficiency of the Customs Service.

On motion of Mr. Estes, the matter was referred to the Executive Committee, with the request that a committee of three be appointed to urge the importance of this suggestion upon the Executive.

On motion of Mr. Wood, it was voted that a like committee be appointed by the Executive Committee to urge upon

* Page 129.

the president the importance of taking all assistant postmasters from the excepted list.

Mr. Rogers, for the Committee on Resolutions, read the resolutions prepared, and submitted them to the League for action. Mr. Wyman moved that the resolutions be considered *seriatim* before being adopted in final form, and the motion was carried.

After some preliminary discussion of the report, the president announced that further consideration would be postponed to the afternoon session in order that the delegates might accept the invitation extended by Hon. W. G. Rice, to meet the Civil Service Commissioners at his residence, at one o'clock. On motion the League then adjourned.

COSMOS CLUB, Dec. 13, 1895.

The President took the chair.

Mr. Justi read a paper on " The State of Civil Service Reform Sentiment in the South." *

Dr. E. M. Gallaudet, president of the Gallaudet College for the Deaf and Dumb, made an interesting address on the peculiar value and necessity of Civil Service rules for the selection of employees in institutions for the deaf and dumb under state control. He offered a resolution, with the suggestion that copies be sent by the secretary to the Executive of each state, urging the importance of maintaining the principle of permanent tenure of office during good behavior in institutions for the deaf and dumb, and protesting against the interference of spoils politics in the affairs of such institutions. Mr. Thorp suggested that the recommendation be extended to cover asylums for the blind and other humane institutions. On motion of Mr. Richardson, the resolution was referred to the Committee on Resolutions to be reported by that committee with amendments conforming to the suggestion made.

Mr. Bonaparte read a paper on " The Reign and Overthrow of an Office-holding Oligarchy." †

Mr. Welsh read a paper on " Civil Service Reform in its Bearings upon the Interests of Workingmen." ‡

------

* Page 81.   † Page 100.   ‡ Page 116.

The president then announced the order of miscellaneous business.

The application of the Civil Service Reform Club of Yale University for admission to the League was submitted by the club's representative, Mr. Lanier McKee. The president stated that without the formality of a vote he might assure the new organization of cordial reception to membership.

The report of the Committee on Resolutions was then taken up, and after having been considered, section by section, was adopted unanimously in the following form:

The past year has witnessed a continued and remarkable progress in the Civil Service Reform. It is attested not only by the large extensions made by the President to the classified service, but by the approbation with which those extensions have been received by the people. The testimony of the heads of Departments and Departmental divisions as to the operation of the Reform system in the conduct of the public service, is concurrent and more than ever favorable, and the press, with few exceptions, has given to the movement a support which indicates that in its judgment the experimental period has passed. There are unmistakable indications also that at last the character of the Civil Service Reform is being recognized in the great cities of the country, and that any attempt to remedy the evils which afflict, and to remove the scandals which disgrace municipal life must be futile so long as its public service is in the hands of spoilsmen. The magnificent popular victory in Chicago for Civil Service Reform is the herald of like victories in all the other great cities of the country. The adoption by the State of New York of a constitutional amendment giving to the competitive system the sanction and security of the organic law has been followed by a marked improvement in the administration of the Civil Service law in that State. Only an honest recognition by appointing officers of their plain duty under the Constitution in the appointment and retention of suitable officials seems now to be necessary, in order to give that great State, with its numerous cities, a thorough and harmoniously working system of appointment to office upon the ground of merit and fitness alone.

The League congratulates the country upon the promulgation of the recent plan of the President and the Postmaster-General to consolidate with the principal post-offices the smaller ones surrounding them, so as to make the latter mere branch offices, and on the recent order to place all persons employed therein, including the postmasters of these branch offices, within the classified service. We trust that this plan may be carried out with energy and courage, so that it may receive a prompt and general application.

The League commends the order of President Cleveland of September 20, 1895, concerning the mode of appointing Consular officers, as an effort to promote the efficiency of the service, and as a recognition of the principle that fitness and qualification should control such appointments and promotion. The League recommends that this order be extended to all purely Consular officers whose compensation exceeds $2,500, and that it also include subordinate officers in the Diplomatic service. The League further recommends, in order that the reform be enduring, and that this executive order may not meet the same fate as the similar executive orders of 1866, 1872 and 1873, that a suitable law be enacted by Congress embodying these reforms; and also that such law provide so far as possible for competitive examinations to be conducted by members of the Civil Service Commission.

The League commends the order of the Postmaster-General requiring that no letter-carrier shall be removed except for cause and upon written charges, and it urges the application of a similar rule to other branches of the classified service.

The League renews it demand for the repeal of the law limiting to four years the terms of certain administrative officers as unjust, impolitic, a prolific source of demoralization and mischief to the public service and to our whole political life, and especially calculated to impair the beneficent effects of recent reforms. "Merit appointments must logically be accompanied by merit tenure."

The League recommends that the present law against soliciting contributions for political purposes from federal employees be so amended as to prohibit such solicitations in any manner or place, and that the Civil Service Commission be given the power to compel the attendance of witnesses, and to put them upon oath or affirmation.

The reforms in the federal and State service already made are in the highest degree important and gratifying, but they are only a part of the work to be done. Municipal maladministration is the deepest disgrace, and one of the gravest dangers of the present time. The great spoilsmen of to-day are plundering our cities. Their power to do so lies in their control of the offices; their overthrow would be the substitution for political influence of the merit system as the test of appointment to office. All Municipal Reform must be based upon Civil Service Reform. We therefore urge upon all seeking good government for our cities the paramount importance of securing the adoption therein of the merit system of appointment.

And we respectfully urge upon Congress the extension of this system by law to the District of Columbia.

Mr. Rogers, for the Committee on Resolutions, reported the resolution offered by Dr. Gallaudet, in the following form:

Resolved, That it is of the utmost importance to establish and maintain the principle of permanent tenure of office during good behavior in schools for the education of deafmutes and of the blind, and in charitable, humane, educational and penal institutions. The League indignantly protests against the interference of spoils politics in the management of such schools and institutions, and it urgently demands that the shameful and disastrous abuses now existing be peremptorily forbidden by legislation.

The resolution was adopted unanimously.

The secretary reported for the Publication Committee that in accordance with the direction of the Executive Committee a plan for the future publication of *Good Government*, in connection with the office of the League, in New York City, had been agreed upon. The plan provided, briefly, that the management of the paper be assumed by the secretary, the more active members of the League to assist in the preparation of purely editorial material, and the news columns to contain information concerning the progress of the civil service reform movement similar to that given heretofore in the abstract of the monthly report of the New York Association. The usual departments would be maintained, with special regard to reports from local associations, municipal reform organizations, the College Civil Service Reform League and other bodies. The Washington office would be continued and regular Washington correpondence furnished. The size of the paper would probably be reduced, but every effort would be made to maintain its character as a journal and as the organ of the League.

On motion of Mr. Wyman, the plan submitted was approved, and the arrangement of further details was referred to a committee consisting of Mr. Cary, Mr. Collins and the secretary.

Mr. Davis, of Cincinnati, referring to a suggestion previously made by Mr. Estes, moved that the members of any local association paying annually a stated sum for the purpose, receive *Good Government* without further subscription. Mr. Bonaparte moved, as an amendment, that the plan proposed be referred with power to the Publication Committee. The amendment was accepted and the motion carried.

The secretary read letters from the Round Table Club, and the Old Oak Club, of Nashville, Tenn., inviting the League.

to hold its sixteenth annual meeting in that city. This invitation was endorsed in very cordial terms in a communication signed by the Mayor of Nashville, the president of the Chamber of Commerce, and the president of the Tennessee Centennial Exposition Company.

Mr. Charles P. Noyes stated that he had been commissioned by the Civil Service Reform Association and the Civic Federation of St. Paul, Minn., to invite the League, on their behalf, to hold its next meeting in that city.

Mr. Justi expressed the hope that Nashville would be selected, and assured the League a hearty welcome.

On motion the invitations were referred to the Executive Committee, and the secretary was directed, in acknowledging them, to express the sense of cordial appreciation in which they had been received.

A communication from the Committee on Civil Service of the National Association of Post-Office Clerks, asking that the League recommend to Congress legislation embodying and extending to all branches of the classified postal service the provisions of Postal Order 235, regulating removals, was read by the secretary. On motion the matter was referred to the Committee on Legislation with power to make the recommendation proposed.

A communication from Dr. C. W. Zaremba, suggesting that the League consider the advisability of the establishment by Congress of a National Academy for the preparation of candidates for the higher branches of the Civil Service, was read, and, on motion, referred to the Executive Committee.

On motion of Mr. Reynolds it was unanimously voted that the president be requested to express, on behalf of the League, a grateful appreciation of the hearty reception and generous entertainment it has received at the hands of the Civil Service Reform Association of the District of Columbia.

On motion of Mr. Foulke the thanks of the League were tendered also to the officers and members of the Cosmos Club for the use of the club's headquarters, and to Rev. Dr. Alex. Mackay-Smith and Hon. W. G. Rice, for the hospitality extended by them to the League.

Mr. Thorp moved that the League express its high appreciation of the eloquent and inspiring address delivered publicly by the president, and that the thanks of the League be tendered him. The motion was carried unanimously.

The League then adjourned.

Attest :

GEORGE McANENY,
Secretary.

On the evening of the 13th a reception was tendered by the Civil Service Reform Association, of the District of Columbia, to the visiting delegates, at the Arlington Hotel. Interesting addresses were made in the course of the evening by Rev. Dr. Alexander Mackay-Smith, who presided, Hon. Carl Schurz, Hon. J. Sterling Morton, Secretary of Agriculture, Charles J. Bonaparte, Hon. Sherman S. Rogers, Hon. Everett P. Wheeler, Hon. Wm. Dudley Foulke, Hon. J. H. Eckels, Comptroller of the Currency, and Rt. Rev. John F. Hurst.

The delegates were entertained at luncheon on the 12th, by the Rev. Dr. and Mrs. Mackay-Smith, and on the 13th by Hon. Wm. G. Rice, meeting on the latter occasion, Mr. Rice's associate Civil Service Commissioners, Hon. John R. Procter and Hon. J. B. Harlow, the Postmaster-General, Hon. William L. Wilson, the Secretary of the Interior, Hon. Hoke Smith, and the Secretary of Agriculture, Mr. Morton.

REPORT OF THE TREASURER.

(Summarized.)

GENERAL FUND.

Balance on hand, Dec. 10, 1894, ...		$1,075.03
RECEIPTS.—Contributions.....................	$1,410.50	
Balance of Anti-Spoils League Fund	32.80	
Sale of documents................	26.06	$1,469.36
		———
		$2,544.39
EXPENDITURES :		
Printing and postage.............	$721.17	
Office rent......................	250.00	
Clerk hire......................	377.00	
Paid to William Potts, under resolution of the League..............	550.01	
Traveling expenses................	97.20	
Freight and expressage............	28.02	
Engrossing......................	3.50	
Congressional Record.............	4.00	
Expenses of collections...........	24.90	
Office expenses..................	138.32	2,194.12
		———
Balance on deposit at Continental Trust Co		$350.27

GOOD GOVERNMENT GUARANTEE FUND.

Balance on hand, Dec, 10, 1894, ...		$56.90
RECEIPTS.—Massachusetts Associations........	$965.02	
New York City Association........	520.00	
Philadelphia " ....,	282.36	
Geneva, N. Y. "	30.00	
Norwich, Conn. "	22.00	
Buffalo, N. Y. "	21.60	
Henry Villard...................	75.00	
Theodore Roosevelt.	26.00	1,941.98
		———
		$1,998.88
EXPENDITURES :		
To F. E. Leupp, Editor...........$1,941.60		
Balance of loan paid New York Association........	50.00	1,991.60
		———
Balance on hand at Continental Trust Co....................		$7.28

E. & O. E.

SILAS W. BURT,
Treasurer.

Address of Hon. John W. Ross,

PRESIDENT OF THE BOARD OF DISTRICT COMMISSIONERS.

THE people of this District extend their welcome to all
true and worthy citizens who visit the capital, but the warmth
of the greeting is intensified when their guests are such eminent and public spirited men as those who compose the Civil
Service Reform League. To my mind the success of the
work in which you are engaged is one of the signs of the time
that this old world of ours is growing wiser and better.
Thoughtful men of all of the political parties have for years
recognized the truth that in selecting employees for municipal,
state or national governments, the same test should be applied
as would be applied in the selection of employees for any great
business enterprise, viz.: fitness for the place, and competency
to return an equivalent for the salary paid. The main differences of opinion have been with regard to how to apply that
test, and so it has taken time to vindicate the system
embodied in the national civil service law. Criticisms
mainly with regard to these details, some just, and many more
unjust, indulged in by men of public standing, have hampered
the cause, but during the years since 1883 the results have
been so beneficent and so satisfactory that the great majority
of the American people, whose chief desire is wise and
honest and economical administration of their affairs, will
never consent to a repeal of this law, nor to any modification which implies a step backward. And from my standpoint the fairest field for the work in which you are
engaged is the municipality. Now, this District, as you are
aware, is a municipal corporation established by an Act of
Congress, and the municipal officers who serve therein, feel a
heavy responsibility in certain directions; they are municipal
officers who are the mere trustees for the people who reside
within their jurisdiction and their business agents. If the
municipal appointing officer is true to his trust, he will, in

making appointments, be governed by the accepted replies to those old fashioned questions with regard to the applicant; is he capable, is he honest? in the same manner as he would if he were a director of a bank, or the proprietor of a great business enterprise. Now the civil service system gives a mode of answering these questions. In this District, while the government is the creature of Congress and subject at any time to its control or to its criticism, it is not such a branch of the general government as would bring it within the purview of the Civil Service law. For many years the teachers in the grades of our public schools have been appointed upon merit wholly. The graduates of our normal school are appointed teachers in the order of their standing in that school. Teachers who have the right to teach because they have passed the examinations, and hold certificates. are appointed in the order of their standing at the examination As a result we have good schools and capable teachers. The commissioners have worked unaided, and enforced a kind of Civil Service system in other respects. They have during the past months held examinations of their own for various positions— for policemen, for clerical positions, and for technical positions of some kinds. They have done the best they could. But we have no funds at our command for such a purpose, and we want you to aid us. You will do so by helping to place us within the strong protection of the law passed by the American Congress, and approved by the President of the United States, giving us the duty as well as the right to have civil service examinations. And this is all the more necessary because every other department of the United States Government is under that protection. What is the result? Our poor little District Government the resort of every man who wants a place, and of every influential government official who asks to have his friends appointed. The result is many times an absolute interruption of the public business. I believe that even the Members and Senators themselves will gladly coöperate to this end. Nobody knows better than they do that what is called "patronage" is a source of weakness and of danger rather than of strength. No one knows better than they that every appointing officer in every appointment is likely to make, in the words of the old saying "Ten enemies and one ingrate."

Now I beg your pardon for bringing a matter so personal as this to your attention, and I beg to express to you the pleasure we feel in the fact that you have selected our city for your meeting place. I know the character of your local committees, and their ability to entertain you, and I doubt not that you will be so entertained that when you leave for your homes it will be with the desire to come again to your own capital city.

The Appointment and Tenure of Postmasters.

By RICHARD HENRY DANA.

It is a curious fact about our so-called "American" Spoils system in politics, that we spoil not a distant enemy, nor even some other race living in our midst, as the Turks do the Armenians, but we despoil ourselves in making spoils of our own institutions. Nowhere is this better illustrated than in the postal service of the United States.

Our post-office department is the largest department in the country, and on its efficient management depends much of our material and intellectual progress as well as our daily convenience, and yet we have been letting our representatives strengthen their political fences by making frequent changes and unfit appointments, in a way that would ruin any business exposed to open competition. As a result, we have the worst postal service of any civilized country in the world. In Tokio, Japan, they had quite recently more frequent deliveries than in New York City, and there are improvements adopted in England, France, Germany and Italy twenty and thirty years ago which we have not yet adopted at all, or only partially and imperfectly. For example, in the large cities of those countries there are numerous branch offices, so numerous as to be for all practical purposes as accessible as letter boxes with us, where stamps or money orders can be bought, where parcels can be weighed, and where matter can be mailed. When with us a note is dropped into a letter box, there it lies untouched for one, two or three hours, till the collector takes it out, and it is not assorted till the collector deposits it at the post-office. When, however, it is mailed in one of these branch offices abroad, it is immediately cancelled and assorted, so that the time which would be wasted in the letter box, is utilized and the note is ready for direct delivery at the first call of the carrier.

This expedites the local city deliveries, so that a note mailed at a branch office is delivered almost as quickly as if sent by a private special messenger, and this again so stimulates the local use of the mails that the extra expense is reported to be more than made up by the increased sale of postage stamps.

For some twenty years or more we did nothing towards adopting this plan, and not only was all the time lost while the mail was waiting in the letter box, but a letter posted within half a mile of its destination often had to be carried two, three, or even four miles to the central office to be assorted, and then to travel all the way back, going over perhaps eight miles in all to accomplish a half a mile. We have very tardily adopted in some of our largest cities a few branch offices, but so few and far between that they do not half serve their purpose.

This is only one of numerous instances that could be cited to illustrate how much our postal system has been spoiled.

Not only in detail has it been thus spoiled, but so much have the postmasters-general and their assistants been occupied with the distribution of patronage that they have not had the time to attend to the organization of the department.

For example, a business man appointed postmaster General writes to some of the model postmasters to consult with him on the business of the service. On account of the pressure of Congressmen he is unable to fix a date before the June after his inauguration in March, but even then these model postmasters get no further than his ante-room, where they vainly wait many valuable hours, while the office-seekers, under the wing of members of Congress, pass in before them. At last, after about a week of waiting, one of these model postmasters gets into the inner room, and finds the Postmaster General engaged in a discussion with a negro postmaster of a small town in the South over the question whether the appointment should not be revoked, not on the ground of unfitness, but because of a rumor that this negro had once attended a Democratic caucus. After some quarter of an hour consumed over this question, so vastly important to the postal service, the Postmaster-General has a moment or two to shake hands and explain that the business consultation must be postponed till the next August, as he is overwhelmed with the pressure for places. This story I tell not as illustrating the work of any one man, but of the heretofore usual duties of this cabinet position in general.

As a result, the organization of the department is on the same basis that it was under Franklin, when there were 75 post-offices in the country. When ordinary business grows large it is subdivided. The express companies, for example, are divided into districts, with a superintendent for each. So with the great railroads and with the post-offices in Great Britain; so with an army. But in the United States postal service there is nothing between the bureau at Washington and the postmasters. It is like an army with no majors, no colonels, no brigadier generals; in fact, with no officers between the general-in-chief with his staff and the captains of companies.

All the questions relating to the wants of the various postmasters have practically to be passed on by two clerks at Washington, who are too far off to be able to judge of the circumstances. Apparently they have to decide by lot in most cases, granting one-fourth or one-eighth of the requests, as it may be, in proportion to the appropriation. For example, from the Boston post-office is sent a request for a New England Directory; price $7.50. The request is denied. As a consequence a clerk at a salary of $750 a year has to be detailed to make out a list of names needing further addresses, go out and look over the directories belonging to some business men, as a favor, and bring back the desired addresses, to the great loss of money to the office and delay to the re-addressed letters.

Again, here are two towns, one 25 and the other 29 miles from Boston, and about four miles apart, with railroad connection between them. The letters from one to the other are sent all the way to Boston, there to be assorted and sent back to the other town, taking on an average about a day and a half. There is much correspondence between the two places. Who is to make the short cut?

The only persons officially charged with changing the routes are in Washington. They have no idea of the merits of the case. The postmasters of these two towns may write to Washington, but it is supererogation on their part if they do, and they are usually told, in reply, to attend to their own business. The only way to have the change made is for the prominent men of both towns to bring pressure to bear on the department and to make the life of their Congressman miserable till, after perhaps two years of agitation, at a great personal sacrifice, the change is at last made.

Indeed it is one of the greatest tributes possible to the versatility and natural business talent of the American people that amid all these frequent political changes of postmasters and this utter want of organization the business of the department is carried on at all.

That the people of the United States do not rise and demand a better service is because they have not seen any better, and do not know of the possibilities of a really good post-office department. It is only a small portion of the small minority who travel abroad that have intelligently observed and compared our postal system and that of other civilized countries.

Let us only hope that the future historian may not judge our present advancement in civilization and intelligence by the workings of the greatest of our national departments. If any proof is required that it is the spoils system which has spoiled our postal service, it is to be found in the records of the railway mail service. For a number of years there has been kept a separate account of the number of pieces correctly distributed in that branch of the service and the number of errors. During the twelve months covered by the last year of the administration of President Arthur, following a previous Republican administration, in neither of which was the railway mail service looted, though the appointments were confessedly political, the number of correct distributions to one error had reached the high number of 5,575. On the incoming of the Cleveland administration many removals were made on political grounds, and the record fell to 3,364, rising again to nearly 4,000, after the men had got used to their work, in the last year of his administration. On the incoming of the Harrison administration, as all will remember, the railway mail service was looted, and that with unprecedented rapidity of removals, as the civil service law was to go into operation a few months after the inauguration. As a result, the number of correct distributions fell to 2,834 to each error, the lowest number on record. Since then the railway mail has been under civil service rules. In two years it reached the highest previous record, the next year passed it, last year came up to 7,831, and this year (1895) to the truly wonderful record of 8,894. To fortify these telling statistics let me quote from the language of the General Superintendent of the Railway Mail Service * the following : " The civil service laws and regulations as applied to the Railway Mail Service accomplish all the most sanguine expected. The eligibles for appointment who have been certified and selected excel in the fundamental qualities, such as suitable age, good physical condition and habits, activity and retentiveness of memory, and prospective growth and length of useful service.

Having such desirable undeveloped material to work upon, the management experience less difficulty in molding it into well-disciplined, industrious, thoughtful, efficient clerks. A much larger per cent. of the probationers succeed in earning permanent appointments, and under the system of development which obtains in the service, they continue to improve during their connection with it; and, as opportunities occur, are advanced in class according to their merits. In the judgment of this office, the present efficiency could not have been obtained under any other method."

Again, the record in the post-offices outside of the railway mail tells the same story. It is well remembered how rapidly the official heads of the postmasters fell under the axe of the headsman Mr. Clarkson. As a result, the number of complaints the next year increased 36 per cent., and the number of "losses chargeable to carelessness or depredation of postal employees" increased 64 per cent., according to the official reports.†

Important as are efficiency and economy in our vast postal business, yet these are not the subjects that concern us most. Were they the only issues, we should not be here. It is because of the corrupting influence of the spoils system on our politics and the danger to our liberties that so many busy persons annually meet to discuss the reform of our civil service. In no branch is the danger to our liberties so great as in the postal service. It composes more than half of our whole civil list. There are over 70,000 postmasters, or about one to every 130 voters; and if every postmaster can muster five friends,

---

* Report P. M. Gen'l 1894, p. 395.
† Reports of the Postmaster General, 1889, p. 167, and 1890, pp. 177 and 179.

they together make 420,000, one in 29 voters, or a clear majority of all persons taking an active part in our nominating machinery. The postmasters, being scattered in every village and hamlet in the country, are from their situation more useful in manipulating delegates to large conventions than the same number of employees gathered together in one or two places. As to corruption, we have seen the bargaining of postmaster-ships at conventions in trade for votes of delegates, to say nothing of selling them by Congressmen or defeated candi-dates for Congress of the dominant party for ready money.

We give special welcome, therefore, to the messenger bring-ing us news that the postmasterships, or any number of them, have permanently been fortified against the raids of the Kurd-ish-like spoilsmen, and the recent order of the President has a peculiar and almost absorbing interest; it cheers the heart and brings hope to the breast.

Those, who have given special attention for several years past to the possible ways of bringing postmasters under the reform system, agree that if the plan contemplated in this order is carried out we shall have the most important, if not the greatest in number, of the postmasters taken out of politics, and incidentally the business organization of the postal depart-ment greatly improved.

In 1889 I read a paper before this League on the subject, "The Post-Offices to be Taken out of Politics." The plan I suggested was, first, dividing the country into postal districts, with a superintendent over each; next, appointing the presi-dential postmasters by way of promotion of other postmasters or of postal employees within the classified service of the dis-trict, putting all fourth class postmasters with a salary above $500. under civil service rules, and for the rest of the places, with lower salaries, to make the declaration by law or executive order that neither removals nor appointments should be made on political grounds, allowing no removals except after a hear-ing and on the reports of post-office inspectors who were then as now under civil service rules, and that appointments should be made under regulations substantially like those incorporated in what has since been called the Lodge Bill for the appoint-ment of fourth-class postmasters.

The plan now proposed by the President and Postmaster General is to consolidate as far as possible neighboring offices with larger ones, as has been so successfully done in Boston and its vicinity, only including many more post-offices, so that all the post-offices in the eastern part of Massachusetts, for example, should be part of the Boston office. In this way the districting of the post-offices is largely effected. Next, all the offices thus consolidated, including the postmasters of the annexed offices, who will henceforward be superintendents, are by the order put under civil service rules. In this way most of those who have heretofore been presidential postmasters of the second and third classes will be appointed by promotion, and the lower positions will be filled by competitive examination conducted by the civil service commission.

By making the postmasters of the subordinate offices into superintendents, our old enemy, the four-year law of 1820, is shorn of more than half its power for ill, for second and third class presidential postmasters made up more than half of all the officers to whom the law applied.

One difficulty, however, still remains, and that is to decide how to treat the fourth-class postmasters with small salaries. In order to understand the situation, it must be remembered that of the 66,500 fourth-class postmasters the average salary is only $167 a year, and about 47,000 have a salary of under $200.

If a clerk with a salary of $750 a year were substituted for each fourth-class postmaster, it would cost the department $39,000,000 a year. By the new order, however, the difficulty seems to be less than it would be under the operation of the Lodge Bill alone. If any fourth-class post-office, consolidated under the order has too small a salary to invite competition, it can be treated just as some other places for which there is no competition are now treated under the civil service rules. If no persons apply for a competitive examination for a position, then none is held, and a pass one is substituted. (Clause 7, section 2, of the civil service law.) The only precaution necessary is not to allow promotion from positions so filled without an examination which is competitive, so as to prevent a well known way of evading the law. This point seems to be at least partly covered by the civil service rules now in force. (General Rule III., clause 2 (c), and Postal Rule 2, clause 6). But I believe many persons would apply for competition for a position under this order, with its possible promotion ahead, who would never do so for the place alone by itself. But few would care to embark in a small boat to cross the ocean, with the additional risk of being tipped out on purpose when not quarter through the voyage, but many will gladly get in a small boat to be rowed to a larger vessel, with a good chance of staying aboard the latter till transferred to still larger.

Again, it must be remembered that many fourth-class post-masters are allowed to supplement their salaries by keeping a store or by being a clerk in a store in which the office is situated, just as is the case with some of the smaller consulates. Indeed. it is the custom the post-office brings to the store that gives the post-office its chief value in many small towns.

Under the order and proposed plan of extensive consolidation we shall have some 3,000 presidential post-offices taken out of the operation of the four-year-term law, and these, together with their subordinates and perhaps at first 5,000 fourth-class postmasters, and later possibly 20,000 more, put under civil service rules. Every one who enters at the lower grades knows he has entered a profession where he may, by faithful and able work, rise to the head of a large consolidated post-office, and we also get a substantial subdivision of the post-offices into districts, with a head postmaster in charge of each.

This is a most important gain. It will eventually bring under civil service rules twice as many new positions as were originally classified when the Pendleton Bill was passed.

On the basis of the present national civil service, the additions under this order will make the whole classified service nearly if not more than one-half the whole civil list.

With this it seems the back of the spoils monster is broken, and it only remains for us to complete the work in good fashion.

To complete the work as far as the post-office department is concerned, for the places above the scope of the present plan the four-year law should be repealed either by law or in substance by establishing an executive custom of reappointing the postmasters at the head of these consolidated offices on the expiration of their terms and filling vacancies among these postmasters by promotion, and also by putting all the positions except those of Postmaster General and his private secretary within the classified service, and, for the places below the scope of this present order, namely, the scattered fourth-class offices with small salaries, too distant from a large office to be consolidated, I should apply the principles of the Lodge Bill* for selection of applicants; and to that I should add that no removals should be made except after giving the postmaster notice of the charges and a chance to be heard, and only on the report of the inspector or other official before whom the hearing took place. By the official report of an "off year" for political changes (1887), it appears that more than one-half the removals were made on reports of inspectors. Why not require that all removals should be made on official reports? Suspension during investigation would cover all cases of need of immediate procedure on account of criminal acts.

When all this is done, and when some more extensions in other departments, now contemplated which, I am informed, will include some 17,000 more places, have been made, we may know that not only is the back of the spoils monster broken, but that the work of extermination is practically completed, and we may prepare to attend the funeral obsequies, keeping, however, our eye open all the while and our hand at the sword hilt, lest some hydra head spring to life again.

* H. R. Doc., No. 7707, 51st Congress, 1st session.

The Important Function of Civil Service Reform.

By F. L. Siddons.

As the movement known as Civil Service Reform gains in the respect and good-will of the American people, and its principles are extended to the various forms of government that exist in this Republic, civil service reformers and friends of good government generally must of necessity busy themselves with the many details involved in the labor of giving legal expression and effect to those principles, which this organization, in a large degree, stands for and represents. But their zeal in the labor alluded to is greatly misapprehended if it is supposed that it is inspired only by the conviction that the system of examing applicants for admission to, or promotion in, the Government service, to test their efficiency, is superior to the old method, which made party or personal reasons alone the "open sesame" to Government employment. For irrational, unjust, and quite indefensible as the old method was, and, alas! still is, it would not in itself, and merely because it was and is irrational and unjust as a method of supplying Government servants, have earned for itself the undying hostility of so many who count country above party and justice above the supposed requirements of political obligation.

No! Back of a mere method of how persons should get into or out of Government service lie questions of far greater moment to the welfare of the country. Questions that indeed claim the anxious thoughts of every lover of our institutions, and upon a right answer to which much of consequence to America depends.

Let us for a moment consider them.

It can hardly be denied that a Government organized upon the theory of the consent of the governed, and which derived all its powers and functions from the people whom it is to protect and rule, must depend for its success and permanence upon the freedom and ease with which its citizens are permitted to give expression to their wishes and desires, and their "consent" obtained in all matters concerning their social and political well-being. It has long been our boast that the United States of America afford to the world a striking example of such a government—a government quickly responding to the needs and aspirations of its people, and knowing no claims but those of equal justice to all within the sphere of its jurisdiction. This is our boast. But can we make it good?

Review the political history of the country for the past seventy years with unbiased minds and we must frankly confess that some of our most cherished institutions have become mere delusions. Who believes to-day that a single important elective office is filled by the free choice of the electors? Who doubts that much of the most needed legislation must be *purchased*, if obtainable at all? And to whom must the people go for permission to elect their servants or to procure the enactment of their laws? To organized bands of political freebooters or to single individuals who have reached a position of political power quite inexplicable, when their education, honesty or ability are borne in mind. What an extraordinary spectacle is presented when a great city is completely dominated for years by a little coterie of ignorant men, who turn out to be, as was long suspected, common thieves, and when the first flood of public indignation has ebbed after engulfing the rogues, the same metropolis in a little while is again in the possession of another set of equally ignorant and corrupt individuals, who, more daring than their predecessors, extend their evil influence and control until a State is in their hands, and they reach up and out for larger spoil. How comes this about? The answer is at hand. By a systematic debauching of the political conscience of the electors. By appeals to their ignorance, cupidity or necessities. *By the bribe of office.* How many leaders of movements for the public good have been tempted and fallen and their cause betrayed by the snare of public place set in their pathway by those who held the key to what has been aptly called a "vast bribery chest." And bribery such as this is not checked by Australian ballot laws or proportional representation.

To destroy the "bribery chests," the one hope of the political striker and boss; to restore the freedom of speech and political action of the voter: to make our public servants truly the servants of the public; to clear the way for those industrial and economic reforms made necessary by the greatly changed industrial and economic conditions of the country; in fine to make our government, in its best and truest sense, "a government of the people," is the *important function* of Civil Service Reform.

Results of Recent Agitation of Consular Service Reform. Their Value. What Next?

By Jonathan A. Lane,

Ex-President of the Boston Merchants' Association.

The invitation, Mr. President, and gentlemen of the National Civil Service League, to take some small part in a discussion of the Consular Service at this, your annual gathering, in the capital of the nation, is something from which the average business man may becomingly shrink. We look to you as men who represent the scholar in public affairs, who unite with patriotic purpose the legal and learned attainments which enable you to present your views in such a, perhaps, academic way, that you command the attention of educated and thinking men at home and abroad. You will, therefore, considerately accept from us only such a way of treating the subject as we are accustomed to in our business and home circles. And also we may be allowed to suggest also that so far as we have anything to say we shall deem it wise to consider mainly the present condition of things in regard to this important part of the great civil service of the country.

The recent agitation directed to this particular cause was begun about two years ago in the city of Boston—it has since been vigorously prosecuted in all sorts of ways in all our country and unmistakably it has produced results. What are they? What is their value? What next?

Action of The State Department.

While the recent action of the State Department has been widely, and I think in general favorably regarded by the press of the country, it does not occur to me that any commercial body has taken specific action thereon except the Boston

Merchants' Association, whose early interest in the subject
made it quite proper they should do so. And at the meeting
of the Board of Directors in November the following votes
were adopted :

" That the Boston Merchants' Association appreciate and approve the
recent action of the Department of State as announced and published in
Consular Reports Oct. 4.

" That the communication to the President by Richard Olney, Secretary of State, upon 'which this action was based,' does great credit to
our fellow-citizen, who, in this transaction, represents the best political
sentiments of Massachusetts and of the country.

" That the order of President Cleveland that hereafter vacancies in
the Consular service below a certain grade shall be filled by the appointment of persons who, by present or past service, or by proper examination, have in character and capacity shown their fitness, is an important
step in the right direction ; and, while it is not a surrender by the Chief
Executive of the nation of his constitutional prerogatives, it should inaugurate a better system of appointments—one which will give to the Consular service a stability and usefulness it does not now possess.

" That this initial action on the part of the Administration will
achieve its best results when the Department of State in conjunction, it
may be with the War Department, to which largely all Consular reports
are referred, shall have such a 'digest' made of every Consular post as
has been recommended in reports emanating from this body and from
the National Board of Trade, and has otherwise been made known to the
State Department. We do not understand that such action would call
for any legislation by Congress or involve any great cost beyond what is
usual in the service, and it is conceded by those who have duly considered it that such full and correct information of the requirements and
possibilities of every field to which our Representatives are sent would be
invaluable to the Administration in making its appointments and to our
Consuls in the discharge of their chief duty, which is to protect and extend the commercial interests of the country they represent.

" That such action as we recommend, supplementing that already
taken, will make a new epoch in the history of our Consular service, will
open new fields to American enterprise, strengthen our national resources,
advance the nation's honor, and give to the Administration which shall
have secured it a high place in the records of our national growth and
prosperity."

These views are a declaration of recent results which are
of great interest, and are also an expression of their value—
together with a recommendation of what in the judgment of
the Boston association should follow. It is quite possible
this league may not it all in the same favorable light. I will
name some of the considerations which had influence with us.

The communication to the President by the Secretary of State contained the admission of that for which we have contended, "That if our Consular service were what it should be, and our officials chosen for their fitness for the duties to be discharged by them, the result to the trade and commerce of the country would be of the most favorable character as is supported by the practice and experience of Great Britain and other countries."

We believe this declaration from the State Department will command attention in every commercial port in the world, and it will be felt that at last our government is getting its eyes open. Every able and useful American Consul will rejoice at the attitude his country has taken, and will become greatly interested in the methods which the Government will speedily apply to correct existing evils in the matter of appointments and length of service. Every public servant abroad who holds his office with utter indifference to and contempt of everything except the political influence which gave him his place, will begin to see "the handwriting on the wall"—a new light shining amidst the semi-obscurity which has so long reigned, and it may constrain him to become a better public servant at once, while there is time, or to prepare to get out.

Again we are grateful that while considerate reference is made to the recent attempts of Congress to reform the service, it is admitted that the Executive branch of the Government should "most naturally take the initial step." This is what we have always felt to be the wiser way. It must be a matter of doubt and uncertainty to what extent a constitutional right can be circumscribed or abridged. The President's oath of office binds him to fidelity in his appointments, and the Senate has the right to reject them. In any new departure, by which this system is to be radically changed, should not the will of the Executive go before? If he stands in the way there can be no progress. If he leads the way, there may be all we require! Again, this action of the President and his Secretary of State, makes distinct reference to the civil service act which authorizes the President to prescribe rules for the admission of persons into the civil service of the United States, and is unmistakably an effort to get the Consular service onto the same footing. If this candidate for admission into our political church is not disposed, as a condition therefor, to be immersed, and is willing to be well sprinkled with civil service reform principles and methods, it would seem to be good policy to take him in, in the hope that later he will fill all the conditions, and get in all over!

And what is perhaps best of all, Secretary Olney admits that the order he recommends " is in no sense final or exhaustive. Experience is to show in what respect it may be amended or enlarged—that it will be a step in the right direction—and a step to be judged of, not by the advance itself makes, but by the advance it may rightly be expected inevitably to lead to."

These words redeem this action from some of its defects, and plainly indicate a spirit and purpose on the part of this Administration to bring us at length to a Consular service which shall not be inferior to that of any nation, and, recalling the past, justifies our exclamation that Massachusetts in Secretary Olney has redeemed herself, and that both the President and his Secretary of State deserve the thanks of all civil service reformers and good citizens.

CONTRARY VIEWS CONSIDERED.

But, as I have already intimated, these views and conclusions are not entertained by everybody. A leading citizen of Boston, hearing that at the time being in Washington, I had expressed to Mr. Olney satisfaction at so much of what the department had done as was then published, called my attention to an editorial in the New York Journal of Commerce—by no means a Republican organ—which condemned the whole scheme as insincere and worthless, and which my friend approved as conclusive and correct.

I suppose the New York members of this body will recall this criticism. It was published Sept. 26, and was entitled " Attempted Reform of Consular Appointments."

It procceds to show " that it only includes a part of the service—with vital modifications of the civil service—the appointing power remains the selecting power, which is the essence of the spoils system, the rules promulgated are made for the President's own guidance, and the matter remains where it always has been in the executive discretion. What is wanted is a President who will refrain from making a clean sweep, and who will not wait till he has filled all the places with his own partisans before he invokes the merit system for the protection of the service."

I think it is true that a serious defect exists in the order of the Secretary of State creating the Board of Examiners This is composed of three persons, entirely within the State Department. If in this respect it had conformed to the Morgan Senate bill of 1894, which provides "that the President shall appoint a board, consisting of five members, who are to be the Civil Service Commission and two officers of the State Department," it would have been such a recognition of the United States Civil Service Board as would have gratified that body and the public generally. It certainly would disarm largely such criticisms as I have cited. I think I am justified, however, in saying that Mr. Olney has some doubts as to the composition of this board, for in his order he says : "Such changes in the membership thereof as experience may prove to be desirable will be dealt with by additional regulations as occasion may require." It would, therefore, be quite in order for this league or the National Board of Trade, or for Congress, in any bill, to endeavor to secure this needed change as something that will greatly advance the contemplated reform and greatly encourage all who feel the importance of sustaining the United States Civil Service Commission and its cause.

But after all it would seem as if the gravamen of this sweeping condemnation is "that the Chief Executive of the nation is still at the head in this business, he will do about what he pleases and the matter remains where it always has been—there is practically no change."

VIEWS OF HON. O. S. STRAUS.

Perhaps some of you may remember a well guarded paragraph in the instructive address of Hon. O. S. Straus, ex-Minister to Turkey, a year ago before this body, as follows:

"The Constitution provides that the President shall nominate and by and with the advice and consent of the Senate shall appoint Ambassadors, other public Ministers and Consuls. It is evident no Congressional enactment can abrogate this constitutional right of the President and perhaps cannot abridge it. The result is possible that any regula-lation made by the President could be entirely ignored by his successor. This fact, however, need not discourage us, for if a President will at the 'outset' of his term adopt regulations for reforming the service and make his appointments accordingly it may be perhaps assumed that public opinion will influence and sustain his successor in following the same course."

The wisdom of these words will not be disputed.

PRESIDENTIAL PREROGATIVES.

The President of the United States by his high office inherits the privilege of these appointments. Under no other limitations or restrictions than his oath of office and the approval of that potential body, the Senate, which very naturally has come into a sort of joint proprietorship in this patronage, by virtue of its authority and power therein. At the "outset" of Mr. Cleveland's Administration, we may perhaps admit conditions were not favorable—the pressure upon the President was very great, and the Department of State was not manned as it is to-day. Therefore no such action as we are discussing did take place. Now, then, I would respectfully submit for the consideration of this body to what extent should the present incumbent of the Presidential office, under these circumstances make rules and regulations concerning the Consular service, which would seem to circumscribe and abridge the privileges and the inherited rights of his successor? Of course it is intended that this policy shall be transmitted to the next Administration, otherwise it would not, or should not, have been entered upon—and upon that excellent rule, good in affairs both national and personal, which in some sense here unite—"put yourself in his place."

Is Mr. Cleveland to be condemned by considerate, fair-minded men for going no further in these rules than he felt it was becoming and proper for his Administration to go? He reserves Consulships above the salary of $2500, for which this New York critic also condemns him. What limitation would this editor suggest, if any? And why not, with equal propriety, demand that he should have gone as far as the Morgan bill in a reformation of the Consular and Diplomatic service? Mr. Cleveland has gone slow in this movement, which, it is to be confessed, is quite in contrast with the too rapid gait which characterized his changes in the Consular service at the beginning of his Administration. It remains for his successor, the incoming President, to show the country that the opportunity reserved for him to make further extension of the civil service system and to do much more, and to do it better, will be eagerly embraced, and that Mr. Straus' admirable suggestion—that it be done at the outset of the succeeding Administration—will not be forgotten! The party in power, which shall in this business take the most liberal non-partisan stand, will earn the lasting gratitude as well as the admiration of the country.

What Congressional Action Next.

What next? is that part of our topic which, no doubt, will the most engage your interest and create the most discussion. A year ago we were all looking to the Senate Committee on Foreign Relations, and the press and commercial bodies were commending the Morgan bill, in which the junior Senator from Massachusetts was greatly interested. Of course, then, the Administration had made no sign, and we knew nowhere else to turn. The report of the Committee of the National Board of Trade in January last, with some hesitation and an inadequate discussion (for the Senate bill to which I have referred was, as finally agreed upon, reported so late that it was impossible to consider it) did recommend such Congressional action as the bill embodied, leaving it to be perfected afterward. It was felt that any bill which promised to take the Consular service out of the " spoils system " must be worth something to the country and the cause, and such was the judgment of our friend, Mr. Roosevelt. Therefore, hoping against hope, and knowing the fate of all bills of this kind in the past, we have urged its passage at that or a succeeding Congress.

This initial action of the President has, however, altered the situation. With the slight change I have suggested in the Board of Examiners, it would seem as if the Consular Service might be lifted at once to a higher level, and the necessity does not exist, as it did, for immediate legislation of such a sweeping character as has been contemplated by Senators Morgan and Lodge. There is certainly more reason and opportunity for calm and considerate action than there was, and the increased uncertainty of any legislation being accomplished in this direction by the present Congress is likely to give us time to see if something better cannot be done. I find the impression is very strongly and widely entertained that Congress does not at the present time, in view of the great civil and commercial changes which are taking place in the world, know enough about the Consular Service of the United States—what it is called upon to do, what it is possible for it to do under present conditions, wherein it is at a disadvantage in the same field with the representatives of other nations and what should be done at once to place it upon an equal footing with them. Pertinent to these investigations will come the question of such a compensation to the United States representative as shall correspond to the service required. We think in this respect there should be a new deal all around, so that it shall not be charged that we are making great demands in regard to the quality of the service we are to receive and quite neglect to follow the simplest rules of justice and right in regard to the equivalent therefor. If the Consular Service is " business," it should be paid on business principles, and the Government "is penny wise and pound foolish" in not demanding in places, too numerous to mention, the best talent and qualifications and paying for them accordingly.

VIEWS OF HON. J. R. LEESON.

The Hon. J. R. Leeson, my successor as President of the Boston Merchants' Association, has been abroad this summer as one of a board of Commissioners appointed by Gov. Greenhalge to investigate the subject of public ownership of docks. They visited seventeen ports in Great Britain and Northern Europe, and Mr. Leeson took special pains to get all the information he had time to get concerning the Consular Service at these seventeen important posts. They were all apparently well manned and all these Consuls were found to be greatly interested and well-informed as to what was being done here to improve the service. Mr. Leeson had a chance to see the conditions under which they were required to do their work, and to contrast it with the pay rendered in this country for corresponding services, and the pay received by British Consuls at the same port, and he returned with very positive views on the whole subject, which I do not wish to anticipate too much, as Mr. Leeson is a delegate to the National Board of Trade, which meets in Washington next month, where the subject will be discussed as it was a year ago.

VIEWS OF HON. P. A. COLLINS.

Our Consul General in London, Gen. Collins, in an interview with Mr. Leeson, was strong in the conviction that Congress should look into the whole business before it undertakes to pass such a bill as that I have referred to. Wise legislation is always supposed to be based upon complete information, and this information we do not now possess.

CONGRESSIONAL COMMISSION.

I am aware that the suggestion of an able Congressional Commission, composed of three from the House, two from the Senate and two from citizens generally, would not be granted cheerfully or at once. But such a body of men, all of them carefully selected for their fitness and fidelity to make such an investigation, is recommended by those who have given the subject much thought, and it could not fail to be worth all it would cost to Congress and the country. We believe that President Cleveland would make such appointments in this case as would be satisfactory to the country, and ensure the best results from the Administration which shall follow him.

SENATOR HENRY CABOT LODGE.

In this connection we venture to express the hope that the junior Senator from Massachusetts—who has spent the summer in Europe, visiting many places—has taken equal pains with my friend in Boston to study the Consular system, at least to some extent, on the ground, where its good and its evil are alike laid bare to the observation of such a student of men and measures as Mr. Lodge's career shows him to be. We think it would help him and us to determine "what next" is needed in this cause.

But you will have observed, gentlemen, that the Boston Merchants' Association makes a very positive recommendation—one which it has urged before—that the State and

Treasury Departments shall, without delay, have made a complete digest of the United States Consulates. This does not mean an expensive, though valuable, commission, nor a Consular inspection, which, as they are ordinarily created, have been of a value less than any cost, whether great or small, which they incur. To express the purpose of a digest in easy terms, we might fairly call it " a still hunt in the Consular field, which will bag more game for the outlay than can be got in any other way," and which we have specially favored because it seemed to be so entirely within the reach and range of the State and Treasury Departments. One of the definitions of this term " digest " so admirably fits this case that we prefer it to any other—"to get an understanding of; to comprehend."

We claim that the Departments of State and of the Treasury, while they have Consular reports in stacks and by the cord, have not reduced to ready use and properly and methodically classified and arranged such knowledge of the chief Consulates, their duties, their conditions and their possibilities, as a good business policy would demand and as would be invaluable in determining the fitness and requirements of the appointee. It is a lamentable fact that oftentimes the applicant for such service is obliged to look abroad for information as to what will be required of him, and were this information available at headquarters, Washington, it would serve often either to deter him from a service for which he was entirely disqualified or to stimulate the applicant either to fit himself for this post or to take one within the range of his capabilities.

We expect Consuls to exercise a wise supervision and judgment upon all invoices to which they give their official approval as to value, etc. How can this be done in a port from which there are large exportations of textile and other fabrics when the Consul is entirely ignorant of all such merchandise, and, by his experience and training is utterly incapable of having any opinion or influence in the matter of values ?

In these days of ad valorem duties the loss to the Government in not having valuations looked into and criticised, where they are made solely in the interests of the foreign manufacturer, is not easily estimated. There can be no doubt it would a hundred-fold exceed the cost of any such looking into the business of these various ports as our scheme for a digest involves. And again what are the opportunities of extending American commerce in such places ? It will be found that the American Consul in some ports has done a great deal in this way, and that in others he is not only indifferent, but is almost a stumbling block in the way. The work of our Consuls should be weighed and measured in this regard, as the great business establishments of this country measure the value of the service of their heads of departments by the results accomplished. Uncle Sam is doing business in all parts of the world, and our Consuls are his representatives, and, in some sense, heads of departments in the fields assigned them. If they do not improve their opportunities to the extent of a reasonable possibility, they are not desirable public servants. If they do, it should be recognized and rewarded.

How to Secure a Digest.

But we must hasten on to this next thought :—How to make the digest. How can such a collection of all the facts and conditions which attach to every important Consular post be thus collated, condensed and made to serve the object we aim at ? It can be done by first finding the man, and then by quietly sending him to do the work. He may be some very able Consul or Consul General in the service. He may be one who has been in the service for a considerable term of years, during which he has illustrated in his own career that fitness required for this special service. We need not say that he should possess the qualities of thoroughness, independence, impartiality and an admirable discretion. That he should know European languages ; that he should have the entrée into the best commercial and social circles by virtue of his personal fitness and reputation ; that he should be a first-class man of business and of affairs ; know about goods, wares and merchandise and their values at home and abroad ; that he should possess no partisan spirit whatever, and be solely animated by a desire and purpose to put the Consular Service of this country, by a complete knowledge of all facts relating thereto on such an elevation as it has never known. All this at a cost to the department so inconsiderable as to call for no special appropriation or legislation.

It could be done by detaching such a party from his post, and detailing him to this service as a part of those contingent expenses which are usual, and which are provided for in both the State and Treasury Departments, and even were Congress to create and make the needful appropriation for such a commission as we have just suggested, there would be a great deal of preliminary discussion and delay, during which the preparation of the digest might go steadily on. Its value to the departments interested can hardly be computed, and in any subsequent looking into this great and important service by a commission or anybody else, this digest would serve as a foundation or base for all future action.

THE PRESIDENT'S MESSAGE.

The reference which the President makes to this subject in his message is of course in accord with the recent action of the State Department. He repeats that the importance of the subject has led the Executive to consider what steps might properly be taken—without additional legislation—which steps he has taken, not assuming that what has been done will prove a full measure of Consular reform. What chiefly interests us is the added declaration by the President that these efforts should be immediately supplemented by legislation providing for Consular inspection to begin with, and a Consular inspection to be followed up in a thorough manner.

This is in entire harmony with all that this paper recommends and suggests. We admit that we do not like the term "Consular inspection," for the reason that while it may be most fitting in itself, and is precisely what our rival nations do, yet with us the favored appointee has simply had a dignified and pleasant outing and exchange of hospitalities with our Consuls abroad, and any such thing as a thorough scrutiny of the entire service in this way we have not known. To get out of these old ruts and reach the result which Mr. Cleveland seeks —by a complete reconstruction and new departure—we decidedly prefer new names and new methods as well.

Certainly at the outset it would seem to be desirable to make an impression that something more, and a good deal more than ever before, is going to be done. But after all, whether it shall be a special commission or a complete digest, or a reinvigorated Consular inspection, the ends we aim at are one, and we must leave to those upon whom the responsibility and duty rests to determine the means by which the result which the President and the people alike seek shall be best and soonest attained.

CONCLUSION.

In conclusion, therefore, gentlemen, whether the "next thing" in this business shall be that the Senate, perhaps stimulated to effort by what the State Department has done, shall revive and revise its action of last winter in the complete success of which, by the passage of a bill through both houses, we have considerable doubt—or whether this Administration shall take other steps such as we have suggested, or wiser and better ones—it is plain enough that the cause which has assembled us here is moving steadily on, at a pace exceeding that to which Edmund Burke refers when he says that the "march of the human mind is slow."

Certainly in view of the political passion and prejudice which this cause has encountered from the beginning, the success which has crowned your efforts, Mr. President and those associated with you, has been surprising. Nevertheless I need not remind any one here that it still remains for us to continue the contest, in which we should not relax a single effort or abate one jot of our zeal and ardor in the good cause.

Superannuation in the Civil Service.

By WILLIAM DUDLEY FOULKE.

John Wanamaker, late Postmaster General, of happy
memory, once wrote by the hand of Marshall Cushing a circular letter to a number of civil service reformers throughout
the country asking why both parties should not discard their
insincere professions for the law and have the patriotism to go
back to the old system.

The devil himself can sometimes put an apposite question
and this letter inquired what answer reformers made to the
objections, that a civil pension list was the logical result of
their system and that the efficiency of the departments would
be seriously interfered with in ten or fifteen years by the old
age of many of the clerks who could not be removed. It was
easy to answer that these clerks ought to be dismissed when
they ceased to be efficient. It was easy to say that when they
accepted employment they knew that no pension awaited
them and that it was their duty to save in the days of their
prosperity enough to support them in the infirmities of age.
It is still true that permanency in office-holding, which the
merit system encourages, makes even discretionary removals
more difficult, and as men everywhere outlive their usefulness,
this so-called tenure during good behavior does sometimes
fasten "barnacles" upon the service. I use the epithet of
another high authority in the camp of our enemies, the late
Mr. Porter, who conducted with such impartial and disinterested fidelity the taking of the last census.

The only objection of our opponents which ever had a
grain of sense in it is that involved in characterizing civil service reform as "the Chinese system," namely its tendency to
crystallization and rigidity. This tendency exists and safeguards are required to ensure flexibility and to maintain constantly that high efficiency which is secured at the outset by

competitive examinations. By these examinations we presumably bring into the service the best men for the places, but other devices are still required to see that these continue to be not only good men but the best men, so long as they remain in the employment of the government.

In the case of appointments we have seen how vain it is to trust the arbitrary discretion of the appointing power. The spoils system has been the outgrowth of that misplaced confidence. Personal and party considerations instead of the good of the service have dictated appointments   But the infirmities of human nature do not stop when the choice is once made, we have no stronger reason to believe that under a discretionary system the best men only will be retained than that the best men only will be appointed.

The competitive plan has indeed removed one great temptation. Men are not dismissed for the mere purpose of appointing to the vacant place a personal or partisan follower. But there are other temptations to retain the inefficient and some of these temptations spring from the best feelings of our nature. Men in prosperity do not always save up their earnings for the hour of need, and the man who has served faithfully for twenty years may find himself when no longer able to perform his duties in a position where dismissal would make him an outcast and a pauper. We may say, that the chief of the department or bureau ought not not to consider this, that his duty is wholly to the State, that he must keep the best men only, and that if a clerk through the weight of years or infirmities becomes inefficient, he must be discharged. We may preach this sort of morality till doomsday, but no man with a heart will do it. Under the present system the government service will continue to be a refuge for the helpless where these have not forfeited their rights by any wilful act of their own. Many of those who are aged and incompetent, but who can point to a record of past usefulness, will stay in place and besides drawing pay for work which is not performed, they will injure the service in other ways. It was the old practitioner who most strenuously resisted the code. It is the old physician who is most reluctant to adopt the new methods recently revealed by science for the cure of disease and it is the old official who is often the greatest obstacle to renovation and reform in the public service. This proposition is too plain for argument. Furthermore it is true that many a man, by mere length of service, comes to believe that he has an indefeasible right to his office. He becomes stubborn and opinionated. He is harder to manage than a new man. Even the judges of our Federal Courts sometimes become arbitrary and disagreeable largely on account of the life tenure upon which they hold their places. A certain insecurity in office is a great stimulus to urbanity, and politeness is an important virtue in public servants especially in those with whom the people are brought into daily contact.

Experience in office is valuable but sometimes enthusiasm is of ten-fold greater value and old age is not enthusiastic. In our great business organizations, our railroads, our banks. our manufactories, the necessity often arises for the infusion of fresh blood. The system of rotation in office every four years was very ridiculous, but because we have avoided Scylla we must not sail into Charybdis. Absolute fixity of tenure is also laden with disaster.

The problem to be solved is therefore to prescribe by some general system of rules an easy and sure method of discharging the incompetent, of providing for the superannuated and of maintaining the service in the highest state of efficiency. Part of this question can be solved, it is true, by a civil pension list. It has been thus solved in other countries, and the expense of such a list, great as it may be, is less than that of keeping incompetent men in the public service. But if we imagine that a civil pension list will, within the life of this generation, be approved by the American people let us speedily undeceive ourselves. The present pension rolls, men think, are long enough. The country will not add to them. Not one man in ten would vote for it. The sentiment of gratitude to our soldiers cannot be stretched far enough to embrace those in the occupations of civil life, no matter how long continued or meritorious their service. The people generally believe, however incorrectly, that these men have easy places and are well paid and multitudes of new applicants can always be found ready to assume their duties without this additional attraction. The people will see no reason why a new burden should thus be laid upon the government. If provision is to be made for the superannuated, the civil service itself which will receive the benefit must bear the burden. I notice that a bill has been prepared by the Letter Carriers' Association for retaining in the Treasury two per cent. from the salary of every carrier for relief against disability by injuries sustained in the service and for annuities for those who have served twenty years and have become incapacitated. By this bill a carrier is not necessarily removed at the end of that time. He is simply allowed to retire on half pay. There would, however, be far less difficulty in removing him if he became inefficient. In the Fire and Police Departments in New York, Chicago and elsewhere, in the railway mail service, among schoolteachers and in other positions, arrangements have been made or proposed for superannuation funds of a similar character. The life, annuity and endowment tables furnish a basis from which the amount to be retained and the annuities to be paid can be determined with reasonable accuracy. The details can be easily adjusted. The greater the number of men embraced in such a measure the more beneficial will it be. A system comprehending the entire classified service would be the most perfect of all.

The next problem is to provide some plan by which the service may be kept from fossilization, even before the period when the members become entitled to the benefits of a superannuation fund, a plan by which some movement can be given to the individuals composing these various corps and by which the efficiency of every department, bureau and office can be maintained at its highest limit.

Now the methods used for this purpose will naturally be the same as those used to secure efficiency at the outset. Examination and probation are the two touchstones by which this is done. A periodical examination then and a constant record of efficiency are the means by which it can be determined what employees should be promoted, reduced in grade or dismissed.

Four years ago I submitted this matter in a communication to Mr. George William Curtis, proposing the following: "Let all grades of the service be open to promotion upon periodical competitive examinations. Let the term of the incumbent of any grade expire at the time of these examinations. Give him the right to re-appoint upon proving his efficiency in competition with all applicants from the grade immediately lower than his own. If any of these men understand how to do his work better than he does himself, the best among them ought to have his place and he ought to go down to theirs. If he cannot hold his own even in the lowest grade, he ought to leave the service. It is evident that this system would inspire the same emulation among those who are in the service as among those who seek to enter it."

This communication was submitted by Mr. Curtis to the Executive Committee of the League. He wrote me that the difficulty with a general competition of different grades was that the clerk who had grown feeble and who ought to be displaced could easily beat any one not in his grade in competitive examination of actual details of review. That the reasons for his removal could hardly be detected by an examination, however evident they might be to observation. Mr. Curtis added: "It is agreed that the question is very important and several of our friends were plainly inclined to approve your suggestions of periodical examinations. We shall keep thinking." The suggestions made at that time ought to be modified in accordance with Mr. Curtis' criticism. A man's ability to advance or retain his grade should be determined not only by examination but also by a constant daily record of efficiency. At the end, say of every four years, let these examinations be made and let the daily record be produced, giving equal weight to each. Begin the examinations at the highest grade and proceed thus downward to the lowest. Let the efficient men of the lower grades move up a step, and let the inefficient men in the higher grades keep moving down a step at a time till they have found their level.

Four years have elapsed since this subject was submitted and nothing definite has been proposed by the League. It is time now not only to keep thinking but to transmute thought into action. The danger of fossilization grows greater year by year. The more the classified system is extended the more the "barnacles" will accumulate and dissatisfaction with a system which permits them will grow in a corresponding ratio. Now is the time for us to see to it that this last objection to our Reform is finally overcome. Let us remove the dead branches of the Civil Service wherever decay appears. The sap must continue to circulate and the foliage must retain its freshness that the tree may bear fruit in greater and greater abundance.

The State of Civil Service Reform in the South.

By Herman Justi.

When the letter of your Secretary was received asking me to give "the status of Civil Service Reform sentiment in the South," my first impulse was to decline the task, for the field appeared, not only vast, but uninviting Some time ago, when one of our local wags was asked for his opinion of the financial condition of the people in a certain section of the South, he replied: " One half of the people are busted and the other half are insolvent." Now I am an ardent believer in the merit system, and yet, I, like many others, often grow impatient at the apathy and indifference of our people regarding this vital issue, and I was almost tempted, in a fit of momentary despondency, to answer Mr. McAneny's courteous invitation after the laconic style of my witty friend, with the simple statement, that one half of our people are opposed to Civil Service Reform and the other half are not for it. But this would be, I am happy to say on reflection, far from the truth. And yet, though the gains to the cause of Civil Service Reform cannot easily be specified, I feel certain that – whatever we may think in times of despondency – public opinion in the South is opposed to the Spoils System. Strict party men and party leaders will stoutly deny this, to be sure ; but it is nevertheless true and, since political parties are subject to that superior power—the will of the people—the politicians must ultimately yield. We are, however. as yet, badly organized ; our demands are not clearly stated and we have taken hold of the issue in a way so half-hearted, that the friends of the "Spoils System" continue bold—even presumptuous. As was so well said by the lamented George William Curtis, "party machines no more favor Civil Service Reform, than kings favor the restriction of the royal prerogative." Party leaders with us, therefore, will not admit the growth of the Civil Service Reform sentiment, because they try not to see it. They wish to ignore its growing power, because to admit it is to give it a tremendous sweep; but we shall keep up the fight at every point and make everybody see that ultimate triumph is sure.

THE OLD SOUTH AND THE MERIT SYSTEM.

In history the South is undeniably committed to the principles of Civil Service Reform. Down to Andrew Jackson's advent to political power her statesmen generally believed not only in its abstract principles, but applied them in fact. As citizens they voted for men of capacity and honesty, and strove and contended for their election. As representatives in Congress, it was their habit to urge the appointment of applicants having the proper qualifications rather than the claims of party fealty. Four of the first six Presidents of the United States were Southern men and they have each left the strongest proof of their attitude on the merit system. They neither appointed men to office as a reward for political partisan services nor removed them because of their political opinions. Nor was nepotism an excuse for bestowing office. On the contrary it was a delicate but strong bar. Even Andrew Jackson was an advocate of the principles of Civil Service Reform until he became President. Then he changed and inaugurated the most unreasonable, unjust and demoralizing political system known to man. Those who respect the past and reverence the memory of Washington, Jefferson, Clay and Calhoun and our ablest statesmen of later days will find, in studying their words and deeds, ample proof to support our contention that the Old South was in favor of the Merit System. The statesmen of the South before the war were our strongest men and no trivial differences with their constituents sufficed to dethrone them. Although known to be opposed to slavery, Henry Clay was never defeated in his own State, in spite of the fact that Kentucky was a slave State. More remarkable even than the continuous public |service of Mr. Clay is the fact that the section of the State in which he lived, which is known as the

"Blue Grass Region," has furnished sixteen of Kentucky's thirty-six representatives in the Senate of the United States, notwithstanding the fact that the different sections of the State have always been. and are now, eager to enjoy this distinction. Still, so long as Henry Clay's old home has offered her strongest and best men of demonstrated ability and power, all sectional or local demands have been gracefully waved in her favor. Is not this example worthy of imitation in every department of the public service, and everywhere throughout the land. The strongest and most abundant evidence may be produced to show the attitude of the South before the war on the subject of selecting officers on their merit. We are by tradition, by character, and by the fair and honorable disposition of our people, unmistakably committed to the principles of Civil Service Reform.

ATTITUDE OF THE CONFEDERATE CONGRESS ON THE SPOILS SYSTEM.

I have been favored since my arrival in Washington with a paper containing what purports to be the record of a debate in the Confederate Congress on a bill that had been introduced in that body, fixing the tenure of a non-political office at four years. Fixing the tenure, it clearly appears, was never contemplated in the passage of other similar bills, but was an inadvertance. The whole debate is intensely interesting and instructive, but I shall content myself with an extract from the remarks of Mr. Semmes, of Louisiana, and Mr. Wigfall, of Texas:

"Mr. Semmes, of Louisiana, asked if we must continue to adhere to a system which was mainly instrumental in the downfall of the old government. It was this that had more influence than anything else, to bring about the present revolution. Our present constitution does not sufficiently provide against it, and we should here set ourselves against it."

"Mr. Wigfall, of Texas. Rotation in office, based upon the party war-cry, ' To the victors belong the spoils,' was undoubtedly the bane of the government of the United States, and exercised the most demoralizing influence. We should show that it was the intention of the Government to select its officers as individuals select their boot-makers and tailors— not to enquire their politics, or to assume that the office was made for the man; not to confer place and position upon him, because he has one child or forty; but for no other reason than because he is capable, efficient, and does the work required ; so soon as he fails in this, turn him out, and not otherwise. The demoralization consequent upon the prospect of distribution in certain periods is very great. It leads hosts of persons to forsake their regular employments, and indulge in all kinds of tricks and schemes and combinations to attain their ends. It is an annoyance to every Congressman, and to every official, from the President down. We should endeavor now to decidedly favor the establishment of the precedent, that so long as a man does his duty he should be kept in office."

WHY THE SOUTH HAS OPPOSED CIVIL SERVICE REFORM IN RECENT YEARS.

Immediately after the War a fairly good reason justified some opposition to the operation of a Civil Service Reform law which seemed devised to keep in office the followers of the party then in control at Washington. But happily that reason no longer exists. Gradually both sides are becoming equal in the possession of minor offices; and, the supremacy of the whites and the undisturbed control of local self government being forever assured, we can and will apply the test of merit in public as we do in private business affairs.

I shall endeavor to state briefly a few of the many difficulties that, in the South, interfere with the more rapid growth of the Merit System which is so just and admirable that it should at once commend itself to public favor. I shall endeavor to give some idea of the manner in which a growing sentiment in favor of that system has manifested itself of late. In the consideration of my subject we must keep in mind several conditions which have been peculiar to the South since the war, namely:

That chaotic state of society which was incident to the Reconstruction period.

The disfranchisement of the negro by devices not strictly legal and his continued presence in the Southern States.

The Solid South and the gradually acquired supremacy of the white race

To bring order out of chaos and to overcome the mistakes and tyranny which were incident to Reconstruction required a period of some fourteen years extending from the close of the civil war. The six years following that period, the first years of local self government since the war, were easily consumed in determining the political status of the negro. In the two or three years succeeding 1885, the supremacy of the whites was fully and forever established. Then came the South's marvelous industrial development, which is universally conceded and commended. The final accomplishment of these great things has served lately to divert the Southern mind from the old conditions and dead issues, to the consideration of vital issues of the present and future. Members of the party now dominant will henceforth freely differ on great economic issues which greatly overshadow the old issues growing out of the war, and of the so-called race problem. The work of dividing the Solid South has fairly begun by disintegrating the great political party which has long and completely controlled that section. The Solid South is now practically broken, in the sense that Southern men consider themselves free to vote for whom they please, and feel safe now that the old issues are no longer pressing, to vote against their old party, should it promulgate false principles or follow faithless leaders or offer unworthy candidates for office. We have just reached a point where we may expect the two main parties to win alternately. As we have now escaped the tyranny of great majorities—as party leaders can no longer count with certainty on success at the polls—we see the prospects for Civil Service Reform both in Federal, State and municipal affairs, grow brighter. We know the day of complete triumph is close at hand.

THE REIGN OF SHAM REFORM.

The first great gain that the Merit System has made in the South is an indirect one and lies in the fact that tens of thousands of voters who, until a comparatively recent date, have firmly adhered to one party, right or wrong, have forever abandoned that practice. This gain, however, has been, in some instances, temporarily offset by the triumph of a dangerous party, conceived in a selfish and unpatriotic spirit, and governed by secret machinations. Mean and self-seeking men, taking advantage of a changing sentiment, have raised an insincere cry of reform and have been supported by many well meaning men who have not at first given due consideration to the principles of the reformers, the character of their leaders, or the merits of their candidates. Recently in a Southern city the so-called "machine" was beaten by a so-called "Reform party." The candidates on both tickets were about evenly matched, both as to character and intelligence. The so called reformers won in spite of the fact that some of the principles promulgated by them were extremely vicious and unpatriotic and their acknowledged leader was positively known to be corrupt. This was most unfortunate, for the *spirit* of true reform has certainly taken hold of the minds of the people, and every rude shock given to it by pretenders, only serves to prolong our misery under the "Spoils System." We have had so much sham reform, so much parading in the livery of reform, that the very name often condemns a really·worthy and meritorious cause. The term is too often synonymous with hypocrisy, and under its banner rascals too frequently march in to power. So often have men that long paraded as great reformers been exposed at last as arrant humbugs, that the bare name of reform provokes suspicion. In a Southern city not long ago, an election for city councilmen was held which resulted in victory for the reformers. These reformers had promised that in filling the offices in their gift they would look solely to the honesty and capacity of the applicants. In due course of time these offices were filled, and on the following day there appeared an article in a highly respectable daily journal which contained this grave charge: "A prominent councilman told the writer a few weeks before the election of city officers that a certain applicant for an important office was in his estimation totally unfit for it—so unfitted that even his candidature was a farce—and yet I observed that this councilman voted for this very candidate on the first ballot. Was it a 'dicker' or a change of heart?" In justice to the public the names should have been given, for, while this was not necessary to satisfy any reasonable mind that it was a "dicker" it would have served a good purpose by making an example there and then of such a rogue. Such affairs are extremely unfortunate at this time but in the end these defeats to party machines—these protests against misgovernment and fraud—will serve as a warning and will prove in the end a decided gain to the cause of good government. Such results tend to breaking up that strict fidelity to party, which in the past has made party leaders so all powerful. A rude shock to politicians now and then makes them realize that they are on trial, that their tenure is frail, that they may at any time go down in defeat.

REVOLT AGAINST BOSSISM IN KENTUCKY.

Recently we have been presented with a splendid illustration of this in Kentucky, where the party leaders expected the people of the State to support a candidate for an honorable and important office, who renounced the party platform. A national issue, the currency, was dragged into a local election. The party in convention adopted a platform of principles that faced one way, and nominated a candidate for Governor who faced in the opposite direction. The result should have been anticipated. Kentuckians would sacrifice much to keep their State in the Democratic line, but not their self-respect. What was the result?

Well, the singular situation of the Democratic party in Kentucky is aptly illustrated by the story of the two Irishmen who occupied berths in a sleeping car on one of our great railway lines. A collision took place in the night and confusion ensued. Both men dressed hastily and when they emerged from behind the curtains Pat, recognizing his friend Mike, said to him "Mike, are you hurted? ' " No," said Mike, who in his haste to dress had gotten into his trousers with the hind part before, " I am not hurt, Pat, but I am fatally twisted."

The Democratic party in Kentucky, my own party in my native State, it is almost needless to remark, is like unto Mike, "fatally twisted."

TIRED OF EQUIVOCATION.

The people of the South are tired of falsehood, of equivocation, of compromise, and hereafter parties must rely upon sound principles without regard to expediency, and make the issues clear. When we act upon this rule we shall deserve to win. Trimming leads to confusion, and compromises lead generally to defeat. We shall learn in time that truth clearly stated, and correct principles consistently and fearlessly advocated, will receive the approval of the masses of voters. In the South, as in the North, we have too often lost sight of the fact that a corrupt party is just as oppressive and just as dangerous as a wicked and cruel monarch. A monarch may be dispatched at a blow but it requires years to destroy or even to displace a corrupt political party. Americans are often heard to ridicule people living under a monarchical form of Government for subscribing substantially to the declaration that "the king can do no wrong" and yet when we come to vote we are no better than they, for we in effect declare that "the party can do no wrong." Professing to stand in awe of a danger that is often chimerical, we rush ahead into difficulties by repeatedly voting for men whom we know to be incompetent, and perhaps dishonest.

No one should fancy for a moment that political parties can be dispensed with. Nor is perfection to be expected from parties and party leaders. Parties and party leaders are necessary, and citizens should therefore stand, if possible, with one of the great political parties in all national issues; should enter into party councils and attend party primaries, advocating correct principles and voting only for good men. Pursuing this course, party leaders would soon be selected from the ranks of our strongest, most honest and most capable citizens. Strong, able, honest men will lift up and influence the weak, ignorant and misguided voter, provided the former appear in respectable numbers at the primary or at the polls. Nothing so delights the soul of corrupt politicians as the absence of a strong representation of intellectual men from party councils.

The importance of the primary cannot be overestimated, for it is the mold, so to speak, in which are cast the party principles and party candidates which we will be expected to support. When this is once sufficiently well appreciated we shall cease our present practice of voting for a choice of evils and vote, as we should have the power of doing, for our choice of candidates, among men known to be honest and capable. Under a system of minority representation, a system thoroughly feasible and perfectly just, this right could be insured to every citizen.

Unless we work with the established parties there is little immediate hope for success. Party machinery is necessary, but capable, faithful managers must be placed in charge.

OTHER CONSIDERATIONS THAN MERIT TAKE PRECEDENCE.

Our too common failing is, that we sometimes vote and otherwise endorse men for public office knowing them to be dishonest or incompetent. Honest and capable men are sometimes opposed in State or Municipal elections because they do not hold our peculiar views in politics, though national politics have nothing to do with the case, We even vote against the admirable candidates for the highest or lowest offices because forsooth we do not like their religious opinions. Could anything be more unjust or contemptible? We sometimes even vote against men because they are our competitors in business or because we dislike their manners! We often vote for men because they belong to our club or church, lodge or guild, or because they trade with us, because they are our clients or patients; or because they treat us or bow politely! Worth alone should control, and yet it is lost sight of in the consideration of trifles.

SENTIMENTAL CITIZENSHIP.

We of the South were once chided for sending "Confederate Brigadiers" to Congress, but they, as a rule, happened to be our leading and most worthy citizens. Now we are going farther and sometimes vote for a man because he happens to be the son of a " Confederate Brigadier," for the same reason that in the North the people vote for the son of a Federal "Brigadier." The Grand Army of the Republic and other associations of old Northern soldiers being better organized and more powerful than associations of old Southern soldiers at the South, and consequently a greater menace to good government, are too much given to caring for their old comrades at the expense of the nation and to the injury of the public service. He may be thoroughly unfit, still there continues to be something potential in that "Strange spell—a name."

The " Brigadiers" at the South, I regret to say, are now nearly all gone and at present it is often the Colonels and the Majors and the Captains for whom we are asked to vote. Many of them are worthy of our suffrages, and when they are worthy, we ought to give them the advantage of their titles honorably won. But it is too often the case that they are elected on account of a mere sentiment. A mere feeling of gratitude for services rendered as soldiers in the war, or for noble work done as physicians during an epidemic of cholera or yellow fever ought not to cause the election of men to civil offices for which they are not qualified. Elected alone upon such a plea, blind to their own weakness or folly, or without capacity for executive work, and too stubborn to accept advice, they usually injure their previously well earned reputation, without doing their State or Country the slightest good. Such men are seldom re-elected and their disappointment is so great that it carries them to the grave, cherishing to the last a feeling of resentment against the whole world because they were not estimated at their own valuation. The toast of an old darkey to a retiring Governor of one of our Southern States, who had secured his election on a mere sentiment, was apt and suggestive: "De Gubner: He went inter office wid very little uppersishun, and he come out wid none at all."

Merit Not Treated as the First Requisite.

At the present time, in many of our larger Southern cities, it would be almost impossible to elect—to a seat in Congress —a man who is only distinguished for exalted virtue, strict integrity and a superior order of intelligence. The fact is, few of our best men possessing these qualities would consent to run for office knowing the silly objections too often raised, not only by the "Common herd," as it is called, but by men in the higher walks of life, whose narrow prejudice and selfishness stand in the way of the common good. Questions that do not in the remotest degree enter into the issues of a campaign are forced into it by rogues and bigots, and rogues and bigots usually stand together. In this contention of the individual or of a faction for the success of the hobby advocated by some man or set of men, the main object sought is subordinated or obscured or possibly wholly ignored. In other words, the main issue must yield to the lesser issue, and if this is not done, a compromise or an emasculated policy, or a weak or a bad candidate is the consequence, and this is why men go to Congress or to the Legislature, who are mere time servers and hand shakers, with wavering convictions, mediocre ability, bad habits and sometimes with little claim to honesty.

Bigots a Serious Obstacle to Unity.

In some Southern cities the A. P. A. is becoming a serious obstruction to every needed reform. It proscribes the able man, who chances to be a Catholic, or who is intimate with, or in any way allied to Catholics. They even carry their proscriptive measures to the extent of using their influence against men holding important business connections. They pretend friendliness to a certain class of foreigners of the Protestant faith; but it is a pretense only. The A. P. A. is after the offices, and to secure them it has adopted unwise, un-American and un-Christian methods and measures. It has struck a blow to the very keystone of reform—*Merit*, which in its creed, is not to be considered. The disgrace of disappearance of the A. P. A. party, therefore, which, let us hope will come soon, is necessary before independent voters can unite upon a proper basis. I do not believe that any one seriously anticipates that it will ever become one of the great national parties, but its dupes do hope to be strong enough to make them the balance of power, trusting that they may effect a favorable bargain with one or the other of the great political parties. In this they must fail surely; for neither one of the great political parties can afford to endorse a secret party that seeks to undermine that religious liberty which is guaranteed by the Constitution. No national party could afford to stultify itself by such alliance and to drive from its ranks an element more numerous, more respectable and more powerful than a combination of the A. P. A. and its sympathizers. This craze and all side issues must be speedily brushed away so that the only tests to be applied to a candidate for public office shall be those laid down by Jefferson, namely:

"Is he honest? Is he capable? Is he faithful to the Constitution?" In this way, and only in this way, can we make our government republican and worthy of the high destiny of America. Only in this way can we make our people thoroughly homogeneous, contented and prosperous, enjoying together every blessing of free institutions and imbued with a well founded, generous love of our common country.

PROHIBITIONISTS AND POPULISTS NOT HELPFUL.

Prohibitionists, too, have been hurtful to reforms in our government. They say that in agreeing to anything less than Prohibition, they will be compromising with wrong, and yet it is clear that much might be gained for the cause of temperance if they would join with those who would be willing to meet them half-way in every reasonable effort to promote their cause. The prohibitionists, however, prefer to sacrifice their whole case and obstruct wise legislation, rather than to accept a little less than they wish. Their cause is, in a large measure, a righteous and wise one, and their motives, we admit, are usually high and noble and they would certainly benefit their party and their country by helping to establish government on a moral, equitable and business-like basis, while slowly erecting bulwarks against the temptations and evils of intemperance.—In like manner the Populists often oppose the most trustworthy and competent men for office, unless he subscribes to their wild and visionary schemes on every subject.

The capacity of great numbers of our voters seems sadly deficient in the power to discriminate between local and national affairs, between the main issues and trifles; and herein we find our problem difficult of solution. The local machine and the national machine are often in the same hands, giving opportunity to party leaders to concentrate national political workers in local elections, and local workers in national elections. Thus the spoilsmen have been enabled to achieve the important victories that might have been prevented by the exercise of a discriminating power upon the part of the intelligent voters.

INVOLUNTARY OBSTACLES.

Strange and contradictory as it may seem, religious, benevolent and fraternal associations have often tended to retard the improvement of our Civil Service. On the other hand, educational, professional and business associations have just as often been helpful in advancing it. It is not intended to reflect upon the good and noble work which religious and benevolent and fraternal societies so admirably perform; (and by religious associations I do not mean the churches). Many religious associations have sprung up in latter years not under the church's jurisdiction. But the very spirit that prompts them to generous and helpful action too often makes them, when not restrained by wise deliberation, unconscious or unvoluntary enemies to the merit system. Bent upon being helpful to the individuals of their order, their zeal makes them blind to the interests of the State. Having perhaps done their full part in supporting improvident members, or not longer caring to do so, they seem to regard these unfortunate ones as natural heirs to public offices and make them expensive wards of the government.

COMMERCIAL AND PROFESSIONAL ASSOCIATIONS LOGICAL ALLIES.

On the other hand, Bar Associations, Medical Associations, Bankers' Associations, Boards of Trade and Chambers of Commerce, School Teachers' Conventions and Alumni Associations, and in fact countless other associations, professional, literary, business and social as well, are bringing together the best minds in all fields of labor with the view of correcting public grievances, in the hope that an exchange of ideas and a free expression of opinion in their meetings may bring out the best thought and the most helpful experience of their members. In these various associations and conventions fair-minded men from all sections of our land and from all parts of the world, of the varying shades of religious and political beliefs, come together with a determination to learn from one another what is most useful and available, and thus they naturally learn and appropriate what is best. They are, in short, the logical allies of good government.

It may be interesting to the League to know that in the " Round Table," a conversation club in Nashville, which meets bi-weekly, Civil Service Reform was the designated subject for discussion at one of its gatherings, and of the fifteen members present fourteen declared themselves straight-out friends of the merit system.

The Old Oak Club, a younger organization of great influence with a larger membership, but devoted to the same objects as the " Round Table," has shown its attitude on the subject by enrolling its entire membership in the " Anti-Spoils League." At an Old Oak meeting, a fortnight ago, there were read two most appreciative papers which treated of one of our greatest apostles of the merit system, George William Curtis. I am sure they would have been heard by this organization with pleasure and satisfaction. At the first meeting of the same club to be held in the ensuing New Year " Civil

Service Reform in the United States " is the subject to be discussed.

Is the Foreigner Responsible for our Woes?

The worker, the trickster, the boss and the foreigner are charged with our political woes. These must bear their share of blame, but how could they continue all the evil practices of which they are accused if our native American population properly discharged their civic duties? The ascendency of the native American population is overwhelming in the South and we should therefore hear little of the complaint so common elsewhere, of the demoralizing and corrupting influence of the alien. The reverse is true, however, and even in the South many intelligent Americans, joining with a set of blatherskites, declaim with great vehemence against the evil influence of an alien population. It is, therefore, clearly our own fault if corruption in political affairs is practiced, for in the South we are clearly a homogeneous people. The truth about the poor alien is that he generally comes to us, owning little more than the clothes he wears, and that he endures at the beginning of his career in a free country many unexpected hardships and privations. He is to some extent the victim of American politicians. The native American spoilsmen who should know better and who do know better, buy his naturalization papers for him or pay his poll tax and thus make him a qualified voter, or buy him straight out. In other words, shrewd native Americans buy the vote of the needy, ignorant and half-fed alien. They know this to be a violation of law, and they know what the alien does not know, that it is this unlawful practice which is undermining the foundations of our government.

Unless the native American proposes to buy, the alien cannot hope to sell his vote. Here then political corruption would end, if Americans so willed it. The truth is, that, when things don't go right and all of those American spoilsmen and office-seekers who have bought votes, have been doomed to defeat, they naturally feel that they must put the blame somewhere and so they make the poor foreigner their scape-goat. Mr. Bryce and other kindly-disposed critics of American institutions are misled by American friends who try to account for the weakness of our institutions and for the ill success of our political affairs by putting all the blame of our failings on our imigrants. At the present time the percentage of foreigners in Tennessee, for example, is less than two per cent., and yet no one claims that our public officials are more honest, capable, public-spirited or patriotic than in States where the percentage of foreigners is far greater. In fact, the manner of conducting public offices in the South is less methodical and business-like, and waste or extravagance in the administration of public affairs is greater than in the North, while our taxes are too high, our public buildings and public works, though expensive, are not beautiful, our streets are poor in construction and often filthy; and yet ninety-eight per cent. of our population is native born. We must be fair to the alien, just to ourselves and look elsewhere for the cause of our trouble.

THE FEE SYSTEM VERSUS OFFICIAL SALARIES.

In the Southern States the salaries paid to State, County and Municipal officers are unequal and unjust, a fact which is a fruitful cause of trouble. The salaries, for example, of our governors, of our judges, of the mayors of our cities and of the members of the boards of public works are inadequate for well-performed services. The public makes unreasonable demands upon them, to which they are expected to respond because of the meagre salaries. It is not fair to expose them to such strains and temptations. The beggarly salaries we pay and the short terms for which our higher officers are elected deter our ablest and best men from entering politics. Prosperous lawyers earn at the bar two or three times as much as the salaries of judges in our State Courts; why, then, should they enter into public service? On the other hand, there are State, County, Municipal officers whose incomes, under the operation of an abominable fee system, are out of all proportion to the value of their services. De-Tocqueville rightly observed: "The minor offices are well paid; the higher offices ill paid." The large incomes derived from the fees in the minor offices account for the liberal contributions made to the corruption funds which are used in our elections. To preserve these large incomes, a

corrupt lobby is maintained in many of our State legislatures. It has unfortunately occurred that where those richly-
paid officers have been appointed by judges, the consideration
of the appointment has sometimes been a participation in the
perquisites. Frequency of elections, short terms, unequal salaries, and election of judges by the people, have been, are
still, and will always be, a curse to us.

RECENT REFORM LEGISLATION.

Many of the evils from which we suffer are receiving attention at the hands of a few wise law-makers, and while recent
legislative enactments are confined to only a few of the
Southern States, and while these enactments may not be sufficiently far-reaching, still they are a decided advance in the
right direction. They at least encourage us to hope for a
wider and more general application of much-needed corrective measures. In Kentucky, for example, the new constitution provides (section 96) that all State officers shall be paid
by salaries and not otherwise, and that (section 240) no public officer, except the governor, shall receive more than five
thousand dollars per annum for his official services. Under
an act of the Kentucky legislature for the "Government of
cities of the first class," some very common complaints against
the police and fire departments of the larger cities are sought
to be remedied, as will be seen from the following provisions:

Section 2893 provides that no officer or member of
police force can be removed or discharged or reduced in
grade or pay for any political reason. No person can be
appointed on account of any political service rendered by
him.

Section 94.—Excepting the chiefs and persons now employed in said departments. and persons who have been employed during the past five years, every officer or employee
shall, before appointment or selection, have the following
qualifications :

First.—He must read and write correctly and fluently the
English language, from dictation, in the presence of examiners
appointed by said board.

Second.—He must pass a satisfactory examination on the
charter and ordinances of the city and such part of the con-

stitution and statutes of the State as relate to the duties of his office.

Third.—He must be at least twenty-one years of age and not more than forty-five years of age.

Fourth.—He must be of sound health and sufficiently strong to be active and able to discharge easily his duties; and

Fifth.—He must be a resident and voter in the city.

Section 99.—No officer or policeman or member of the Fire Department shall be called on for any contribution or assessment by any official superior or political organization or committee. No officer or member of said Police or Fire Department shall be allowed to solicit any contributions or funds or to sell any tickets or procure money by any devices from the public. Any persons violating the provisions of this section shall be fined in a sum not exceeding one hundred dollars or imprisoned for a period not exceeding two months, or both so fined or imprisoned.

COLLEGIATE INFLUENCE.

We shall now begin to feel the great advantage resulting from the work that has been done in the last ten years by our colleges and universities for reforms in our government. The course in political education is now an essential part of the curriculum of every college. Every year hundreds of young men go forth from these institutions of learning, imbued with correct ideas of government and animated by an honorable ambition to be useful citizens. It is they who will be stanch allies of the advocates of good government and who will certainly help to make a successful fight in favor of the merit system. Professor Thornton of the University of Virginia in speaking of the college-graduate's position in life, wisely and truthfully observed that " in politics, at the bar, in the medical profession, in business, he stands for cleanness and honesty and is the hated foe of the bribing lobbyist, the unjust judge, the quack and the cheat."

The influence of this class of men is now clearly seen in many localities, and each year their number and power increase. The sense of civic duty, as well as the necessity for exercising it, will be stimulated by their contact with the masses, and their increasing familiarity with the principles of government and with the elements of administrative machinery will not only enable them to exercise their rights as citizens but to impart their knowledge and their spirit of patriotism to others. We need an army of just such men who are to be the leaders and the teachers of the people. Strong, able, honest men, who are willing to come out of their shells and mingle with their fellow citizens, rubbing up against them, and showing that none are too good for practical politics in its best sense, pointing out to the people both their rights and their obligations. The people always want to learn, but they won't learn unless met in a straight-forward, manly way,— not as unfeeling creatures devoid of self-respect, honesty and intelligence.

Benefits to Southern Men Under Civil Service Reform.

The impression widely prevalent in the South that Civil Service Reform is designed to favor the highly educated and the wealthy is erroneous. It is also not true that under its operation the South fares unequally with other sections. Through the operation of the reform law, employment in the Civil Service was thrown open to the people of the South for the first time since the breaking out of the War of the Rebellion. Poor men and men of limited education but ambitions and resolved to learn, have risen to distinction in our Civil Service. It is well known that during Mr Harrison's administration Commissioner Roosevelt made it a special object to encourage young Southerners to go into the examinations and to see that, when appointments were made, the full quota of each Southern State was allowed. It ceased to be a novelty for Southern Congressmen to meet young constituents on the streets of Washington and to learn that they were there under a Republican administration. Nothing of this sort had been known for a generation. Thirteen Southern States, including Maryland and Kentucky, are, under the operation of the Reform law, entitled to thirty per cent. of the positions in the classified Civil Service. Of the eleven Civil Service Commissioners appointed up to Jan. 1st, 1895, four were Southern men, viz.: William L. Trenholm and Hugh S. Thompson of South Carolina, George D. Johnson of Louisiana and John R. Procter of Kentucky. What more had we a right to ask?

What fairer treatment could we expect? It should also be borne in mind that an appointment now in the civil service means an opportunity for an official career. This is impossible under the spoils system. As a plain business proposition, for government is only another name for business, what could be better for both the citizen and office holder?

The Southern press is fast falling into line and it is now definitely known that at least twenty-five daily papers, over one hundred weekly papers, and eight monthly publications are known to be entirely friendly to the merit system and are championing its cause with zeal and intelligence. In fact few Southern newspapers now openly and enthusiastically support the "Spoils System," a sure indication of the tendency of public opinion on that subject. The advocates of the merit system, steadily increasing in numbers, aer each year becoming more active and aggressive and ultimately must hold the balance of power in determining the fate of candidates and of parties.

As a Southern man, both by the accident of birth and as the result of my deliberate choice, proud of the past of my section and confident of its future glory, with that of the Nation, I declare it to be my honest conviction that the Southern people are tired of the iniquities of a vicious public policy which has always been condemned by her wisest statesmen, who have ever taught that the greed of the spoilsman, and the corruption of elections are the greatest dangers threatening the perpetuity of our government. Their words of warning were once heeded; these words are now again being driven home with telling force to the Southern heart and mind, and he who seeks shall find unmistakable evidences of an awakening patriotism, of a higher sense of public duty and of a healthier political life and spirit abroad in the land.

The Reign and Overthrow of an Office-holding Oligarchy.

By Charles J. Bonaparte.

The Pendleton bill was reported to the Senate on December 12th, 1881, just fourteen years ago. In the debate which followed, Senator Brown of Georgia expressed grave apprehensions regarding the effects of its enactment on our free institutions. His words were:

"I say it is not compatible with our very form of government. It is one step in the direction of the establishment of an aristocracy in this country, the establishment of another privileged class. * * * It builds up a powerful class supported out of the Treasury of the United States, out of the taxes of the people, and places in their hands the power, if they choose to exercise it—and there is a great deal of human nature in man, so that they probably would exercise it—the power to do much to control the future rulers and destinies of this government.

I am not very fresh from my reading of Roman History; but as I recollect it there was a period in the history of that government when it became necessary to establish the praetorian guard to protect the ruler against the populace.

It would naturally enough have been claimed that that guard would take no part in the politics of Rome, and yet in the workings of time that praetorian guard became the master of Rome, and assumed control of the government. As they protected the sovereign, they dictated who should be the sovereign, and for a large enough amount of money they would displace one sovereign to make room for another. How do we know that we may not build up a similar class here, when we build up a lifetime aristocracy in office, or when we establish a lifetime tenure of office? It is contrary to the very genius and spirit of our government."

The fears thus expressed by this eminent statesman had haunted many others of our public men from the time when legislation looking towards Civil Service Reform was first suggested by Mr. Jenckes. the "old war horses" and "old wheel-horses" who flourished in his day snorted suspicious defiance

at a measure destined, in the language of one of the best
known, at that time, of their number "to create a pampered
aristocracy." It is not my purpose to discuss how far these
patriotic forebodings have been justified by the event; the
dangers to our liberty lurking in the insidious proposals of
Jenckes and Pendleton have had every opportunity to become visible since the Senator from Georgia depicted them in
prophecy. In one of the Ingoldsby legends, the hero remarks:
" I did not see my little friend, because he was not there."
Such blindness as we may exhibit to these perils admits, perhaps, of the same explanation.

I have lived, however, for some twenty or twenty-five
years under a government marked by not a few of the charac-
teristics which these sages saw in vision defacing that of our
nation. In Baltimore we have had a powerful class supported
out of the taxes of the people holding "in their hands the
power, if they choose to exercise it" (and they most undeni-
ably did choose) "to do much to control the future rulers and
destinies" of the City and State. We have had an organization by no means unlike a "praetorian guard" which "protected the sovereign," at least the sovereign *de facto*, "from
the populace" when this "populace" endangered his safety or
continued rule at the polls, and it "protected" him, on the
whole, very effectually. Moreover, this "guard," had occasion offered, would have readily "dictated who should be the
sovereign" and, "for a large enough sum of money, displaced
one sovereign for another;" indeed, it actually did these
things whenever and in so far as it had the opportunity.

In Baltimore that "first step towards the establishment of
a privileged class," which Senator Brown saw in the Pendleton
bill, and a good many succeeding steps as well, had been
taken a number of years before the bill was heard of, or its
author heard of as a Civil Service Reformer; it is, perhaps,
doubtful whether the late rulers of my native city could
appropriately be called "pampered," for the adjective at least
suggests indolence, and to charge them with this fault would
be certainly unjust; nevertheless, they no less certainly constituted a "privileged class" in every sense of the term; a
class of men in many respects *legibus soluti*, privileged to do
wrong (or what would be wrong for others) with impunity and
even with profit; superior themselves to the laws as well as

able to make the laws for those of inferior station; in my trespass on your attention this afternoon I shall depict a few features of their rule, and describe briefly some of the causes and incidents of their downfall.

It will be noted that I have not called them "an aristocracy." Mr. Freeman observes in his Comparative Politics:

" I need hardly say that the vulgar use of the word 'aristocracy,' to mean, not a form of government but a class of society, has no countenance from Aristotle or from any other writer who attends to the meaning of the words which he uses."

And in another passage:

" Aristocracy, I need hardly say, in its strict sense, is the rule of the best : indeed aristocracy would be the rule of the ideally best, those who are really wisest, bravest and most upright. Any other standard, be it that of age, of birth, or of wealth, is simply a substitute which is accepted because, in an imperfect world, the rule of the ideally best is something which may be talked about, but which will never be found in actual being."

In accordance with his views, I might describe our recent government as an aristocracy wherein the imperfection of the world was recognized by accepting, as the standard substituted for ideal wisdom, courage and uprightness, exceptional skill in ballot stuffing and kindred crimes and marked ability in the advantageous sale of legislation and various other forms of bribery. But, as Mr. Freeman is himself obliged to admit, in common parlance " aristocracy " is used in the sense whereof he and Aristotle disapprove; and I fear lest its employment in this paper might lead the unthinking and ill-informed to suppose that our late rulers constituted a hereditary caste, looking down, regardless of individual merit, upon all born without its pale : a reproach to which they are not fairly open.

I had, however, another, perhaps a better reason for avoiding the term. The same author from whom I have just quoted tells us further :

" I should rather say that it is only in a republic that a real aristocracy can exist. Corinth and Rome, Venice and Genoa, Bern and Nürnberg, bear out what I am saying. The nobles who cringed at the court of the Great King of Paris, or at the lesser courts of his imitators in the petty despotisms of Germany and Italy, had no right to the name of an aristocracy. Aristocracy is the rule of the best ; they were not the best, and they did not rule."

And again :

" I maintain then that aristocracy, in its true sense, is something essentially republican, something to which a monarchic state can present only a faint approach."

Now the government which has lately fallen in Baltimore was distinctly monarchical, at least, in its tendencies. Under it, power was not always, indeed it was never, quite concentrated in the hands of one man, but our rulers were never truly equal, *inter sese ;* their mutual relations rather resembled those of the several Augusti and Cæsars of the later Roman empire : these always tended towards, and within the past eight years had well nigh definitively settled into the dominion of a single ruler surrounded by a group of more or less powerful, sometimes more or less mutinous, but always distinctly subordinate, lieutenants.

There were, however, already indications that in this case, as in those of all other privileged classes known to history, there would have been in time developed a theory of hereditary right to public office, as the nobility of the Roman Republic was gradually formed of descendants of office holders, claiming by custom a monopoly of all posts of trust and honor. Thus in the Seventeenth Ward of the City, there bore sway a magnate whose merits as a "praetorian" had been proven by an almost incredible number of assaults, arrests and indictments for crimes of violence, whilst his influence was no less clearly illustrated by his prompt acquittals and the steadiness with which, throughout his eventful career, he retained the apparently modest, but really important position, of Superintendent of Street Cleaning for his District. However useful as a drill master for recruits, advancing years and frequent wounds had, in a measure, impaired his personal prowess, but during the past year public attention has been called to three worthy sons, displaying at once their father's decided inclination towards public employment, and his characteristic methods of deserving this. They " did good work " at the last election ; unfortunately their services can hardly receive the recognition they expected, although it is not impossible that another may await them.

A slight symptom of that spirit of social exclusiveness which will be certainly shown in time by any ruling class, although it is but just to say that the oligarchy of Baltimore, so far, at least, as my personal observation can be trusted, was, as yet, but little affected by it, may, perhaps be found in the title chosen for a little book to which I would direct your attention. I believe that the names and residences of the local "Four Hundreds" in our several cities are usually to be found in compilations entitled "Blue Books"; this reason may have caused "Colonel" Edward O'Mahony to choose the same title for a work headed by the suggestive query: "Do you Want an Office?" and said on the cover to contain: "An Accurate List of Every Position in the State and City with their Duties and Salaries." The author is widely known in Baltimore, and has held, according to general and uncontradicted report, the responsible position of "Wiskinkie." I do not vouch for my orthography in this instance, and confess ignorance as to the origin or meaning of the name, but the duties of the office are well understood; its incumbent collects, or collected, the assessment levied on the salaries of all office holders under the state and municipal governments, which defrayed the expenses of keeping at each successive election the sovereign in power, and, it has been sometimes whispered, if not all needed for this purpose, afforded occasionally a partial compensation for the cares of State to those burdened with them. The peculiar experience of its author may, perhaps, explain an apparent (but only apparent) misstatement in what he says of his work; it contains not one word as to the "duties" of the several positions enumerated, except so far as these are intimated in their respective names. This, however, is but seemingly inconsistent with the promise of the cover; the only *official* duty of any real consequence connected with a public position in Baltimore under the late *régime* was that the holder should regularly draw his salary so as to promptly pay the assessments on this: if he did so much, whatever more he did for the State or City was, in great measure, a work of supererogation, which would scarcely, if at all, affect his retention in office, and his duties to the Boss the "Blue Book" does not profess to describe. I will partially repair this omission, but must first say a word as to the number and compensation of the officials mentioned.

To understand the system of government which has existed for nearly a generation in Baltimore, we may glance at three departments only of the City's public service, those headed in the book respectively: "City Commissioner's Office," "General Superintendent of Lamps" and "Superintendent of Streets and District Superintendents." These were composed as follows:

CITY COMMISSIONER'S OFFICE.

One City Commissioner	$4,000
Three Assistant City Commissioners	2,000
One Bridge Engineer	2,400
One Chief Clerk	1,500
One Assistant Clerk	1,200
Five Engineers, each	1,500
One Clerk	1,200
Eighteen Foremen of Gangs	1,200
Five Engineers	1,200
One Sand Inspector	1,080
Six Draughtsmen, each	900
One Clerk	1,100
Eight Rodmen, each	900
Three Rodmen, each	700
One Keeper, Belair Lot	800
Twelve Watchmen, each	720
Two Superintendents of Annex, each	1,000
One Superintendent of Light Street Bridge	1,200
Six Assistants at Light Street Bridge, each	600
Fourteen Superintendents of Cobble Stone Gangs	600
One Paymaster	1,400
One Assistant Paymaster	900
Fifteen Tally Clerks, each	750
Twelve Carpenters, each	900
Eighteen Assistant Foremen of Gangs, each	600
Two thousand Laborers and other minor positions when working full force, *per* week	10

GENERAL SUPERINTENDENT OF LAMPS.

One General Superintendent	$2,000
One Clerk	1,000
Two Inspectors of Electric Lights, each	900
Two Inspectors of Repairs, each	900
Five General Utility Men, each	520
Five District Superintendents for City, each	600
Two District Superintendents for Annex, each	936

Twenty-one Lamplighters, Western District, each... 416
Twenty-two Lamplighters, Northwestern District, each........ 416
Twenty-two Lamplighters, Southern District, each............ 416
Twenty-two Lamplighters, Northeastern District, each........ 416
Twenty-four Lamplighters, Eastern District, each............. 416
Thirty-four Lamplighters, Annex, each..................... 416

SUPERINTENDENTS OF STREETS AND DISTRICT SUPERINTENDENTS.

One General Superintendent......... .... $2,000
One Clerk................. 1,000
Seven District Superintendents, each...................... 1,000
Four Tally Clerks at Dumps, each........ 600
One Foreman of Street Cleaning Wagons.................... 700
Five Drivers of Street Cleaning Wagons, each............... 550
Twenty-seven Drivers of Street and Garbage Carts, First District,
    each.. 935
Thirty-seven Drivers of Street and Garbage Carts, Second District, each.................................... 935
Twenty-seven Drivers of Street and Garbage Carts, Third District, each....... 935
Thirty-seven Drivers of Street and Garbage Carts, Fourth District, each... 935
Thirty-six Drivers of Street and Garbage Carts. Fifth District,
    each... 935
Thirty-eight Drivers of Street and Garbage Carts, Sixth District,
    each.......................... 935
Nineteen Drivers of Street and Garbage Carts, Seventh District,
    each... 935

In these three departments alone there were employed, when that of the City Commissioner was "working full force," and, it is needless to say, that such was always the case when elections were held and might be, if needful, at the time of primaries, 2,540 men; 95 per cent. of these discharged functions for which any ordinary laborer was qualified; all, except perhaps a dozen of those highest in rank, received a compensation greatly in excess of that paid for similar services by private employers; and all of them, without exception, were selected for reasons of political expediency or personal favoritism.

The last remark, although strictly accurate, may be somewhat misleading; I do not mean that in these departments or any others, the subordinate employees of the city, or that those of the State, where chosen capriciously or without reference to their capacity to discharge the *real*, as distinguished from the merely *nominal*, duties which they had to perform. On the contrary, every man of them, with exceptions altogether insignificant in number, was selected because he had shown, or was expected to show, marked fitness for service in the "praetorian guard," to which I have alluded, and, if he fulfilled these expectations during a period of probation of reasonable length, he was assured of a fixity of official tenure far greater than any contemplated by the Pendleton bill or any similar measure, since it was, under ordinary conditions, unaffected by the merits of his official conduct. As an illustration the Seventeenth Ward chieftain to whom I have alluded, was first called to my attention as an office holder (he was already well-known in other capacities) in 1883, when he was desperately wounded in a shooting affray at the very door of the City Hall, his assailant being afterwards acquitted on the ground of self defence. He had then held his present position for some time, and, unless my memory be at fault, he has retained it uninterruptedly during the twelve years which have since elapsed. Nor is his case in any wise exceptional; such services as his,—I mean, of course, as a praetorian, not as a District Superintendent of Streets,—were too valuable to be lightly lost.

If the character of these services be asked, I can best answer by giving the dry facts of an event which deserves a more worthy and perhaps a more sympathetic historian. To return to Mr. Freeman, every reader of his Norman Conquest must share his regret that the legend of the battle of Stamford bridge is proven baseless and its history is lost; that it is only in imagination :

"We may see the golden Dragon, the ensign of Cuthred and Aelfred, glitter on high over this its latest field of triumph. . . . . We may call up before our eyes the final moment of triumph, when for the last time Englishmen on their own soil had possession of the place of slaughter."

There is even greater reason to deplore the probable loss to the world of any adequate narrative of the Special Election held in the Fifteenth and Sixteenth Wards of Baltimore on March 26th last, when, probably for the last time, our veteran praetorians returned with sundown victors to their camp, a loss almost certainly irreparable, for the relations of our late rulers towards that class of the community known to them as "damn literary fellers" were so far from cordial that it is eminently unlikely any Freeman will be hereafter found to lovingly chronicle the deeds of might which preceded their downfall.

It may be well to explain that one member of the Second Branch of our City Council is chosen every second year for each two Wards of the City; this election was held in the present year and, therefore, next previously in 1893. Towards the end of last winter the gentleman representing the fifteenth and sixteenth Wards died. The circumstances under which his successor was chosen are thus set forth in a report of the Standing Committee on Elections of the Baltimore Reform League, presented, after a very careful investigation, to the Executive Committee on July 11th last:

"It will be remembered that at the election of the first Branch of the City Council in November, 1894, the combined Republican vote in the Fifteenth and Sixteenth Wards was 2851 and the combined Democratic vote was 2,338, a Republican majority in the two Wards of 513. It is a fact of public notoriety that a victory for the Democratic management at the Special Election in March following was regarded by Democratic politicians as a supreme necessity to arrest the party demoralization which followed upon the November election. It is accordingly significant that we find that at the Special Election in the following March, about five months after the Democratic defeat of 1894, and without any apparant change or occasion for change in popular political sentiment, the combined Republican vote in the two wards was declared to have fallen to 2444 and the combined Democratic vote was declared to have increased to 2471—a declared Democratic majority of 27."

The result thus attained is the more worthy of note because at the election held last month, the Republican candidate for the same office received in the two Wards 3812 votes, a gain of 961 over that cast in 1894 and of 1368 over that cast (or at least returned) in the previous spring, whilst the Democratic vote was 2447, only 109 more than in 1894, and actually 24 less than at the Special Election. No one will seek to detract from the hard-earned glory of our prætorians by pretending that any real change in public sentiment could have converted, or even aided materially to convert, into a minority of 27 a majority of 513, which at the next succeeding election became one of 1365. Nor, it is but just to say, has any one attempted seriously to dispute their claim to full credit for the achievement. It is true that, in the language of the report from which I have just quoted:

"The Democratic candidate was seated by the Democratic majority in the Second Branch in the City Council, notwithstanding the protest of his Republican competitor, which was tabled without discussion, and without pretence of investigation of the truth of its allegations."

But the report goes on to say:

"The evidence before your Committee, however, shows that the declared Democratic majority of 27 was wholly fraudulent, and that the Democratic candidate probably received the benefit of 188 fraudulent votes, and perhaps of 259 such votes, thus converting the declared majority of 27 into a minority of probably 232 votes, and certainly of 161."

Of the correctness of the conclusion thus expressed, except in so far as it is a great and evident understatement, no one who has examined this report and its appended exhibits can entertain any doubt. A few extracts from the report of the League's counsel, constituting one of these exhibits, may illustrate the efficient causes of the result. He says:

"The result of this investigation is to make certain that at least 188 names voted on were voted on by persons to whom they did not belong. There are 71 other votes, each of which it is practically certain was cast by repeaters, although it would not be possible to prove to absolute demonstration that they were. These votes were cast on the names of persons about whom nothing can be learned at their registered address, and whose names were either originally placed upon the registration list for fraudulent purposes, or of persons who since their registration have removed entirely from the City, leaving no trace of their present whereabouts. . . . .

"Both colored and white repeaters were engaged in the perpetration of these frauds. Of the votes, each of which was without the possibility of a doubt cast by a repeater, 105 were cast upon the names of colored men and 83 upon the names of white men. Of the 71 votes which to a moral, though not a legal certainty, were cast by repeaters, 52 were cast upon the names of white persons, and 19 upon those of colored persons. . . .

"The gangs or companies of repeaters were relatively large at the openings of the polls in the morning, but later in the day they seem more frequently to have consisted of 2 to 5 persons, though, of course, occasionally a repeater came to the polls alone. . . . .

"In addition to the fraudulent votes actually polled, there were a great many attempts to vote fraudulently. These attempts failed because the challengers representing the candidate, who, on the face of the returns, was defeated, were able to show that the person offering the vote could not possibly be the person registered. . . . .

" The efforts made to prevent the fraudulent reception of voters not infrequently attended with serious risks to the persons making them. Thus, in the Ninth Precinct of the Fifteenth Ward a colored man, who had lived in the precinct practically all his life, and he is now a man of 44 years of age, noticed in line before the polls opened a number of colored men whom he knew not to be residents of the precinct. He himself was at the head of the line, and, having voted, he stepped out of the polling-room and warned Mr. Robert E. Fisher, a resident of the Ward and an officer of the First Branch of the City Council, that there were a number of colored repeaters in line. While talking to Mr. Fisher on the subject, a white man, whose identity I have been unable to discover, struck him with such force as to knock him down and break his right lower jaw in two places. . . . .

" In the Third Precinct of the Fifth Ward the Republican challenger states that, while insisting upon the arrest of a man of 30 years of age, who had offered to vote on the name of a man of 54 years of age, he was knocked down by persons in the room, and, when he got up, was again struck, the repeater making his escape during the scuffle. . . . .

" At the late election in three of the Precincts persons, while engaged in peaceful attempts to prevent election frauds, were assaulted, and more or less seriously beaten. In no one of these cases was the perpetrator of the assault arrested, and in the only case in which an arrest was made in connection with these assaults, the persons arrested were the victims of the attack and not the persons making it. . . . .

" Of all the persons voting illegally and attempting to vote illegally —the aggregate number of both classes of which must have certainly exceeded 300 in the Wards—only seven were arrested. . . . .

" The result has been that out of the, as before mentioned, 300 attempts, successful and unsuccessful, to vote illegally, only two men were indicted upon charges laid on election day, or by any officers of the law."

I have said thus much of the special election of last March because, although otherwise of comparatively little importance, it serves to illustrate with special clearness one of the principal causes of the Ring's long lease of power in Maryland; this is simply that, through its absolute control of the State and Municipal patronage, it was able to maintain in Baltimore, at the people's cost, a small standing army of experts in election frauds and professional ruffians, unreservedly subject to its order and prepared to furnish any reasonable majority which could be required for its safety under normal conditions; whilst it could likewise assure them almost certain immunity from punishment for their crimes committed in its in-

terest. But this alone would not have availed it much : even
if we suppose the number of fraudulent votes cast at the special election to have been (as it very possibly may have been)
twice as great as the Reform League's Committee reported,
still at least four-fifths of those received by the Ring's candidate must have been legal votes, and, with all its facilities for
successful fraud, its reign would have been short-lived but for
its unqualified and, of late years, undisputed dominion within
the Democratic party. Indeed, it fell at last, not because it
either couldn't or wouldn't cheat, but because, although it
would, it couldn't cheat enough to overcome the widespread
revolt within that party against its domination. A few words
then as to the instrumentalities which rendered that nomination permanent and irresistible.

The Venetian oligarchy maintained its rule through a
Council of Ten, that of Baltimore may have been said to
reign through one of Nine, bearing the modest and outwardly
innocent title of City Members of the Democratic State Central Committee. There was one marked difference, however,
between the two bodies : in Venice the Doge was a figurehead and not a member of the Council, in Baltimore his ana-
logue, the reigning Boss, was a Member of the Council and
very decidedly not a figurehead. Moreover, the Council itself
was differently organized : our rulers may not be, I think, the
probabilities are very strong that they are not, familiar with
the writings of the late John Stuart Mill, but they have practically endorsed his recommendation of the organization given
by the East India Company to its Councils. Of these
bodies Mr. Mill says :

" These Councils are composed of persons who have professional
knowledge of Indian affairs. . . . . As a rule, every member of Council
is expected to give an opinion, which is, of course, very often a simple
acquiescence. . . . . . In ordinary cases the decision is according to the
sense of majority ; . . . . . but if the Governor-General or Governor
thinks fit, he may set aside even their unanimous opinion. . . . . . The
result is that the chief is, individually and effectively, responsible for
every act of the government. The Members of Council have only the
responsibility of advisers."

In like manner in all the various deliberative bodies, and
there were several which, with more or less formality of procedure, were permitted to share in the government of our oli-

garchy, whilst the Sub-Bosses had the right to speak and even to swear, freely, the last word, the effective decision, lay always with the Supreme Boss.

The authority of the body to which I have referred as of decisive weight in the party organization, seems at first sight simple and harmless, being limited substantially to selecting the times, places and officers of the Democratic primaries; but this had come to include the determination in advance of their results upon the principle stated succinctly by one of the witnesses in Commissioner Roosevelt's investigation of the Baltimore Post Office, that, in primaries in that City, "whoever gets two judges" (out of three) "wins." In fact, so fully was this recognized, at least as to Democratic primaries, that for the past eight years both these and the subsequent conventions have been pure forms; invariably the fate of all candidacies has been determined by one man, or, at most, by two or three men, before a vote was cast on them, and the idea of running an opposition ticket has not even occurred to any one. I might give my illustrations of this singular situation, but one of the most recent and most striking will suffice.

For the Democratic nomination as Governor there were several candidates, and had been in some of the counties of the State an animated contest: the subject attracted universal attention and aroused no little feeling. Yet at the city primaries and at the subsequent District Conventions which chose delegates to the State Convention there was not even a ripple of excitement. At the former every body voted, that is to say, every body who voted at all, for the prescribed candidates whose names were first known when seen on the tickets; the latter remained in session but the few minutes needed to organize and unanimously elect the appointed delegates regarding whom there had been as little antecedent publicity. And when the Convention was held, a gentleman received the nomination, who had not been thought of, or, at all events, mentioned as a possible candidate until every primary of the State had been held. The history of his choice was thus given in the Baltimore *Sun* of the day following:

"Here is the way the nomination for Governor came about: Senator Gorman had said in effect to Mr. Rasin, 'I will not accept as a candidate Governor Brown, Judge Robinson or Judge Fisher.'

"Mr. Rasin had said in effect to Senator Gorman: 'I will not accept as a candidate Thomas G. Hayes, Spencer C. Jones or John Walter Smith.'

" Then came the question : ' On whom can we unite ?'

"Several gentlemen were considered, and finally Mr. Hurst was decided upon. Friends of Mr. Rasin and friends of Senator Gorman were sent to Mr. Hurst separately, so as to make the offer of the Governorship look like a spontaneous movement. Mr. Hurst consented ; Gorman and Rasin did the rest."

The last few words are slightly misleading; when the two potentates had agreed upon a man for the place, and he had agreed to take it at their hands, "the rest" was done already.

We may glance for a moment at the composition of the body which could and, indeed, can still, control, without the possibility of effectual resistance, the action of the party organization. Of course, this has varied from time to time, but there is nothing abnormal in its present *personnel.* This included, when it was chosen, a Police Justice, the Clerk of the Superior Court, a Court Bailiff, the Insurance Commissioner of the State, a Member of the City Council, the City Examiner of Titles, the Warden of the Penitentiary, the Superintendent of Streets. and the Clerk of the Criminal Court. Every one of these and, with a single exception, every one is still a public officer, although several more will probably lose their places as the result of the late election ; moreover, all but possibly one or two have been continuously or nearly so in public employ, "supported out of the taxes of the people," to use Senator Brown's words, for from ten to thirty years. For the most of them rotation in office has meant emphatically "rotating out of one office," city, state or federal, " into another," and the same is no less true of the great bulk of those who hold and have recently held the offices catalogued by Mr. O'Mahony. It is not surprising that Mr. Roosevelt should have found reason to say in his report of the investigation to which I have alluded :

" All of the office-seeking or office-holding ward-workers who came before me, evidently believed that the business of managing primaries, and in fact the business of conducting politics generally belonged of right to the office-holding caste. They were as thorough believers in a system of oligarchical government as if they had lived in Venice or in Sparta, only the names enrolled in their ' Golden Book' were those of the men who through political influence had been fortunate enough to get government place or who hoped to get it."

That these men should think this is the more natural because, as I have already said, they not only enjoyed a monopoly of political power, but were granted a practical license to violate the law. I spoke of this feature of our polity at the first Conference for Good City Government, held in Philadelphia nearly two years ago, and as I may safely presume that those among my present hearers who either heard or read what I then said, have wisely forgotten this, I may be pardoned the vanity of quoting my own words:

"Article 9 of the Bill of Rights in the Constitution of Maryland declares :—

" ' That no Power of suspending laws or the execution of laws, unless by, or derived from, the Legislature, ought to be exercised or allowed.'

" ' *Nous avons changé tout cela*,' and a power of suspending laws or their execution exists in Baltimore, which is in no wise 'derived from the Legislature,' although the political existence of members of the Legislature is often 'derived' from those who exercise this power. On our statute book are laws which seem to describe penalties for election frauds, for various forms of gambling and of swindling disguised as gambling, for illicit liquor selling and for maintaining or advertising resorts for immorality, but practically all these pretended crimes are licensed, except the one first named, and that is rewarded. In an address which I delivered some years since at one of the annual meetings of our local Society for the Suppression of Vice, I said, and I now and here repeat : It is no exaggeration of language to say that saloons and gambling houses and brothels are here nurseries for statesmen, that the active hostilities of their keepers is, if not fatal, at least a grave impediment to success in public life ; and that men and women who gain their living by habitually breaking laws have a potent voice in selecting the public servants who make, interpret, and execute those laws."

It must be further remembered that I could then also say truly :

" A very important condition of municipal government in Baltimore is the 'Grandmother's Fund.' As I am away from home, it may be well to explain that this is not a particular sum of money committed to a designated custodian, but represents the aggregate proceeds of various kinds of tribute levied upon the community by its real, as contradistinguished from its nominal rulers. This tribute includes assessments on office-holders and candidates for office, 'benevolences' from contractors doing work or furnishing supplies of any kind to the City or State or institutions under public control, the price of franchises and privileges and special legislation of every kind, whether from the City Council or the General Assembly, the amounts contributed by corporations when sub-

jected to a process known technically as 'plugging,' and the ransom
paid by criminals of all sorts, and especially, as I have endeavored to explain by policy players, brothel-keepers and offenders against the liquor
laws, for impunity,"

The oligarchy of Baltimore is a thing of the past. When
I commenced this paper, I expected to tell, at least briefly,
the tale of its downfall, but when I had written what I have
now read, I realized that ere this my time and your patience
would be alike exhausted. It has fallen, I hope and believe,
never to rise, at least in its old-time shape or strength. As to
the causes of its fall, I would say but one word. The underlying theory of its system cannot be better expressed than it
has been by Mr. Roosevelt in the same report, when he
says :

"Resolved into its ultimate elements, the view of the spoils politician is that politics is a dirty game, which ought to be played solely by
those who desire, by hook or by crook, by fair play or by foul play, to
win pecuniary reward, and who are quite indifferent as to whether this
pecuniary reward takes the form of money or of office. . . . At present
the ordinary office-seeking ward-workers, and a very large percentage of
office-holders have grown to believe that it is a part of the natural order
of things that those who hold or seek to hold the offices should exercise
the controlling influence in political contests."

After all, in a free country, a system of government founded
upon such a theory was doomed to die. Accidental or personal causes might hasten, as they might retard, its fate, but
nothing could have finally averted this. Such a political
structure was indeed "contrary to the very genius and spirit
of our government."

Civil Service Reform in Its Bearings Upon the Interests of Workingmen.

BY HERBERT WELSH.

When Mazzini, the great Italian patriot, addressed the workingmen of his country in 1844, he chose as the title of his essay "The Duties of Man," in sharp antithesis to the great cry which heralded the French revolution — "The Rights of Man." No reformer certainly was more sensitive to the rights of man, in the recognition of which liberty was cradled, but with true religious intuition he perceived that rights were an empty possession, even to the freest of us, unless the heart that rejoiced in them were alive to the obligations they conferred, unless the mind which discerned and demanded them humbly recognized them as the mother of duties. Mazzini pointed out to his fellow countymen how barren to the world had been the possession of rights gained by the ʹrevolution, where the advance was followed by no recognition of duties to one's self and one's fellows. He claimed that the recognition of individual rights must be followed by a sense of universal obligation. He appealed to his hearers with a breadth and simplicity of spirit which must have at once erased the line which separates the workingman from man, and have reached directly his hearers, for the heart leaps artificial boundaries. "I intend to speak to you according to the dictates of my heart," he said; "of the holiest things we know; of God, of humanity, of the Fatherland and the family." And so, in speaking to-day, out through this audience, to those workingmen whom I may be able to reach, of the appeal which Civil Service Reform should make to them, I do it with these four great human relationships which Mazzini enumerates firm in my mind—God, humanity, the Fatherland and family, and not so much to workingmen as men of a

separate and distinct class do I speak as to them as members
of the great human family. But this nobler point of view will
not exclude the consideration of those especial points in which
Civil Service Reform is of peculiar benefit to those whom we
call wage-earners.

The true American workingman, and the true American of
whatever trade or work in life he be, are one in this: That
both desire the full benefits of American institutions; both
desire to see the Government of these United States stand for
liberty, for equal laws, under which men may not be tempted to
change their conceptions of God as a just and loving Father,
of humanity as the great family of mankind, throughout whose
extent some day may be realized the idea of universal brother-
hood, and under which the family may be made a holy and
true relationship, the fountain of domestic virtue, the support of the State, which I, for one, believe that it was ordained
to be. We are one, workingman and other man, in desiring
that America shall be a nation in which these ideas, which
appeal to all hearts, shall be nurtured and have sway. I take
it that the true American workingman will be quite content if
the Government under which we live be honest and true, if it
will truly seek those great principles of liberty and justice to
rich and poor alike, to obtain which its great founders gave
their life; and to preserve its entirety and its integrity, to prevent a rupture that would have been fatal to the realization of
its ideas, its saviors of thirty years ago shed their patriot
blood.

If I mistake not, at the bottom of industrial discontent,
whose mutterings and moanings create at times vague uneasi-
ness and concern in the business of the country, which flashes
out occasionally into revolt, showing fierce tooth and claw, as
at Homestead and Chicago, is the feeling, reasonable or
unreasonable, that there exists to-day some dangerous disloca-
tion between a real Christianity and American political ideals,
on the one hand, and practical existing American Christianity
and existing American politics, on the other. A more or less
vague idea exists in the minds of American workingmen that
capital and wealth have influence with the political machinery
of the country, with legislatures and executives, that they do
not possess; that monopolies and great corporations can, by
corrupt and dishonest methods, so control the conditions of

wealth-getting that enormous and unjust profits accrue to them, out of all proportion to their merits, with total disregard to the rights of those who are dependent upon their pleasure for daily bread. The workingman feels that more and more is the possibility increasing for capital to organize itself into trusts and monopolies, by which the necessaries and the luxuries of life may be put at a price which will bring enormous wealth to the beneficiaries of the monopoly and a correspondingly heavy burden upon the people. Believing this, is it to be wondered at that the American workingman organizes in self-defense, that he forms trades unions and labor organizations, of various kinds, for operations, offensive and defensive, against those whom he believes to be hostile or indifferent to his liberties, his rights, his opportunities? Or is it marvelous that the method by which he defends himself should often lack in wisdom, that it should be sometimes violent and often criminal, therein being akin to the methods which have been more than once adopted by his opponents? Truly, the workingman would be much less then human if he never shared in human folly. The question for the American citizen to ask, as he witnesses the growth of this gigantic conflict, should not be "Is the American workingman always justifiable in his choice of weapons?" By no means, since we know that neither he nor his foe are so; but "Has he any just ground of complaint?" And if so, let us who have such especial time for thought and study of these questions show him, if we know any rational, safe means for reaching the root of the trouble.

To those American workingmen who care to listen to me, may I make the plainest possible confession of my political faith, the simplest statement of those principles and methods which are wholly American in spirit, and which need especially to be enunciated and practiced at this crisis, principles which we all have equal need of for the preservation of our rights, for the right-working of the great national institutions which we enjoy by inheritance.

This is the era in the United States of a great movement to secure honest and sound administration. This era began when the civil war closed; when it will end we cannot say; not at least until what we seek be attained. But that the agitation for sound administration, observable throughout the country, is spreading and strengthening we feel assured. What we want to secure is a perfectly sound political fabric, not a rotten, worm-eaten one, which will not bear the strain of the fierce storms that may come upon it. We want in our legislatures, national, state, municipal legislatures, honest and wise men, men faithful to the people who elected them, not corrupt or foolish men who can be bought by the highest bidder. We need such men in power so that American institutions may resist the attacks made upon them by lawless men who have everything to gain and nothing to lose in times of civil commotion, who imagine they see in law, which should be their protection, and in the representatives of law, enemies to liberty and instruments of oppression. At these they would strike with blind and savage fury. With such anarchists the American workingman has neither part nor lot, for his wages and welfare depend upon stable capital and public security which cannot even exist where the red flag floats. Law, liberty and security are the indispensable conditions of commercial prosperity, and commercial timidity or commercial disaster touch with their blight the wage-earner first. His tiny sails are struck first and fiercest by the ill-wind of financial storm. But there is another form of anarchy with which we, as a nation, are much more likely to be threatened than that which shouts its challenge to our civilization from ignorant and inebriated minds, and, for the most part, in foreign tongues. The anarchy which threw its bombs at the police in Chicago seems juvenile malicious mischief compared to that which illustrated its purpose and methods in the famous, or infamous, oil monopoly of Cleveland, which, by immoral and illegal secret compact with great railways controlling the highways from the oil regions to the markets of the world, stifled an industry on which the prosperity of communities rested, drove towns and cities to desperation in gaining for itself such wealth as imagination can scarcely compute. The oil monopoly, with its merciless destruction of industry in that especial department of business, is but an example of numerous other monopolies which tend to pursue similar purposes by similar methods in every branch of business. Their wealth is so great, running up into untold millions, their advance is so remorseless, uncontrolled by conscience or scruple, that laws, legislatures, courts, colleges and church cannot withstand them. I ask not alone workingmen, but all men who believe in the unreserved application of moral principle, of justice and righteousness to all affairs of life, whether the Republic has faced so strong an enemy since slavery fell, if, indeed, in that institution, she faced one as dangerous? Examine the evidence piled up in the reports of State and Federal investigating committees of the practices and results of the great monopolies—Whiskey Trust, Oil Trusts and the like—which has been so effectually marshalled in a notable recent publication, Lloyd's "Wealth Versus Commonwealth," and tell me whether, in this shameless and audacious history, we have not sufficient evidence of a force for evil in the present business world, which, in subtle sagacity, in breadth of operation, in its ramifications of influence, and in the infernal splendor of its designs, is certainly an industrial Lucifer of the first magnitude. It stands to-day as the most astute and majestic enemy of the Republic, already subjecting our institutions to their severest test, as it is testing the gold of an individual and national character, by the severest analysis, in its fiery crucible. It has debauched our politics from the primary to the Senate. It has so long had our legislatures in its pay that their servility has ceased to astonish us. It has swayed our courts, and its shadow still rests upon some of them. Its operations have infused moral malaria into the atmosphere of our entire business world, making men listless and nerveless in the presence of crimes, which, if committed by individuals or in other spheres of life, would have roused them to swift activity. But now we have seen the demand for investigation of corruption charged upon a member of the Senate of the United States voted down under the influence of one great trust; we have seen in that body party interests betrayed openly and shamelessly under the influence of another, exciting, apparently, but little public indignation. Turn to nearly any of the great cities of the country to New York, Chicago, to Philadelphia, New Orleans, Baltimore or others, and you will find the most flagrant violations of all rules of honesty and sound government plotted, executed and persisted in by a corrupt combination of great corporations, great monopolies and a political machine manned by mercenary politicians and commanded by mercenary bosses. We see corrupt councilmen and aldermen, corrupt police force, ill-enforced or unenforced laws, places of prostitution and liquor saloons in known alliance with the very authorities that should suppress them. We see public franchises of enormous value sold for a song or given away to such corporations by men whom we know to be their creatures, bought with their money. Many of these corporations have a curious, illusive, double nature. They play the Dr. Jekyll and Mr. Hyde rôle to perfection. Their presidents and directors are our leading and influential men, prominent in our best society, in our churches, trustees of our hospitals, colleges and charities. But they have a man, or men, well adapted for the purely practical part of their business, who know how to "see" to good purpose legislators and councilmen who have legislative favors to grant. These prominent railroad men, these captains of industry, do not believe in mixing politics and religion, nor do they believe in allowing their ministers to mix religion with politics. They believe in what they call "a pure Gospel," which means impure politics. They do not believe in the simple application of ethics to daily business and political life. If our colleges will not teach such application rigorously, if they will not question the methods by which much of their patrons' wealth has been obtained, they will enormously endow institutions of learning. Such men, if the pulpit will keep silent upon the eccentricities and irregularities of their business methods, will endow churches and support charities by liberal gifts, and send their ministers and their families on excursions at home or abroad. If cities and society will courteously receive them and not look too curiously at the foundations of their fortunes, they will raise statues to great men, enrich art galleries and beautify parks, and in all, perhaps, but in one vital respect, play the part of the generous patron and good citizen.

Anarchy means confusion, chaos, unrepressed violation of law, the overturning of law. Is not, then, this conspiracy between corrupt business and corrupt politics, notwithstanding its elegant veneer, a death's head hidden beneath gems? Is not this, to the impartial judgment, anarchy? Is it not, moreover, the most potent provoker of the conventional anarchy, with which we are so familiar? Have not wage-earners, workingmen and all other true Americans reason to fear it? Is there any David, with shepherd's sling and smooth stone out of the brook, who dares meet this Goliath? Civil

Service Reform, if left free to do its full work, will overcome the champion of the Philistines.

I believe that the spirit of Civil Service Reform and its practical application to our politics by reasonable methods will prove the most fundamental corrective for the evils of which we complain. Civil Service Reform is the name which covers a great principle; that principle is honesty and sound sense in the use of non-political appointive offices. Civil Service Reform rules are the practical application of that principle to politics. Civil Service Reformers ask a very simple and practical thing—that every non-political appointive office in the Union, whether in the Federal, State or municipal service, should be filled in accord with principles of rigid honesty. This reform asserts that all such offices are not concerned with carrying out party policy, but only with an honest and efficient performance of duty, on the part of their incumbents, in the interest of the entire body of citizens for whom that duty is done. To effect this purpose these reformers say a proper and reasonable test should be applied to every applicant for such office, which test should be open and competitive, and fitted to show whether the applicant really possesses the required qualifications or not. Thus, for example, to a person seeking a postion the duties of which were astronomical in their nature, questions in astronomy and mathematics would be applied, while to one seeking a humble position—we will say in the labor service of a great city—would be given the most simple and rudimentary form of examination possible, an examination, possibly, which would not embrace any form of book learning, or even writing, but which would simply relate to the applicant's physical strength, his experience and his character. Such an examination might give the applicant a certain preference over others, if he had served his country in the army or navy, and if he had a family to support. I mention these differences in the character of examinations in order to show their complete adaptability to differing circumstances and to meet the criticism often made that they cannot really test practical fitness. Persons who had passed such an examination at the hands of an impartial commission, whether national, state or municipal, would then have their names registered on a list called the eligible list, the list from which men may be chosen. Then the appointing officer, whether the head of a great national department or the head of a city bureau, when he had a vacant place to be filled, would have the right to choose one from the three highest names on the list to fill it. Then if, for any reason, the person chosen, after trial, proved unsuited to his work, he would be removed and the next on the list substituted, and so on until the right man was found. See how simple, reasonable and practical this plan is, and how wide its application, and how great the advantages flowing from it. 1st, it affords an orderly and systematic way of doing business instead of a disorderly, slipshod way. 2d, it relieves the appointing officer of the intolerable pressure for appointment to which he is subjected by a crowd of importunate and often very unsuitable office-seekers. You know how great this pressure often is at Washington, upon the beginning of a new administration, so that the President and his Cabinet are nearly distracted by it, having no time for their real duties. Under the tyranny of this selfish system, these, the highest executive officers of the government, whose time and energies should be devoted to the consideration of the serious national problems which confront them—questions of finance, of administration, of foreign policy—have been obliged to fritter away much of their time in the ignoble and corrupting practice of dispensing offices; and to do this, moreover, under conditions which usually forbade any full inquiry into the rival claims of applicants, compelling a favorable decision mainly by clamor or by force of partisan service. Do you not see how this system is not alone foolish and unsatisfactory, but that it is, at the bottom, false and dishonest? Its falseness and dishonesty infused themselves into the entire fabric of American politics, not in one sphere alone, but in all. Honest men, men who have strict ideas regarding public duty and public work, have been more and more put to a disadvantage by it. They have found the public service distasteful to them, and, indeed, that it was harder and harder to enter it. Proper protection and rewards were not held out to duty; the sacrifice to conscience, character and independence were too great. Reasonable and honorable party organizations, honorable and inspiring party leadership, such as were observable in the early days of the Republic, were given way to the unscrupulous machine, the unscrupulous boss. These were the conditions, these the men which naturally invited the alliance of great trusts and monopolies, whose gigantic operations and enormous fortunes, swiftly and dishonorably gained, have alarmed thoughtful men. It was the existence of such evils as these, which had buried their roots deep in the spoils system, drawing their main power and sustenance from it, that led, some twenty-five years ago, Mr. George William Curtis, that purest of American patriots, and with him a corporal's guard of like-minded men, drawn from both parties and from different States, to become aggressive champions of Civil Service Reform. Their weapon against this giant of corruption was apparently as insignificant as that of the Hebrew youth. They said simply make American government perfectly honest in its beginnings, and it will become honest in its ends. Lessen the chances for bad men to control politics by stopping their control of spoils, and good men, finding their work both more inviting and easier to perform, will begin to make their wholesome influence felt in public life. Make the machinery which creates executives and legislatures by controlling nominations true and right, and corruption will of necessity be driven out of executive chambers and legislative halls. Remove from the itching fingers of the political boss the great bribery chest which contains approximately 200,000 salaried Federal offices, not counting the vast number of State and municipal offices, and you will largely have destroyed his power for evil. You will have cut off the motive power which drives his machine.

Through long years of popular indifference and misunderstanding and, in the face of contempt, ridicule and of open and secret opposition of politicians, Mr. Curtis and those about him fought that good fight. A Federal Civil Service Bill was passed, a commission to superintend the details of its enforcement was created. Group after group of appointive offices were brought under the restraining sway of the law. These offices were rescued from the brutal ravage of political spoilsmen and restored ·to the honorable possession of the entire people. Offices have ceased to be coin in the purse of a powerful Senator, or of a party boss, which he may throw to a relative, a favorite or a vassal. Under a fair competition they have become open to the use of all. To-day, approximately, 55,000 out of the 200,000 Federal appointive offices are covered by the Civil Service rules. It is but a question of time, and of not very long time, when the entire number will be so covered, and when one of the most serious elements of the corruption of American politics will no longer exist. I ask every thoughtful, intelligent workingman if that is not a consummation that he and every other lover of the country must desire.

But Civil Service Reform has another application which is only now beginning to be seriously considered. It is to the administration of our great American cities, in which—for various causes it is not necessary now to discuss—vast populations are centering; where wealth, intelligence, enterprise, commerce and manufactures, the homes of the rich and the poor are focused. Here every question affecting human life and happiness—questions of sanitation, of sewerage, of water supply, of transportation, of public parks and libraries, of taxation, of the care of the poor, assume accentuated importance. To deal intelligently, honestly and economically with these questions requires intelligence, honesty and experience on the part of the public officers, the Mayors and heads of departments to whom they are committed. Every citizen's interest, his health and his happiness, and that of those near and dear to him, are bound up in the right handling of these matters; but, above all others, will the workingman, the wage-earner, the man of slender means, of hand-to-mouth existence, be sensitive to the excellence or folly of the government of the great city in which he lives. A few cents difference in his car-fare may be sufficient to unbalance his small account at the end of the year. A very small rise in the rate of taxation, due to municipal extravagance or dishonesty, will be keenly felt by him. Public advantages, such as free libraries, public parks and the like, to the poor man mean much, while the man of ample means is virtually independent of them. The sanitary condition of the city, of which the rich man is measurably independent by his ability to go elsewhere during the summer, or to obtain at all times protections which are impossible to the poor man, to the latter are matters of vital import. But how is the city to be well governed if the boss and the machine control it, whose interests are selfish interests, who, by an invariable law of their being, will be as selfish and dishonest in their government of the city as the relative indifference and partisanship of its citizens will permit? How can the city be well governed, I ask intelligent workingmen, whose interests in this question are the interests of us all, only doubly, trebly accentuated, if the 10,000 or 15,000 or 20,000 offices of the city are to be filled by boss and machine, not on proved merit, and held not for faithful performance of duty, but as partisan rewards of the unworthy, and so as to compel partisan service? How, I ask sensible workingmen, can any intelligent and satisfactory city government be conducted on these corrupt and foolish lines? And for the folly of all this, for the pickings and stealings, the losses and blunders, for the costly, unfulfilled contracts, the man who pays most is the workingman. These were the principles which gave us the Tweed ring in New York, with its $15,000,000 to $17,000,000 direct theft, its debauched judiciary, its carnival of spoils. It was the spoils system where there should have been civil service reform, which made Tweed and his fellow conspirators possible. This truth he himself confessed, before he died in prison: That unless some way were found to remove the control of patronage of great cities from the grasp of politicians, there would be recurring scandals, such as his.

Civil service reform is the narrow pass where the defenders of good government may mass their feeble strength so that it shall count in value out of all proportion to their numbers. We must make this reform, in our struggle for good government, the Thermopylae of the present crisis.

Cannot the workingmen of America see how, for every good and honorable purpose which they have in view, their influence should be concentrated to establish this reform, in all its practical details, in the administration of our great cities, in whose slums, in whose saloons, in whose brothels, in all these foes to family life and welfare, the roots of corrupt politics find their nourishment. Let them insist upon the passage of a good civil service law in every State legislature, if one does not already exist. Let them apply it to every city of the State, that every smallest office may be removed from the curse of boss patronage, and so that it shall be filled by suitable test. See that a State Civil Service Commission exists in every State to superintend the practical application of the law, a commission with such men upon it as Theodore Roosevelt and his colleagues, and Colonel Procter and Major Harlow have proved themselves to be on the Federal Commission—

honest, experienced, courageous men, who will see that under the law the humblest, least protected applicant gets his rights and a fair chance to show what is in him. See that every city of your State has the same great American principle of justice and fair play, as opposed to privilege, applied to its labor service, just as to-day is in successful operation in the city of Boston, in Cambridge, in New Bedford and in New York and Brooklyn. The same labor system has won the approval of naval officers of high rank in the Federal service.

Let us set to work, then, promptly, practically, to correct the evils of our city government, as of our broader politics, at their source, remembering that "the corruption of the city is the menace of the State." I use the word State not to signify a narrow geographical expression, but the State in its supreme signification—the Nation. Let us, in approaching this great work, understand that even its details can best be mastered by taking, first, a broad view of its entirety. Let us rest our eyes, tired with watching only the complex machinery under our fingers, for a moment on the peaceful blue of a broad horizon. We must go to this great work of American political reform catching the grand inspiration of its ultimate purpose. It is to make America strong for her future work, a larger work than we now surmise, that we struggle. As Mazzini, a weary exile in a foreign land, wrote, reminding the workingmen of Italy, we must not be content with asserting our rights; we must also remember that we have duties to perform—duties to God, to humanity, to the family and ourselves. I emphasize duties in antithesis to rights, not with the intention of trying to persuade any workingman within this land, who asserts rights that he thinks have been withheld from him, to refrain from demanding their recognition. Indeed, I have fully admitted, in the opening part of this address, that I think wrongs of a most serious nature have been perpetrated by unscrupulous capital, acting in conjunction with unscrupulous political machines, on us all, wrongs which should be opened to the full light of day, carefully considered and fully righted; but I believe the most effective way to secure these rights and to cure these wrongs is to approach the whole question from the point of view of duty, to recognize the wrong which is perpetrated upon our entire country, upon the humanity which it embraces. We must recognize evils, not as inflicted by one class upon another, which will lead us to divide into warring and embittered factions, but we must regard them, if we would be both just and strong, as the product of bad men and bad methods, which do not spring from any one class, and which inflict their injury upon all men and upon a common country. Against an anarchy springing partly from beneath, from ignorant or perverse men, who would overthrow all law to obtain what they misname their rights, and against that anarchy which comes from above, which would draw to itself all wealth by corrupting public life, against these twin foes of the Republic we must unite, not in the spirit of hate, but of love and of duty, on the basis of uncorrupted law and sound political life, with the consciousness of a divine purpose guiding us and of an unselfish labor to perform. Our keenest weapon in the conflict is the spirit of Civil Service Reform and its practical application throughout the range of our public service, and our battle ground is the great cities of America.

Status of the Civil Service Reform Movement in the District of Columbia.

By CHAS. W. STETSON.

The immediate practical object which the Civil Service Reform Association of the District proposed to itself on its formation was the extension of the classified service of the National Government to the municipal offices of the District. The District municipal service comprises about two thousand positions. No law existed applying the tests of merit or fitness to appointments, promotions or removals in this service. It has been the object of the Commissioners of the District in the main to keep the service out of politics. But their situation was often a trying one, and the greater number of appointments made by them in recent years have been in deference to political pressure. Members of Congress who failed to find "berths" for constituents in the national civil service have turned on the Commissioners of the District and demanded that the latter discharge congressional obligations to party-workers by appointments in our municipal service; and worse still, necessary and legitimate appropriations for the District have been imperilled by the reluctance of the Commissioners to barter offices for legislation.

As an instance of the trials to which the Commissioners have been subjected this may be told: Several years ago a newly-appointed commissioner, a republican in politics, found himself mysteriously in possession of a complete list of all the employees of the district government, with the names of the republicans in black ink and the democrats in red, the latter color being used, he conjectured. to signify it was their blood that was wanted. Broad hints as to the proper use to be made of the list were followed by a determined onslaught on him by the so-called local politicians, assisted by their congressional allies, but the commissioner, now an ex-commissioner and a member of our association, sent them away in the same hungry condition as they came in.

The immediate object of the association then was to se-cure some executive or legislative action which would take the District service entirely out of politics; to strengthen the Commissioners' hands by enabling them to say to congres-sional and other importunists, " We cannot do what you ask without violating the law." But I need hardly say that the Association conceived itself to have larger reasons for exist-ing than its effort to secure the extension of the classified ser-service to the District municipal offices. We wished to take our part in the great work of creating a public sentiment which shall realize the all-corroding influence of the spoils sys-tem on our national life and politics, and to set up in our com-munity a visible protest against the false and vitiating concep-tion, so prevalent yet, that it needs the bribery of office to arouse a healthy interest in political questions. What we may have accomplished towards this end cannot, of course, be ac-curately determined, but if the increased attention to the gen-eral subject of civil service reform in our local newspapers be anything of a test, we have real cause to feel gratified.

Our first effort was to induce the President to extend the provisions of the civil service law to the District by executive order. In this we had the co-operation of the District Com-missioners It was ascertained that the President was inclined to act favorably, but doubted whether the general civil service law gave him authority to deal with the municipal offices of the District. The question was referred by him to the Attorney General, and in the course of the winter the President informed a committee of the Association that the Attorney General held under existing law that the extension could not be made and that legislative enactment would be necessary to accomplish what was desired. The short session of Congress was already far advanced, but a bill was thereupon introduced into the House of Representatives by Mr. Everett of Massachusetts, having for its object the removal of the diffi-culties supposed to exist in the way of executive action, and this bill was referred to the Committee on Civil Service Re-form. Earnest efforts were made by several officers and members of the Association to secure action on it, but the

crowded condition of the House calendar and the indifference
of the majority of the members of the Civil Service Reform
Comittee made it impossible to secure any action. Senator
Lodge stood ready to introduce a similar bill in the Senate,
but the fruitlessness of our endeavors to secure consideration
of the House Bill led us to think it best to postpone the matter to the present long session of Congress.

During the winter the Board of Trade of the District
took up the matter of municipal civil service reform. After
some discussion a resolution of approval was passed almost
unanimously and a committee appointed to co-operate with
our Association in an effort to secure proper legislation in
this Congress.

The Commissioners, however, have not waited for Congress
to act, but have themselves taken a step in the right direction. On June 17th, 1895, this order was issued by them:
"All appointments to positions in the District Government
shall be made under civil service rules to be adopted and
promulgated as soon as practicable." The rules for carrying
this order into effect have not yet been formulated for lack
of appropriation, but as a declaration of policy which the
Commissioners propose to follow in filling positions at their
disposal, the order is very encouraging.

A bill enlarging the scope of the Everett bill will be introduced in the House early in the present session; its progress will be carefully watched by the Association and no effort
will be spared to secure its passage. If passed by the House
and Senate, the Association has every reason to believe it will
receive the President's signature.

Report of the Special Committee

On Extension of the Civil Service Rules and the Adoption of Rules for the Consular Service.

In compliance with the following resolution adopted by the Executive Committee of the National Civil Service Reform League at its meeting of September 23. "That a special committee be appointed to report on the additions to the classified service made by the President, with special reference to the order concerning the Consular Service," the Special Committee beg leave to report as follows:

Extension of the Classified Service.

From information published in abstracts of the monthly reports of the Secretary of the New York Civil Service Reform Association it appears that the following extensions of the classified service, and reductions in the list of excepted places within the classified service, have been effected by executive order during the present administration:

By Classification.	Dates of Executive Order.	Number of Employees Affected.
Post Office Dept.:		
Clerks and Post Office Inspectors	Nov. 2, 1894	29
Sea Post Office Clerks	Dec. 3, 1894	14
		—— 43
Treasury Dept.:		
Customs Districts having as many as 20 and less than 50 employees	Nov, 2, 1894	647
Employees in Customs Districts having more than 50 employees with compensation of less than $900	Nov. 2, 1894	860
Internal Revenue Service (exclusive of 913 deputy collectors)	Dec. 12, 1894	2,939
		——4,446

By Classification.	Dates of Executive Order.	Number of Employees Affected.
INTERIOR DEPT.:		
Assistant Teachers, Indian Service.......	May 11, 1894	89
Employees at Indian Warehouse, N. Y...	July 25, 1894	2
Pension Agency Clerks.................	July 15, 1895	505
		596
DEPT. OF AGRICULTURE:		
Bureau of American Industry: Inspectors.	May 28, 1894	69
" " " " Microscopists, 7; Asst. Microscopists, 212; Taggers, 162; Clerks, 18; Agents, 2; Live Stock Agents, 27; Stock Examiners, 113.	May 24, 1895	541
Weather Bureau Messengers, outside of Washington	May 24, 1895	170
Supt. of Quarantine Station.............	May 24, 1895	2
Supt. of Veterinary Experiment Station...	May 24, 1895	1
Veterinary Inspectors	May 24, 1895	4
		787
MISCELLANEOUS:		
Messengers, Watchmen, etc., in Departments at Washington	Nov. 2, 1894	868
Employees of Government Printing Office.	June 13, 1895	2,710
Firemen in the Departments	July 15, 1895	100
		3,678
		9,550

By Transfer from Excepted to Competitive List.	Dates of Executive Order.	Number of Employees Affected.
POST OFFICE DEPT.:		
Superintendents, Custodians of Money, etc., at Post Offices..............	Nov. 2, 1894	2,267
Steamboat Clerks, Railway Mail Service..	Nov. 17, 1894	25
Transfer Clerks " " " ..	Nov. 17, 1894	139
Superintendents of Post Office Stations at which Carriers are employed	Jan. 3, 1895	128
		2,559
DEPT. OF AGRICULTURE:		
Appointment Clerk....................	Mar. 20, 1894	1
Professors of Meteorology..............	May 1, 1894	3
All Chiefs and Asst. Chiefs of Divisions..	{ July 9, 1894 } { Mar. 24, 1895 }	44
Topographers, etc., Geological Survey....	Dec. 4, 1894	78
Various Scientific positions, Geological Survey.................................	July 15, 1895	100
Experts in Washington.................	May 24, 1895	53
Experts outside Washington.............	May 24, 1895	25
Statistical Agents.....................	May 24, 1895	20
		324

By Transfer from Excepted to Competitive List.	Dates of Executive Order.	Number of Employees Affected.
MISCELLANEOUS :		
Engineers and Asst. Engineers in the Departments	June 25, 1895	40
Bookbinders.........................	Sept. 5, 1895	25
Compositors and Pressmen.............	Aug. 16, 1895	100
		——— 165
		3,048

Since these figures were compiled one further extension has occurred, affecting 46 employees of the Department of Labor. There have therefore been added to the competitive list during the present administration, 12,644 positions—9,598 by original classification and 3,048 by transfer from the excepted list.

The additions thus made to the classified service are of high value, and the country may therefore be congratulated upon a very appreciable advance of the cause of Civil Service Reform.

The Consular Order.

The executive order concerning the consular service is as follows:

"It being of great importance that the consuls and commercial agents of the United States shall possess the proper qualifications for their respective positions to be ascertained either through a satisfactory record of previous actual service under the Department of State or through an appropriate examination.

"It is hereby ordered that any vacancy in a consulate or commercial agency now or hereafter existing, the compensation of which (whether derived from salary or from official fees), exclusive from notarial and other unofficial receipts, does not exceed $2,500, nor fall below $1,000, shall be filled (a) by a transfer or promotion from some other position under the Department of State of character tending to qualify the incumbent for the position to be filled ; or (b) by appointment of a person not under the Department of State, but having previously served thereunder to its satisfaction in a capacity tending to qualify him for the position to be filled ; or (c) by the appointment of a person who, having furnished the customary evidence of character, responsibility and capacity, and being thereupon selected for examination, is found upon such examination to be qualified for the position.

"For the purpose of this order notarial and unofficial fees shall not be regarded, but the compensation of a consulate or commercial agency shall be ascertained, if the office is salaried, by reference to the last preceding appropriation act, and, if the office is not salaried, by reference to the returns of official fees for the last preceding fiscal year.

" The examination herein provided for shall be by a board of three persons designated by the Secretary of State who shall also prescribe the subjects to which such examination shall relate and the general mode of conducting the same by the Board.

" A vacancy in the consulate will be filled at discretion only when a suitable appointment cannot be made in any of the modes indicated in the second paragraph of this order."

This order affects 196 of the 320 positions in the Consular Service at the time it was issued, as follows:

Salaried officers—Consuls and Consuls General—above. $2,500   53

Salaried officers between $2,500 and $1,000 :

	CONSULS.	COMMERCIAL AGENTS.		
$2,500	30	1	31	
2,000	52	4	56	
1,500	69	6	75	
1,000	13	0	13	
			175	

Feed officers less than $1,000 (a):

	CONSULS.	COMMERCIAL AGENTS.		
	9	12	21	196

Feed officers below $1,000 (b).   71

320

(a). The maximum compensation by fees is $2,500, and the minimum compensation by salary is $1,000.

(b). The places that pay less than $1,000 are generally filled by foreigners or residents of the locality. It is not practicable to extend the new system to them, as the examinations are to be held in Washington.

The following table of subjects on which candidates for consular offices are to be examined has been published:

1. General education, knowledge of languages, business training and experience.

2. The country in which the consul or commercial agent is to reside, its government, chief magistrate, geographical features, principal cities, chief productions, and its commercial intercourse, and relations with the United States.

3. The exequatur, its nature and use.

4. Functions of a consul or commercial agent as compared with those of a vice-consul or consular agent—relation of former to latter, also to the United States Minister or ambassador at the capital of the country.

5. Duties of a consul or commercial agent as regards :

    a. Correspondence with State Department and the form thereof.

    b. Passports, granting and viséing.

    c. United States merchant vessels in a foreign port and their crews, whether seeking discharge, deserting or destitute.

    d. Wrecks within the jurisdiction.

    e. Wrongs to United States citizens within jurisdiction.

    f. Invoices.

    g. Official fees and accounts.

6. Treaties between the United States and the foreign country.

7. Relations of ambassador and minister to laws of the country to which they are accredited, as compared with those of consul or commercial agent to those of the country where they reside.

8. Acts of ambassador or minister, how far binding upon his country.

9. Diplomatic, judicial and commercial functions of consuls or commercial agents.

10. Piracy, what it is, and where punishable.

11. Consular regulations of the United States (copy of which to be returned to the department) will be supplied to each candidate upon application.

12. Such other subject or subjects as the board may deem important and appropriate in any particular case.

These subjects appear to be well chosen.

The Secretary of State has also appointed a commission to conduct the examinations, which is composed of men thought to be thorough believers in the principles and aims of Civil Service Reform.

All this permits us to hope that, after having in so unequivocal a manner recognized the necessity of improving the consular service by promoting meritorious officers from lower to higher positions, and by subjecting candidates for appointment to comprehensive examinations calculated to test their general intelligence and their knowledge of things which a consular officer should know—an official recognition which is, as such, of great value, the administration will faithfully endeavor to secure from the system thus initiated the best possible results. Nor do we doubt that a strict and consistent enforcement of this order would lead to a considerable improvement of the consular service.

But we cordially agree with the Secretary of State, Mr. Olney, when in his letter on this subject addressed to the President he says that the order should be considered as "in no sense final or exhaustive," but rather as a mere "step in the right direction" which "will inevitably lead to a further advance." In the first place, the insufficiency of a mere executive order to secure a permanent improvement in the methods of making appointments to places in the consular service is strikingly exemplified by the history of such executive orders set forth by Mr. Olney in his letter. The executive orders of 1866, 1872 and 1873, requiring all applicants for consular offices to be examined as to their qualifications, were, no doubt, well meant, and attempts were made to put them into execution. There is as little doubt that, had they been faithfully observed, they would have brought about material improvements in the consular service. The reason why they soon fell into complete disuse is very obvious. They were regulations which the appointing power adopted for its own guidance. It kept the machinery for enforcing those regulations under its own control. The same power that had issued those regulations by a mere exercise of its own discretion, could, by a mere exercise of the same discretion, stop their enforcement. The regulations were naturally distasteful to influential politicians, members of Congress or other party leaders, who wished to obtain from the administration appointments to consular offices as rewards for their henchmen. So long as the executive resisted the urgencies of these politicians the regulations were observed. As soon as the Executive yielded to that pressure, the regulations were dropped. And in every instance they were dropped very soon after they had been issued, because the Executive very soon again yielded to political pressure. Even admitting, for the sake of argument, that the present administration may resist that pressure with greater firmness than its predecessors, and that public sentiment demands reforms in the consular service more loudly now than it demanded them at the time when the former executive orders were issued, yet we are not san-

guine enough to hope that members of Congress or other
party chieftains will cease to ask for consulships in their hunt
for spoils, and that all Presidents and Secretaries of State will
henceforth be proof against all pressure coming from their
party friends. We see, on the contrary, great reason for ap-
prehending that before very long the present executive order
will fall a victim to the same influences which have proved
fatal to its predecessors.

In our opinion Mr. Olney, therefore, in the letter to the
President recommending the issuance of the order, wisely
guarded against its being considered as "final or exhaustive."
We presume that he does not mean that it should stand in the
way of bills touching the same matter which have been introduced in Congress, but looks for a further advance. The history of the executive orders mentioned proves clearly that this
advance, to be lasting in its effect, must come in the shape of
legislation. Only when the resistence of the Executive to
political pressure is fortified by a law, can it with any degree
of certainty be expected to be enduring. We believe, therefore, that the present executive order does not give the friends
of reform in the consular service any reason for relaxing their
efforts to obtain legislation to that end on the basis of the
Lodge and Morgan bills, On the contrary, it should stimulate those efforts, and it is to be hoped that they will have the
support of the administration. Such legislation should provide, as far as practicable for open competitive tests of fitness,
and place the conduct of the examinations necessary to that
end under the control of the National Civil Service Commission; for nothing can be more certain than that just so long
as the appointing power reserves to itself the discretion for
designating the candidates to be examined, and thus to point
out to examiners under its own immediate control the persons
it wishes to be found fit—just so long the political pressure
and the danger of relapse will continue, and in the same measure there will be popular distrust as to the fairness and impartiality of the proceeding.

Examinations for public employment are not intended
only, or even principally, to test the capacity of applicants;
they do indeed fulfil incidentally this important and salutary
function, but the one peculiar and transcendant merit of
fairly conducted competitive examinations is that they furnish,

as nothing else as yet devised furnishes, a real and effective safeguard against the abuse of the powers of appointment and removal for partisan or personal reasons. After all, the vital obstacles to the organization of a faithful and efficient consular service for this country are the frequent desire and established custom among our public men to use such offices as a bait or reward for campaign assistance, or as a means of support for friends and dependents. No proposed remedy for existing evils can be recognized by sincere reformers as genuine and thorough which fails to make this form of bribery and breach of public trust impossible for the future.

(Signed)   Carl Schurz,
           Charles J. Bonaparte,
           Richard Henry Dana,
                Committee.

CONSTITUTION

OF THE

National Civil-Service Reform League.

I.

The name of this organization shall be the National Civil Service Reform League.

II.

The object of the National Civil Service Reform League shall be to promote the purposes and to facilitate the correspendence and the united action of the Civil Service Reform Associations.

III.

The League shall consist of all the Civil Service Reform Associations in the United States which signify their willingness to become members thereof. Any association hereafter expressing such willingness shall become a member of the League upon its being accepted as such by the League or the Executive Committee. Any member of any such association may be present at any meeting of the League and take part in the debates or discussions as the by-laws may provide.

IV.

At any meeting of the League, each association belonging to it shall be entitled to one vote upon every question coming before the League; such vote may be cast by a personal representative designated by each association, or by proxy, as the by-laws may provide. If no such designation be made the delegates from such association present at such meeting, or a majority of them, may cast the vote of such association.

V.

The officers of the League shall be a President, Secretary, Treasurer and nine Vice-Presidents; and there shall be a General Committee and an Executive Committee. The officers and the committees shall hold office until their successors are appointed or elected.

VI.

The President and Vice-Presidents shall be elected by ballot at the annual meeting of the League.

The Secretary and Treasurer shall be chosen, and may be removed, by the General Committee.

The General Committee shall be chosen annually, and shall consist of one delegate from each association belonging to the League; and one additional delegate for every two hundred members, or major fraction thereof, of such association as certified by its secretary. Each association shall elect its own delegates in such manner as it may determine.

The members of the Executive Committee shall be ex-officio members of the General Committee.

Any member of the General Committee may act by proxy.

The General Commitee shall keep a record of its proceedings, and shall make a report to the League at the annual meeting. A vacancy in any office, except that of Vice-President, may be filled by the General Committee for the remainder of the term.

The General Committee may delegate to the Executive Committee any of its powers; provided, however, that it may at any time resume the powers so delegated.

The Executive Committee shall consist of twenty-one members to be elected annually by the General Committee and shall have power to fix its own quorum. And any member of the Executive Committee may act by proxy.

VII.

The General Committee may, subject to these articles, manage the affairs of the League, direct and dispose of the funds, and may, from time to time, make and modify by-laws for the League and for its own action.

No debt shall be contracted, nor shall any appropriation of money be made, by the League or by the General Committtee, beyond the amount in the hands of the Treasurer.

VIII.

There shall be an annual meeting of the League at such time in each year, and at such place as the General Committee may determine, at which officers shall be elected for the ensuing year, and other appropriate business may be transacted.

A meeting of the League may be called at the discretion of the General Committee whenever any association belonging to it notifies the Secretary of the League of its desire to have such meeting, and the President may at any time call a meeting of the League.

IX.

Any provision of this Constitution may be suspended or amended by a vote of two-thirds of the members present at any meeting of the General Committee, due notice of such proposed suspension or amendment having been given at a previous meeting. Any association belonging to the League may, through its representatives, propose amendments to the Constitution which may be approved under the same conditions.

Purposes of the Civil-Service Reform Association. Per copy, 5 cts.

The Beginning of the Spoils System in the National Government, 1829-30. (Reprinted, by permission, from Parton's "Life of Andrew Jackson.") Per copy, 5 cts.

The Spoils System and Civil-Service Reform in the Custom-House and Post-Office at New York. By Dorman B. Eaton. 136 pages, 8vo. Per copy, 15 cts.

Term and Tenure of Office. By Dorman B. Eaton. Second edition, abridged. Per copy, 15 cts

The Danger of an Office-Holding Aristocracy. By E. L. Godkin. Per copy, 5 cts.

Daniel Webster and the Spoils System. An extract from Senator Bayard's oration at Dartmouth College, June, 1882.

A Primer of Civil-Service Reform, prepared by George William Curtis. (English and German Editions.)

The Workingman's Interest in Civil-Service Reform. Address by Hon. Henry A. Richmond.

Annual Reports of the C. S. R. A. of New York for the years 1883-1895 inclusive.

Constitution and By-Laws of the New York Association.

MISCELLANEOUS.

The "Pendleton Bill." Bill to Regulate and Improve the Civil-Service of the United States, as approved January 16, 1883.

State Civil-Service Reform Acts of New York and Massachusetts.

Decisions and Opinions in Construction of the Civil-Service Laws. Per copy, 15 cts.

The Competitive Test. By E. M. Shepard.

The Meaning of Civil-Service Reform. By E. O. Graves.

The Selection of Laborers. (In English and German Editions). By James M. Bugbee late of the Massachusetts Civil-Service Commission.

The Workingman and Civil-Service Reform. What Can He Do About It.

Report of Select Committee on Reform in the Civil Service (H. R.), regarding the registration of laborers in the United States Service.

Report of same Committee regarding selection of Fourth-Class Postmasters.

George William Curtis. A commemorative address by Parke Godwin. (Published by the Century Association). 10 cents per copy.

(A charge is made only where the price is given.)

11 d h GEORGE McANENY Secre-

PROCEEDINGS

AT THE ANNUAL MEETING OF

The National Civil-Service Reform League

HELD AT

PHILADELPHIA, PA., DEC. 10 AND 11, 1896.

WITH THE ADDRESS OF THE PRESIDENT,

HON. CARL SCHURZ,

AND OTHER MATTERS.

NEW YORK:

PUBLISHED FOR THE

NATIONAL CIVIL-SERVICE REFORM LEAGUE.

1896.

PRESS OF GOOD GOVERNMENT.

CONTENTS.

ANNUAL MEETING

OF THE

NATIONAL CIVIL SERVICE REFORM LEAGUE.

- - - - -

DECEMBER 10 and 11, 1896.

Pursuant to call duly issued, the sixteenth annual meeting of the National Civil Service Reform League was held at Philadelphia, Pa., on the 10th and 11th of December, 1896. Among the delegates in attendance during the several sessions were the following:

BALTIMORE: Charles J. Bonaparte, John C. Rose, Daniel Coit Gilman, Cleveland P. Manning, Wesley M. Oler, J. I. Cohen, G. Wm. Sattler, George A. Pope, Daniel Miller.

BOSTON: Moorfield Storey, Harvey W. Shepard.

BROOKLINE, MASS.: Dana Estes.

BROOKLYN: William G. Low.

BUFFALO: Sherman S. Rogers.

CAMBRIDGE, MASS.: Richard Henry Dana, J. G. Thorp, W. W. Vaughan, Morrill Wyman, Jr.

CHICAGO: John W. Ela, W. K. Ackerman.

CINCINNATI: Nathaniel Henchman Davis, Charles B. Wilby.

CONNECTICUT: William A. Aiken, Charles Amos Johnson.

DISTRICT OF COLUMBIA: John R. Procter, William G. Rice, John Joy Edson, Francis E. Leupp, Frederick L. Siddons, Adolf G. Wolff.

GENEVA, N. Y.: Arthur P. Rose.

INDIANA. Lucius B. Swift.

NEW YORK CITY: Carl Schurz, Silas W. Burt, Theodore Roosevelt, Dorman B. Eaton, Everett Case, Alfred Bishop Mason, William Jay Schieffelin, George McAneny, Charles Collins, William Potts, S. P. Avery, Richard Watson Gilder, Robert Shaw Minturn, Henry Villard, A. S. Frissell, J. H. C. Nevius, George R. Bishop, Horace E. Deming.

Women's Auxiliary: Mrs. W. H. Schieffelin, Mrs. Charles Russell Lowell, Mrs. Winthrop Cowdin, Miss Schieffelin, Mrs. Sylvanus Reed.

PHILADELPHIA: Herbert Welsh, Charles Richardson, J. G. Rosengarten, Stuart Wood, James G. Francis, W. W. Montgomery, R. Francis Wood, Edward S. Sayres, Clinton Rogers Woodruff, William Waterall, Dr. John B. Roberts, Joseph Lapsley Wilson.

ST. LOUIS: Henry Hitchcock.

ST. PAUL: Rev. W. R. Lord.

HARVARD UNIVERSITY: John R. Procter, Jr.

PRINCETON UNIVERSITY: Henry Mears Stevenson.

YALE UNIVERSITY: Edward E. Garrison, J. M. Gerard.

In response to invitations issued by the League to Municipal Reform Associations, and other bodies having the reform of the civil service among their objects, delegates were present from a number of such organizations as follows:

BOSTON.—*Massachusetts Reform Club:* Andrew Fiske, Samuel Y. Nash.

CHICAGO.—*Municipal Voters' League :* Edwin Burritt Smith.

CLEVELAND.—*Chamber of Commerce :* William E. Cushing.

NEW BRUNSWICK, N. J.,—*City Improvement Society :* Mrs. Nicholas Williamson, Mrs. M. H. Hutton.

NEW YORK CITY.—*City Club :* Robert Shaw Minturn.

PHILADELPHIA.—*Civic Club :* Mrs. Cornelius Stevenson, Mrs. J. P. Mumford, Mrs. Matthew Baird, Mrs. Alfred Harrison, Miss Frothingham, Mrs. R. Francis Wood, Mrs. Hampton L. Carson, Mrs. Theodore M. Etting, Mrs. Thomas S. Kirkbride, Mrs. J. P. Lundy, Mrs. Edward Longstreth, Mrs. N. Dubois Miller, Miss Ida Cushman, Mrs. Clinton Rogers Woodruff, Mrs. C. Stuart Patterson, Miss Hallowell, Miss Nina Lea, Miss Mary Channing Wister, Mrs. Charles A. Brinley, Mrs. Charles Richardson, Mrs. W. M. Salter, Mrs. Joseph May, Mrs. R. Blankenburg, Mrs. Chancellor C. English, Miss Jane Campbell, Mrs. William F. Jenks, Mrs. Talcott Williams, Miss Edith Wetherill, Mrs. Leverett Bradley, Mrs. Richard Harte, Miss Frances Clark, Mrs. William Channing Russel, Mrs. E. C. Hewitt.

Women's Health Protective Association : Mrs. Anna Townsend Scribner, Miss Elizabeth F. Elder, Mrs. D. Stuart Robinson, Mrs. H .M. Pancoast, Mrs. James Irwin, Mrs. Morris Jastrow, Mrs. Henry L. Childs, Mrs. Charles Richardson, Mrs. William Henry Kennedy, Mrs. J. F. Sachse, Mrs. Finley Acker, Mrs. Walter Erben, Mrs. H. L. Wayland, Mrs. Charles S. Hinchman, Mrs. John R. Whitney, Mrs. Rudolph Blankenburgh, Miss Lizzie Esterick, Mrs. Anna M. Green.

Municipal League : George Burnham, Jr., Charles Richardson, J. Roberts Foulke, Joseph P. Mumford, John H. Converse, Clinton Rogers Woodruff.

PITTSBURG.—*Citizen's Municipal League :* D. D. Bruce.

WASHINGTON.—*Civic Centre :* Mrs. Frederick L. Siddons.

The morning session of the 10th, commencing at 10.30 o'clock, was occupied by a joint meeting of the General and Executive Committees, held at the Hotel Walton.

At 2.30 o'clock in the afternoon an open meeting of the League was held at the Hotel Walton, at which the President presided, and the following papers were read:

"Civil Service Reform in Philadelphia." Charles Richardson.

"The New System in New York." Hon. Silas W. Burt.*

"Post-Offices as Party Spoils." Richard Henry Dana.†

"The Self-organizing Power of the American People." R. R. Bowker, (read by Horace E. Deming).

"Lo, the poor Spoilsman: His days numbered in the Indian service." Francis E. Leupp.

"Results of the Merit System in the New York Police Department." Hon. Theodore Roosevelt.

The annual address of the President, Hon. Carl Schurz, "Encouragements and Warnings," was delivered at the Musical Fund Hall, at 8 o'clock on the evening of the 10th. It is as follows:

---

* Page 47. † Page 59.

ENCOURAGEMENTS AND WARNINGS.

*An Address delivered at the Annual Meeting of the National
Civil Service Reform League at Philadelphia, Pa., December 10, 1896.*

By Hon. Carl Schurz.

THE year which has elapsed since our last annual meeting
has been, in various ways, one of extraordinary prosperity to the cause of civil service reform. The recent election
campaign has served to exhibit in a singularly clear light
some of the remarkable and beneficial changes which the
merit system has wrought in our political life, and to expose
in their whole futility many of the fallacies, deceptions and
superstitions, which the reform movement has had, and, in
some measure, still has to overcome.

There are many among us who remember the time when
the heads of our larger custom houses, post offices, navy
yards, internal revenue offices, and so on, were looked upon
as great party potentates responsible not merely for the
business conduct of their respective offices, but for the political
conduct of the districts over which they held sway—nay,
whose political duties were not seldom regarded as paramount to their strictly official functions. I have frequently heard
it said that the collector of customs for the port of New York,
was second in political importance only to the President of
the United States inasmuch as he had to control the politics
of the great Empire State, whose vote was usually decisive in
presidential elections. It was owing to the political importance of this office that the country had to witness the grotesque spectacle of a United States Senator resigning his place
because his advice was slighted in an appointment to the col-
lectorship. The collector of the port of Boston was regarded

as the political representative of the national administration
not only for Massachusetts, but for New England, and it was
therefore, not deemed requisite, that, although officiating in
Boston, he should be a Massachusetts man. Similar offices in
Pennsylvania, and in other states were held in similar consideration as partisan satrapies.

The heads of such offices commanded in their subordinates
and satellites large and well drilled forces of party workers
most of whom owed their official positions and salaries only to
their influence or efficiency as political menials. The approach
of an election set these forces into feverish activity. At the
command of the chiefs they tumbled over each other in their
zeal to pack primaries, to secure the election of reliable delegates to conventions, to serve as drummers or shouters in such
bodies, and during the campaign to get up meetings, to ar-
range demonstrations, and to manufacture enthusiasm. While
all this was going on, the public business was a matter of second-
ary consideration. It may be doubted whether it was a matter of first consideration at any time. The election over, the
great chiefs presided over the distribution of the spoil—a business requiring much attention, work, and ingenuity. In the
meantime the preparations began for the next campaign in the
way of setting up pins and laying wires. So it was from the
beginning of the office term to the end—politics with official
business by way of incidental interruption—and frequently a
very unwelcome and irksome interruption, too.

Does not this sound like a reminiscence of days long, long
past ? There are probably in the city of New York many
otherwise well informed citizens, taking a lively interest in
public affairs, who do not to-day even know the name
of the collector of the port—not as if that gentleman were not
an excellent officer, but *because* he is an excellent officer, devoted solely to his official duties, and not meddling with public affairs beyond those duties. He not only does not consider
it to be a part of those duties to send out the employees of
the Custom House to look after the primaries, or caucuses, or
conventions, or to run campaigns, but he would be more apt
to reprove such things as " pernicious political activity " and
punish it, especially if it in any manner interfered with the
official business of the employees in question. It is even quite
probable, if not absolutely certain, that about the political

associations of many of his men he knows nothing and cares nothing, but that he is interested only in the weighers weighing, the gaugers gauging, the inspectors inspecting, the accountants accounting, and so on, and in their conducting themselves before and after office hours as respectable persons and good citizens.

Far from being an exceptional case, this has so much become the rule that the re-appearance of the old practice anywhere would be a public scandal. I do not mean to say that the service in this respect is in an ideal condition, and that there are not sporadic cases of officers or employees of the national government still too much given to partisan activity. But these expose themselves not only to unfavorable criticism on the part of the public, but also to the danger of being severely disciplined by their superiors. Surely our custom houses, post offices, revenue offices, navy yards, and so on, have thoroughly ceased to be mere barracks for the housing and feeding of the janissaries of the ruling political party, who are to be let loose on the community as the exigencies of party interest might require. This we owe altogether the introduction of the merit system. In making those offices what they now are—business establishments in the conduct of which business principles are the ruling motive power—it has not only given the people a more honest and more efficient service, but it has also made a vigorous beginning of that moral reformation of our political life, which is its ultimate and its most important object.

How persistently have the adherents of the spoils system been telling us that the reform of the civil service we proposed, was incompatible with democratic institutions, because without the organization of regular party troops on the spoils basis, and without the incentive of the spoils of office in prospect it would be impossible to keep alive the popular interest in public affairs! And how completely and conclusively has since the introduction of the merit system each successive presidential election refuted that slander upon the character of the American people! In no instance, however, has this refutation been more striking than it was in the election just behind us. A campaign more earnest we have never had. The number of citizens with whose earnestness the possession of office or the hope of spoil had anything to do, was no doubt un-

precedentedly small. But I shall hardly be contradicted when
I say that the party most earnest in its work and most active
and enthusiastic in its efforts, was the one which fought without any prospect of a partisan victory and into whose hopes
the winning of office or other selfish advantage did not enter
in the slightest degree.

I mean the sound money Democrats, for whom the struggle
had no victory but the victory of the cause which they believed
to be the cause of the national honor and welfare. Truly, the
slanderers who asserted that it requires the promise of reward in the shape of official spoil to inspire Americans with
an earnest interest in the affairs of their country and to stimulate them to patriotic exertion have never more impressively
been put to shame, and their disgraceful pretence ought not
to be heard of again. It is a significant fact that those whose
zeal' in the late campaign was most conspicuously unselfish,
put forth the most emphatic pronouncement in favor of civil
service reform, while the party whose cause was condemned
by the verdict of the American people, was the only one
which sought to inspirit the efforts of its adherents by opening
to them the prospect of unlimited official plunder.

I' am, of course, very far from asserting that civil service
reform played an important part in the late campaign as a
political issue. The popular mind was absorbed with other
things. But I do say that spoils politics suffered a double
defeat in the election: The party to whose cause and to
whose prospects the spoils idea was most foreign proved itself
in political action the most enthusiastic and efficient, while the
party which invoked the spoils spirit to its aid, found the
promise of spoils utterly impotent to avert its discomfiture.

This moral triumph, however, is by no means the
only auspicious event upon which we may congratulate
ourselves. The hope expressed a year ago that President
Cleveland would, as to the extension of the classified service
so far as it could be effected by executive action alone, leave
to his successors but little to do, has been fully justified. The
executive order promulgated by him on May 6th, 1896, marks
one of the greatest and most important onward strides in the
history of the reform movement. This order added to the classified service and subjected to the merit system at one stroke
of the pen more than 40,000 places, so that the number of posi-

tions in the national service placed under the civil service rules, which was 15,000 under President Arthur twelve years ago, has now risen to nearly 90,000, while the number of excepted places in the branches of the service covered is reduced to less than 800. That order provided for promotion examinations in all the departments. It put an end to the old controversies as to whether such positions as those of chiefs of division in the government departments, and of deputies of various sorts, could or should be entirely withdrawn from the reach of party politics, and it dispersed the charm by which certain places of a very ordinary sort were sought to be consecrated to the spoils idea by simply calling them "confidential." That order condensed the large and somewhat confused aggregation of civil service rules which in the course of time had accumulated, into a simple, clear and practical code. And—more than all this—that order established the general principle that it is the natural and normal status of persons serving under the executive departments of the national government to be under the civil service rules—in other words, that it shall not require a special edict to put them there, but that they shall be considered and treated as being there unless exempted by special edict.

What this is worth only those will fully appreciate who, during these long weary years of struggle, have witnessed the ingenuity displayed by the spoils politicians in conjuring up difficulties to every extension of the merit system, and the tricks and stratagems employed in changing the names and in mixing up the duties of various offices, and in other disreputable ways, to steal places already classified, from the realm of the merit system for the benefit of the spoilsmen. All this is now over in the national service; the merit system is unequivocally recognized as the general rule, and, I am sure, I am speaking the sentiment of every member of this League and of every sincere friend of good government in the country when I say that, had he never done anything else to advance it, the name of President Cleveland would for this order of May 6th alone for ever stand pre-eminent in the annals of the civil service reform movement.

Nor should we fail gratefully to remember the valuable services rendered by the National Civil Service Commission, which has proved itself conspicuously faithful, judicious, and efficient, and the loyal enforcement of the law in the several Government departments, especially that of the Post Office, which has resolutely sought to rescue the country Postmaster from the reach of spoils politics, and that of Agriculture, which has carried the domain of the competitive rule to the very top of its organization.

It is not only in the national service that we find evidence of gratifying progress. The establishment and maintenance of the merit system in the various State and municipal governments is next in importance. The complete expulsion of the spoils spirit from the national service can hardly be expected so long as that spirit is kept alive and fostered in the services of our states and municipalities. As you are aware, the constitution of the State of New York contains a clause making the introduction of the competitive merit system in the service of the State and municipalities obligatory. That the genius of the spoils politicians in New York—for there are such in that community—should at once have applied itself to the task of circumventing that constitutional provision, you will readily believe without the production of affidavits. But there are judges in Israel, and the Court of Appeals, the highest tribunal in the State of New York has construed the civil service section of the constitution according to its meaning and intent, holding that the constitutional provision is self-executing, and that, while the existing civil service statutes may be used so far as they go in enforcing it, the courts would be obliged even in the absence of such statutes to pronounce all appointments made without competitive examinations to positions for which competitive examinations are practicable, to be illegal. This decision has been practically enforced by the competent authorities refusing pay to persons who had, according to the Court of Appeals, been illegally appointed. The spoilsmen, finding this to be serious business, for their favorites for whom they attempted to steal places dislike as much to serve for nothing as their patrons are loath to pay salaries out of their own pockets, have now conceived a new plan of campaign, of which I shall speak later.

In the mean time Mr. Morton, the Governor of New York, mindful of his constitutional obligations, and having learned from practical experience the value of the merit system, instructed the State Civil Service Commission to prepare for his consideration a revision of the classification and of the rules that would carry into full effect the constitutional mandate as construed by the Courts. The new classification and the revised rules have recently been promulgated by the Governor who by this act entitled himself to that honor which a public duty well performed deserves. It is no exaggeration to say that this is the completest embodiment of the civil service reform idea so far attempted in any State.

In the city of New York, too, the Mayor, Mr. William L. Strong, has greatly extended the operation of the civil service rules, excepting only 75 positions in a total number of about 15,000, and confining the exceptions to deputies, private secretaries, and a few professional places.

Also in the cities of Buffalo and Rochester there has been decided progress, while in the city of Brooklyn whose Mayor belongs to that class of reformers who approve of the merit system in theory, but would rather not be bothered with it in practice, the Courts have had to be invoked to secure proper respect to the constitutional mandate. A test case is now pending.

Especially gratifying is the triumph recently won by the sturdy mayor of Baltimore, Mr. Hooper, over the Republican spoils politicians of that city who had sought to turn into a carnival of plunder last year's victory of the reform movement, overthrowing the Democratic machine. The reformers have, indeed, failed to carry a general civil service law through the Maryland Legislature, but a constitutional provision, similar to that of New York, is to be voted upon by the people next year.

In my last annual address I had to deplore the fact that in Massachusetts a vicious blow had been struck at the merit system by the passage of a bill, over the governor's veto, providing that veterans should be appointed without any examination whatever to any vacant place for which they might apply—a bill no less obnoxious to the self-respect of the veterans than to the public interest. But the Supreme Court declared the law unconstitutional, basing its decision upon the old Bill of Rights which discountenances class privileges. Thereupon the legislature has passed another veteran bill continuing the provision of the previously existing law, which merely *permits* the appointing officers to appoint veterans

without examination if they deem such appointments proper.
This act the Supreme Court has held to be constitutional.

In Pennsylvania, too, the adoption of a civil service law is
in prospect. A committee of the Civil Service Reform Association has drafted a bill, and that bill has been substantially
endorsed by the Republican State Committee as well as the
State Convention of the same party. Let us hope that it will
pass unscathed the snares and pitfalls of legislative action and
place this old commonwealth in the front rank of reform States.
Civil service bills are also likely to be introduced this winter
in the legislatures of Minnesota, where a bill presented by
Senator Ozmun passed at least one House at the last session,
and in Colorado where the civil service reform cause has the
advantage of strong and active sympathy among the women
voters.

Nothing could be more encouraging than the fact that in
several States the people of individual cities, without waiting
for general acts of legislation, have secured civil service reform
by means of amendments to their charters. In Louisiana the
city of New Orleans has obtained a charter embodying provisions for the application of strict civil service rules to every
municipal department. In Seattle and Tacoma, the principal
cities of the State of Washington, in the extreme Northwest
of the country, similar rules have been placed in the charter
by popular vote. Evanston in Illinois has also adopted the
merit system by a vote of the people under the provision of the
Illinois State act, thus following the example of Chicago. In
San Francisco and Los Angeles, California, in Wheeling, West
Virginia, in Galveston, Texas, in Denver, Colorado, and in St.
Louis, Missouri, steps have been taken toward the same end.

Thus North and South and East and West, from the
Atlantic to the Pacific, and from the Rio Grande to the Northern frontier, the seed of the reform sentiment which so long
seemed to have been sown in vain, is vigorously pushing and
promising a harvest which not a few years ago was beyond the
most sanguine flights of expectation.

But let us not indulge in the delusion that what has been
gained can be preserved intact and that more can be won without a continuation of incessant watchfulness and militant effort.
The tactics of the spoils politicians have indeed changed from
the direct to the indirect attack. The theoretical argument

against civil service reform has in a great measure ceased to be resorted to. The merit system has so conspicuously commended itself by its practical results to the enlightened opinion of the country, as to make the old objections to it appear simply foolish or spiteful. When we are now told that our competitive examinations may indeed exhibit the scholastic acquirements of a candidate for place, but not his practical business capacity, his industry, or his aptitude as a worker, the overwhelming answer is found in the established fact, that wherever the competitive system has been properly carried out, it has immeasurably improved the service in its practical efficiency. When we are told that our competitive examinations can, in any event, not prove the moral qualifications of the candidate, his truthfulness, his honesty, we can point to the unquestionable fact, that many thousands of places have for many years been filled under the merit system, and that in the places so filled the number of cases of dishonest conduct has been infinitesimally small. When the threadbare objection is repeated that our competitive exminations will give an undue advantage to college-bred men and exclude the humbler classes of the people, the statistical showing presents itself that since the competitive system was introduced in the national service, only a little more than twelve per cent. of the men appointed under it were college-bred men, and outside of the places demanding scientific acquirements hardly more than six per cent.—that in fact the service is more open than ever to persons of the so-called humbler classes. And so we might go through the whole list of the hackneyed criticism, and at every step the theoretical objector would find himself utterly discomfitted by the evidence of practical experience.

The argumentative fight against civil service reform has, therefore, very largely ceased. It is true that this year for the first time since the enactment of the national civil service law, a national convention of one of the great political parties, that held at Chicago, made in its platform an attack upon the merit system. But nobody will maintain that this attack bore any vestige of a reasoned motive. The pretence of that platform, and of Mr. Bryan as its expounder, that there is " a life tenure being built up at Washington which excludes from participation in the benefits the humbler members of society," simply flies in the face of well-known fact. And the demand for " fixed terms of office," which meant nothing else than that not only the places heretofore usually changed with a change of party in power, but the classified service, too, should be thrown open to a general spoils debauch every four years—this demand was in fact like a mere war whoop of Goths and Vandals preparing for the assault of a town and eager for the loot. It is according to the eternal fitness of things that of national conventions, this should have been in our days the only one to characterize itself by such an utterance. The barbarous foray has happily been averted, and a repetition is not likely ever to occur.

The dangers threatening civil service reform come no longer from open assault upon the merit system, but from insidious attempts to destroy its substance, while preserving its forms. You may hear many a politician who all his life has trained with the old spoils guard, now deliver himself in this wise: "Civil service reform? Certainly. An excellent thing. But it should be practical civil service reform. Examinations? Certainly. But they should be sensible, practical examinations. The trouble is, these professional civil service reformers do not know how to manage this business. They are mere theorists, one-sided, unpractical, unreasonable fanatics. In one word, whether they call themselves Republicans or Democrats, they are Mugwumps. They ought to be reformed themselves. And we can do it. We are the men to give the country the reform it wants. Let us have an opportunity to try our hands at it." And with this preface various schemes are proposed that may appear plausible to the unwary. But when the Greeks come bearing gifts, it behooves us to keep our eyes open.

In order clearly to gauge and to appreciate the character of such designs, it is expedient that we should at all times keep before our eyes the essential principles, without the observance of which no true reform of the civil service is possible. There are certain things which cannot be repeated too often. The object of civil service reform is twofold: to improve the character and efficiency of the public service, and, by the abolition of the spoils system, to elevate the intellectual and moral character of our political life. To attain either part of this object, the very first and absolutely imperative requirement is that office cease to be an article of patronage, a .

thing to be bestowed by way of arbitrary personal or political favor and, therefore, that appointments to office be made *exclusively* upon the ground of impartially ascertained fitness for the discharge of official duty.

The exclusion of favoritism evidently requires that in making selections for appointment personal or political influence count for nothing; and this can be accomplished only if such selections are made according to *the degree of fitness* respectively shown by the different candidates. This again requires two things—first, that whatever tests for the ascertainment of that fitness be established, they be, as a rule, accessible to all persons possessing certain qualifications as to good repute, and, perhaps, as to age and physical condition; and, secondly, that those tests be competitive; that is to say, that the candidates showing themselves best qualified shall have the best claim for appointment. The competitive feature of these tests is, therefore, not to be looked upon as something merely desirable for this or that practical reason; but it must be regarded as the most essential prerequisite, as the absolute *sine qua non* of the merit system. Without it there will be no exclusion of favoritism from appointments; and without this there will be no true and lasting civil service reform—at least not in a country in which the spoils system has prevailed and formed part of the political habits of the people.

There is here and there in the popular mind—even among those who on the whole favor the merit system—a lack of appreciation of just this point. We still hear reasoning like this: "You wish the public service to be conducted on business principles. Now, would not any practical business man be better satisfied with some less restrictive method of ascertaining the qualifications of those he has to employ? Will he not be the best judge of those qualifications? Will he limit the freedom of his choice by any competitive system?" The answer is simple. Yes, we do wish the public service to be conducted on sound business principles. But we have to recognize the fact that in one respect the situation of a public officer wielding the appointing power is essentially different from that of a private business man. The public officer is exposed to a peculiar pressure of political influences and importunities of which the private business man knows nothing. Of this pressure only those have a just conception who have actually experienced it.

It is a remarkable fact that many men in politics who are otherwise always mindful of the public interest, seem to lose all sense of responsibility whenever the patronage comes into question. I do not speak here of the professional spoils monger who makes the providing of places for his henchmen or the building up of a party machine his principal business in public life. But I speak of men ordinarily conscientious in their conduct who will, perhaps moved only by the generous desire to help or please, or sometimes only to get rid of importunity themselves, not merely perfunctorily recommend and even earnestly and persistently urge the appointment of— pardon the vulgarism—the veriest " deadbeats " to positions requiring not only superior ability but a nice sense of honor. From my own official experience I might quote instances which would make you stare. There seems to be something in the pursuit of office, either for oneself or for others, that benumbs all moral feeling as to means and ends, and tempts men to do things which they would in private life be ashamed of, and to make common cause with persons whom they would not socially recognize as fit to associate with. There are, of course, some public men who will never propose any-body for office of whose worthiness they are not personally convinced. But, alas, they are in the minority. On the whole, I feel myself warranted in saying that recommendations for office generally are among the most untrustworthy, aye, the most treacherous of human utterances, even if signed or spoken by men otherwise ever so respectable.

From this incessant, imperious, and deceptive pressure which forces itself mercilessly upon the appointing officer, the private business man is wholly exempt. In selecting his employees he is permitted to act upon his best judgment, while the appointing officer in the public service is not. Resistance to the con-straining forces bearing down upon him requires a firmness of purpose and a fearlessness of consequences which but few public characters have proved themselves possessed of. His freedom to make his selections for appointment according to his sense of duty and his knowledge of the requirements of the service, of which we hear so much, is therefore a myth. In a large majority of cases, if apparently left free, he himself does not make those selections at all, but they are made for him and forced upon him by political influences with the impelling motives of which the public interest has ordinarily nothing to do. And you may be assured that most of those who clamor to have the appointing officer entirely free in his choice, do so only because they wish to make him their slavish tool. What they are struggling for is their own freedom to impose their choice upon him. Against these 'incessant efforts to enslave him to influences foreign to the public interest the appointing officer needs protection; and that protection he can find only in a law, or in a rule having the force of law, which restricts the choice to a limited number of candidates found most fit for the performance of official duty by impartial test.

Will this protection be given—in other words, will favoritism be excluded, by non-competitive, mere pass examinations, in which a minimum of requirements is established and the choice is from all the candidates whose proficiency is above that minimum? This question is answered by long and varied experience. There were such examinations in the government departments in Washington many years before the enactment of the civil service law, without in any appreciable degree affecting the evils of the spoils system. Why was this the result? . In the first place, those examinations were not open to all qualified persons. Only candidates designated for that purpose were admitted. Who designated such candidates? In name the appointing officer; in fact the politicians of influence who wanted places for their favorites. Thus favoritism entered into, nay, controlled the proceeding before the examination began. If several candidates for the same place passed above the minimum requirement, who received the appointment? Not the man who had passed highest but he who was selected—in name by the appointing officer, in fact by the politician who had the largest influence. Thus favoritism controlled the consummation of· the proceeding. I will not say that it absolutely always happened so; but it was the rule, and exceptions were rare. Is it a wonder that the spoils system with all its scandals flourished under this system without substantial restraint?

I am well aware that under certain conditions such pass-examinations may be made to do good service. Given a small number of places to be filled, one at a time—places requiring certain specific qualifications of a superior order—and then given an appointing officer of moral courage and firmness in resisting pressure, and even this scheme may work well. It has, for instance, brought forth some good fruit with regard to the consular service under the present administration. This is gratefully acknowledged. But have we any assurance that it will steadily continue to bear good fruit ? We should not forget that rules to govern appointments to consular places very similar to those at present in force, had been introduced before and had fallen into abeyance. They were revived again and again, but have heretofore always, after a short period of observance, become useless by the failure of the appointing power to resist the political pressure hostile to them. Is it not to be feared that what has happened before, may happen again—that, while these rules may work beneficially under the present administration and under the next, the time will come again when, with a less vigorous will-power in the Presidential chair, the wave of influence will wash down the feeble breakwater of the pass-examination once more ? Secretary Olney was therefore entirely right when he characterized the present rules covering the consular service as only a "step in the right direction," which, as we hope, will before long be followed by a measure of reform bottomed upon the competitive principle and thus offering greater guarantees of consistency and endurance.

But even if the system of pass examinations could be maintained in successful working when applied only to a small number of conspicuous positions, it would under our conditions inevitably and speedily become worthless, a mere cloak for arbitrary favoritism and spoils politics, when applied to the thousands upon thousands of places in the national service which are less in the public eye, and even with the smal'er number under our state and municipal governments. Actual experience in this respect is so general and uniform as to extinguish all doubt. There is no teaching of history and no process of reasoning that will not unfailingly lead us to the conclusion that the element of favoritism and of spoils politics can be excluded from the public service at large only by the establishment and maintenance of competitive tests to which every qualified person has free access, and which secure to the best merit properly demonstrated the best title to appointment.

The competitive principle, I repeat, is the very soul of civil service reform. Without it there can be no true merit system on a large scale. Without it every reformatory attempt of a general nature will eventually become a sham and result in failure. I am sure I am not going too far in saying that whenever you find a man who presents himself as a friend of civil service reform, but who stops short of the competitive principle as a general rule admitting but few exceptions, you have before you one who is either ignorant of the fundamental principle, or a pretender with evil designs. And whenever political parties or politicians speak of reforming the civil service and offer to that end a general measure of legislation not containing the competitive rule, you may set them down as either deceiving themselves or as seeking to deceive the people.

There is another essential point which must never be lost sight of. The conduct of the competitive examinations should present every possible guarantee of impartiality and should therefore be independent of the appointing officers, that is to say, out of the reach of the pressure of political influence to which the appointing officers are exposed. In other words, while the President of the United States, or the Governor of a State, or the Mayor of a city may exercise the power of determining the rules under which the competitive examinations are to be conducted, and of appointing the persons who are to conduct them, those persons, when so appointed, should, in conducting those examinations, not be subject to be directed or influenced by the officers by whom. or for whose departments of the service, the appointments are to be made. For, if they were, the impartiality of their action would in many cases be gravely endangered, and in many more cases be generally suspected.

To illustrate this point you will pardon me for relating what is at present said to be going on in New York. I have mentioned the fact that the Constitution of that State makes the introduction of the competitive merit system in all branches of the service obligatory; that the Court of Appeals has given the broadest construction to that constitutional mandate, that public employees appointed in contravention of that mandate are deprived of what their hearts most yearn for, their pay, and that therefore the soul of the spoils politician is seriously disturbed. He has to deal with the fact that the competitive examination cannot be gotten out of the way. But he does not despair. His inventive genius is equal to the emergency. To him the problem is simple. What does the spoils politician care whether the competitive system controls the appointments if he can get control of the competitive examinations? The party machine hopes to coerce Governors and Mayors into putting machine men at the head of the different departments of the service—places not subject to competitive examination. It has succeeded with this coercion so often that it may hope to succeed again. Why not, then, transfer the conduct of the competitive examinations from the general State Commission appointed by the Governor, and from the city commissions appointed by the Mayors, who took the competitive business more or less seriously, to the different departments of the service, at the head of many of which the party machine hopes to have its tools? The constitutional mandate will then, in point of form at least, be complied with. There will be competitive examinations. The courts will have nothing more to say. But what a roaring farce these competitive examinations would become under the control of examiners chosen, for instance, by the present State Superintendent of Public Works in New York, who has made it one of his favorite studies, how to "beat" the civil service law, or by that member of the Charities Board in New York City, who loudly advocates the transfer of the examinations because under the present system he "cannot get the men we want!"

The ostensible reason for such a transfer will undoubtedly be that the heads of departments know best what qualifications are required for the positions under them, and that they are therefore best fitted to adapt the examinations to those requirements. This is plausible but futile under our circumstances. It is a matter of universal experience that the heads of departments are most severely subjected to pressure for changes in their force immediately after their accession to office, that is to say, when in an overwhelming majority of cases they are least acquainted with their own duties and least fitted to form a clear judgment of the qualifications their subordinates should have. I speak here from my own experience, for I have gone through it all. Another one of my personal observations may be of equal interest. I have known several heads of public departments who were indifferent, or even hostile, to civil service reform when they went into office but became thorough converts to it before they had been there long. Some of them frankly confessed to me that, had they had their way at the beginning of their respective administrations, they would have freely used their power of appointment to take care of their supporters, to oblige their friends, and to look out for their party; that they would have yielded to the pressure for place, sometimes willingly, sometimes because they could not resist it; that they chafed at the civil . service rules restraining them; that, had they been permitted, they would gladly have disregarded them; but that as they gained better knowledge of their duties and of the requirements of the service under them, they became aware how discreditable to themselves and how hurtful to the public interest would have been the things they had at first wished to do, and that they could never be too grateful to the civil service rules for having saved them from ignorantly or improvidently falling into errors, the consequences of which would have plagued them throughout their whole administration.

Here I speak, of course, only of public officers to whom, their early misconceptions notwithstanding, the public interest was the supreme consideration. But what will happen if men who persist in regarding public place as the mere spoil of party warfare, and their official power as a legitimate means for serving the "machine," are put at the head of public departments and entrusted with the management of civil service examinations? Can there be the slightest doubt that they would eagerly embrace every opportunity to disembowel the merit system, to make sport of the examinations, to give the freest possible play to spoils politics, behind the empty forms of the competitive rule, and to make the constitutional mandate a laughing stock for the "boys"? If anybody doubts, let him consider what has already happened. Last year the majority of the Fire Commission of New York city was composed of men of the spoils persuasion. Owing to the watchfulness of the City Civil Service Board they failed, in spite of their efforts to circumvent the civil service rules, in "getting the men they wanted." They forthwith engineered through the Legislature a bill turning over the management of the civil service examinations for the Fire Department to the Fire Commission itself. What they aimed at was no secret. The bill failed to become a law in consequence of some peculiar provisions of the State Constitution concerning bills relating to cities. Meanwhile, the majority of the Fire Commission has fallen into the hands of men who are not given to spoils politics, but are true to the public interest. These men are perfectly satisfied with the control of the examinations by the City Civil Service Board, and protest emphatically against the transfer of that control to the department on the very ground that, in the long run, it would mean a return to the spoils system. The same opinion is expressed by other heads of departments for the same reason. Here is the object lesson.

Will it be said that men may be put at the head of the departments who will be as conscientious in the management of the examinations as the independent Civil Service Boards? The answer is that if the examinations are put under the control of the departments the chances for spoil are increased and the spoils politicians will make redoubled efforts to secure the chief places for men who will do their bidding. On the other hand, the more the departments are stripped of the chance for spoils the more they will lose in interest to the spoils politicians, and the easier will it be to put them under the control of men who look only to the public interest.

I am, therefore, not going too far when I say that this scheme of transferring, in whole or in part, the management of the examinations from the independent Civil Service Boards to the departments means a deliberate attempt to destroy the substance of the merit system while preserving some of its forms, and that it has no other purpose than to return to the old spoils practices. No Legislature can pass a bill embodying such a scheme or anything akin to it, and no Governor can sign such a bill, without becoming responsible parties to this plot. I call upon all friends of good government in the country to watch with keen attention the developments which are likely to take place this winter in the State of New York. If they hear of the introduction in the Legislature of such a bill as I have described they will understand what it means.

It is the duty of this League to see to it that, if such an attempt is made, the responsibilities which it involves shall not escape the judgment of the American people.

Neither should the friends of good government in those States in which civil service laws are in preparation permit themselves for a moment to overlook or to underestimate the universal experience that, unless bottomed on the competitive principle, no civil service reform will be lastingly effective, and that unless made independent of the control of the appointing officers, no system of competitive examinations can maintain its integrity. Our duty to our cause demands that we should be careful not to let anything pass as true civil rervice reform that does not answer its essential requisites.

The rapid progress of our cause during the last few years has not only gladdened its friends, but also exasperated its enemies. Until a recent period the spoils politicians have looked upon the civil service reform movement as a mere whimsey of theorists which would have its day and then pass by. They have at last become aware that it is a substantial force seriously threatening to annihilate their trade, unless effectively checked. They will be incessantly busy, if they cannot hope to overthrow it by open assault, to destroy it by a warfare of underground sapping and mining. And this warfare will not cease until the victory of civil service reform is complete—that is to say, until the whole public service, national, State and municipal, excepting only the few distinctly political offices, has been taken out of politics by being brought under the merit system, and until this general rule of the merit system has become so fully identified with the political habits and ways of thinking of the American people as to exclude altogether the old idea of public office as the spoil of party victory from our party contests.

True, this is a large programme. But why should not that which has been actually accomplished elsewhere be possible here? As a remnant of feudalism, as a monarchical and aristocratic institution, the distribution of public offices as mere patronage, the spoils system, flourished in England as much as here. Owing to the progress of the democratic idea in government in England the patronage abuse has been completely supplanted there by the democratic merit system, as it is gradually being supplanted here. In consequence of this, the idea of public office being a matter of patronage or spoil—aye, almost the very memory of that idea—has completely disappeared from politics in England, while party struggles are there as vigorous as ever. Thus, the consummation has actually been reached there, proving that it can be done. Let us measure the distance which still separates us from the goal.

Of the public servants under the national government who should still be put under civil service rules the minor postmasters are the most important class. Of these there are about 67,000. Nothing has done so much to keep the spoils idea alive in the popular mind as the change of the village postmaster with every change of party in power. Nothing will do more to disinfect the popular mind of the spoils idea than the taking of the village post office out of politics. Nothing has brought more torment and trouble, socially and politically, often amounting to political ruin, to members of Congress than the use of the village post office as their personal patronage. And there is nothing, it seems, for which the ordinary member of Congress is more determined to fight, even with complete disregard of the public interest, than for the privilege of appointing the village postmaster. Of this the defeat in Congress of Postmaster-General Wilson's reform proposition, which I mentioned in my last annual address, furnished a striking illustration.

The plan adopted by Postmaster-General Wilson, pursuant to an executive order amending the postal regulations, contemplates the consolidation of smaller and contiguous post offices with the free delivery offices in such manner that, when such a consolidation has been effected, the smaller office becomes a mere station and its postmaster a superintendent or clerk, as the case may be, and he is, together with his subordinates, if he has any, brought within the classified service. Under this plan the Postmaster-General during the year 1895, actually effected about a hundred consolidations, which resulted not only in a very considerable simplification and improvement of the service, but also in an annual saving of $43,-000. But to enable him to extend this reform the Postmaster-General needed the transfer of funds from the appropriation for postmaster's salaries, to that for clerk hire. This required Congressional action. The Postmaster-General applied for it. He explained the scheme in an elaborate letter to Mr. Loud, the

chairman of the Committee on Post Offices and Post Roads of
the House of Representatives   He indicated that during his
administration of the post department the consolidation of
a few thousand post offices might be effected.   He did not ask
for more money; he asked for less.   He recommended that two
millions of dollars be taken from the appropriation for the salaries
of postmasters, and that in place of this an increase of only one
and one-half million be added to the appropriation for clerk
hire—a clear saving of $500,000.

Well, what happened?   Of course, Congress jumped at
the chance of saving this sum—a sum certainly not to be despised in this time of harrassing deficits, when every dollar
counts?   Of course, Congress made haste to encourage the
Postmaster-General in such a measure of economy, which, at
the same time, was shown to be of great benefit to the efficiency of the service?   Oh no, Congress did not jump at the
chance.   The plan was received with chilling aversion.   In
vain was the Postmaster-General's plea that the extensive
realization of the plan would strengthen and improve the
postal organization by introducing competent local supervision, responsibility and control;   that it would insure a
prompter and more intelligent accounting for public funds
with less bookkeeping, less correspondence, fewer requisitions
for supplies, and less call for inspection from the department;
that it would increase and improve the postal facilities of the
people, and thereby augment the postal revenues; that it
would lessen, by a large amount, the necessary expenditure
for the postal service, with the certainty that this saving would
swell into millions of dollars annually—all of which nobody
has denied, and nobody can to-day.   All in vain.   The House
turned a deaf ear to the appeal.   The transfer of appropriations asked for was not granted.   And when the matter turned
up in the Senate, that body, led by the well-known statesman
Mr. Gorman of Maryland, not only did not further the reformatory and economizing work of the Postmaster-General,
but expressly *curtailed* his power by resolving to prohibit the
consolidation of post offices beyond five miles from the cor-
porate limits of any city, and providing that even within those
limits no consolidation should affect a post office located at
any county seat.   This is the law now.

Look at this spectacle.   The representatives of the people in Congress, charged with the duty and entrusted with the power of taking care of the people's convenience and of the people's money, deliberately put aside a proposition submitted to them by a faithful officer of the government to promote the people's convenience and to save the people's money—nay, they tell that officer that he shall not go on promoting the people's convenience, improving the people's service and saving the people's money. Is it too much to say that this means robbing the people of that money which might be saved and is now unnecessarily expended, and of the accumulating millions henceforth to be unnecessarily expended? And why all this? The reason is notorious. This was done because the consolidated post offices would pass under the civil service rules and members of Congress would have fewer postmasterships to distribute among their hangers-on. The plan was arrested, *because* it was good.

This is spoils politics in characteristic efflorescence. But how long will the people tolerate such nefarious sport with their interests? Are they not civilized enough to want the best facilities for the transmission of intelligence offered to them? Are they so reckless as to permit, with eyes open, the squandering of their money at the rate of millions a year merely that their Congressmen may have more post office plunder at their disposal? Is it not time that good citizens should unite to tell the politicians in language vigorous enough to be heeded that this outrageous trifling with the people's service and the people's money must stop? Indeed I trust that the day is not far when the enlightened public opinion of the country will compel what several Postmasters-General have already suggested and what common sense as well as the public interest urgently demand—the complete taking out of politics of the whole postal service, including every position belonging to it. And in your name I express the hope that legislation enabling the Postmaster-General to carry out the admirable consolidation plan to the greatest possible extent, and to bring the smaller post offices which cannot be so consolidated, under effective civil service rules, will be pushed with the utmost energy, and will not cease to be pushed until the post office is what it was intended to be and always should have been: merely an efficient servant of public convenience, and no longer the booty of party warfare and a source of political demoralization.

We have on occasions like this so frequently reiterated our demand for the repeal of the pernicious four year's term law, and supported that demand with elaborate argument that I might abstain from anything more than a passing notice of that subject had not the principle involved in the four year's term law been recently recognized by the enemies of civil service reform in the Chicago Convention as the surest means to destroy the merit system. With the natural instinct of the spirit of mischief they hit upon the poison which, if injected into the body of the public service at large, would most unfailingly kill every reform that has been accomplished in it. The general introduction of "fixed terms of office" which the Chicago platform calls for, and which, as already mentioned, means nothing else than a general change in public places, large and small, in the departments at Washington, as well as in the country, with every change of administration, would result in a quadrennial spoils debauch so monstrous—more and more monstrous as the government machinery grows—it would bring forth a demoralization in the service and among the people so far-reaching and rank, and it would injure the public interest so disastrously, that the imagination fairly recoils from the picture. Happily the defeat of the plotters removed the danger of its realization. But the fact of the fixed term principle having again been proposed as the surest anti-reform poison most forcibly recalls the attention of all friends of good government to the actual existence of a law embodying this very principle of evil—a law which, although fortunately applying only to a comparatively small number of offices, has done more than any other act of legislation to develop the evils of the spoils system and to demoralize the service, and has for this reason been emphatically condemned by almost all the great statesmen of the past, from Jefferson and Madison to Webster and Clay. Having been thus impressively reminded again of the utter viciousness of the principle embodied in that law, may we not hope that a new effort may succeed in bringing about its annulment?

The party which was victorious in the late national election stands upon this platform: "The Civil Service law was placed upon the statute books by the Republican party which has always sustained it, and we renew our repeated declaration that it shall be thoroughly and honestly enforced and extended wherever practicable." The Republican candidate, Mr. McKinley, in his letter of acceptance spoke thus: "The pledge of the Republican National Convention that our civil service laws shall be sustained and thoroughly and honestly enforced, and extended wherever practicable, is in keeping with the position of the party for the last twenty-four years, and will be faithfully observed. Our opponents decry these reforms. They appear willing to abandon all the advantages gained after so many years of agitation and effort. They encourage a return to methods of party favoritism which both parties have often denounced, which experience has condemned, and which the people have repeatedly disapproved. The Republican party earnestly opposes this reactionary and entirely unjustifiable policy. It will take no backward step upon this question. It will seek to improve, but never degrade the public service."

Nor is this clear and emphatic declaration a mere perfunctory endorsement of the party platform. It expresses Mr. McKinley's own honest sentiments, for, to his honor be it said, he has never failed as a member of Congress to give the civil service law a hearty and effective support. It was he who, in 1890, when some members of his own party sought to overthrow it, indignantly exclaimed on the floor of the House of Representatives: "If the Republican party of this country is pledged to any one thing more than another, it is the maintenance of the civil service law and its efficient execution—not only that, but to its enlargement and its further application to the public service. The merit system is here and it is here to stay." And nobody who knows him doubts that Mr. McKinley meant what he said and that he is honestly determined to act, as President, according to that meaning.

Thus the party in power and the new President have both solemnly promised, not merely to maintain the merit system as now embodied in the civil service law, but to extend it. How are they to extend it? As to the strictly ministerial part of the national service President Cleveland has left them little to do. It is true, the excepted list may still be somewhat reduced by classifying the assistant postmasters, the deputy collectors, and so on. Also the employees of the District of Columbia may, and should, be brought under civil service rules. Likewise would the two Houses of Congress do themselves, and by

way of reducing expenses also to the people, a valuable
service by putting their own employees, excepting perhaps the
private secretaries, under the merit system; nor would the judicial branch be injured in dignity or in comfort, by having its
employees classified too.

But these are comparatively small matters compared with
what has been done, and with what is still to be done. Every
administration since the enactment of the civil service law, has
signalized itself by some conspicuous advance of the merit
system. If the incoming administration wishes to follow this
rule, its ambition cannot permit itself to be satisfied with merely
adding to the competitive schedule a few more hundreds, or
thousands of clerks. It will have to aim much higher. It
will have at least to accomplish the solution of the postmaster
problem, which is the next in order. Indeed, supported by a
strong public opinion in favor of thorough administrative reform, it will have the power, and it may consider it its duty,
to complete the work of eliminating the spoils virus from the
whole of the national service altogether. Only then will it
fully equal the precedents set by its predecessors who, one
after another, advanced the merit system in constantly increasing progression. And when the national service stands
there purged of the spoils blemish, a living proof of the beneficent effects of civil service reform, me may expect its example presently to become irresistible to those of the State and
municipal governments that are now lagging behind the onward march.

What I said of the dangers still besetting our cause may
have shown you that I underestimate neither the strength nor
the cunning of our opponents. But I am nevertheless convinced that their striving will be in vain. They may fight
skillfully and stubbornly, but already their cause is morally
ost. The question is only, if they fight on, how many dead
and wounded they will leave on the field, and how many captives in our lines. Civil service reform has carried position
after position, at first against apparently overwhelming odds,
and with each advance its force has grown stronger and the resistance weaker. But yesterday we were only a handful, ridiculed and neglected. To-day we count well-nigh the whole
intelligence and moral sense of the nation as an earnest ally
of our cause. I do not say that the contest is already ended,

but I do say that it is no longer doubtful. There were nearly two years between Gettysburg and Appomattox. But after Gettysburg, Appomattox was sure to come. Thanks to the executive order of the 6th of May, 1896, our cause won its Gettysburg under the leadership of President Cleveland. We have reason to hope that it will win its Appomattox under the leadership of President McKinley. If the opponents of civil service reform, instead of saving time and trouble by a speedy surrender, continue their hostile efforts, it may mean to its friends a longer struggle but none the less a certain victory.

MEETING OF THE LEAGUE.

HOTEL WALTON, December 11, 1896,
10.30 A. M.

The President opened the meeting, and called Mr. Henry Hitchcock of St. Louis to the chair.

The Secretary called the roll of delegates.

The first business in order being the election of a President and Vice-Presidents for the ensuing year, the Chairman called for the report of the Committee on Nominations, appointed by the General Committee. Mr. R. Francis Wood of Philadelphia, for the Committee, submitted a report placing in nomination the following:

For President : —Hon. Carl Schurz of New York.

For Vice-Presidents :—Charles Francis Adams of Boston, Henry Hitchcock of St. Louis, Henry Charles Lea of Philadelphia, Augustus R. Macdonough of New York, Franklin MacVeagh of Chicago, J. Hall Pleasants of Baltimore, Rt. Rev. Henry C. Potter of New York, William Potts of New York, and Rt. Rev. P. J. Ryan of Philadelphia.

Mr. Bonaparte of Baltimore moved that the Secretary be directed to cast one ballot for the election of the gentlemen named, and the motion was carried unanimously. The Secretary cast the ballot and the nominees were declared duly elected.

Mr. Collins for the Auditing Committee, appointed by the General Committee, submitted the following :

We have examined the accounts of the Treasurer, comparing them with the vouchers, and find them correct ; the amount to the credit of the League being $171.97, and to the GOOD GOVERNMENT account, $164.87.

(Signed) CHARLES COLLINS,
WM. A. AIKEN.

On motion, the report was accepted and ordered filed.*

The Secretary made a verbal report, outlining the extensions of the Federal classified service during the year, and the extensions that may still be made, substantially as follows:

Since our annual meeting of 1895, President Cleveland has added to the classified service approximately 35,000 positions, the greater propor-

---

* Page 46.

tion of these having been brought in by the Executive order of May 6.

There are now in the Executive civil service 178,717 officers and employees, and of these 87,117 are in the classified service ; 79,212 are subject to competive examination, 5,063 are employees in the Navy Yards, selected through the registration system, 2,061 are Indians employed in the Indian service, for whom non-competitive examinations are allowed, and 781, only, of whom 592 are Assistant Postmasters, are on the excepted list.

In the unclassified service there are 4,815 officers appointed subject to confirmation by the Senate, 8,854 common laborers below classification, 66,725 fourth class Postmasters, and 11,206 miscellaneous employees, excluded from classification under the rules, the greater number of whom clerks at unclassified post-offices, or persons receiving less than $300 annually, in other departments.

These figures do not include the members and employees of either the Legislative or Judicial branches of the government, the Diplomatic and Consular Service or the municipal service of the District of Columbia.

The extensions of the merit system in the Federal service still to be effected will be discussed during this session, and it may be of use to have them mentioned briefly at the outset. The principal extensions for which the League will now contend would seem to be as follows :

(1) The further reduction of the excepted list by the transfer of all Assistant Postmasters to the competitive class.

(2) The repeal of the laws limiting to four years the terms of officers appointed subject to confirmation by the Senate.

(3) The reorganization of the Consular Service on a competitive basis, and under permanent rules.

(4) The development of the plan of consolidating fourth class post-offices with larger free-delivery offices, thereby bringing fourth class postmasters and their clerks within the classified service.

(5) The classification of certain branches excluded under the new rules, including particularly the force of the new Congressional Library.

(6) The application of the civil service rules to the Municipal Service of the District of Columbia.

(7) The application of the rules to the employees of the Legislative and Judicial branches of the Government.

With these things accomplished, exceptions to the operation of the rules would be confined to those officers having to do with the political policies of the government, and the establishment of the merit system would be complete

At the invitation of the Chairman, Hon. John R. Procter, President of the United States Civil Service Commission, addressed the League, reviewing the extensions mentioned in the Secretary's report, and adding much interesting information respecting the practical working of the merit system, in the departments to which it is now applied, and its effect on the efficiency and economy of administration.

In response to questions, Mr. Procter stated his belief that the employees of the new Congressional Library are properly within the Executive Service and subject to classification. He added that their classification would probably be effected before the new force is organized.*

The Chairman then announced that reports would be received from representatives of States and localities where local movements for civil service reform are in progress.

Mr. Wilby, of Cincinnati, reported for Ohio as follows:

In responding for Ohio I regret that I cannot report more substantial progress. Among the first local Associations to be organized was that of Cincinnati, but after the passage of the Federal law its members seemed to think that their work had been finished and the Association remained dormant until 1895. In that year, Mr. Roosevelt gave us the benefit of his inspiring presence, and under the influence of an address which he delivered in Cincinnati the Association was revived, and a bill prepared by its executive committee was introduced in the Ohio Legislature. It was drawn on the lines of the Illinois law, applying the merit system to the largest five cities of the State after a vote in its favor by the people of either of those cities. This plan was adopted because it was feared the country members could not be convinced that the economy of the system would offset the expenses of a State Commission. The bill was endorsed by the Chambers of Commerce of Cincinnati, Cleveland, Columbus and Toledo, and by other non-political associations including the leading labor organization of Cincinnati, the President of which appeared with other representative citizens before the Committee to which the bill had been referred. To the surprise of the spoilsmen the bill passed the Senate, but was subsequently reconsidered and defeated through the efforts of a henchman of our Cincinnati boss who has since been rewarded for this and other misdeeds by an election to Congress. Another bill will be introduced at the next legislative session.

Mr. Cushing, of Cleveland, supplemented Mr. Wilby's report as follows:

There are many signs that the importance of the merit system and the need of its adoption are felt in Ohio to-day more generally than ever before. Our Legislature is not to meet again until 1898, and in the interval the friends of the reform will have an opportunity, which they mean to improve, to agree upon a bill to be presented at that session, and we have many grounds for hope that it will pass.

Rev. W. R. Lord, of St. Paul, read a letter addressed to the League by Senator Ozmun, of Minnesota, reviewing the movement for civil service reform in that State.

* Page 98.

Senator Ozmun reported, in part, as follows:

At the last session of the Legislature, held in 1895, I had the honor, as Senator from one of the districts of St. Paul, to introduce a measure designed to place the Civil Service of the State of Minnesota and of the cities thereof, under the merit system. This bill, which was drawn by and with the advice of your Secretary, met with considerable opposition in the Senate, as it was supposed to be a very stringent and comprehensive measure; but by persistent effort I succeeded in getting it through the Senate in almost the identical form in which it was introduced. In the House it was reported back from the proper committee with the recommendation that it be passed. The prospects for final passage of the bill, for a time seemed to be good, and it undoubtedly would have passed had not the Mayor of a large and neighboring city come down with a powerful lobby and accomplished its defeat. The objection raised to the measure by this lobby and by those who were induced to speak and vote against the measure in the House, were so trivial that they deserved little, if any, consideration. The main objection was that it placed too great a power in the hands of the Governor of the State, and that by appointing improper men as Civil Service Commissioners, the proper working of the law could be easily perverted. Those who would naturally object to a measure of this character, found themselves supported in their opposition by many, who, under other circumstances might have been favorably disposed, and the bill was defeated.

As I am still a member of the Senate, I intend, at the coming session, which opens in January next, to introduce two bills for the placing of the Civil Service of the State, counties and cities under the merit system, adopting so far as practicable the plan carried out in Illinois two years ago. I shall first introduce a bill relating to cities only, and providing for its approval by the people of the respective cities before it can be put in operation. After the passage of this bill, which I think can now be brought about without a great deal of difficulty, I intend to introduce a bill for the application of the system to the civil service of the State and counties, relying upon the sentiment already secured in support of the principles of civil service reform, to pave the way for the passage of such an act also. Although the Mayors of some of the largest cities of this state are, to my personal knowledge, still unfavorably disposed toward civil service reform, I hope, nevertheless, to secure the passage of both bills, though it may be necessary to provide in the first instance that the Commissioners serve without salary.

Following the reading of this letter, Rev. Mr. Lord reviewed briefly the plans of the Civil Service Reform Association of St. Paul with relation to the promotion of Senator Ozmun's proposed bills.

Mr. J. G. Thorp, of Cambridge, reported for Wisconsin as follows:

Although I come from Massachusetts, I represent Wisconsin as the proxy of Mr. C. N. Gregory, the member of the general committee from that State. I am always pleased to stand for Wisconsin, as it was my old home. I am proud to represent her just now in this body of reformers because of the magnificent showing she made in the recent national election. I am especially proud to represent Mr. Gregory, who is one of the most earnest and intelligent reformers in the North-west.

Mr. Gregory writes me that while the organized efforts for reform the coming winter will be directed toward securing the passage of a Corrupt Practices act for Wisconsin (an excellent draft bill, by the way, has been made by Mr. Gregory himself, who is a recognized authority on this question), an effort will be made to secure the passage of a civil service reform act. A bill for this purpose has already been drawn and will be urged upon the Legislature. It is not expected, however, that it will pass this year ; but it will be presented in a way to keep the subject before the public, and to create public opinion in its favor. It will have the support of at least two influential newspapers of the State. The work being done to secure the passage of the Corrupt Practices act has been so thorough that they have strong hope of securing such legislation, which will in itself help toward our special reform.

Mr. R. H. Dana, of Cambridge, reported as follows for Massachusetts :

On December 3d the civil service rules of Massachusetts were, by the approval of Governor Wolcott, extended so as to include messengers in the cities of the Commonwealth, certain superintendents and assistant superintendents, civil engineers, draughtsmen and the like and the aids of the State Fire Marshall, which positions had heretofore been excepted.

The economy of the civil service reform system is well illustrated by the messenger service in the city of Boston. When the reform was introduced in 1884 the number of messengers in the city of Boston was small and the pay such as would hardly invite competition. On the classification of clerks and other employees, there developed an inclination to increase the number of messengers and their salaries. In 1890 the number of such messengers in the city of Boston had already been increased beyond any legitimate demand, but since 1890 the number was still more increased and the annual pay for this additional increase of messengers, to $27,000. A Boston Alderman frankly admitted that the messenger places were being used for patronage purposes, and that if they were taken away from the Aldermen and put under civil service rules there would be no place left in which to put their political friends. By putting these messengers under civil service rules this whole $27,000 will doubtless be saved to the city of Boston, while the annual expense of the Civil Service Commission for the whole Commonwealth of Massachusetts and all its cities, and some of its towns, is only $25,000,

The Secretary read a letter from Mr. Charles Janvier, President of the Citizens' Municipal League of New Orleans,

reviewing the recent reform movement in that city, ending in a victory at the polls for the candidates of the League for municipal and legislative offices, and the subsequent establishment of civil service rules. Mr. Janvier wrote, in part, as follows:

We have secured the enactment by the State Legislature of an Australian Ballot Election Law (the nearest approach to the real article at present in force in this country), and also a new Charter for the city of New Orleans, containing civil service rules modelled upon those now in operation in Chicago. Our law is, however, broader than the Chicago statute, the powers of the Commissioners being much greater. Under our law the Commissioners cannot hold any public office during their incumbency, and are ineligible for any municipal office for five years after they have ceased, either by resignation or expiration of term, to be Commissioners.

It is yet to early to say anything about the Charter, and Civil Service reform, while provided for, is not yet an accomplished fact, owing to the opposition, on the score of expense, manifested by some of the Councilmen. We hope to be able amicably to overcome this opposition, and to have the Civil Service Commission at work by the first of the year. We feel that we have accomplished much, but we fully realize that more remains to be done. It is, of course, of the first importance that the advantage thus gained shall be neither lost nor wasted. We should not only hold steadfast to what we have, but with unfaltering tread move forward to further successes. Genuine reform cannot be reached and established by spasmodic endeavor. It is the fruit of steady, unceasing and progressive effort. The mistake of disbanding when the first spasm is over and thus leaving the field clear to influences for evil which never disband, has heretofore proved fatal to lasting reform, and we do not propose to repeat that mistake.

We propose to maintain a permanent organization and to see that the fences around our municipal prosperity are kept up so that the wild cattle we drove out shall not break in again and "make havoc of our works."

Mr. John C. Rose, of Baltimore, reported for Maryland that the proposed constitutional amendment passed by the Legislature of that State at its last session, had been approved by the Maryland Civil Service Reform Association, and that the Association would make strenuous efforts to secure its ratification when submitted to the people at the fall election of 1897. The Chairman announced that a report for Missouri would be submitted after the luncheon recess.

The Secretary stated that besides the States from which specific reports had been received, he is in correspondence with the promoters of local movements in Pennsylvania, West

Virginia, Iowa, Texas, Colorado, California and Washington.

Mr. Welsh and Mr. Richardson referred briefly to the movement in Pennsylvania. Mr. Siddons, of Washington, suggested that the members of the Pennsylvania Association use their influence with Mr. Brosius, Chairman of the House Committee on Reform in the Civil Service, and a representative from this State, in favor of the bill providing for the application of civil service rules to the official employees of the District of Columbia.

Mr. Bonaparte, for the Committee on Resolutions, presented and read the resolutions prepared, and moved their adoption by the League. Mr. Wyman moved as an amendment that the resolutions be considered seriatim. The amendment was accepted by Mr. Bonaparte and carried.

At the suggestion of Mr. Welsh, discussion of the report was postponed to the afternoon session, and the League then adjourned.

HOTEL WALTON,
December 11, 1896, 2 P. M.

The League reconvened at 2 o'clock P. M. Mr. Hitchcock in the chair. On motion the consideration of the report of the Committee on Resolutions was resumed. The resolutions submitted were taken up seriatim, and after full discussion were adopted unanimously in the following form:

(1) The National Civil Service Reform League assembled in this its sixteenth annual meeting is compelled to notice the fact that during the past year, for the first time since its organization, its principles were openly repudiated, and a revival of discarded abuses threatened, in the platform·put forth by a National Convention, and in the public declarations of a candidate for the Presidency. The League cordially endorses the protest published during the contest by its Executive Committee against these mischievous and misleading utterances. It congratulates the country that the purpose thus foreshadowed to undo the good accomplished by persistent effort during a generation's space have failed of consummation, and records its hope that it may be called upon to meet no similar assault in the future.

(2) The League heartily congratulates the country on the truly remarkable progress of the reform under the second administration of President Cleveland, and especially during the past year, a progress which can be best appreciated if we remember that less than 15,000 positions were included in the original classification under President Arthur, and that

in the ten years following, only some 28,000 had been added, while under this administration the whole number therefore included has very nearly been doubled, many thousands being added by the single order of May 6, 1896. So that now, while some 90,000 positions are embraced in the classified service, there is left without the protection thus afforded against the abuses of she spoils system, beside the 70,000 postmasters, only a small fraction of the whole executive Federal Service, consisting of about 1,000 positions subject to confirmation by the Senate, about 8,600 laborers not yet included in the registration system, some 2,000 Indians employed as policeman or in other capacities on the Reservations, about 6,000 positions with very small salaries, mostly under $300 a year, and 781 offices specially exempted from the rules, being for most part those of Assistant Postmasters. For this great achievement, advancing as it does the fundamental principles of free government, President Cleveland deserves the sincere and heartfelt thanks of all good citizens.

(3) The League recognizes in the President-elect a friend to civil service reform who has rendered eminent service in the past to our cause. His record assures all other friends of the reform that it will be his desire as well as his duty to end what remains of the practice of using Federal offices to reward personal or party service.

To this end, the League, having in mind the instructive experience of past administrations, ventures to hope that he will refuse to recognize individual Congressmen as a part of the appointing power, and that he will adopt as soon as may be practicable, aided, if need be, by the judicious advice of the Civil Service Commission, a plan which may enable him to base his nominations for non-political presidential offices, such as those of Postmasters, and Consuls, upon ascertained fitness and efficiency, regardless of party or other affiliations, and in accordance with the principles of competitive selection. The League hopes that a satisfactory system of classification may be devised and applied to fourth-class and other small post-offices; but until such system is in practical operation the League further suggests to the President-elect that the public interest would be advanced if no removals were made of fourth-class Postmasters except for cause; and it also respectfully submits for his consideration the advisability of extending the system of registration of laborers to all departments of the public service in which laborers are employed.

The League earnestly urges upon him the advisability, and indeed necessity, of adopting these salutary measures at the threshold of the incoming administration, and it pledges him its support, and that of all good citizens in the efforts it confidently expects at his hands toward the betterment of the public service and the cleansing of our National politics.

(4) The League congratulates the State of New York upon the recent classification of its State and departmental service. This important administrative act attests in the clearest and strongest manner the loyalty of Governor Morton to the obligations of the Constitution, and has been hailed with satisfaction by the friends of Civil Service Reform throughout the Union.

(5) The League renews its recommendation that the legislation requisite to place the municipal government and other local offices of the District of Columbia within the operation of the civil service law, be enacted without delay, and it respectfully requests that such executive or legislative action be taken as may be needed to extend the provisions of that law to the employees of the National Library.

(6) At its last annual meeting the League heard with pleasure of the commendable attempt of the Postmaster-General to extend the benefits of the classified service to many postmasters of smaller post-offices, by consolidating their offices with those of the larger cities in the vicinity. This measure held out the promise of a considerable saving of public money and a market increase in mail facilities, beside applying the merit system to a portion of the public service wherein its introduction is at once most desirable and attended with serious difficulties. The League has since seen with regret and indignation the practical frustration of this judicious measure through the selfish and unscrupulous hostility of certain Senators and Representatives, a hostility cloaked under various frivolous pretexts, but which could be inspired only by a desire to use the public patronage as rewards for personal adherents or party workers, and it urges upon Congressmen that this eminently practical reform be no longer delayed.

(7) It cannot be too clearly and generally understood that the principles of civil service reform in no wise countenance any tenure of office other than during merit and fitness. The League fully recognizes the importance of preserving to responsible superior officers the power of removal of their subordinates, whenever in their judgment this power should be exercised in their public interest, but the League deems it no less important that the officer exercising this power should do it with full and trustworthy information as to the facts, and that reasonable safeguards should be afforded to employees against the loss of their livelihood for personal or political causes. As a means to these ends it commends the requirements of General Order No. 235 of the Postal Department issued by Postmaster-General Bissell, whereby letter carriers are informed of charges made against them and afforded an opportunity for written explanation or defence, before the power of removal is exercised in their cases ; and it would see with pleasure the salutary and conservative provisions of this order extended to other branches of the public service, believing that this course would tend to strengthen discipline and increase efficiency besides removing opportunities for injustice and possible abuse of authority.

(8) The League observes with peculiar satisfaction the remarkable increase in the number and activity of the agencies working for better government throughout the country and it calls attention to the significant fact that these agencies, without exception, recognize the principles of Civil Service Reform as fundamental in all well considered movements for improvement in the public service and the purification of our political life.

Mr. R. Francis Wood, of Philadelphia, presented a proposed bill regulating the removal of employees in the classified service, for which the endorsement of the League had been asked by a Committee representing the National Association of Letter Carriers. He moved that the matter be referred to the Executive Committee, with power, and the motion was carried.

Mr. Potts, of New York, then moved that the report of the movement for the adoption of the merit system in the municipal service of St. Louis, postponed from the morning session, be received, and that the Chairman of the meeting, Mr. Hitchcock, be invited to address the League. The motion was carried unanimously. Mr. Hitchcock called Mr. Dorman B. Eaton to the chair, and reported substantially as follows:

The situation in St. Louis, with reference to the introduction of the merit system in the civil service of that city, is a peculiar one. In any other State, that end would probably be sought by procuring the passage by the State legislature of an Act, either amending the city charter, or substituting a new charter ; or, as in Illinois, of a general law authorizing such an amendment to the city charter to be submitted to popular vote. Under the present Constitution of Missouri, adopted in 1875, neither of those methods can be pursued. Under a special provision of that constitution, the present charter of St. Louis was framed, in 1876, by a board of thirteen freeholders elected for that purpose by the voters of the city, and was adopted by popular vote. Other provisions directed the legislature to enact general laws providing for the organization and classification of cities and towns, in not more than four classes, all municipalities of the same class to have like powers and be under like restrictions, and authorized any city having a population exceeding 100,000 to frame and adopt by popular vote a charter for its own government, consistent with the constitution and laws of the State. Another provision forbade the legislature to amend any municipal charter by special Act. The legislature having passed such general laws, Kansas City, in 1889, framed and adopted a new charter, substantially similar to that of St. Louis. Before the constitution of 1875 was adopted, the Missouri Legislature, like some others, had a way of passing laws directly amending municipal charters, and since then from time to time enacted laws, general in form, but designed to have that effect. During the past twenty years the validity of such laws has been frequently tested in the courts, with varying results. In 1895, the Supreme Court, in construing a general law which, if valid, abrogated a portion of the Kansas City charter, reviewed all its previous decisions on that subject and held, in substance, that under those constitutional provisions the legislature could not, even by general law, amend a city charter framed and adopted pursuant to the constitutional provisions in question, unless such amendment was made either (1) in pursuance of some duty imposed upon the legislature by the constitution, for example, that laws shall be passed for the registration of voters in cities, or (2) in reference to some matter which concerned the relation of the city to the State at large, for example, a revenue Act ; but that as to matters of purely municipal concern, such charters could be amended only by vote of the citizens themselves. In other words, that court construed those constitutional provisions as establishing municipal home rule in cities having such charters.

The pending movement for municipal reform in St. Louis grew out of a paper on that subject read in March last before the St. Louis Commercial Club, an influential organization of prominent business men. The club referred that paper to a special committee of five, of which Colonel James C. Broadhead is Chairman, and which, in April, reported in favor of action by the club, looking to an amendment of the city charter, introducing the merit system. They further reported that, under the decision of the Supreme Court above mentioned, this could not be done by the legislature, but only by the adoption by vote of the citizens of an amendment submitted by the Municipal Assembly ; for which purpose an amendment must be framed and recommended to the Municipal Assembly by the Charter Amendment Commission, an advisory body established by ordinance, and consisting of the Mayor, President of the Council, Speaker of the House of Delegates, President of the Board of Public Improvements, City Comptroller and City Counsellor. This report was unanimously approved, and the committee was continued, with full power to urge the adoption of such an amendment. No active steps were taken during the presidential campaign. In October the committee appeared before the Charter Amendment Commission and obtained leave to submit such an amendment, which was submitted to the Commission in December and is now under consideration by them with other important amendments to the charter.

The proposed amendment contains sixteen sections, to be added to the article of the charter concerning the administrative department. Without going into details, I may state that the proposed amendment follows the general plan now in force in the Federal service. It provides for a Civil Service Commission of three members, to be appointed and removable by the Mayor, and to serve for three years, one going out each year. They are to classify the entire civil service, with the usual exceptions, conduct or supervise all examinations of applicants, and, as vacancies arise, certify the three names highest on the list of eligibles for such duties, also providing for promotion on the basis of merit. They are not authorized to remove incumbents, the existing provisions of the charter as to removals being left unchanged, but are required to make annual reports to the Mayor, with suggestions as to the working of the system.

The Charter Amendment Commission received this plan favorably, and we have good reason to believe that they will recommend its substantial adoption by the Municipal Assembly. The Assembly has power by ordinance, to submit any amendment to the charter to popular vote, at a general or special election ; and any amendment so submitted and

44

receiving three-fiths of the votes cast at such election will thereupon
become a part of the charter. All that can be said at present is that the
friends of the merit system are hopeful of success.

Mr. Hitchcock then resumed the chair.

Mr. Mason, of New York, moved that the Executive Committee be requested to take into consideration the best
methods of enlisting in the cause of civil service reform the
labor organizaiions of the country, and the motion was
carried.

Mr. Collins, of New York, moved the adoption of the following:

RESOLVED : That the League expresses its grateful sense of the
generous hospitality extended to it by the Pennsylvania Association, the
Civic Club, and the Citizens of Philadelphia.

The resolution was seconded by several members and carried unanimously.

The following papers were then read:

" The Relation of Women to the Movement for Civil Service Reform," * by Mrs. Charles Russell Lowell, of New York.

" Civil Service Reform in the West," † by Hon. John W.
Ela, of Chicago.

" Four-Year Tenure," ‡ by Lucius B. Swift, of Indianapolis.

" Civil Service Reform in the Constitution of New York
State," by Hon. Sherman S. Rogers, of Buffalo.

A paper by Hon. Dorman B. Eaton, of New York—" Civil
Service Commissions Essential to Civil Service Reform " §—
was not read owing to the lateness of the hour. Mr. Eaton,
however, made a brief extemporaneous address summarizing
his subject.

On motion of Mr. Bonaparte it was voted that the Secretary be authorized to incorporate in the printed report of the
proceedings of the meeting the annual address of the President, together with the papers read by Mrs. Lowell and Mr.
Eaton, and such others as the Executive Committee shall
deem it practicable and advisable to publish.

On motion of Mr. Storey it was voted that the President's
address be printed also as a separate pamphlet and circulated
as widely as possible.

* Page 66. † Page 73. ‡ Page 84. § Page 89.

Col. Burt, of New York, moved that the thanks of the League be extended to the Acting Chairman for his valuable and courteous services as presiding officer. The motion was carried unanimously.

The Chairman expressed his appreciation in a brief response and, on motion of Mr. Low, of Brooklyn, the League adjourned.

Attest: GEORGE MCANENY,
Secretary.

———————

On the evening of the 11th, a banquet was tendered the visiting delegates at the Hotel Walton, by the citizens of Philadelphia. Mr. Herbert Welsh, President of the Civil Service Reform Association of Pennsylvania, presided, and addresses were made by Hon. J. Sterling Morton, Secretary of Agriculture; Hon. John R. Procter, President of the United States Civil Service Commission; Hon. W. L. Strong, Mayor of New York; Bishop Cyrus D. Foss, of the Methodist Episcopal Church; Charles J. Bonaparte, of Baltimore; Lucius B. Swift, of Indianapolis, and Sherman S. Rogers, of Buffalo.

The delegates were entertained at luncheon at the Hotel Walton on the 10th and 11th, by the Pennsylvania Association, assisted by a Committee of members of the Philadelphia Civic Club.

REPORT OF THE TREASURER.

GENERAL FUND.

Balance on hand, Dec. 10, 1895, ... **$350.27**

RECEIPTS.—From subscriptions.................$2,145.00
    "   contribution of Newton Assn...   60.00
    "   sale of pamphlets.............   11.40
    "   interest on deposits..........   15.84 **$2,232.24**

                                            2,582.51

EXPENDITURES :

    Account of Secretary's salary........ **$950.00**
    Clerk hire...................... 660.00
    Printing... .... 306.25
    Postage 114.75
    Paid to F. E. Leupp, account of ex-
      penses of " Good Government,"
      for six months ending December,
      1895............... ...... 200.00
    Traveling expenses.............. 87.70
    Congressional Record............ 8.00
    Expenses of Finance Committee... 27.70
    Office expenses, stationery and sup-
      plies....................... 55.14 **$2,409.54**

Balance on deposit at Continental Trust Co....... ....$172.97

GOOD GOVERNMENT GUARANTEE FUND.

Balance on hand, Dec. 10, 1895, ... **$7.28**

RECEIPTS.—From Maryland Association........ **$197.25**
    "   Buffalo   " 45.00
    "   Massachusetts subscribers...... 5.20   247.45

                                            $254.73

EXPENDITURES :

    Paid to F. E. Leupp, Manager, ac-
      count of year ending July 1, 1895 **$254.73** **$254.73**

E. & O. E.

WM. JAY SCHIEFFELIN,
Treasurer.

The New System in New York.

By Silas W. Burt.

THE State of New York has, probably with some reason, borne the odium of nourishing if not of engendering the spoils system in the early history of our nation. It was a senator from New York, who later, in debate, uttered the oft-quoted phrase, "To the victors belong the spoils." It must be accepted as some counterpoise to this bad distinction that in the same State was organized the first great movement against the spoils system and that on its statute-books was inscribed the first civil service law applicable to State and municipal governments.

This law, as was also the present United States law, was drawn by a committee of the New York Civil Service Reform Association, and both were largely the work of Mr. Eaton, to whom the cause of reform owes so much. The United States law was enacted on January 16th, 1883, and the New York law on May 4th of the same year and both were wrested from reluctant legislators by that audacity which has proved to be the most potent instrumentality in the arsenal of reform.

The New York law was approved both officially and personally by Governor Cleveland who, on the day he signed it, named an admirable Commission to administer it, consisting of two well-known friends of the reform, Andrew D. White and Henry A. Richmond, and Augustus Schoonmaker, who though not then known prominently as a reformer proved to be a most cordial and useful one. Mr. White, having declined the appointment, John Jay, an eminent member of the New York Association, was appointed in his place.

Everything was thus auspicious for the successful inauguration of the new system, so far as the machinery was concerned, but there were three impediments to be considered: the hostility of a large number of the appointing officers; ignorance as to how far popular sentiment sustained the law and a consequent fear that there might be a repeal or serious impairment of the statute by the next Legislature. It is now evident that this fear was unfounded since in the later years when the law was, so far as its enforcement was concerned, a mere dead letter, no one dared to press its repeal.

While these deterrent considerations were not controlling, they suggested the tentative character of the law and such an administration of it as would clearly though gradually demonstrate the benefits of the merit system and insure its popular appreciation and support.

The administration of the State law could not be modelled upon that of the United States law, though almost identical in expression, because of the radical difference in the framework of the two services. In the National Government the President is the executive head of the whole service which almost wholly falls within the domain of the eight great departments, administered by the official chiefs who comprise the Cabinet This comprehensive organization and the classification of the clerical force under the act of 1853 enabled a systematic application of the rules from the outset in the field first occupied.

In the State government the Governor holds no such supreme position as the President—he does not appoint the heads of the great departments, who on the contrary are elected in the same manner and by the same constituency as himself, and so are independent in their respective spheres. And again—only a very small part of the service is comprehended within these departments—the far greater part is scattered through the State in the prisons, reformatories, asylums, hospitals, public works and buildings, normal schools, agricultural stations and many other branches, all of which are distinct, and even in these there is a general lack of union and system.

Another marked difference obtains in the classification of the subordinate force in the National service, and the fixed salaries of positions in the several classes and the allotment in the appropriations of definite numbers of clerks of each class or, when outside the classes, definite numbers and salaries of the persons to be employed. In the State service the head of each department or office is given a "lump" appropriation and subject to its limits employs such number of persons and at such salaries as he in his discretion may determine. This lax method not only breeds extravagance, but its lack of system prevents proper organization, leads to harmful and unjust discrepancies in the compensation of persons in different offices performing like duties and impedes the free operation of the civil service rules.

In this chaotic domain, the first Commission addressed itself to the application of the law so far as practicable and sustained by the sympathetic support of Governor Cleveland, had made some progress when the latter was elevated to the Presidency and was succeeded by David B. Hill. It is not purposed to give an account of the mal-administration of the law by Governor Hill, who in December, 1886, removed Commissioners Jay and Richmond, Judge Schoonmaker having previously resigned. For eight years or so the active friends of the merit system saw with mingled grief and shame the practical suspension of the law. In 1894 they secured a special committee of the Senate for an investigation that laid bare the many violations and evasions of the law, known and suspected, during those dreary years.

But this year of 1894 is conspicuous for two other most important achievements. First, the passage of an amendment to the law making it unlawful for the State Comptroller to draw his warrant for the payment of any officer or person in the classified service who has not been certified by the Civil Service Commission, as appointed or employed in pursuance of the law and the rules, and giving any qualified tax payer the right to maintain an action in the Supreme Court for the recovery from the Comptroller of any such unlawful payment and the return of the money to the State treasury. A similar provision applies to the like unlawful payment for services of uncertified persons by the fiscal officers of cities. This has proved to be a most efficient means of enforcing an obedience to the rules and it should be comprised in all laws establishing the merit system.

The second achievement in 1894 was the incorporation in the new State Constitution, then being framed, of a mandate in these words: " Appointments and promotions in the civil service of the State, and of all the civil divisions thereof, including cities and villages, shall be made according to merit and fitness, to be ascertained, so far as practicable, by examinations, which, so far as practicable, shall be competitive," and which Constitution by a majority of 83,000 votes became operative on January 1st, 1895. The history of this great attainment and of its broad results will be presented to you by a distinguished member of the League to whose advocacy and efforts we are largely indebted for this unique triumph.

I would add that since the Constitution went into force nearly two years ago the civil service section has been construed on several points by the higher courts and the decisions have invariably sustained a strict adherence to it both in letter and spirit. The expression of this purpose in the opinion by the Court of Appeals in the McClelland case is most noteworthy. The Court says: "It is apparent that a new principle, far reaching in its scope and effect, has been firmly imbedded in the Constitution. Like many other reforms, this work has not been accomplished without a long and persistent struggle. The friends and opponents of the measure have debated its merits and the difficulties in the way of its practical and harmonious operation, before the public for years. The considerations which entered largely into this debate are no longer pertinent, since the principle has become an accomplished fact and placed by the people beyond the possibility of any substantial change in a contrary direction. This court, upon more than one occasion, has, with entire unanimity, expressed its approval of the principle, and exercised all its powers in every proper case in aid of the laws intended to carry out the idea which was always at the foundation of the question. Whatever doubt or distrust may exist with respect to the possibility of obtaining for the law an honest and fair execution, there is none and can be none, at least among thinking men, with respect to its ultimate beneficial effects upon the service. That it must, if fairly and honestly administered, go far to suppress very grave evils and abuses that have become peculiarly rife and active in our political system, few intelligent people who have given the subject much attention can doubt. In so far as its administration may depend upon the action of the judicial department it is entitled to, and doubtless will, receive a fair and liberal construction, not only according to its letter, but its true spirit and the general purpose of its enactment."

The civil service provision in the Constitution directed that "Laws shall be made to provide for the enforcement of this section." Two sessions of the Legislature have occurred since the Constitution became operative and no such laws have been passed, but on the contrary bills prepared by the Associations of the State have at each session been defeated.

This failure has been repaired so far as the State service is concerned by the act of Governor Morton in directing the

State Commission to revise the rules and classification so as to make them accord with the provisions of the Constitution and their construction by the Courts. The rules so revised were promulgated by the Governor on the 8th instant and this closing act in his administration deserves and will receive the hearty applause of all those interested in good government.

It was intended that these rules should include every valuable means to secure the perfect working of the merit system so far as devised through experience gained in every field. In the new rules prepared by the United States Commission and promulgated by the President on May 6th last, whatever was deemed applicable to the State service has been borrowed and the same liberty has been taken with regard to the rules and practice elsewhere adopted. Of course the controlling motive has been to put in practical execution, so far as possible under existing laws, the mandate of the new Constitution.

Our League has concerned itself rather in the promotion, establishment and enforcement of fundamental principles than in the details of their administration, but these latter points have aroused greater interest since the merit system has been extended to so many fields. At the risk of repeating what to some here present may be trite, I will briefly give the general outline of the new rules just promulgated by Governor Morton and mention their novel features.

The rules begin with a definition of the civil service of the State as comprehending all offices and positions of trust or employment the incumbents of which receive compensation for services or expenses from the treasury of the State or that of any civil division thereof or official fees, except military and naval officers. This broad and sweeping interpretation is intended to indicate that merit and fitness as enjoined by the Constitution shall govern all appointments whether made under the rules or not.

As usual this integral service is divided into the unclassified and classified, the former comprising all positions filled by the Governor and Senate, or by joint ballot by the Legislature or by name in any statute, or appointed by the Governor alone, and all the officers, employés and attachés of the Legislature. All the residue constitutes the classified service subject to the rules and distributed to four classes,

The first class comprehends the positions exempt from examination, being the lawful deputies of chief officers, the secretaries of State boards and commissions, one chief cashier in offices where the receipt and disbursement of public funds is a function and confidential positions—every position in the class being named. The great number of distinct and independent offices, commissions and boards makes this class number about 265, of which, however, 115 are attachés of the courts including the confidential stenographers, etc., of the 76 judges of the higher courts. The inclusion of quite a number of places hitherto ignored has increased the number of these exemptions but not excessively as compared with previous classifications. It is probable that the present aggregate will be reduced from time to time by transfers to the next class.

The second class includes all positions to be filled by competitive examinations, being the great bulk of the service, and is the residual class as embracing every position not specially comprised by name in the other classes. It is divided into fourteen groups, based upon the respective duties and functions of the several positions, as follows:

A.—Clerks.
B.—Cashiers.
C.—Custodians and Messengers.
D.—Engineers.
E.—Inspectors.
F.—Special Agents.
G.—Law Positions.
H.—Medical Positions.
I.—Mathematicians.
J.—Scientists.
K.—Agriculturists.
L.—Instructors.
M.—Mechanics and Craftsmen.
N.—Miscellaneous Positions.

And these in turn are subdivided in accordance with the importance and special character of the duties—for instance Group D.

Engineers:—
Subdivision 1.—Civil Engineers.
    2.—Levelers, surveyors, rodmen.
    3.—Chainmen.
    4—Architects.
    5.—Draftsmen.
    6 and 7.—Electrical engineers—dynamo tenders.
    8 and 9.—Steam and mechanical engineers.

Again, for the purpose of orderly arrangement and of regulated promotion, the positions in the subdivisions are graded upon the basis of their rates of annual compensation. There are ten of these.

All this, as presented here, may seem to be a complicated disposition, but the plan has been suggested by long experience and will very greatly abridge the work of examination. The distribution of places among the groups without regard to their titles, compensation or office, but solely in accordance with their respective duties is also devised to prevent evasions by novel appellations, or otherwise, designed to throw them out of the classification.

The rules repeat the formula that all examinations shall be of a suitable and practical character. That body of our citizens who have, for obvious reasons, always looked askance at the merit system, have been from the first supersensitive regarding the character of the examinations. In New York they have been recently reiterating the old complaint that the tests are too scholastic and that they should be practical and pertinent to the duties of the positions. As the expression on this point by both the enemies and friends of reform is identical it follows that the difference of ideas lies in a corresponding variance in the significance of words.

We, who adhere to the merit system, use the adjectives "practicable," "suitable" and "pertinent" when qualifying the noun "examinations" as having reference to the whole service to be rendered as a result of such examinations. While the greater weight should rest on the questions testing fitness for the immediate duties to be performed, they should also test probable ability to meet the additional duties in such emergencies as occur in all public offices, and what is more important should test the candidate's docility and aptitude for promotion, since it is from such of these candidates as are selected for admission to the service that the greater number of the higher places are to be replenished.

It is also to be remembered that we have always insisted that our system is the *merit* system and the New York Constitution links "merit" with "fitness" as the two sole and indispensable qualifications for the service of the State and that of all its civil divisions. That State, like its sisters in the Union, provides free education for all and spends annually millions of dollars to that end. This free education is not a bounty to the individual but in a higher sense that of the German universal military service is a civic obligation and so has been made compulsory. The State insists that all, unless otherwise educated, shall avail themselves of its gratuitous means of preparation for the duties of citizenship—and among these duties is the service of the State when selected for that purpose. Those who have utilized these means merit the recognition of the State when in need of good service and the relative degrees of their merit are to be ascertained by competitive examination. In fact the merit system is the natural and logical sequence of our free school system and the latest statistics show that 89 per cent. of those competitively examined have been educated in the free schools and in the academies receiving State aid, and the same ratio holds in the appointments.

It follows that our examinations may properly, and indeed should, test the candidates general intelligence and acquirements by a few simple questions—not to define the boundaries of Zanzibar or the diameter of the moon, or to answer any of the other absurd and fictitious queries our opponents are ever fabricating and quoting as facts; but it is certainly no hardship for a citizen of New York to be asked to solve a few problems in fundamental arithemetic or to name the more important of the geographical features of his own State. These questions in elementary education are abhorrent to our critics who, when not inventing preposterous falsehoods about them, are harping on the word " practical."

In New York City an ardent reformer has recently arisen in the person of Mr. Abraham Gruber, who calls his scheme " progressive civil service " though so far as revealed it indicates retrogression to the times and methods when the main questions asked the candidate for public appointment were "To what organization do you belong ? " " How did you vote at the last primary ? " " Who are your backers? " and all the other searching and intensely practical queries of the spoils catechism.

There is of course the liability that untrained and zealous examiners may ask questions too scholastic and recondite, but such cases are infrequent and their harmful influence greatly exaggerated, but as affording pretexts for criticism they should be prevented by a more careful supervision.

In some of the State departments there are positions where

the service is not continuous through the entire year, but regularly recurs in each successive year—for instance the great majority of the places in the Department of Public Works require actual service only during the period of canal navigation. These places are filled by competition as the others in this class and the incumbents are entitled to re-employment at the beginning of each recurring annual season as if their service had been uninterrupted.

Whenever the Commission deems it advantageous to the public interest the territory of the State may be divided into distinct districts for examination and appointment. For general purposes the examinations are held at ten or fifteen different points several times in each year.

In this class the appointing officer may select from the three persons certified as standing highest upon the proper eligible list, thus retaining the principle that such officers must exercise a limited discretion in order to conserve their authority and consequent responsibility.

The period of probationary service is three months, and liberal but guarded provision is made for temporary employment, transfers and reinstatements.

What are believed to be adequate provisions have been made to prevent the evasions and abuses that have hitherto weakened the operation of the merit system in New York, though past experience warns us not to underrate the ingenuity and activity of the spoils-mongers, which grow sharper as they see that the whole service is being gradually but surely wrested from their grasp.

The Constitution couples promotions with appointments in its injunction that merit and fitness as ascertained by examination shall govern them. In framing the new rules it has not been considered that such examinations for promotion should be necessarily the formal written ones applicable to appointments. The reasons for reform as regards the original admission to the service are not so cogent when applied to promotion. As in this respect these rules differ from those adopted elsewhere, this divergence demands some explanation.

So far as competition is concerned, that of daily actual service is incomparably superior to any short inquiry—which, in the nature of things, must be incomplete. This common service, side by side, for a long period is a genuine, thorough and practical competition that even Mr. Gruber could not carp at. Some qualities of such service can be comparatively recorded such as attendance, accuracy and general conduct. But the main qualifications on which promotion may properly depend are not stable and may differ widely in different offices and under different conditions—thus it might be expert ability, scientific or otherwise—or knowledge of precedents—or power of systematic record,—or that of clear and comprehensive expression—or administrative and executive ability—or tact in treating the external official relations, or critical or detective ability, or a score of other diverse qualities, even including technical skill and manual dexterity, few of which could be adequately tested by a written examination or even comparatively recorded. All these qualities, however, that may not be demonstrated in a formal inquisition of a few hours are exhibited under the daily observation of the superior officers. It also often happens that some signal display of ability in a difficult and complicated matter or in an important crisis may indicate promotion as the proper and perhaps the only possible reward.

I think, however, that the controlling argument is that in the ardor for reform, we must not seriously weaken that administrative authority and responsibility that form the essential framework of the public service and without which it would collapse. The tendency in this direction seems to me to be the most dangerous menace to our work in establishing permanently the merit system. Any impairment of official responsibility invites insubordination and consequent inefficiency. These promotion examinations are almost invariably made by fellow-subordinates which in itself is a demoralizing influence so far as discipline and respect for the head of the office is concerned.

The new rules give the appointing officer discretionary power to promote for ascertained merit and fitness, giving due weight to seniority, but he must certify to the Commission his reasons for the promotion and these shall be of public record in his office open to the scrutiny of any one concerned. Publicity is the most valuable, conservative and beneficial agency in securing the proper administration of public affairs and I believe this will be demonstrated in this new scheme for promotion.

The principal objection urged against this discretionary method is that it permits the practical operation of undue favor or prejudice; but certainly this liability is greatly reduced through the requirement of public reasons by the officer. It, however, suggests another menace to the stability of the merit system and that is the growing disposition of its beneficiaries to think they must be protected against the contingencies in private life where employees must run the risk of prejudice and neglect.. The civil service must not be coddled nor led to believe that this League and its friends will strive to make them that privileged class the opponents of reform talk so much about. There has been a strong inclination by some portions of the service to organize for the purpose of securing legislation to abridge hours of labor, increase pay and obtain a tenure in most cases incompatible with good government. The League should strongly oppose this tendency towards such questionable class-organizations.

To resume the classification—Class III embraces all mechanics and skilled laborers receiving an annual compensation of less than $720, and other minor positions the greater part of which are in the many isolated asylums, hospitals, reformatories and other corrective and charitable institutions. These places are, as hitherto, filled by non-competitive examination, but whenever it is deemed practicable to fill any of them by competition the Commission is bound to transfer them to Class II.

Class IV includes all unskilled laborers who are to be employed at discretion. Under favorable conditions a system of registration based upon the approved Boston plan would have been established for this class, but almost without exception the only unskilled laborers are those casually employed upon the canals. All construction work on these water-ways is done by contract and it is only when breaches in the banks require repair that such laborers are needed, and these unforeseen casualties may occur at any point on several hundred miles of the canals. It is obvious that no scheme of registration could be applied in such a field.

As the Constitution, while providing for regulated appointments and promotions, does not mention removals, the rules do not restrict the power to remove. The only such restriction that seems consistent with the views expressed here regarding promotions would be the extension to removals of the filing of reasons therefor as a public record. Many cogent arguments plead against other restraints proposed.

The rules do not apply to the service of the civil divisions of the State since existing laws provide for distinct action by the mayors of cities and they do not confer upon the Governor authority to regulate the service of counties, towns and villages. It is probable that future legislation will confer such authority as to counties and also that the respective cities will continue to have control of their municipal service. The Massachusetts system under which the State Commission exercises supervision over the regulation of the service in the cities has many advantages and is adaptable to the conditions existing in many of the States. But New York contains many very large cities whose internal affairs have been so frequently and intolerably interfered with by the Legislature that the principle of home-rule is accepted as the only safeguard against such misrule and any apparent infringement of the principle is strenuously resisted.

The New York law, however, does require that all regulations prescribed by the mayors of cities shall be subject to the approval or veto of the State Commission which also has full power of investigation. While these powers should be extended so as to ensure a uniform and close adherence to the mandate of the Constitution, it is probable that the general and immediate control will remain with the cities.

Such are the present conditions in New York, though how long these will retain their pleasing aspect seems doubtful. There is much agitation among the "progressive" reformers whose leader has been mentioned and there are rumors of legislation of a more *practical* character at the coming session. Great confidence is felt, however, that public opinion will prevent any impairment of the principle enunciated by the Constitution that merit and fitness ascertained by open competitive examination shall be the general rule for appointments and promotions.

The Post Offices as Party Spoils.

By Richard Henry Dana.

One year ago I had the honor of delivering an address before this League on the appointment and tenure of postmasters. In that address it was pointed out how, under our spoils system, we had spoiled our greatest government business, how the one department which should most administer to our business convenience and social intercourse was in very many respects less efficient than in other great civilized countries and all because we had allowed it to be looted for party purposes; and how we had done this not for our own advantage or our better government, but to aid one party against another, and more often to allow one faction or individual within a party to keep some other faction or individual of his own party out of power, and usually with the purpose and effect of thwarting the public will and depriving us of self-government. In short, Uncle Sam has allowed the boys to play base ball all the season over his vegetable garden and then wondered that his vegetables have not thriven as well as his neighbor's.

It was pointed out how several important improvements which had been adopted in other countries twenty or thirty years ago hád not yet been introduced into the United States, or only in a partial degree, and how our post office department was wholly without efficient organization, having no divisions or division superintendents, but was like an immense army with no majors, no colonels, no brigadier generals, with no officers between the captains and the general in chief. It was shown that this want of organization had been officially recognized in the reports of every postmaster general for the past ten years or so.

Since this address was delivered, one critic complains of one or two instances of apparent slowness in some European post office, but no one fully acquainted with the system in this and other countries has denied our lack of efficiency. One person questions whether some civilized country, say Spain, may not have as bad a postal organization as we, but no one well informed on the question has doubted that we are behind the greater civilized nations in our postal development and even Spain, as is shown by its last admirable post office report, does not give much comfort to those who would like to find some civilized country worse off than ourselves in this respect. Several writers have argued that the newness of our country is the sufficient cause for our postal deficiencies, but post offices are not ancient affairs. There was no government post office in England before the landing of the Pilgrims. The modern system grew up under the inspiration of Sir Rowland Hill. He was born nineteen years after the declaration of our national independence and he first secured cheap postage in England only in 1840. Our railroads and express companies and telegraph and telephone companies are all new, newer than the postal department, and yet in comparison they are admirably organized.

I have seen it given as an excuse that our country is large, and in many places our population sparse. That is a curious excuse for want of organization. As a rule the larger the business and the larger the country over which it extends the greater is the need of thorough organization and not the less. On a one mile branch railroad with but one engine and train of cars the President of the road may light the fires and collect the fares, but the efficiency and financial success of the Pennsylvania, the New York Central and the C. B. & Q., require most thorough organization. As to the finances, many of the improvements in which we are deficient in our thickly settled districts are such as have been proved, where adopted, to be sources of additional net income, while it has been clearly demonstrated that it is the abuse of our franking privilege and the want or proper laws and rules regulating second class mail matter, that causes our annual deficiency in the postal revenues.

In setting forth our postal short comings and stating the true relation of our post office department with those of other countries I have been accused of being unpatriotic and of unduly admiring what is foreign, Now while I trust I am free from Anglo-mania or Europo-mania I also hope and pray to be delivered from the inability to see anything good beyond the Eastern shores of the United States. Soberly and seriously, is it not the part of a patriot who finds anything superior in another country to urge its adoption in his own, and if he is aware of glaring defects in any of his institutions to try and find the remedy and call attention in no unmistakable terms to both the ill and the cure, that in the end everything in his country may be of the best.

It is plain we cannot let a complicated piece of machinery made for one purpose be used also for wholly different and inconsistent purposes and get good results. We cannot expect the immense postal department with its one hundred to two hundred thousand employees be made a dumping ground of political henchmen and to have its officials changed from top to bottom just as they are beginning to learn the rudiments of this very complicated business and at the same time get the good results of business-like appointments and tenure of office. You cannot expect your children can play go-cart in the mud with your gold chronometer watch and have it keep perfect time.

There is, however, a marked unwillingness to face the plain facts and admit the deficiencies and the want of organization and business methods in our postal system. In short, both good natured Uncle Sam and the boys who have been playing all the spring deny that the vegetables are any less flourishing than in other gardens, notwithstanding their capers, but add, with beautiful consistency, that the reason for the deficiencies, which they say don't exist, are the atmosphere, or the distance of the sun. No, Oh dear me, no! It is not the dragging the watch in the mud that made it stop.

But for all this we are by no means in a hopeless condition. As was pointed out last year, the very fact that we have as good service as we have under such demoralization of all business methods is conclusive proof of the natural adaptibility to circumstances and the business instincts of the average individuals who from time to time have had a short try at some part of the job. An eminent postal authority from Germany expressed himself as very much struck with the alertness and diligence of the employees in one of our larger post offices then under civil service rules and headed by a postmaster believing in the reform.

Experience in the railway mail service continues to illustrate what can be done for the benefit of the postal service by abolishing the spoils system and introducing civil service reform methods. As I showed last year, the best record ever reached in the railway mail service under the spoils system was at the end of President Arthur's administration, when for a longer time than usual very few partisan changes had been made. The employees though then appointed as party spoils were each submitted to a thorough "case" test, a sort of half examination pending probationary employment. The record showed the number of correct distributions to one error had reached the high number of 5575. On the incoming of the first Cleveland administration there were many changes for political reasons and the record fell to 3364. After the looting of this part of the service in the first few months of the Harrison Administration with absolutely unprecedented rapidity of removals, the record fell to 2834 and, after that, under six years of civil service reform, had risen to the remarkable record of 8894 a year ago last June. During the last year the improvement has continued and as more and more of the present employees have been brought in under civil service reform examinations and are continued in the department during good service, the record of correct distributions has come up to the still more remarkable figure of nearly ten thousand to one error. It is said to be the best service of its kind in the world. In the general postal service, too, the adoption of civil service principles in so many of the post offices has had the effect of diminishing the number of letters sent to the dead letter office, notwithstanding an actual increase of mail matter during the same time.

Possibly, if our shortcomings arose from incurable national deficiencies, our duty might lie in concealment, but when we know that the cause is curable and that while it lasts it is also demoralizing and corrupting to our politics, our duty is plainly disclosure.

At our meeting a year ago we were greatly encouraged by the new plan of consolidating the fourth-class post offices with larger central ones, by the order bringing the smaller offices thus annexed, with their former postmasters, into the classified civil service, and also by the promise of very considerable extensions of the civil service law soon to be made. These extensions have since been carried out, so that the post office department at Washington is practically on a basis of merit appointment and tenure of office. We shall, therefore, soon have a trained body of officials at the centre of the department with a better understanding of the needs of the service and consequently a gradual improvement. In fact as far as the postal department at Washington goes, and also the post offices where the reform is applied, the reform has been carried about as far as it can be, with the exception of the postmasters themselves and perhaps some 570 assistant postmasters who are excepted.

The plan of consolidating smaller post offices was, however, effectually blocked in the United States Senate last spring by amendments to the Post office appropriation bill so that no post office can be consolidated if it is over five miles from the boundary of the city or town having the principal office, and not even then if the town of the subordinate office happens to be either a county seat (with the exception of Cambridge, Massachusetts and Towson, Maryland) or is of less than 1500 inhabitants. Even the small amount of consolidation that might still have taken place under these amendments was prevented by the refusal of Congress to allow salaries to be paid postmasters after they had become heads of branches, although it has been proved that such consolidation actually saves money. That this consolidation and reform of post offices, much needed also for the better organization of the department into districts, should have been blocked mainly by the efforts of Senator Gorman, of Maryland, the spoilsman who has notoriously put incompetents and criminals into the government employ, was most fitting. It is still possible to remove these obstacles to consolidation with the next post office appropriation bill, but it would then be too late to do much in this way of reform before the incoming of the next administration, so that Mr. McKinley will have to meet the full pressure for these numerous offices without the aid of any established system of appointment on merit.

What would be the consequence of the change of administration on the service already classified, it is impossible to doubt. Mr. McKinley's attitude is, too, well known. His able defence of civil service reform in Congress in 1890, the platform on which he was elected and his explicit letter of acceptance make it clear that he will uphold the system already established and will make any required extensions along the usual lines. To think differently would be putting Mr. McKinley among the most insincere of the "catch-vote" poli-

ticians. But how about the postmasters? As I have
said, they are not classified under the civil service rules and
they can only be brought under its principles by the adoption
of some new and unusual method. There are now 70.238
postmasters, according to the report for June 30, 1896. Of
these, 3,635 are presidential and 66,303 are fourth-class.
They man the military outposts, they are the pretorian guards
of the boss system in every city, town and village of the
United States. They are the chief resources in the Federal
service now left for the mere wire-pulling politicians. Their
salaries, with those of the consuls and a few other officials,
form the only remaining national bribery fund for private use,
at public expense, for controlling primaries, caucuses and conventions. Theirs are the only large number of positions
which congressmen and defeated candidates for Congress of
the dominant party can continue to sell for cash payments, by
way of commissions on the salaries secured. Consequently
the crowding for these places promises to be very great. The
scramble has already begun. According to press interviews,
many a Congressman is planning how to divide this patronage
carcass within his district. Shall we be subjected to another
disgraceful scene with this incoming administration or has the
time and the man come to put an end to it all? Mr. Mc-
Kinley has certainly shown enough interest in and compre-
hension of the reform to wish to put a stop to this remainder
of the vicious system. He has been enough in Washington
to see the danger of yielding a little. He must be aware that
if he should yield one office to one congressman, he would
have to yield another to another, and so on, yielding one after
another, he would fall with increasing rapidity into the old
spoils method. The times, however, have come to Mr. Mc-
Kinley's aid. Every other election has been distinctly a party
victory. It has been hard for the President to resist party
claims, but this time it was not a party victory but a national
one. Under the condition of this year's vote the sound money
democrats alone insured Mr. McKinley's election, and if I do
not misunderstand the sound money democrats, they are not
asking for a division of the patronage. Then why is this not
the time and why is not Mr. McKinley the man to take the
firm stand and to say "No" to every partisan demand for a
postmastership? If he should do this, Mr. McKinley will be

added to the list of those Presidents who have done so much to advance the cause of civil service reform. Nay, more, he will go down to history as the one President who has completed the reform and the only one who has in no respect yielded to the spoils system since the days of Washington and Adams, and who has at last put American politics on a higher level, where purity and honor will have a fair chance to win. Is this too much to hope? I trust not. Before our next annual meeting, one way or the other, it will be writ in History.

The Relation of Women to the Reform of the Civil Service.

By Mrs. Charles Russell Lowell.

It was natural that the first Association for the Reform of the Civil Service should have been formed in New York, because New York has the unhappy distinction of having originated the "spoils system." In 1832 Van Buren's nomination as Minister to England was opposed by Webster, Calhoun and Clay because of his attempts to persuade the President to adopt the " New York System " of party removals.

" It is a detestable system," cried Henry Clay " drawn from the worst period of the Roman republic, and if it were to be perpetuated—if the offices, honors and dignities of the people were to be put up to a scramble and to be decided by the results of every Presidential election—our government and institutions, becoming intolerable, would finally end in a despotism as inexorable as that of Constantinople."

But Van Buren prevailed, President Jackson adopted the " New York system " and Federal politics quickly became poisoned, while in New York the corruption of United States office-holders was added to the already existing corruption of the Civil Service of the State, and "machines " of both parties exercised a power which was irresistible, because there was no attempt to resist it.

The "inexorable despotism " prophesied by Henry Clay was a fact, and there was no organized plan of revolt until 1877, when the first Civil Service Reform Association was formed in New York, at the suggestion of Mr. Dorman B. Eaton, and a constitution adopted of which the second article reads as follows:

" The object of the Association shall be to establish a system of appointment, promotion and removal in the Civil Service, founded upon the principle that public office is a public trust, admission to which should depend upon proven fitness. To this end the Association will demand that appointments to subordinate executive offices, with such exceptions as may be expedient, not inconsistent with the principle already mentioned, shall be made from persons whose fitness has been ascertained by competitive examinations open to all applicants properly qualified, and that removals shall be made for legitimate cause only, such as dishonesty, negligence or inefficiency, but not for political opinion or refusal to render party service; and the Association will advocate all other appropriate measures for securing integrity, intelligence, efficiency, good order and due discipline in the Civil Service."

The Woman's Auxiliary to the Civil Service Reform Association of New York was formed only a year ago, and it is not to the credit of women that it should have taken them so long to realize that they had a duty in this matter, and that, so far, the example of the New York women should not have been followed in any other State.

The New York Auxiliary was the result of two suggestions, both coming from persons from outside the State—Mr. Herbert Welsh, of Philadelphia, and Miss Cleveland, of Washington; and the hope of both was, I believe, that an Auxiliary to the National League should be formed at once. It was thought best, however, to begin with the local organization and to trust to the natural development of the federation as soon as there should be local organizations enough to form it.

The Woman's Auxiliary has, strangely enough, been obliged to explain the reasons for its existence—one good Civil Service Reformer even going so far as to object to its formation as unnecessary, because the cause of reform was already won. That objection, unfortunately, we know not to be valid—however great may be the cause for gratitude for many victories, the war is by no means over yet, and the spoilsmen, driven to bay, are (in New York at least) preparing for a determined attack on the very life of the reform. I will not, therefore, stop to answer an objection to which the continued existence of the National League itself is an all-sufficient answer, but will proceed to the other objection which has been made to the Woman's Auxiliary, which is that there should not be a separate *Woman's* Association, but that women should join the Civil Service Reform Association and work with the men.

This seems to the Executive Committee of the New York

Women's Auxiliary to be a mistake simply because they believe, and they think they have already proved by their year's experience, that by having two Associations more interest can be aroused than by having only one. There is no doubt that women are very much more ready to join a *Woman's* Association than one composed of both men and women ; partly because the very name leads them to feel that the matter involved is their business, partly because it seems to them less public and aggressive; partly because the meetings and other methods of any joint organization must be arranged to suit the convenience of men, and do not therefore equally suit the convenience of women.

It would have been possible, of course, for the women who undertook to form the Women's Auxiliary to have simply offered their services as individuals to the Executive Committee of the Civil Service Reform Association, but under those circumstances they could not have made any special appeal to women to come forward to help the cause, and I doubt if their efforts would have resulted in getting a quarter of the members or of the money for the Association that they have secured by the other method.

Whatever argument there may be for forming Students' Civil Service Reform Associations in colleges, instead of trying to draw the students in as individuals to existing local or State Associations, is equally strong for forming Women's Auxiliary Associations in all the cities where Associations already exist. The human mind is so constituted that an appeal to associate one's self with a distinct class of persons to which one naturally belongs (whatever the distinguishing characteristic of the class may be) is much more attractive than an appeal to join mankind at large, and it is to this natural tendency that the Woman's Auxiliary appeals.

One mistake, I think, we may have made—that is, in fixing the membership fee at $5—and I should advise women in other States to consider whether it would not be wiser to make it $2, or even $1. Five dollars is sufficient to keep out many persons who otherwise would join, and a large membership is more important than any other consideration.

The methods of the Auxiliary are extremely simple—it was established, according to the constitution, " to assist the Civil Service Reform Association in promoting the objects of the Association . . . and to raise funds to assist the Association"—and it has sought to accomplish both objects by holding parlor meetings, by circulating literature and by personal appeals.

Some women have objected to becoming members, because there was nothing especial to *do* ; but to study the whole subject of Civil Service Reform thoroughly enough to be able to advocate it intelligently and help to form a public opinion favorable to it, to fit one's self to answer conclusively the objections raised to it, will be found to furnish quite enough work for any one anxious to take an active part in the fight, while the giving of money to the Auxiliary is a most important means of *doing* something to advance the cause.

As to the special service which women should render this reform, it is the one which they should render to all reforms—that is, the maintenance of *uncompromising ideals*. Men, when they are required to put ideals into practice, finding it necessary to give way a little here, to adjust a little there, are constantly in danger of lowering their standards, and of thus gradually surrendering the very essence of reform, of becoming, indeed, traitors to the highest ideal while they still believe themselves true to it. Women, on the other hand, removed from political life and having nothing to do with the difficult and bewildering task of accommodating the ideal to the possibilities of the actual, are not exposed to the temptations to be "practical" which beset men, and can therefore with much less difficulty uphold the ideal, and refuse all suggestion of compromise. This, then, is their especial function. They must prepare themselves to resist everything that tends to lower the standards and ideals of the reform—they must strengthen the hands of the idealists against the "practical" men, they must point to the eternal laws of right, and encourage those who are battling for them against compromise.

And just at the present moment such aid is especially needed. We have reached a point in the fight for the reform of the Civil Service when our success is the cause of our greatest danger—when we are threatened with actual and total defeat in the guise of victory, and when the new allies can be of the greatest service because as I have said they are peculiarly fitted to protect the weakest point in our defences.

Any reform is safe while it remains so far in its ideal stage that its supporters and defenders, whether men or women, are necessarily idealists, but as soon as it becomes successful enough to attract the support of "practical" men, then its very life is imperilled, and the astounding progress made by Civil Service Reform during the past two years exposes it to a danger, which though it seems to be double and though it makes its attack both from within and from without, is in fact one and the same. The friends of reform are in danger, on the one hand, of accepting an empty shell, failing to recognize that the substance has been stolen from them, and the foes of reform, more keen-witted, are ready to give up the shell if they are only allowed to enjoy the substance in peace. A constant watchfulness is needed to make sure that, under the new laws and new forms, the old spirit does not obtain control and render our apparent victory vain and fruitless.

The Spoils System is directly responsible for political dis-honesty and for the false view of public office which obtains in the United States and it is impossible to be satisfied with the destruction of the former until the two latter are also removed —indeed it is impossible that the Spoils System should really be destroyed while the other evils continue, for a vicious circle has been created whereby the spoils system, political dishonesty and the view that public office is intended for the benefit of the officer, and not for the service of the public, alternately assume to each other the relation of cause and effect, so that the final and effectual reform of the Civil Service cannot be even hoped for until after the education of the American people in honest and correct views of politics and of public office.

To show how far these false views extend, it is only necessary to recall the fact that there are very few persons even among reformers who do not think it rather unfair that the examination for any office should be made so hard that persons of average ability should be unable to compete—but does not this simply mean that they forget what is the real end of the public service ?

If the object of the public service is the *best* service of the public, it is above all things desirable that the person best fitted shall be found to fill it, and also that only those best fitted should try for it, and difficult examinations accomplish this.

If, however, the public service is to be regarded as a means of support for the public officers, then it is desirable that everybody should "have a chance" and easy examination will bring this about, but this view, if acted on at all, will result, and must result, in all the old evils of the spoils system.

There can be no mixture of motives; either the public good or the good of the office holder must be the object in view, for, there is no doubt that, if it is the good of the office holder which is sought even remotely a good public service is impossible. In that case his need and not his fitness will be considered, and if an appointment is made because of the need of the appointee, it would be unreasonable to dismiss him because of inefficiency, since that was a matter of course, as, had he been efficient, the office would have sought him instead of his seeking the office. Thus by allowing the theory that public office is a means of benefiting the office holder, to have any weight at all, an extravagant and inefficient service naturally results in addition to the other evils.

The point to which this theory will lead even reformers was painfully exemplified last year when a man who had within a month finished his second term in an inebriate asylum was appointed to an important office in New York City, and the action was defended by two gentlemen high in official circles, by the one on the ground that it was charitable to give him the opportunity to reform, and by the other on the ground that the public was more interested than any individual could be in his reformation. In the minds of both, the fact that the public required a certain service to be done, which this man's previous life rendered him quite unfit to perform was entirely forgotten, and the public service was regarded by each as if it were his private property which he had the right to use for charitable purposes, and which, indeed it was a virtue so to use.

Before women can be of much use, however, in this great field where they are so much needed, they must educate themselves, and I can recommend no more instructive and inspiring book for the purpose than Mr. Dorman B. Eaton's "Civil Service in Great Britain; a History of Abuses and Reforms and their bearing upon American Politics." In that book Mr. Eaton did a service to the cause of Reform which is incalculable, and one which all reformers should constantly remember. He and George William Curtis (for I shall not allow the fortunate circumstance of my near relationship to the latter to prevent my offering my tribute to him) are the two men to whom the reform owes most, and I cannot more appropriately close than with the closing words of an address on "The Relation between Morals and Politics" delivered by Mr. Curtis before the Unitarian Conference in 1878:

" * * * Children as we are of men who founded a State on the Moral Law, and resolved as we are that it shall not swerve from that eternal foundation, holding that in the moral order of the Universe the right is always the politic, and pledged by our patriotic hearts to keep unstained the high ideal of our America, I appeal to you whether the moral purification of our public life is not a work of vital Christianity, and whether a wise and reasonable reform of the Civil Service would not tend to unite more closely American Morals and American Politics."

Civil Service Reform in the West.

By John W. Ela.

An account of Civil Service Reform in the West naturally begins at Chicago,—the starting point and center not only of this reform, but of the general movement which is gradually remodelling primitive political machinery and introducing business methods into local government throughout the middle West.

The action of the Illinois Legislature in passing the civil service bill a year ago last spring was by no means as spasmodic as it seemed to you gentlemen of the East. It had its history. The relation of cause and effect was plainly visible to those who were in the thick of the fight. A succession of purely political administrations had applied the old-fashioned spoils system so faithfully and successfully that the city found itself burdened with an enormous debt, with little or nothing to show for it. Administrations changed politically, now and then, but the system never changed. A change in administration simply meant that the names of the horde of political workers of the defeated party went off the pay-rolls and were replaced by those of the successful horde. Each new administration inherited the debt from the old one, struggled with the banks to carry it along through the two-years term, added generously to it, and passed it on to the next. Nearly the entire energies of the Mayor became concentrated on the continuous efforts to pay his political debts with the city offices and stave off payment of the floating debt of the city until the next unfortunate should step under the yoke. Meanwhile streets and alleys were not cleaned, taxes were getting higher and more uneven, expensive town offices which had become outgrown and meaningless could not be abolished because it would take fat places from the spoilsmen, and the gentlemen who had accepted offices under the administration, having paid for them with services rendered before the elec-

tion, were taking their ease in the comfortable places provided
for them or were getting ready for the next campaign.

Four years before the passage of the civil service bill an
organized movement was inaugurated to apply the merit system to the conduct of our city affairs. A non-partisan city
ticket was nominated on this basis which polled twenty-five to
thirty thousand votes. The *Daily News* was the only newspaper which supported the ticket, but the educational effect of
the lively campaign was apparent two years later, when the
reform sentiment had grown so strong that a citizen's ticket,—
nominated on a platform of which the sole plank was the application of the merit system of appointments to every department of the city,—was put into the field by leading citizens of
both parties, was endorsed be the Republican Convention, was
supported by every newspaper, except one, and was only defeated by a narrow majority in favor of an exceptionally popular candidate. It looked then like a defeat for civil service
reform, but it proved to be a long step towards victory; for
before the next biennial election (in April, 1895) the spoilsmen
had surrendered unconditionally.

In November, 1894, Mayor Hopkins appointed three members of the Civil Service Reform League of Illinois a commission to report a plan for putting the police force of the city on
a civil service reform basis. The committee reported a set of
rules applying the merit system to this department, which
were substantially the same as those provided for in the present civil service law. These rules were adopted and were, by
order of the Mayor and Superintendent of Police, put in operation by the Commission, and they continued in operation until
the end of that administration, April, 1895.

The National Civil Service Reform League, on invitation
of the Illinois League, held its first annual meeting in the
West in Chicago the middle of December 1895; and its Proceedings, and especially the admirable address of its president,
were given wide circulation. By these instrumentalities,—to
say nothing of the efforts of the local league and other citizens'
organizations,—the sentiment for the reform was greatly intensified.

At the opening of the Legislature in the following January
the civil service bill was introduced. By that time the demand
for reform had become irresistible, and soon afterwards the

committees of both political parties in Chicago declared in favor of civil service reform and endorsed the bill pending in the Legislature. I will not go over the interesting history of the passage of that bill and its adoption by the city in the election of April 1895 by 50,000 majority ; interesting to you, probably, because it was the passage of the first civil service reform bill in the West. But we are chiefly concerned here as to the results.

About the first of July, 1895, the Mayor appointed an excellent commission, and it is enforcing the law intelligently and thoroughly. Every man who has been appointed to office, or has been employed, in any department of the city government, since the appointment of the commission, has been subjected to an examination calculated to ascertain his fitness to perform the duties of the place sought to be filled, and the man who passed best got the place. Of course the ideal thing would have been to have had the law go into operation with the coming in of the new administration, in April 1895. It was a change of administration from one party to the other; there was the usual cleaning out of the city offices, which were largely filled with the appointees of the old administration. If the law could have taken immediate effect all these vacancies would have been filled by competitive examination and the reform would have been in operation in a few months throughout a large proportion of the city service. The bill so provided when it went down to the Legislature, and its friends consented very reluctantly to the amendment which allowed the Mayor ninety days within which to put the law into operation. But it was argued that the bill could not pass without the amendment, and we had waited too many years to haggle now over another three months. The law now only applies to vacancies as they occur, but they are occurring in some of the departments, with refreshing frequency.

There are eight thousand places under the city government, including officers and laborers, to which this law is admitted to be applicable. That does not include the Board of Education which, however, has recently appointed a committee to apply the merit system to most of the places within the jurisdiction of that Board, excepting teachers. In the seventeen months since the law went into force the Commission has subjected over four thousand men to competitive examinations for various official positions. Of these nearly twelve hundred have successfully passed the examinations and over five hundred of them have been certified to fill vacancies and have been appointed. Between two and three thousand laborers have passed an examination to test their fitness for the labor applied for, and nearly eight hundred of these have been put to work. About four hundred men in office have been promoted to a higher rank, as the result of examinations to determine the men in the lower rank best fitted for the higher.

Under the clause for investigation of the departments the Commission is breaking up one of the worst and most expensive frauds of the spoils system, viz.:—"Stuffing the pay-rolls," —by which political workers, who do not work except to draw their weekly pay, are kept on the city rolls for campaign purposes. The Civic Federation looked up the evidence and instituted the proceedings before the Civil Service Commissioners and the Citizens' Association furnished the funds to pay the expense of the investigation. As a result several men holding important positions have been discharged by the administration and two were indicted by the grand jury, convicted and sent to jail.

The Commission also prosecuted a vigorous investigation into the assessment of office holders for political purposes, with the result that the practice has been rendered so hazardous that it will probably be dropped hereafter as part of the political machinery, so far as the city offices are concerned.

It used to be a convenient instrument for manipulating majorities to largely increase the police force just before an election. The excuse for this was the alleged necessity for extra policemen to maintain order at the polls. But, by a singular interposition of political providence, the men taken on for this temporary purpose were always of the same political stripe as the existing administration. Now, the Civil Service Commission has always on hand a large eligible list of applicants for police positions,—those who had passed the examinations and are waiting for vacancies,—and all requisitions for these temporary appointments are filled from this list, without regard to political affiliations or fitness for campaign work. It is remarkable how complaints of police intervention in elections for partisan purposes have disappeared under this operation of the civil service law. Four hundred of these special policemen,—from the eligible list,—were employed at the election last month, and not a complaint has been lodged of interference or improper action, and the election was noticeably quiet.

Perhaps one of the most notable effects of the law is that the offices in the City Hall are no longer crowded with politicians after places for themselves and friends; and so all the officers, from the Mayor down, are allowed to devote themselves to the interests of the city; whereas formerly a very considerable portion of their time,—at least during the first half of their term,—was absorbed in parcelling out the plunder.

Again, the execution of the law by the Commission is effectually breaking up the "Padrone" system—the custom, which had gradually secured a strong foothold, by which a large proportion of the ignorant foreign laborers employed by the city paid a portion of their small wages every week to padrones under the belief that these men secured, or preserved, their places for them.

Although the change in the personnel of the service may be comparatively slow so long as there is no change in the politics of the administration, still the law, and its thorough execution, are gradually clearing the atmosphere and strengthening the moral tone in every department of the city government. It took time for even public officials to realize that there was a practical phase to the reform. Some of them have only recently discovered that there is such a law. Within the year, it is said, men elected to the City Council have walked over to the City Hall and submitted a list of names of their quota for appointment in some of the departments, and were apparently astonished to learn that there was a set of disagreeable officials, called the Civil Service Commissioners, who were interfering in an exceedingly obnoxious manner with this time-honored prerogative.

The intelligent politicians,—the leaders,—favor the law. The leading men of the committees of both parties have assured me that they were for the law, and do not want it interfered with. They have become disgusted with the spoils system. They say that it has proved a conspicuous failure; that it has defeated each party in succession in the last dozen years. The men who oppose the reform are those who know they would never get an office if the test were simply their fitness to perform the duties of the office. The higher grade of politicians,—politicians in the best sense—those who formulate the policy of party—rely upon their individual merit for political preferment; and this law clears the field for such men. And so while the coming Legislature will be the first since the passage of the law, and while the lower grade of partisan workers undoubtedly find the reform atmosphere a little too rarified for comfortable respiration and will probably make some clamor, I have no fear that there will be any serious attack on the law. It is the desire of its friends, including the Civil Service Commissioners in Chicago, that the law shall stand just as it is, without any attempt to amend it in any particular; and I believe that desire will be respected. I believe that the men who are going to the Legislature this year, are, as a general thing, satisfied with the law, and they know that the leaders of their respective parties are satisfied with it. I am sure the people of Chicago, of every party, regard it as advancing our city to a distinctively higher grade of civilization; that they are proud of having presented to the great West what promises to be a solution of the most puzzling civic problem of our time, viz.: the government of the modern city; in the struggle for which republican progress on this side the Atlantic has encountered disastrous failure; and I believe that at the first menace to the existence or the efficacy of this law, in any form or from whatever quarter, these people will express themselves in a manner that will be absolutely conclusive.

The merit system is also being applied to some of the County institutions in Chicago, and is unquestionably working out a very desirable reform in the conduct of those institutions. This county law applies only to the County Hospital, Insane Asylum, and employees in the County buildings and in the offices of the Superintendent of Public Service and County Agent,—where the poor relief is distributed. There are about seven hundred and fifty officers and employees altogether, men and women, to whom this applies. And, as many of these are nurses and attendants on the sick and insane, the field is peculiarly fit. The principal difficulty in the administration of this law is the small appropriation. The law only allows five thousand dollars, and as the salaries of three commissioners, at fifteen hundred dollars each, and the compensation for a stenographer, come out of that, there is little or nothing left for other purposes. The commissioners, however, prepare and conduct the most of the examinations, and where experts are required they obtain the voluntary services of professionals in good standing. They have competitive examinations of physicians, nurses, attendants, engineers, etc., and keep eligible lists from which persons are certified for appointment as required by the law, which is similar in that respect to the city law. Although there was considerable criticism as to its execution at first, the effect of this law is plainly perceptible in the improved condition of that part of the county service which comes under its jurisdiction. But the principal county offices, like the Sheriff's, County Clerk's, County Treasurer's and Recorder's offices, await the passage of a general county civil service law, which will be one of the next steps in the reform. There are constitutional reasons why these other county offices could not be covered by the present county law.

The city law has been adopted by Evanston, a city of twenty-five thousand inhabitants, twelve miles from Chicago, and it is working to the satisfaction of everybody. When applied to small cities the machinery of the law is very simple and inexpensive, and there are already movements under way for its adoption in others of these cities. A bill for a state law, applying the merit system to all the state institutions, was introduced in the Legislature of Illinois at the last session, by Honorable W. G. Cochran, one of the ablest members, and afterward Speaker of the Special Session. Mr. Cochran is a good friend of the reform, and as he will be a leading member of the next legislature,—probably Speaker,—we may expect a strong effort, at least, to pass this bill.

In several other western states the reform is making continual progress. At the last session of the Minnesota Legislature a civil service bill passed the Senate but failed to pass the House. The local civil service league led in the effort to pass this bill; a large mass meeting was held in the Representatives' Hall at St. Paul, in the middle of the session, to promote the bill, and a strong public sentiment in its favor was aroused. The prospect for its passage at this winter's session seems promising. In St. Louis the local civil service league has been active; there is considerable enthusiasm there over the reform and charter amendments applying civil service rules to the city government which are to be submitted to a vote of the people of the city next April. The Civic Federation, the Commercial Club and other citizens' associations have joined the local civil service league in St. Louis in its efforts for this reform. The Mayor and the President of the City Council are members of the local league. The citizens of San Francisco have also been agitating for the reform, to the effect that a new city charter containing a provision for civil service rules was submitted to the people at the late election, and was defeated by the small majority of 1,806. The defeat was due principally to other provisions of the new charter, and the civil service proposition will be again submitted at the next election. In Indianapolis are some of our leading civil service reformers. Civil service rules are now provided for in the charter of that city, but they have been temporarily set aside by the present Mayor. In New Orleans similar rules have been recently adopted by the people, applying to every department of the City Government. In the grand reform revolution, which was so magnificently successful in the New Orleans election of last spring, the adoption of the merit system was the principal demand. In Seattle also the citizens united on a demand for this system and it has been adopted by vote of the people of that city. Milwaukee and Portland, Oregon, have made a beginning; they have rules applying the merit system to certain departments only. Tacoma also adopted these civil service rules by amendment to the city charter, but the amendment has been declared void by the Courts on a technical point and the proposition will be again submitted to the people in proper form. In Ohio a bill applying the reform to such cities as adopt it passed one house. If a strong effort is made it can probably be carried in the next Legislature.

You will observe that the movement has developed concrete results in these Western states, and nearly all of them since the passage of the Illinois law. And this movement in the West is not alone along the lines of civil service reform, but is broadening into that other reform, non-partisanship in local elections, which is the logical sequel of the application of the merit system to the local appointive offices. With the elimination of the spoils system, the gang, which depends on the spoils for its existence, gradually disappears. The local gang is by far the most obnoxious fruit of the old system. It is composed wholly of the petty politicians who take no interest in what they are pleased to call "politics" unless there looms up very distinctly at the end of the campaign a chance to divide the local offices. When a city has adopted the policy of appointing to the local offices only the men who pass examination as to fitness,—in which ability to carry "de Fift Ward" cuts no appreciable figure,—these patriotic gentlemen incontinently retire from the business of regulating the governmental policy of their country to some other field of labor, where a fair compensation is still paid for an honest day's work. Without a local gang,—that is, without the power to pay a local gang out of the public funds,—the other patriotic gentlemen who are running for the local elective offices are compelled to run on their merit, and so, naturally, the best men,—the men best fitted for the elective offices,—are brought to the front. The question of fitness governs here as well as in the appointive offices. Party politics are seen to be out of place where the question is,—Who shall take charge of a great business corporation like a city? Already parties,—where they still make nominations for the local offices,—are running business men for candidates, and are running them on the basis of their business ability. Scarcely a word of party politics is heard in the campaign; and the spectacle is presented of a political campaign with no politics in it. While I do not say that we have reached this advanced stage in political science throughout the West, there are evidences that we are well on the way.

In the municipal elections of last year, in cities in several of the western states,—Illinois, Ohio, Iowa, Wisconsin and others,—there were citizens' tickets, based upon the merit system, and in nearly every case they were successful. These cases are undoubtedly increasing from year to year. Although in many of these states there is as yet no civil service law, still these citizens' movements are distinctly on the merit system and on the line of this reform; the candidates are run on their fitness for the office and on the promise to apply the merit test in appointments to office. In fact, these organized efforts to exclude party politics from local government are an expansion of the civil service reform idea, and the public sentiment which makes them possible is the result, largely, of the spread of that reform. In communities where a civil service law continues in thorough operation it seems to me that non-partisanship in local elections must necessarily follow, and is merely a

question of time. The Voters' League of Chicago last Spring
began the regeneration of the City Council—a job which they
propose to finish with neatness and dispatch in the coming
spring election.

In conclusion, I know you will permit me to say,—without
implying any discourtesy whatever,—that the atmosphere of
the West seems more congenial to the growth of civil service
reform than that of the East. I know that you of the East
have fought those bitter battles for a foothold, which are so
peculiarly thankless, for many years ; and that your experience
has not only furnished us with material for a quicker develop- .
ment, but has, to a large extent, opened the educational feature
of the campaign all over the country. I mean, therefore, to
give you full credit for your share in bringing about this unusual susceptibility of the people of the West to take kindly to
civil service reform.

In the West the growth of the sentiment for the reform, in
all its aspects, seems to be rapid and continuous, and yet
healthy ; and it is already cropping out in practical legislation
in many of these states. In Chicago we shall get the entire
city service under the rules within five years after the passage
of the law,—even if we have to change the political complexion of an administration sometimes on purpose to do it. A
business proposition like that which lies at the base of this reform, and its application to matters which have heretofore been
thought to be political,—in the worst sense of the word,—is
readily apprehended in the West. The reign of precedent
is not so imperious as in the East. The perception of the
useful is keener, and the determination to test it, regardless
of its youth or want of respectability, is swifter and more tena-
cious. Civil service reform in the West, although slow in
getting its start, has had no steps to retrace; no experience
with unfortunate results. Its wide significance,—its absolute
necessity as the foundation of safe municipal government,—
has now gained the recognition of the people,—especially those
of the cities. Movements in its behalf are already becoming
the tests of progress in the large western towns; the standard
by which the grade of popular intelligence is judged. I believe
it is only a question of time when the merit system will be permanently applied to the filling of all places in our municipalities, and when we shall be ashamed to acknowledge that there

was a period in our history when men got positions as inspectors of our drains, or assessors of our property for taxation, on the sole ground that they had rendered questionable assistance to some ward politician in his personal campaign for a more important office, for which he was equally unfit.

Four-Year Tenure.

By Lucius B. Swift.

THE late Bryanite platform declared against a life tenure, charged as being built up in the public service; and Bryan himself in his letter of acceptance, and in one of the slight variations of his speech, showed that no after-thought had brought him new light. No one in America is in favor of a life tenure. It is contrary to republican government and to the spirit of American institutions. If a life tenure is being built up here, it is the duty of every one to turn in and pull down the structure. But it is well first to be sure of the fact.

A boiler-maker works through the week in the shops and at the end draws his pay. The next week is the same, and this may continue through months and even years. It might continue until from old age or other disability he is no longer able to work. The requirements are that there shall be work for him to do and that he shall be faithful and efficient. While these exist it is manifestly to the detriment of his employer to dismiss him. He may, however, be dismissed at any time because there is no work, or for any kind of misconduct, or for lack of efficiency, or for no reason whatever. Clearly, this is not a life tenure. Turning to the public service, a railway mail clerk obtains his place by competition. Having obtained it and proving himself faithful and efficient, he may work on for weeks, months and years, and even until old age or other disability renders him unfit. He may be dismissed, however, at any time because there is no work, or for any impropriety or misconduct, or for lack of faithfulness or efficiency, or for no reason whatever. This is not a life tenure, as Bryan and his convention knew. The declaration of his platform was a falsehood, fitly set with other falsehoods to aid him and other demagogues in a scheme of plunder so comprehensive that it left no interest untouched.

There is no difference between the tenure of the boiler-maker and of the clerk. The work which has been accomplished in the thirty years of the struggle for the merit system, largely under the leadership of this League, is the transfer from the field of politics to the field of the wage-earner of about 100,000 of the best places in the federal service. This is a tremendous fact to wage-earners. The former occupants went into these places political heelers. They had nothing at the beginning nor more at the end. It became a proverb that a place was a curse and place-seeking a guaranty of poverty. What do these places mean now ? · They mean the retention of manhood in getting them ; they mean comfortable support of families, the acquirement of a home, the education of children and peace of mind; they mean a better and more economical public service and a great elevation of public morals. That the men who attacked and would have overthrown this system have met with overwhelming and humiliating defeat, is the most gratifying fact that has appeared in the history of civil service reform. And the unhampered power of dismissal which should be kept unhampered, except by the requirement of a written reason, is not only the guaranty of discipline and efficiency, but it is and will remain the complete answer to the charge of life tenure.

The victory and final establishment of the merit system has left much of the federal service in a curious condition. It may be described as light-headed. Most of the offices under the merit system have under-employees of long experience and high skill and efficiency. The heads have less, for the reason that they were generally appointed within four years and almost universally without knowledge of their duties or of the work to be done. The process was to go upon the street and pick up active politicians or take some beneficiary of an active politician. President McKinley will soon be asked to repeat this process because four years have elapsed since the present holders came in. Your county chairman of the party committee is expected to become post-master; your state chairman in a close state, a greater consul; your state secretary a lesser consul; your state committeeman, collector of internal revenue; your chief wire puller, district attorney, and so on; but always a place to reward actual or alleged service in carrying the election.

I wish to say a word for campaign services. I have seen them rendered for years but I have never seen them so necessary or so well rendered as on the victorious side in the late campaign. An intelligent and sleepless county chairman was a most comforting assurance. Nevertheless the question of campaign service is easily settled. Much of it has always been done and always will and ought to be done without hope or expectation of reward. All which cannot for good reason be so done, and there is much, should be paid for openly and publicly out of the campaign fund; much already is so paid for. The close of the campaign should leave the account between the workers and the party balanced. It is not now regarded as balanced, and every place not within the civil service rules will be demanded of Mr. McKinley to complete the payment. The demand will be made in entire confidence that it will be acceded to on the ground that the incumbents have been in four years; and where the law does not so limit the term, it will be claimed that custom amply does.

I cannot find that in dividing spoil any distinction has been made between offices where the commissions run four years and where they run indefinitely. The fourth-class postmasters are an overwhelming evidence; with every change of party 50,000 of them have gone in and out. It is most desirable that Congress repeal the laws which seem to fix the tenure at four years. It would show that Congress had at last come up even with the progress of the reform. But it would be a serious mistake to admit that rapid and steady progress can be interrupted by the failure of Congress to perform its duty. The completion of the reform in the federal service must not be made to depend upon this repeal. Congressmen do not have us in their eye; that space is entirely occupied by party managers and workers at home. There is no longer doubt but that Congressmen are glad of the great number of places we have taken away from them and that they would be glad to see the rest taken if it could be done without their seeming to have a hand in it. But they know that primaries and conventions are still managed by a mere fraction of the party and that that fraction never forgives a shrinkage in patronage. It is well to remember also that the repeal if accomplished would not stand in the way of a President or a party intent upon destroying the merit system.

The reform can be completed in spite of the four-year laws. In all the years of this agitation I have believed that the one unfailing source of progress and success was the will of the President acting under the powers conferred upon him by the Constitution. That is now our ample resource. Once inaugurated, the President has but to take his stand and the thing is done. The rock-bottom of that stand is that Congressmen are not part of the appointing power. There was a time when custom furnished some shadow of excuse, but in the light which accomplished reform in the federal service throws, any attempt by individual congressmen to "name" persons for places, is a presumptious and impertinent interference with the duties of the President. Time has been when Presidents were afraid of congressmen and felt that they must yield to them. Such yielding now in face of the general contempt in which office-brokers are held could not plead any kind of necessity.

It does not make any difference how many times or how many years it is said that you can with propriety go upon the street and pick up a politician and make him the head of an office filled with skilled and experienced employees, numbers of them more fitted for the place than himself, it is not true and will never be true. Such a practice would wreck any private business. It is a fraud upon the public and it is a gross injustice in depriving under-employees of a chance of promotion. The practice will not continue because the interests of business and good sense and fairness cry out against it. Mr. McKinley is not free in the matter. He is bound by his platform and by his own repeated utterances. It will not do for him to leave his sincerity to be questioned; he must take up the work where his predecessor leaves it and go forward to the end. To urge that four-year commissions or four-year custom stand in the way would be a childish excuse. The first principle to be laid down by President McKinley is that there are no offices to be divided as spoil. The second principle is the same and the last is like unto it.

There are some 65,000 fourth-class post offices. These are destined to pass away as little political centers and except in sparsely settled districts their places will be taken by sub-stations under the control of a neighboring central authority which will bring the benefits of free delivery and good service to nearly all of the people and the employees will be within the classified service. The plan has been developed under the present administration and the new administration has but to occupy the ground. If it is said that legislation is needed, the administration should answer that it will leave things as they are until such legislation is had. If the gross injustice of transfering so many positions of one party to the classified service should be urged, it should be answered that no such transfer is to be made but that the present incumbents have only the right of competition for the new places.

The presidential offices are a much easier problem. The President may nominate whom he will to be postmaster. He has but to direct the Civil Service Commission to prepare a scheme of promotion which under competitive tests shall bring to him out of the postal service names of men fit to be postmaster, and from these names send his nominations to the senate. This practice may be applied to every non-political office : it is not new for it is now applied in some portions of the consular service.

I desire to add that I am not wedded to a plan for any branch of the service. When there is a will there is no difficulty about a way. We can not expect congressmen to take the lead. Already the four-year signs which have been familiar to us for a life-time are re-appearing. The petition of the place-seeker is on its rounds and careful calculations are being made as to what patronage the representative of the right party stripe will control, and what senator or party leader will "name" men for places in districts of the wrong stripe. Men are working with members elect of legislatures to secure their votes for senatorial candidates and the federal offices which the successful candidate will control are having their usual weight in the contest. Congressmen willing or unwilling seem to acquiesce and participate in this old-fashioned movement for a division of spoil and in such ways as deciding whether or not elections shall be held for post masters have assumed the air of ownership. It is unsafe to rely upon their voluntarily voting themselves to be law makers and nothing more. It will be President McKinley's duty to break this practice up. There would be some opposition ; the opposition would be noisy, but after all it would only embrace a small fraction of the President's party, and would be helpless against the President sustained by the ample power of the constitution and by the approval of the great body of the people.

Civil Service Commissions Essential to Civil Service Reform.

By Hon. Dorman B. Eaton.

The enemies of civil service reform in the State of New York are preparing for a combined assault upon her reform system at the next session of her legislature. This assault will be novel in kind, highly plausible in theory, and well calculated to deceive the friends of reform who do not understand the practical methods essential for its success. Yet, if it shall prevail, it is sure to be—as it is intended to be—disastrous to the reform policy of the State.

The direct object, and only avowed purpose of the assault, is to deprive the state commission of essential power over the examinations—if possible to supersede the Commission altogether—and substitute for the present examinations under it, a series of detached and miscellaneous examinations under which the official head of every department and great office—State and Municipal alike—will have a special examination to be devised and controlled by himself, which will be the only one required for entrance to the part of the public service over which he presides. Though it is not admitted to be a part of the scheme to allow every head of a bureau and division—in State and city departments—to have an examination to suit himself, the logic and tendency of the proposed new system of disintegration and feebleness will make this result, which every boss, spoils-system politicians, greatly desires—both inevitable and speedy.

We shall be told that, under the new plan proposed, the examinations upon which we insist will continue, that merit and fitness will be tested by them, and that there will be the competition which is required by the New York constitution of 1895. This constitution proclaims a noble reform policy in these memorable words: "Appointments and promotions in the civil service of the State and of all the civil divisions thereof, including cities and villages, shall be made according to merit and fitness to be ascertained, so far as practicable, by examinations, which, so far as practicable, shall be competitive."

The leaders of this assault will declare their object to be, not to defeat this constitutional policy, not to suppress anything of real value, but merely to improve the agencies by which Civil Service reform and this policy are to be made effective, without the incumbrance and expense of a civil service commission. In fact, our assailants present themselves as advanced reformers, who merely seek to improve the methods of the old reformers.

For mere scheming politicians, patronage mongering party managers, and bosses to pretend to seek the advancement of civil service reform, which they have always opposed and now detest, and the more efficient execution of this new constitutional policy, which they have bitterly resisted, and which now threatens the speedy extinction of the spoils system by which they prosper, is a piece of audacious and mendacious impudence as incommensurable as it is grotesquely ridiculous. The appetite of the tiger and the shark may doubtless be greatly modified, but before we can trust them, it is prudent to have some evidence of a change of taste.

The leaders of this assault have for two years in succession refused—despite the exhortations of the Governor—to discharge their plain duty to enact a law in aid of the execution of this high constitutional policy. This refusal to enact such a law, which the Constitution in express terms requires, is, in substance, a violation of their oaths of office, a deliberate and treasonable defiance of their duty to obey the Constitution, and a cowardly rebellion against the form of government under which they live. That this treacherous policy has been pursued —in conspiracy with the Tammany leaders—in the hope of defeating the purpose of the constitution and the will of the people —is a fact too plain to be doubted.

The simple fact that the enemies of reform seek to suppress commissions is, in substance, an avowal of the further facts that they find them an effective force in restraint of the spoils system, and very troublesome bodies in the way of all those who seek, under that system, to grasp and distribute patronage and spoils for personal and party gain. If bosses, politicians, and thrifty patronage-mongers do not think they could more easily enforce party tests at the gates of office, more readily foist their ignorant and unworthy favorites upon the public service, more easily extort political assessments for party purposes from the public servants, under the new examinations they propose than under examinations controlled by commissions, why do they combine for a common assault upon these bodies ? . . . It is certainly possible that they have become reformers. But has any of them the courage to declare it to be their object, to make civil service reform methods more effective, to put men into the public service upon their merits irrespective of party opinions, to arrest political assessments, or to restrain the despotic domination of the boss or the partisan majority ?

Every person acquainted with the methods of the spoils system,—especially if he has had experience as a Civil Service Commissioner—knows that there are three main sources of hostile influence which civil service reform and every commissioner must encounter: (1) the selfish efforts of individuals who seek offices and gain for themselves and their relatives at the cost of the people; (2) unpatriotic and unscrupulous public officers, who prostitute their power over appointments and removals for paying their political debts, for conferring benefits upon their favorites and henchmen, and for placing their party managers under obligations to advance them to higher offices; and, (3) —and most potent of all—debased political parties, their bosses and leaders who constantly exert their power, in violation of the civil service law and rules, for enforcing party tests, for conferring office by favor, for evading the examinations—for coercing and deceiving civil service commissioners, and for extorting assessments from the public servants and compelling them to be servile to party electioneers.

The new system of examinations proposed would, with most grotesque absurdity, give the direct control of them to the second class of these irrepressible enemies, who are chosen by the third class. The very forces and persons whom the examinations most need to restrain would be given direct control of them. The wolves would be chosen to protect the sheep. Every civil service commissioner has given a very large portion of his exertions—I certainly gave one-third of mine—to resisting the pressure and defeating the conspiracies of these enemies. It is difficult to say which has been the most frequent and the most difficult to defeat, the machinations and corrupt efforts of party bosses and managers out of office, for evading and cheating the examinations, or the frauds and perversions of unworthy politicians, in office for the same purpose. Therefore to hand over to them—or either of them—the control of the examinations would be the merest stupidity and madness, sure to be fatal to the cause of reform.

The salutary utility of commissions results very naturally from their organization, powers and duties. Adherents of different parties must be among their membership, which makes party favoritism nearly impossible; the entire proceedings of commission must be public and a matter of record; they have everywhere to deal with the rival and suspicious competitors, who are interested and ready to expose every fault; they are required to disregard party opinions and resist party pressure; they are constantly liable to be called to account in Congress and legislatures by hostile politicians anxious to discredit them; commissions have a duty to investigate and expose frauds and the use of partisan influence in the examinations and in all administrative offices, which naturally inclines all unworthy officers and professional politicians to dread them, and to try to discredit them by false charges; they have a duty—essentially judicial—to enforce a great, salutary, non-partisan principles of equality and justice according to stringent provision of laws which impose grave penalties for infidelity; they are required to submit detailed reports of all their proceedings, which makes it very difficult to conceal their own faults; they are supported by the power and prestige of Presidents and Governors—so far as the latter are faithful to their duty, instead of prostituting their power for party ends.

It should, therefore, be no matter of surprise that both the moral and the legal power of commissions has been much greater for good administration than most people have supposed. It is perfectly natural, therefore, that they should be both feared and hated by the whole class of ringsters, unworthy officers, and patronage mongering politicians.

Though all these enemies of reform who see with dismay their vicious patronage diminishing have done their utmost to discredit the commissions and arrest the reform of which they are an essential support, their efforts have been a dismal failure—especially in the National service and in that of the State of Massachusetts. Every one of their attacks has been utterly repulsed. They have not proven an offense committed by any Commissioner. They have not shown a single one of hundreds of thousands of questions to be unfit. It is true that Congressmen have sometimes, in cowardly secrecy, voted against appropriations for the work of reform, but the dread of public opinion has compelled them to change their votes when the public record of them would expose their authors to the indignation of the people. These enemies have seen with alarm, the examinations, which in 1883 extended to only about 14,000 places in the National service, now extending to about 85,000 such places. They have seen the cause of reform within that period grandly triumph and pass out of the sphere of controversy in the State of Massachussetts. They have seen this —to them mysterious—advance with all the more anxiety because it has everywhere marked the triumph of non-partisan public opinion over party opinion and party managers, and they can form no conception of the possible potency of this victorious opinion in the near future.

Is it any wonder, then, that these enemies in New York are alarmed,—that they are resolved to suppress the existing examinations and to provide for others which they can manage for their own advantage, without being obstructed by a commission, or exposed by its reports? They as naturally dread a Civil Service Commission as a criminal dreads a court, or a heathen dreads a missionary.

The enemies of reform see, with wonder and alarm, more than a hundred grades of examinations in the National service, and perhaps two-thirds as many in that of New York, carried forward harmoniously and economically under Commissions, everywhere bringing men and women of superior character and capacity into the public service and raising it in the estimation of the people; everywhere disregard party and sectarian opinions; everywhere rejecting party tests and withstanding party influence; everywhere diminishing the patronage and limiting the vicious influence which strengthen the spoils system, and make the positions of the party boss and the party managers both potential and profitable. Should we be surprised if they are angry and arm for a desperate assault.

The people are more and more clearly seeing that the ex-

aminations as conducted under commissions, are as favorable
to true party action as they are to the common school system
and to the suppression of the patronage and spoils by which
voters are bribed and party managers are made despotic and
rich.

These examinations facilitate the choice of members of the
legislature who represent not a boss, or mere factions, but the
people, and the true interests of every district—members who,
in that body, will dare say what they think well. Among the
2613 persons examined under the Massachusetts Commission
in the past year—and the ratio is much the same everywhere
—2,578 of them had only a common school education, while
only 35 of them had attended college. In such relations with
the common schools and the people who support them we may
see one of the sources of that potential public opinion—likely
to be much stronger in the future—which makes civil service
reform irresistable.

In managing machine politics and the spoils system the
enemies of reform can see the advantages of centralized organization and combined power, and they use them to the
utmost in every locality and at every point where their system
is attacked. The duty of feudal obedience on the part of
every local organization to the central State machine—and
even to the boss at its head—is constantly inculcated. The
freedom of local representation has been thus impaired, and
every local candidate for the legislature feels the need of de-
ferring to the State boss. The Briarian arms of the central
machine—a sort of political octopus—are thrust out and made
potent in every county, town and village election; its power
curtails the freedom of every member of the Legislature, making it nearly impossible, save under servile conditions, to procure the passage of any law in the interest of his constituents.
This same central power largely dictates local appointments
and removals, and degrades the public servants into party
electioneering vassals.

Yet, with astounding audacity, the supporters of the spoils
system—the men who are themselves the very embodiment of
centralized control—insist that the friends of non-partisan justice and reform and the supporters of the State constitution
shall, in their contest with these enemies, have no central organization, no commission to see that the examinations are every-

where just and reasonable, and to repel the attacks and expose the misrepresentations of their combined enemies. They seek to divide and isolate the examinations, and deprive them of salutary supervision and support, so that the whole horde of their confederated assailants may attack and defeat them in detail.

If the general of one of two armies arrayed for battle should propose to the other that he and the members of his staff should be at once taken off the field, and that his army should be divided into many separate detachments, the proposal must be thought sublimely impudent—but is it any more so than the proposal of our assailants?

It would be far better for the ultimate and speedy triumph of reform to repeal at once all laws upon the subject rather than to allow deceptive and fraudulent examinations to bring its very name into contempt.

Every one familiar with civil service examinations knows how easily, in charge of their enemies, they could be prostituted for personal and party advantage. At least one Governor of New York has strikingly illustrated this fact, and our enemies hope to make another follow his disgraceful example.

Yet, these evils, sure to result from examinations not supervised by a Commission, are hardly the worst. If every head of a department and great office is to have examinations to suit himself, he must be allowed to make the rules for regulating them, to fix the conditions of entering them, and the kind of character and the measure of capacity necessary for passing them, and for gaining appointments. He will select the one he prefers from among all those examined. True and honest competition such as the New York Constitution requires will no longer exist. The examiners must be appointed by him, and they will be compliant to his will. Thus every such officer will, in substance, fix the conditions of entering and remaining in the public service under him.

Inevitably, every one who is standing as a candidate for an office having this power apendant will be regarded by the voters and party leaders as having the ability, when elected, to give him an office—if need be, by making a removal to create a vacancy. Here we should have the establishment of the spoils system by law—the very thing our assailants seek. The office-seekers and spoilsmen would demand promises of office as the condition of giving the candidate their support. Such promises would be made and would be fulfilled. The examinations would be so manipulated—as they could easily be if there was no commission—that these election pledges could be redeemed. It is obvious that such a system would favor the most unfit and unscrupulous candidates, for they would promise the easiest admission to office and the most unjustifiable removals, and they would thus win the basest voters. More and more the examinations would tend to become a sham and a fraud. There would, we repeat, be no real competition, such as the constitution of New York requires, but a mere scrub-race between bribed voters and the local favorites of factions, bosses and heads of departments— the effective competing forces being party influence, boss power and miscellaneous pulls.

Let us turn from theory and reasoning to the admonishing lessons of history on the subject. The intolerable evils in English civil service, which resulted from allowing the heads of departments and offices—largely dominated by partisan members of Parliament and great politicians—to select their own subordinates, began to arrest the serious attention of statesman as early as 1820.

Examinations were introduced in various departments and offices, soon after 1841, and they had become known in the United States before 1853. They were isolated examinations for each department and office, though to a limited extent they were competitive in theoiy though not in fact. The conception of a Civil Service Commission, or the need of it had not apparently been developed. A very resolute patriot or reformer in office might without a commission enforce effective examination subject to his control for entering the service under him. But the ordinary officer controlling such examinations could and did easily make them serviceable to himself, his favorites, his relations, and his party. It soon appeared that he would not withstand party pressure. Patronage mongering members of Parliament and party managers could concentrate their combined influence for controlling these isolated examinations, and they soon began to do so effectively. As a result, the most unfaithful officers readily yielded, and consequently they were most liked, and were aided by the spoilsmen, ringsters, and corrupt party leaders. The examinations—unaided as they were by any commission—could not arrest unworthy party favorites and consequently the examinations became steadily degraded—lower and lower standards for admission prevailing until they became, in large part, a farce and a false pretense. In the words of Mr. Mill they excluded " only mere dunces." They demoralized administration. Only members of the ruling party were admitted to the examinations at all.

The English for more than half a generation tried these isolated examinations—to which our New York politicians now wish to revert—when the government had become convinced of the indispensable need of a strong civil service commission for devising and taking charge of all examinations. Such a commission was provided in May, 1855. It withstood the politicians from the first, and made the examinations everywhere just and effective. Its popularity increased, and its jurisdiction was more and more extended. It has continued down to this time, without scandal, discharging its duties with great advantage to the public service of Great Britain, and to the cause of popular education. The commission and its doings soon ceased to be subjects of controversy ; party tests were everywhere excluded from the administrative service ; men of high character and capacity readily entered it ; parties and politicians soon ceased to attempt to obstruct the commission. Yet legitimate party contests over party principles are—to say the least—as vigorous and salutary in Great Britain as in any other country of the world. So completely has mere partisan influence, and patronage-mongering been excluded from its administration that, at the last change of ministry, there were, save as to a very few unimportant places accidentally left out of the examinations—as the Author of the American Commonwealth has declared—less than a hundred changes made altogether for party reasons, or on account of political opinions. No postmaster, no collector, no heads of bureaus or divisions and no clerks are changed in Great Britain as the result of a new administration coming into power.

Experience in this country may teach us a similar lesson.

The old party spoils system had become unendurable here before 1853. The original examinations in England had attracted attention in the United States. Laws enacted in 1853 and 1855 provided for the classification of clerkships in the great departments, and in some of the local offices, and exam inations were required before appointments could be made to these clerkships. But, unfortunately, these examinations were under the control of the heads of the departments and offices; they were in no true sense made competitive, and there was no commission to take charge of them. Parties and their managers as they had done in England—as well as members of Congress, combined their attacks upon the officers having charge of the examinations, who were unable to make any effective resistance to their demands. Parties and their leaders took care that no man should be placed at the head of one of these departments or offices who was not likely to comply with their demands in regard to examinations. The new system soon became a source of official degradation. The experience of England was repeated. Soon every applicant for a clerk-ship not belonging to the party in power—if not everyone not belonging to the ruling faction of this party—was excluded from the examinations; there was no true competition; and from among those examined, those were appointed who were backed by the strongest party and official influence, and who were likely to be the most useful for doing party work. As in England, these isolated examinations excluded mere dunces, but they soon became, in the main, a farce and a fraud. Col. Silas W. Burt,—now a New York Civil Service Commissioner, and a veteran, to whom the cause of reform is greatly indebted for invaluable services in its behalf—has kindly supplied me with an interesting and characteristic illustration from his own experience. He applied for admission as a clerk at the Naval Office, in New York, in 1869. The only questions asked him were these: " What is the capital of the United States?" " How much is eight times eight?" He was admitted to the office he sought. Is it unkind to suggest that our assailants would be satisfied with examinations like this? We have no space for tracing further the evils or the uselessness of this kind of examinations which our New York spoilsmen now seek to re-establish.

As in England, this experiment in the United States led to the development of an intelligent reform sentiment, and to a clear conception of the indispensable need of a Civil Service Reform Commission which should have charge of all examinations. We can now clearly see that the whole contest for civil service reform in this country has been in substance for the establishment of a kind examinations which will exclude party tests and make true non-partisan competition of capacity and character possible. The primary purposes of seeking to suppress the Commission and to establish feeble and isolated examinations, are obviously these: (1) that no one not a member of the dominant party shall be admitted to the examinations; (2) no one who passes the examinations shall be appointed unless he belongs not only to the ruling party, but to the ruling faction of this party.

We cannot too much emphasize the fact that the noble advance in the cause of non-partisan administration in the two great English speaking nations has in the main been achieved through competitive examinations under the charge of commissions sustained by public opinion rather than party opinion. For more than 40 years, they have been tested on a grand scale in England, and for more than 13 years in the United States; and never, in either country, were they more popular, more potential for good, or apparently more certain to overcome all enemies than they are at this moment. In Great Britain the methods of civil service reform have long since ceased to be matters of controversy and its few enemies are regarded as curiosities, and as bourbons. The rapid advance of the reform in the national service of the United States—a service under which a single commission has charge of all examinations, has astonished its friends as much as it has dismayed its enemies; the new president is its sincere supporter, and is likely to do whatever wise things in its behalf, the patriotic achievements of President Cleveland have left undone. In Massachusetts, where a single state commission—which every Governor has supported—controls all examinations, even those in cities, the reform policy is supreme, and is questioned only by a small class of benighted spoilsmen and besotted partisans who are powerless for evil and without hope in the future. The city of Chicago—suddenly springing to the lead of many cities in the west well advanced in the cause of reform—has by popular vote established a powerful commission in control of all examinations, which is enforcing the reform system with great usefulness and promise. Over against these records our assailants have nothing which they can cite, but the history of the spoils system degradation under their proposed method which we have set forth. If they refer to the independent examinations for the police force of New York city, they are condemned by President Roosevelt—a most competent judge—and Mayor Strong has refused to allow independent examinations for the New York Fire Department. The State of New York, under a worthy Commission appointed by Governor Cleveland, entered upon the work of reform as auspiciously as did the State of Massachusetts. But the next two Governors of New York—very much unlike Governor Cleveland, and their contemporaries in Massachusetts—yielding to the base elements of their party, gave the Commission no adequate support, which led to its powers being perverted for party advantage. Governor Morton has done much, by revising the rules and enlarging the powers and duties of the commission, to enable it to fitly discharge its functions, and to much advance the cause of reform. There is now every prospect—save for the proposed assault—that the State of New York will make a creditable record and become a leader in the cause of reform. If Mr. Morton could be Governor for two years more, the struggle of the spoilsmen for supremacy would be made hopeless, and the abiding triumph of reform would be achieved. Much now depends upon whether Mr. Black, the new Governor of New York, shall decide to lead the higher, or shall prefer to yield to the lower forces of his party, whether he shall take patronage-mongering Governor Hill for his model, and court his shameless and ignominious fate and the disruption of his party, or shall rise to the level of Governor and President Cleveland, of President Harrison, Governor Morton—and of all the Governors of Massachusetts—the latter of whom have vetoed every bill which has threatened the reform in the state. I do not believe that the new Governor will accept orders from any boss, yield to the demands of the spoil system faction of his party, or fail to comprehend the duty of a governor to support the policy of the constitution. He was elected in the faith that he had the capacity and independence of a statesman, and that he would comprehend the rare opportunity—such as hardly any Governor of New York has ever had—to make his administration a great honor to himself and an abiding blessing to his State and the nation. The majority of the voters never imagined that—under the lead of a politician who, fifteen years ago, tried to subjugate a President of

the United States to the rebellious Senators from New York—
the new Governor would aid a traitorous attempt of the spoils
system factions of both parties to defeat a constitutional provision—adopted by the people—by means of rebellion and hostile action in the legislature—a rebellion in no wise less dangerous and flagitious than would exist if the spoilsmen, in that
body, should with arms in their hands prevent the competitive
examinations which the Constitution of New York requires.
Well may it be asked, What is the use of constitutional requirements if Governors and partisan majorities may, by conspiring together, defeat their policy and the will of the people ?
Tens of thousands of Democrats—with a patriotic sense of
duty of which our assailants seem to have little conception—
swelled the majority of the new Governor and helped save
the country from peril and disgrace. It would be strange in-
gratitude and meanness to connive at a change in our
system of examination—a retrogression to partisan barbarism
—which is intended to, and would, probably, cause the removal of every democrat who, upon his superior merits, has
won an appointment, and which would certainly prevent any
more democrats being appointed through the examinations.
These are primary objects of our assailants. Under such conditions it is the imperative duty of the friends of reform and of
every one who cares for the honor and political civilization of
New York to make his influence felt to the utmost against the
assault now threatened. If the conspiring spoilsmen, now led
by the bosses of both parties. shall be defeated at Albany this
winter, the spoils system will be crushed, and the noble principle of the constitution of New York, and the will of her people, will be permanently established.

It does not come within the scope of this paper to deal
with the constitutional question which its subject involves
But, in conclusion, I wish to say that I think the new examinations proposed would not provide for the competitive examinations which the constitution of New York requires, and
that the old spoils system is not likely to be re-established by
law, for the very purpose of defeating its provisions, until they
have been interpreted by the highest court of the State, which
has given significant evidenceof its purpose to uphold them.

Efficiency and Economy Under the Merit System.

REMARKS OF HON. JOHN R. PROCTER,

President of the United States Civil Service Commission.

IT was held by Senators and Representatives in Congress, when the civil service law was under debate, that the federal service under the patronage system was inefficient, more or less corrupt, and extravagant; that unnecessary positions were created and unnecessary salaries paid on account of pressure for office under that system. It was also promised that the merit system would, if adopted, result in a more economical administration of the Government. The two systems have been working side by side in Washington for more than thirteen years, and it is practicable to make comparisons of their relative advantages and disadvantages. There are thousands of positions included under the merit system, subject to competitive examinations provided by the Commission. There are also thousands of positions which were not classified until recently, and other thousands over which the Civil Service Commission still has no jurisdiction. It may easily be demonstrated whether the one system is extravagant and the other economical. I will give you figures showing the increases and decreases in numbers and salaries in the legislative, executive and judicial branches in the City of Washington since the organization of the Commission. It has not been practicable as yet to prepare statistics for those branches of the service outside of Washington, but it is believed that they would not differ materially in the results they would show:

THE LEGISLATIVE BRANCH.

(Unclassified.)

	1883.	1896.
Number of subordinate officers and employees in the Senate	154	326
Total amount appropriated for salaries	$276,044.60	$432,228.90

Increase in number of employees........		172
Per cent. of increase...................		112
Number of subordinate officers and employees in the House of Representatives............................	197	591
Total amount appropriated for salaries...	$364,028.20	$624,022.91
Increase in number of employees........:		394
Per cent. of increase.................		200

JUDICIAL BRANCH.
(Unclassified.)

Number of subordinate officers and employees...........................	6	89
Total amount appropriated for salaries...	$15,000.00	$114,150.00
Increase in number of employees........		82
Per cent. of increase.................		1383

EXECUTIVE BRANCH.
(Unclassified portion.)

Number of positions requiring appointment by the President and confirmation by the Senate (Departmental)........	88	107
Total amount appropriated for salaries for Presidential positions in Washington...	$345,200.00	$456,590.00
Increase in number of Presidential appointees..........................		19
Per cent. of increase................		22
Number of unclassified and other positions (not subject to competitive examination)..........................	7,847	10,760
Total amount appropriated for unclassified positions.......................	$6,792,377.00	$9,764,252.00
Increase in number of unclassified positions...........................		2,913
Per cent. of number in unclassified positions...........................		37

EXECUTIVE BRANCH.
(Classified portion.)

Number of classified positions subject to competitive examination by original classification......................		5,530
Total amount appropriated for competitive positions.....................	$7,035,820.00	$6,960,602.00
Number of original competitive positions still existing......................		5,414
Decrease in number of original competitive positions.....................		116

Per cent of decrease in number of original
  competitive positions................

Decrease in appropriations for salaries for
  original competitive positions........ $75,218

Percent of decrease in appropriations for
  salaries for original competive positions   1

The statement of unclassified Executive positions includes the positions which have from time to time been
added to the competitive list by extensions of the classified
service. More than 4,000 (?) of these were added to the
competitive list by the recent extensions, which have reduced
the positions at Washington not subject to competitive examination approximately to 4,821 (?).

It will be seen, therefore, that every branch of the Federal
service at the Capital has increased largely since the organization of the Commission, except those positions which are
subject to competitive examinations, where the increases have
occurred not by extra appropriations but by extensions of the
competitive list to cover existing unclassified and other positions not open to competition, until at present there are over
11,000 (?) positions in Washington subject to competitive
examination. The statistics show that the number of classified clerkships and copyist positions in Washington have decreased 3.9 per cent. in number since 1883, effecting a saving
of $228,200, while the unclassified positions of messengers,
the employees of the Government Printing Office, and others
recently added to the competitive list, together with the positions which remain unclassified by law, increased 37 per cent.
in number, involving an extra yearly expenditure for salaries
of $2,971,875, an increase of 43 per cent. If the patronage
system had continued unchecked, and the positions originally
made competitive had increased in the same proportion as the
unclassified positions, as a result of additional appropriations,
it would require an extra yearly expenditure of $3,100,620
for salaries in Washington alone.

There are numerous specific instances in which the saving
in the cost of administration effected by the merit system
has been demonstrated. A few of these I will cite by way of
illustration.

The last report of the Superintendent of the Bureau of Engraving and Printing shows that while the work performed has increased more than 77 per cent. since the application of the rules, the force has increased during the same period not more than 11 per cent. The Government Printing Office is another instructive exhibit. A year ago, before the rules were applied, the number of employees was 3,500. At the present time, with 35 per cent. more work, the total is 2,600. The Secretary of Agriculture in his recent report shows that as a result of the operation of the rules in his Department, while the work has been increased and extended in many new directions, there has been a reduction in the force of 280 employees, and that during the period since March 7, 1893, more than $2,000,000 out of a total of $11,000,000 of appropriations has been covered back into the Treasury.

Another striking instance is found in the comparative records of efficiency in the Railway Mail Service. The latest obtainable figures show that while the number of pieces of mail matter distributed per clerk has increased from 1,222,762 in 1885 to 1,779,759 in 1896, the ratio of errors to the number of pieces distributed correctly has decreased from one error to each 5,575 distributed correctly in 1885 to one for each 9,843 pieces distributed correctly in 1896. It is to be noted, too, that the year 1885 was, up to that time, one of exceptional efficiency in distribution. The ratio of errors in 1887 dropped to 3,364, and in 1890, following the numerous removals made just prior to the application of the civil service rules, to one in 2,834. The increase in efficiency since the adoption of the rules, as indicated by the ratio of errors, has been, therefore, about 400 per cent.

Another evidence of the superior results secured under the merit system is found in the comparative record of removals. In the classified departmental service at Washington the removals from competitive positions for all causes have been less than 2 per cent. a year, while in the unclassified and excepted branches the changes have aggregated, in the four years past, probably 50 per cent. From these figures the conclusion must be drawn that either the persons brought in through the examinations are far more efficient than the others, or that the removals from the unclassified positions have been made for causes other than the good of the service.

The decrease in the proportion of employees appointed after competitive examination, and rejected during the probationary period, is very significant. In the Railway Mail Service in 1890 there were 150 such rejections; in 1892, 70; in 1894, 18, and in 1896 only 5.

The results of the work of the Commission during the last thirteen years ought, in fact, to be more than gratifying to the advocates of civil service reform. Their claims for the merit system have been fully realized. Wherever the civil service rules have been applied the service has been improved, extravagance has been checked, and the chances of corruption in office by the sale of positions, or by their disposal for considerations other than those of merit and fitness, have been removed. With the extension of the classified service to cover practically all positions in the Executive service which under the existing statute can be included, efficiency and economy should, and doubtless will, become the underlying principles in the administration of the Government.

Results of Reform in the Department of Agriculture.

Address of Hon. J. Sterling Morton.

It is related of a certain American citizen that he arrived at the age of fifty years without having indulged in any marked peculiarities or frivolities, except a too constant attendance upon the theatre. He was always foremost among "first-nighters," and loudly laughed or silently wept as the play went. Each succeeding drama, tragedy or comedy, was to him more realistic than its predecessor. His satisfactions and enjoyments were consummate and intense. But at last an unwise friend induced him to attend a "rehearsal" and there he saw all the mechanism of the stage and listened to the uninteresting recital of the parts. His illusions were dispelled. He never again enjoyed a play or an opera.

And now, in the presence of the members of the Civil Service Reform League of the United States, the foregoing comes to my mind, because it somewhat illustrates my past and my present position relative to the public service. Arriving in Washington early in March, 1893, with a very indefinite knowledge of the Departmental positions and the services which they require, I was inducted to office entertaining the idea that the old system of appointments was probably well enough and good enough for practical as well as political purposes. Those views were the result, no doubt, of the patriotic esteem in which Senators and Representatives in Congress had been held by me and those with whom I came in daily contact. It never then occurred to me that any American citizen was in public life purely for personal ends or personal gains. It had never dawned upon my mind that the patriotism exhibited upon the stump was stage, and not real love of country. No suspicion had permanently lodged in my mind that statesmen ever sought offices for their relatives and friends and billeted them upon Departments for the mere sake of relieving themselves of the duties of kinship and friendship.

But my illusions and delusions were suddenly dispelled by the innumerable collusions which I detected between statesmen and those relatives and retainers whom they sought to impose upon the public service without considering their efficiency, fitness or adaption for that service.

My primary experience was in regard to the position of Appointment Clerk in the Department of Agriculture. The incumbent of that office had been appointed by my predecessor, Secretary Rusk, and had held the place about two years. He was a man more than fifty years of age, thoroughly qualified, punctiliously exact and conscientious in the performance of all his duties. He had faithfully kept the records, as far as they could have been made up under the patronage or political system, of the merits of each employee. He knew the day and hour when each came into the service, when each had been promoted or demoted, and the salary of each. He knew how many days of sick-leave and how many days of vacation had been given to each every year. The archives of the office of the Appointment Clerk were as complete and perfect as they could have been made under the then existing spoils system of appointments. But immediately upon induction to office I was assailed with the importunities of Representatives in Congress from the State whence came this Appointment Clerk, to displace him, because he was a Republican, and to put a gentleman whom they named into the position, because he was a Democrat. No Congressman or Senator suggested educational qualifications or peculiar personal merits as factors in the case. Then I began to see the importance of a Classified Service.

In the very beginning of my duties as Secretary of Agriculture I had been solicited, importuned, imperatively ordered, in short, to deprive myself and the Department of a faithful, honest and efficient officer, and thus to cripple my capabilities for intelligently managing the Department, and to minimize the value of its public service, by accepting for that clerkship a person utterly ignorant of the details of its duties.

The importunities continued; the importunists were put

off from day to day, until my official life became burdensome to such an extent, that I could see only one way of extricating myself from the torments which the spoils system provides for those who may have Departmental places at their disposal. And that way led up to and through the Classified Service. Therefore, I asked the President to place the position of Appointment Clerk, by special order, within that service. This was readily accomplished, because, as you know, there is no more genuine or courageous advocate of the reform of the Civil Service than President Cleveland.

Soon after the classification, the statesmen from the West who were so anxious to provide me with a raw recruit, by displacing a skilled veteran, called again. They were informed politely that, while I could remove the incumbent, they could not name his successor, nor could I name his successor, because the position had been placed in the Classified Service. They were amazed; they were indignant. And when informed that the Secretary of Agriculture had secured the classification of this position, their indignation was such that it found vent only through the door and out of the Department.

But, as the Executive branches of the federal Government have no right to demand appointments from the Legislative branch, it is difficult to determine upon what law or alleged right, Representatives and Senators may claim to place their favorites in departmental service and then hold the heads of Departments responsible for results.

Permit me, briefly, to give you an epitome of the relation of the United States Department of Agriculture during the last twelve years to the classified service. The Department was first placed under the operation of the civil service law on December 12, 1884, by the inclusion of 118 persons and the positions they occupied, in the classified service. That was by order of President Arthur. On June 30, 1888, the service was extended by order of President Cleveland, and 116 more positions were included. On January 5, 1893, President Harrison ordered observers and local forecast officials employed outside the District of Columbia in the Department of Agriculture, numbering 314, into the classified service.

On March 20, 1894, the position of Appointment Clerk of the Department was added to the list of classified places.

July 1, 1894, the classified service in the Department was

extended so as to include all inspectors and assistant inspectors in the Bureau of Animal Industry, numbering at that time 67 men. The duty of these inspectors is to examine and pass on the sanitary condition of live animals, first, and afterwards to examine all carcasses of slaughtered animals which are intended for interstate or foreign trade. They either accept or reject, after determining sanitary conditions by ante-mortem and post-mortem investigations. It occurred to me that this inspection, carried on by laymen who were entirely unversed in veterinary science, was a waste of money and a farce. Inspection should inspect. Only those learned in the pathology of domestic animals and skilled in veterinary science, could render service in this line worth paying for or commensurate with the require-ments of the public health and the good name of American meats, intended, either at home or abroad, for human con-sumption. Therefore, at my suggestion, this classification was made, and as a condition precedent to securing an examina-tion for an inspectorship or assistant inspectorship before the United States Civil Service Commission, all applicants must exhibit diplomas from reputable veterinary colleges. Thus be-gan the building up of an inspection system which has been of inestimable advantage to American meats in the home market and also in foreign markets. The certification of the health-fulness and wholesomeness of edible meats by inspectors of the United States Department of Agriculture has credit in all markets, co-equal with that certification of a United States mint which assures the fineness and weight of a gold or silver coin.

On June 6, 1894, the professors of meteorology in the Weather Bureau were brought into the classified service.

It will be seen that up to this time, after my conviction of the error which I had entertained as to the possibilities of car-rying on departmental work honestly and efficiently under the old spoils system, my conversion had steadily evolved until now I began to feel the value and necessity of the saving grace of a classified service in every division and bureau of the Depart-ment. Consequently, on July 12, 1894, the chiefs and assist-ant chiefs of Entomology, and of Ornithology and Mammal-ogy, were included in the classified service, and on November 6, 1894, the chief and assistant chief of Pomology were like-wise included.

On November 2, 1894, messengers, assistant messengers, plant-mounters and folders were added to the list, by order of the President. These numbered 117.

On July 1, 1895, having been taught by the experience evolved under the satisfactory operation of previous Presidential orders classifying positions in the Department, and having become fully convinced that the business of the Government could be properly conducted only by a system and a discipline such as obtained in a private business,—the chief and assistant chief of the Bureau of Animal Industry, all chiefs and assistant chiefs of all divisions, experts, artists, state statistical agents; microscopists, assistant microscopists, taggers, stock-examiners, clerks and agents of the Bureau of Animal Industry, numbering 754 persons, were, by the order of the President of the United States, brought into the classified service.

On May 6, 1896, by the same process, all persons assigned to do any kind of clerical work were brought into the classified service,'and on June 10, 1896, *all persons doing any kind of classified service work not previously brought into the classified service were then included;* so that the private secretary to the Secretary of Agriculture is the only person excepted from the Civil Service rules in that Department, who is not a mere manual laborer.

It is only fair to state, in this connection, that the first private secretary employed by the present head of the Department of Agriculture was furnished him by a political friend and that after a short service that private secretary resigned the position, which remained vacant for more than a year, when the present incumbent, Mr. John Nordhouse, of Chicago, Ill., an expert stenographer and typewriter, was selected from the classified service. His appointment was made because of his merit and fidelity as a stenographer and typewriter to the Secretary, during a service of nearly two years, in which he had proved his worth, industry, discretion and efficiency.

Reviewing the last four years, we find the status of the classified service in the Department of Agriculture as follows:

March 4, 1893, there were two thousand four hundred and ninety-seven (2,497) men and women upon the pay rolls of the Department. But on November 1, 1896, there were only two thousand two hundred and seventeen (2,217) on the rolls; that is—notwithstanding an increased amount of work—there had been a reduction in the force of two hundred and eighty (280).

In the classified service, March 4, 1893, there were 698. Of that number there were excepted from competitive examination 80, subject to non-competitive examination 12, total 92 ; leaving subject to competitive examination 606.

On November 1, 1896, there were in the classified service 1,658, excepted from competitive examination 1, leaving subject to competitive examination 1,657. Thus an increase of 1,051 persons subject to competitive examination has been made between March 4, 1893, and November 1, 1896.

The remaining 556 persons on the rolls of the Department, on the latter date, were laborers, workmen, charwomen, and others in a subordinate grade, not more than 40 of whom were employed in Washington, D. C. A great proportion of these 556 are rainfall and river observers in the Weather Bureau, at salaries ranging from $3 to $25 per month, and their employment is intermittent. Every person ranking as a skilled laborer or skilled workman is classified.

A classified service is disciplined merit. Disciplined merit renders a steady and efficient service, and steady and efficient service is economy.

Good government is the chief conservator of the welfare of all legitimate business and gainful undertakings. It must, therefore, if it is to be made better and perpetuated, be itself administered in harmony with business principles and methods. Just government is economical—not wasteful; frugal, and not extravagant. An ounce of economy in executive affairs is worth more than a pound of revenue. More economy, through a judiciously organized and efficiently directed departmental service, will bestow upon this Government and American citizenship far greater benefits than more revenue

By the aid of a completely classified service to which there is no ingress, save through competitive examinations by the United States Civil Service Commission, the Department of Agriculture—the smallest and youngest of the Executive Departments—has demonstrated the truth that the Civil Service law, regulations and rules, vigorously carried out, are the best forces for economy yet tested in this form of Government. In four years' trial of the merit system more than two millions of dollars have been saved to cover back into the Treasury out of appropriations made during that period for that Department. And as employees become more skillful, more expert and adept from experience in the service, the labor-cost of administration will continue to decline. My successor will find a fairly well equipped and decently disciplined force at his command, and the members of that force from the highest to the lowest will, as a rule, prove their allegiance to their duties by constant and efficient industry. Thus it will be easy to continue, proportionately with the growth of the Department of Agriculture, a reduction of expenditures and an enhancement of the value of its work in behalf of that, advanced and successful agriculture upon which all other callings depend for existence.

Sneeringly the practical politician denounces Civil Service Reform as an illusion of doctrinaires, theorists and schoolmen —a theory from Utopia. But what great movement for the elevation and improvement of humanity ever came from any other than a scholary or thoughtful source? And can there be a more sincere tribute to the merit system in the public service than its vituperation by those who have no merit? Only those political pirates who by retrospection, introspection and prospection are convinced that with a firmly established merit system in the civil service of municipal, state and federal government their calling as plunderers of the public has been abolished, now openly denounce the reform. Therefore, it will win its way to greater victories for honesty, economy and efficiency, and its triumphs will be equally enjoyed by all good citizens upon whom rest the responsibilities and burdens of maintaining for this Republic a Government which " will *sell* to no man " and " will not *deny* to any man, either Justice or Right."

CONSTITUTION

OF THE

National Civil-Service Reform League.

I.

The name of this organization shall be the National Civil Service Reform League.

II.

The object of the National Civil Service Reform League shall be to promote the purposes and to facilitate the correspondence and the united action of the Civil Service Reform Associations.

III.

The League shall consist of all the Civil Service Reform Associations in the United States which signify their willingness to become members thereof. Any association hereafter expressing such willingness shall become a member of the League upon its being accepted as such by the League or the Executive Committee. Any member of any such association may be present at any meeting of the League and take part in the debates or discussions as the by-laws may provide.

IV.

At any meeting of the League, each association belonging to it shall be entitled to one vote upon every question coming before the League; such vote may be cast by a personal representative designated by each association, or by proxy, as the by-laws may provide. If no such designation be made the delegates from such association present at such meeting, ro a majority of them, may cast the vote of such association.

V.

The officers of the League shall be a President, Secretary, Treasurer, and nine Vice-Presidents; and there shall be a General Committee and an Executive Committee. The officers and the committees shall hold office until their successors are appointed or elected.

VI.'

The President and Vice-Presidents shall be elected by ballot at the annual meeting of the League.

The Secretary and Treasurer shall be chosen, and may be removed, by the General Committee.

The General Committee shall be chosen annually, and shall consist of one delegate from each association belonging to the League; and one additional delegate for every two hundred members, or major fraction thereof, of such association as certified by its secretary. Each association shall elect its own delegates in such manner as it may determine.

The members of the Executive Committee shall be ex-officio members of the General Committee.

Any member of the General Committee may act by proxy.

The General Committee shall keep a record of its proceedings, and shall make a report to the League at the annual meeting. A vacancy in any office, except that of Vice-President, may be filled by the General Committee for the remainder of the term.

The General Committee may delegate to the Executive Committee any of its powers; provided, however, that it may at any time resume the powers so delegated.

The Executive Committee shall consist of twenty-one members to be elected annually by the General Committee and shall have power to fix its own quorum. And any member of the Executive Committee may act by proxy.

VII.

The General Committee may, subject to these articles, manage the affairs of the League, direct and dispose of the

funds, and may, from time to time, make and modify by-laws for the League and for its own action.

No debt shall be contracted, nor shall any appropriation of money be made, by the League or by the General Committee, beyond the amount in the hands of the Treasurer.

VIII.

There shall be an annual meeting of the League at such time in each year, and at such place as the General Committee may determine, at which officers shall be elected for the ensuing year, and other appropriate business may be transacted.

A meeting of the League may be called at the discretion of the General Committee whenever any association belonging to it notifies the Secretary of the League of its desire to have such a meeting, and the President may at any time call a meeting of the League.

IX.

Any provision of this Constitution may be suspended or amended by a vote of two-thirds of the members present at any meeting of the General Committee, due notice of such proposed suspension or amendment having been given at a previous meeting. Any association belonging to the League may, through its representatives, propose amendments to the Constitution which may be approved under the same conditions.

Purposes of the Civil-Service Reform Association. Per copy, 5 cts.

The Beginning of the Spoils System in the National Government, 1829-30. (Reprinted, by permission, from Parton's "Life of Andrew Jackson.") Per copy, 5 cts.

Term and Tenure of Office. By Dorman B. Eaton. Second edition, abridged. Per copy, 15 cts.

The Danger of an Office-Holding Aristocracy. By E. L. Godkin. Per copy, 5 cts.

Daniel Webster and the Spoils System. An extract from Senator Bayard's oration at Dartmouth College, June, 1882.

A Primer of Civil-Service Reform, prepared by George William Curtis. (English and German Editions)

The Workingman's Interest in Civil-Service Reform. Address by Hon Henry A. Richmond.

Annual Reports of the C. S. R. A. of New York for the years 1883-1896 inclusive.

Constitution and By-Laws of the New York Association.

MISCELLANEOUS.

United States Civil-Service Statutes and Revised Rules of May 6, 1896.

State Civil-Service Reform Acts of New York and Massachusetts.

Decisions and Opinions in Construction of the Civil-Service Laws. Per copy, 15 cts.

The Competitive Test. By E. M. Shepard.

The Meaning of Civil-Service Reform. By E. O. Graves.

The Selection of Laborers. (In English and German Editions). By James M. Bugbee late of the Massachusetts Civil-Service Commission.

Report of Select Committee on Reform in the Civil Service (H. R.), regarding the registration of laborers in the United States Service.

Report of same Committee regarding selection of Fourth-Class Postmasters.

George William Curtis. A commemorative address by Parke Godwin. (Published by the Century Association). 10 cents per copy.

(A CHARGE IS MADE ONLY WHERE THE PRICE IS GIVEN.)

Orders for the publications will be filled by GEORGE MCANENY, Secretary, 54 William St., New York, or by G. P. PUTNAM'S SONS, 27 and 29 West 23d St., New York.

(c.IV,56)

PROCEEDINGS

AT THE ANNUAL MEETING OF

The National Civil-Service Reform League

HELD AT

CINCINNATI, OHIO, DEC. 16 AND 17, 1897.

WITH THE ADDRESS OF THE PRESIDENT,

AND OTHER MATTERS.

NEW YORK:
PUBLISHED FOR THE
NATIONAL CIVIL-SERVICE REFORM LEAGUE.
1897.

Publications of the National Civil-Service Reform League

Proceedings at the Annual Meeting of the National Civil-Service Reform League, 1882, with address of the President, George William Curtis. Per copy, 8 cts.

The same, with address of the President, for '84, '85, '86, '87, '89, '90, '91, '92, '93, '94 '95, '96 and '97. Per copy, 8 cts.

Civil-Service Reform under the present National Administration. By George William Curtis. (Address of 1885.)

The Situation. By George William Curtis. (Address of 1886.)

Party and Patronage. By George William Curtis. (Address of 1892.)

Civil-Service Reform and Democracy. By Carl Schurz. (Address of 1893.)

The Necessity and Progress of Civil-Service Reform. By Carl Schurz. (Address of 1894.)

Congress and the Spoils System. By Carl Schurz. (Address of 1895.)

Encouragements and Warnings. By Carl Schurz. (Address of 1896.)

The Democracy of the Merit System. By Carl Schurz. (Address of 1897.)

Civil Service Reform as a Moral Question. By Charles J. Bonaparte. (1890.)

The Influence of the Spoils Idea upon the Government of American Cities. By Herbert Welsh. (1894.)

The Reform of the Consular Service. By Oscar S. Straus. (1894.)

The Interest of the Workingman in Civil-Service Reform. By Herbert Welsh. (1895.)

The Appointment and Tenure of Postmasters. By R. H. Dana. (1895.)

The Republican Party and Civil-Service Reform. By Henry Hitchcock. (1897.)

The Democratic Party and Civil-Service Reform. By Moorfield Storey. (1897.)

An open Letter to Hon. C. H. Grosvenor, in reply to recent attacks on the Civil Service Law and Rules. George McAneny. (1897.)

Constitution of the National Civil-Service Reform League.

Good Government: Official Journal of the National Civil-Service Reform League. Published monthly at 54 William St., New York. One dollar per year. Ten cents per single copy.

For other publications, see third page

PROCEEDINGS

AT THE ANNUAL MEETING OF

THE NATIONAL CIVIL-SERVICE REFORM LEAGUE

HELD AT

CINCINNATI, OHIO, DEC. 16 AND 17, 1897.

WITH THE ADDRESS OF THE PRESIDENT,

AND OTHER MATTERS.

NEW YORK:

PUBLISHED FOR THE

NATIONAL CIVIL-SERVICE REFORM LEAGUE.

1897.

9384,40

N.Y. Civil Service Reform Association

PRESS OF GOOD GOVERNMENT

CONTENTS.

ANNUAL MEETING

OF THE

NATIONAL CIVIL SERVICE REFORM LEAGUE.

DECEMBER 16, AND 17, 1897.

Pursuant to call duly issued, the seventeenth annual meeting of the National Civil Service Reform League was held at Cincinnati, O., on the 16th and 17th of December, 1897. Among the delegates in attendance during the several sessions were the following:

BALTIMORE: Charles J. Bonaparte.

BOSTON: Charles Warren, Samuel Y. Nash.

BUFFALO: Sherman S. Rogers, Henry A. Richmond.

CAMBRIDGE: Morrill Wyman, Jr.

CHICAGO: John W. Ela, Edwin Burritt Smith, Ralph M. Easley, Adolph Nathan, John A. Roach, W. K. Ackerman.

CINCINNATI: Nathaniel Henchman ·Davis, John W. Warrington, Leopold Kleybolte, Rufus B. Smith, Herman Goepper, C. B. Wilby, Max B. May, L. C. Black, Henry C. Urner, William C. Herron, Larz Anderson, J. G. Schmidlapp.

CLEVELAND: William E. Cushing, James R. Garfield.

DAYTON: Lewis B. Gunckel, L. H. Patterson.

DISTRICT OF COLUMBIA: John Joy Edson, Frederick L, Siddons, Adolf G. Wolff, A. J. Glassie.

FORT WAYNE, IND.: Henry N. Williams.

INDIANAPOLIS: Lucius B. Swift, Noble C. Butler, Frederick W. Dewhurst, J. H. Halliday.

INDIANA UNIVERSITY: Samuel B. Harding.

NEW YORK: Carl Schurz, George McAneny.

PHILADELPHIA: Herbert Welsh, Clinton Rogers Woodruff.

RICHMOND, IND.: William Dudley Foulke, Jesse Reeves, Stanley C. Hughes.

ST. LOUIS: Henry Hitchcock, A. L. Berry, A. R. Verdier.

ST. PAUL: Rev. W. R. Lord.

In response to invitations issued by the League to Municipal Reform Associations, and other bodies having the reform of the civil service among their objects, delegates were present from a number of such organizations, as follows:

ANN ARBOR:—*University of Michigan Good Government Club :* F. V. Byam.

BOSTON :—*Massachusetts Reform Club :* Charles Warren, Samuel Y. Nash.

CHICAGO:—*Municipal Voters' League :* Edward Burritt Smith.

CHICAGO:—*Civic Federation :*—Adolph Nathan, R. M. Easley.

CLEVELAND :—*Chamber of Commerce :* William E. Cushing.

LOUISVILLE:—*Good City Government Club :* F. N. Hartwell, Lafon Allen.

PITTSBURG :—*Citizen's Civic League :* Edward D. Frohman.

ST. LOUIS :—*Civic Federation :* A. L. Berry, Henry Hitchcock, A. R. Verdier.

VINELAND, N. J. :—*Citizens' Committee :* R. B. Moore.

WASHINGTON :—*Board of Trade :* John Joy Edson.

The morning session of the 16th, commencing at 10.30 o'clock, was occupied by a joint meeting of the General and Executive Committees, held at the Burnet House.

At 2.30 o'clock in the afternoon an open meeting of the League was held at the College Hall.*

The annual address of the President, Hon. Carl Schurz, was delivered at the Odeon at 8 o'clock on the evening of the 16th. It is as follows:

---

* Page 35.

THE DEMOCRACY OF THE MERIT SYSTEM.

*An Address delivered at the Annual Meeting of the National
Civil Service Reform League, at Cincinnati, Ohio,
December 16, 1897.*

By Carl Schurz.

AT our last annual meeting I had occasion to congratulate
the country upon the extraordinary advance the cause
of civil service reform had made during the preceding year.
President Cleveland's executive order of May 6, 1896, had
not only added many thousands of positions to the classified
service, but it had also established the general principle that
it is the normal condition of public servants under the executive departments of the national government to be under the
civil service rules, and that they should be considered and
treated as being there, unless excepted by special regulation
—a gain of incalculable consequence. I was also able to report signal progress of the reform in various States and in the
municipal service of various cities. At the same time I expressed the apprehension that the advocates of the spoils system would not cease their hostile efforts and that, although the
final result could not be doubtful, we might still have a period
of arduous struggle before us. This apprehension has proved
to be well founded.

The American people have hardly ever beheld a rush for
the spoils of office more tumultuous than that which followed
President McKinley's accession to power. Nor have we ever
heard a more furious, and, I may add, a more disgraceful
clamor from party men for the breach of party faith than that
of Republican politicians demanding the repeal, or at least
the disembowelment, of the civil service law by a President
and a majority in Congress solemnly pledged to its maintenance and extension.

Recall to your memory some of the almost incredible
scenes we have had to witness. The Republican national

convention in St. Louis had put these words in its platform: "The civil service law was placed on the Statute book by the Republican party, which has always sustained it, and we renew our repeated declaration that it shall be thoroughly and honestly enforced, and extended wherever practicable." When the Republican national convention adopted that pledge, President· Cleveland's executive order of May 6th had been in operation for several weeks. It had not gone into force unobserved. The friends of good government had praised it, the spoilsmen of both parties, Republicans and Democrats, had denounced it. It was thus with full knowledge of its being an integral part of the civil service system then existing, that the Republican party in national convention assembled made its pledge. Neither could anybody pretend that it was a mere haphazard promise made inadvertently; for one national Republican platform after another had repeated the same declaration for many years. Nor could there be any doubt as to the meaning of the pledge. Nothing could be plainer. It was to enforce, honestly and thoroughly, the civil service law wherever it was then in operation, and to extend, wherever practicable, the operation of the law beyond the limits within which it operated at the time when the pledge was made. And then Mr. McKinley, the Republican candidate for the presidency, made the pledge of the party his own in the letter of acceptance by which he asked for the votes of the people. He accused the opposition party of "decrying this reform"; of being willing "to abandon all the advantages gained after so many years of agitation and effort"; of "encouraging a return to methods of party favoritism which both parties have denounced, which experience has condemned, and which the people have repeatedly disapproved"; and he assured the country that "the Republican party earnestly opposes this reactionary and entirely unjustifiable policy"; and that "it will take no backward step upon this question, but will seek to improve but never degrade the public service." And when introduced in his office as President, Mr. McKinley reiterated the vow in his inaugural address.

If there ever was a party pledge clear, unequivocal, and specific—if there ever was one sanctioned as a definite party policy by constant reiteration, it was this. And yet no sooner was Mr. McKinley seated in the executive chair than a countless swarm of Republican spoils seekers swept down upon him, struggling to force the barrier of the classified service. Had that swarm consisted only of—pardon the vulgarism—the "deadbeats" hanging around the Republican camp as they hang around every other, or of members of Congress driven to mad despair by the pitiless persecution of hungry supporters insisting upon their reward, the spectacle might have been regarded as a mere after-play of the old barbarism which has brought so much humiliation and shame to our patriotic pride, but is gradually to pass away. But of more sinister portent was it when President McKinley was waited upon by a delegation pretending to come from the "League of Republican Clubs" in whose name they demanded that the President should forthwith rescind the executive order by which his predecessor had enlarged the scope of the civil service law, and that he should thus open again the places covered by that order to appointment by favor, that is, to the invasion of spoils politics.

It is worth while to contemplate that scene. There stood the President of this great republic with the solemn vow honestly and thoroughly to enforce the civil service law and, wherever practicable, to extend it—with that vow still warm on his lips; and, facing him a group of persons pretending to represent a great organization "embracing the young and active men of the party," coolly insisting that this President should by one of his first official acts break and dishonor his party's and his own pledge and thus before the American people and all the world declare his party to be a cheat and himself a dishonest man. Did it not occur to those persons that in approaching the President with such a request and in professing to think him capable of so disgraceful an act, they offered him just as deadly an insult as if they had asked him to forge a bank check or to embezzle a trust fund, with the expectation that he would do it? Did not one of them feel that after so outrageous an affront the President would have been justified in treating them as persons not to be recognized as gentlemen, and as base slanderers in falsely pretending to represent the young men of the Republican party? Could they forget that if it really were true that the young men of the Republican party can be inspired to strenuous effort only by the prospect of spoil, and that to obtain that spoil they would have their party dishonor itself by breaking a time honored vow, and by repudiating its faith, the moral vitality of that party would soon be gone? It was indeed a repulsive exhibition of the effect which the spoil system has exercised upon the moral sense of men, and the young men of the Republican party cannot too soon repel the calumnious imputation cast upon them by their pretended representatives.

I know the excuse that is given for this amazing demand. It is that President Cleveland's administration had filled a great many positions which were not in the classified service, with Democrats, and then covered them with the civil service rules in order to protect the new incumbents against removal. The civil service reformers have not been sparing in criticism and remonstrance when under the Cleveland administration removals or appointments were made which appeared improper. But I do not hesitate to say that the objection to Mr. Cleveland's great executive order made by the Republican spoils politicians is utterly futile. That order did not protect any public servant covered by it against removal—proof of which is the simple fact that a considerable number of them actually have been removed. The effect of the order simply was that, if any of those places were vacated they could not be arbitrarily filled by way of political or personal favor with incompetent or otherwise unsuitable persons; for the order subjected candidates for such places to competitive examinations. And this is the thing that troubles the Republican politicians of the spoils persuasion. Their souls are in patriotic agony not because some Democratic party hacks were kept in their places by the civil service rules, which they were not, but because those places can not be filled at pleasure with Republican party hacks. Not in order to improve the honesty and efficiency of the service, but to turn over those offices as plunder to their own men they insist that their party shall repudiate its pledge and the President shall dishonor himself by breaking his word.

Besides, there has never been any advance of civil service reform that did not call forth the same flimsy charge. The civil service law was enacted in 1883 when the whole service with very few exceptions, was filled with Republicans. By direction of Congress and with the approval of President

Arthur about 14,000 places were classified. It might have been charged by the Democrats, in accordance with the argument used against Mr. Cleveland's order, that President Arthur protected about 14,000 Republican placemen in their positions. Under President Cleveland during his first term about 6,500 places were added to the classified list. A similar charge might have been brought by the Republicans. Under President Harrison's administration, including the growth of the service, the executive extensions, the railway mail clerks, and the navy yard employees classified by Secretary Tracy, about 26,000 were added; and in this case the Democrats brought the same charge with more color of justice, as the execution of the order extending the civil service rules over the railway mail service was stayed for several weeks, giving the Postmaster-General time to stock that branch of the service thoroughly with Republicans before the rules were permitted to take force. About 2,500 vacancies were created by removals, and corresponding appointments of railway mail clerks were made in a hurry. And I may add that when during the Democratic administration following an attempt was made to re-open by law to the persons thus removed the way to their former positions without examination, that attempt was sternly resisted by this league for the reason that, if successful, it would have served as a precedent for further unsettling and demoralizing movements in the future. Then came President Cleveland's second administration when by several successive executive orders and through natural growth over 39,000 places were added, more than 11,000 of which, however, had already been subject to the examination system under separate departmental orders, or were field employees of the war department.

This is sufficient to show that if there were any ground for the charge concerning the alleged protection of appointees by extensions of the civil service rules, that charge would apply to both parties alike. But during the operation of the civil service law there has been no ground for such a charge, for the simple reason that really no operative limitation of executive discretion as to removals existed. It was not until the appearance of Mr. McKinley's recent order that any effective limitation was put in force.

Every self-respecting American will prefer to assume, that

the Presidents who ordered those extensions, did so from patriotic motives. But even if partizan considerations had at times intruded into their action, the practical result would, after all, have been only the enlargement of a system which ministers to the public interest without in the end giving either party any advantage at all. Nor should the Republican spoilsmen forget that, had not President Cleveland made the extensions they complain of, President McKinley would have been in honor and duty bound to make them himself—for according to the pledge of the Republican party and his own, he has not only to enforce the civil service law honestly and thoroughly, but to extend it *wherever* practicable. And that these extensions have been practicable, is proved by the fact of their successful operation. He will soon have to go beyond them, according to the Republican platform, wherever further practicability appears.

True to his honor as a gentleman, to his vows as a Republican, and to his duty as President of the United States, Mr. McKinley stoutly held his ground against the fierce foray which was set on foot to overwhelm him. It may be said that to resist pressure, especially pressure from party friends aiming at a wrongful object, is the first and most obvious duty of the head of the State, and that its simple performance does not call for extraordinary praise. But when faithfully performed against unusual urgency, as it was in this instance, it deserves a tribute of gratitude, and this tribute should be heartily paid to President McKinley by every true friend of good government.

The first onset has been repulsed, but the fight is not finished. The clamor of the place-seekers still resounds with lusty vociferation. In three Republican State conventions resolutions have been adopted hostile to the merit system. An association has been organized to agitate for the repeal of the civil service law, and Republican members of the Senate of the United States and of the House of Representatives are loudly threatening to bring the matter to an issue at the present session of Congress. Two of them, Representative Grosvenor of Ohio, and Senator Gallinger of New Hampshire, have already been designated by one of the spoilsmen's organs as the anti-civil service reform candidates for the presidency and the vice-presidency. It seems that the rapid progress of the merit system had put its enemies into a desperate state of mind and that, seeing their case in deadly peril, they have resolved to rally their whole force for a final effort. The hour has come for them to do or die.

The weapons employed by the champions of this reactionary movement are characteristic of their object. Whoever has attempted to argue the subject of civil service reform with one of its opponents, will have gathered this experience: You ask him whether it is not true that the public service was originally intended, not for the benefit of this or that political party, nor of influential politicians, nor of the public servants themselves, but solely for the accommodation and benefit of the people, and he will have to admit it.—You ask him, whether the people are not clearly entitled to the best—that is, the most honest and efficient service attainable, and he will have to admit that too.—You ask him whether, in order to secure to the people the best attainable service, it is not most reasonable to select public servants with a sole view to their fitness for the work to be done, and to ascertain that fitness by the best available method, and he will admit that also, in theory at least, although with some reluctance.—But when you ask him whether the fitness of a candidate—say, for a clerkship— cannot be better ascertained by examining him as to handwriting, orthography, ciphering, abstract making, tabulating, simple composition, and the like, and by obliging him to exhibit testimonials from some reputable citizens as to his moral character, than by inquiring whether he can claim reward for having served the party by drumming up voters, or by having helped to pack or run a caucus, or by money contributions coming either from himself or his relatives or friends,—and when you ask further, whether the best attainable service cannot most surely be secured by giving every one who considers himself fit for such public employment an opportunity for proving his fitness by assembling the candidates together in a competitive examination or test, which will be apt to point out those best fitted, the best man to have the best chance for appointment—when you ask him these questions,—questions which would be answered by every disinterested citizen of ordinary common sense with a hearty, " Yes, of course,"—then the brow of your champion of the spoils system becomes clouded with an angry gloom, and he tells you with fierce emphasis, that those are outlandish notions, utterly un-American, British, Chinese, or what not, and that you are an impracticable theorist, a visionary, a dude, a pharisee, a "holier-than-thou" man—in short a mugwump, who has no business to interfere with practical politics at all.

You try to appease him by showing him your willingness to hear what *he* has to say, and give him the floor. He tells you that in a free country there must be political parties and that, without them, the government cannot be carried on. This you do not deny.—He goes on telling you, that without the distribution of patronage in the shape of offices among its workers, a political party cannot exist. You answer him by pointing out the fact, that political parties do exist without patronage in ever so many foreign countries, and that they did exist in this country without the use of offices or patronage before the spoils system was introduced, and that they were then as full of life and energy as ever since.—He excitedly asks you whether you really think that a party can win without patronage, and whether the popular interest in politics can be kept up without holding out to the people the prospect of a large distribution of offices if their party wins. You answer by reminding him of our own experience that in the last four presidential elections that party which possessed the patronage was regularly beaten; that therefore the patronage has certainly not proved an element of strength sufficient to save a party from defeat; that it is rather an element of weakness in creating disappointments and animosities, and in making, by its inevitable abuses, the party possessing it odious to public spirited citizens. And as to the necessity of the patronage for keeping up the popular interest in politics, you turn upon him with this question: Is it not a foul slander npon our national character to say, that, while in England, Germany, Italy, France, Belgium, Switzerland, Norway, the popular interest in public affairs does not need the stimulus of office plunder, the American people have become such a lot of mercenary wretches, that only the promise of reward, the prospect of official salaries will inspire them to maintain political parties, and keep them alive to the honor and the welfare of this great republic?—This staggers our spoilsman somewhat but he does not give up. He asks whether it is not true after all that many of the busiest workers in party organizations depend upon office as a reward of their activity and that without the stimulus furnished by patronage, their useful zeal would be wanting. You answer that this may be so, but that the zeal which needs the stimulus of patronage is after all a mercenary zeal; that the mercenary element in political parties will grow the more powerful, the more it is stimulated by spoil; that the moral spirit and tone of a party organization will sink the lower, the more powerful the mercenary element in politics grows; that the pushing intrusion of that mercenary element will naturally serve to drive persons of self respect and high ideals from public life; that the patriot for revenue only is the bane of our politics and can best be spared; that if he drops out, he will only make room for a better class of men; that the spoils system has enabled persons whose statesmanship consists in distributing patronage, and hardly in anything else, to maintain themselves in public life, and to organize the so-called machine consisting of patronage mongers and place hunters; that the machine tends to make political parties wholly subservient to selfish ends, to crowd out that statesmanship which is inspired wholly by high patriotism, and to turn our political contests into sordid squabbles about personal advancement and public plunder.

In saying this you have touched a sore point; for the statesman you address is likely to be himself one of those public men whose statesmanship consists mainly in the handling of the patronage and who would be in danger of speedy extinction, were that resource of political sustenance taken from him. It is a delicate matter for him to discuss, and he therefore changes his tack and begins to impeach the efficiency of the merit system itself. He will tell you of absurd questions being asked in the examinations—how a candidate for a letter carrier's place had to give the exact number of the killed in the battle of Marathon, or a candidate for a clerkship the distance of the moon from the planet Mars, and so on. Your answer is that these ridiculous stories are simply not true— mere inventions of the enemy—and that, if the examinations have in any cases not been sufficiently practical, the obvious remedy is, not to abolish the whole merit system but to instruct the examiners to make the examination more pertinent.—He will tell you that under the civil service law only college graduates have a chance and that the whole system is,

therefore, aristocratic. You confute him by authoritative statistics proving that in Massachusetts there were during the
last eight years among 9323 successful candidates only 157
college men, and that even in the federal service the college
graduates form less than 10 per cent. of the successful candidates, and in those branches of the service which require no
scientific education, only 6 per cent.—He will tell you that
under the merit system a life tenure of office prevails in the
public service which is obnoxious to our institutions. Your
answer is, that according to the fundamental principle of the
merit system, the tenure of the public servant is determined by
the efficiency with which he performs his duties, and that his
tenure is therefore not a life-tenure, but a merit tenure; and that
merit tenure is the vital principle of a good service.—Your
spoilsman further insists that a man at the head of a public
office knows best what kind of men he wants to do the work
under him, and that it is therefore most reasonable to permit
him full liberty in the choice of his help. You reply that this
rule may hold good as to the conduct of private business
where the head of an establishment enjoys real freedom in the
selection of his clerks or agents; but that according to universal experience, a public officer under the spoils system is not
permitted that freedom; that whenever he has any place to fill
he is instantly set upon by party managers, or bosses, or other
politicians of influence, who urge upon him their creatures or
favorites; that he is apt to be compelled by a fierce pressure
to accept men as his subordinates whom his own judgment
would have rejected; that the so-called freedom of the head
of an office to select his help really means nothing but the
freedom of influential politicians to select that help for him
and to keep such favorites in place not so long as *he* likes, but
as long as *they* like; that against such pressure he can find
effective protection only in a law or rule making competitive
examinations of candidates obligatory, thus excluding favoritism and influence; that the more conscientious an officer is
in his desire to serve the public good, the more heartily he
welcomes such a law; and that this is not mere theory or
guess, but a stubborn fact to which every candid man who has
had the experience of official life will unqualifiedly bear his
testimony.

Being thus baffled at every point in detail, your antagonist will again take refuge in general assertion and say that the public service is no better now than it was before the civil service law was enacted, and that the boasted merit system is therefore a practical failure.—To this daring allegation—daring I call it, for he who alleges this will have the courage to allege anything—you are able to oppose the crushing fact that since the enactment of the civil service law every President, whether Republican or Democrat, has in his official utterances borne the most ample testimony to the signal benefit the merit system has conferred upon the service in efficiency as well as in moral tone; that one Secretary after another, without distinction of party, has pronounced the merit system the only method by which the business of their departments could be carried on in an honest and proper manner; that ever so many executive officers who entered upon their duties with a prejudice against the merit system, have become ardent converts to it after some practical experience; and that, as the undisputed statistics of the service incontestably prove, wherever the merit system prevailed, more work was done by a smaller force and for less money than before, while, where it did not prevail, the old wastefulness in the multiplication of offices and salaries for little and frequently poor work continued; and that he who disputes this, might as well dispute the multiplication table.

And what has your spoils politician still to say after this? He then thinks it expedient to let others speak for him and brings on his witnesses. Here is the sorely aggrieved patriot who has been accustomed to be taken care of by influential politicians, who finds himself debarred from the public crib by the merit system, and who insists that a boss, or a party committee, or a member of Congress is a better judge of a man's fitness for office than an examining board. Here is the unfortunate who has failed in his examination and thus concludes that the whole system of examination is a cranky contrivance. Here is the man who knows of a case in which the spirit of the merit system has not been, honestly enforced, and who therefore denounces civil service reform as a delusion and a snare. Here is the appointing officer who thinks that any restriction of his power to grant favors is an insult to his dignity, or who occasionally cannot get "the man he wants," and who therefore concludes that the whole system is utterly impracticable. And so on. But when the investigation is carried further, and the overwhelming preponderance of the testimony sustains the practical as well as moral excellence of the system, your spoils politician falls back upon his last resource which is indeed inexhaustible—his power of imaginative invention. It is not too much to say that " the lie well stuck to " has become a favorite weapon with the ordinary stripe of the enemies of civil service reform; and this weapon is employed with the loftiest confidence in the assumed ignorance or gullibility of the public, and the most reckless disregard of consequences as to the character for truth and veracity of the person using it.

During the long period that I have been an attentive observer of public affairs, I have witnessed many heroic dealings with the truth. But I have seldom seen men of prominent position commit themselves to statements which everybody in the slightest degree conversant with the subject knew to be untrue, with such wild imprudence as some of them do in their struggle against civil service reform. It is almost incredible, but literally true, for instance, that Senator Gallinger, of New Hampshire, with whom I have had some public correspondence, would, among other equally astounding things, stubbornly insist upon it, that under the civil service rules every candidate for the position of compositor or printer in the Public Printing office was required to hop a certain distance on one foot, as part of his examination ; that all official inquiries had proved the civil service system a dead failure, and that President Cleveland had issued his order of May 6th, 1896, making large additions to the classified service, only after he had been informed of the Republican victory of the Presidential election, which took place on November 2, 1897. No wonder the organ of the spoils politicians put that Senator forth as their candidate for the vice-presidency.

Nor is it easy to believe that a member of the House of Representatives, hailing from this State, too—the Hon. C. H. Grosvenor, should, at the last session of Congress have made a speech against civil service reform which contained scores of statements of fact flagrantly untrue or misleading. Of their quality you may judge from this representative specimen : He positively asserts that the civil service law " was never intended to cover anything but the departments in Washington, and that alone in its application to the clerical force," while at the very time when the law was enacted, the competitive system was in actual operation in the Custom House and the Post office in New York, and while the law itself provided in terms that the merit system prescribed by it should be introduced throughout the country in every post office and custom house having 50 employees, and that the President and the several department chiefs should from time to time revise the classification so as to include places theretofore not classified, excluding only from the scope of such extensions offices not in the executive branch, offices to be filled by the President with the consent of the Senate, and common laborers. No wonder Mr. Grosvenor was nominated by the organ of the spoils politicians as their candidate for the presidency.

While thus almost all the objections to the merit system brought forward by its enemies are easily and conclusively refuted either by the public record or by the simplest reasoning, there is one which has a certain plausibility for those who form their judgment upon superficial impressions. It is, that, one American citizen having as much right to public employment as another, a system making appointments dependent upon the result of examinations removes public offices from the reach of the people and confines them to a privileged class, which will bring forth an officeholding aristocracy. The idea of a great American aristocracy consisting of Treasury clerks, or letter carriers, or customs inspectors, or even of such magnates as revenue collectors or presidential postmasters, or Indian agents, must appear laughable not only to the people but to the employees themselves. But there are, indeed, many persons who think that appointment to office as a reward for party service, or upon the recommendation of an influential politician is more apt to give everybody a chance, and, therefore, more democratic than a system requiring a proof of fitness. What a preposterous idea! Subject the essential features of the spoils system to a simple analysis and compare them with those of the merit system, and you will find, as I argued before the Governor of New York last spring, and as recently the Secretary of the Navy, Mr. Long, has forcibly set forth, that the merit system furnishes the only method of appointment that is really democratic—the only one that is truly just to the people.

Here is the ordinary course of things under the spoils system.

John Smith, a carpenter, or a bricklayer, who sustains himself and his family by industrious work and does his duty as a good citizen by voting according to his honest convictions, has a bright boy. That boy has received a good common school education and sharpened his intellect and increased his knowledge by personal effort in various ways. He is a young man too, of correct habits and excellent character. He wishes to enter the government service as a clerk. How must he go about it? The spoils system prevails. He finds that government clerks are appointed only upon the recommendation of somebody. He can easily obtain testimonials from a number of highly respectable persons who know him, but he is told that he will need the recommendation of some politician of influence, best of all that of the member of Congress—that, in fact, without the good will of the member of Congress nothing can be accomplished. He approaches the member from his district and exhibits the testimonials as to his ability and to his character. "Oh, that is all well enough," says the honorable gentleman, "but to what party do you belong?" If poor young Smith happens not to belong to the party of the honorable member, there is, of course, the end of it at once. But let us suppose, he does. Then the great man continues the examination. "What claims have you?" he asks. "Claims?" replies young Smith —"why, here are my testimonials as to my ability and character, and I am willing to undergo any test to prove that I can well perform a clerk's duty." "Oh, hang all that," exclaims the member of Congress, impatiently,—"what claims have you politically, you or your father? I have never heard of either of you during the campaign." The young man is obliged to confess that they were too poor to contribute money to the campaign fund, and too busy with their daily work to do more in the election than cast their votes and occasionally discuss politics with their neighbors. The examination is finished. "Well," says the great man languidly, "you may leave your papers here and I will consider them in time." This ends the interview.

When young Smith passes out of the great man's door, two other persons pass in—Mr. Brown, a wealthy manufacturer with hundreds of operatives in his employ, and his nephew, young Mr. Green, a youth of questionable parts and uncertain character. Mr. Brown is tired of taking care of this unthrifty poor relative and finds it most convenient to unload him upon the government. The member of Congress receives the two most cordially, and asks what he can do for them. "I want a government clerkship for my nephew," says Mr. Brown. "You know what I did for you in the campaign—my contribution to the war chest and the votes of all my people.—" "Of course," interrupts the member of Congress, "I know what recognition I and the party owe you. Your nephew seems to be a splendid fellow, too!" "Well," says Mr. Brown, "as to that, I don't think he knows much, but he may learn." "Never mind that," says the member of Congress, smilingly, "that will be all right. Send him on to Washington." In Washington he takes young Mr. Green to one of the Departments. "I must have a clerkship for this young man," he says to the Secretary, "and a good one, too. He is the nephew of one of my most powerful constituents whom I am bound to oblige." The Secretary sees the necessity.

There are pass examinations held in the department—that is to say, examinations conducted by the appointing power itself, to which only candidates with influential recommendations behind them are admitted, not seriously to compete with each other, but, at best, to show that they are not absolute dunces or idiots. These examinations are a mere hollow form, as influence rules it all. The member of Congress asks that they be made easy to young Mr. Green. He receives a knowing wink in reply, and the thing is made easy. Mr. Green is asked to add up two and two and to give the name of the capital city of the Union—questions which were once actually asked within my knowledge. Mr. Green issues triumphantly from the ordeal.

But there is no vacancy. What of it? A vacancy must be made. It is found that some clerk in the Department has "lost his influence," that is, the member of Congress on whose recommendation he was appointed has died or dropped out of politics. The clerk is indeed very meritorious and valuable, but having lost his influence, and no new influence turning up, he is removed to make room for young Green. Young Green soon shows a fondness for strong drink and neglect of duty, and he is threatened with dismissal. He complains to his member of Congress who rushes at once to the Secretary, exclaiming: "If you dismiss young Green, it will offend Mr. Brown, my most powerful constituent, and my district may be lost. I must insist that Mr. Green be kept." Young Green is kept in the service, and his duties are made light so that there is not much to neglect. In the meantime young Smith is still waiting for a favorable consideration of his testimonials, which, of course, never comes.

This is no caricature. Not that in every instance, or in a majority of cases the favored individual was a scapegrace or a dunce—for it is true, able and decent men got into public employment that way. Not that every drunkard or drone was kept in the service by political intercession, for some were really turned out. It is also true that there have been conscientious Congressmen who would not recommend unworthy persons. But the story I have told was rendered not only possible by the spoils system, but it has actually so happened hundreds of times. While there was indeed much variety as to the qualifications of the persons appointed, one rule was universal—without influence no appointment; without influence no security of tenure of office.

Now mark the course of proceedings under the merit system. Here is young Smith, the bright son of the carpenter again, wishing to obtain a clerkship in a government Department. He finds an announcement in the papers that at a certain time and place a competitive examination will be held to test the qualifications of candidates for appointment. He finds that admission to that competitive examination is open to him. He has only to satisfy certain requirements as to age, health, and a certificate of good character, to be signed by two reputable citizens. No questions are asked as to his politics, or his creed, or his origin. No claims based upon party service, no recommendations by influential politicians are called for. The examination is held, and the carpenter's son meets there young Green, the nephew and protegé of Mr. Brown, the rich manufacturer who had made a heavy contribution to the campaign chest and has power enough to command ever so many votes. The examination being competitive the candidates examined are graded according to the degree of their success in answering the tests of merit and fitness proposed to them, those who are most successful to have the best title to appointment. Now, suppose young Smith, the carpenter's son, appears at the head of the list, and young Green, the rich manufacturer's nephew and protegé, far behind. The carpenter's son, without political claims, without influence, will get the clerkship, while the young man with all the power of wealth and political pull at his back will have to look to his rich uncle or to honest work outside of the government service for support. Young Smith will first receive a probationary appointment for, say, six months, to prove his practical capacity and adaptation to the work he is to do. If that probation is successfully passed, his appointment is made definitive, and then his tenure of the office will not depend upon the influence or power of anybody ever so powerful, but entirely upon his own merit. He will hold his place with undisturbed self-respect so long as he performs his duties efficiently and faithfully and maintains a character befitting a public servant.

This is the merit system in its purity. It is true, the civil service rules provide that the appointing power shall not be bound to appoint the one highest on the list, but to have his choice among the highest three—thus being permitted some discretion where the difference of merit may be trifling. But, as a rule, the first of the three gets the place. It is also true that unscrupulous appointing officers sometimes try, by circumventing the spirit of the system, to give an advantage to political favorites, or that removals in the classified service have sometimes been made for political reasons. But such transgressions are strictly forbidden and punishable by dismissal. Thus it may truly be said, that while in the administration of the civil service law influence and favoritism may creep in, they can creep in only through fraud or violation of duty, and that the system opens as a rule to every citizen, rich or poor, without distinction of party or creed or social station, the road to public employment through the gates of simple merit.

Now I ask any unprejudiced and candid man, which of the two systems is most apt, not only to give the republic an honest and efficient service, but to put public employment most impartially within the reach of everybody? Which of the two is the most democratic? On the one hand we behold the group of political magnates, the bosses, the Senators and the Representatives, the party leaders—the dukes, the earls, and the barons of politics—doling out by way of favor their recommendations, which are usually equivalent to appointments, among the applicants for office who appear as petitioners before them, the favored petitioner to feel himself under constant obligation to the political magnate to whom he owes his place, knowing that he will be secure in his place only so long as that favor continues. Is not this a political aristocracy with something like a feudal retinue in full bloom?

On the other hand we behold the American citizen, the freeman, no matter whether rich or poor, whether backed by the influence of the powerful or not, independent of the favor of anybody, claiming and obtaining the right to compete for public employment upon equal terms with other freemen, the poorest with the richest, the lowliest with the most powerful, the best man to have the best chance. Is not this the equality of opportunity which forms the very life element of true democracy? On the one side the aristocracy of influence which grants or withholds as a favor what merit may claim as its right. On the other hand the democracy of equal opportunity which recognizes in all citizens alike the right of merit by giving the best man the best chance.

It is a significant fact that in England, so long as the government was essentially aristocratic, the spoils system flourished—that is to say, public employment was bestowed by the favor of the powerful. But as the government became more and more democratic, the merit system took the place of favoritism and public employment was thrown open to free and public competition.

I say, therefore, that in contending for the merit system we contend for the right of the people to the offices instituted for their benefit. Whoever opposes it, fights against true democracy. Nothing is more ridiculous than the manner in which the spoils politicians seek to obscure this feature of the question. They carry the word "people" constantly at their tongues' end and mean only those for whom *they* want public places and salaries. Mr. Grosvenor loudly protests that the men who "in 1896 marched thousands and thousands of miles to hear the words of encouragement and instruction from the President as he stood upon the steps of his home in Canton" shall not be excluded from places in the department by troublesome civil service tests. He will admit that, there being untold thousands of them, they cannot all have offices, unless we create an office with a salary for every applicant of that kind. Who, then, is to select from among the untold thousands of patriotic wanderers those who are to be blessed with place and pay ? Why, Mr. Grosvenor tells us that the members of Congress are the fittest men to make that selection, and of those members of Congress Mr. Grosvenor is one. Their " people," therefore, are those whom this aristocracy of influence find it convenient to favor.

Does not Mr. Grosvenor think that President McKinley, to whom those thousands came to listen, had a much more correct conception of what is really due to the people, when in his letter of acceptance he sternly rebuked those who " encourage a return to methods of favoritism which both parties have denounced, which experience has condemned, and which the people have repeatedly disapproved ?" Is he not much more just to the confidence of the people who made him President, and more conscientiously mindful of the people's rights when he firmly tells the clamorers for the " return to methods of favoritism " that, faithful to his recorded vow, he will to the utmost of his power protect the people in the enjoyment of the right freely to compete on equal terms for public employment?

I repeat, it is the aristocracy of influence on one side and the democracy of merit on the other. And I cannot too strongly impress upon the mind of everyone concerned that every public employment unnecessarily withdrawn from the domain of the democracy of merit and turned over to the aristocratic rule of influence is an encroachment on popular rights. There is constant urgency on the part of so-called practical politicians, and sometimes also from executive officers who are exposed to political pressure, for the withdrawal of this or that class of positions which are now in the classified service, from the competitive rule. In hardly any case has my examination of the reasons for such a demand convinced me of the necessity of the withdrawal. In almost every instance we find the same or a similar class of offices elsewhere successfully administered under the competitive rule, and nothing can be more certain than that the withdrawals asked for would result simply in turning over the positions concerned to the abuses of patronage mongering and spoils politics. Those in power should never permit themselves to forget that when an office, the subjection of which to the competitive rule is at all practicable, is withheld from the domain of that rule, or whenever an office already under the competitive rule is without the clearest necessity withdrawn from it and is thus made a matter of patronage commanded by influence, the people are robbed of their right of free competition for that public employment. That right cannot be too jealously guarded, especially by the men and women who are poor, or without influential backing, or too self-respecting to make themselves dependent upon the favor of the powerful instead of their own work, and who, when serving the public, will not make themselves anybody's political slaves. It is in the competitive rule alone that they find a guarantee of a fair and equal chance, and they have every reason to hold to stern account any man in power and any political party that is weak or wicked enough to participate or acquiesce in any attempt to subvert or only to curtail the right of the people to that equality of opportunity, that independence of influence and favoritism, which true democracy demands. And the efforts of certain politicians to repeal the civil service law or to restrict its operation, are clearly a war upon this right.

The first practical attack was made in New York where Governor Black sounded the keynote by proclaiming his desire to "take the starch out of civil service," whereupon the Legislature followed with a law making an artful distinction between "merit" and "fitness"—a distinction without a difference, never heard of before—and providing that each candidate for a place in the classified service shall have to pass two examinations,—one for "merit" to be conducted by the established civil-service boards, and the other for "fitness" to be conducted by the appointing officers themselves in such manner as they may see fit to adopt, oral or in writing, public or secret. Inasmuch as the value of such examinations is shown by experience to rest upon the independence of their management from the appointing power, it was safe to predict that the practical result of the operation of this law would be the virtual annihilation of the competitive system prescribed by the State Constitution of New York. And this has substantially been the case wherever the dual examination system was applied, while some public departments appointed the existing civil-service boards as their examiners, which in so far set a limit to the restoration of the spoils system. But the new law stands in such glaring antagonism to the evident spirit and intent of the constitutional mandate that a test case which is soon to be carried before the courts, is most likely to bring forth a judicial decision declaring it unconstitutional. Meanwhile there has been an election in the State of New York, which proved quite intelligibly that the Republican party has, to say the least, not been strengthened by the attempted relapse into spoils politics. It is the old experience.

Of the efforts being made to rally the whole army of spoils politicians for a general assault upon the national civil-service law, I have already spoken. The first onset has been bravely beaten back by the President. Instead of breaking his word by rescinding all the extensions of the rules made by his predecessor, he issued an executive order on the 27th of July by which he exempted from the competitive rules certain classes of positions in the revenue service, extended the rule over a few others, and then directed that "no removal shall be made from any position subject to competitive examination except for just cause and upon written charges filed with the head of the department or other appointing officer, and of which the accused shall have full notice and an opportunity to make defence." Of the exceptions from the competititive rules made in the first part of the order, it may be said that after full consultation they were agreed upon between the Secretary of the Treasury and the Civil Service Commission, both being known to have the cause of civil-service reform seriously at heart. Candidates for the places thus excepted are subject to examinations to be prescribed by the Secretary of the Treasury, with the approval of the Civil Service Commission, which is also to conduct them. It is to be said, however, that if this arrangement succeeds in keeping the positions concerned out of reach of spoils politics, it will accomplish more than has usually been accomplished by mere pass examinations before. Nor is there any risk in predicting that further experience will prove not only the practicability, but also the desirability of returning those positions to the domain of the competitive rule.

But the clause of President McKinley's order which attracted the greatest attention is that concerning removals. It is no exaggeration to say that its appearance was greeted with a round of applause that resounded all over the country. The best part of the public press was enthusiastic in its praise, and the hearty acclaim of all the true friends of good government in the land fairly drowned for a while the savage clamor for spoils which since the presidential election had filled the air. When he witnessed that spontaneous outburst of approbation, President McKinley cannot have failed to feel that he had the true public opinion of the country on his side, and that the motley crowd of spoils hunters pressing upon him to force dishonor on himself and his party, was only a small minority making up in noise for what it lacked in good sense as well as in numbers. What was it that called forth that loud and general applause? It was that the American people felt themselves after all the confusing rumors and speculations that had disquieted them, suddenly relieved of all uncertainty as to whether President McKinley would surely meet his own and his party's pledges. The American people like an honest man. They admire a man of courage in the right, who will stand firm as a rock against the pressure even of his friends when they demand what is wrong and dishonorable. And the people saw in President McKinley's order a vigorous manifestation of his patriotic purpose to make true his words: "Civil Service reform has come to stay."

Besides, the intelligence of the country recognized in the order concerning removals a decided progress of that reform. The time had come for this step and President McKinley responded to a wise public sentiment in taking it. Thoughtful citizens had long been disgusted at the reckless disregard of the public interest as well as of private justice with which meritorious public servants had been turned out of their places merely to make room for the favorites of influential politicians. It was, indeed, thought at first by civil service reformers that arbitrary removals would cease whenever the competitive system made arbitrary appointments impossible. As our lamented leader, George William Curtis, happily expressed it "if the front door is well guarded the back door will take care of itself." It was, therefore, believed best that the discretion of the chiefs of executive departments in the matter of removals should be left entirely unlimited. But this sanguine expectation did not stand the test of experience, and Mr. Curtis himself, toward the close of his life, was inclined to abandon it. The introduction of the competitive rule in certain branches of the service did not at once produce the effect of wholly curing all appointing officers of the widely prevailing spoils disease.

It was found that those of them who were unscrupulous enough to care more for party politics than for the public interest, as well as others who had not courage enough to stand up against the pressure of political influence, would make arbitrary removals for the purpose of opening a chance for some trick by which, in spite of the competitive system, they might put the favorites of power into the vacated places,—and not seldom they succeeded, either by way of arbitrary promotions, or of emergency appointments, or by other devices. And it may be said that nothing has done more to shake the popular belief in the good faith of the merit system than such dishonest practices.

To such artful violations of the spirit of the civil service law President McKinley's order is intended to put a stop. It does not make a removal subject to a formal judicial proceeding. It does not limit the discretion of the executive officer to an extent prejudicial to the discipline of the service; but it does make the reason assigned for every removal as well as the answer thereto a matter of public record, and it will thus render the executive officer for every removal from a place under the competitive rule amenable to the judgment of public opinion as well as to the judgment and the corresponding action of his superiors. The new rule, if carried out with fidelity and firmness, will thus be well apt to rid the service of a very offensive and dangerous abuse, and President McKinley fully deserves all the praise he has received for this achievement.

To secure the enforcement of the order the Secretary of the Treasury, Mr. Gage, with recommendable promptness issued excellent instructions to executive officers under the Treasury Department prescribing an appropriate mode of procedure, and containing the important injunction that reductions in grade and salary should be treated in all things like removals—this to put a stop to the tricky device followed by some unscrupulous executive officers, of forcing worthy public servants to resign by arbitrarily reducing them to a lower grade which they could not accept with self-respect —a practice most objectionable on account not only of its injustice, but also of its peculiarly sneaking character. This action on the part of the Sectretary of the Treasury was most praiseworthy, and it is greatly to be hoped that his instructions will be made a uniform rule for all the executive departments that have not yet adopted them.

Nothing would gratify me more than to be able to add that the President's order had already borne all the good fruit which it is expected to bear. But I regret to say that so far it has not. Many reports have come to us from Washington as well as from other parts of the country which represent executive officers as making or recommending removals or reductions without assigning any just cause, or any cause at all. There is no doubt that some of those reports will, upon careful examination, turn out to be unfounded, or at least exaggerated. But it must also be admitted that some of the cases that have come to our knowledge, bear an exceedingly ugly look and leave scarcely any doubt that the President's order has in those instances been treated with wanton defiance. It is hardly necessary to say that public officers doing this not only violate their official duty, but are basely disloyal to their chief; especially if they count upon the goodness of his heart to let their offence pass with impunity. For they must know that such leniency on his part would only serve to encourage further defiance and turn the praise he has received for issuing the order into scorn and reproach for permitting it to fall into contempt. It is confidently to be expected that the President, as such offences come to his notice and the facts are fully ascertained, will enforce respect for his order by duly punishing the offenders.

A matter in which not only the civil service reformer, but the whole commercial community takes a lively interest, is the improvement of our consular service. As is well known, certain rules were established under the last administration for the examination of candidates for consular offices drawing $2,500 or less down to $1,000 salary. It is reported that this system is being continued by the State Department, but in what manner and with what effect I am unable to say. Inquiries addressed to the State Department by the officers of this League as to the scope of the examinations and the relative number of those who have succeeded and those who have failed in them, have been answered to the effect that such things are treated as strictly confidential by the Department and that the information cannot be furnished. I can only repeat what I said in former annual addresses, that a system of mere pass examinations may do some good when conducted with particular conscientiousness and courageous independence from political influence, and may then, as Secretary Olney called his measure, be " a step in the right direction," but that, as all experience has shown, pass examinations are apt to degenerate into a mere matter of form, a mere pretense of a test of qualifications, in which as a rule those succeed who have the strongest backing, and those fail who have none. Pass examinations for the consular service have been tried at various periods, and they have always taken that course. Whether they have or not in the present instance, I am unable to tell, the matter being strictly confidential. But this I may say with assurance: If our commercial community wants a real reform in the method of appointment to consular positions, it must insist upon three things: *competitive* examinations for admission to the lowest grade of the consular service, promotion only for merit, and removal only for cause. From this rule should, at most, only those few consular positions be excepted that have a diplomatic character.

The postmaster, too, is receiving promising attention. It is a hopeful sign that the Posmaster-general, a business man not suspected of being a civil service reform theorist, has from a mere business point of view found it expedient to advocate the removal, by Congress, of those restrictions by which the consolidation of minor offices with those which are central, had been hampered. And altough the subjection to proper civil service rules of the fourth class post offices, which so far have furnished the material for the most widespread spoils scandals, may as yet seem ever so far away, still it is approaching and may be nearer than even the most sanguine among us now apprehend.

" The system has the approval of the people, and it will be my endeavor to uphold and extend it." These are the closing words of the paragraph touching civil service reform in the President's annual message. In his endeavor to uphold and extend the merit system the President will have a larger majority of the people on his side than any of his predecessors ever had, for what formerly seemed to be only a dream of idealists, is now a practical fact, well understood and recognized in its beneficial effects by the enlightened public opinion of the country. As I pointed out in my last annual address, not one of President McKinley's predecessors has, since the enactment of the civil service law, failed to distinguish his administration by large and important extensions of the domain of the merit system. It would be doing injustice to his motives as well as to his powers to fear that in his achievements President McKinley might remain behind the best of them. He has signalized the very beginning of his administration by an advance of exceeding importance. And now, considering that wellnigh the whole clerical part of the governmental machinery was already under the merit system when he took office, and need only be protected against the wily attempts of spoils politics to invade it, we may hope that President McKinley may recognize it as his part of the great work, to carry the reform beyond those limits. There is good reason for believing that the necessities of the consular service have already engaged his care; and whoever undertakes seriously the task of putting that, as well as any other, branch of the government service upon a footing of thorough efficiency, will soon recognize that the first requirement is its absolute emancipation from the influence of the patronage mongers.

There is a force working for civil service reform which is now far more effective than ever before. It is the character of the opposition to it. As the number of good citizens favoring our cause increased and grew into a majority, the opposition became numerically weaker but far more desperate and vociferous. And the more it becomes desperate and vociferous, the more recklessly it discloses its true nature and its aims. Civil service reform is now gaining in the esteem and friendship of the people, not only by the recognition of its correct principles and in good results, but also " for the enemies, it has made." The very shamelessness with which certain Republican politicians now clamor for the repudiation of their platform pledge to enforce and extend the civil service law— a pledge of which Mr. McKinley in the House of Representatives once said that "if the Republican party is pledged to one thing more than another it is the maintenance of the civil service law, and its enlargement and further application to the service "—the very vehemence with which they rush upon the President they have just elected, to force him to break his word and to proclaim himself a dishonest man—the very audacity with which they seek to deceive the people with the most barefaced falsehoods about the civil service system—and all this for the palpable purpose of looting the government for party spoil—these very exhibitions of unscrupulousness and fury make unprejudiced men, who never cared much about civil service reform, stop and ask: "What does this all mean? Can a fight carried on so indecently be a good fight? Must not the right be on the other side?"

There was a rumor in the newspapers that the opponents of civil service reform planned a national convention to be held in this very city of Cincinnati for the purpose of organizing a grand movement for the overthrow of the civil service law. This plan is very much to be commended and I fervently hope that its promoters will strain every nerve to insure its execution. Nothing could be a more striking object lesson than a grand muster of the enemies of civil service reform in bodily exhibition. Nothing could be more edifying to the people of Ohio than an open denunciation of the honored son of their State who now stands at the head of the republic, by members of his own party for doing his manifest duty as President and patriot. Nothing could be more generally instructive than clear avowals by themselves of their principles and aims.

Their leading statesman, Representative Grosvenor, has already sounded the keynote of their movement by a cry of exultation with which, in a letter to a Washington newspaper, he recently greeted the triumph of that nest of political pirates, Tammany Hall in the city of New York. Mr. Grosvenor says: "The battle cry of Van Wyck (the Tammany candidate for Mayor) is a liberal political education to the people of the United States. He won a victory unprecedented, and he gave out but one great battle cry, and that thrilled through the hearts of a great body of the American people and an echo will be heard. That battle cry was: 'I will put none but Democrats into office in New York.'" Mr. Grosvenor can hardly ignore the fact that there was, accompanying this, another and kindred Tammany battle cry: "To hell with reform!" the two watchwords being inseparably united. And then, after this enthusiastic greeting to Tammany Hall, Mr. Grosvenor admonishes the Republican party to follow Tammany's example, thus: "We must teach the members of the Republican party that it is responsible for the administration of the government when it is in power, and to that end we must teach the people that the instrumentalities of government from highest to lowest during Republican administration shall be placed in the hands of Republicans." There can be no doubt of what this means: A clean sweep from top to bottom, from Cabinet minister to scrub woman, with every change of party in power! The battle cry from which political parties are to receive their strongest inspiration, is to be: "To the victors belong the spoils, and every government employment shall be spoil!" The kindred battle cry: "To hell with reform!" will soon follow. And the result? A great Democratic Tammany on one side and a great Republican Tammany on the other fighting for public plunder and casting lots for the garments of the crucified republic.

What spectacle could be more significant than that of the Republican enemy of civil service reform jubilantly congratulating the Tammany Tiger upon his triumph and proclaiming to the world their common ideal of government! Let this ideal be soberly contemplated by an intelligent people who wish to be proud of their country and to preserve its institutions. Such are the hostile forces the friends of civil service reform has to contend with. Can our victory be doubtful? The enemy being desperate, the struggle now before us may be arduous and bitter. But it is likely to be the last. General Grant's Wilderness campaign of 1864 was the bloodiest of the civil war. But when it began the rebellion was in fact already broken and doomed. Whoever still fights for the spoils system sacrifices himself for a lost cause. The final victory cannot fail to be with sound democratic principles, reason, and civilization.

MEETING OF THE LEAGUE.

The President took the chair.

The Secretary made a verbal report covering the work of his office during the year, and reviewing the course of Congress, and of the present administration, with reference to those matters having to do with reform in the federal civil service. On motion the report was accepted.

The President announced the next business in order to be the reception of reports from representatives of local Associations.

Mr. Clinton Rogers Woodruff, for the Pennsylvania Association, reported as follows:

"When in August, 1895, the State Republican Convention of Pennsylvania, composed of delegates from every county in the State, adopted resolutions favoring civil service reform with scarcely a dissenting voice, civil service reformers were justified in a reasonable hope that the spoils system existing in this State was likely to be abolished in the near future. Such an utterance was on a basis entirely different than that of a promise of a candidate—it was the carefully prepared and formally expressed pledge of a great party of forty years standing, representing a large majority of the voters of the Commonwealth.

"Thus it will be seen that the Republican party in Pennsylvania was solemnly pledged to the enactment of certain greatly needed reform legislation, and as the bills providing for these reforms had been drafted by a committee of the State Convention, and formally endorsed and made a part of the Republican platform, it was reasonably expected that their passage by the Legislature when it assembled in January, 1897, would take but a short time. There was no doubt in the minds of any one that United States Senator Quay, who had been responsible for the insertion of the reform planks in the platform, and who was successful in his fight for the control of the party machine because he had unequivocally espoused the cause of reform, was in supreme control in the Legislature.

"When Mr. Quay made his peace with certain ward leaders in Philadelphia, signs began to multiply with great rapidity that notwithstanding the great Republican majority in the Legislature, and the explicit Republican pledges, reform legislation would have as thorny a path in the Pennsylvania Legislature as it had had at any previous session. In the meantime the Civil Service Reform bill had passed the Senate and was sent over to the House for concurrence. It was referred to a committee from which, after a very considerable delay, it was reported. Once on the calendar it was delayed and postponed for various reasons, and then sent back to the committee for amendment; really to have its vital features eliminated. Here it remained until within a week of adjournment, late in June.

"A proposition was made by the civil service reformers, while the bill was in committee, under advisement and waiting orders from Washington, to introduce a local option feature, so that it could become operative in those counties expressing, by a majority vote, their desire to have the provisions of the law apply. Upon a careful examination of adjudicated cases it was found that such a provision would be unconstitutional. Then the proposition was made to submit the whole question directly to a vote of the people. This the professional politicians were afraid to do, and they would not consent to such a plan. Finally the bill came out amended; or perhaps we would more appropriately describe the process as emasculation.

"This altered bill proved a grotesque burlesque of civil service reform. How its sponsors could advocate its passage, in view of their platform pledges, it is difficult to understand. It provided for a Commission composed of three State officers; for a four year tenure of office, and for an examination at the end of every four years conducted by the Department of Education. Thus it was proposed to fulfill the solemnly declared pledges of a great party, but those sincerely interested in genuine civil service reform were not misled by such a trick and they bent their energies to encompass its defeat. They succeeded, after a hard fight.

"We are not discouraged nor cast down because of this betrayal. We believe that the cause of civil service reform at present has a deeper and more abiding hold on the voters of the State than at any previous time. The prospect is that there will be a reaction in favor of better government and more decent politics in the State, as well as in Philadelphia, the result of which will be the elimination of those leaders and bosses who have so long prostituted the Republican party to their own selfish personal interests."

Mr. Hitchcock, of St. Louis, introduced Mr. A. R. Verdier as representing both the Missouri Civil Service Reform Association and the Civic Federation of St. Louis. Mr. Verdier said:

The Civic Federation of St. Louis, of which I have the honor to be the Secretary, was organized for general Municipal Reform; its efforts not being confined to, but including the introduction of the Merit System in our Municipal offices. Last year we undertook the reform of our Board of Education, that being looked generally upon as the most corrupt of our city departments. We succeeded in securing the passage of a new school law in our State Legislature, against the combined opposition of the entire St. Louis delegation in the lower House, abolishing the old Board and providing for a new one, consisting of twelve members, elected at large. Sixty days after the passage of this bill, at a special election, we elected a ticket composed of eminently capable men, and under their direction in July, 1897, was held, what was probably the first competitive examination in St. Louis for public place, when two hundred applicants were examined for positions as Janitors.

At the first regular meeting of our association in the fall of this year, after an adjournment during the summer months, a large variety of work was outlined and conferred to committees. Among the subjects was that of Civil Service Reform, and after careful consideration the Executive Committee fixed upon this reform as the most important one to be taken up, in view of the fact that our City Council was preparing a set of amendments to our City Charter to be submitted to the Citizens at an election in 1898. A petition asking that a Civil Service provision be included in them, was prepared, and is now being circulated and hundreds are signing it. We find nine out of every ten men enthusiastically in favor of the proposition, although the misrepresentations made by its enemies in Congress and elsewhere are not without their effect. However, we hope to secure twenty-five or thirty thousand signatures before presenting our petition and by keeping a careful record of the name and address of every signer, to be in a position, in case of necessity to make an issue of this question at the next election, and carry the day.

As our Charter can only be amended by vote of the people, we are seeking to secure a broad provision modeled on the New York State Law, leaving the details of application to city ordinances. With a machine administration the odds are against us, but still we hope by the time of the next meeting of this League to be able to report the enactment of a law which shall place St. Louis in the van rank so far as the management of her public offices are concerned, through the introduction of the Merit System.

Col. John W. Ela, for the Civil Service Reform League of Chicago, reported as follows:

There has been a change of administration in Chicago since the last annual meeting of the League. As the law was only put into operation by the last administration after many discharges and appointments in the different departments, and as the present administration is of different politics, the law is now having its principal test. While the present Mayor declares himself in harmony with the spirit of the law and says it shall be enforced, he desires several changes and his chief law-officer and many of his active supporters are opposed to the law and to the principle upon which it is based. The Civil Service Commission (appointed by the present Mayor) is composed of good citizens, and its President has been known for some time as an advocate of the merit system. A considerable proportion of the friends of the law believe that the Commissioners are endeavoring to do their duty, as they see it. There is tremendous pressure brought to bear upon them by people who demand their reward for political service, as is usual at a change of administration, and who are surprised and indignant at discovering that there is actually a law in force which takes the offices out of the spoils-pot. Many friends of the law have felt like standing by the Commission and giving them the benefit of their encouragement, so long as they appeared to be honestly doing all they could to resist these attacks and to carry out the provisions of the law.

Our Civil Service Reform League has a Committee to watch the execution of the Civil Service Law in Chicago, call the attention of the Commissioners to any matters which require it, and proceed to enforce their requirements, through the courts or otherwise, if they deem necessary. If it should at any time be discovered that the law is not being enforced in good faith, I think there will be no hesitation with any of its friends in compelling its strict enforcement.

There is a suit now pending in the State Supreme Court in which the constitutionality of the law is involved. A decision is expected in this case very soon now, and we feel quite certain that the law will be sustained. There is also a suit by the Commission against the Board of Education to compel that Board to come under the law, in which suit the Circuit Court has decided that this important Board is a Department of the City Government, and therefore subject to all the provisions of Civil Service Law. This case has been appealed by the Board to the Supreme Court. The appeal is now pending.

There is also a proceeding by the Commissioners for a mandamus to compel the Secretary of one of the general departments of the city to testify in an investigation by the Commission. The defendant in that proceeding attacks the constitutionality of the provision of the law, allowing the courts to compel the giving of testimony before the Commission. The case has been argued and is held under advisement by the Circuit Court.

The atmosphere is clouded in some respects by all this litigation, but will probably be cleared when we get the decision of the Supreme Court sustaining the law in all its essential provisions, which we confidently expect within a very short time.

Brief reports were also made by Mr. Charles J. Bonaparte, for the Maryland Association; Mr. Sherman S. Rogers, for Buffalo; Rev. W. R. Lord, for St. Paul; Mr. William Dudley Foulke, for Indiana; and Mr. F. L. Siddons, for the District of Columbia.

Mr. Foulke then made a verbal report for the Committee on Congressional action appointed by the Executive Committee at its meeting of October 4. He stated that the Committee would be represented at Washington during the remainder of the winter, and that the programme already submitted to the Executive Committee, and by them approved, would be followed as closely as might prove practicable.

Mr. Siddons, of Washington, addressed the League with reference to the proposed exemption of the force to be employed in connection with the taking of the Twelfth Census, from classification under the civil service rules. He urged that a special report be prepared and circulated by the Committee on Congressional action, showing the unsatisfactory results of the organization of the Census Bureau in 1890 on a patronage basis, and proposing legislation that would insure the classification of the Bureau, before its reorganization, for the highly important work now to be undertaken.

The Secretary, on behalf of the Special Committee on Reform in the Consular Service, made a verbal report concerning the changes among Consuls made under the present administration. The results of such changes he summarized as follows:

There are at present in the Consular Service, 284 Consulates and Consulates-General, and 30 commercial agencies, having practically the rank of Consulates—314 in all. Of these, 9 are filled by Diplomatic officers who serve in a dual capacity; 15 are vacant. There are thus 290 officers of the class in question now in the service, as follows:

(1) Between the grades of $2,500 and $1,000 annual salary. (Subject to non-competitive examination) 186

(2) In grades above $2,500 annual salary. (Exempt from examination)... 55

(3) In grades below $1,000 annual salary, paid by fees. (Exempt from examination) 49

—————
290

The proportion of changes in each of these classes since March 3, 1897, and the proportion of previously appointed incumbents remaining on December 1, is shown by the following:

	Changes.	Percent-age.	Officers retained.	
(1)	103	.55	83	186
(2)	45	.81	10	55
(3)	12	.24	37	49

—————
290

It will thus be seen that during the first nine months of the administration, fifty-five per cent. of the Consular officers coming within the scope of the examination system established by President Cleveland, in September, 1895, have been changed, and that among the salaried officers of all classes the percentage of changes has been sixty-one, or nearly two-thirds. There is no appreciable difference, so far as proportion is concerned, between the changes under the present administration and those made by Assistant Secretary Quincy during the corresponding period of the previous administration. The service has been deranged as seriously as before, and changes continue to be made daily. The examination system, lacking as it does the competitive element, has proven to be practically no barrier to the removal of competent officers, or the appointment of those lacking in personal fitness. The examinations, conducted by the State Department, are private; none of the papers pertaining to them are public, as in the case of examinations under the Civil Service Commission. While in some respects the treatment of the service has been more orderly than has at times been the case, the need of radical reform in methods of appointment, as well as in tenure, is as apparent as heretofore.

On motion the report was received.

A paper: "Civil Service Reform in Municipal Government," prepared by Dr. Albert Shaw, of New York, was then read by Mr. Welsh, of Philadelphia.*

The Secretary presented a paper prepared by Mr. Horace E. Deming, of New York, treating certain phases of the same subject.†

On motion the League then adjourned.

COLLEGE HALL,
December 17, 1898; 10.30 A. M.

The League re-convened at half-past ten o'clock.

The business in order being the annual election of officers, the President called Mr. Rogers, of Buffalo, to the Chair.

Mr. Woodruff, of Pennsylvania, nominated Carl Schurz for President of the League for the ensuing year. The nomination was seconded by various gentlemen, and Mr. Schurz was unanimously elected. In a brief address he thanked the League for the continued confidence it had manifested, and resumed the chair.

On motion of Mr. Wilby, of Cincinnati, the Secretary was directed to cast one ballot for the re-election for one year of the gentlemen now serving as Vice-presidents, as follows: Charles Francis Adams, Boston; Henry Hitchcock, St. Louis; Henry Charles Lea, Philadelphia; Augustus R. Macdonough, New York; Franklin MacVeagh, Chicago; J. Hall Pleasants, Baltimore; Rt. Rev. Henry C. Potter, New York; William Potts, New York: Rt. Rev. P. J. Ryan, Philadelphia.

---

*Page 120.   †Page 132.

The Secretary cast the ballot, and the gentlemen named were declared elected.

Mr. Siddons for the Auditing Committee appointed by the Executive Committee, submitted the following report:

December 17, '97·

To the National Civil Service Reform League:

The undersigned, constituting the Auditing Committee, respectfully report that we have examined the accounts of the Treasurer,* comparing them with the vouchers. We find them correct, and that the amount in the treasury at this date is $366.13.

> John W. Ela,
> Fred'k. L. Siddons.

On motion the report was accepted and ordered filed.

Mr. Bonaparte, for the Committee on Resolutions, read the resolutions prepared and submitted them for the action of the League.

Mr. Foulke, of Indiana, moved that the resolutions be considered and acted on seriatim, and the motion was carried.

The resolutions were then re-read, and after some discussion, were adopted unanimously in the following form:

(1) The National Civil Service Reform League, assembled in this, its seventeenth annual meeting, reminds the country of the specific and emphatic pledges of the last Republican National Convention thoroughly and honestly to enforce the present Federal Civil Service Law, and to extend its operation wherever practicable. The League confidently expects from the President, and demands from every Republican Senator and Representative, a faithful fulfillment of this distinct and solemn pledge.

(2) The League denounces any attempt on the part of Republican members of either House or Congress, to repeal the law or embarrass its administration, or in any way to modify of its provisions, except to the end that the merit system of selection for public officers and employees may be extended, and personal or partisan favoritism in their choice more thoroughly eradicated; and declares such attempts, not only unpatriotic and unwise, but gross and shameful breaches of party faith, of which no man of honor would be guilty.

(3) The League recognizes in the order of President McKinley forbidding removals in the classified service unless for good cause and after due notice to the person accused, a wise and just measure, fully endorsed by an enlightened public opinion, and it demands for this order a fair

*Page 45.

construction and a practical enforcement, with adequate punishment for any officials who disobey or seek to evade its provisions.

(4) The League respectfully urges upon the President and upon those members of his Cabinet and of either House of Congress who also desire to preserve and extend the merit system of appointment in the Federal service, the importance of an unflinching resistance to the impudent demands of men who wish its destruction. The least concession to demands inspired by such motives will greatly encourage these men and increase their greedy clamor, while making resistance to such pressure more difficult in the future.

(5) The League calls attention to the fact that in those states where the party now dominant in the Federal government has sought in the resolutions of its State Conventions to qualify or evade the unequivocal utterance of its National platform as to civil service reform, the results of the late elections have clearly indicated the disapproval of honest and patriotic citizens. The League further recognizes with pleasure the steady and rapid growth of sympathy with its principles and purposes among enlightened and conscientious Americans of all classes.

(6) The League indignantly stigmatizes the mendacity with which the enemies of good government and pure politics, both in and out of Congress, have misrepresented the practical working of the merit system, and their persistent repetition of gross and ridiculous falsehoods, clearly and frequently exposed, as insults at once to the intelligence and the conscience of the American people.

(7) The League demands that the employees of the Census Bureau be selected for merit and fitness, to be determined by fair, practical and thorough competitive examinations under the direction of the Civil Service Commission. With the warning example of the last census before its eyes, it protests against any enactment which may prevent or impede such selection, as involving a scandalous waste of money and a sacrifice of the country's interest. It were better to have no census at all in 1900 than one taken by incompetent or untrustworthy political proteges, selected according to the well-known methods of so-called practical politics.

(8) The League renews its previous declarations in favor of the repeal of the law prescribing four year terms for many Federal offices, the extension of the merit system to the Consular Service and the municipal civil service of the District of Columbia, and the consolidation of outlying with central post offices. It expressly disclaims any advocacy of civil service pensions as a part of the merit system, which contemplates such pensions no more than did the system of appointment and removal by favor, prevailing before the merit system was introduced; on the contrary the protection which an assured tenure during efficiency affords to public servants, should enable them by the exercise of the frugality and forethought displayed by all prudent persons, to provide out of their current earnings for the ordinary contingencies of age and infirmity.

Mr. Swift, of Indiana, called the attention of the League to the desirability of giving the widest possible circulation to the address delivered by the President on the evening of the 16th inst.

Mr. Wilby, of Cincinnati, moved that a special Committee, of which the Secretary shall be a member ex-officio, be appointed and charged with the printing and circulation of the address in question. The motion was carried unanimously.

On motion of Mr. Richmond, of Buffalo, it was voted that the Resolutions adopted by the League be also printed and circulated as widely as practicable.

A paper: " The Legal Situation—The Right to Compete for Public Employment," was then read by Mr. Edwin Burritt Smith, of Chicago.*

Mr. Wilby announced that the Women's Club of Cincinnati would entertain the visiting delegates at luncheon, and extended the invitation of the Club to all present.

On motion the League then adjourned.

COLLEGE HALL,
December 17, 1898, 2.30 P. M.

The League reconvened at half past two o'clock.

The President called Mr. Rogers, of Buffalo, to the chair, and the following papers were read:

"The Municipal Situation in Ohio." Rufus B. Smith, of Cincinnati.†

"The Republican Party and Civil Service Reform." Henry Hitchcock, of St. Louis.‡

"Do the American People Want Civil Service Reform." Charles J. Bonaparte, of Baltimore.‖

A paper prepared by Mr. Moorfield Storey, of Boston: "The Democratic Party and Civil Service Reform,", was presented by Mr. Charles Warren.§

At the conclusion of the reading of papers, Mr. Welsh, of Pennsylvania, moved that the grateful thanks of the League be tendered to the Civil Service Reform Association of Cincinnati, and to the Women's Club, for the courteous and

*Page 104.   †Page 138.   ‡Page 46.   ‖Page 83.   §Page 70.

bountiful hospitality received from each during the period of these meetings.

The motion was carried unanimously.

The League then adjourned.

Attest:

GEORGE McANENY,

Secretary.

On the evening of the 17th, the visiting delegates were entertained by the Civil Service Reform Association of Cincinnati at a banquet given at the Hotel St. Nicholas. Justice William R. Taft, President of the Cincinnati Association, presided, and addresses were made by Carl Schurz; Senator James R. Garfield, of Cleveland; Gustav Tafel, Mayor of Cincinnati; Herbert Welsh, of Philadelphia; Col. John E. Ela, of Chicago; Lucius B. Swift, of Indiana; Lewis R. Gunckel, of Dayton, and Charles J. Bonaparte, of Baltimore.

ANNUAL REPORT OF THE TREASURER.

Balance on hand, Dec. 10, 1896, ...			$172.97

RECEIPTS:

Subscriptions from	members of Massachu-			
		setts Associations....	$1,400.00	
"	"	Cambridge (additional)..	71.90	
	"	Newton, " ..	50.00	
	"	Mass. Reform Club....	250.00	
	"	Philadelphia	725.75	
	"	New York.............	630.00	
	"	St. Louis.............	221.50	
	"	Cincinnati............	55.00	
	"	Washington...........	150.00	
	"	Buffalo...............	27.00	
	"	Chicago	375.00	
"	"	Miscellaneous.........	100.00	
Pamphlets sold........................			15.83	4,071.98

$4,244.95

DISBURSEMENTS :

Proportion of Secretary's salary............	$1,200.00	
Clerk hire	598.75	
Rent of office	150.00	
Printing.................................	637.00	
Postage	129.00	
Traveling expenses	296.15	
Expenses of Washington Committee.......	94.77	
" " Finance Committee..........	42.80	
Congressional Record, and Documents......	21.29	
Office furniture..........................	29.00	
Office expenses, miscellaneous.............	180.06	
Paid F. E. Leupp, on account of *Good Gov-*		
ernment..............................	500.00	3,878.82

Balance on hand $366.13

E. & O. E.

A. S. FRISSELL,
Treasurer.

The Republican Party and Civil Service Reform.

By Henry Hitchcock.

Fifteen years, less one month, have now elapsed since the statute was enacted, which embedded in the framework and administrative policy of the national government the wholesome doctrine that public office is a public trust, and that public servants, charged with subordinate administrative duties, ought to be appointed, not because of political opinions, nor as a reward for partisan service, but for merit and fitness alone. That great legislative event was thus recorded in the Address of President Curtis, at the second annual meeting of this League:

" On the 16th of January, 1883, upon the earnest recommendation of the President, and by overwhelming majorities in Congress, the Pendleton bill became a law, and on the 16th of July, 1883, amid the general applause of the country, it went into effect."

That doctrine was not new. The fathers of the republic not only proclaimed but practiced it, as an axiom of political morals. Washington required of applicants for office proofs of ability, integrity and fitness. "Beyond this," he said, " nothing with me is necessary or will be of any avail to them in my decision." In at least one historic instance he preferred for appointment an avowed political opponent to a valued personal friend, upon the express ground that the latter did not possess the business qualifications of the former. Jefferson proclaimed it on the threshold of his first administration, declaring that of the thousands of officers in the United States a very few individuals only,— probably not twenty — would be removed, and these only for doing what they ought not to have done. Again, in his famous letter to the merchants of New Haven, he declared that the only questions concerning a candidate should be,— " Is he honest? Is he capable? Is he faithful

to the Constitution?" And Madison, Monroe and John
Quincy Adams so faithfully followed their example that the
Joint Congressional Committee upon Retrenchment reported, in 1868, that after having consulted all accessible
means of information they had not learned of a single
removal of a subordinate officer except for cause, from the
beginning of Washington's administration to the close of
that of John Quincy Adams,— a period of forty years.

It is not the purpose of this paper to trace the steps by
which, during the succeeding forty years, a very different doctrine gained ascendency and an opposite practice came to
prevail. The history of the spoils system, its corrupting
tendencies and the menace which it involves to the perpetuity
of our government, are unhappily familiar to every student
of American politics, — to none more than the members of
this League, whose privilege and delight it was, year by
year, to listen to the annual addresses of our lamented
President, distinguished alike for their historic accuracy and
fullness, their persuasive and manly eloquence and their
captivating literary form. Those addresses, and other
papers, not less brilliant and memorable, prepared by Mr.
Curtis from the year 1869 up to the organization of this
League, in August, 1881, contain also — and not only contain but to an important degree constitute,— the history of
the struggle to overthrow the spoils system which began in
1867, and after fifteen years of determined effort, of varying success and frequent disappointment, was crowned with
the sanction of law in 1888.

That Act, substantially unchanged, and, as we rejoice to
know, honestly enforced, stands upon the statute book to-
day. But the struggle and the conflict are not ended.
Both before and since its enactment, in Congress and
among the people at large, able men of all political parties
have enlisted on one or the other side of the controversy.
During all these thirty years, in presidential messages and
declarations of policy, in Congressional debates and in the
successive platforms of the great political parties, the
reform of the civil service, the mischiefs and dangers of the
spoils system and the methods by which they ought to be
prevented, have been conspicuous topics. In Congress
efforts have again and again been made, hitherto always

unsuccessful, to repeal the Civil Service Act of 1888, or to destroy its efficiency by refusing the necessary appropriations, in which members of both the great parties have joined.

In March last, a new Administration assumed the reins of government, and within the past ten days the 55th Congress has assembled for its first regular session. The election of its candidate for President in 1896, and of a large majority in the House of Representatives, assures to the Republican party, if not the absolute control of the legislation of this Congress, at any rate the power to prevent the repeal or modification of any existing law. Scarcely had that Administration assumed the responsibilities of office, and while the new Congress was occupied with questions of revenue legislation whose urgency had induced the President to call an extra session, when the formation of an anti-civil service reform league was loudly announced. During that extra session speeches were made, both in the Senate and the House, by members of that party, elaborately and savagely attacking and misrepresenting not only the methods and provisions of the Civil Service Act, but the principles upon which it is based. And, if the press reports are correct, on the second day of the regular session which begun last week, the deliberations of the House as to the proper reference of the various portions of the President's annual message were interrupted and delayed by speeches from two members, one a Democratic representative from Alabama, the other elected as a Republican from Ohio, both bitterly denouncing the Civil Service Act, advocating the abandonment of the merit system, and taking issue with the President's statement that it has the approval of the people.

Under these circumstances, the actual relation of the Republican party to civil service reform and the probable or even possible attitude of that party towards the system now established by law, are questions not only germane to the objects of this League but which may well receive the earnest consideration of its members, and of the people at large.

How shall those questions be answered? By what rules may we reasonably forecast the attitude of any political party? By what test may we fairly determine the obligations and gauge the fidelity of its members, especially of those whom it has placed in office,— above all, those who have been elected to the State or National Legislature, as fit and loyal representatives of the party policy? Obviously we must look, we can only look, to the formal declarations of its policy publicly made by that party through its authorized or official representatives, and to the public or official acts of its recognized leaders. Thus only can the policy of any party be made known. Only by accepting that test can any party organization reasonably or honorably claim public confidence or support. Doubtless any political party may change its policy; for party organization is only a means to an end, and every citizen, under a government of the people, is free at any time to adopt in good faith whatever political views or principles may commend themselves to his judgment and to support whatever party best represents those views. These are mere truisms. But it follows from them that no political party which has come into power by professing certain principles or proclaiming a given policy as its own, can consistently or honorably abandon those principles or repudiate that policy and still hold fast to the power or deserve the confidence and support thus gained. And what is true of the party is true of each one of its official representatives, since it can speak and act through them alone.

Above all is it true of the legislator who owes his seat, and his share in the law-making power, to the confidence of the people in the pledges of his party. When the question is not merely of methods, as to which a large discretion must be allowed, but of the substantial fulfillment or the repudiation of those pledges, the man of honor can have but one choice,— he must fulfill those pledges or he must resign.

What position, then, has the Republican party of the United States publicly taken in respect of civil service reform? What policy has it announced, what pledges has it given through its authorized representatives?

The platform, or formal declaration of its policy, adopted by the National Republican Convention at St. Louis, on June 18, 1896, by a vote of 818½ to 105½, leaves no doubt on that point.

I quote from that platform as follows:

"The Civil Service law was placed on the statute book by the Republican party, which has always sustained it, and we renew our repeated declarations that it shall be thoroughly and honestly enforced and extended wherever practicable."

The concluding paragraph of that official document, referring to each and all of the declarations which preceded it, was as follows:

"Such are the principles and policies of the Republican party. By these principles we will abide, and these policies we will put into execution. We ask for them the considerate judgment of the American people."

That Convention having nominated William McKinley as the Republican candidate for the Presidency at the election in November, 1896, this declaration of the party policy was officially communicated to him with the tender of said nomination. On August 26, 1896, he formally accepted the nomination in a letter to the Notification Committee, in which he considered in detail the "questions at issue in the pending campaign." From that letter I quote as follows:

"The pledge of the Republican National Convention that our civil service laws 'shall be sustained and thoroughly and honestly enforced, and extended wherever practicable,' is in keeping with the position of the party for the past twenty-four years and will be faithfully observed. Our opponents decry these reforms. They appear to be willing to abandon all the advantages gained after so many years' agitation and effort. They encourage a return to methods of party favoritism which both parties have often denounced, that experience has condemned, and that the people have repeatedly disapproved. The Republican party earnestly opposes this reactionary and entirely unjustifiable policy. It will take no backward step on this question. It will seek to improve, but never to degrade the public service."

The National Democratic Convention which met at Chicago on July 7, 1896, accepted the issue thus tendered. The civil service plank in that platform, while characteristically ambiguous, denounced what was called, " Life tenure in the Civil Service," and it is a matter of political history that the Democratic candidate for President and his supporters proclaimed their determination, if they should obtain control of the Government, to abolish the system established by the Civil Service Act of 1883. There was no doubt in the public mind, when the general elections of 1896 were held, what was the position of either party upon the question of civil service reform.

Upon the issues thus made up, the contending parties went to the country. The American people responded by electing William McKinley President of the United States by a plurality of 573,000 and a clear majority over all opponents of about 258,000 votes. The unqualified promise of the Republican party, not only to sustain but to honestly enforce and extend the existing civil service law, was accepted by the people.

On March 4, 1897, President McKinley, on taking the oath of office, made the customary Inaugural Address, setting forth the policy of his Administration. From this I quote the following passage relating to the civil service :

" Reforms in the civil service must go on, but the change should be real and genuine, not perfunctory, or prompted by a zeal in behalf of any party, simply because it happens to be in power. As a member of Congress I voted and spoke in favor of the present law, and I shall attempt its enforcement in the spirit in which it was enacted. The purpose in view was to secure the most efficient service of the best men who would accept appointment under the government, retaining faithful and devoted public servants in office, but shielding none under the authority of any rule or custom who are inefficient, incompetent or unworthy. The best interests of the country demand this, and the people heartily approve the law wherever and whenever it has been thus administered."

These declarations, I need hardly remind you, are in complete harmony with the utterances and the votes of President McKinley during his long and distinguished service in the House of Representatives. Of those utterances, one illustration will suffice. In 1890, the most strenuous attempt of all was made to cripple the operation of the Civil Service Act by cutting down the appropriations necessary to carry it into effect. Mr. McKinley, then Chairman of the House Committee of Ways and Means, successfully led the opposition in a speech from which I quote as follows:

" Mr. Chairman, if the Republican party of this country is pledged to any one thing more than another, it is the maintenance of the civil service law and to its efficient execution — not only that, but to its enlargement and its further application to the public service.

" The law that stands upon our statute books to-day was put there by Republican votes. It was a Republican measure. Every national platform of the Republican party, since its enactment, has declared not only in favor of its continuance in full vigor, but in favor of its enlargement so as to apply more generally to the public service. And this, Mr. Chairman, is not alone the declaration and purpose of the Republican party, but it is in accordance with its highest and best sentiment — aye, more, it is sustained by the best sentiment of the whole country, Republican and Democratic alike."

It is well known that since his inauguration the President has carried out these pledges with characteristic integrity. It is said that strong efforts have been made to induce him to modify the civil service regulations in a sense unfriendly to genuine reform: but if so, such efforts have failed. Suggestions respectfully submitted to the President, on behalf of this League, touching the practical working of the Act and apparently desirable amendments to the civil service rules, have been received and considered in a frank and cordial spirit most gratifying to your representatives. Two important amendments to the civil service rules have been promulgated by the President.

Rule II, relating to dismissals from office, has been amended in a very important respect by adding the following:

" No removal shall be made from any position subject to competitive examination except for just cause and upon written charges filed with the head of the Department, or other appointing officer, and of which the accused shall have full notice and an opportunity to make defense."

This amendment has met the hearty approbation of the friends of the reform. It is manifestly just, and is an additional safeguard against the arbitrary dismissal of meritorious employees, really for political reasons, but upon some other pretext, while avoiding the opposite danger of restricting the indispensable power of prompt removal where just cause exists.

Rule VI, which prescribes exceptions from the requirements of examination or registration, is amended, as to the custom-house service, by extending to all customs districts and to each sub-port or station, the exemption of one chief or principal deputy or assistant collector, heretofore confined to customs districts whose employees numbered one hundred and fifty or more; and as to the internal revenue service, by extending the exemption, already in force, of one employee in each internal revenue district who shall act as cashier or chief deputy or assistant collector, so as to include also one deputy collector in each internal revenue district where the number of employees in the collector's office exceeds four, and one deputy collector in each stamp or branch office. But this rule as amended, further provides that all appointments to the positions in the customs and internal revenue service excepted by this rule shall be subject to an examination to be prescribed by the Secretary of the Treasury, not disapproved by the Civil Service Commission, equal to the examination held by said commission for positions of like grade, such examinations to be conducted by the Commission, in accordance with its regulations:

All the amendments above mentioned were recommended by the Secretary of the Treasury, and approved by the Civil Service Commission.

In entire harmony with these official acts and declarations, the first Annual Message of President McKinley, received by Congress on the 6th of this month, included among other topics the further improvement of the civil service, renewing his pledges to that end. And while referring to the power of removal for incompetency or inefficiency as a vital safeguard to the reform, the President again declared his conviction that the system has the approval of the people, and his purpose to uphold and extend it.

If, as I have assumed, the true attitude and policy of a great political party, and the obligations to the people at large which it accepts by seeking and gaining success at the polls, are to be judged by the formal declarations and pledges of its authorized representatives, by the political issues which it tenders to its opponents and by the official acts and declarations of those who, in its name and through its support, have been charged with the responsibilities of government,— then the inquiry as to the present attitude and obligations of the Republican party of the United States, in respect of the conduct of the civil service, the honest enforcement and extension of the existing civil service law, the faithful application of the merit system to appointments and removals from administrative offices, and the unflinching opposition to the spoils system which that implies, is fully answered by the acts and declarations above stated. If the Republican party, and the men who on the faith of its promises have been entrusted by the people of the United States with the conduct of the government, are not pledged to these things, to what are they pledged? In no partisan spirit, but as a citizen who values the immense power of party organization in proportion as it is honestly used for worthy ends, I rejoice that such an answer can be made to that inquiry,— still more in the assurance afforded by the exalted personal character and honorable public career of the President, that these pledges will be faithfully kept.

Such is the present attitude of the Republican party in relation to civil service reform. But the history and traditions of a great party count for much in any horoscope of its future. As we have seen, that party, at the opening of the campaign of 1896, in submitting its principles and policy to the considerate judgment of the American people, not only claimed for itself the authorship of the Civil Service Act of 1883, and the credit of having always sustained it, but referred to its repeated declarations, once more renewed, that it " shall be thoroughly and honestly enforced and extended wherever practicable."

It may be of interest to briefly recall the facts which support that claim, with some reference to events which preceded them, in which prominent Republicans took part. And in so doing, I desire to acknowledge with sincere thanks the valuable data furnished me by the indefatigable and thoroughly well-informed Secretary of the League.

As already stated, the enactment of the civil service law of 1883 was the culmination of a struggle which really began in Congress in 1867. Three years earlier, in 1864, that eminent Republican, Charles Sumner, of Massachusetts, introduced in the Senate the first civil service reform bill; but it was not seriously discussed or acted upon in either House.

In January, 1867, Thomas A. Jenckes, an able and prominent Republican member of the House from Rhode Island, presented an elaborate report from the Joint Committee on Retrenchment of the 39th Congress, embodying a vast amount of authentic information, including the experience of foreign governments, concerning the proper conduct of the civil service, and advocating its reform substantially on the lines since adopted. In May, 1868, in the 40th Congress, Mr. Jenckes presented a second report, accompanied by a bill to regulate the civil service, which was made a special order for a subsequent day. The facts and principles set forth in these two reports, covering three hundred printed pages, were supported by Mr. Jenckes in speeches of great force, and furnished data of great value to the Civil Service Commission of 1871: but it was seed time, too early for harvest, and his party did not commit itself to the measure. But the seed was sown, the education of public sentiment began, and one of its earliest and most valuable lessons was contained in the masterly address of George William Curtis before the American Social Science Association in October, 1869, upon civil service reform.

In March, 1869, President Grant's first term began. In his annual message of December, 1870, he earnestly called the attention of Congress to the necessity of a reform in the civil service, declaring that no duty so much embarrassed the executive and heads of departments as that of appointments, that no such arduous and thankless labor was imposed upon Senators and Representatives as that of finding places for constituents, that the existing system did not secure the best men, and often not even fit men for public places, and that the elevation and purification of the civil service would be hailed with approval by the whole people of the United States.

During the last week of that session of Congress, ending March 3, 1871, Senator Trumbull, of Illinois, introduced a bill which went to the House in the form of an amendment to the pending appropriation bill. It passed both Houses, and was approved by the President on the same day, March 3. This bill, now known as Section 1753 of the Revised Statutes, was as follows:

"The President is authorized to prescribe such regulations for the admission of persons into the civil service of the United States as may best promote the efficiency thereof and ascertain the fitness of each candidate in respect to age, health, character, knowledge, and ability for the branch of service into which he seeks to enter; and for this purpose he may employ suitable persons to conduct such inquiries, and may prescribe their duties, and establish regulations for the conduct of persons who may receive appointments in the civil service."

It may fairly be said that in passing this bill, the Republican party, under the leadership of President Grant, whatever its subsequent shortcomings, distinctly took ground in favor of the reform, and President Grant during the next three years gave it his earnest support.

On March 4th, 1871, he appointed an excellent commission, with George William Curtis at its head, to prescribe rules for carrying the Act into effect. On December 18, 1871, the Commission presented its report, prepared by Mr. Curtis, with appropriate rules, which the President adopted, at once transmitting the report to Congress by special message, announcing his purpose to faithfully execute the rules, and asking for all the strength which Congress could give him to carry out the reforms proposed.

In April, 1872, the Advisory Board appointed by the President under these rules made a further report, grouping various offices, and accompanied by further regulations, which were at once adopted and promulgated by executive order. In his annual message in December, 1872, the President, referring to the abuses which had grown up through appointments to office as a reward of political service, again declared his purpose to apply these rules so as to secure the greatest possible reform in the civil service, and recommended legislation to make them permanent. In his annual message of December, 1873, he again commended the reform to Congress, recommending the appointment of a committee of Congress to act with the Civil Service Board in devising permanent rules, "which will secure the services of honest and capable officials and which will also protect them in a degree of independence while in office."

In his annual message of December, 1874, the President again commended the reform to Congress, stating that the effect of the civil service rules was beneficial, and tended to elevate the service, but that it was impracticable to maintain them without direct and positive support of Congress: further stating that if Congress should adjourn without positive legislation on the subject he would regard such action as a disapproval of the system and that competitive examinations would be abandoned. Congress did adjourn without such action, and for the time the progress of the reform was arrested.

Meanwhile the growth of public sentiment in favor of the reform produced its effect upon the Republican party at large and even among certain of its leaders who would gladly have seen it fail. The National Republican platform of 1872 contained the following declaration:

"Any system of the civil service under which the subordinate positions of the Government are considered rewards for mere party zeal is fatally demoralizing, and we therefore favor a reform of the system by laws which shall abolish the evils of patronage and make honesty, efficiency, and fidelity the essential qualifications for public positions, without practically creating a life tenure of office."

The Republican platform of 1876, reported by Senator Hawley, of Connecticut, and unanimously adopted, contained the following:

"Under the constitution the President and heads of departments are to make nominations for office; the Senate is to advise and consent to appointments, and the House of Representatives is to accuse and prosecute faithless officers. The best interest of the public service demands that these distinctions be respected: that Senators and Representatives who may be judges and accusers should not dictate appointments to office. The invariable rule in appointments should have reference to the honesty, fidelity and capacity of the appointees, giving to the party in power those places where harmony and vigor of administration require its policy to be represented, but permitting all others to be filled by persons selected with sole reference to the efficiency of the public service, and the right of all citizens to share in the honor of rendering faithful service to the country."

In March, 1877, President Hayes was inaugurated. In his Inaugural Address he dwelt upon the paramount necessity of reform in the civil service, referring to the platforms of both the Republican and the Democratic parties in 1876, as expressing the united voice and will of the whole country and virtually pledging both parties to give it their unreserved support. His first annual message in December, 1877, dwelt at length on the subject and urged an appropriation to enable the Civil Service Commission to continue its work. Mr. Curtis having resigned from the Commission in 1875, Mr. Dorman B. Eaton was subsequently appointed its chairman, and in May, 1877, at the request of the President, but at his own expense, visited England, studied the civil service system there, and subsequently published the result of his researches in his well-known and valuable Report entitled, " Civil Service in Great Britain." But that Congress failed to respond to the President's request, and his annual Message of December, 1879, again urged, at still greater length, the necessity of the reform, strongly denouncing the evils of a partisan spoils system, and referring to the repeated recommendations of President Grant, the salutary results of the competitive system established by the Civil Service Commission of 1871, and the additional testimony in favor of that system furnished by the reports of the Secretary of the Interior, the

Postmaster General, and the postmasters and collectors in New York and other large cities, where it was still maintained. I need not remind you with what firmness and complete practical success the Secretary of the Interior under President Hayes, now the honored and worthy successor of George William Curtis as President of this League, exemplified the methods and the benefits of genuine civil service reform throughout his department, during his entire term of office.

In June, 1880, the Republican National Convention adopted, without a division, as part of its official declaration of party principles and purposes, the following:

" The Republican party, adhering to principles affirmed by its last National Convention of respect for the Constitutional rules covering appointments to office, adopts the declaration of President Hayes that the reform of the civil service should be thorough, radical and complete. To this end it demands the co-operation of the Legislative with the Executive Department of the Government, and that Congress shall so legislate that fitness, ascertained by proper, practical tests, shall admit to the public service."

President Hayes' last message, in December, 1880, again recommended the reform of the civil service, especially in the method of appointment and removal by legislation; but no responsive legislation was had.

President Garfield, in his Inaugural Address, on March 4th, 1881, declaring that the civil service could never be placed on a satisfactory basis until it was regulated by law, announced his purpose, at the proper time, to ask Congress, for the good of the service and the protection of executive officers and employees, to legislate concerning appointments and removals. This purpose was defeated by his untimely and tragic death in September following. But his deliberate and public utterances in Congress and elsewhere, long previously made, leave no doubt as to what his recommendations would have been. Seldom, in brief compass, have the evils of what he described as " the corrupting doctrine that ' to the victors belong the spoils,' shamelessly announced as an article of political faith and practice," been more clearly pointed out than by General Garfield in an elaborate article entitled "A Century of Congress," published in the *Atlantic Monthly* for June, 1877.

The first session of the 47th Congress began on December 5th, 1881, the Senate being composed of 37 Republicans, 37 Democrats, 1 Independent and 1 Readjuster; and the House, of 290 members, of whom 150 were Republicans and 140 Democrats, with three vacant seats. President Arthur's first message, received on December 6th, discussed at length the plans proposed for the reform of the civil service. Conceding the success of the competitive system in Great Britain, he expressed doubts as to the applicability of some features of that system to the civil service of the United States. But he stated that if Congress should establish competitive tests for admission to the service, no such doubts would deter him from giving the measure his earnest support, and earnestly recommended the appropriation of $25,000.00 per annum for the enforcement of the Civil Service Act of 1871; promising, with such aid, to execute the provisions of that law according to its letter and spirit. Congress responded by appropriating only $15,000 for that purpose, under circumstances graphically told by Mr. Curtis in his first annual address as President of this League. To that address I must refer you for a characteristically brilliant sketch of the condition and prospects of the reform at that time, my present purpose being solely to state, as briefly as possible, the position of the Republican party through its representatives with reference to the reform.

On December 6, 1881, Mr. Pendleton, of Ohio, a Democrat, introduced in the Senate a bill bearing his name, but drafted by the Committee on Legislation of the New York Civil Service Reform Association, of which Mr. Dorman B. Eaton was chairman. And in January, another bill was introduced by Senator Dawes, of Massachusetts, a Republican, also looking to the substitution of merit for favor in minor appointments. These bills were referred to a committee, of which Senator Hawley of Connecticut, a Republican, was Chairman, which in May reported the Pendleton bill, somewhat amended, supporting it by a statement of the evils of the spoils system, a sketch of the movement for reform, and an appendix containing important testimony concerning the reformed methods pursued in the New York Custom-House and Post Office. At the same session, bills of like character were introduced in the House and referred to a select committee on reforms in the civil service, but not reported on; nor was the Pendleton bill further discussed in the Senate at that session.

During the summer and fall of 1882, the friends of the reform, notably the President and members of this League, redoubled their efforts to arouse public sentiment, in view of the general election to be held in November. The result is a matter of history, and was thus tersely described by Mr. Curtis in his Annual Address at your meeting in August, 1883:

" The issue was plainly made and an appeal taken at the polls. The result of the election was startling and impressive. The most conspicuous enemies of reform were dismissed by their constituents from the public service, and although it is not always easy precisely to define the significance of a general election, it was universally conceded, that, whatever else the result might mean, it was a clear and decisive demand of the country for civil service reform. The response of Congress was immediate and never was the flexibility of a popular system more signally displayed."

The significance of this statement lies in the fact that the Republicans elected in November to the 48th Congress numbered only 119, as against 150 in the 47th, while the number of Democrats rose from 140 to 201. I must again refer you to Mr. Curtis' address for an account, sparkling with characteristic humor and delicate sarcasm, of the progress of the Pendleton bill in both houses when the 47th Congress re-assembled. From the moment that Congress met, the mandate of the people still thundering in their ears, this question took precedence over all others. The President's message frankly urged its passage and promised his hearty co-operation in enforcing it. Within a week it was taken up in the Senate, and was passed on December 27th by 38 yeas to 5 nays; 23 Republicans, of whom Benjamin Harrison, of Indiana, was one, 14 Democrats and 1 Independent voting for, and 5 Democrats against it. In the House, on January 4th, Mr. Kasson, of Iowa, a Republican, and Chairman of the Civil Service Committee, reported the bill as passed by the Senate, without amendment. It was taken up under a suspension of the rules, thirty minutes debate allowed, and passed by 155 yeas to 47 nays; the affirmative vote being 100 Republicans, including William McKinley, 51 Democrats and 4 Independents: and the negative vote 39 Democrats, 7 Republicans and 1 Independent. Unquestionably the Republican party adopted and passed the Pendleton Bill, and by passing it, they fulfilled, at last, the promises which Republican National Conventions had constantly made for ten years preceding.

President Arthur promptly fulfilled his own promise to give the reform system fair play by appointing as Commissioners Mr. Dorman B. Eaton of New York, Dr. J. M. Gregory of Illinois, and Judge L. D. Thoman of Ohio; the gentleman first named being well described by Mr. Curtis in the same address as " one of the ablest, sincerest and most devoted friends of the reform." On March 9, 1883, the Commission was organized, and in July the system went into operation: the places originally included in the classified service, by direction of the President, numbering 13,924.

The Republican National Convention of 1884 met at Chicago on June 3, after a year's experience of the working of the system. The platform unanimously recommended by the Committee on Resolutions, as reported by William McKinley, Jr., of Ohio, and adopted without dissent, contained the following:

" Reform of the civil service, auspiciously begun under Republican administration, should be completed by the further extension of the reform system already established by law to all the grades of the service to which it is applicable. The spirit and purpose of the reform should be observed in all executive appointments, and all laws at variance with the objects of existing reform legislation should be repealed, to the end that the dangers to free institutions which lurk in the power of official patronage may be wisely and effectively avoided."

By the election of Mr. Cleveland as President in November, 1884, and of a clear majority of 21 in the House of Representatives of the 49th Congress, the Democratic party became responsible for the enforcement of the Civil Service Act during the next four years. The conduct of the civil service during that period is not within the scope of this paper, but it may be noted that the number of classified places which during President Arthur's term had increased by natural growth to 15,573, was nearly doubled under President Cleveland: 7,259 being added by his orders, and 4,498 by natural growth, making a total of 27,320 at the close of his term. And the Democratic National Convention which, on June 5, 1888, at St. Louis, re-nominated Mr. Cleveland for the Presidency by acclamation, declared in its platform that "honest civil service reform has been inaugurated and maintained by President Cleveland and he has brought the public service to the highest standard of efficiency."

Two weeks later, on June 19, 1888, the Republican National Convention, at Chicago, met this challenge by nominating for President, Benjamin Harrison, who as a senator from Indiana had voted for the Pendleton bill in 1883, and against all subsequent efforts to repeal or cripple it, and by unanimously adopting a platform, from which I quote as follows:

"The men who abandoned the Republican party in 1884 and continue to adhere to the Democratic party, have deserted not only the cause of honest government, of sound finance, of freedom and purity of the ballot, but especially have deserted the cause of reform in the civil service. We will not fail to keep our pledges because they have broken theirs, or because their candidate has broken his. We therefore repeat our declaration of 1884, to wit: The reform of the civil service, auspiciously begun under the Republican Administration, should be completed by the further extension of the reform system, already established by law, to all the grades of the service to which it is applicable. The spirit and purpose of the reform should be observed in all executive appointments, and all laws at variance with the object of existing reform legislation should be repealed, to the end that the dangers to free institutions which lurk in the power of official patronage may be wisely and effectually avoided."

General Harrison, in his letter of acceptance, cordially

approved "the clear and forcible expression of the Convention upon this subject," advocating further legislation to include other branches of the service, and declaring his sincere purpose, if elected, to advance the reform. He was elected President in November, 1888, and the Republican party, having a majority in both houses of the 51st Congress, again became responsible for carrying on the reform.

President Harrison's first annual message, of December 3, 1889, discussed at length the operation of the Act and certain criticisms thereon, suggesting certain improvements and recommending appropriations for an increase in the clerical force. In his subsequent messages the subject was discussed in a like spirit. During his term of office 15,598 places were added to the classified service, 8,690 by his orders and the remainder by natural growth. In 1891 the merit system was also applied by General Tracy, Secretary of the Navy, to the employees of the Government Navy Yards, by an admirable and effective order, which removed more than 5,000 places from the sphere of politics. It should be remarked here, to the credit of the succeeding administration, that in 1893 this order was continued in force by Secretary Herbert, and President Cleveland's order of May 6, 1896, which greatly enlarged the classified service, brought these and many other places for the first time within the civil service rules.

That the Republican party had not changed its position was manifested by the action of the Republican National Convention in June, 1892, over which Wm. McKinley, Jr., presided, in nominating Benjamin Harrison for re-election, and unanimously adopting as part of its platform the following:

"We commend the spirit and evidence of reform in the Civil Service, and the wise and consistent enforcement by the Republican party of the laws regulating the same."

To this the Democratic National Convention, meeting a few days later, responded by again nominating Mr. Cleveland for President, upon a platform declaring that public office is a public trust, affirming former demands for the reform of the civil service, and calling for the honest enforcement of all laws regulating the same. So far as platforms and public pledges went there was nothing to choose between the two great parties. In November, 1892, Mr. Cleveland was again elected President and the Democratic party once more became responsible for the reform. During his administration about 44,000 places were added to the classified service, including, however, the 5,000 Navy Yard employees affected by Secretary Tracy's order above mentioned, and 2,412 by natural growth.

At the date of the 13th annual report of the Civil Service Commission, January 30, 1897, the total approximate number of positions in the civil branch of the government, as stated in that report, was 178,717, of which 87,107 were in the classified service and 91,610 in the unclassified service; but of the number last mentioned about 5,500 are not classified, for reasons deemed best for the service, 4,800 are appointed by the President and confirmed by the Senate, and nearly 8,900 are persons employed merely as laborers or workmen, leaving 72,371 places considered as classifiable but not yet classified, of whom 66,725 are Postmasters of the fourth class, who are appointed, and may be removed, by the Postmaster General. And this was in effect the status of the civil service in November, 1896, when both the great parties last went before the country, with the results already mentioned.

Well might the Republican candidate for the Presidency, in accepting his party's nomination for that great office, declare that its latest pledge was but in keeping with the position it had taken for the past twenty-four years. Each one of the six Republican National Conventions which during that period announced the party policy, emblazoned this reform upon its banner. Every President, whose candidacy was supported during that period by that party, urged upon Congress the necessity of the reform, and the legislation necessary to make it effective,— Grant, Hayes, Garfield, Arthur and Harrison. True it is that within the party lines, especially before 1883, were men whose reluctant support, still more their avowed hostility, obstructed the reform. But, as we have seen, while they could obstruct, they could not control the party: though, as we have also seen, their unfaithfulness to its pledges bred a popular distrust which brought it to disaster and defeat. "Sweet are the uses of adversity." The disastrous rout of the Republican party at the polls in November, 1882, was swiftly followed by the enactment of the Pendleton bill, under a suspension of its rules by the Republican majority in a House in which, three months earlier, that bill was not deemed worthy of a Committee report.

It would seem incredible, alike on grounds of party sagacity, of fidelity to party pledges and to the honored leader who urges their fulfillment, and, I do not hesitate to add, of personal honor, that any Republican member of Congress should take part in repudiating the principles and policy of the Civil Service Act. And yet if the press reports are true, not only was the opening of the present session signalized by attacks upon the Civil Service Act,— not merely it methods and its administration, but the policy it embodies,— but later reports state that on the evening of the 11th, a conference of Republican members of the House was held for the purpose of securing changes in the Act, at which a Committee was appointed, with Mr. Grosvenor, of Ohio, as Chairman, who were instructed to examine the bills pending before the Civil Service Committee and report thereon: and that the expediency of attacking and opposing the civil service items in the pending appropriation bill was considered, though not determined on.

These statements await confirmation, and it would be premature to comment upon them now. If the assaults upon the merit system, so often defeated, are to be renewed, its friends in and out of Congress will be heard from at the proper time. They welcome every honest inquiry into its operation, for in the end the truth is sure to prevail. Indifference, not inquiry, reckless and false assertions, not sincere investigation, have been the obstacles to the reform.

But a certain interest attaches to such statements, in view of a speech made by Mr. Grosvenor, published in the Congressional Record of August 11, 1897, as part of the proceedings of the House on July 19th. It reads like one of those explosive and ephemeral contributions to political literature which, doubtless to the relief of the author, certainly to the comfort of his colleagues, from time to time find vent through the safety valve of a "leave to print." It contains many assertions of a kind familiar to the advocates of the merit system: assertions which — to continue the simile — resemble the clouds and wreaths of vapor which escape from an overcharged boiler, not only in their noisy emergence, extreme tenuity and lack of propelling power, but in their sudden collapse and condensation into harmless drizzle when brought into contact with the pure cold atmosphere of truth.

For example, a letter of George Washington is quoted in which he declined to appoint to "*an office of consequence*" a man whose political tenets were adverse to the measures the general government were pursuing, because, in the judgment of Washington, he would thereby certainly be enabled to embarrass its movements — which "would be a sort of political suicide." And then follows a denunciation of the Civil Service Act, as contrary to the views of Washington. In fact, that letter (Sparks' Writings of Washington, Vol. XI, p. 74) expressly states that the office which Washington then had in mind was that of *Attorney General* — a Cabinet office, which neither the Civil Service Act nor any scheme of reform yet proposed has ever included. Why did not Mr. Grosvenor mention that fact? The answer to that question is obvious.

But the author of this essay, still speaking in Washington's behalf, further assures us that—

— "little did he ever dream that the hour would come · in American history when the President would have been [*sic*] *forced by law to yield the appointing power given him by the terms of the Constitution* to a bureau independent of the President, whose orders, if he shall violate them, *will lay him liable to indictment and impeachment*."

Mr. Grosvenor, by profession at least, is a lawyer. Does he really imagine, or is he only trying to persuade his confiding constituents, that by any provision of the Civil Service Act the President's appointing power *under the Constitution* is or can be in the slightest degree affected or impaired? There is not the least ground for asserting that any bureau or commission or officer under the Civil Service Act can issue any order which can possibly trench upon the President's appointing power under the Constitution. Is he really ignorant that if that Act did contain any provision inconsistent with that power it would be simply void?

And how shall we reconcile this learned jurist's solicitude for the President's dignity with the following assertion, replete with adjectives, but quite ignoring the fact that every occupant of that office during the past twenty-four years has earnestly advocated the merit system?

" There has never been a cold, deliberate, dispassionate and candid or just argument made by these men why this law should be upheld and vindicated. They have never yet dared to touch the true test of the efficiency or inefficiency, the beneficent or non-beneficent character of the administration of this law in the United States."

This sentence follows an uncomplimentary reference to Mr. Logan Carlisle and to Mr. Procter, the present Chairman of the Civil Service Commission. It would probably amuse Mr. Logan Carlisle should he ever learn that Mr. Grosvenor had challenged him to defend the Civil Service Act. Mr. Procter, as we all know, has effectively vindicated it by reference to facts for the absence of which this essay is conspicuous. But the implication is clear that the law is not susceptible of a candid and just defense, and that no proof has been offered by any one, no test has been made, of its efficiency or its beneficent operation. In fact, after making the sneering charge that Mr. Jenckes, in 1867, " played to the public galleries," he ventures upon the assertion (I quote his words) —

" At that time Mr. Jenckes was challenged over and over again to bring forward any reason why such a law was to be passed. *He was never able to do it*, and finally, after his defeat, as above stated, he abandoned the field, so far as Washington and the Departments were concerned and undertook to try and reach inefficiency, as he called it, in the customs and internal revenue service."

This is history, as she is wrote — by Mr. Grosvenor. No one has told him, apparently, that President Grant and his successors, Hayes, Garfield, Arthur, Harrison and McKinley, have made some official declarations upon that subject. He has not, perhaps, had time to read the voluminous and cumulative testimony, year by year, of Cabinet officers, heads of departments, collectors and postmasters in the great cities, gladly given in favor of the greatly increased efficiency and economy in the public service which this Act has produced. Yet the library of Congress is open to him.

But enough of these samples of statesmanship, culled from a few of the fifty-three closely printed columns devoted to the denunciation of that iniquitous and indefensible law. Still assuming that the press reports of the debate in the House on Tuesday of last week may be trusted, not the least significant feature of it, as reported, is the statement that Mr. Bailey of Texas, the leader of the Democratic party in the House, commended Mr. Grosvenor's utterances against building up an office-holding class in this country — "a doctrine,— he said,— which was almost literally embodied in the Chicago platform." One is distantly reminded of the Arabic proverb — though I should be far from applying it to any person so estimable as Mr. Bailey and his Democratic colleagues — "The blessings of the evil genii, which were curses, were upon him."

It has been the purpose of this paper to show the true relation of the Republican party to civil service reform, by setting forth the principles and policy to which it stands publicly pledged, as declared by the official representatives of that party. The record speaks for itself. The American people, who, in 1896, accepted the pledges of that party, will sit in judgment upon its fulfillment, or betrayal, of their trust.

The Democratic Party and Civil Service Reform.

By Moorfield Storey.

It may properly be said that the Democratic Party is under a peculiar obligation to promote the reform of the civil service; the obligation felt by every honorable man, to repair a wrong which he has done. It was the Democratic party under the lead of Andrew Jackson which first treated the public offices as plunder and which under him and his successors cherished the spoils system so lovingly as to make it a cardinal principle of our government. In thirty years it had become so well established that even President Lincoln in the midst of our civil war recognized its binding force. He could say in his despair, "I wish I had time to attend to the Southern question, but these office seekers demand all my time. I am like a man so busy letting rooms at one end of my house that I have not time to put out the fire which is burning in the other," but he could not escape from degrading bondage to the barbarous maxim, "To the victors belong the spoils."

It is not perhaps surprising that a party, devoted to the support of slavery as the Democratic party then was, did not clearly see how inconsistent with true Democratic principles was a system which made every officeholder a slave, whose acts, whose words and whose opinions, even, must be subject to the will of his patron and master. The slavery contest was in fact a war, in which, as in every war, God was forgotten. In the struggle to retain the control of the government the Democratic leaders used every weapon that opportunity offered, and did not stop to reconcile their practice too nicely with the traditional principles of their party. In the heat of that tremendous conflict the American people had no time to consider administrative reform.

When however the contest was over and the smoke of the battle had cleared away, the scandals of the spoils system, which like every other abuse had flourished amid the disorders of war, forced themselves upon the public attention. The evils which had been tolerated under the first administration of General Grant had made men think, and many of the most earnest Republicans were beginning to waver in their allegiance to an organization, which seemed determined to ignore or condone the corrupting practices of party leaders.

The Democrats saw the weak point in the record of their opponents and sought to attract dissatisfied Republicans by espousing the cause of reform. The party needed new issues and new leaders, and it did not shrink even from the desperate step of nominating a life-long enemy, in the person of Horace Greeley, as its candidate for President.

The reform of the civil service was already commanding strong support. President Grant had commended it to the attention of Congress in his message of December 5th, 1870, and on March 3d, 1871, the first civil service reform law received his approval. The experiment had begun when the National Democratic Convention was held in 1872, and the Democratic party took an unequivocal position on the question. Its language was clear and distinct.

" The civil service of the Government has become a mere instrument of partisan tyranny and personal ambition and an object of selfish greed. It is a scandal and reproach upon free institutions and breeds a demoralization dangerous to the perpetuity of Republican government. We therefore regard a thorough reform of the civil service as one of the most · pressing necessities of the hour."

This is strong language, but it only expressed the unanimous opinion of the American people at the time, if we may judge from platform professions, for the conventions of all parties made similar declarations. The spirit of independence was abroad in the land, and independent votes were in demand.

The result of the election in the autumn of 1872 gave the Democratic party no opportunity of proving its sincerity. The war was too recent. The Republicans retained power by an overwhelming majority, but used it so that in 1876 the people found themselves engaged in the most doubtful political contest which the country had known. The Democratic party selected as its candidate a Democrat and undertook in its platform to state the principles of the Democratic party. Among these was included the reform of the civil service, and no party ever made a stronger and clearer declaration on this subject than the following statement, which is said to have been written by Mr. Tilden, then fresh from his victory over the spoils system in the City and State of New York.

"Reform is necessary in the civil service. Experience proves that efficient economical conduct of the governmental business is not possible, if its civil service be subject to change at every election, be a prize fought for at the ballot box, be a brief reward of party zeal instead of posts of honor, assigned for proved competency and held for fidelity in the public employ: that the dispensing of patronage should neither be a tax upon the time of all our public men nor the instrument of their ambition. . . . President, Vice-President, Judges, Senators, Representatives, Cabinet officers, these and all others in authority are the people's servants. Their offices are not a private perquisite: they are a public trust."

Taught perhaps by adversity, but with every prospect of power before it, the Democratic party returned to the principles of its founders. It recognized the great truth that the spoils system rests upon patronage, and that patronage is aristocratic and not democratic. No man should owe the privilege of serving his country to the favor of another. All are entitled to equal opportunities, and the country, another name for us all, is entitled to the best service. The equal rights of all and the greatest good of the greatest number, these are the corner stones of Democracy and of civil service reform. The Democratic party, freed from the blight of slavery, became again a great power in the nation when it re-asserted its fundamental principles in the language just quoted.

In 1880 the party in general language pledged itself "anew to the constitutional doctrines and traditions of the Democratic party, embodied in the platform of the National Convention of the party" including "a general and thorough reform of the civil service." This must be interpreted as reiterating the language which has been quoted from the earlier platform, though in itself less specific.

It is not, however, from party platforms that the purposes of a party are to be gathered. In the same year Mr. Pendleton, of Ohio, a Democratic leader, introduced in the Senate of the United States " a bill to regulate and improve the civil service of the United States," which was referred to a select committee of the Senate. This bill was modelled upon the earlier measure of Mr. Jenckes, but before any action was taken upon it, a carefully framed bill prepared by several gentlemen who had the subject much at heart, among whom that early, devoted and unwavering friend of our cause, Mr. Dorman B. Eaton, was most active, was laid before Mr. Pendleton and by him readily accepted as a substitute for his own less perfect measure. This bill was reported by Mr. Pendleton on February 16th, 1881, and he presented with it an admirable report, in which he took the most advanced ground in favor of the reform.

This bill was not reached during the session, but he introduced it again and on December 13th, 1881, supported it with a powerful speech, closing with an appeal to his party associates, in which he said, "We are not in majority. We have no offices now. The chances of time will sooner or later put them in our grasp. Let us now declare that we will have none of their offices except those which may be won by merit, let us give this earnest of our sincerity in a great reform, let us give this token of the purity and patriotism of our coming administration of the government, let us convince the people, even our opponents, that we contend for power not that we may enjoy the emoluments of office, but that we may lead the country in the pathways of advancement and beneficence under the inspiration of a true democracy. The patronage, however pleasant for the moment, is a snare and a curse to any man or party."

Thus by a Democratic leader, in a speech which states the true principles of his party, was launched for a second time the great measure, which was to become the law of this country.

It was referred again to the committee and carefully considered. On May 15th, 1882, it was reported by Mr. Pendleton to the Senate with a recommendation that it pass, and the report which accompanied it contained a statement of evidence and facts, which was of the greatest value. The bill did not come up for a consideration during that session. The Republican party controlled the government and their President had urged the reform, but the House had refused to appropriate even the modest sum of $25,000 for the support of the civil service commission, and only on the motion of Mr. Holman, a Democrat, appropriated $15,000. This was the era of Jay Hubbell, and in this company I need say no more. The atmosphere of Congress when he was the chairman of the Republican Congressional Committee was not favorable to civil service reform.

The people, however, were not blind, and when Congress met again December, 1882, the Democratic party had swept the country. In many districts it was Republican hostility to civil service reform that defeated their candidates. Theodore Lyman in Massachusetts was elected on that issue and so were others, though less clearly. Congress understood the lesson. The session began on December 4th, 1882, and on the 12th Senator Pendleton brought his bill before the Senate, which entered upon its consideration with such diligence that on the 27th of December it passed the Senate by a vote of thirty-eight to five. The five were all Democrats, to their shame be it said, but the leaders of the party, Bayard, Pendleton, Lamar, Vest, Garland and even Gorman supported the bill, and that just after their triumph at the poll seemed to assure them the control of the offices in the near future.

The House was more expeditious. On January 4th the Senate bill was reported, and after thirty minutes' debate was passed by a vote of one hundred and fifty-five to forty-seven. Neither party was unanimous, but only a small minority of either was found to oppose the bill. This result conspicuously shows the salutary effect of defeat upon a party, and the lesson may well be taken to heart. Congressmen are quick to see what votes really mean, and out of many issues discussed they select with unerring accuracy the real cause of their defeat. The change of heart wrought by adversity was quick and complete. Even Jay Hubbell did not record his vote against the bill.

Such is the part which the Democratic party took in laying the foundation of the merit system. It was a Democrat who led the contest, he was supported by the leaders of his party, and it was a Democratic victory which persuaded Congress to pass the bill. The statute then enacted has since held its place, and every year has furnished fresh evidence that it was framed wisely.

Since the passage of this act the the duty of carrying on the work by extending and perfecting the national system has devolved upon the executive. There is much that the legislature can still do, but to-day the pressure is rather to undo than to do. Our efforts are needed to hold the ground which we have won. The President now, as ever since the reform was inaugurated, is more enlightened than Congress.

It was in 1884 that, for the first time since civil service reform became a burning issue, a Democratic President was elected, and the party had an opportunity of proving the sincerity of its professions. The nomination of Grover Cleveland in itself pledged the party to civil service reform, for his record was known. He had signed the first State reform law. He had appointed an admirable commission headed by John Jay. He had seconded their efforts, and was thoroughly committed to the cause. The declarations in his letter of acceptance were full and explicit. I may perhaps quote a few sentences to remind you with what distinct promises the Democratic party returned to power.

" The selection and retention of subordinates in government employment should depend on their ascertained fitness and the value of their work, and they should neither be expected nor allowed to do questionable party service. The interest of the people will be better protected. The estimate of public labor and duty will be immensely improved. Public employment will be open to all who can demonstrate their fitness to enter it, . . . and the public departments will not be filled with those who conceive it their first duty to aid the party to which they owe their places, instead of rendering patient and honest return to the people."

Ante-election professions are notoriously unreliable. The ordinary politician accepts as a political axiom the remark of the eminent English statesman, " However much a party may gain by making promises, it always loses by fulfilling them." President Cleveland, however, took the earliest opportunity to renew in office the pledges he had made as a candidate. In his inaugural address he said with emphasis : " The people demand reform in the administration of the government and the application of business to public affairs. As a means to this end, civil service reform should be in good faith enforced. . . . Those who worthily seek public employment have the right to insist that merit and competency shall be recognized instead of party subserviency."

The President gave the most striking proof of his sincerity when at the very outset of his term he reappointed Henry G. Pearson as Postmaster of New York. We all remember how good men of every party hailed this act and how it excited the politicians, though as Mr. Schurz then said, ".This is probably the only civilized country on the face of the globe where the reappointment of a very efficient capable public officer, regardless of political opinion, would be looked upon as anything extraordinary." Yet we must confess with shame that in this country it was an extraordinary thing, and it afforded us extraordinary pleasure, not only for itself, but because we thought we saw it in the determination to apply the true rule in all appointments.

The standard, however, was too high, not merely for Democrats, but for some civil service reformers. It was not long before the specious suggestion of dividing the offices equally between the two great parties began to find favor, as if the object of civil service reform was only to insure a fair division of spoils. Others urged that if an officer was allowed to serve out his term, it was quite right then to fill the office for political reasons, as if civil service reform meant only a gradual distribution of spoils,—a postponement of plunder. There seemed to many a crying injustice in perpetuating an official force from which Democrats for years had been carefully excluded, and the people were not sufficiently educated to understand the true faith. The Democratic party was not unselfish enough to find sound principle attractive, when it triumphed at its cost, and when the pertinacious efforts of spoilsmen were met in a spirit of compromise by the friends of reform, it is not perhaps surprising that the standard was lowered. The breach once made, it was hard to defend the fort. Within the classified service the rules were applied with reasonable fidelity, but other offices were filled with little regard to the principles of reform. I need only allude to the changes in the Postal Service and the Indian Service. Facts and figures might be given in tedious detail, but it is enough to quote the summing up of Mr. Curtis in his address to the National League on August 3, 1887, when he said:

" Practically there has been a very general partisan reconstruction of the national civil service," and " It wóuld be a great wrong to the cause of which the League is the authorized national representative if it did not plainly and emphatically declare that it does not regard the administration, however worthy of respect and confidence for many reasons, as in any strict sense of the words a civil service reform administration."

We cannot doubt that the President was entirely sincere in his promises of reform. He was a reformer by conviction, and his courage and strength of will were beyond question. That he failed so completely to realize his promises shows how great was the pressure and how slight the assistance which he got from the public. The education of the people was not complete.

But while he failed conspicuously to realize our hopes, he satisfied the Democratic party, which in its national platform of 1888 declared that " Honest reform in the civil service has been inaugurated and maintained by President Cleveland." This was a practical interpretation by politicians of Democratic promises.

Yet the President, while falling far short of our hopes, advanced the reform materially while in office. He found some fourteen thousand offices covered by the rules when he was inaugurated, and he extended the rules so as to add many more, including that important branch of the public service, the Railway Mail Service, and the Bureau of Engraving and Printing. In all some thirteen thousand six hundred places were added to the classified service during his first term. He also, by ordering various investigations, made office-holders feel that the reform law was in active operation and that its provisions could not be neglected with impunity. During his term the civil service reformers were organized and militant, and public education progressed rapidly. Perhaps nothing helped to make men realize the hold which the spoils system had taken upon our people more than the fact that a man so courageous, so sincere and so strong as President Cleveland, had been overborne so completely by the pressure for office.

The Republican party, with the strongest professions in its platform and the most specific promises by its candidate, came into power, largely helped by the votes of civil service reformers, who had been disappointed by Mr. Cleveland and who turned with hope to Mr. Harrison. It is not for me, however to record in this paper how far their hopes were realized. It is enough to say that when the next Presidential election came Mr. Cleveland and Mr. Harrison again led their respective parties.

Four years of adversity had quickened the zeal of the Democratic party for reform. Their declaration in national convention was distinct. "Public office is a public trust. We reaffirm the declaration of the Democratic National Convention of 1876 for the reform of the civil service," which was quoted, "and we call for the honest enforcement of all laws regulating the same." President Cleveland in his letter of acceptance commended "an honest adherence to the letter and spirit of civil service reform," and made other public declarations which gave reformers great reason for hope that his singularly independent position would enable a man of his high purpose and great courage to carry his principles into practice.

The loot of the consulships which immediately followed his return to power was a bitter disappointment. This, with the removals of fourth class postmasters and other departures from sound principle, excited indignant comment at the time, and nothing has occurred since to make us retract anything that was said in condemnation of the removals then made. We must not forget, however, that in his own time and in his own way President Cleveland showed his earnest purpose to advance the reform by extending the classified service almost to the possible limit. By his order of May 6, 1895, he placed under the civil service rules some 30,000 more positions, making the total of classified positions 87,098, and reducing the exempted places from over 2,000 to 775. This order also swept away many opportunties for abuse and made the entire code of rules much more simple and effective. No greater service to the cause of reform has been rendered by any President, and his party should remember that in doing what he did Mr. Cleveland simply fulfilled their promises, recognizing perhaps that the true Democratic party was the many million voters who made him President, and not the few thousand office seekers for whom no votes were cast. The impudence with which these pestilent persons assume that a battle upon great issues is fought only to provide them with salaries is amazing, but it is even more amazing that the real nature of their pretensions and their relative unimportance are not seen more clearly by intelligent men.

Nor was this all. During the same administration Post-master-General Wilson put into operation the best scheme that has yet been devised for extending the merit system to the fourth class offices,—the gradual consolidation of neighboring offices by making them stations of a central office. This change, which increased efficiency and diminished expense, was too serious a blow at the patronage of Senators and it was accordingly prohibited by law. One Democratic spoilsman who was prominent in the work has lost his re-election and he perhaps now recognizes that to the civil service reformers whom he has long contemned, his defeat is in great part due. We may well tender to our friends in Maryland our congratulations upon a victory which crowns one of the most determined and persistent struggles that our movement has seen.

And so if, at the end of May 1896, we had taken a retrospective view of our struggle, we should have seen the Democratic party as soon as it recovered from the strain of the war pledging itself to civil service reform. We should have seen the present law introduced and championed by a Democratic statesman with the support of his party's leaders. We should have found in a Democratic victory the impulse which carried it through Congress, and we should have seen the system which the law established carried to its highest development by a Democratic President. We should have seen that at every step in its progress Democratic " Bosses " and Democratic office-seekers have opposed reform as much as they dared, and that their concentrated and persistent efforts had proved so powerful as to make a Democratic President concede much that his party's promises forbade. None the less these influences had not availed to change the position of the party as a whole. Whenever it met in National Convention it had reaffirmed more or less clearly its allegiance to the reform, which had by repeated declarations become firmly established as a cardinal article of Democratic faith.

A few weeks later the situation changed, and the Democratic organization turned its back upon the leaders who had carried it to victory, and renounced the essential principles of Democracy which are the source of its marvellous vitality. Among other great Democratic causes which it abandoned was the cause of civil service reform. The declaration of the Democratic Convention of 1896 was a model of that perverted dexterity which is able to " keep the word of promise to our ear but break it to our hope." This is the language :

" We are opposed to life tenure in the public service. We favor appointments based upon merit, fixed terms of office, and such an administration of the civil service laws as will afford equal opportunities to all citizens of ascertained fitness."

This may seem to promise reform but the first sentence is the key to its true meaning. There *is* no life tenure, and this attempt to mislead is in keeping with the demagoguery of the whole Bryan movement, which brought the Democratic party to defeat at the polls, as overwhelming as it was richly deserved.

But even then men were found who, without hope of political preferment, held to the faith and rallied round the standard of true Democracy. These men made at Indianapolis the strongest declaration of devotion to our cause and their sincerity is doubted by no one. They stand to-day the only representatives of the true Democratic party.

From this retrospect it appears, and perhaps the lesson is worth teaching, that the strength of the Democratic party at the polls has increased and decreased with its support of reform. When it has taken the highest ground on this question, it has won. When it has receded or faltered, it has lost. While there was in the country a strong body of voters, not tied by partisan feeling to either organization, but considering only the welfare of the country, their votes were the prize for which each party bid. A distinct declaration in favor of civil service reform was necessary to win their support. Each party *out* of office, and seeking to regain it, has been willing to promise more than the same party *in* office and expecting to retain it. The disappointed office seekers of a Presidential term have had influence enough in the next national convention of their party to lower the standard. When this surrender of public interests to private demands has been followed by defeat, the standard rises again.

The activity of Republican spoilsmen to-day is readily explained by the disorganization of the compact force which has stood for reform so long. With the Democratic party committed to the spoils and to heresy of every kind, the Republicans feel that no reform voter can support a Democratic candidate. Believing that the votes of reformers are secure, Republican politicians feel it safe to take a little risk of disgusting them for the sake of reviving the good old days when every Congressman was a patron, who could buy his election with the money of the people, ostensibly spent for the public service, but really to pay for personal support. If we would influence either party, we must still stand a compact body, ready to vote for either which will best help our cause, or better still form a new party, organized to promote by active work what we have at heart. The practice of Hobson's choice, the election between two evils, has gone too far. Let us hope for a party which will give us a positive good.

The real feeling of the two parties can best be judged in the States where each has undisputed sway. If this field is examined, it will be found that in proportion as their power is unquestioned, their zeal for civil service reform has languished. Men who are in earnest use their power to accomplish their real ends, and the failure to use established power in our cause shows that the earnest purpose is lacking. Those of us who have enlisted for the war must stand together, must increase our efforts, must rally to our banner new recruits and must become an organized force, which both parties will fear. The organization of the Gold Democrats is heartily with us, and where independent action is needed we can unite our force with theirs; but the lesson of our whole movement, the lesson which Grosvenor and Gallinger are teaching us to-day is that our strength lies in independence, and that unwavering allegiance to either party is inconsistent with true devotion to civil service reform.

To the Democratic party we may commend the study of their own history. They will find that their principles, their consistent declarations for twenty-five years, and the teachings of their great leaders all support our cause, and that the spoils system is undemocratic. They will find that when they have been strongest in their support of reform, they have been strongest in the country, and that as they have faltered, they have lost ground. Wherever civil service reformers have been strong they have been prompt to punish any treachery to their cause. The party must return to Democratic principles, if it is ever again to be trusted with power, and it must abandon a course which drives from its ranks the men who have led it to victory. Whenever it is ready in all sincerity to say again with Pendleton, "We contend for power, not that we may enjoy the emoluments of office, but that we may lead the country in the pathways of advancement and beneficence under the inspiration of a true Democracy," nothing can keep it from the lasting control of the government. Till then it deserves and will meet only defeat.

Do the American People want Civil Service Reform?

BY CHARLES J. BONAPARTE.

My attention was called some three or four weeks since to a letter addressed to the President by a Mr. J. L. Kennedy* of the "Anti-Civil Service League" (a gentleman of whom my own obscurity had doubtless prevented my hearing sooner), in which occurred the following passage:

" There is not one grain of comfort for the civil-service reformers in the late elections. Look at Maryland! The Legislature of the State submitted a proposed constitutional amendment to the people to be voted on at the recent election. It proposed to erect a State civil-service establishment, patterned after the National Civil Service Commission. As an issue in the campaign, it, like all others, was subordinated to the greater one, which Mr. Gorman's personality brought into the canvass. Nevertheless, the people kept it in mind, and had their eyes on it when they went into the booths to mark their ballots. A Baltimore Republican of some fame, who was in the city Saturday, informed me that the proposed amendment was buried under an adverse majority of 75,000, and that it did not carry in a single county in the State. This, too, notwithstanding the fact there is a strong civil service reform organization in Baltimore, the leading spirit of which is Colonel Charles Napoleon Bonaparte."

Upon the interesting information thus vouchsafed the President by Mr. Kennedy and the "Baltimore Republican of some fame," the Washington correspondent of the *Philadelphia Star*, to whom I should say, I am indebted for knowledge of the measure of "fame" so accorded to myself, comments as follows:

---

*Since this paper was first published I have had some correspondence with Mr. Kennedy : he denies that he belongs to the Anti-Civil-Service League or that he wrote any letter to the President, and says the words I quoted were "exultant remarks" contained in an interview published in the Washington "Post." I congratulate Mr. Kennedy on thus avoiding disreputable associates and refraining from an exhibition of ridiculous presumption ; my authority for both statements was, as I say above, the Washington correspondent of the Philadelphia "Evening Star," whom he calls "Honorable James Rankin Young." I have no acquaintance with this "honorable" person.

"Col. Bonaparte and his confreres were strong enough to go to the Legislature of Maryland and have such a proposed amendment submitted to the electorate ; but they were very weak with the people. It is always thus with the civil-service reformers. They can go before small bodies like Legislatures and conventions, and exert an influence, as Senator Lodge and a few others of them did in St. Louis, when they had a mugwump plank inserted in a Republican platform, but they have little influence with the people."

In point of accuracy these statements rival the well-known definition of a crab mildly criticized by Cuvier. His colleagues of the Academy having described the animal as "a little red fish that walks backwards," his only comments were that it "wasn't a fish, wasn't red and didn't walk backwards." The suggested amendment did *not* "propose to erect a State Civil Service establishment patterned after the National Civil Service Commission," or propose to erect a "State Civil Service establishment" of any sort, kind or description whatsoever. My "confreres" and I were *not* "strong enough to go to the Legislature and have such an amendment submitted to the electorate;" the bill which they and I *did* ask that body to pass it refused to make law, and I did everything in my power to prevent the enactment of the measure actually adopted. In this matter I was most emphatically *not* the "leading spirit" of the "Civil Service Reform organization in Baltimore," for I retired from its presidency a few weeks after the act had been passed because it would not be "led" by me into openly repudiating the proposed amendment. Whatever may be my "weakness" or however "little" my "influence" with the people of my native State, the result of this particular election certainly did not tend to show such weakness or lack of influence, for as I voted on the amendment so voted an overwhelming majority of my fellow citizens. Finally, my middle name is not "Napoleon" and I am not, and have never been, a "Colonel" or a soldier at all.

A very eloquent and plausible preacher of my acquaintance. when privately questioned as to effective, but rather sweeping, statements in his sermons, had the habit of saying : "Now don't let's be too accurate." In this respect (but, it is fair to say of him, in no other) he would have been well qualified for membership in the "National Anti-Civil Service League." The editor of "City and State" said recently of that great body :

" By the way, we desire to inquire of those distinguished gentlemen, Mr. Grosvenor and the rest, why they call their organization by the name which indicates the very opposite of their purpose ? They are *Anti*-Civil Service Reform, but surely not *Anti*-Civil Service. It cannot really be their wish to abolish *the service* which contains all the offices and the salaries these gentlemen are so keen after. How could the League possibly exist if it succeeded in gaining its ostensable purpose,—the abolition of the Civil Service of the United States ?"

I cannot, for once, agree with our good friend of " City and State " as to this. Macaulay was probably mistaken in saying :

"A man who has never been within the tropics does not know what a thunderstorm means ; a man who has never looked on Niagara has but a faint idea of a cataract ; and he who has not read Barere's Memoirs may be said not to know what it is to lie."

Probably " those distinguished gentlemen, Mr. Grosvenor and the rest," have not, for the most part, read Barere's Memoirs; I believe these have only recently been translated and it is likely that few of them have had leisure for foreign literature. For some reasons this may be regretted; they would doubtless read with sympathetic pleasure of Barere's sentiments and actions; it might be hard to find any more commendable if tested by their standards of morality and honor; but for the particular purpose indicated by Macaulay they have no need to read these Memoirs or anything else; however imperfect it may be otherwise, in this respect their education is complete: they may be ignorant of many things, but certainly they cannot "be said not to know what it is to lie." If, therefore, the title chosen for their association embodied a lie, I at least should regard this as in every way appropriate.

But I do not think it does: on the contrary, in choosing their name, they seem to me (for once only and, of course, unwittingly) to have told the truth. These men would convert the public Service of the United States into an asylum for political bums, they would have the Federal offices throughout the country serve as currency wherewith politicians may pay their debts and their bribes ; they would see official salaries once more taxed to pay real and pretended, legitimate, and illegitimate campaign expenses, and the departments at Washington again crowded with men who had known how to make themselves useful, with women who had known how to make themselves agreeable, to Senators and Representatives. Entertaining these purposes, it is, to my mind, eminently fitting that they should proclaim as their end "the abolition of the Civil Service of the United States:" for they would indeed abolish everything in that service worthy of a civilized and Christian Nation.

If, however, these ornaments to our politics told the truth on this occasion, their so doing was beyond question a pure accident, and wholly without precedent on their part, nor have they subsequently given the public the slightest reason to doubt their unfaltering and boundless confidence in the adhesive qualities of unadulterated mendacity: to furnish another illustration of this attractive trait, whether displayed by Mr. Kennedy or by his friend of the *Star*, would scarcely justify a trespass on the limited time of the League; but their reckless talk, as above given, suggests two enquiries of real interest and to which very different men have anxiously sought and still seek answers reassuring as to the future of popular government. Is it true that honorable and disinterested men, for, whatever I may be, such men are my "confreres" among the reformers of Maryland, " can exert an influence before small bodies like Legislatures and Conventions," but "have little influence," are "very weak" with "the people ?" Is it true that "there is not one grain of comfort for the Civil Service Reformers in the late elections ?" or rather that these elections or any other events in our recent history show or suggest that the American people do not want Civil Service Reform?

I will answer the first question from experience, from the experience of the very men to whom the sages of "Anti-Civil Service" refer as my "confreres." Since they formed themselves in 1885 into the Baltimore Reform League they have thrice appealed to the people; in each one of these cases they, or those in sympathy with their purposes, had previously attempted to " exert an influence " on "small bodies " of politicians or public officials to the same end. In 1885 and 1886 they laid before a Democratic President and Secretary of the Interior and afterwards before a Republican Senate overwhelming and practically undisputed proofs of the unfitness for the public employment of a man nominated as Inspector of Indian Agencies; but before these "small" (*very* small) "bodies" they were indeed "very weak." But in 1888, when, emboldened by his "vindication," and perhaps yet more by the prevailing partisan excitement, inseparable from a Presidential campaign, he offered himself as a candidate for an elective local office, though he secured an enthusiastic "endorsement" from another "small body," *i. e.*, the Democratic City Convention, and though his party carried both the City and State, the Reform League was strong enough, had sufficient "influence with the people," to defeat him and defeat him so thoroughly and significantly that since then he has well nigh disappeared from notice in our politics. In 1891 certain of my "confreres" with the help of some other gentlemen who would perhaps disclaim the title, not having yet outgrown a youthful belief in the possibility of "reform within the party," attempted to prevent the continuances in his office of State's Attorney of another man, personally far more estimable, but whose official course had provoked grave and authoritative censure, by remonstrances addressed to the leading politicians of his and their common party then dominant. I have narrated elsewhere the suggestive and ludicrous incidents of this very well meant but very ill-judged effort to "exert an influence" for good on a "small body," made up of the Supreme Boss and his lieutenants; its outcome was a complete and ridiculous failure. Three years later, however, when the same influences which had kept the State's Attorney in his office of public prosecutor secured his nomination as Judge, the "weakness" of the Reform League "with the people" was again tested through its earnest public protest against his election; and again these weaklings in popular favor proved strong enough to administer a decisive defeat to the highly "practical" politicians who had derided their warnings. Some six months since the same feeble organization exposed and censured grave abuses in the office of the Clerk of our Criminal Court, whereby the acceptance of "straw-bail" had become a frequent incident in prosecutions for certain offences. A "small body" of twenty-three men, that is to say, the Grand Jury then serving in that Court, or, to speak more accurately, a still "smaller body" of uncertain number, constituting a majority of the twenty-three, cheerfully accorded the incriminated official a comfortable coat of whitewash, and another "small body," the City Convention of his party, promptly renominated him for the office he so worthily held and which would be filled by the people in November. The Reform League accepted the challenge, and we have a new Clerk at the Criminal Court.

I have cited facts in the history of Baltimore as an answer to the first question, not because the experience of that City in this respect has been exceptionally significant or striking, but because the newspaper correspondent whose words I quoted selected my "confreres" and myself as types of the class he believed to be "weak" and destitute of "influence" with "the people." Innumerable illustrations of the falsehood and even absurdity of his statement could be furnished from almost every part of the Union. It has been demonstrated everywhere, and again and again, that "with the people" the advocates of good government are strong; that with politicians, whether in or out of office, they are pitiably weak. This is not only because the practical and thoroughgoing application of their principles to the conduct of public business would oblige our professional officeholders and office seekers of high and low degree to starve or change their calling and that neither prospect pleases: in truth, an American politician of to-day lives in so dense and unwholesome a moral atmosphere, his views on all questions of conscience or honor are so false and distorted, that he can hardly conceive of a party, or a political organization of any kind, with other ends than to secure support at public expense for as many as possible of its members; that citizens should combine for any other purpose seems to him visionary and absurd. To his mind a political party is kept up for purposes as strictly interested as a railroad or life insurance company: the sentiments of its platform mean no more than the devotion to the public to be found in the prospectus of the former, or the longing to care for the widow and orphan professed in the circulars of the latter; they are advertisements and nothing more; and he openly or secretly believes the "fine talk" of avowed reformers to be, what it would be if uttered by him or his like, mere sham and cant. It is when we break out from this dismal malarial fog of paltry passions and vulgar selfishness into the broad life-giving sunlight of our orderly freedom that we find among Americans, men who yet love justice and hate iniquity.

To answer satisfactorily the second question, we must first state it clearly; in other words, to decide whether the American people want Civil Service Reform, we must understand what is meant by "the American people" and what is meant by "Civil Service Reform," and this is the more needful because there is no little confusion of thought and language, partly wilful but in great part also stupid and careless, as to both subjects. Within the delivery of every faithful and competent letter carrier in the country there could doubtless be found to-day fifty bummers of his own party and as many of the other who would see him removed with delight if through his removal each of them might hope, immediately or at the next turn of the political wheel, for a chance to loaf in his place at the taxpayer's cost : there could also be found a thousand or more men and women, of all shades of political opinion, ready to protest against a change which might turn over their mail to the tender mercies of a rowdy or a drunkard or, at best, a greenhorn. Now when President McKinley says that the people are friendly to Civil Service Reform, he is thinking of the thousand respectable citizens who, in every such district, are quietly attending to their legitimate business; when Gallinger and Grosvenor and *their* " confreres " talk of the people as hostile to Civil Service Reform, they are thinking (at least, it is charitable to suppose that they may perhaps be thinking) of the hundred political mendicants within the same space who are clamoring or whining for " recognition," and who, if tenfold less numerous, are a hundredfold more noisy and obtrusive than their decent and busy fellow countrymen. Indeed, although judging them by their records, there is a fair enough presumption that any allegation of fact made by one of these eminent persons is a deliberate falsehood, it is not improbable that, in thus defaming the people, they may enjoy the sensation, which must have all the charm of novelty, of believing themselves to speak the truth. A well known French statesman was said to be so thoroughly in sympathy with the public sentiment of his country that, to know what France thought on any subject, he had only to ask himself what he thought about it : few of us may have as good grounds as he had to claim that, as we think so think the people, but in conjecturing the thoughts of that vast mass of humanity which we so name, every one, more or less consciously, generalizes from his own opinions and wishes and those of the men among whom he lives, with whom he is brought into hourly contact. These men are themselves professional politicians; they live surrounded by other professional politicians and when they speak or think of " the people's" wishes, sentiments and opinions, they really mean their own wishes, sentiments and opinions and those of their fellows in the craft. Do then the views of American politicians fairly reflect the views of the American people ? That we may judge, let us further ask what manner of men are they and how do they live ?

The typical American politician, as developed by the spoils system of politics, earns his living by holding, when he can get it, a public office (usually of subordinate importance and purely ministerial functions) in return for past or expected party work. He is liable at any moment to be thrown out of employment for no other fault than being less useful to his party, or faction or special patron than some one else who wants his place, and his chance of promotion depends on his ability to supplant in like manner somebody else; in no legitimate way can he ensure himself and his family a continued subsistence, much less make a provision for the future: that he should be usually dishonest is a logical sequence of his conditions of life. He passes his time in an atmosphere of intrigue and dissimulation, concealing or exaggerating his sentiments, amplifying his importance, striving to arouse hopes and fears he knows to be groundless, and to gain a confidence he will be strongly tempted to abuse: it is therefore a law of his being to deceive in words and actions. He is regarded by the community, and especially by the classes who usually fix its standards of thought and conduct, much as usurers were in the Middle Ages, feared and occasionally courted for their power, but hated and despised. Although fortunes are no doubt made in it, politics regarded as a way to make money, is, after all, a poor trade: the proportion of really prosperous politicians is very small compared with the vast number for whom a needy and anxious life ends in a dishonored and miserable old age. It has consequently few attractions for men of character and ability, and such men, with rare exceptions, shun it: it is recruited from the failures and outcasts of all honorable professions, those too dull, indolent or vicious to hold their own in any field of worthy competition. Its low-

est stratum is made up in no small measure of habitual criminals: we may truly say that our Botany Bay is the political arena. Among so many thousands a certain number of
men of ability will, of course, be found, but I believe the
very general impression that politicians are usually acute and
ingenious, though untrustworthy, is wholly groundless; the
vast majority of them are men of the most moderate natural
abilities, and the most limited acquirements. The relations
between the prominent and the ordinary members of this
calling closely resemble those between the robber barons and
their men-at-arms: the "bosses" are noted for skill in obtaining plunder and liberality in its distribution among their followers; while the latter believe in their patron's star, that is
to say, feel confidence in his continued ability to find them
places, they adhere to him with unscrupulous fidelity, but he
will be deserted in an instant if another proves, or is thought,
better able to reward effective service at the people's cost.
With little exaggeration it may be said that our professional
politicians constitute that class of the community which is
universally and unhesitatingly pronounced the least worthy of
confidence in any of the relations of private life.

It follows that, not only have they no special aptitude to
gauge public opinion, but they are peculiarly clumsy and un-
lucky in their efforts to forecast a public verdict. The blunders made by American politicians of more or less prominence
as to the results of impending elections have been so gross
and frequent of late years as to seem at once incredible and
incomprehensible to observers who know public men in other
countries or who knew our public men in other days. Innumerable instances of these blunders could be furnished: I
will give three from my personal experience. In October,
1892, I was opposed in a case at our Court of Appeals to a
lawyer, better known as an active Democratic politician than
professionally. On the way to Annapolis he shook his head
sadly over Cleveland's prospects: the latter's nomination
"had been a great mistake;" he "had no strength with the
people;" his defeat "was certain;" the discourse was a perfect jeremiad. Two years later, under very similar circumstances, I was favored by a Republican lawyer, a member of
the Committee in charge of the campaign then in progress,
and himself very active in its management, with prognostica-

tions as to the outcome. " It will go against us, as it always does in Maryland. They will elect their Congressmen and their Judge, and take everything else in sight; but I don't believe they'll get any fancy majorities." His views were not, indeed, of a tint so nearly indigo as those of his brother across the way had been, but he was no less incapable of seeing the prodigious turn in the tide, than had been the latter to feel the great wave of popular favor which was sweeping Mr. Cleveland a second time into the White House. Two years yet later another very prominent Republican politician actually trembled when he told of the likelihood that Bryan would be elected, and said, as for Maryland the only hope was in rolling up (just how, he didn't *say* clearly) such a majority in Baltimore City as might swamp the inevitable hostile majorities in every rural district of the State. When I told him I considered Bryan already beaten in the country and particularly · badly beaten in our State, and that I believed the farmers, in Maryland at least, were in favor of sound money, he thought I did not know much about politics : what he thought a few days later when the papers told him McKinley had eleven thousand plurality in Maryland outside of Baltimore City and carried twenty-one counties out of twenty-six, I never cared to enquire.

But surely there has been no more striking exhibition of blindness as to indications of popular sentiment, than when Mr. Kennedy referred the President to the results of the election just held to show, in substance, that the Republican party might safely and profitably repudiate what his friend the correspondent calls "the Mugwump plank" in its National platform. That plank was in the words following :

" The Civil Service law was placed on the statute book by the Republican party, which has always sustained it, and we renew our repeated declarations that it shall be thoroughly and honestly enforced and extended wherever practicable."

· Both of these " honorable men," and all the other " honorable men " confederated with them to obtain the laudable ends of the " Anti-Civil Service League," proclaim that in the " repeated declarations" which their party thus " renewed', it simply displayed the most barefaced hypocrisy; that it' intentions, or at least those of its leaders and candidates wers precisely the contrary of those it thus explicitly avowed. The

morality of such professions combined with such purposes,—
how far such a party would deserve, how long it could hope
to retain, the allegiance of any honest man, I need not here
discuss; for, after all, the sentiments and conduct of honest
men must be matters both unfamiliar and indifferent to the
"Anti-Civil Service League." Its shining lights, however,
may be more interested to know and better able to discuss
how far this hypocrisy (if such it was) has paid, and whether,
as some of them seem to think, the time has now come when
the party can throw off its supposed mask with impunity.
Experiments in that line have, indeed, been tried; let us note
their results.

In this State, the Republican party, standing on its "Mugwump plank" and presenting as its candidate for the Presidency a citizen of Ohio who had always spoken and voted
as though he believed in that plank and thought his party
sincere in its adoption, obtained last year nearly 50,000 plurality. This year its State Convention improved on the National platform to the following effect:

"We denounce the violation of the spirit of the Civil Service Act
by President Cleveland, and those orders which extended its operation
beyond its purpose and intent. We demand such revocation of orders
or modification of the law as will accomplish its manifest purpose."

Will Mr. Kennedy or the *Star's* correspondent or that great
apostle of their common cause, Mr. Grosvenor, tell us what
addition has been made by this change of front to the 50,000
plurality? And, by the way, since I am so near the home of
that illustrious man, may I ask his admiring neighbors whether
his campaign against Civil Service Reform has strengthened
or weakened the Republican party in his own district?

Across the river to the South, the doctrine of the "Mugwump plank" was this year diluted to the strength indicated
by the following formula:

"The Republican party is pledged to wise and just civil service,
but is opposed to the unwise and partisan civil service of the late Democratic administration, and will ask for a modification of the civil service
laws of President Cleveland. We believe that this should be done in
order to protect the rights and interests of the American people."

Kentucky's electoral vote was cast for McKinley, but this
year it went Democratic by seventeen thousand, or, more accurately, if we add the vote cast for the Sound Money Demo-

crat nominated for Clerk of the Court of Appeals, by over twenty-six thousand majority.

The Republican State Convention of Pennsylvania went farther yet. It had this to say about Civil Service Reform:

"We adhere to and renew again the pledges of the Republican party to maintain a just, reasonable and equitable system of civil service, but we denounce President Cleveland for his partisan abuse of its powers and his manipulation and unjust extension of its provisions beyond that which was originally contemplated by the law or required in the interest of good government, so as to protect the unfit appointees from his own party from threatening non-partisan competition.

By his violation of the spirit and intent of the law the offices of the Federal government have been filled with representatives of a single party; the standard of efficiency has been degraded; veterans of the late war have been dismissed to make place for political favorites without just or reasonable cause; promotions and transfers have been made for partisan reasons, regardless of merit and in disregard of the spirit of the Civil Service Law.

With an earnest desire to sustain the principles of the law and secure an honest, economical and efficient administration of the affairs of the government, we demand that the President of the United States, by executive order, and Congress, by legislative enactment at the approaching session, shall establish a Civil Service system that shall meet the approval of the better judgment and common sense of the American people."

Apparently, the "Civil Service system" established under that law which the National Convention said "shall be thoroughly and honestly enforced and extended wherever practicable," already met "the approval of the better judgment and common sense of the American people," for the suggestion that it be changed, reduced Mr. Beacom's plurality as State Treasurer to less than 130,000 from over 300,000 for McKinley and converted the latter's majority of 262,000 into 10,000 minority.

In New York the Republican platform contained no reference to Civil Service Reform, and none was needed: Senator Platt and Governor Black and Chairman Quigg were in themselves a platform as to this question, indeed as to any question of decency and good morals among public men. Its eloquent silence, however, was no less effective than the utterances in other States of statesmen recognizing the like principles and standards as those models: it availed to transform a Republican plurality of 268,000 into a Democratic plurality of 61,000 and we should be unreasonable if we asked more.

Mr. Kennedy, however, bids the President "Look at

Maryland!" Well, let him look. He will see that with his
"Mugwump plank" and his record as a friend to Civil Service
Reform, he carried Maryland by over thirty-two thousand
plurality, and that this year, when the Republican Convention, like that of New York, said nothing on the subject, an
exceptionally strong candidate was elected Comptroller by
barely eight thousand. If he can and will look a little below
the surface of our recent history, he will see further that only
the fact that, in the language of Mr. Kennedy, all other issues
"were subordinated to the greater one which Mr. Gorman's
personality brought into the canvass" enabled the Republicans to carry Maryland at all. Senator Gorman is entitled to
their thanks for another Republican legislature at Annapolis,
for another Republican City government in Baltimore: heav-
ily as they were handicapped by their own follies, he, this
noted enemy of Civil Service Reform, fatally overweighted his
own party.

I know well that these features of the result in Maryland
were not those at which Mr. Kennedy invited the President to
"look:" it may be safely assumed that when one of his stamp
asks a public officer to look at anything, he means that the
latter shall look with one eye shut, shall see what is pointed out
to him and see no more. Since I do not propose to imitate such
people as Mr. Kennedy, in this respect or any other, I will
deal with the matter to which he specially refers, and deal
with it frankly. It is true that the politicians who controlled
the last General Assembly submitted to the voters of Maryland an amendment to the State Constitution which they called
a "Civil Service Reform," or more usually (and, in this instance, more accurately) a "Civil Service," *without* "Reform," amendment: it is also true that the voters at the late
election rejected this amendment by a very great majority.
To this majority I personally contributed one vote, and, on
the day after election, I said for publication:

"I expected its defeat and thought, and now think, as I showed by
my vote, that it deserved defeat. Its rejection shows that the people of
Maryland know the difference between a real and a humbug merit system, and are not going to vote for the latter because called by the name
of the former."

Did I thus state fairly the significance of this popular vote?

The amendment submitted read as follows:

" Appointments in the civil service of the State in the municipalities
and counties of the State, shall be made according to merit and fitness, to
be ascertained so far as practicable by examination, which shall be competitive, except appointments which are subject to confirmation by the
Senate, and the General Assembly shall pass all such laws as may be
necessary more fully to carry into effect the provisions of this section."

It was offered in pretended satisfaction of the following
promise made by the party's last preceding State Convention :

"We pledge ourselves to the enactment of such legislation as shall
permit the people of the several counties and the municipalities of this
State to decide for themselves by popular vote whether appointments to
the police, fire or other departments of public service shall be in accordance with the principles of the merit system."

That the submission of the amendment in no wise fulfilled
the pledge must be obvious to the most careless reader: evidently the people of Baltimore City, for instance, were not
thereby "*enabled* to *decide for themselves* by popular vote"
whether partisan or personal favoritism should be banished in
the choice of their public servants, without regard to the
opinions or wishes of the people of Frederick or Elkton, West-
minster or Annapolis or the more remote Counties of the State.
But a more careful reading of the amendment discloses more.
An officer of the State *located within* the territory of a municipal or other public corporation is no more an officer *of* that
corporation than a Federal officer so located would be : therefore *all* County or Municipal officers and employees, the very
classes mentioned in the platform, were excluded from its operation; it could apply only to persons strictly in the employ
of the State.   And, if we examine it yet more closely, we shall
see that, if adopted, it would have affected the selection of very
few among these, perhaps of none at all.   To the words "in
the Municipalities and Counties of the State," however obscure
and *apparently* artificial the phrase may be, *some* meaning
must be given, and the only intelligible meaning which can be
given them, further limits the scope of the provision to such
civil servants of the State as are necessarily confined in the
discharge of their public duties to the territory of some particular County or Municipality.   This would have certainly left
out two branches of "the Civil Service of the State" to whose
selection the merit system might be applied with the greatest
facility and benefit, namely, the Oyster Police and the employees of the Tobacco Warehouses.   Of the former, the same

convention had said in the very next plank of its platform:

"We condemn the partisan management of the Oyster police force of this State."

Among the latter the Governor has been since obliged to dismiss several of his own appointees, after an investigation which disclosed the existence of grave abuses, undoubtedly of long standing. These branches of the public service would have been excluded from the protection afforded by the amendment, if adopted: to what offices would it have extended? This question no one has been able to answer with any certainty; when, after these exclusions, we further leave out all civil officers of the State either confirmed by the Senate or elected by the people, and also those whose choice by competitive examination would be impracticable, the residuum is almost one of those "least things whereof the law takes no heed."

The bill submitting this amendment to the people was originally introduced in the House of Delegates by an enemy to Civil Service Reform as bitter as Gallinger or Grosvenor or any member of the "Anti-Civil Service League," and, whatever may have been, in fact, its genesis, no one of these worthies could have suggested a more cynical evasion of party pledges, or have proffered to the friends of good government a test of strength, in all outward appearance, more impudently devised upon the time-honored principle of "heads I win, tails you lose."

I called the possible fruit of this measure a "humbug merit system;" it remains for me to define the genuine article, and I deem this the more material because I think whatever reasonable doubt may exist as to whether the American people want Civil Service Reform arises from some difference of opinion or rather some confusion of thought as to what Civil Service Reform means.

Civil Service Reform means simply the application of morality and common sense to the choice of public servants. A public office belongs to the people; its duties are fixed by the people's laws; its salary is paid with the people's money. In the words of the Court of last resort in my State:

"In this country a public office cannot be the property of the incumbent, because it belongs to the sovereign people who created the government. In the declaration of organic principles, prefixed to the instrument creating the government of this State, those holding the most important offices are declared to be 'the trustees of the public.' The same designation necessarily applies to all public functionaries. Therefore, every office, created either by the Constitution or by the laws authorized by that instrument, is a public trust created for the public benefit."

It follows logically that if a President or Governor or Mayor uses the patronage which he holds in trust for the Union or his State or his City to strengthen himself in his faction, or his faction in his party, or his party at the polls, his conduct is indistinguishable in morals from a guardian's who would use his ward's money in his own business or in the business of some firm or corporation of which he is a member. It is not enough that he may not choose unfit subordinates; but he must choose them *solely* because of their fitness; if he allow any other consideration whatever to influence his choice he is *pro tanto* unmindful of the duty which he has promised, nay sworn, to perform. In words thus much is admitted by everyone: even Governor Black would have civil servants chosen for " merit and fitness" of some sort. Moreover, the great mass of the American people see clearly enough that political opinion no more affects the merit or fitness of an applicant for a non-political office than does his religious faith. Macaulay says:

" The points of difference between Christianity and Judaism have very much to do with a man's fitness to be a bishop or a rabbi. But they have no more to do with his fitness to be a magistrate, a legislator, or a minister of finance, than with his fitness to be a cobbler. Nobody has ever thought of compelling cobblers to make any declaration on the true faith of a Christian. Any man would rather have his shoes mended by a heretical cobbler than by a person who had subscribed all the thirty-nine articles, but had never handled an awl. Men act thus, not because they are indifferent to religion, but because they do not see what religion has to do with the mending of their shoes. Yet religion has as much to do with the mending of shoes as with the budget and the army estimates."

And politics has as much to do with the mending of shoes as with the keeping of books or the collection of mails : the points of difference between Republicanism and Democracy have very much to do with a man's fitness to be a President or a Congressman, but they also have nothing in the world to do with his fitness to be a letter carrier or a department clerk. It is true that, as we have among us A. P. A. who would exclude men from office because they profess a particular form of Christianity, so we have professional office seekers who

clamor for the like proscription on grounds of political sentiment or party allegiance; but, in the one case no less than the
other, we deal with a small minority, thoroughly discredited
among their fellow citizens. If any proof were needed for a
proposition so obviously true the hearty and practically unanimous approval accorded to President McKinley's order forbidding merely partisan removals by all newspapers having
the least claim to be regarded as exponents of public opinion
would furnish this proof.

It is true that when we come to the question how "merit
and fitness" for appointment to subordinate and ministerial
positions in the public service shall be tested there is not the
same unanimity: to the mind of the average American it is
not self-evident that these can be best determined through
competitive examination, but, wherever opportunity offers, he
is rapidly acquiring, or has already acquired, this conviction
through experience. In 1887, the Baltimore Reform League,
in a letter to the Secretary of the Treasury, which received no
reply, informed him that the then Collector of Internal Revenue in that City had appointed to positions of trust one man
who had passed two months in jail for keeping a gambling house,
another who had been indicted, although never punished, for
shooting a ruffian like himself in the very station house where
the latter was in custody and about to answer for a murderous
assault on the future appointee, and a third who had been imprisoned five years, as an insufficient penalty for perhaps the
most unprovoked murder ever committed in the City. These
were fair specimens, but specimens only of the class of men
who then made up the *personnel* of the Internal Revenue
Department there; a Department not then under the merit
system. Now, however it may be with politicians, the average citizen, ninety-nine American citizens out of a hundred,
would like to keep such men out of public employment: and
what will keep them out? Is it the want of recommendations
from reputable citizens? But every one obtains recommendations; the most notorious though not the worst, of these Internal Revenue Clerks, said, and I have no doubt said truly,
that he had been recommended by some who professed to be,
not only respectable but reformers as well. Is it the fear of
exposure? But these men were exposed, not in Maryland
only, but throughout the length and breadth of the Union, and

what harm did it do them? It didn't stop their salary, and, while that was paid, for what else did they care? Is it their incompetency to discharge their legitimate duties? But they were not appointed to discharge those duties: they were appointed to do other work for which they were thoroughly competent, and which they had often done already to the satisfaction of those who secured their appointments. The one effective barrier which will keep such men out of the service is to make their appointment depend, not on favoritism, but on merit, and on merit tested by a method which radically excludes favoritism; and competitive examinations, whatever their theoretical merits or defects, furnish practically such a test. The Civil Service rules may not give us ideal public servants, but they shut out gamblers and assassins. These gentry are not good at examinations, they share the distaste of their present Senatorial and Congressional patrons for the merit system, and will have none of it. Note well, that, not only in Baltimore, but elsewhere, all scandals such as these have occurred in the departments of the Service not subject to the rules: the convicted murderer I have mentioned passed a Civil Service examination in the Custom House, but took so low a mark that he despaired of appointment and turned his attention to a field of labor where such methods of selection were not then in vogue.

We had simultaneously in our Post Office a very striking object lesson as to the difference in results between a reasonably fair, though unfriendly, observance of the rules by the Postmaster and his fraudulent evasion of them. There was for a year in that office a gentleman who, having no doubt heard that office is a trust, consistently administered his public office as he did his private trusts, that is to say, shamefully abused both. Finding the Civil Service rules in his way, he introduced a scheme of certification and appointment, the practical result of which was that the protection of the rules was reduced to that afforded by a pass examination of candidates. Under this system he was able, as he boasted, to replace many Republican clerks and carriers with Democrats, but what was the character of the latter? From the report of his successor, as strong a partisan as himself, to the Postmaster-General, it appeared that the latter had been obliged, notwithstanding their political orthodoxy, to remove in less than two

years no less than one hundred and nineteen of this gentleman's appointees. "To be more specific as to causes," said
the succeeding Postmaster, "they have been as follows: inefficiency, discourtesy, general stupidity, want of activity,
drunkenness, indifference as to their duties, want of cleanliness,
having dangerous associates, dishonesty, and others in whom
I did not have confidence as to their trustworthiness, honesty
and competency (the majority having been removed for drunkenness.)" The grammar of this statement may not be fault-
less, but its meaning is clear, and, taken in connection with
the history of his predecessor's proceedings, very significant.
When Civil Service Reform had been practically eliminated by
the latter's ingenious devices, the door was opened to the
drunken, dirty, disreputable, dishonest and stupid hangers-on
of influential politicians who wished them supported at public expense, men just able to stumble through an examination,
and whom the new Postmaster had for his own protection and
comfort to get rid of. And yet the latter was no more of a
reformer than the man he succeeded; for his chief assistant he
chose a person whom the President had been deterred by
earnest remonstrances, based on his antecedents, from making
United States Marshal. Such then was the order: real civil
service reform, respectable men as officers, sham civil service
reform, drunkards and slovens as officers, no civil service reform at all, gamblers and assassins as officers. These were the
lessons of Mr. Cleveland's first term in Maryland.

We should find, if we sought them, the same conclusions
established by similar facts in many, if not all, other States:
for example, there were in the year 1896, one hundred and ten
dismissals for drunkenness from the public service of New
York City: of those dismissed *two* had been appointed after
competitive examination, *one hundred and eight* had been appointed without examination; but the length to which this
paper has grown forbids my alluding to more than one other
aspect of the matter, an aspect unsuitable for presentation in
great detail, but too vitally important to be wholly neglected.

Before the days of Civil Service Reform, or, at least, before
the Pendleton bill became law, it was my very unpleasant professional duty to take part in the trial of a suit brought against
the then Postmaster of Baltimore by a young woman formerly
employed in the office and whom he had dismissed. Of the

disclosures made in that trial it is sufficient to say that they caused the removal of the defendant from office and practically closed his political career, but they had another result which was of greater significance: the succeeding Postmaster dismissed within a few months every woman employed in the office (except two very old ladies), and publicly announced that he would never employ another. When he had a successor of different politics the latter adhered to the same policy, and, in conversation with me, defended it by saying, in substance: "The women in whom politicians are sufficiently interested to urge them for these places, are often of such a class that, if I were obliged to discipline one of them, I should never know what story she might tell about me." Those acquainted with the departmental services in Washington before the introduction of the merit system and especially for the ten years next succeeding the close of the war, will understand his allusion and appreciate its force.

In this matter we must indeed avoid exaggeration: the vast majority of the women then employed by the government were undoubtedly virtuous and estimable, I should be very reluctant to believe that it was then, or would be now, possible to find in any legitimate occupation, a considerable number of American women of whom the majority, or even a large minority, should be otherwise; but, as every one so employed had then gained his or her position through influence of some sort, and almost invariably through the influence of some politician interested in the employee, the origin and nature of this interest became matters of suspicion and gossip and, in view of the character and habits of some among our public men, of suspicion not always unreasonable and of gossip not always groundless, in the case, not only of the comparatively few towards whom this involved no injustice, but of well nigh every woman who entered the public service of her country. It may be that to some the abating of this nuisance through Civil Service Reform seems a matter of small moment; it is even possible that some of the statesmen now posturing as enemies to the merit system and all of its fruits regard the loss of a *Parc aux Cerfs* maintained at the taxpayers' cost for their benefit as a legitimate grievance: but need I ask twice if the American people, having seen this ordure washed away, would knowingly suffer its renewal?

In closing this long trespass on your attention I will ask the "Anti-Civil Service" champions in Congress to "look at Maryland" and note something which even they can understand in the results of the late election. The breach of ante-election promises on the part of the legislature chosen there in 1895, and particularly on the part of those members of the House of Delegates from Baltimore city who voted against the real, not the bogus, civil service reform measure submitted to them, was not quite so shameless as what they urge on their party in Congress; but it was bad enough: of the eighteen city members, but one has been re-elected this Autumn, but one of the delegation has been promoted to the State Senate; he introduced the bill prepared by the Civil Service Reform Association of Maryland, conducted the debate on its behalf and voted for it to the end: does this look as though the people of Maryland didn't want Civil Service Reform? They seem, at all events, to want its friends. And are its enemies in the national legislature quite sure that, like the voters of Baltimore, their enraptured constituents may not insist on keeping them at home next November? So much for the benefit of the "Anti-Civil Servicers:" to the really responsible politicians of the Republican party let me say something more serious. Public men who would have their party shamefully violate the pledges of its platform may be readily believed if they say these pledges, on their own part, at least, were hypocritical and mendacious, but the fact affords them no justification; their moral standards may be those of poker sharps and confidence men, but it is not for them to say so: if their party has obtained power under false pretences, I warn them that they will not be heard with patience when they tell a duped people: "You ought to have known that we lied."

The Legal Situation:—The Right to Compete for Public Employment.

By Edwin Burritt Smith.

George William Curtis stated the purpose of civil-service reformers, as early as 1869, in these words: "What we want is to intrench the principle and practice of Washington in the law." (II Orations and addresses, 9.) The pioneer step to this end had been taken in Congress two years earlier when Thomas J. Jenckes presented his report on the condition of the civil service, accompanied by a bill to regulate the civil service of the United States and to promote its efficiency.

This early desire to embody the proposed reform in the law of the land found its first expression in the ninth section of the sundry appropriations bill of March 3, 1871. This measure authorizes the President "to prescribe such rules and regulations for the admission of persons into the civil service of the United States as will best promote the efficiency thereof, and ascertain the fitness of each candidate in respect to age, health, character, knowledge and ability for the branch of service into which he seeks to enter." It also authorized the President "to employ suitable persons to conduct said inquiries, to prescribe their duties, and to establish regulations for the conduct of persons who may receive appointments in the civil service."

This prompt recognition that the proposed reform must find expression in the law, shows how clearly its pioneers comprehended the nature of the mighty task to which they had set their hands. The story of what followed their first success in securing legal recognition of the reform—of the appointment by President Grant of an admirable commission headed by Mr. Curtis, of the active opposition by the spoilsmen, of the indifference of public sentiment, and finally in 1875 of the refusal of appropriations by Congress and consequent suspension of the rules—is too well known to need recounting here.

The early leaders of the reform movement, in seeking "to intrench the principles and practice of Washington in the ‖law," made no mistake in the remedy for the monstrous evils of the spoils system. They failed for the moment sufficiently to realize that law, to be effective under free institutions, must be the command of popular opinion. However, to them the failure of the act of 1871 was only a repulse. They at once appealed from Congress to the people. By a few years of well-directed agitation they aroused and informed public opinion. The direct results were the national act of 1883, the New York act of the same year, the Massachusetts act of 1884, the New York constitutional provision of 1894, the Illinois act of 1895 and recent charter provisions for various cities. These achievements mark the progress of a rising and active popular sentiment in support of the merit system, which gives bright promise of its early extension to our entire civil service, national, state and municipal.

The legal situation is just now of peculiar interest. In Massachusetts, where the reform of course found a congenial atmosphere, it has been accepted as part and parcel of the orthodox faith. This happy result was not reached without some difficulty and even litigation. The appointing officers and the courts were for a time much perplexed by the veteran preference legislation; but a way has finally been found to recognize two privileged classes, women and veterans, under legislation the general purpose of which is to open public employment to the free competition of all. The Supreme Court, in the case of *Brown vs. Russell*, 166 Mass., 14, early in 1896 held the act of 1895, which required the appointment of any veteran to any position for which he and three citizens of his selection might certify him to be qualified, to be unconstitutional. Thereupon, by act of 1896, it was provided that veterans found to be qualified upon examination shall be preferred in appointment to

all others, except women. The act also permits appointing officers to appoint or employ veterans without
examination. This act the court, by a majority of four
to three, has sustained, on the ground that the legislature may have considered that veterans, otherwise qualified, are "likely to possess courage, constancy, habits
of obedience and fidelity, which are valuable qualifications for any public office or employment; or that the recognition of the services of veterans in the way provided
for by the statute would encourage that love of country
and devotion to the welfare of the state which it concerns the commonwealth to foster." The minority of
the court refuse to concede that the fact of being a veteran bears such relation to the duties of a present office
or employment in the civil service that it can be made
a decisive test in the selection of persons for employment, or that service in the army or navy in the late
war is the only way to acquire special fitness for public
employment. They say: "The important matter is
to get the best possible service, and the selections should
be made with reference to the qualifications or fitness
for the performance of the duties which are to be performed. And, since this is so, it is not within the constitutional power of the legislature to fix as a decisive
test anything which does not bear such a relation to the
duties to be performed as to show special fitness for the
performance of those duties;" 166 Mass. 589. It is evident that the act thus sustained has at least gone to the
extreme limit in securing a class preference by law.

The legal situation in New York shows that the fully
evolved spoilsman is not awed even in the presence of
a constitutional provision. The constitution of 1894 requires that "appointments and promotions in the civil
service of the State, and of all civil divisions thereof,
. . . shall be according to merit and fitness, to be ascertained, so far as practicable, by examination, which, so
far as practicable, shall be competitive." The Court of
Appeals, in the case of *People v. Roberts*, 148 N. Y.
Rep., 148, broadly says: "The principle that all appointments in the civil service must be made according

to merit and fitness, to be ascertained by competitive examinations, is expressed in such broad and imperative language that in some respects it must be regarded as beyond the control of the legislature, and secure from any statutory changes. If the legislature should repeal all the statutes and regulations on the subject of appointments in the civil service, the mandate of the constitution would still remain, and would so far execute itself as to require the courts, in a proper case, to pronounce appointments made without compliance with its requirements illegal."

The same court, in the case of *Chittenden v. Wurster*, 152 N. Y. Rep. 345, 358, holds that the question whether the examination of a candidate for a public position is practicable, is judicial and depends upon the nature and character of the duties of the position. This case presented the question whether a clerk to the committees of the Brooklyn board of aldermen, an assistant warrant clerk, a dockmaster, a chief clerk, a law clerk, a surveyor, a finance clerk, a license fee collector, a department secretary, a commissioner's clerk and a deputy license clerk, are within the constitutional provision, it appearing that they had been appointed without competitive examination. The plaintiffs produced a mass of evidence, including examination papers, reports and various civil service regulations, to show that competitive examinations for the appointments in question are practicable. The defendants produced no evidence to show that they are impracticable. The trial justice held "that it was and is practicable to ascertain the merit and fitness of a person to be appointed to each of said positions by competitive examinations." The Appellate Division of the Supreme Court held that "none of these appointees fall within the debatable class, but were plainly susceptible of being filled by competitive examination." (14 App. Div. Reps., 497.)

The Court of Appeals, by a majority of four to three, reversed the lower courts, holding generally, that where the duties of a position are not merely clerical, and are such as especially devolve upon the head of the office, which by reason of his numerous duties he is compelled to delegate to others, the performance of which require skill, judgment, trust and confidence and involve the responsibility of the officer or the municipality which he represents, the position should be treated as confidential. (152 N. Y. Rep., 360).

The conclusion of the majority of the conrt was strongly contested in dissenting opinions by Judges Gray and O'Brien, in the first of which Chief Judge Andrews concurred. They pointed out that the six Justices below were unanimous in finding, upon uncontradicted evidence, that it was practicable to fill all the places in question by competitive examinations, and that "the obvious effect of the constitution was to remove the eleven places in question from the non-competitive schedule since it was practicable to fill them all by competitive examination." (152 N. Y. Rep. pp. 386, 393.) Judge O'Brien, in his very able dissenting opinion, correctly stated the situation in these words: "The future of the law which now rests upon the basis of the constitution is dependent upon the decision of this court. The decision in this case will either place the reform upon a reasonable and just basis, and command the approval of all good men, or it will be a step backward." (Id. p. 389.) While the majority of the court frankly announce that "Should time and experience prove that we are in error . . . we shall not hesitate to carry out the spirit and intent of the law" (Id. p. 360.), it is to be remembered that the Court of Appeals must alone determine what the spirit and intent of the constitution require.

The prevailing opinion in the *Chittenden-Wurster* case must be regarded as a loose construction of the constitutional requirement that appointments and promotions shall be according to merit and fitness, to be ascertained by competitive examination, so far as practicable. It is "a step backward," by a great court, which had from the outset led in judicial support of the merit system. In the presence of a judgment so favorable to the spoilsmen, resting as it does upon the opinion of four of the Judges, against that of three others unanimously supported by the six Justices of the Supreme Court who passed upon the case below, the Court of Appeals can no longer truly say, what it said in the Roberts' case in speaking of the reform : "This court, upon more than one occasion, has, with entire unanimity expressed its approval of the principle, and exercised all of its powers in every proper case in aid of all laws intended to carry out the idea." (148 N. Y. Rep., 364.) If the majority opinion of the court is finally to prevail, the constitutional provision of New York, requiring competitive examinations so far as practicable, falls far short of the Illinois statute which provides that all applicants for positions in the classified service, from which but few places are excluded, "shall be subjected to examination, which shall be public, competitive and free to all citizens of the United States, with specified limitations as to residence, age, health, habits and moral character."

The Legislature of New York under anirresponsible dictatorship, has persistently neglected, since the adoption of the constitutional provision of 1894, to provide appropriate legislation to give it full and affirmative effect, as commanded by the constitution itself. This neglect was emphasized by the passage, at the last session, of an act providing for two examinations to ascertain the "merit and fitness" of candidates for appointment, one by the civil service commission to determine their relative "merit" and one by, or under the authority of, the appointing officer to satisfy him as to their "fitness." Each examination is to cover one-half of the rating of candidates. It is not in fact required that the so-called "examination" to ascertain "fitness" shall be competitive, or that it shall be public or made matter of record. It may be conducted by "some person or board designated by the person holding such power of appointment." In plain words, this so-called examination may be held at the party headquarters, on the street, or in the corner saloon, and may be conducted by a political committee, the party boss, or a convenient barkeeper.

Mr. Schurz, in his powerful address of protest to the governor, properly suggested that holding two examinations to ascertain "merit and fitness" is like requiring two examinations by physicians to find whether one is "hale and hearty," one as to whether he is "hale" and the other as to whether he is "hearty."

The act in question is the clumsy device of spoilsmen to nullify the constitution of the State. That a conspiracy so transparent and subversive of public order can succeed, is of course impossible. There is nothing in the history of the courts of New York to give any promise of success to an unlawful purpose so obvious. In the prevailing opinion in the *Chittenden-Wurster* case, written after the passage of this measure, the Court of Appeals significantly say: "It is said that each officer having appointments to make could himself examine the applicants for position, and in that way determine who should be the appointee by a competitive examination. Undoubtedly, but it will readily be seen that this system would practically nullify the civil service law and bring it into disrepute." (152 N. Y. Rep. p. 356.)

The submission of the "Black Bill" to the scrutiny of the courts, which is soon to be made, can have but one result. The certain defeat of this transparent attempt to nullify the constitution ought to prepare the way for the legislation which it commands.

The change of administration in Chicago last April has subjected the Illinois statute to a crucial test. Unfortunately, the act did not go into effect until the July following its adoption at the city election of 1895. That election resulted in a change from democratic to republican control. The new mayor promptly turned out "the gang," as his followers not inappropriately called the democratic host, and installed "the boys" who were expected to control in his interest the republican machine, now enuphonetously known as "the organization." This clean sweep and substitution even extended to some six hundred members of the police force. Having thus strikingly illustrated the need, and prepared the way, for reform, Mayor Swift appointed an excellent commission and thereafter cordially supported it. This seeming inconsistency on his part is perhaps traceable to a desire to mark the introduction of the merit system by a conversion as dramatic as that of St. Paul. Possibly he sought at the outset of his administration to put temptation behind him, or to create a sort of solitude in which the new commission might learn its duties and formulate the rules required by law. Whatever the truth, the mayor thereafter sustained the commission while it worked out a thorough classification of the service, prepared adequate rules, held many examinations and certified a few eligibles for appointment. Under such conditions came the change from republican to democratic rule in the election of Mayor Harrison last spring and a clean sweep of Mayor Swift's personal appointees.

The Illinois statute is based on the national, New York and Massachusetts acts. It differs from the earlier legislation in that it is more inclusive and stringent in its provisions. The excluded "head or heads of any department" of the New York act gives place to the "heads of any principal department" in the statute of Illinois. Unrestricted removals under all prior legislation give way in Illinois to removals only for cause, to be ascertained upon written charges after opportunity to the person charged to be heard. The Illinois act also provides that vacancies shall be filled by promotion where it is practicable, that promotions shall be "on the basis of merit and seniority of service and examination," and that "all examinations for promotion shall be competitive."

The commissions under the Illinois statute are continuous and independent bodies. Mayor Harrison, however, assumed the Chicago commissioners to be his subordinates, and that a majority of them should be in political and personal accord with himself. Upon the refusal of the majority of the old commission (the other member having been appointed comptroller) to accept his construction of the words, "heads of any principal department," used in naming the excluded officials, to include some fifty heads of bureaus in the departments, inspectors and captains of police and various foremen and others, the mayor removed the two remaining members on frivolous charges afterwards trumped up to comply with a provision of the statute requiring him to file his reasons for such removals. The new commission promptly published an opinion construing the words, "heads of any principal department," so as to exclude from the classified service most of the desirable positions claimed by the mayor as spoils, thus giving him (to use their words) "the benefit of the doubt" as to the positions which "should be taken out of the classified service." The mayor was thus enabled to fill the higher places in the service with avowed and active enemies of the merit system, an opportunity which he promptly improved. His appointees, with some honorable exceptions, in co-operation with the council, are doing what may be done to place the civil service law in a false light before the public, and—so far as practicable—to render it inoperative.

The statute excludes from the classified service "officers .... whose appointment is subject to confirmation by the city council." When the act was adopted but few officials, some of them of minor importance, were subject to such confirmation. Upon the accession of Mayor Harrison, it was feared by some of the best friends of the law that it is especially vulnerable at this point. Its enemies quickly sought to avail themselves of their apparent opportunity. The council promptly created a considerable number of new positions, making them all subject to confirmation by itself. The committee on civil service, on June 14, 1897, reported forms for four ordinances, recommending their passage. By these measures it was gravely proposed to designate as "'heads of principal departments,' as said term is used in section eleven" of the civil service act, numerous "public officials" and "all employees of the City of Chicago, receiving $3 or less per day, as compensation for work;" to make "the head of each and every department, bureau or division of work in the public service of Chicago," and certain experts, private secretaries, head assistants and others, subject to confirmation by the council ; and to make "all transfers, appointments, discharges and promotions in the fire and police departments" subject to the order of the mayor and approval of the council. These extraordinary proposals were opposed by the administration which was not prepared to attempt the complete nullification of the statute. Two weeks later the council passed, as an administration measure, an ordinance which provides that a considerable list of "officials" named "shall be designated as 'heads of principal departments,' as said term is used in section eleven" of the civil service act.

Some of the friends of the law, fearing these attacks were aimed at a vital point, deemed it wise to endeavor to save something by acquiescence. Others, and notably the Citizens' Association, held that the way to save the law was to defend it against all comers. The Citizens' Association retained special counsel and procured the Attorney-General to file petitions, on behalf of the people, in the Supreme Court for writs of *mandamus*, to obtain an authoritative and final interpretation of the law and of the power of the city council in respect to it. These cases were fully presented to the court in October last, and early decisions are expected. The new commission only contended for a liberal construction of the words, "heads of any principal department." The corporation counsel boldly attacked the constitutionality of the act, and defended the ordinance which seeks to make subordinate officials "heads of principal departments" merely by thus designating them. The writer's relation to these cases renders improper here any prophecy in regard to the result. It must suffice here to say, that we hope for a judgment by the court strongly sustaining the act, with a finding that the ordinance is void as unreasonable and in conflict with the statute.* The law is supported by public opinion. The penalties for its violation are severe. If fully sustained by the court, it will be at least reasonably enforced.

The President, by his executive order of July 27, 1897, directing that removals shall be made only for just cause, upon written charges and opportunity to be heard, has raised the question whether removals should be controlled by law. Civil service reformers have hesitated to place any legal restraint upon the power of removal by the appointing officer for any cause satisfactory to him. They have assumed that such officers will not be apt to remove efficient subordinates to make way for unknown successors to be taken from the eligible list. As early as 1881, in his address before The American Science Association, Mr. Curtis said:

"Removals for cause alone means, of course. removal for legitimate cause, such as dishonesty, negligence, or incapacity. But who shall decide that such cause exists? This must be determined either by the responsible superior officer or by some other authority. But if left to some other authority the right of counsel and the forms of a court would be invoked; the whole legal machinery of mandamuses, injunctions, certioreris, and the rules of evidence would be put in play to keep an incompetent clerk at his desk or a sleepy watchman on his beat. Cause for removal of a letter-carrier in the post office or of an accountant in the custom house would be presented with all the pomp of impeachment and established like a high crime and misdemeanor." (II Orations and Addresses p. 190).

Mr. Curtis, in his second annual address as President of the League in 1883, also said: "We do not plead for fixed permanency in public place, nor assert

---

* The Supreme Court of Illinois on December 22, 1897, handed down a strong opinion in these cases, holding the Statute to be constitutional and the ordinance in question void for unreasonableness. The court, in effect, holds that the Council has no power to add to the list of exclusions from the act. This decision places the Illinois act on a firm basis.

a vested right in public employment. Due subordination and discipline are essential to all effective organized service, and, therefore, dismissal for proper cause should be prompt and sure. To this end the power of removal should be left as free as possible, provided that motives for its illegitimate exercise are destroyed. Such a provision secures both proper discipline and a just tenure." (Id. p. 248.) Again, in his sixth annual address, he said : "The power of removal no less than that of appointment is a public trust, and it cannot be rightly used arbitrarily or for any other cause than the public interest. Such cause should be publicly assigned and recorded, that the people may clearly understand the reason of the change in service." (Id. p. 340.)

These passages indicate what has been the generally accepted view of reformers. Aside from the prohibition of removals for political reasons, there was no attempt until recently to limit the power of removal by appointing officers. The framers of the Illinois act took the first step in advance by providing that "no officer or employee in the classified service . . . shall be removed or discharged except for cause, upon written charges and after an opportunity to be heard." From this provision laborers and "persons having the custody of public money, for the safe keeping of which another has given bond," are excepted. "Such charges shall be investigated by or before said civil service commission, or . . . some officer or board appointed by said commission to conduct such investigation. The finding and decision of such commission, or investigating officer or board when approved by such commission, shall be certified to the appointing officer, and shall be forthwith enforced by such officer." (Act 1895, Sec. 12.)

These provisions, it will be observed, make no attempt to define what causes shall be sufficient to justify removals. It is not believed that the act confers upon those in the classified service any vested right to continue in public employment, or to call upon the courts to determine whether any alleged cause of removal, except it be political, is sufficient to justify it. The intention is to protect the classified service from arbitrary and unjust removals by appointing officers, and to prevent removals for other than causes that will bear public record, after opportunity to make defense. Under this act the commission is made publicly responsible for every removal from the classified service.

The question involved in the recent decisions of United States courts, whether the President's order in respect to removals has the force of law, is less important than the question whether it ought to have such force. The answer to the first depends upon the extent of executive power under the civil service act to make rules that shall have the force of law. The answer to other must be sought in the further inquiry, whether public employment can be the subject of vested right, —whether office is a place of public service, or a castle to be privately held and enjoyed.

The merit system of appointment recognizes and protects the right of all to compete for public employment, the right of freedom of contract with the largest employer of skilled and unskilled labor. The Massachusetts act provides for the punishment of officials and others who shall "defeat, deceive, or obstruct any person in respect of his or her *right of examination.*" (Sec. 18). The constitution of New York requires all appointments to be made upon "examination which, so far as practicable, shall be *competitive.*" The Illinois act provides that "all applicants for offices or places in said classified service . . . shall be subjected to examination, which shall be public, *competitive and free to all citizens of the United States,* with specified limitations as to residence, age, health, habits, and moral character." (*Sec.,* 6.)

The Supreme Court of Massachusetts, in the case of *Commonwealth vs. Perry,* 155 Mass., 117, said: "There are certain fundamental rights of every citizen which are recognized in the organic law of all our free American States. . . . The declaration of rights in the constitution of Massachusetts enumerates among the natural inalienable rights of men the right 'of acquiring, possessing and protecting property.' The right to acquire, possess, and protect property includes the right to make reasonable contracts, which shall be under the protection of the law."

The Supreme Court of Illinois, in the case of *Braceville Coal Co. v. People*, 147 Ill. 66, 70, said:

"The fundamental principle upon which liberty is based, in free and enlightened government, is equality under the law of the land. It has accordingly been everywhere held, that liberty, as that term · is used in the constitution, means not only freedom of the citizen from servitude and restraint; but is deemed to embrace the right of every man to be free in the use of his powers and faculties, and to adopt and pursue such avocation and calling as he may choose, subject only to the restraints necessary to secure the common welfare."

The same court, in the great case of *Ritchie v. People*, 155 Ill., 98, 104, also said: "The privilege of contracting is both a liberty and property right. . . . The right to use, buy and sell property and contract in respect thereto is protected by the constitution. Labor is property, and the laborer has the same right to sell his labor, and to contract with reference thereto, as has any other property owner. . . . The right to labor or employ labor, and make contracts in respect thereto upon such terms as may be agreed upon between the parties, is included in the constitutional guaranty."

Thus it follows that the right of freedom of contract with the largest employer of labor, is a property right which is protected by the fundamental law. (*See also Stimson's Handbook to the Labor Law of U. S., p. 10, etc.;*) that all citizens, having the proper requirements of age, health and character, have a property right to compete for public as well as private employment. It is the great purpose of the merit system of appointment to give force and effect to this fundamental right of free men.

We are now ready for the inquiry, whether the right to compete for public employment extends, on behalf of

the successful competitors, beyond the threshold of such
employment, there to become a vested property right in
the office itself. Unless offices exist to be held, the
answer must be in the negative. A fundamental principle of civil service reform is that public office is a public
trust. It is an opportunity to render a public service,
and whatever of personal honor and profit attach to it
is but incidental. The public has a right to the most
efficient and devoted service, and to this end to continue
competent and faithful officials in its employment.
Thus the public need, not personal interest, becomes
and is the basis and measure of a just tenure. Only in
this view can "the public service be, indeed, the public
service," (Gladstone)—the property of the nation, not an
asset of a party boss or machine.

We may, therefore, conclude that the right of competition for public employment is a property right of
all; that this right is part and parcel of the fundamental
right of freedom of contract; that a right of such importance ought to be given full force and effect by positive
law. We have seen that this is the great purpose of all
civil service legislation. It also follows, that public
office is not properly a subject of vested right; that
official position is an opportunity for public service,
not a private property interest; and that its control is
an executive, not a judicial, function. If these conclusions are sound, it remains for the executive to forbid
removals except for just cause. It does not follow that
the President's order is less wise because it is not properly enforceable by the courts. It will be to the lasting
honor of the present administration if it shall firmly
establish a rule of executive action to prevent removals
without just cause.

The evolution of modern democracy is from the
simple and primitive groups of kinsmen, known to us
as village communities. The crude democracy of these
isolated communities gave way to the despotic feudal
monarchy which molded them into the great nation
having a definite territory, uniform laws and comparative freedom from local disorder. Then came the long

struggle for a democracy which should combine the great advantages of a wide national authority with as much as practicable of the local self-government and personal freedom of the village community. This struggle is marked by a long succession of popular victories over despotic privilege. The spoils system in our day is a mercenary survival of feudal privilege. Its destruction will remove another barrier that stands between the people and their government. The merit system, in its purpose "to intrench the principle and practice of Washington in the Law," seeks to recover a fundamental right of free men. To such a purpose, complete success is sure. It may be here and there delayed, but it will come.

Civil Service Reform and Municipal Government.

FIRST PAPER.

By Albert Shaw.

We have been talking much in this country of Municipal Reform ; and that phrase, when applied to existing conditions in various cities, embraces obviously, a great range and diversity of specific needs. But it is well for us that we should understand clearly that, in the present stage of our progress, Municipal Reform means before all else civil service reform, and that the abolition of the personal and party spoils system from our municipal administrations is the one and only remedy for the worst of our present evils in city government.

Good government in itself is a fit and desirable thing, and patriotism demands it ; for how can the citizen love his country as he ought if its administration is habitually corrupt and inefficient, and if there is altogether lacking in the exercise of public authority the attributes of disinterestedness, of dignity, and of equal beneficence towards all citizens, regardless of party, race, or other distinction ? Nevertheless, while I do not fail to appreciate the fitness and the moral beauty of good government as an abstract consideration, I have always, in the application of government to local and municipal affairs, preferred to think of government as a means to an end rather than an object in itself.

Municipal government in our day has come to be Collectivism, on a vast and ever more diversified scale. I am familiar with the abstract discussions, current nowadays, dealing with the question whether or not municipal government may be rightly termed a matter of business. These discussions deal only with definitions. They play with words and phrases. I am not able to see that they bear upon the real work that we have before us in this country.

Nor do I see anything practical to be gained at present by arguments, either for or against the extension of the working functions of municipal government in the direction of local Collectivism, or, as some people prefer to put it, Socialism. The principles of municipal collectivism were established long ago. What we have to deal with now is the practical working out of those principles in concrete instances, as such instances arise.

Inasmuch as we are not going to revive the system of private wells and town pumps, but are universally committed in all enlightened cities to a public water supply, it clearly behooves us to see that the public supply is procured and distributed upon the best possible engineering, financial, and sanitary principles. Inasmuch as we have no intention of going back in this country to the very recent period of private cesspools and open drains, it behooves us to deal in the most enlightened way with the problem of drainage, to the end that the sewer system may perfectly fit the local situation, and that the ultimate sewage disposal may meet the requirements of sanitary science, with a due regard to the economic principles involved. Since good streets, well made and well kept, are a public necessity, and we have no intention of relapsing to primitive conditions in that respect, it plainly devolves upon us to make the paving as good and as durable as engineering experience can devise, and to clean the streets as perfectly as the health and comfort of the community would require. Inasmuch as we do not intend to revert to the period when vagrancy, common begging, street rowdyism, and a great variety of ordinary nuisances and minor misdemeanors were freely tolerated as a matter of course, but on the contrary do intend to maintain conditions of order, decency, and safety throughout the bounds of the community, it needs no argument to show that we ought to avail ourselves of the best possible methods in the organization and management of the police service, and of the establishments that have to do with the detention and correction of offenders and with the relief of distress. Since, furthermore, we have long ago accepted the principle that it is both the right and the duty of the community to make provision for the instruction of all children, to the end that our average standards of civilization may not decline in the process of transmission from one generation to the next, it is plain enough that our public schools ought to be as good as they can possibly be made, and that their methods ought, from time to time, to be adjusted to meet the new needs of a changing situation.

These statements are the merest commonplace. The man who in our day would argue against good water, good drainage, good streets and good schools, as proper things for a community to secure by collective action, would be looked upon as a mere anachronism, or else as an after-dinner theorizer whose views have nothing to do with those practical concerns that belong to the working hours of the day.

And yet, while everybody believes that these things belong to what may be called the irreducible minimum of a modern city's public necessities, how many of our cities actually possess them ? Certainly not many. If the water supply suffices in quantity, in too many instances it falls short in quality. If the ramification of sewers is sufficient to collect liquid waste, it too frequently happens that proper provision is not made for the disposal of sewage. If the street system is judiciously laid out, it is seldom the case that good paving extends beyond a few streets, or that there is any efficient system for keeping the streets clean. If the school houses provide places enough for the children who ought to attend, which is not the case in the great majority of our large towns, it is seldom that the system or the methods of instruction come anywhere near meeting the proper demands of the present day.

Now I am well aware that I have sometimes been accused of presenting an unduly favorable view of contemporary conditions in European cities. I have only to reply that what I have said about cities abroad is in plain print and is true. In many things that belong to the functions of the modern city, most of the European towns are relatively in advance of our own. Nor is it true that the better municipal appointments of European cities are to be attributed either to their greater age or to their superior wealth ; for they are not so rich as our cities by any means, nor, considered as modern urban communities, are they any older. All cities of the modern type belong to the existing regime of steam transportation and industry. For all purposes that municipal administration has now to concern itself with, the modern city is nowhere fifty years old. Considered as a great urban centre, Chicago is of about the same age as Berlin ; and Boston, New York and Baltimore are as old as Glasgow, London and Hamburg. Considered for purposes of modern improvements, Cincinnati, for example, is as old as any city of its size in Europe, and richer than almost any that could be named.

Why, then, to cut short these comparisons, have European cities accomplished more than our own in these practical, concrete directions ? I have thought about the matter a good deal, and have investigated it very considerably, studying home conditions quite as carefully as I have those abroad, although I have written more about European cities. And I have reached one firm conclusion, which is that with anything like as good administration in this country as in Europe, we should have been not simply as far advanced in our municipal appointments, but vastly further advanced than the European cities, because all the material conditions have been so much more favorable in our own country.

We have done many things extremely well in this

country, for the reason that private initiative possesses intense energy and high efficiency. And it has happened once in a while, by a stroke of luck, that some department of public administration has for the moment borrowed the personal resources of private enterprise. Now, it happens that in England, France and Germany, municipal work is carried on under a system which normally gives the public the benefit of the best efforts of the best trained men. With us, public work is carried on under a system which normally gives the public something less than the best efforts of men who average far below the best.

Previous to 1890, New York had spent vastly more money for street paving than any city of comparable size or conditions in Europe ; and yet New York had only one or two well-paved streets. And this is typical. No language can well exaggerate the frightful losses that American communities have suffered in the thirty years since the civil war through bad administration. Thousands of millions of dollars would only begin to express the tangible losses. And I hold the spoils annex of the American party system as chiefly responsible for this waste of resources and of opportunities.

Certain American visitors, who have recently taken a glance here and there at politics in Europe, have come home to sneer at the demands of those in this country who advocate administrative reform in our cities and who sometimes cite European experiences as affording instructive lessons. These scornful personages have in their turn sought to convince the people of this country that partisanship prevails in precisely the same way in European cities, and particularly in those of England, as we have been accustomed to see partisanship prevail in our American cities.

I absolutely deny that this is true. It is true, that,— to an extent which would seem to me to be unfortunate, —the annual elections which fill one-third of the seats in the municipal councils of England have recently been fought to an increasing extent upon the Liberal and Conservative lines of the national parties. Nevertheless, it is worth while here to observe that in the recent elections held on November 1st, there were as usual a very great number of non-contested seats, which simply means that the councilman for a given ward, regardless of his preferences in national politics, had served his constituents in local matters so well that nobody opposed his re-election for another term ; and thus his unopposed nomination gave him another three years of office without the expense or trouble of holding an election in his ward. The revolt of the Liberal Unionists in England, which made an intense feeling between the Gladstonians and the followers of Mr. Chamberlain, was to a considerable extent responsible for the infusion of national politics in the municipal elections. But even in Birmingham, where these November elections for the town council have often been most stubbornly contested, I have not been able to discover that there is the slightest taint of partisanship in appointments, or in the practical work of administration.

In one-fourth of these English municipalities holding their regular elections last November, the polls were not opened in a single ward, for the reason that only one candidate was presented in each division. In the remaining three-fourths of the English municipal corporations there were also of course a great number of uncontested wards. In many instances where contests did occur, it is true (as I have taken pains to ascertain), that there was no question of party politics involved, but only local or personal questions.

In Liverpool, on the other hand, the fight was a very spirited one on party lines, although even there in seven wards, one-fourth of the whole number, no contest was made. It happens that just now the advanced Liberals in England are trying in every way to show that the tide of national feeling is turning against the existing Tory government. For this reason the Liverpool Radicals contested nineteen Conservative council seats. But in eighteen cases out of the nineteen, the public preferred to endorse things as they were rather than to make a change.

In another English town, every one of the retiring members was a candidate for re-election, and every one of them was defeated ; but this was because public opinion was in favor of a new municipal water supply, and elected new men who were committed to the desired policy. In the great town of Sheffield there were contests in only two wards. But the great and significant point that I wish to enforce is that in not one of all these English towns was there involved, even incidentally, the idea that the result could in any wise affect the appointive offices, either for or against members of any political party.

If the chief of police, the superintendent of water supply, the head of the public library, the superintendent of the municipal gas works, the manager of the great sewage disposal establishment, or any other of the principal working heads of departments, should resign, it is almost inconceivable that the party results of an election for the municipal council would have the slightest effect upon the appointment of a successor to such a department head. Far less is it conceivable that the victory of one party or the other in a municipal election should result in the removal of an efficient head of a department for the sake of giving the place, for partisan or personal reasons, to someone connected with the victorious element. It is absolutely agreed on all hands in England that the discretionary heads of administrative municipal departments shall be selected for their fitness, regardless of their party affiliations, and that they shall be retained so long as their conduct is good and their services are efficient. And if this is true of heads of departments, it is hardly necessary to add that it is also true of the entire ramification of subordinate appointments.

So far as practical every-day administration is concerned, a large part of the difference between the English municipal system and the system established by the new charter of the Greater New York lies in the fact that in England the municipal council exercises the appointing power, while in New York the appointing power is exercised by the mayor. The working administration is carried on in England by a number of appointed heads of departments, and the same thing may be said of the government of the Greater New York. In England those heads of departments are chosen by the municipal council, working through its committees. In New York they are to be chosen by the mayor. If the very large Tory majority in the Liverpool municipal council should decide to dismiss existing heads of departments in order to appoint Tories to succeed them,—selected on the New York plan with special reference to private and personal as well as political affiliations,—such an act would involve a greater change in the actual system of government in England than would be involved in changing the constitutional monarchy to an absolute monarchy like that of Russia. The repudiation of a non-partisan civil service on purely business principles under the merit system, would signify a change incomparably more vital than any possible variations in the mere outward structure of municipal government,—such for instance as appear when one compares the typical English municipal system with the French, the German, or even that which the Greater New York Charter provides

Further than that, the making of partisan appointments to office would be deemed in English towns not merely a blow at the efficiency of administration, but also a violation of every principle of civic justice and equality, a proscription of half the tax-paying community by the governing authorities,—in short, an act of hostility, which carried on to its logical end would mean the denial of civic rights to all citizens not adhering to a single political party, or, in a word, civil war. At least the sharp drawing of political lines in municipal appointments in England would now be deemed by public opinion to be practically as objectionable as political discrimination in courts of justice, or as the exemption from taxation of all the adherents of the party in power. And the same thing may be said concerning the generally excellent public service that one finds in French,· German, and other continental cities.

When therefore American politicians return from their brief vacations in Europe to tell us that they find party lines recognized in municipal elections abroad, they have told us only a very limited part of the truth. There is no such thing in England, or France, or Germany, as a *partisan management* of municipal public works. I have known such a thing in an American city as ninety-nine per cent. of the common labor employed (to an extent of hundreds of. workmen on streets and other public work), adhering not only to the national party, but also to the local faction of the party that held the reins of municipal power· for the time being. And I· have known, as everyone else in this country has, of more than one city where at least nine-tenths of the public appointees holding positions requiring skill or the exercise of discretion have also been filled in the same way by the henchmen of a political boss or faction.

As our civilization advances further, and as the necessary functions of a municipal government become more varied and elaborate, this American system of partisanship in appointments becomes more and more intolerable. Favoritism to the extent of a partisan appointment or two in the health service may mean a great epidemic, with paralysis of business as well as loss of life, where the European system of non-partisanship would have meant perfect safety.

Just now there is much agitation throughout the United States touching the question of the proper regulation in the general interest of such quasi-public services as the supply of illumination and the provision of transit facilities. One hears the advocacy of public ownership even in strange and unexpected quarters. The workingmen of the City of New York have of late especially identified themselves with the demand for a great extension of the functions of municipal government. Yet they have elected as mayor, a gentleman who approached the assumption of his official duties with the one bold and unqualified announcemenc that nobody could even be considered for an appointment, unless he belonged to the Democratic party,—by which he meant Tammany Hall and its affiliated organizations. Surely the workingmen of New York ought to have intelligence enough to understand that a non-partisan administration, based strictly upon reasonable assurances of long tenure and of promotion on principles of fitness, must be the *sine qua non* of any successful extension of municipal functions.

They have learned something of successful experiments abroad in the municipalization of lighting supplies, and even of street railroads; and they are clamoring for a radical advance in such directions by our American cities. But if they care for these things they should have learned also that there is no partisanship in Glasgow's municipal transit,—which has been made successful through the meritorious labors of Mr. John Young precisely as street-cleaning in New York has been made successful through the meritorious labors of Colonel Waring.

How has it happened that a place like Glasgow has proceeded to increase the range of its important municipal activities? The answer is perfectly plain. That city was emboldened to try new ventures because its non-partisan administration of earlier ones had been thoroughly satisfactory. John Young had been the Colonel Waring of Glasgow for a good many years. That is to say, he had been superintendent of the cleansing department, and had worked out and administered a remarkably perfect system for the cleansing of the streets and the collection and disposal of garbage. If anybody knows John Young's politics, certainly nobody cares. He has been allowed to organize and manage the municipal street railway service on strict business principles, and has promptly made a success of it,—precisely as Colonel Waring, if commissioned to organize and manage a municipal lighting service, or a transit service, would have no difficulty in carrying the matter out as successfully as any like services elsewhere.

If the workingmen of New York had really wanted to take the short cut to enlarged municipal ownership and operation, they ought to have voted for Seth Low, for the simple reason that Seth Low was pledged to organize a municipal administration on strict business principles, free from the taint of politics, precisely as Glasgow or Berlin is organized. Tammany, in its latest platform, professes to have become converted to the principles of enlarged municipal ownership of natural monopolies of supply. But in the very same breath Tammany informs us that a municipal lighting plant, for instance, if established in New York, shall not be managed by a man selected solely for his fitness to manage such a business, but must be managed in any case by a politician belonging to Tammany Hall.

Nothing more ignominious in all the history of American municipal government has ever been witnessed than the recent confession on the part of the city government of Philadelphia that it was incompetent to manage the lighting supply, and its transfer by lease for a long term of years of the municipal gas plant to a private corporation. Nearly every large city in Europe conducts the business of supplying light as a municipal department. Under any ordinary decent system of administration, there is probably no department of municipal business so simple in its nature and so perfectly easy to finance and to administer as a gas supply. The European cities have been conspicuously successful in this particular branch of their municipal business. They have justified the experiment of the municipalization of lighting supplies by making the venture financially beneficial to the public treasury, by greatly improving the public lighting of the streets, and above all by a greatly diffused and cheapened supply to private citizens. Where European cities have been so successful Philadelphia has confessed failure; and the sole reason lies in the fact that the party spoils system, rather than the merit system, has dominated the city government.

The police, the fire department, the care of the

streets, the erection of public works, the water supply, the sanitary services, and all the varied practical business of carrying on a modern city,—these are not properly matters of party politics. Such public interests should, in their every-day working, be as free from the bias of partisan politics as the administration of justice. Most people in this country admit that school teachers ought not to be appointed for party reasons ; and we shall in time come to see with perfect clearness that all other departments of local administration, not less than the schools, must for efficiency's sake be put on the basis of pure merit. When that time arrives it will be safe for the municipality to extend its functions, if such extension should seem desirable.

But on the other hand it might then appear to make very much less difference. For example, I do not find that in a German city it signifies much one way or the other whether the municipal government itself provides an electrical plant and runs it, or gives a charter to a private company. This is because in Germany the municipal governments are efficient enough to take full care of the rights of citizens. And so, if a private company is to manage the electrical supply, it will proceed under the terms of a franchise that exacts everything that is right, both for the municipal treasury and also for the private user of electric light or power. But where, as in this country, municipal administration is on a party basis, and the party is locally controlled by a clique or a boss, there is no one who is looking out efficiently for the rights of the city or of the citizens. The corporation seeking a franchise is looking out for its own interests, and the politicians in control of the municipal situation are looking out for themselves and their party machine. The consequence is that the city and the citizens are usually betrayed. Those who ought to serve the community are traitors to it. The treasury of the city goes empty, while the treasury of the party machine is enriched. In Europe, with permanent non-partisan administrative and law officers in positions of authority, franchises are always carefully drawn in the interest of the public, and it is practically impossible for a private corporation to obtain any public privilege that is not paid for at its full worth. Under our system, on the contrary, the party spoils administration breaks down public ownership as in Philadelphia, and makes it easy for private ownership to rob the community of valuable franchises, as in New York.

In conclusion of the whole matter, it would seem to me that all honest citizens,—whatever their point of view regarding such questions as public ownership or the extension of municipal functions,—ought to be able to unite upon the indispensable prerequisite of administration upon business principles, whether the work of the municipality is to be enlarged or whether it is to be diminished. A more practical issue cannot be named. And so long as the existing political parties decline to accept the principle of non-partisanship in the making of municipal appointments and the carrying on of municipal business, there will of necessity be a field for independent action in city elections. When, as in England or on the European continent, our political parties shall have abandoned the local spoils system frankly and in good faith, they may strive for victory in municipal campaigns as much as they please and without reproach.

SECOND PAPER.

By Horace E. Deming.

Political partisanship may properly be roused to most intense activity in determining whether there shall be high tariff or low tariff, protection with incidental revenue or revenue with incidental protection; but there is no proper place for political partisanship in collecting the revenue honestly. The country may be storm swept by the contending political policies of the single gold standard and a dual gold and silver standard at a fixed ratio; but whichever policy wins the work at the government mint demands not political partisanship, however pure or however intense, but plain every day honest work for honest wage.

A wide gulf lies between questions of public policy on which men divide into opposing political parties and questions that involve merely the honest and efficient administration of public business. Civil Service Reform has nothing to do with the former questions. It does not concern itself with them. With questions of administration it does and must concern itself until all appointments to government positions having nothing to do with determining questions of public policy on which men divide into political parties are made solely for merit and fitness without regard to any partisan political considerations whatsoever.

In short, civil service reform is an administrative reform, not a political reform. It seeks to exclude " politics " altogether from the business-side of the government's operations. Civil service reform means that all employees of the government having merely to do with matters of administration shall be appointed, shall hold their places, and shall be discharged not because they or their sponsors have or have not done political party service but because the employee is personally fit or unfit for his position.

This principle is aptly called the merit principle. How far is it an important factor in the solution of the problem of municipal government? To those who have investigated the . nature of the municipal problem the answer is almost too self evident. To others it may be of service to be reminded for a moment how some of the chief activities of a municipality, those which concern most intimately the daily life of its citizens, have come into existence.

When a trail has become a cartroad the cartroad a highway, the highway a constantly traveled and closely thronged city street, the proper maintenance and care of the latter is an administrative problem of the greatest importance to scores of thousands and it may be to hundreds and hundreds of thousands. It is often also a problem of the greatest difficulty. Experience has demonstrated that the streets cannot even be kept clean without the aid of the merit principle.

The isolated house on the prairie or the hill-side is kept healthy by the simplest sanitary measures and its location may be such that it remains healthy in spite of a reckless disregard of even ordinary sanitary precautions. The building in the congested tenement region of a crowded city not only breeds enfeebled vitality and too often death among its own occupants unless extraordinary sanitary precautions are enforced, but becomes a radiating centre of disease. The enforcement of these precautions is a matter of administration; and the lower the death rate of a city the higher the appreciation and the more rigid the enforcement of the merit principle in the administration of the city's health ordinances.

A sparse population may be sufficiently served by a single teacher in a one roomed school house and the teacher may build the fire, sweep the school room and teach his score or two of scholars. When each school house must accommodate a thousand pupils and there must be hundreds of such school houses, the administrative problem becomes one of the first magnitude. Without the merit system the problem is insoluble. Go to any city in the land; if its public school system is successful, you will find the merit principle actively enforced by the department of education; if its public school system is a failure the merit principle is absent or but lamely recognized.

Wherever there is a multitude in a limited area good order must be enforced, laws in the interest of public morals must be observed, peace must be preserved and a special group of the citizens must be set apart from the rest and charged with the duty and the responsibility of enforcing the laws and preserving order and peace. Is this class corrupt? Does it sell protection to vice and overlook violations of law for its own private gain then there is no merit principle in the police administration. When you find the wives of police captains large landlords and the brothers or cousins of chiefs of police yacht owners, the "starch" has been taken out of police civil service.

What we have said of streets, of the public health, of education and of the police is equally applicable to each of the departments of municipal public service. Each is largely, if not chiefly an administrative problem, and good administration whether of private or public business depends in its last analysis upon the selection of its agents solely with reference to their personal merit and fitness. In the public service the

recognition and enforcement of this truth are incomparably
more important and its disregard more far reaching in evil results than in private business.

It is not alone that the private employer must pay in his
own person and out of his own pocket the loss occasioned by
his unwise selection of employees, while in the public service
the public treasury pays the bill and the official superior may
even profit pecuniarily and politically by the incompetence or
dishonesty of his subordinates, but the public administrative
service is subjected to a new master as each change of political policy brings a new party into power. If now the personnel of the purely administrative service is to shift with each
change of political policy efficient administration is impossible
no matter how lavishly the public funds may be spent to secure
it. It is as if the Pennsylvania Railroad Company should
change its directors every two or three years on questions of
policy such as extending its lines by lease or purchase, con-
structing new lines, acquiring additional terminals or coal
fields, furnishing through transportation, and the like, and with
each change of directors should call into its service an entirely
new set of station agents, trainmen, superintendents, machin-
ists and civil engineers. The directors' policy might be never
so good, the administration would be unspeakably bad. No
one doubts or denies these obvious truths as applied to ordinary business affairs, why should there be any doubt of their
being equally truths and equally obvious in the case of municipal government.

It is not surprising therefore that there is not a well governed city anywhere whose civil service is not based upon the
merit principle and not an ill governed city in whose civil service the evil effect of neglect or positive disregard of this principle do not serve as an example and a warning. These propositions are true of the cities of France and Spain of Germany and England under their widely varying forms of government as well as of the cities in our democratic republic.
Municipal government whatever its form and in whatever
country is an attempt to meet the common needs of a considerable population concentrated within a limited area. What
factor is or can be so important in the solution of this problem
as administrative skill and honesty? And the more populous
the city the more imperative the demand for honesty and skill

in administration. Whatever the plan of municipal government, however carefully devised, and by whomsoever attempted to be carried out, it is always and everywhere a failure unless the merit principle obtains in the municipal public service and the measure of the failure is the extent of the violation of this principle.

But while it is true that civil service reform is an administrative reform, the existence or absence of the merit principle in the public service is also a decisive factor indetermining important questions of purely municipal policy. Shall the city own or operate its system of intra mural transit? Shall it provide its own system of lighting? Shall it undertake on an adequate scale the economical and sanitary disposition of the city's waste? Shall it establish museums and libraries? Shall it have an intelligent system of large and small parks? Shall the management and improvement of its water front be a matter of public or private enterprise? The mere aggregation of population within a small area creates innumerable sources of revenue; shall these be utilized for the profit of the public treasury? Shall the city go on indefinitely giving away to private individuals the income its own existence creates and which its own needs require? Must the tax rate go ever higher while the almost exhaustless streams of the city's wealth forever flow into private coffers? These are some of the questions confronting the policy determining authority of every considerable city in this and other countries. Where the merit principle prevails we know what are the answers to these questions. Where the merit principle is absent or is but lamely applied we also know the answers. And in a democratic country these answers are breeding a popular unrest and a political discontent that may well make thoughtful men pause. The baleful compact between the political "boss" and the corporation which exists by public favor and lives by or on the public revenue, if it continues, means the sure destruction of our present form of government, and what may then take its place let wiser men than I foretell.

The powerful forces underlying modern industrial civilization are driving a larger and larger proportion of the population into the cities. In our older States the city dweller already constitutes the majority in the electorate. The City vote chooses the majority of the State legislature. The boss of the most populous city in the State aspires to be and often is the boss of the State. What makes this possible? Is there any doubt that not the least important reason is the fact that the merit principle is not rigidly enforced in the municipal civil service? Imagine, if you can, a city boss without patronage or hope of any, with nothing to give and nothing to promise save at his own personal expense. Is it not true that so long as the merit principle is absent in municipal administration a corrupting political force is steadily at work producing the political boss and that not only successful municipal government is impossible but the unclean municipal politics begets unclean state politics and steadily tends to create a national government after its own kind? On the other hand, imagine New York City, Buffalo, Troy, Albany, Syracuse, Rochester and the lesser cities of New York State each a city without political patronage within its limits, each a city in whose public service the merit principle wholly prevailed. Municipal government in the State of New York would no longer be a problem.

Civil Service Reform is not by any means the only reform needed, nor will good government be accomplished without the aid of other vital reforms; but every stride forward in Civil Service Reform brings their accomplishment nearer, makes their success more sure; and it is certain that a successful municipal government without the observance of the merit principle in its civil service is unthinkable.

The Municipal Situation in Ohio.

By Rufus B. Smith.

When the forefathers of this republic wrested this country
from European and monarchical domination and established the people of the country as its sole rulers, they
doubtless believed that no time would arrive when in the
slightest degree the people would cease to eagerly and diligently participate in the management of its public affairs.

The country, however, has rapidly developed large cities
whose material interests are large, varied and complex, whose
government requires the constant employment of thousands
of persons, whose annual expenditures run into the millions,
but the majority of whose citizens give but little, if any attention to its affairs; either because their private affairs require
their almost exclusive attention, or, as said by Mr. Bryce, because "The population is so large that the individual citizen
feels himself a drop in the ocean, his power of affecting public
affairs seems insignificant, and his pecuniary loss through
overtaxation or jobbery or malversation is trivial in comparison with the trouble of trying to prevent such evils."

The result has been what naturally would be expected.
The political power of the cities has passed into the control of
the few who are willing to make a business of politics, and to
devote a large part, and in some cases their entire time and
energy to it.

That the citizens of the large cities of the United States are
dissatisfied with the government which this few gives them, is
a proposition which is so generally conceded that it seems
almost unnecessary to affirm it. If denied, one has to read
only casually any of the metropolitan journals with the
charges and counter charges they contain of maladministration, with the abundant evidence they furnish in most cases to
support the charges; to observe the frequency with which legislatures change the form of city governments, in the hope of find-

ing some form which will obviate all evils; to observe the apparently fickle and bewildered manner in which the people vote into power first one party and then another party or one set of men under the name of a party and then another set, and again return to those at first voted out and back again, progressing always in a circle and never forward; to note the public expressions of opinion in all assemblies of men that are not partisan in character; or to hear the expressions of opinion on every side in private life.

The large cities of Ohio constitute no exception in the matter of municipal government to the other large cities of the Union. The same conditions surround them that surround the other cities of the country. They are no better and they are no worse.

It is believed, however, by those who are in sympathy with the purposes of this association that the great, underlying radical cause of the mis-government of American cities, is their failure to recognize and apply the principles for which this association contends; and that if the people of the large cities of Ohio will recognize this fact they will find in it a solution of this vexed and unsettled problem of municipal government.

What is the vital principle of civil service reform? To what extent has it been applied in the large cities of Ohio? Has the failure to apply it been a potent cause of their mis-government? Is there any reason why it should not be generally adopted as a part of a permanent municipal policy in Ohio? These and kindred questions are pressing for solution in this State.

The vital principle of civil service reform is simply this: That the person in the community best fitted to discharge the duties of a subordinate non-elective position and who is willing to serve shall be appointed to the same, and that he shall continue to serve until death, old age or other sufficient cause affecting his competency to discharge the duties of the office disqualify him from longer service.

To what extent has this principle been applied in the municipalities of Ohio?

Generally speaking, it may be stated that it was early recognized by the people of Ohio that the teachers in the public schools and the subordinates in the fire departments must not be changed at every municipal election if the degree of efficiency which is necessary to make such departments successful is to be secured. Consequently, long before any laws had found their way upon the statute books, permanency of tenure, with removal only for cause, came to be demanded by public opinion, and constituted a sort of unwritten law which officials dared not, at least, openly or generally, violate. Within recent years, however, this public opinion has found partial expression in the statutes, and in 1895 a law was passed which declared that all teachers who shall have served seven successive years in the public schools of cities of the first grade of the first class, whether before or after or partly before or after the passage of the act should when appointed hold their positions until removed by death, resignation or for cause.

This act has placed several hundred of the teachers of this city upon a legal basis of permanent tenure and every year adds many to their number.

It is also provided by law that no teacher shall be employed in any public school of the State who has not shown himself or herself qualified by passing a required examination, and receiving a certificate of competency; but unfortunately the selection from those holding a teacher's certificate is entirely a matter of favor with the appointing power.

As respects the fire departments, it is also now provided by law that in this City and in Cleveland, Toledo and Dayton, no subordinate can be removed except for cause, although the power of removal is with the board that appoints and no examination of competency is required by law before an appointment can be made.

It will thus be seen that the statutory provisions with respect to the public schools and the fire departments are not as complete or as wide in their application as the true principles of civil service reform would demand; yet many of these deficiencies are supplied by an enlightened public opinion which makes a certain unwritten law in regard to the same.

As a result of this written and unwritten law the appointees in these departments abstain from active participation in politics and are never openly, at least, a part of any political machine; and the departments, especially when compared to the other departments of municipal government, may be said to be upon a fairly satisfactory basis, with much to be hoped for, it is true, but with a steady development in the right direction, which development in the course of time, it is hoped, will result in the adoption of all the principles of civil service reform, when any evils that now exist in the departments will disappear.

Up to within a comparatively recent period, however, the police departments of the large cities, as is still true of the smaller municipalities of the State, were overhauled with the incoming of every new mayor. All who were either politically opposed to the new mayor, either because of affiliation with the opposite party or with an opposing faction in his own party, were put to the sword, and a new force mustered in, whose main, and generally whose sole claim to position, was that of loyalty to the political fortunes of the new mayor. As municipal elections are frequent in this State and the terms of officers short, the police force was in an almost constant state of demoralization. It necessarily became a huge political machine, bent upon selfish ends, yet wearing the cloth and invested with the baton of the police power of the State.

When a mayor was to be nominated the police force of the city filled the convention hall of their party clamoring and insisting as individuals and officials for the nomination of their favorites; and when the election came on they surrounded the polling booths, electioneering for their candidate, assuming to be guardians of the peace, yet arresting upon mere pretence, intimidating under color of office, and resorting to acts of fraud and violence to elect their candidate.

This conduct finally became so scandalous and notorious that public opinion became aroused and demanded their retirement from active participation in politics. A reform police law was enacted. Applicable at first only to the City of Cincinnati, it was subsequently followed by other laws substantially similar, which were applicable to many other large cities of the State. The law as applied to this city may be briefly stated as follows: The mayor has power to make appointments as a matter of favor subject to the approval of a nonpartisan board of police commissioners, appointed by the Governor, and no removal can be made except for cause upon charges filed before and heard by the board. While not required by law so to do, the board, nevertheless, compels a practical examination of an appointee to determine his fitness before it gives its approval to the appointment.

In this city, by reason of the civil service features alluded to, as if by the touch of a magician's wand, the demoralized and lawless police force gave way to a splendid body of men of superb physique, upright conduct and great efficiency, the only faults which the system has shown arising from the power of the mayor to appoint as a matter of favor. Yet the system as a whole has been so great an improvement over the old one, that no public man to-day would venture to suggest a return to the old system. Such a suggestion would encounter the hearty and unanimous condemnation of all citizens, irrespective of party.

The principle, however, of selection and promotion for merit, and retention during good behavior, which, to the extent I have described it, prevails in the administration of the school, fire and police departments of this and many other large cities of this State, as yet in no degree has been applied to the other subordinate positions in our municipal government. In all other departments, in the main, what is known as the spoils doctrine has prevailed, borrowing its title from the famous declaration "To the victors belong the spoils."

The fact that a different system has prevailed in the other departments is not due to the fact that the public mind, having been directed to the subject, and having been advised in regard to it, and having considered the arguments for and against it, has decided upon its adoption, but is due to the fact that the people have not heretofore realized the dangers of the system when applied to departments other than the police, fire and school departments, and to a vague feeling that the merit system is undemocratic and un-American and that the spoils system is absolutely essential to the maintenance of political parties.

The advocates of the merit system are convinced that these objections are not well founded, and so far as the members of this association are concerned, no arguments are necessary to confirm those convictions; but in as much as the local association at the next session of the Ohio Legislature, which meets in January, will present for enactment a bill which looks towards placing all the subordinate positions in the large cities under the operation of civil service reform laws, the occasion seems to be opportune, pertinent and important for a submission to the people of this State, under the auspices of the meeting of this association of a brief statement of the reasons why the civil service in the large cities of the State should be reformed along the lines suggested by the advocates of this movement.

What is the purpose of the organization of a city? What is the mission it is called upon to perform? It has little, if anything, to do with questions affecting the political rights of its citizens; those questions upon which his rights to person and property depend. Such as, for instance, questions relating to the creation and punishment of crimes, except mere minor offenses, the mode of acquiring and transferring and the devolution of property, of making and discharging contracts, or of recovering for injuries to person, property or character. Such questions and questions of a kindred nature fall strictly within the domain of Federal and State legislation.

A municipal corporation is organized for business purposes, of which the following are illustrations: to furnish adequate police and fire protection: to provide good streets and sidewalks and to keep them clean and in repair; to provide good schools, pure water, sufficient parks, and proper sewer and sanitary arrangements; to determine as to the proper manner of laying gas and water pipes, of erecting telegraph and telephone poles, and of laying rails for street railroads; and to determine whether the municipality shall own and operate its own gas works, water works, and street railroads, and if not, upon what terms such franchises shall be granted to private persons or corporations.

In the discharge of its various functions as a business corporation, in large cities, a great number of persons must necessarily be constantly employed in non-elective positions.

In the city of Cincinnati the number of such persons runs into the thousands, and the annual expenditure in salaries and wages, runs into the millions. Thus, in the city of Cincinnati, in the year 1896, there were employed in non-elective positions 5513 persons; and in the county of Hamilton, of which the city of Cincinnati in population and wealth constitutes the main part, there were employed 262 persons, making a total employment, in both the city of Cincinnati and the county of Hamilton, of 5771 persons. The amount thus expended in salaries and wages in the city of Cincinnati was $2,830,555.94; and in the county of Hamilton, $303,659.00; making a total annual expenditure for both city and county of $3,144,214.-94. In this estimate the judges and clerks of election are considered city employees because appointed by a city board, but the compensation for the same is part of the expenditure of the county as they are paid by the county.

Excluding, however, the election judges and clerks and employees of the school, fire and police departments, there still remains a total of 2400 persons, with an annual expenditure for the salaries and wages of the sum of $1,525,229.28.

From these figures it will be readily seen that the question as to the manner of securing employees in this and other large cities in Ohio, and of making the expenditures for the same, is one of the most vital interest.

The principle of selection adopted by every large private business concern in determining upon its employees is to select those persons who, for the salary or wages fixed, are best fitted to discharge the duties of a position and to retain them in such position as long as their service is satisfactory, promoting them from time to time as vacancies may occur in superior positions, provided they have shown themselves qualified to fill such vacancies. Such a system secures the highest efficiency because it secures the best qualified persons: inspires them to their best efforts, by making retention and promotion dependent solely upon such efforts; and fills them with enthusiasm and ambition by holding out the reward of promotion as a consequence of the faithful discharge of duty. As the system secures the greatest efficiency, it is necessarily the most economical.

What would be thought of the business foresight of a private business concern which, in place of the system of selection of subordinates, just described, every six months would take a vote of its employees upon the questions that divide the great political parties of the nation (as is the case with the municipal corporations of Ohio), and each six months would reorganize its force of employees, retaining only those who hold the same political views as the proprietor, discharging those who differ and substituting for them strangers who know nothing about the business? Does any sensible man suppose a business run on those lines could be successful or that it would be anything more than a question of time when the business would go into bankruptcy.

It is true that unsuccessful municipal corporations are not wound up in the courts of bankruptcy (although an application was recently made to an Ohio court by a tax-payer of one of our populous and wealthy cities to have a receiver appointed for the City). A municipal corporation must continue its existence. A failure, however large or disastrous, must be continually met by the tax-payers; and whatever indebtedness may have been incurred by officials in the past, from the very nature and purposes of the organization of a municipal corporation, its officers are continually authorized to and must make further expenditures. Otherwise the community lapses into a state of anarchy.

Considered, therefore, merely in the abstract as a question of business principle, the mode of selecting the employees of large cities in Ohio violates the first and most elementary principle of business; and ordinary foresight (if the lessons of experience were lacking, which they are not) could predict the following evils as a result of its adoption.

FIRST: A large part of the time following the election of the officers elected by the people which should be devoted to the consideration of questions of municipal policy is occupied in hearing and deciding as to which one of twenty applicants shall receive the appointment to each one of the subordinate positions under him. In this city a recently elected official who has the appointment of sixteen subordinates stated to me that for these sixteen positions there were seven hundred applicants, all of whose claims, together with those of their numerous supporters, were heard and considered by him.

SECOND: The appointments being temporary and the appointees frequently changing, a considerable time is occupied in each administration in learning the duties of the position; a larger force of persons is therefore required to discharge the duties of the office, increasing thereby the expenses of the departments; and at each municipal election, which may determine the tenure of office of the employees, a demoralization more or less wide spread and extending over a considerable period of time and affecting the efficiency of the service, necessarily follows.

THIRD: A large number of persons is continually attracted by the hope of getting into the public service and devote valuable time and energy to this end only at last to be disappointed; while those who are successful and secure positions retain them generally only for a length of time sufficient to take them out of the current of legitimate business, finding upon their effort to return that during their absence the business current has swept by them and from the fact that they have held public office business men look askance or with positive disfavor upon their applications.

There are other evils of the spoils system, however, which could not be foreseen in advance of its adoption by the large municipalities, but which practical experience in Ohio has demonstrated to be an inseparable concomitant of it. The most important of them may be enumerated briefly as follows:

First: The business of our large cities has become so complex and vast and requires so much attention that the average man in a large city finds it impossible to keep informed in regard to it. Sooner or later, therefore, it is found that one man or set of men who devote a large part and in some cases their entire time to politics, will come into the control of the party machinery, then of the conventions, and if the party is successful at the polls then of the offices, and with the offices of the subordinate positions in the same. The method by which this control is secured is well understood. The influence of such men quickly becomes sufficiently great to nominate for one of the principal offices some one who is satisfied with the salary of the office, and in order to secure the same, is quite willing to agree that those who secure him the nomination may appoint the subordinates under him; then another office is added upon the same terms; and then another, until all the subordinate positions, for all political purposes, are in control of the oligarchy.

If these appointments to the subordinate positions are judiciously made with reference to the ability of the appointees to be elected delegates from their respective precincts, the control of such men becomes riveted. Nothing short of a popular uprising can affect it. Once having secured control, all manner of persons and corporations who wish to use the combination flock to its support; but these latter influences are only aids and not the main support of the combination which is founded upon patronage, with which the army of followers are supported. Cut off the patronage and you destroy the army; for without patronage the leaders could neither attract or retain such a following. You can not cut off the patronage by abolishing the positions, for a large number of such positions is required to discharge the business of the city. But once let the subordinates know that they can retain their positions until discharged for cause, and that their only hope of advancement is through the faithful discharge of the duties of the positions they are filling and the call or order of neither leader nor leaders will give them any concern. From that moment the army is disbanded.

It may be inquired whether there is anything criminal or unlawful in this seizure of power by a few men? And whether such seizure is not one of the prizes of politics? The answer is, that there is not necessarily anything either criminal or unlawful in it, and that it is the legitimate and inevitable result of the spoils system applied to the offices of a large municipal corporation. But this very argument in justification of those who possess the power is a condemnation of the system which permits it: and the belief has ripened into a conviction in the minds of the electors of the large cities of Ohio, that the temptations to use such power for personal and sordid ends in one or all of the many avenues which such a power opens to its possessors, are too great to be entrusted with safety to them.

That civil service reform will destroy and prevent such control of a party is illustrated by the effect of the Federal Law upon the politics of this city. Prior to 1883 when that law was passed, the men who exerted the largest control over the nominations and conventions of the party were found in the Federal offices. Since 1883 such office holders have had but little more influence, if any, than they would have had if they had not held office.

Second: An inevitable result of the spoils system as demonstrated by its operation in Ohio, is that it increases the number and salaries of the subordinates, but decreases their efficiency. The explanation of these facts is that the greater the number of places and the more attractive the salaries, the greater the power of those in control: consequently there is a constant tendency to increase the number of employees: and as appointments are made mainly upon the ground of political service to the appointing power and not upon the ground of ability to discharge the duties of the office, the service is necessarily inferior to what it should be.

It is not contended that all subordinates under the spoils system are either dishonest or inefficient. Undoubtedly in this city there are many subordinates possessing both these qualifications. What is contended is, that under the merit system it will be found that as a general rule a larger percentage is found in the possession of these qualifications: and therefore the expense of running the office is correspondingly less.

Third : The influence of those in control of a party and assuming to speak for it is not limited to their own locality, but extends throughout the State, the legislature of which if in control of the same party grants any legislation that may be asked, excusing itself upon the plea that the legislation asked is a mere local matter in regard to which they must seek the advice of party leaders: whereas in fact the real reason is that most of the legislators, being ambitious of State honors, which must be secured through their party, are afraid to offend so overpowering a force in the party: or give their vote in exchange for votes in favor of local schemes which they wish to put through for their own localities.

Fourth : It is the practice of all parties in Ohio, on the occasion of each election, through the regularly constituted party committees to levy assessments upon those occupying subordinate positions for the purpose of raising a fund to assist the party in its contest at the polls. The ground upon which these assessments are levied is that the subordinate owes his position to the favor of a political party, and good faith to the party as well as self-interest requires that he should assist the party to maintain itself and win victories.

However effective the aid rendered to the party by the subordinate in the past may have been, no temporary disapproval of candidates or party policy or even personal poverty will be accepted as an excuse for omission to pay the assessment. An assessment levied must be paid or the penalty of a discharge from the position is rigidly enforced.

This practice is a legitimate result of the spoils system which regards the power of appointment and discharge as the perquisite of a political party instead of an attribute of government to be exercised solely in its own interest.

If it be conceded that a true public spirit would induce the subordinate as it would induce every other person in the community to contribute to his party such an amount as he could afford ; yet certainly it will not be contended that assessments are levied by political committees to enforce this moral obligation resting upon the subordinate; for the assessment is made without any inquiry as to whether the subordinate favors the candidates or the policy of the party which levies the assessment; and even if he is in sympathy with the candidates or the party policy it will not be seriously contended that the assessments are delicately adjusted by political committees to enforce the duty upon the subordinate, to which each citizen whether in office or out should respond. The assessments always go far beyond that limit. In Ohio in recent years they have been annually four per cent. of the salary.

If the subordinate can afford to pay these large assessments, then the salary or wages are beyond what they should be and the assessments in effect come out of the public treasury.

If the subordinate cannot afford to pay them they are an imposition and by decreasing his earnings tend to promote peculation and theft to reimburse himself.

Fifth. The evils of the spoils system heretofore considered, whether with respect to the government or the subordinate are of a material character.

There is, however, a moral aspect of the question which should not be overlooked.

The spoils system tends to lower the standard of patriotism by placing it on a mercenary basis. It teaches that the government is something to prey upon, that office is party plunder intended to benefit a party and the individual who fills the office; not an honorable distinction whose object is the serving of the whole people.

It tends also to destroy free thought and open expression of opinion and makes mere automatons of a large part of the young and old men of the nation or turns them into hypocrites lest they may fail to enjoy the fleshpots of office. Thus upon a republican government whose every institution should cultivate the spirit of patriotism and democracy is fastened a system which is constantly at work to destroy such a spirit.

But it is insisted that notwithstanding these objections to the spoils system we must bear with it because the objections to the merit or civil service reform system are even greater. These objections are mainly of two kinds.

The leaders and managers of the political parties in Ohio

have continuously insisted at all times and places, by argument and persuasion, by taunts and sneers, by charges of party disloyalty and by threats of party resentment and ostracism, that the spoils system is absolutely essential to the support of a political party and that without its existence political parties cannot maintain themselves or secure victories and therefore cannot accomplish the purpose of their organization.

As was said by Mr. Schurz, in his masterly address last night, this argument should be spurned by every true American as an insult to his patriotism. If the American people cannot be aroused to an interest in those great party questions which mark our political campaigns, unless a certain portion of them, in case of the success of the party with which they ally themselves, are to be paid for their interest by an office, then patriotism among the American people is a thing of the past, popular government in America is a failure, and the American Commonwealth is on the rocks.

The truth, however, is that instead of the appointing power being a source of strength, it becomes, in course of time, a source of weakness to any official or party that may exercise it; for the disappointments outnumber the appointments twenty to one. In this city the principal administrative board which has an immense civil patronage within its control, within the last ten years, sooner or later has defeated every party that controlled it, and, as the pendulum of popular disfavor swung to and fro, has been successively called the Board of Public Works, the Board of City Affairs, the Board of Public Improvement, the Board of Public Affairs, and the Board of Administration.

The last two elections in this city and county illustrate the same truth. In the Presidential election of 1896 Hamilton county gave McKinley 19,000 majority. Six months after at the municipal election in Cincinnati, without any reason for a change of view upon the political questions which had been the issues at the Presidential election the Republican candidate for mayor was defeated by 7,000; and at the election of this fall the entire Republican ticket including the legislative ticket, whose election might decide the fate of a United States Senator, was again defeated. Yet in this city and county the spoils system had been carried by the Republican party to perfection; and if one of the great virtues of the spoils system is that it wins party victories, certainly when the election of a United States Senator was at stake it should have vindicated its claim in this respect. On the contrary the system here having worked out its inevitable and logical result in investing the absolute control of the party in the hands of a few men, the popular indignation and resentment was so great at the possession of such power that, coupled with the disappointments for office, the entire party was disastrously defeated.

Yet so accustomed has the community become to these political revolutions that many seem unable to comprehend the significance of the same; and upon each occasion assert that the defeat is due to the persons who happened to be in control and not to the system that makes such control possible. Consequently new men in the Republican party and the old leaders in the Democratic party are pushing themselves to the front, appearing to think that in the last two elections they recognize a call long delayed to take charge of their respective parties and through the parties of the people; and that this city is rapidly passing into the control of another set of men, is too apparent for denial. The first act of the new administration was to discharge forty-six City Hall employees, including fifteen women who scrubbed the floors, without the slightest inquiry as to whether any of such employees were efficient or not. The same course will undoubtedly be followed with respect to all the other departments of the city as soon as the newly elected officers secure control; and from the ruins of one political machine will arise another.

What profit is there in all this for the people? Can they not see that if they wish to free themselves from political machines change of persons is immaterial? What is necessary is a change of system.

Recurring again for a moment to the argument that the spoils system is necessary for party success—Is it not true that if the spoils system is necessary to party success, and as all the great political questions of the day are largely determined by a contention between opposing parties, that the people of this community are recreant to their duty as citizens and patriots in allowing any part of the municipal government to be removed from the operation of the spoils system, and ought there to be any delay in placing the public schools, the fire and police departments upon the spoils basis? Surely the logic of the argument requires this result and the advocates of it should not shrink from the result to which their argument inevitably leads them.

I come now to consider the remaining objection to the merit system, viz., that it is un-American and aristocratic both in principle and practice. In principle, for the reason that rotation in office is the only system which gives an opportunity to every one in the community to aspire to and hold office, whereas the merit system excludes all but those who are so fortunate as to have had the advantages of a higher education and by continuing them in office builds up an aristocratic class in the community; and un-American in practice, for the reason that the examinations are not adapted to making a fair test of the qualifications of applicants but are impractical, technical, pedantic and scholastic, discriminating in favor of the few and beyond the reach of the plain people.

I fear that this objection has great weight in the minds of a very large number of well-intentioned people in this community and that they must be convinced that it is erroneous before the merit system can be assured of popular support. Fortunately the objection, like every other one that is made to it, is found, upon examination, to be fallacious and unfounded.

Our government is founded upon the principle that no man shall be born to office nor receive it as a favor from the powerful or privileged, but shall hold it because he has demonstrated by his ability or character that he is entitled to it. The merit system is simply an application of this principle to the minor non-elective positions of the government and is, therefore, the only true American system; the only one worthy of a true democracy. Instead of being a system that discriminates in favor of any particular class it is the only one that is entirely free from that objection. Political, religious or social influences count for nothing. The applicant must vindicate his right to the position for which he applies by his superior fitness to fill it. If he does that he receives the appointment. If he does not and another man does, what right has he to demand of the public that the latter shall be put aside and the public be compelled to accept his inferior service.

The contention, too, that the system builds up a privileged class and creates an aristocracy in the community, would be laughable if it were not seriously urged by well-intentioned persons. The average annual compensation of the subordinates in the large cities of Ohio would probably not be over $700 or $800 a year. Imagine an aristocracy, most of whom have families to support and educate, with an income of $800 a year. What luxurious practices borrowed from the effete monarchies of the old world and what insolence of office we should be compelled to endure from such a class! What an aristocracy the teachers of the public schools and the members of the police and fire departments in this city now constitute! What a demoralizing influence in our community is their extravagant and purse-proud mode of life!

As to the impractical character of the examinations—it is not true that the merit system necessitates impractical examinations. In support of this statement I wish to quote from the report for 1896 of the Civil Service Commission of Chicago, a city which a few years ago, by a popular vote, adopted the merit system. The report says:

" In regard to the competitive examinations provided for in the act, grave misunderstanding has existed in the public mind, which the commission would be glad to dispel. For this purpose, and as a matter of general information, there will be found attached to this report a number of examination papers taken at random from those that have been used in examinations held by the commission for different positions in the public service. It has been supposed by many that these examinations were in all cases made to test the *education* or *scholarship* of the applicant. Nothing could be further from the truth. The law requires that the examinations ' shall be practical in their character.' In all examinations for laborers, or for positions where only strength or mechanical skill is required there is no educational test whatever. For clerical and professional positions educational and technical tests are applied, but in every case, as the law requires, the examination is adapted to the requirements of the position to be filled and the advice and the assistance of men practically acquainted with the duties of the position is availed of in preparing the papers and in conducting the examinations."

Is not this method of examination fair and just to every one ?

Has a man ignorant of engineering—or, if not entirely ignorant, not possessed of sufficient knowledge to discharge the duties of the position—any right to demand of the public that he be employed as an engineer? Or a man who has no knowledge of drugs or their application a right to demand a position in the sanitary department which requires such a knowledge; or a man who reads and writes imperfectly, that he be employed as a clerk or accountant? And does not the standard adopted by the Civil Service Commission of Chicago open a wide field for employment in which the selections are not made by any test which requires either education or scholarship. We must learn to accustom ourselves to the idea that appointments should be made to benefit the public and not the appointee, and that a municipal government is neither a training school nor an infirmary. When that is done the difficulties that many minds seem to have with this question will disappear.

The contention, too, that under the merit system the men and women of college education will monopolize the best subordinate positions by reason of their greater ability to pass difficult examinations is found in practice to be illusory and without foundation; either because very few persons with a college education make application for these positions or because if they do they meet with no greater success than other persons. A good illustration of this fact is the one given last night by Mr. Schurz when he stated that in Massachusetts out of 9,323 persons successfully passing the examinations during eight years, only 157 were college graduates.

An argument quite commonly made in defense of the spoils system is that an officer elected by the people, and held responsible for his office by force of that circumstance and by analogy to a private business should be allowed to select his own subordinates; and that the merit system forces upon him men who are not of his own selection.

It is true that an officer is held responsible for the failures of his office so far as those failures are attributable to him, and no further. If any subordinate forced upon him is incompetent the merit system provides for a method of discharge, and if the subordinate unexpectedly proves dishonest, such dishonesty, where the merit system prevails, is not charged to him, nor is he compelled to bear the burdens of the same.

So far as the right of the elective officer to select his subordinates as the owner of a private business selects them is concerned, it is a sufficient answer to say that under the spoils system while in theory he has such·right, in practice he has not, because in practice his subordinates are selected for him by the managers of the political party to which he belongs.

To judge from the arguments that are urged to-day in this State against the adoption of civil service reform, one who was not informed on the subject would suppose that its advocates were attempting to impose upon the State a theoretical, utopian system, born only in the minds of dreamers, and advocated only by those who believe in "lunar politics." The truth, however, is that with the exception of Turkey and Morocco and certain South American Republics, the only civilized nation upon the face of the globe which adopts the spoils system, with respect to municipal government, is the United States; and it is one of the remarkable inconsistencies of the present American situation that on a subject which is largely practical in its nature, the American people, whose progress in the last century has shown them to be the most practical people of the world, possessing what may be termed a very genius for practical work, should be found in this department of practical life to be so far behind the civilized world as to rank with Turkey and Morocco.

The States of Massachusetts and New York, both of which have adopted the merit system, and the City of Chicago, have begun the advance. In these places, with the exception, I believe, of New York City, where the law has not been faithfully enforced, the new system has given the greatest satisfaction. Shall Ohio lag behind? Shall a State whose boast is that it contains more colleges than any other state in the Union still continue to do business upon Turkish principles?

At the last session of the Legislature in 1896 a civil service bill prepared by the local association was presented to the Legislature but was defeated. It passed the Senate, but was reconsidered there and defeated and never reached the house.

Another bill will be presented this winter. It does not impose the merit system upon the municipalities but leaves it to popular vote in each municipality to determine whether it shall be adopted. Can the Legislature of Ohio give any valid reason why the people of Cincinnati, Cleveland and the other cities of Ohio should not be permitted to vote upon this question and if they deem it best to adopt · the merit system? If the majority are opposed to it the measure will be defeated. In either event the popular will only will prevail. And whatever may be true of any other measure whose advocates are urging that it be submitted to a vote of the people, there is no danger in this case that any corrupt influence or influences will be exerted to secure the adoption of the merit system.

I have not time to go into the details of the bill. It may be that its advocates may be compelled at first to make concessions which they would regard as important. It seems to me that it would be the part of wisdom to make many concessions, provided they are not of a vital character, in order that the system may secure a foothold trusting to its merits to rapidly bring it into popular favor when amendments to the law may be easily secured. Our experience in Ohio has demonstrated that one of the vital features of the bill is that when once appointments are made they shall continue until the appointees are removed for cause relating to the competency or efficiency of the appointees upon charges filed before and heard by a tribunal different from that which has the power of appointment to the vacancy. It is the absence of this provision that in many cases has made non-partisan boards so unpopular in this state. For with the power of appointment and removal in the same board, even though it be non-partisan, unless public sentiment is such that it will not tolerate a removal other than for cause, it is found that one of two results follows: Either two political machines are built up, or what is the more usual result, by the appointment of men from the opposing party who are willing for the salary of the office to subordinate themselves to the political wishes of the appointing power one huge political machine is built up which embraces all parties in its wide embrace.

The fate of the bill in any form is problematical. It remains to be seen whether the people of the State require further and more disastrous object lessons in the spoils system before they realize its nature and effect. You may be " babblers to your own times " but the " prophetic voice " will yet be heard. Selfish interests, loose reasoning, ignorance and prejudice may delay the adoption of the principles of civil service reform; but its principles are founded in truth and justice and in the end they must prevail—their ultimate triumph is assured.

The subject invites to further discussion, but the limit of time forbids.

In closing I desire to express to the local association my appreciation of the honor shown me by its invitation to address the National Association upon this occasion. The names of many of the members of the National Association and the work of its members are familiar to every one who watches the progress of the better forces in American life. The distinguished services and high purposes of the association pursued with no motive but that of a patriotic desire of its members to benefit their fellow countrymen, gives assurance that in the future as in the past, the time will never come to this nation when the political abuses of the day will not find in opposition to them a disinterested and fearless class of men against whom "the gates of Hell shall not prevail." Upon such men the taunts and sneers which every movement for reform encounters, seem only to strengthen their arms and purpose and to clarify their brains. If at any time there come to such persons moments of depression, let them remember the words of a former president of this association now dead, but whose soul is marching on,—George William Curtis,— who, in reply to the sneers against the Pharisees of reform said:

"No American, it seems to me, is so unworthy the name as he who attempts to defend any national abuse or tries to hide it or who derides as pessimists and Pharisees those who indignantly disown it or raise the cry of reform. If a man proposes the redress of any public wrong he is asked severely whether he considers himself so much wiser and better than other men that he must disturb the existing order and pose as a saint. If he denounces an evil, he is exorted to beware of spiritual pride. If he points out a dangerous public tendency or censures the action of a party, he is advised to cultivate good humor, to look on the bright side, to remember that the world is a very good world, at least, the best going, and very much better than it was a hundred years ago. Undoubtedly it is, but would it have been better if everybody had then insisted that it was the best of all possible worlds, and that we must not despond if sometimes a cloud gathers in the sky

. . . When the sea is pouring into the ship through an open seam, everybody is aware of it. But then it is too late. It is the watch who reports the first starting of the seam who saves the ship.

"It is an ill sign when public men find in exposure and denunciations of public abuses evidences of the Pharisaic disposition and a tendency in the critic to think himself holier than other men.

＊　＊　＊　＊　＊　＊

"To the cant about the Pharisaism of reform there is but one short and final answer. The man who tells the truth *is* a holier man than the liar. The man who does not steal *is* a better man than the thief."

CONSTITUTION

National Civil-Service Reform League.

I.

The name of this organization shall be the National Civil-Service Reform League.

II.

The object of the National Civil Service Reform League shall be to promote the purposes and to facilitate the correspondence and the united action of the Civil Service Reform Associations.

III.

The League shall consist of all the Civil Service Reform Associations in the United States which signify their willingness to become members thereof. Any association hereafter expressing such willingness shall become a member of the League upon its being accepted as such by the League or the Executive Committee. Any member of any such association may be present at any meeting of the League and take part in the debates or discussions as the by-laws may provide.

IV.

At any meeting of the League, each association belonging to it shall be entitled to one vote upon every question coming before the League; such vote may be cast by a personal representative designated by each association, or by proxy, as the by-laws may provide. If no such designation be made the delegates from such association present at such meeting, or a majority of them, may cast the vote of such association.

V.

The officers of the League shall be a President, Secretary, Treasurer, and nine Vice-Presidents; and there shall be a General Committee and an Executive Committee. The officers and the committees shall hold office until their successors are appointed or elected.

VI.

The President and Vice-Presidents shall be elected by ballot at the annual meeting of the League.

The Secretary and Treasurer shall be chosen, and may be removed, by the General Committee.

The General Committee shall be chosen annually, and shall consist of one delegate from each association belonging to the League; and one additional delegate for every two hundred members, or major fraction thereof, of such association as certified by its secretary. Each association shall elect its own delegates in such manner as it may determine.

The members of the Executive Committee shall be ex-officio members of the General Committee.

Any member of the General Committee may act by proxy.

The General Committee shall keep a record of its proceedings, and shall make a report to the League at the annual meeting. A vacancy in any office, except that of Vice-President, may be filled by the General Committee for the remainder of the term.

The General Committee may delegate to the Executive Committee any of its powers; provided, however, that it may at any time resume the powers so delegated.

The Executive Committee shall consist of twenty-one members to be elected annually by the General Committee and shall have power to fix its own quorum. And any member of the Executive Committee may act by proxy.

VII.

The General Committee may, subject to these articles, manage the affairs of the League, direct and dispose of the

funds, and may, from time to time, make and modify by-laws for the League and for its own action.

No debt shall be contracted, nor shall any appropriation of money be made, by the League or by the General Committee, beyond the amount in the hands of the Treasurer.

VIII.

There shall be an annual meeting of the League at such time in each year, and at such place as the General Committee may determine, at which officers shall be elected for the ensuing year, and other appropriate business may be transacted.

A meeting of the League may be called at the discretion of the General Committee whenever any association belonging to it notifies the Secretary of the League of its desire to have such a meeting, and the President may at any time call a meeting of the League.

IX.

Any provision of this Constitution may be suspended or amended by a vote of two-thirds of the members present at any meeting of the General Committee, due notice of such proposed suspension or amendment having been given at a previous meeting. Any association belonging to the League may, through its representatives, propose amendments to the Constitution which may be approved under the same conditions.

Publications of the New York Civil-Service Reform Ass'n

The Beginning of the Spoils System in the National Government, 1829-30. (Reprinted, by permission, from Parton's "Life of Andrew Jackson.") Per copy, 5 cts.

Term and Tenure of Office. By Dorman B. Eaton. Second edition, abridged. Per copy, 15 cts.

Daniel Webster and the Spoils System. An extract from Senator Bayard's oration at Dartmouth College, June, 1882.

A Primer of Civil-Service Reform, prepared by George William Curtis. (English and German Editions.)

Address of Hon. Carl Schurz in opposition to the bill to amend the New York Civil Service laws, commonly known as the "Black Act." May 6. 1897.

Report on the Operation of the "Black Act." March 21, 1898.

Annual Reports of the Civil Service Reform Association of New York for the years 1883-1898 inclusive, Per copy, 8 cts.

MISCELLANEOUS.

United States Civil-Service Statutes and Revised Rules of May 6, 1896.

State Civil-Service Reform Acts of New York and Massachusetts.

Decisions and Opinions in Construction of the Civil-Service Laws. (1890) Per copy, 15 cts.

The Meaning of Civil-Service Reform. By E. O. Graves.

The Selection of Laborers. (In English and German Editions). By James M. Bugbee late of the Massachusetts Civil-Service Commission.

Report of Select Committee on Reform in the Civil Service (H. R.), regarding the registration of laborers in the United States Service.

Report of same Committee regarding selection of Fourth-Class Postmasters.

The Need of a Classified and Non-Partisan Census Bureau— Report of a Special Committee of the National League. (1898)

George William Curtis. A commemorative address by Parke Godwin. (Published by the Century Association). 10 cents per copy.

(A CHARGE IS MADE ONLY WHERE THE PRICE IS GIVEN.)

Orders for the publications will be filled by GEORGE MCANENY, Secretary, 54 William St., New York, or by G. P. PUTNAM'S SONS, 27 and 29 West 23d St., New York.

PROCEEDINGS

AT THE ANNUAL MEETING OF

The National Civil-Service Reform League

HELD AT

BALTIMORE, MD., DEC. 15 AND 16, 1898.

WITH THE ADDRESS OF THE PRESIDENT,

AND OTHER MATTERS.

NEW YORK:

PUBLISHED FOR THE

NATIONAL CIVIL-SERVICE REFORM LEAGUE.

1898.

Publications of the National Civil-Service Reform League

Proceedings at the Annual Meeting of the National Civil-Ser. vice Reform League, 1882, with address of the President, George William Curtis   Per copy, 8 cts.

The same, with address of the President, for '84, '85, '86, '87, '89, '90, '91, '92, '93, '94 '95, '96, '97 and '98. Per copy, cts.

Civil-Service Reform under the present National Administration. By George William Curtis. (Address of 1885.)

The Situation. By George William Curtis. (Address of 1886.)

Party and Patronage. By George William Curtis. (Address of 1892.)

Civil-Service Reform and Democracy. By Carl Schurz. (Address of 1893.)

The Necessity and Progress of Civil-Service Reform. By Carl Schurz. (Address of 1894.)

Congress and the Spoils System. By Carl Schurz. (Address of 1895.)

Encouragements and Warnings. By Carl Schurz. (Address of 1896.)

The Democracy of the Merit System. By Carl Schurz. (Address of 1897.)

A Review of the Year. By Carl Schurz. (Address of 1898.)

Civil Service Reform as a Moral Question. By Charles J. Bonaparte. (1890.)

The Influence of the Spoils Idea upon the Government of American Cities. By Herbert Welsh. (1894.)

The Reform of the Consular Service. By Oscar S. Straus. (1894.)

The Interest of the Workingman in Civil-Service Reform. By Herbert Welsh. (1895.)

The Appointment and Tenure of Postmasters. By R. H. Dana. (1895.)

The Republican Party and Civil-Service Reform. By Henry Hitchcock. (1897.)

The Democratic Party and Civil-Service Reform. By Moorfield Storey. (1897.)

An open Letter to Hon. C. H. Grosvenor, in reply to recent attacks on the Civil Service Law and Rules. George McAneny. (1897.)

The Need and Best Means for Providing a Competent and Stable Civil Service for Our New Dependencies. By Dorman B. Eaton. (1898.)

Constitution of the National Civil-Service Reform League.

Good Government: Official Journal of the National Civil-Service Reform League. Published monthly at 54 William St., New York. One dollar per year. Ten cents per single copy.

For other publications, see third page

PROCEEDINGS

AT THE ANNUAL MEETING OF

The National Civil-Service Reform League

HELD AT

BALTIMORE, MD., DEC. 15 AND 16, 1898.

WITH THE ADDRESS OF THE PRESIDENT,

AND OTHER MATTERS.

———

NEW YORK:

PUBLISHED FOR THE

NATIONAL CIVIL-SERVICE REFORM LEAGUE.

1898.

PRESS OF GOOD GOVERNMENT.

CONTENTS.

ANNUAL MEETING

OF THE

NATIONAL CIVIL SERVICE REFORM LEAGUE.

DECEMBER 15 AND 16, 1898.

PURSUANT to call, duly issued, the eighteenth annual meeting of the National Civil Service Reform League was held at Baltimore, Md., on the 15th and 16th of December, 1898. Among the delegates in attendance during the several sessions were the following:

BALTIMORE: Charles J. Bonaparte, Daniel Coit Gilman, Joseph Packard, Jr., William Reynolds, William Keyser, W. Hall Harris, John C. Rose, Edwin G. Baetjer, Henry W. Williams, T. Erskine Carson, Cleveland P. Manning, George Reuling, George Pope, John J. Dobler, Skipwith Wilmer, G. W. Gail, Fabian Franklin, John Helmsley Johnson, Alex. Y. Dolfield, Dr. Samuel Theobald, Edward Stabler, Jr., John M. Glenn, Lawrence Turnbull, Wm. T. Brigham.

BOSTON: Richard Henry Dana.

BROOKLINE: Dana Estes.

BUFFALO: Sherman S. Rogers, Henry A. Richmond, Frederick Almy, Charles B. Wheeler.

CAMBRIDGE: Morrill Wyman, Jr.

CHICAGO: John W. Ela.

CINCINNATI: Charles W. Wilby, Max B. May.

CONNECTICUT: W. A. Aiken, Robert P. Keep, Norwich.

DISTRICT OF COLUMBIA: John Joy Edson, Frederick L. Siddons, Henry Heywood Glassie, John T. Doyle, Charles Lyman, Theodore De Land, Adolf G. Wolf, Charles W. Stetson.

HARVARD UNIVERSITY: F. C. Sutro.

INDIANA: William Dudley Foulke, Richmond.

NEW YORK: Carl Schurz, Silas W. Burt, Everett P. Wheeler, William Potts, Dorman B. Eaton, Edward Cary, J. Lawrence McKeever, Cornelius B. Smith, George Haven Putnam, Charles W. Watson, Charles Collins, Samuel P. Avery, Frederick H. Allen, George McAneny.

GENEVA, N. Y.: Francis O. Mason, J. Lawrence Slosson, Theodore J. Smith.

PHILADELPHIA: Herbert Welsh, Charles Richardson, R. Francis Wood, Clinton Rogers Woodruff, George Burnham, Jr., W. W. Montgomery, John Field, Enoch Lewis.

ST. LOUIS: Frederick N. Judson, Albert L. Berry.

VIRGINIA: H. B. Frissell, Hampton.

In response to invitations issued by the League to Municipal Reform Associations and other bodies having the reform of the civil service among their objects, delegates were present from a number of such organizations, as follows;

CHICAGO:—*Citizens' Association:* Murray Nelson, Jr.

CLEVELAND:—*Chamber of Commerce:* William E. Cushing.

BOSTON:—*Massachusetts Reform Club:* Charles Warren, William C. Wait.

WASHINGTON:—*Civic Centre:* Dr. Murray Galt Motter.

The morning session of the 15th, commencing at 10.30 o'clock, was occupied by a joint meeting of the General and Executive Committees, held at the Assembly Rooms, Music Hall.

The annual address of the President, Hon. Carl Schurz, was delivered at Lehmann's Hall at 8 o'clock on the evening of the 15th. It is as follows:

A REVIEW OF THE YEAR.

An Address delivered at the Annual Meeting of the National Civil Service Reform League, at Baltimore, Md., December 15, 1898.

By Hon. Carl Schurz.

It was in this hall that, six years ago, my predecessor, George William Curtis, whose memory is reverently and affectionately cherished by us all, delivered the last of his annual addresses—addresses which never failed to instruct our judgment, to strengthen our faith, to inspire our efforts, and to lift us up to a higher conception of patriotic duty. After having, with the peculiar grace and force of his eloquence, discussed the evils and dangers flowing from the use of official patronage as party spoil, he proceeded, as had always been his wont on similar occasions, to review the conduct of those in power, as that conduct had served to advance or to hinder the reform of the civil service; and in doing so he pronounced praise or censure, according to the facts before him, in a spirit of justice and fairness, without fear or favor. In his annual address of 1886 he declared:

"This League is the only organized and authentic national representative of the reform sentiment. I challenge any man to show that it has in any degree, or at any time, betrayed the trust voluntarily assumed by it, with the approval o, the locally organized friends of reform, of honestly and adequately representing that sentiment, and its criticisms and demands upon political parties and public men. The League has pandered to no personal ambition, to no party purpose. It has been no man's instrument, nor has it been the organ of any faction."

I trust the League deserves this definition of its character and attitude to-day as much as it deserved it twelve years ago, and that it will always deserve it while it lives. Indeed, if it ever ceased to be perfectly non-partisan as between political parties, and perfectly impartial as between persons, it would forfeit all claim to public confidence, and all possibility of public usefulness. And this I am confident it never will, so long at least as you and I have any part in its direction.

Our record will bear me out when I say, that we have always been heartily glad to praise and heartily sorry, even reluctant, to blame, when our duty demanded it. And so we are now. But at present we find ourselves, much against our liking, compelled to recognize the fact that in the year now ending the cause of civil service reform has been less prosperous than in the year which preceded it. In saying this, 1 have the national service especially in mind.

President McKinley, was elected on a platform which declared that: "The civil service law was placed on the Statute book by the Republican party, which has always sustained it, and we renew our repeated declaration that it should be thoroughly and honestly enforced, and extended wherever practicable." In his letter of acceptance and his inaugural address he emphatically accepted this platform, and pledged himself that under his administration there should be no backward step. These pledges clearly covered the extension and the scope of the civil service rules made by President Cleveland, which had long been published and sufficiently discussed by the public press to bring them to the knowledge of every intelligent person in any manner interested in public affairs. At our last annual meeting, at Cincinnati, the League whenever opportunity offered, was profuse in its praise of the fidelity with which President McKinley had withstood the pressure of the spoils politicians urging him to rescind President Cleveland's order, and with which he had upheld the integrity of the merit system as far as it then existed; and gladly were some delinquencies of minor importance overlooked which, occurring here and there, it was hoped would be promptly corrected by the administration as soon as its attention were invited to them. In short, the League in every possible manner expressed its confidence in the President's intention to make good the solemn pledges of his party, as well as his own, and it left nothing undone to assist him in doing so, by offering such information as was at its disposal, and such suggestions as occasion seemed to demand. And it must be added that the President uniformly received such information and such suggestions with great courtesy, and with the assurance that they would have his earnest consideration.

But some time ago he gave us to understand that he purposed to issue an order excepting certain important classes of offices from the operation of the civil service law, against which we thought it our duty respectfully to remonstrate, hoping to convince him that such exceptions were unnecessary and would be injurious to the public interest. When the report that such an order would after all be issued continued to appear, the League thought it proper to submit to him a more formal protest, which has been spread before the public, together with elaborate briefs showing in detail how uncalled for, as we thought, as well as how hurtful, such curtailments of the merit system would be.

So far the order in question has not appeared, but we have no assurance of any sort that the President has changed his mind as to his intention to issue it. Under these circumstances I can only repeat the appeal made to him by the General and Executive Committees of the League in these words:

"We believe that changes, whereby positions and classes of positions are now removed permanently from the classified service, will be accepted not only as a step backward, but as proof that the system is not regarded by the present administration as here, and here to stay, and will inevitably awaken doubts as to the sincerity of repeated declarations of the party now dominant in national affairs that the law establishing it shall be thoroughly and honestly enforced and extended wherever practicable. How far this view of the action said to be contemplated would be just or reasonable, we do not think it need ful to discuss: we lay before you our conviction that it would be the view taken, in fact, by the intelligent public, that it would impair the confidence of many patriotic Americans in the honor and good faith of their government, and that it would encourage the pernicious activity of men interested in our politics principally as a means of securing selfish advantage. We urge earnestly, that these grave evils may be guarded against." And I may add that if the President should after all decide to abstain from issuing such an order that decision would be welcomed by the advocates of civil service reform with hearty gratitude.

It is not supprising that the frequent recurrence of the announcement coming from Washington, that the President was resolved to except certain classes of officers from the operation of the civil service law, should have had a somewhat unsettling effect upon those branches of the service which were reported to be most concerned. It being, for instance, taken for certain that the Deuputy Internal Revenue collectors would be excluded from the classified service, many Internal Revenue collectors proceeded to remove their deputies and appointed others without the slightest regard for the civil service rules, defending their lawless conduct by the pretense that they were only anticipating an Executive order, which they believed was sure to come.

The Treasury Department, indeed, in one or two cases, addressed to the officers concerned a mild remonstrance against so flagrant a breach of discipline, apt to demoralize the whole service by contagious example, but when the remonstrance proved unavailing, no further steps to punish the offenders or to prevent repetition of the same offence were taken.

The Department of Justice did the same thing, in a considerable number of cases, and utterly ignored the remonstrances made by the Civil Service Commission.

Now, I would respectfully ask whether the circumstance that an order of exception was merely foreshadowed in newspaper reports, should be regarded as a valid excuse for violating the rules in anticipation of it, and whether these Departments should have permitted such violations to pass with impunity ?

In the Interior Department likewise many appointments, especially in the inspecting and examining forces of the General Land Office, were made with entire disregard of the principles of the civil service law and the rules under it.

The plea in justification was in many cases that there were no eligible lists available at the time when the appointments were made, but the flimsiness of that excuse appeared from the fact that when examinations might have been held, and eligible lists might have been formed, that means of keeping the offices in question practically within the classified service was not resorted to; and that the cause of this is to be found not in any unwillingness or unreadiness on the part of the Commission, but rather in an indisposition of the Secretary of the Interior to take the officers or employees concerned from such lists, or to co-operate with the Commission in holding the examinations for forming the lists.

It has also been urged that many of the offices in question require special qualifications, which could be better ascertained by the appointing power than by examination. This is a well-known plea urged by the opponents of civil service reform. How much that plea holds good is strikingly exemplified by the fact that the officers who by their misconduct helped to bring on the recent Indian outbreak in Minnesota, belonged mostly to that identical class which we are told must be excluded from the merit system because of peculiar fitness required for the performance of the duties imposed upon them, and which, we are told, can be secured only by the Department exercising an untrammelled discretion in the selection of candidates. It is hardly necessary to say that in this, as in almost all similar cases, the discretion exercised by the head of the Department is a ghastly myth, and that he exercises hardly any discretion at all, but that the appointments are simply imposed upon him by influential politicians, usually members of Congress, who seek to quarter their tools, or dependents, or favorites, upon the public purse, without much, if any, regard to their fitness for the duties to be performed.

This applies with equal pertinency to the forest rangers who have been appointed to protect the public timber lands against devastation by fire. These officers, too, required in the opinion of the Secretary of the Interior peculiar qualifications, which made it impracticable to confide their selection to the methods of the merit system, and demanded the exercise of personal discretion by the head of the Department. A searching investigation of the results will undoubtedly convince him that the " discretion " of the politicians who usually succeed in obtaining appointments for " their men " in such cases, is the last thing to be depended upon, if really conscientious and efficient persons are desired for so important a branch of the public service.

The President's order of July 27, 1897, that no removals

from positions subject to competitive examination shall be made without assignment of cause in writing, and without giving the person to be removed an opportunity for being heard in his defence, was at the time hailed by public opinion as a reformatory step of great value. And such it unquestionably was, not only inasmuch as it established a rule desirable in itself, but also as it served to confirm the popular belief that it was the President's settled purpose to advance the progress of civil service reform so far as his power would go. I am sincerely glad to say that the order *did* have the effect of making arbitrary removals more rare, but there have been enough of such arbitrary removals—and a great many of them of sufficiently flagrant and conspicuous a character—to attract public attention.

In my last annual address it was my duty to mention the fact that in some cases the President's order had been set at defiance with great boldness; that such instances had been duly brought to the President's notice, and that it was hoped the President would, after satisfactory ascertainment of the circumstances, deal with the offenders according to law, and make of some of them warning examples by dismissing them from the service. I sincerely wish I could report that this had been done, but I am compelled to say that it has not, and that so far the offenders have escaped with impunity. This is deplorable in two respects. In the first place it is apt to encourage in the service itself a spirit of insubordination and contempt for the law and the rules. When the spoils politicians in public place, or public officers who are subject to the influence of spoils politicians, are made to understand that they can trample upon the law and upon the regulations laid down by the Chief Magistrate, without danger of being held to account for it, what can be more natural than that in constantly widening circles the law should become an object of sport for those who desire to circumvent or to subvert it? But we observe another effect of that toleration of insubordinate conduct which is hardly less important. There is not one of those occurrences which, as soon as it came to public knowledge, did not call forth from the enemies of the merit system the customary cry—"See there another proof of what an unmitigated humbug civil service reform is!" Indeed, such cries are extremely unjust; but who will deny that they have a most undesirable effect upon those who do not take the trouble to discriminate? Do we not know that most people judge others rather by their faults than by their virtues, rather by their failures than their successes?

There are ten commandments. A man will be less praised for observing nine, than he will be blamed and discredited for breaking one. Nor has he any right to complain of this. The observance of the nine commandments is a simple duty, the performance of which should be regarded as a matter of course. By the breach of one he forfeits his virtue, and lays himself open to the suspicion of being capable of breaking more of them. So it is with the government in its administration of the civil service law. One conspicuous dereliction in its enforcement going unpunished will cause a widespread belief that there may be many similar derelictions not so conspicuous, and that the whole system is a hypocritical farce. And such a suspicion is especially dangerous and deplorable in view of the fact that the permanency and the extension of the merit system depend very largely upon the popular belief in the honesty of its advocates and the trustworthiness of its enforcement.

Equally deplorable in its spirit, as well as in its effect is the manner in which the reform of the Consular service has been treated. You will remember how the rushing rapidity with which, at the beginning of President Cleveland's second administration, Consular officers were removed and new men put in their places, was at the time resented by public opinion, and how severely it was denounced by this League. In all parts of the country not only civil service reformers, but almost the whole business community, through its representive commercial organizations, joined in the demand that the Consular service should be taken out of politics, that Consular offices should cease to be treated as the spoil of party warfare, or to be used as the mere reward of partisan activity, that capable and efficient Consular officers should be kept in their places without regard to their party standing, and that vacancies in that branch of the service should be filled only upon proof of the specific fitness of the candidates for the duties to be performed. President Cleveland's administration, recognizing this demand as just, made an effort, no doubt an honest one, to comply with it. Mr. Olney, as Secretary of State, proposed, and President

Cleveland issued, in 1895, an order that no person should be appointed to a Consulship, the salary of which was between $1,000 and $2,500, both inclusive, without having been subjected to a rigid examination on the following subjects:

(1) General education, knowledge of languages, business training and experience.

(2) The country in which the consul or commercial agent is to reside, its government, chief magistrate, geographical features, principal cities, chief production and its commercial intercourse and relations with the United States.

(3) The exequatur, its nature and use.

(4) Functions of a consul or commercial agent as compared with those of a vice-consul or consular-agent, relation of former to latter, also to the United States minister or ambassador at the capital of the country.

(5) Duties of a consul or commercial agent as regards:

    (a) Correspondence with the State Department and the form thereof.

    (b) Passports, granting and visaing.

    (c) United States merchant vessels in a foreign port, and their crews, whether seeking discharge, deserting, or destitute.

    (d) Wrecks within the jurisdiction.

    (e) Wrongs to United States citizens within jurisdiction.

    (f) Invoices.

    (g) Official fees and accounts.

(6) Treaties between the United States and the foreign country.

(7) Relations of ambassador and minister to laws of the country to which they are accredited, as compared with those of consul or commercial agent to those of the countries where they reside.

(8) Acts of ambassador or minister, how far binding upon his country.

(9) Diplomatic, judicial, and commercial functions of consuls or commercial agents.

(10) Piracy, what it is and where punishable.

(11) Consular Regulations of the United States—copy of which (to be returned to the Department) will be supplied to each candidate upon application.

(12) Such other subject or subjects as the Board may deem important and appropriate in any particular case.

These examinatious were to be conducted by a Board consisting of the Third Assistant Secretary of State, the Solicitor of the State Department, and the Chief of the Consular Bureau.

Secretary Olney, himself, pronounced this order at the time of its promulgation, not a final measure, but a "step in the right direction." As a step in the right direction, as a proof of good intentions, and as an official recognition of the necessity of withdrawing the Consular service from the reach of spoils politics, this League hailed the measure with hearty applause. But we could not conceal our apprehension that inasmuch as the system of examinations proposed did not contain the feature of open competition, and that it permitted the selection by the Department, or by those exercising influence upon the Department, of the candidates to be put through a mere pass examination, it would eventually meet the fate of similar experiments that had been made before; that is to say, that the examination would degenerate into a mere formality, and as before, almost all Consular appointments would again be ruled by political favor. To this apprehension I gave expression in my annual address of 1896, when I predicted that eventually " the waves of influence will wash down the feeble breakwater of the pass examination once more."

I must confess, however, that when I said this I did not expect that my prediction would be verified so soon. The character as well as the rapidity of the changes in the Consular service, which were made during the first months of President McKinley's administration—the number of such changes even exceeding the number made during the corresponding period of the Cleveland administration—startled many people also among those who were not as warmly interested in the cause of civil service reform as the members of this League are. Many things happened which excited suspicion as to the seriousness of the examinations to which, under the Olney order, candidates for consulships were to be subjected, and officers of the League thought it their duty to make, from time to time, enquiries of the State Department as to the scope of the examinations, and the relative number of the successful and unsuccessful candidates.

Such inquiries until lately were met with the answer that the information so called for could not be furnished, for the reason that such things were treated by the State Department as strictly confidential. But the veil of mystery has been lifted since the new Secretary of State entered upon the discharge of his duties.

I have had before me two examination papers for consulships of more than ordinary importance—one in France and one in England. The questions therein proposed to the candidates conform in appearance to most of the subjects enumerated in the Olney order. But they are so put that any person

of ordinary intelligence and average memory ean prepare himself for such a trial of his faculties and attainments by a very
brief study of the consular instructions. The requirement that he
should know the language of the country to which he wishes to
be sent, need not embarrass him; for the candidate for the
consulship in France is not asked to write a letter in French,
but simply to write a letter in English " in regard to his knowledge of the French language." He may answer that he thinks
he has enough even if he can say only "*oui*" and "*non;*" and
that may be considered satisfactory by the appointing power.

Moreover, excepting two or three points, the questions on
the two examination papers are not only substantially but lit-
terally the same, so that by frequent repetition they are certain
to leak out. Indeed, it would be a perfect wonder if the
coaching schools for examinations, which no doubt exist in
Washington, were not, under such a system, in full possession of them, and thus enabled to send every candidate
into the examination with a complete assortment of answers
securely in his coat pocket. It is therefore not surprising that,
of 112 candidates for consular offices examined during the
first year of this administration, only one failed to pass, and
that this one did not pass can be explained only upon the assumption that his must have been an obtuseness of extraordinary pathological interest, or that he must have fallen a
victim to political intrigue, which misfortune would entitle
him much to public sympathy.

At any rate, the facts ascertained leave no doubt as to the
mode of procedure by which this great Republic receives its Consular representatives abroad, under this so-called reform system.
It is this: A useful party worker who is to be provided for, or a
person of some local political influence who is the favorite of a
powerful political patron, conceives the idea that it would be
pleasant to him to have some comfortable salaried position
abroad, either because he has no other paying job on hand, or
because his wife's health needs a change of climate, or because
he wishes his daughters to have good and cheap music lessons,
or because he wants to be "vindicated" or raised in the social scale
by means of recognition on the part of the Government. The
United States Senator from his State, or his representative in
Congress, or both, find it desirable for what they call the public
interest—that is, their own interest, in keeping their political ma-

chine in order—that the ambition of this person should be gratified, and they assail the President with suitable urgency, telling
him that the people of their respective States or districts demand
just this thing, and that unless it be done the consequences to
the party will be awful.

The President is impressed. It may happen that the candidate presented to him is a very improper person, and that
the respectable part of the community from which he comes
make, with more or less indignation, their protest against the
appointment, as happened in the case of the notorious Saylor,
of Pennsylvania, whose appointment to a consulship even
standing above the $2,500 level was successfully demanded by
Senator Quay. Now the President considers that he needs the
support of this Senator or Representative for whatever policy
he may wish to put through Congress, and, if the candidate
aspires to a consulship subject to an examination, he orders him
to be examined. The candidate then passes the examination,
as a matter of course, and the appointment follows. It is the
old story.

Now, I do not deny that in this way some meritorious persons have been appointed—be it that their congressional patrons were uncommonly conscientious, or that they happened
to find that they could by presenting such a person do themselves a good turn. But in view of the fact that in the same
manner many inefficient and generally improper persons have
found their way into the Consular service, and that this method
of appointment encourages, with every change of administration, sweeping removals of Consular officers, when after some
years of service they have acquired a certain desirable degree
of experience and efficiency, it will be admitted that this is
certainly not a system calculated to give the American business community as good a Consular representation abroad as
it should have. It is our duty to call things by their right
names, and that duty compels me to acknowledge the fact that,
Secretary Olney's step in the right direction notwithstanding,
the method of selecting and appointing Consular officers is
substantially what it was under the frank and open old
spoils system. The business men and the commercial bodies
that have petitioned and memorialized for the reform of the
Consular Service with so much energy, and who were made to
believe that by the Olney order at least a beginning of that

reform was to be made, must understand that their efforts have
so far been in vain, and that, very thinly disguised, the old
spoils methods in the appointment of Consular officers are in
full flower. They seem to acknowledge this, for they have begun to petition for reform of the consular service once more,
with Cleveland, Ohio, in the lead.

I am sure I am expressing the feelings of every member of
this League—indeed of every honest and self-respecting citizen the country over—when I say that we should prefer the
dropping of the disguise. If men of unsuitable character and
acquirements must, at the dictation of Senatorial or other bosses,
be put into the Counsular Service of the country, let it at least
be done frankly and courageously under the old spoils flag,
and not under the cover of a so-called reform system.

The new Secretary of State, Col. John Hay, has done a
good service to the country by permitting the truth about
the Consular examinations to emerge from the veil of mystery
in which they had been shrouded. The public obligation
to him will of course be much greater if he employs his
official influence to the utmost, as I earnestly hope he will,
toward accomplishing what the business community of the
country has so long and so vainly been praying for—that is a
system of examinations for Consular positions that will really
rescue the Consular service from the deleterious touch of spoils
politics, and bring to it the best attainable ability and character.

I have no doubt that he is the man to do this, and that he
has the honorable ambition to earn this title to the gratitude of
the country. But if he makes the attempt he will, in order to
succeed, have to take the experience of the past earnestly to
heart. Why have all similiar attempts failed? Not necessarily
because the men making them acted in bad faith, but because
they contented themselves with mere pass examinations.

The first consequence regularly was that presently admission to these examinations was granted only by way of
political favor and influence ; and the second, that the political favor and influence which had secured to the favored
the admission to the examination, then also proved strong
enough to have the examination so arranged that the favored
could easily pass. And thus appointments were controlled by
influence and favor, just as they had been before. Now I
admit that in countries in which spoils politics have never

prevailed, as in Germany, or in which, as in England, they have long ceased to prevail so as to have entirely disappeared from the habits and even from the memory of the people, pass-examinations may more easily be maintained in practical efficiency, although even there,—as John Stuart Mill forcibly set forth in a well remembered dissertation—even there they were apt to deteriorate. But in a country, in the politics of which the spoils system has long been the rule, is still struggling for existence, and has a majority of active politicians still on its side, and those spoils politicans constantly scheming how to prevent every arrangement that might wrench any office with a salary worth having from their grasp, or how to subvert or circumvent existing barriers in order to get hold of those offices again—in such a country mere pass examinations can answer the purpose only when they are conducted by exceptionally conscientious and competent persons under an administration so indomitably resolved to maintain them in absolute integrity, as to be perfectly proof against all political influence and pressure An administration fully answering this requirement we have not had yet. It is therefore necessary that in such surroundings the administration should protect itself with as strong a bulwark as possible against the pressure of influence, and the strongest bulwark as yet discovered is the competitive system of examination, open to all, which gives the best man the best chance for appointment without regard to party affiliations. In this respect I can only repeat what I said in my last annual address:

"If our commercial community wants a real reform in the method of appointment to Consular positions, it must insist upon three things: competitive examination for admission to the Consular service; promotion only for merit; and removal only for cause."

Nor can it be said that competitive examinations are inapplicable to Consular offices, appointments to which are subject to confirmation by the Senate; for it is wholly within the power and discretion of the President to order, for his own guidance, open competitive examinations for the candidates presenting themselves, and then to nominate to the Senate, as his own choice, the man who comes out best. If then the Senators systematically refuse to confirm such nominations in order to save their patronage, they will do so on their own responsibility to their constituents. But I have no doubt that if the President introduced such a system, and the Senate sought to break it down by systematically rejecting the candidates so selected, the commercial community would rise up in its might, and the public opinion of the country would teach the Senators a lesson not likely to be soon forgotten.

I said that the competitive system is the strongest bulwark so far devised against the pressure of political influence. I do not pretend, however, that it is an absolutely safe bulwark when those whom it is to protect collude with those who assail it.

It appears that the smuggling of persons into places subject to competitive examination without such an examination has been developed into a fine art in various branches of the service, and that the "beating" of the law and of the rules is extensively carried on with much ingenuity and system.

Some of these practices, as they occured in the Revenue Service, and in the Internal Departments, I have already discussed; but more is to be said. The Pension Commissioner circumvented the law in the appointment of Examining Surgeons by appointing in localities where Boards already existed, new Boards, and sending all applicants to these. As the personnel of such Boards become classified only when the amount of fees received is $300 annually, the new appointees were invariably treated as unclassified, and the old classified Boards were practically driven out of business. In the Post-Office Department it has become a not infrequent practice to appoint persons without examination as clerks in offices that are about to be made free delivery offices becoming thereby classified, and then to transfer such persons, immediately after they have thus been "covered in," to other positions in other parts of the Post-Office department, or even in other departments. Four persons have been transferred in this way to the important classified position of Post Office Inspector, four have been sent to the Treasury Department, and others to the San Francisco Mint, the Government Printing establishment, and other offices.

The method followed in the field force of the Interior Department, whereby persons have been employed temporarily in the absence of eligible lists, and all efforts to hold examinations to secure permanent appointees have then been discouraged, has been referred to.

As the Civil Service Commission depends on the department officers for a statement of the duties for which specific qualifications are desired, and for other information necessary in fixing the scope of an examination, it will readily be seen that where the department refuses utterly to co-operate, the provisions of the law cannot be enforced. The Department of Justice has followed this same plan in the appointment of clerks and others made in the offices of United States District Attorneys and Marshals. In other departments and offices, notably in the San Francisco Custom House, persons have been appointed to positions nominally in the "excepted" list and then assigned to other duties, while the "excepted" duties are performed by old employees under classified titles.

The tricks employed in getting rid of employees whose places are desired, have been quite as various. In many cases men have been laid off, ostensibly "for lack of work," while immediately afterward their positions have been filled by others who perform the identical duties. In other cases the reasons stated in nominal compliance with the President's order of July, 1897, have been so plainly of the "trumped up" sort as to call forth indignant protests not only from the Civil Service Commission but from the inspecting officers of the departments themselves. In still others employees have been given an "indefinite furlough without pay," and their places quickly filled by persons appointed to do the same work "in the absence of eligible lists."

These are not secret matters. Many of these occurrences are reviewed in the last published annual report of the Civil Service Commission, 127 pages of which are devoted to them. The most serious fact is that such cases, remaining uncorrected, are permitted to stand as precedents of the most vicious and demoralizing sort.

This is an unwelcome exhibition which I should be most happy not to be obliged to spread before you. But however unpalatable that duty may be, it must be done. The President's good intentions are not to be questioned. But those intentions are evidently treated with reckless disrespect by some of the officers under him who by their evil practices burden him with responsibilities which he must find extremely irksome, and which he should not be willing to bear.

Let us now turn to the brighter side of the picture. I believe I can say with perfect assurance that the public opinion of the country has never been so strongly supporting the cause of civil service reform as it is now. Among the great newspapers of the Republic, that is to say among those which have the largest circulations, and command the most influence, there are avowedly opposed to it hardly more than you can count upon the fingers of one hand. A large majority of them are advocating and sustaining it with more or less fidelity and force. Discussion on the usefulness of the merit system as it affects the administration of the public business has substantially ceased. On the whole, the spoils politician in assailing civil service reform confines himself to certain hackneyed ribaldries, and to the fierce exclamation that he and his kind *must* have the offices as a reward for party service. I have of late observed only one argument against the merit system, which, although not new, has recently been advanced by an adherent of the Republican boss of Pennsylvania in the tone of a wail of despairing virtue clad in a garb of politico-philosophical reasoning. It appeared in one of our journals in these words:

"The amount of jobbery and corruption which pervades all parties and all factions is enough to make a man who knows anything about it sick and skeptical concerning the future of the country. I call it horrible. I will tell you what has done more than anything else to debauch American politics. It is this civil service reform business. Before the Chinese system came in, whenever you wanted a man to work for you in politics, all you had to do was to promise to find him a place in Washington if you were successful and your party got into power. If you did not win he did not expect anything. To-day, if you are running for an office, and ask a man in town to round up the voters at the caucus for you, he stands back and asks: 'What am I to get out of it?' You cannot give him a place in Washington now, and if this civil service business is allowed to go on the day will come when you cannot give him anything in the line of office anywhere. The result is now that he wants money, and in plain English, you have got to hire and pay for whatever you want done.

The outcome, then, is that an aspirant for political power must either be very rich or must work the corporations which are seeking favors. If he can turn legislative privileges to profit, and so make himself indispensable to somebody, he will have money to do business on. One man cannot run this alone, for one man does not make a Legislature. Hence we must have leaders or 'bosses' as you would call them, so that whenever a great corporation wants something which it is willing to pay for, it can go directly to the boss, and he in turn can parcel out the money to such of his followers as are willing in state Legislatures, city Councils, and the national Congress to vote as he directs, or to earn the money. This is a plain business proposition."

Thus we are asked to return to the spoils system in the interest of the public virtue, and strange to say, I have known cases in which this appeal has had some effect upon otherwise sensible persons. Their reasoning is this. We must have political parties. A party must have an organization. An organization must have workers to get out the vote. The workers must have reward. That reward must be either in the shape of office or of money. If you take away the offices, only money remains. And then it will require more and more money.

This reasoning is not without plausibility to a certain point. We must have political parties, and a party in order to be effective must have an organization and workers. This is true. But what kind of an organization and what kind of workers must a party have? Is it necessary that the organization and the workers should consist of a lot of mercenaries who put themselves to party work only for the purpose of making politics profitable to themselves personally? Some people will say that only that class of persons can be found willing to devote themselves to the drudgery of party work. This is plausible. But is it true? We have had political parties in this country before the offices were distributed among party workers with every change of administration, and before much money was used in elections to bring out the voters; and yet parties were as active and party contests as spirited, and the vote was as full then as now. We know that in other contries which have constitutional government, and . political parties, and elections, but no distribution of offices as party spoil, and no bands of mercenary party workers living on politics, party contests are as energetic as they are here.

Must we then admit it to be a fact that while in other countries parties can be maintained without official spoils, and while in this Republic, too, they have in former times been so kept in energetic vitality, the American people have become so mercenary and degraded that they will not give any time or work to their public interests unless they are individually bribed to do so? Have we sunk so low? But if we had, would the substitution of one kind of bribe for another furnish any remedy for this appalling evil? For the distribution of money in the guise of official salaries to party workers is no less a bribe than cash itself. Would not the result of the complete restoration of the spoils system be that those who now demand money for their patriotism, would then demand money and offices, too? Do they not do so now, wherever the offices are still attainable? Is it not true, as a matter of history, that it was the use of offices as a means of bribery that gradually developed the mercenary spirit in our politics? And will not this mercenary spirit, started and stimulated by the partisan use of the patronage, necessarily spread more widely the more it has to feed upon? The spoils system offered the mercenaries offices. The offices presently proved insufficient to satisfy their greed. They then exacted money in addition. They received money, together with the offices. Then certain classes of offices were withdrawn from their grasp, and they demanded more money. And now they simply want the offices back on the ground that they otherwise must insist upon still more money. Is it not certain that the return of the offices to their constantly widening greed would not satisfy, but only sharpen, the appetite?

The suggestion that under existing circumstances we cannot keep our political parties in effective activity without systematic bribery and corruption of some sort, and the fact that such a theory can be advanced with the expectation of its being accepted by good citizens, should only serve to open our eyes to the frightful character of the condition confronting us. It should convince us that the true remedy must be found in the direction of the complete abolition of political pelf.

We must not seek to satisfy the mercenary element, bnt to get on without it. We must not endeavor to attract the mercenary element to political activity, but do everything we can to drive it out of that political life. We must strive to convince the popular mind that while political parties must have organization, party machines consisting of patronage-mongers and bribe-givers as leaders, with hordes of patronage-hunters and bribe-takers at their command, are not only not necessary to the existence or efficiency of political parties but will deprive parties of their moral vitality, and turn them into mere agencies of general robbery and spoliation.

Nothing could be more deceptive and dangerous than the doctrine that if one party has such a machine, the other one must have one, too, in order to fight the devil with fire. If the observance of this doctrine were carried to its logical consequences, it would turn our party contests simply into something like two or more devils fighting each other with fire. Where two bosses, at the head of two parties respectively, fight one another, this is actually and visibly the case. The peculiarity of these pyrotechnical contests is that not the devils themselves but the people are scorched and roasted.

To put an end to this abominable state of things, there is no other effective means than to deprive the devils as much as possible of their fuel—that is, of their means of bribery; to strip them of their patronage by the greatest practicable extension of civil service reform, and then also to restrict the use of money in elections to the narrowest attainable limits by corrupt practices laws. The latter has been tried, so far with little success, but it is to be hoped that experience will suggest more effective methods, and that the moral sense and the enlightened opinion of the people will compel their introduction and enforcement, as it has compelled the establishment, and is compelling the maintenance of the merit system in the National civil service against all the open assaults and hidden intrigues of spoils politicians.

How strong on our side that moral sense and public opinion have become was strikingly manifested by the signal failure of the anti-civil service reform campaign in the last session of Congress. Every imaginable enginery of warfare was set in motion. There was a committee to investigate the practical working of the civil service rules, by which the enemies of the merit system expected to bring to light its uselessness, or at least striking abuses in its administration. There were speeches made, some of which resembled in their fierceness of denunciation the wild fury of Indian war-whoops. But the investigation served only to show that the working of the merit system had been most beneficial wherever the civil service regulations had been most faithfully enforced; and the boisterous oratory served only to expose the futility of the intent to hide the absence of argument by vituperate epithets and frantic exclamations. The result was the utter failure of the legislation hostile to the merit spstem, which had been intended, and that result was unquestionably due to the restraining power of that public opinion which sternly condemns any backward step from the position gained by the advance of civil service reform. It must be emphasized that the President himself also earnestly discountenanced legislation of that kind, and assiduously used his influence to discourage and prevent it.

We have indeed to admit that under cover of the pressure put upon the Government by the breaking out of the Spanish War, some things were done during that session which looked like real successes of spoils politics. The War Department, as well as the Navy Department demanded, to satisfy the exigencies of the time, many additions to various classes of the service under them. The additions were certainly needed, and needed without much delay. The question was only whether the persons needed could be taken from existing eligible lists, or through examinations that might have been speedily held. This question was raised when the Emergency Bill. appropriating money for such positions, was up in Congress. The chairman of the Committee on Appropriations in the House, who had charge of the bill, asked that the additional force be appointed without regard to the civil service rules, for the reason that the Civil Service Commission was utterly unable to cope with the emergency,—that is to furnish a sufficient number of men in accordance with the regulations. This was a remarkable mistake—all the more remarkable as the chairman of the House Appropriations Committee had never taken the trouble to inform himself by application to the Civil Service Commission as to what that Commission was able to do.

The fact is, that the Commission had eligible lists ready to hand from which a large majority of the additional force needed might have been taken, and that there was enough time for holding more examinations, and for preparing additional lists, before all that force would have been needed. These facts were actually communicated to the Senate Appropriations Committee after the Bill had passed the House, but without effect.

It has been ascertained that of the emergency appointments under the War Department without examination, about 560 were made in the Washington offices directly. It is an interesting fact that a large proportion of these persons, so appointed, were incompetent, and generally ill-suited for the work to be done. That was at the point where political pressure was strongest. On the other hand, the appointments made " in the field," outside of the Department at Washington, were of better character. That was where the political pressure was weakest. The emergency appointments without examination made by the Navy Department were much less in number than those made by the Department of War, but on the whole, of great efficiency. The popular impression is not wrong, that, in the Navy Department, political pressure had the least effect.

While the emergencies of the War were thus taken advantage of to foist into the civil service a large number of persons without examination, the same emergencies, and the events of the War generally have really served to put the necessity of a consistent and vigorous enforcement of the merit system, wherever there is any possibility for it, into a clearer light.

The finest illustration of the virtues of the merit system is furnished by the American Navy, in its administrative as well as in its fighting force. If there be a person in the land who would favor the injection of spoils politics into that splendid organization, the American people would surely set him down as an idiot, or as a traitor. And there is hardly less unanimity of opinion as to the fact, that had there been as general an adherence to the merit principle in the management of the various branches of the military service, the heroic efforts of our soldiers would have achieved their triumphs far more easily, and been attended with far less loss and suffering. This lesson is so obvious that it should penetrate even the dullest understanding, and disarm the most plausible advocacy of spoils politics.

Can the most inventive ingenuity produce any valid reason

why the whole public service—National, State and Municipal—should not be organized upon the simple and self-evident principle which in our Navy has proved so brilliantly successful? Can there be any excuse that would really satisfy the conscience and the common sense of any patriotic citizen, for not conducting the management of our Revenue service, our Consular Service, our Postal Service, our Land and Forestry Service, our Indian Service, the taking of the Census, and every other branch of our administrative machinery, on the basis of the same simple principle? Should not, in the face of these palpable and convincing experiences, the President, and every head of department, and every Senator and Representative in Congress, make haste to break through the vicious notions and habits with which the traditions of spoils politics have surrounded them, and to recognize not only in theory, but by corresponding action, the self-evident truth that as mere skill or unscrupulousness in carrying a caucus, or mere zeal and dexterity in electioneering, or mere liberality in contributing to a party campaign chest, or mere energy in bringing out the voters, would not by any sane person be considered sufficient qualification for the command of a ship, or even for the humble position of a gunner or boatswain on a man-of-war, so it should not be considered a sufficient qualification for a consulship, or a post-office, or a revenue place, or an Indian agency, or even the humblest clerkship; but that wherever any work is to be done for the public, the people are entitled to the best work, and that the work should be given only to those who by the best available method prove themselves best fitted for that work?

There is much talk about the new obligations which the results of the recent war have thrust upon us. This is indeed not the place for discussing the question whether it is desirable or not for this Republic to possess colonial dependencies. But it is certainly pertinent to say that if this Republic should charge itself with such dependencies, the question of their government will be to us one of the gravest problems of the future. Now, however opinions may differ on other points, will anybody deny that if such colonial governments were run on the spoils principle, they would inevitably bring upon us not only disastrous failures, but unbearable disgrace? I think I am not going too far in saying that the intelligence and the moral sense of the country should in that event be united in demanding for these dependencies a civil service organized upon merit rules as strict, and upon examinations as exacting, as are those of the India Service of Great Britain, that is, rules and examinations far more strict and far more exacting than those which at present govern our classified service.

Now, if the merit system in its fullest development should be considered indispensable for the government of the colonies, in case they come, will there be any hope of obtaining it unless it be considered equally necessary for our home service? I may therefore be permitted to point out in what manner the system we have may still be improved and extended. In the first place all public officers who have any power over their subordinates in the way of promotion or reduction in grade, or of appointment or removal, should be made to understand that they will not be permitted to take any liberties with the civil service law and the rules. In this respect nothing would seem to be more desirable, in order to restore that necessary discipline which in some quarters seems to have become dangerously lax, than the removal of offending officers, by way of warning example. This would prevent much mischief in the future, and save the President himself much otherwise inevitable and exceedingly vexatious tribulation. Secondly, in accordance with the pledge contained in the Republican platform, that the operation of the civil service law should not only not be restricted, but, on the contrary, extended wherever practicable, it would be fitting, and greatly to the public interest, that the assistant postmasters, the employees of the District of Columbia, those of Congress, those of the Congressional Library, the fourth class postmasters, the whole clerical force of the Census Bureau, and the laborers, should be brought into the classified service—the unskilled laborers by means of registration.

Nor should we fail to repeat that, for reasons often set forth by this League, the four-years-term laws, which have been denounced by almost every one of our prominent statesmen in the first half of this century, from Jefferson down, as a prolific source of favoritism, profligate intrigue, and political demoralization, should at last be repealed.

It is gratifying to observe that in several States and municipalties the cause of civil service reform is prosperously advancing.

The story of that Governor of New York who undertook to take the starch out of the civil service of his State, is familiar to you all. He did indeed succeed in taking out of the civil service much of the starch it contained, although, thanks to the watchful energy of the friends of civil service reform in the State, by no means as much as he had intended. But now, having been dropped by those whom he had sought to serve, but, it seems, whom after all he did not serve enough to keep their favor, he will be succeeded by a new Governor, Col. Roosevelt, who in whatever other respects some of us may differ with him, is hailed by all of us as a champion of civil service reform, who in many a hard fought contest for that cause has amply proved that in his composition there was starch in almost limitless abundance. We may therefore confidently expect that, so far as his power reaches, we shall not only recover the ground temporarily lost under his predecessor, but advance beyond it to new fields. At any rate, in the co-operation between Governor Roosevelt and the civil service reformers of the State, good faith and energy will not be wanting, and as there is no doubt that the best part of the intelligence and respectability of that great Commonwealth stands behind them, a happy outcome may surely be hoped for.

From Illinois, too, where since the adoption of the merit system in Chicago, long and somewhat confused struggles have been going on concerning its scope, we have the welcome news of important victories won by the civil service reformers in the Courts.

In far-away San Francisco also, a new city charter has been adopted by a majority of 4,000 votes, after a contest carried on mainly on the civil service issue; and from many other cities we are receiving evidences of hopefully rising interest in our cause.

The present situation may therefore, be summed-up thus: The national administration has so far failed to redeem the pledge contained in the platform upon which it was elected—not only to "enforce the civil service laws honestly and thoroughly," but also to "extend it wherever practicable;" and various abuses have been allowed to creep into the conduct of the civil service which have had the effect of nullifying the spirit and intent of the law and of the rules in a considerable number of cases. It is gladly acknowledged that the number of such cases is still so limited that it may be spoken of as exceptional. But it has been large and conspicious enough to impair the confidence of many people in the honest enforcement of the merit system, and to justify the apprehension that, if the abuses complained of be permitted to continue and to spread, they will undermine the discipline of the service and bring back many of the worst evils which the introduction of the merit system was designed to remedy. On the other hand, recent events have served to put the necessity of the maintenance and of the greatest possible extension of the merit system in a stronger light than ever, and still more to invigorate that patriotic public opinion which, steadily increasing in righteous power, will not only not tolerate any backward step but never cease to press on until the work of reform is wholly accomplished and firmly founded.

We are indeed at this annual meeting not so fortunate as to have fresh conquests achieved during the past year to celebrate. But it remains nevertheless true that the main strength of the enemies of civil service reform is broken, that their arsenals of argument are exhausted, and that in the intelligence and virtue of the people we possess a reserve force growing stronger every day. The attacks we have now to beat back from the ground we have won, are after all those of mere marauding parties seeking lodgment in ill guarded positions of ours, and trying to pick up what there may be within their reach, for a living. While they are not without power of mischief, they will be really dangerous only if there be negligence, or pusillanimity, or bad faith in our own camp.

Our duty, always the same, is clear and peremptory. It is to hold aloft with a firm hand the standard of genuine civil service reform; to permit nothing to pass under that name that does not truly satisfy its test; to repel without regard of person or party, without fear or favor, whatever attack may be made upon it, and to press on with indomitable perseverance toward the final consummation of the work If that duty is fulfilled, as I am fully confident it will be by the League and its patriotic allies, with the old fidelity, truthfulness and courage, a complete and final victory of our cause will surely come, and come at a day not far distant.

MEETING OF THE LEAGUE.

MUSIC HALL, December, 15, 1898.

2:30 P. M.

The President took the chair.

The Secretary made a verbal report, reviewing the work of his office during the year, and the relations of the League with Congress and the Executive, in matters pertaining to the reform of the national civil service. On motion the report was accepted.

The following papers were then read:

"Colonial Administration—A Warning from Spain," by Henry Haywood Glassie, of Washington.*

"Criminal offences among Federal Civil Servants in Maryland under the Spoils and under the Merit System," by John C. Rose, of Baltimore.†

Mr. William Dudley Foulke, of Indiana, as Chairman of the Special Committee on Congressional Action, appointed by the Executive Committee at its meeting of October 4, 1897, presented and read a report on the organization of the Census Bureau. The report showed the virtual failure of the Census of 1890, a result due principally to the selection of the working force for political reasons, and without examinations as to special fitness under the civil service rules. It recommended that immediate action be taken by the League toward inducing Congress to make proper provision for the classification and examination of persons to be employed in the taking of the Twelfth Census, through amendment of the bill to reorganize the Census Bureau now pending in the House.

Some discussion followed, in the course of which Mr. Rose of Baltimore, asked whether in the judgment of the Special

---

* Page 55.
† Page 68.

Committee it would be practicable to select supervisors and enumerators through competitive examination. The Secretary, for the Committee, replied that it was not the intention to recommend the selection of enumerators in this manner, but that the appointment of Supervisors for special fitness, and without regard to political considerations seemed to be of the highest importance. As the enumerators are selected by the Supervisors, they too would be chosen as a rule for other than political reasons, if the supervisors themselves were unhampered by political ties. The provision of the pending act that not more than two-thirds of the enumerators should be of the same political party would require an inquisition as to the personal politics of every applicant, and, in the judgment of the Committee, would inevitably produce results of the most pernicious character.

After further discussion Mr. Bonaparte of Baltimore, moved the adoption of the following:

RESOLVED.—That the League cordially endorses the conclusions and recommendations of the Special Committee on the Census.

RESOLVED.—That a new Committee of five members be appointed by the President to take whatever steps they may deem to be advisable to secure the adoption of the merit system in the selection of the force to be employed for the taking of the Twelfth Census, and that such Committee be authorized to print the report here submitted, and to send the same to Members of Congress.

Mr. Bonaparte explained that the original committee would be superseded in its general field by the Investigating Committee created by the Executive Committee at its session of this date, and that a separate Committee to deal exclusively with the matter of the Census seemed desirable. The resolutions were then adopted unanimously.

Mr. Bonaparte announced that the members and visiting delegates would be entertained at luncheon by the ladies of the Arundel and Arundel Good Government Clubs, and the hour of one having been reached, the League then adjourned.

Music Hall, December 16, 1898.

10:30 A. M.

The League re-convened at half-past ten o'clock.

The business in order being the annual election of officers, the President call Mr. Cary of New York to the chair.

Mr. Wood, of Pennsylvania, moved that the Secretary be instructed to cast the vote of the League for the re-election of Hon. Carl Schurz as President for the ensuing year. The motion was seconded by a number of members and carried unanimously. The Secretary cast the ballot, and Mr. Schurz was declared elected. In a brief address the President thanked the League for the renewal of confidence it had expressed, and resumed the chair.

On motion of Mr. Bonaparte the Secretary was instructed to cast one ballot for the re-election for one year of the present Vice-Presidents, as follows: Charles Francis Adams, Boston; Augustus R. MacDonough, New York; Rt. Rev. Henry C. Potter, New York; J. Hall Pleasants, Baltimore; Henry Hitchcock, St. Louis; Henry C. Lea, Philadelphia; Franklin MacVeagh, Chicago; Rt. Rev. P. H. Ryan, Philadelphia; William Potts, New York.

The Secretary cast the ballot, and the gentlemen named were declared elected.

Mr. Siddons for the Auditing Committee appointed by the Executive Committee, submitted the following report:

To the National Civil Service Reform League :

The undersigned, constituting the Auditing Committee, respectfully report that we have examined the accounts of the Treasurer, and compared them with the vouchers.* We find them correct, and that the amount in the Treasury at this date is $62.57.

Respectfully submitted,
F. L. SIDDONS,
JOHN W. ELA.

The report was received and ordered filed.

The President announced the business next in order to be the reception of reports from representatives of local Associations.

---

* Page 54.

Reports were then received as follows:

For New York State, Mr. Sherman S. Rogers, of Buffalo—

There is little to add to what the President said in his address last evening about the reform in the State of New York. It is making its way there surely but with occasional reverses. We must not expect to have favoring gales always. We shall have our ups and downs. Civil Service Reform will never be securely established till a generation shall have grown up under its teachings and the young men who are now coming into the life of the citizen have taken on the belief that the offices are to be acquired by personal merit and fitness and without regard to political influence and pull as naturally as the generations preceding them took on the opposite ideas. Just now the reform in our State has come into an extraordinary experience of good fortune in the election of a true Civil Service Reformer to the Governor's chair.

This follows something of a very different sort. When Governor Morton's term of office expired he left the law and the general rules and regulations in reasonably good shape, and a Commission, the dominating member of which was that tried and able friend of Civil Service Reform whom we know so well, Col. Silas W. Burt. His associates had been appointed from political life and for political reasons, and were not very active reformers, but our friends throughout the State felt very hopeful. The only element of doubt in the situation was the new Governor, who was an unknown quantity in the matter of Civil Service Reform.

You all know how he developed, and that, too very soon. The story of the Anti-Starch Bill need not be repeated. It was Governor Black's own and was driven through by him. It threw the civil service in the State into confusion, but in the cities its worst effects were averted by the appointing officers refusing to exercise the fifty per cent. power of examination, and turning it over to the local Civil Service Commissioners. But two years have passed and the *Starch* has disappeared from the Governor, and his bill was amended last winter so as to leave the examinations in the cities where they were before its passage.

And now, following Governor Black, we have as Governor-elect, a man who has been known for years as a Civil Service Reformer of the best type—able, sincere, intelligent, aggressive, combative. Col. Roosevelt's election may well be regarded as a fact of the highest importance. It has a national interest. He will give to the State of New York, I believe, a commission of his own type. And we are hopeful of the very best results.

For Massachusetts, Mr. Richard Henry Dana, of Boston.

During the year the Massachusetts Civil Service Reform League and the Associations of Boston and Cambridge, have repelled several attacks made in the Legislature by means of attempted amendments to the Civil Service statutes. The associations were taken by surprise, and were unable to present any opposition until after these measures had progressed several stages without their knowledge. The opposition when ogranized, however, was effective. In order to guard against the recurrence of covert attacks at the coming session, arrangements have been made for the employment of an agent at the State House, a reliable newspaper reporter, who will watch the proceedings of the Legislature and give immediate notice of matters requiring attention.

An effort will shortly be made to extend the operation of the law to the County offices within the State, which were excluded from the scope of the original Act of 1884, as most of the subordinates were then mere contractors with the registers of deeds and probate. By subsequent statutes these persons have been made regular employees of the county.

The Boston Association secured something over $800 for the purposes of the National League, in reply to a circular sent to its members. The Cambridge Association raised for the same purpose about $250, by sending canvassers among its members and other citizens likely to be interested in the same. An especial effort has been made to interest younger men in the purposes and work of the League.

For Connecticut, General William A. Aiken, of Norwich:

The fact that Connecticut contains no large cities, in the modern sense, and that so large a proportion of local administrators are elective rather than appointive, owing to the survival of its ancient town and school district jurisdiction contemporary with, but separate from those arising under its city charters, is adverse to the growth of militant local Civil Service Reform Associations.

While no comprehensive law exists making the open competitive test the basis for municipal appointments throughout the State, reformatory movements are now going on in several localities.

Some of these are of more interest to the League for Municipal Reform than, directly, they would be to ours; yet Civil Service Reformers must note with approval all movements for the general welfare within the cities.

The movement to which I wish especially to call your present attention is that in our largest city, New Haven. Under its new charter of 1897 sweeping provisions were made against corrupt and improper influences in elections or appointments, with the penalty of imprisonment for violation. Thereunder, no appointments can be made for political considerations, no questions can be put to applicants for positions, designed to disclose political or religious views, and applicants are forbidden to make known such views or affiliations to examiners. In scope the system embraces all positions in the city government, including the Police and Fire Departments, excepting elective officers, commissioners, officials appointed by the Mayor, and superintendents, principals and teachers employed by the Board of Education. It should be said, in passing, that the Mayor's appointive powers are very limited as compared with those of the Mayor of Greater New York. The charter creates a Civil Service Board, which has very broad powers. I am indebted to Prof. Henry W. Farnam, of Yale University, the very able president of this Board, for a summary of its workings, upon which I shall largely draw for what follows.

The present Board, supplanting one of very limited powers under the previous charter, consists of three well-known citizens, and, ex-officio, of the chiefs of the Police and Fire Departments. Immediately after its organization it drafted a complete set of rules, and has thus far held examinations for positions in the Fire and Police Departments, clerks, engineers, drawbridge tenders, janitors, etc., and also for promotions therein. Regarding the success of the system, the president of the Board expresses himself as confident that it commends itself to the great mass of city officials, if not to them all. The candidate passing the examination with the highest mark has, generally speaking, been appointed and has proved himself competent. The rules are, in general, similar to those adopted in New York, Boston and elsewhere, except that the classifications and examinations are adapted to a city of the size of New Haven.

The physical tests for members of the Police and Fire Departments are now conducted in the Yale gymnasium, by the director of physical training, thus saving the city the expense of a special examiner and apparatus for this purpose.

One excellent and novel feature that this Board has introduced relates to the appointment of special constables, to which office many unfit persons had previously been appointed by the Common Council. It having been ruled by the Corporation Counsel that special constables were subject to the rules of the Civil Service Board, they decided that, inasmuch as they were not paid by the city nor subject to the discipline of the Police Department, a formal examination would be absurd. A rule was made, however, exacting conformity with certain requirements as to citizenship, habits, etc., and providing that they must show some good reason, non-political in character, that there was ground for their employment. The appointing power as to special constables vests with the Police Commissioners, who have, in every instance, followed the recommendation of the Civil Service Board, and they have effectually weeded out the unfit.

The New Haven experiment will be watched with much interest in the smaller cities of our State, and excellent results may reasonably be hoped for through the labors of the painstaking and excellent Board which is furnishing so valuable an object lesson in our leading city.

It was announced that the Committee on Resolutions was prepared to report, and on motion the order of reports from local associations was suspended.

Mr. Cary, of New York, for the Committee on Resolutions, read the resolutions prepared, and moved their adoption.

Mr. Wyman, of Massachusetts, moved that the several paragraphs be considered seriatim, and the motion was lost.

Some discussion followed, during the course of which certain changes of language were suggested and accepted by the committee.

Mr. Watson, of New York, moved that the preamble of Resolution III be amended so as to state more definitely the fact that the terms of the Civil Service law had been violated in certain branches of the Federal Service. Attention was called to the fact that this was implied by the specifications contained in the resolution in question, and the motion was lost.

Mr. Montgomery, of Pennsylvania, moved that the vote on the motion to pass on the resolutions seriatim be reconsidered. A division being called for, there were 24 ayes, and 24 nays, so the motion was lost.

The resolutions were then adopted unanimously in the following form :

I.

The National Civil Service Reform League congratulates the country upon the entire failure of the attack on the merit system in Congress at the last session—a result due to the advancing sentiment of the nation and to the firm attitude of the President in that crisis.

II.

The League, however, has heard with concern the report that it is the intention of the President to withdraw important positions and classes of positions from under the civil service rules. We believe that such action, if taken, would be contrary to the interest of the public service, and we can but repeat the conviction already respectfully expressed to the President, that such changes would be accepted not only as a " step backward," but as proof that the system is not regarded by the present Administration as "here and here to stay," and would inevitably awaken doubts as to the sincerity of the repeated declarations of the party now dominant in National affairs that the law establishing it shall be thoroughly and honestly enforced and extended wherever practicable.

III.

There are none in the country who have wished more earnestly for the success of the present Administration in carrying out its declared principles with regard to the reform of the civil service, and none who have been more jealously anxious that in this particular its record should be consistent and unimpeachable. The League, however, in the discharge of the duty of watchful and impartial criticism—a duty more than ever imperative at this critical period in the development of our administrative system—is forced to recognize certain grave departures, within the present year, from a strict observance of the civil service law and the principles underlying it. As to these, it can be shown by detailed evidence:

(1.) That the order of July 27, 1897, regulating the method of removal, has been violated in both letter and spirit in various branches of the service, and that in many localities the whole system of civil service administration has been discredited in consequence.

(2.) That in the Internal Revenue Service, and in the offices of United States Matshals, appointments have been made altogether in violation of the law, and that such appointments have been made openly for political considerations.

(3.) That appointments have been made in the same manner in the General Land Office, in the Forest Reserve force, and in other branches of the service of the Interior Department.

(4). That through appointments and removals for political reasons the efficiency of the Indian Service has been seriously affected, and that certain of such changes have been made against the protest of those engaged most earnestly in the work for Indian improvement.

(5.) That the operation of the rules in the Pension Examining force has been nullified by an adroit system of evasion practiced by the Commissioner of Pension, against the protests of the Civil Service Commission, and of many prominent individual surgeons interested in the honesty and efficiency of this peculiar important service.

(6.). That in certain Customs Houses, and in the departments at Washington, many persons have been employed without examinations as "laborers" and assigned to various kinds of classified work.

(7). That through these and other methods, the proportionate number of persons appointed in the classified service, under this administration, in full conformity with the civil service rules, when compared with the number not so appointed, has been materially decreased.

(8). That hundreds of appointments to civil positions in the Washington offices of the War Department, and in certain bureaus of the Treasury, were made, during the recent war, without reference to the civil service rules, although the lists of the Commission contained the names of several thousand persons eligible for appointment, and within easy call; and, further, that the persons so appointed were in many cases illiterate and otherwise incompetent and unfit.

(9.) That changes in the Consular Service have been more sweeping than at any previous time, exceeding in number those made under the preceeding administration, and amounting, in the salaried grades, to a total of 237 out of 272, or nearly ninety per cent. of the whole; and that the system of non-competitive examination, established for certain grades of the Consular Service has been so modified as to be practically ineffective.

IV.

The League also calls attention to the fact that the pledge of the party now in power in the National government to "extend the system wherever practicable," is yet to be redeemed with regard to the assistant postmasters at free delivery offices, the fourth class postmasters, the force of the Congressional Library, the employees of the Census Bureau, the municipal service in the District of Columbia, and—by registration—the labor service, in all of which branches extension is not only clearly practicable, but urgently required.

V.

It is the profound conviction of the League that the rule of outlying dependencies by the United States would inevitably result in disaster and disgrace to the nation if conducted upon the plan of spoils politics; and that success in such an experiment would be impossible without the strictest and most exacting application of both the spirit and method of the merit system.

The regular order was resumed.

Mr. Wood, of Philadelphia, reported for the Pennsylvania Association as follows:

The experience of our Association during the past year corroborates the statements made by President Schurz in his Annual Address to the League last night as to the demoralization in the United States service.

This began in the Post Office after the appointment of the present Postmaster. The attempts of that officer to evade the Civil Service Law became so notorious, and the complaints made to our Association were so frequent, that the President of the Association requested the aid of a committee of the National League to assist in an investigation which was made in the month of January, and a report was subsequently presented to the President of the United States, showing the result. While, so far as is known, no public action was taken, it came to the knowledge of the Secretary that the Postmaster received some intimation from Washington, which put an end to his attempts to ignore the Civil Service Law.

Later came the appointment of a new Collector of Customs, who, like the Postmaster, had been a man in active political life, and who had already shown his dislike to Civil Service Reform. Early in the Summer

complaints began coming to the Secretary of the Association from employees of the Custom House to the effect that men were discharged on
the plea that there was not sufficient work for them to do, but that soon
afterwards other men were appointed who did the same work, though in
some cases their offices were given different titles. These complaints
were laid before the United States Civil Service Commission, which instituted an investigation and laid several of the matters complained of
before the Treasury Department, which, however, has either attempted
to justify the action of the Collector or has ignored the complaints, and
the Commission seems powerless to stop these proceedings.

At the December meeting of the Executive Committee of the Association information was laid before it to the effect that the Collector
was making temporary appointments and upon the expiration of the
period renewing these appointments for another temporary period instead
of making appointments from the eligible list. One specific cause was
mentioned—that of T. Larry Eyre, and it was said, in addition, as to
this man, that he spent very little time at the Custom House, but was engaged mostly in collecting political assessments at the head-quarters of
one of the Campaign Clubs. This information came so direct that the
Secretary was instructed to call the attention of the Civil Service Commission to the facts, and ask for a further investigation.

With regard to local conditions in Philadelphia, there is nothing new
to be reported. There are still in effect the defective rules applying to
admissions to the municipal service, and these have probably brought
about the admission of a somewhat better class of men, but have not removed the service from politics.

A new Association has been started by a member of the Pennsylvania Association at Wilkes-Barre, and this organization has become a
member of the National League.

It is the intention of the Association to again introduce a State
Civil Service Bill in the coming session of the Legislature, but it is the
feeling among reformers in Pennsylvania that the most important legislation to be sought for is a new ballot law, and as this Association
started the agitation for the Australian Ballot System, it will probably
take an active interest in the effort to have the present imperfect law
improved.

Mr. Bonaparte then moved that the order of reports from
local associations be suspended until following the reading of
papers at the afternoon session. The motion was carried and
the League then adjourned.

MUSIC HALL, December 16, 2.30 P.M.

The League reconvened at half-past two o'clock.

The following papers were read:

"The Murrain of Spoils in the Indian Service," by Herbert Welsh, of Philadelphia;*

"The Need and Means of Providing a Stable and Competent Civil Service for Our New Dependencies," by Dorman B. Eaton, of New York;†

"Can We Trust Our Army to Spoilsmen?" by Charles J. Bonaparte, of Baltimore.‡

The order of reports from local associations was then resumed as follows:

For Maryland, Mr. William Reynolds, of Baltimore:

The year which is now drawing to a close has not proved an eventful one for Civil Service Reform in Maryland. No legislation bearing directly upon the introduction of the Merit System into the State government has been enacted by the General Assembly which met in January, but that body did enact a new Charter for the City of Baltimore which, among other needed reforms, provided for a reorganization of the Department of Education, and for the nomination of all teachers of the public schools being made from graded lists, which are to be prepared by the Superintendent of Public Instruction and his assistants by placing thereon the names of all accepted candidates in the order of their relative qualifications, as ascertained by competitive examinations, which shall be open to all who desire appointment. If these requirements of the new Charter are faithfully carried out, the result will be the application of the Merit System to the appointment of all teachers of the public schools of Baltimore City, a consummation most devoutly to be wished for.

The coming into power of the Republican party, which was, in a large degree, attributable to the abuses of the Spoils System under its predecessors, has had the usual effect upon the spoilsmen of the victorious party in stirring them up to denounce most vigorously what they are pleased to denominate "Civil Service;" but the result of the election last month for Congressmen, by which the Republican plurality in Baltimore City of over 17,500 at the Congressional election of 1896 was reduced to very little more than 500 in 1898, has been calculated to throw somewhat of a damper upon all vaporings of this description, and has encouraged many good citizens to hope that the uncertainty of the result will put both political parties upon their good behavior, so that

* Page 83.
† Page 73.
‡ Page 98.

the coming municipal election in the Spring may be controlled by independent votes cast in the interest of honest government rather than
by the cohesive power of public plunder manipulated by the rival
machines.

This association has, like many of its sister members of the League,
united in a vigorous protest against any action being taken by the President to reduce the area of the competitive system, which it would regard
as a backward step in a great reform, the value of which is becoming
day by day more thoroughly appreciated by the great body of the
American people.

For the District of Columbia, Mr. F. L. Siddons, of
Washington.

As may be remembered, in the last Congress, the Civil Service Reform Association of the District of Columbia procured the introduction
of a bill, which had for its object the extension of the provisions of the
Civil Service Law to the municipal government of the District of
Columbia. The bill was introduced in both Senate and House and referred to appropriate committees, and a hearing was given representatives of our Association, the Board of Trade, and other organizations, by
the committee of the House of Representatives, to which the bill was referred, but we did not succeed in having the bill favorably reported.
The chairman of the committee, Mr. Brosius, frankly told representatives of the local Assoc ation that the bill would, if reported
to the House, simply provoke a fight, which it was his belief
the best interest of the reform should not hazard at that time.
In the present and last sessions of Congress, the hostility towards
the cause that we represent has been so pronounced that to ask for consideration of our bill was simply to invite defeat, and the Association has
deemed it wise not to press their measure at this time. It is undoubtedly
true that the District Commissioners, who constitute our local government, have the power to adopt any regulations that they please affecting
the appointment to, promotion in, and removal from office, so far as the
employees of the District government are concerned, but this they have
never done, for the reason, as it is believed, that they would be constantly
asked to make exceptions or to ignore their regulations by members of
Congress, who do not hesitate to make it a *sine qua non* to District appropriations that their demand for offices in the local government should
be recognized. The President also could indirectly exercise a power in
the matter of such regulations by requiring persons whom he was about
to appoint as Commissioners to pledge that they would make such rules
and regulations and adhere to them, or to remove Commissioners who
refused to carry out such a wish if expressed by him. It is sufficient to
say that no President has ever taken this position. Our hope is that at
no distant time, we can go to Congress for the needed legislation, with
the hope and expectation that our wishes will be gratified.

For Ohio, Charles B. Wilby, of Cincinnati.

There is but little that I can say as to the progress of our cause in the State of Ohio, and in that little there is not much good news.

As you will remember, our first Civil Service bill failed to become a law at the session of the Ohio Legislature held before the last meeting of this League. The member of that Legislature to whose efforts the defeat of the bill was chiefly due, has been rewarded, for this and other services to him who dispenses the political spoils of southern Ohio, by a seat in Congress.

At the next session of the Legislature, we introduced a second bill. The first had been prepared after the Chicago plan, with no State Commission, covering only the Civil Service of four or five of the larger cities, whenever the voters of such cities should ask to have its provisions applied to them.

We had adopted this plan, notwithstanding the advice which we had received from our friends of the Home Office at 54 William Street, as well as from other friends in the East, that we should follow the plan of the New York and Massachusetts laws, because the Legislature of Ohio at that time was having a spasm of economy, and we determined to go to the country members with a bill which would impose no expense upon the State at large ; so that we could say to them : "Here is a bill which only touches the Civil Service of the larger cities, where it is most needed, and which takes nothing from the State Treasury." Our hopes thus to escape the opposition of the country members were realized too well. They not only did not oppose our bill, but they declined to take any interest in it and turned it over to the tender mercies of the delegations from the larger cities which were controlled by spoilsmen who realized that the passage of the bill meant the end of their power, and by them it was killed. Our first bill had been prepared by the Cincinnati Association. Our friends who are represented here by Mr. Cushing, had preferred a bill providing for a State Commission, so that when we came to prepare our second bill, the Cincinnati idea as expressed in the original bill was abandoned and a bill on the State plan was introduced at the next session of the Legislature which met soon after the meeting of this League held in Cincinnati a year ago. The effect of that meeting had been very marked in arousing general interest favorable to our cause, not only in Cincinnati, but throughout the State.

Those of you who were at the dinner which closed that meeting, will remember that there were present the entire Legislative delegation from our County, who then were able to hear the gospel of our cause as it is preached by its best expounders. When the Legislature met, we entered upon the work of securing the passage of our bill filled with hope. The first business the Legislature undertook was the election of a United States Senator, and the feeling which that contest aroused disturbed all of our arrangements, so that we were never able even to get the bill to a vote during the session.

Since that time two new Associations have been formed in Ohio, and we expect to get together again and to agree on a new bill, probably on the plan of the last, with a State Commission, and shall introduce it at the next session of the Legislature and do what we can to have it passed, and shall continue to introduce such a bill at every succeeding session of the Legislature until we have secured this indispensable aid to good government in our State.

For Illinois, Col. John W. Ela, of Chicago:

The vicissitudes experienced by the Democrats in Cook County at the last election will probably not encourage them to repeat the blunder of putting an anti-Civil Service Reform plank in their platform. In an "off year," when any kind of an opposition party is generally successful, they lost most of their county candidates by decided majorities. The only ones elected were two judges and one assessor, who succeeded only because they were tried men, were satisfactory to the public and were endorsed, the judges by the Bar Association, and the assessor by the Real Estate Board Committee ; while the leader of the avowed enemies of the law, whose campaign was run expressly on that issue, was not only defeated,but received the smallest number of votes cast for any candidate on the ballot. Such legislative candidates as they elected were in districts where they were always elected, regardless of the platform, and this year their old majorities were considerably reduced.

This plank was probably put into the platform to catch the votes of the "gangs" and the incompetents of both parties; and it undoubtedly did catch some of them, although it is now claimed that some of them were too utterly incompetent to comprehend that by voting the Democratic ticket they might get rid of the law altogether and so they did not vote at all. But that a much larger number of their best men voted against the ticket on account of this plank the result shows beyond question. It was claimed by some of the leaders that the existence of the civil service law lost them many votes. Their explanation of this phenomenon constitutes one of the strongest arguments in favor of such a law that I have ever encountered. The explanation was, that, in some of the Democratic wards, many voters, knowing that they could not pass the examinations provided in the law were "tired of the civil service law," and so refused to vote. Could there be any more conclusive proof of the success of the Civil Service Reform legislation in this county ? Here is a law passed for the purpose of excluding from public employment those men who are incompetent to perform the duties of the position; and in the fourth year of its history a considerable number of this very class of men "throw up their hands," so to speak, admit their incompetency, and the futility of further attempts to loot the city treasury. It is not quite the same as if the inmates of the State penitentiary should pass resolutions denouncing the laws against larceny and expressing their intention to abandon their perennial fight with the police force and the deputy sheriffs, but the elements of encouragement to the so-called reformer would be somewhat similar in both cases.

It will not do to say that the complaint of these tired voters is based upon the unreasonable examinations required by the law and not upon their incompetence, for the requirement of the law is that the examinations "shall be practical in their character and shall relate to those matters which will fairly test the relative capacity of the persons examined to discharge the duties of the position to which they ask to be appointed;" and the enforcement of this law, the character and conduct of the examinations, is absolutely in the hands of the city administration; the leaders of which are making this highly satisfactory statement of the effect of the proper enforcement of the law.

Of course, this statement involves a direct compliment to the administration. It assumes that the law is being properly enforced in Chicago. And I believe that the compliment was intended; for some of these gentlemen believe in the law, and favor its enforcement notwithstanding the disagreeable effects of which they complain. And I believe that some of them are endeavoring to enforce the law, under circumstances so discouraging, from the standpoint of the average politician, that their action seems almost heroic.

The circumstances are, briefly, these: The bill was passed by a Republican legislature just before the commencement of a Republican city administration ; it was adopted by the city at the same election which put that administration in power; and yet, instead of putting in immediate operation the law which their party had enacted, and the people of the city so emphatically demanded, they, taking advantage of a three months' option in the law, postponed its enforcement until most of the places had beeen filled by Republicans, under the old system. So that when the present administration came into power it found nearly all the offices and places held by Republican political workers, and a civil service law on the statute book, passed by a Republican legislature, and which has been in existence for two years, during a Republican city administration. It is true that an excellent Board of Commissioners was appointed by this administration who did admirably such work as was given them to do, and made a set of rules, to be executed by a Democratic administration, which were so nearly perfect that they have remained almost wholly unchanged up to the present day.

There was certainly nothing in the moral or political aspect of the situation to encourage an incoming Democratic administration to undertake a rigid enforcement of this law, the spirit of which had been substantially repudiated for two years by the party which claimed the credit of its enactment. By any ethical standard which has obtained in Cook County politics since the time when the memory of man runneth not to the contrary, the new administration would have been justified in " throwing down" the law, at least until it had "evened up" the political complexion of the City Hall. An opposite course would be regarded by the local politicians of both parties as an attempt to inaugurate a theory of political ethics much too fine for common use.

It is probable that some of the leaders in the new administration, and many of their followers, took this view of the situation, for they have persistently disregarded the law and obstructed its operation from the first.

On the other hand, the mayor and the heads of some of the principal departments, notably the departments containing much the largest

proportion of the city employees, are business men who know the value
of the merit system and who believe in the necessity of its application
to city affairs and the conscientious execution of this law.

It will appear in the annual report of the Civil Service Commissioners next month that seven thousand two hundred and seventy persons have been examined and certified for appointment, under the law,
during the past year; and something over ten thousand since this administration came in. It will also appear that three hundred and
seventy-five examinations have been held so far in this administration,
and that only fifty-nine remain to be held. These fifty-nine examinations are required in order to cover the positions of that number of
"sixty day men," and will be held before April first, after which, as the
report will show, there will be no sixty day men (men holding temporary
appointments) in the city service.

The Supreme Court of Illinois has sustained the civil service law in
all its important features. This court is composed of eminent lawyers,
some of them from sections of the State where the doctrine of Civil Service Reform is as unfamiliar as the Hebrew language. Every objection
that a sleepless hostility could frame has been hurled at this court in the
last two years, and. without regard to previous condition of political
servitude or present considerations of political policy these judges have
unanimously confirmed the constitutionality of the law, both State and
National, and approved its principle and its scope. So comprehensive
and so well-reasoned are these decisions that I predict their adoption by
the Supreme Court of the United States whenever a civil service law
reaches that tribunal.

The latest decision of the Illinois Supreme Court (rendered within
the last few weeks) puts the employees in the four important offices of
the City Clerk, City Collector, City Comptroller and City Treasurer,
under the provisions of the act. To the surprise of the friends of the
law a decision appeared in the morning papers one day, rendered by two
Judges (of the Circuit and Superior Courts) holding that these four
offices are not covered by the law. This decision appeared to have been
made in a "submission" case between the incumbents of two of those
offices. The Civil Service Commissioners, notwithstanding this decision, immediately instituted proceedings in the Supreme Court to test
the question, and that Court has decided that the offices in question are
covered by the law, and has issued a writ of mandamus commanding
these officers to follow the provisions thereof in the appointment of their
employees. Since that decision examinations have been held, and the
vacancies in those offices have been filled, under the law.

There will be, probably, a decision soon in the case brought by the
Civil Service Commissioners, and now pending in the Supreme Court,
to compel the Board of Education to come under the provisions of the
law.

For St. Louis, Mr. Albert L. Berry:

I come from a city which was settled by the French, is inhabited by
Americans, guarded by the Irish, and ruled to-day by the Germans.

You see how difficult, yet how necessary that such a city should have Civil Service Reform. The organic laws which form the frame work of our city government, emanated from a party of freeholders, about a quarter of a century ago, and are known as the Scheme and Charter of the City of St. Louis, which placed our city in the hands of its own people, free from the interference of State Legislature or State officials. All amendments to our City Charter must be recommended by its legislative bodies, and receive the approval of the people at a special election.

As there were to be submitted last Spring a number of amendments to our City Charter, a movement was inaugurated by the Civic Federation, early in the Winter, to have an amendment known as the Merit System Amendment, submitted with other amendments, then in the hands of the Council, to a vote of the people.

A Citizens' Committee was formed, composed of such representative bodies as the Merchants'Exchange,the Business Men's League,the Central Trades and Labor Union, the Commercial Club, the Civil Service Reform League, and some twenty other bodies, representing every commercial, industrial, civic and social organization of prominence in the city. An amendment was drafted under the supervision of Mr. Henry Hitchcock, whom you all know rocked the cradle of Civil Service Reform in this country, has been godfather to its principles and godmother to its needs.

The amendment was submitted to the City Council, and while we waited for the decision, as to whether that body would allow the people to vote upon a question, which by voice, petitions and resolutions, they had so strongly appealed, a good deal of work was done, especially among the trades and labor unions, who saw at once its need and benefit, and rendered us valuable and efficient aid. By their assistance and the assistance rendered us by the business men, in allowing our literature to be circulated through the medium of their pay envelopes, and by the aid of the press and the mail, we were able to make known to almost our entire reading population, what was meant by the Merit System, and the needs and benefits to be derived by its adoption into our City Charter.

Both bodies of our Municipal Assembly had recently been elected by quite large majorities, and thought themselves so strong that they could defy public opinion, and carry any measure they desired. Both of these bodies refused to allow the Merit System Amendment to be submitted to a vote of the people; but the amendments which they did submit were so dangerous and oppressive, that we would have been placed in the awkward position of having to defeat our own measure if it had been submitted, as we could not have supported our own amendment in company with those submitted, for fear of passing both. When the amendments the Council did submit came before the people for adoption, the Citizens' Committee opposed them, and made a vigorous fight against their adoption, and they were defeated by a vote of three to one. The Merit System has now become so well known and endorsed that I am confident that at next Spring's election, when six new members are elected to the Council and a new House of Delegates is chosen, that new amendments will be submitted to the people which all citizens can endorse, and you can rest assured that any amendments to our Charter, which will receive sufficient support from our people to be adopted, will embrace the amendment known as the Merit System.

For Harvard University, Mr. F. C. Sutro.

The Civil Service Reform Club of Harvard University differs from those organizations from which we have just heard such gratifying reports, in that, unlike these, it has no immediate field for action ; but must devote its efforts solely and purely in the line of education. This object, however, may not be overlooked. Harvard University, ever first in accomplishing the immediate purposes for which men visit her, tries also to be first in keeping them in close and continuous touch with the things that are going on in the world about her. In line with this policy, the Civil Service Reform Club was founded about five years ago, remained for a year or two in a flourishing condition, and then, partly through lack of sufficiently large membership, partly through the adoption of an inefficient and unprogressive policy, gradually, I regret to say, fell into insignificance. This year, however, several members of the class of Ninty-nine have taken up the cause energetically, and the presence of a delegate in this impressive assembly is the best evidence of their success that I can offer. We hope in the course of the year to restore the organization to its original vigor.

Mr. Murray Nelson, Jr., of the Chicago Citizens Association, reported as follows with regard to legislation in the matter of civil service reform, successfully conducted by that organization and other relevant matters :

Illinois may well be proud that she is among the very few States having a merit system in municipal government. The Illinois Civil Service Law has this year survived the combined attack of its whole souled enemies and its half hearted friends. The law has been sustained by the Supreme Court of Illinois in an opinion of the greatest scope and completeness, which, upon review, the Court at Washington did not disturb. An interpretation has been given of value to all students of the subject.

The Citizens' Association of Chicago, which I have the honor to represent, through the able and efficient Attorney-General of Illinois, Mr. Edward C. Akin, is entitled to all credit for its expenditure of time, money and energy in this cause. They succeeded in Chicago where the present municipal authorities are either the avowed opponents of the Merit System or its timid friends.

The present Mayor at the earliest opportunity removed without cause the very excellent Civil Service Commission selected by his predecessor and appointed a new commission, who proceeded to "interpret" the law in accordance with the opinion of the Mayor's Corporation Counsel, a zealous and sincere advocate of the Spoils System, to the end that the unclassified list of the City of Chicago might take in as many active spoilsmen as possible. This interpretation the Illinois Supreme Court has swept away.

No ideal situation has been realized; the Merit System is young and the spoils system is very old, but it has been fairly demonstrated in Chicago, at least, that vigorous action, strict and just interpretation of the law are not damaging to the cause of Civil Service Reform.

A rightful law however unpopular at the outset, if properly and strictly enforced makes hearty friends. Lax enforcement and loose interpretation may avoid the antagonism of enemies, but active friendship in a cause like this far outweighs the advantage got by concessions to the enemy. This statement may seem inconsistent with practical politics. We are advised not to seek enforcement of the Civil Service Law lest it be repealed. I for one believe that the advocacy of the Merit System is part of the most practical politics. The result of the November election in Chicago tends to sustain this belief.

In that election the democratic platform contained the following language: "We pronounce the present civil service law inefficient, mischievous and hostile to the regnant principles of popular government. The enforcement that this law has had in Cook County has abundantly proved to us that it greatly adds to the burdens of the taxpayers, destroys the sense of responsibility in the heads of governmental departments, tends to create an official class to the exclusion of other equally deserving and capable citizens and utterly fails to secure the best men for public service. We believe that the people should be allowed through the ballot to select officers who shall be wholly and unqualifiedly responsible to the electors for success or failure in their several offices; and believing that this law, an exotic imported from monarchic governments beyond the seas, prevents such responsibility, we demand its repeal."

The Republican platform condemned the City administration for its "palpable attempts to evade the provisions of the Civil Service Law."

After the election, Mayor Harrison, one of the party leaders in Illinois, in an interview published in several Chicago papers, ascribed the defeat of the democrats to the Civil Service Law, which, he said, had prevented the rank and file, who were too ignorant to pass examinations, and so were without hope of holding office, from taking an interest in the election. This from an opponent of the Merit System is perhaps as good an argument for it as the most ardent advocate could wish.

The people are for the Merit System and whenever the people vote they vote for it. The people in Chicago voted for its adoption by a majority of two to one. The small politicians are hostile, but it has been demonstrated often enough that the people outvote the small politicians. The small politicians in their caucuses and ward clubs may declare the Merit System unAmerican, monarchical or hypocritical, but to take their declaration as expressive of the popular will is the narrowest and stupidest politics.

I believe in practical politics, and I believe also that the most practical politics consults rather the many who do not seek public office than the few who do.

Mr. William E. Cushing, representing the Cleveland Chamber of Commerce, reported respecting the recent activity of that body in the movement for the reform of the Consular Service as follows:

Last year the Cleveland Chamber of Commerce passed resolutions expressing its desire that the Consular service of the United States should be put on a merit basis, and requesting Congress to take action in that regard by passing either the Lodge bill or the Morgan bill, or some other equally effective measure.

About two weeks ago the directors of the Chamber reaffirmed these resolutions and sent delegates to Washington to urge affirmative action on the part of Congress and of the administration. The delegates were courteously received by the President, and are now taking steps to obtain an opportunity for a hearing before the House Committee on Foreign Relations.

Our action has attracted public attention to a degree that we did not anticipate. A good deal of mention has been made of it in the press despatches and in the editorial columns of newspapers, and letters are beginning to come to us from other chambers of commerce saying that they have heard of our action, and that they approve of it and propose to imitate it. If the business organizations of the country will seriously undertake to impress upon the authorities their wish that this reform, so important to the business interests of the country, be instituted, it may be that something will be accomplished sooner than we expect.

Hon. John R. Procter, President of the United States Civil Service Commission, responding to the invitation of the president, then made an informal address, in the course of which he read to the League certain highly interesting extracts from advance sheets of the annual reports of bureau officers, testifying to the value of the merit system in technical branches of the service. Mr. Procter stated that the commission has met with difficulties in conducting its examinations only in those branches where the officers in control have shown their hostility to the system, and failed properly to co-operate in the preparation of the necessary tests.

At the conclusion of the regular order, Mr. Potts, of New York, moved that the cordial and grateful thanks of the League be extended to the Civil Service Reform Association of Mary land, and to the ladies of the Arundel and Arundel Good Government Clubs, for the courteous and generous hospitality extended by them to the visiting delegates during the period of these meetings.

Mr. Wilby moved that the same acknowledgment be made of the hospitality received from Mr. William Keyser, of the Maryland Association.

The motions were carried unanimously.
The League then adjourned.

Attest :

GEORGE McANENY,
Secretary.

———

On the evening of the 16th, the visiting delegates were entertained by the Civil Service Reform Association of Maryland, at a dinner given at the Hotel Rennert. Mr. Charles J. Bonaparte, President of the Association, presided, and addresses were made by Carl Schurz, of New York; John R. Procter, President of the United States Civil Service Commission; Representative James R. Fleming, of Georgia; Representative W. H. Gillett, of Massachusetts; and William Dudley Foulke, of Indiana.

ANNUAL REPORT OF THE TREASURER.

Balance on hand, Dec. 16, 1897, ... **$366.13**

RECEIPTS:

Subscriptions from members of the Pennsyl-
vania Association.... $1,118.00
" " Boston " 814.00
" " Cambridge " 239.65
" " Newton " 50.00
" " Massachusetts, Miss.... 285.00
" " New York Association.. 320.00
" " Cincinnati " 545.00
" " St. Louis " 45.00
" " Chicago " 50.00
" " Washington " 75.00
" " Buffalo " 95.00
" " Norwalk " 65.00
" " Baltimore " 168.00
Pamphlets sold........................ 16.12   3,885.77

$4,251.90

DISBURSEMENTS:

Salary of Secretary...................... $1,687.50
Clerk hire....... .... 690.50
Rent of office......................... 150.00
Printing............................... 564.95
Postage and stamped envelopes............ 213.88
Travelling expenses...................... 385.80
Office Expenses, miscellaneous........... 169.70
Paid F. E. Leupp, on account of *Good Gov-
ernment*............................... 100.00
Expenses of Investigating Committee...... 227.00   4,189.33

Balance on hand, December 15, 1898.................... $ 62.57

E. & O. E.

A. S. FRISSELL,
Treasurer.

Colonial Administration: A Warning From Spain.

BY HENRY HAYWOOD GLASSIE.

Flushed with joy and gratitude at the prospect of empire beyond the sea, Spain hastened to add to the newly granted arms of the discoverer, the lofty and sonorous legend—

Por Castilla y por León
Nuevo Mundo halló Colón.

The simple Saxon name of our Admiral of the Indies does not lend itself to verse. It may be said of him, nevertheless, that he found for America a new world. For it is to the victory of Manila, coming with such dramatic force from the end of the earth, that we owe the new passion for empire which has already extended our sway over Porto Rico and the Philippines, and is stretching out our hands against Cuba herself.

It is idle for advocates of imperial expansion to run back from precedent to precedent—Alaska, California, Texas, Florida, Louisiana. Why not Tennessee, Kentucky, Michigan? For all of them were alike parts in the orderly development of our destiny on this continent. The settlement of Texas, no less than the settlement of Tennessee, was a stage in the expansion of our vast democracy over the free land of a virgin world. Both belong to the history of the Frontier, in which we are beginning to recognize the history of the Nation. But neither is a precedent of Empire.

The idea of empire, which has every where transcended the idea of nationality, has come in modern times to signify, above everything else, dominion beyond the sea—" dominion over palm and pine." It brings to our minds distant lands, strange speech, foreign faces. Its outward signs are "far-called navies,"

"Or embassies from regions far remote,
In various habits."

Nothing but these can give that strange expansion of the national consciousness — that sense of a people called to rule—which is the secret of the true imperial passion.

We shall have to date our titles, then, from the battle of Manila. Thenceforth we enter a new world; a world of new races, new manners, new customs, new tongues; a world of provinces and the governers of provinces.

In the difficulties and perils of our novel situation, it would seem that much might be learned from the experience of Spain herself, the last fragments of whose colonial domain are to be the corner-stones of ours. It is not, of course within the scope of this paper to review the history of Spanish colonization, even if the subject did not require an equipment which I do not possess. Nor is it my intention to enter into the controversies between Spain and her rebellious subjects. My object is simply to present, from sources either official or at least not unfriendly to Spain, some aspects of her rule in Cuba, which, it seems to me, disclose the indispensable basis for a sound and vigorous colonial administration.

I take Cuba as an example rather than Porto Rico, partly because it is better known to us, and partly because Cuba, owing to the wide difference in the economic and social organization of the two islands, shows more completely than Porto Rico the operation and effect of the Spanish colonial system.

In a memorial upon the state of Cuba addressed to the Spanish Government in 1850, Governor-General Concha sketched with admirable skill the causes which had within a few years wholly transformed the social and political life of the island. The abolition of the old colonial system, the opening of the ports to the world's commerce, the consequent influx of foreigners, the rapid progress in wealth and civilization, the new contact with the outside world, and particularly with the great democratic community of the West— all these, he said, had combined to awaken new desires, new ambitions and moral needs which, being unsatisfied and even thwarted by the government, were everywhere creating an irresistible current towards separation from the mother-country.

One thing, indeed, he continued, might have counteracted this tendency—" a sound, upright and enlightened administration." But alas! the defects, the grave and scandalous abuses, the immorality of that very administration had done more than everything else to infuriate Cubans, to exalt their ambitions and to make them look forward to the inevitable rupture with confident satisfaction rather than anxiety. The prestige of the mother country was being destroyed. The judicial officers, taking advantage of a vicious fee-system, were making the very name of justice odious by their insatiate rapacity. As a single example, the advocates and assessors of the revenue had managed, within a few months after taking office, to secure as private perquisites 30,000 or 40,000 pesos from trial fees alone ; digging out of the files and reviving for that purpose suits long since abandoned and forgotten. To make things worse, these officials were being replaced at shorter and shorter intervals. Not content with the old profits, the new men were bent on making as much in two years as their predecessors had in twelve. The civil government presented the same distressing and disheartening spectacle. The deputy governors were men appointed through influence and favor rather than for any merit or fitness for the task. They brought to their posts in general a strong desire to get rich ; this was indeed the sole purpose for which most of them had come to the island. With superiors like these, it was needless to comment upon the subordinates. Things were drifting speedily towards a violent and ruinous catastrophe. " When a people," said the General, " see in their rulers, nothing but an everlasting purpose to advance their private fortunes in complete disregard of their duties, they will seize the first means which misery offers to free themselver from the society which oppresses them." What must be done, then, to restore the ancient prestige of Spain and regain the loyality of this people, bound to her even yet by ties of kindred, faith, speech, and the tradition of a common glory ?

" Now is not the time in my opinion," concluded General Concha, " to start any political question. . . . . . The urgent thing is to enter heart and soul into administrative reform and the right choice of employees for every branch."

Twenty years after these words of warning, the island being on the verge of bankruptcy and economic collapse, Señor Mariano Cancio Villa-amil was sent as Intendant of the Treasury, upon a special mission to reorganize the Cuban finances. Two months after his arrival he wrote to the Minister of the Colonies: "The hopes born of my good intentions I doubt now whether I shall be able to realize. In my staff I have hardly a man who is intelligent and who inspires confidence. . . . . . . Everything must be reorganized, or rather created anew. The task is immense."

The language of his subordinates was equally strong. "I proceed next to report," says the Chief of the Division of Account in the Central Bureau of Inland Revenue, "the present state of general administrative Account in this bureau. It is nothing at all. There is no Account—*no existe contabilidad.*" We learn from the same sources that there was hardly an office in the whole administration having a clerk who knew enough double entry to keep the books in the manner required by law. The Chief Administrator of Taxation and Statistics wrote: "It was well known what was the state of this office when I took charge of it. The force was then altogether new. Within two months that force was succeeded by another. While the office as a whole has suffered two complete changes of personnel within six months, the position of Head of the Custom Division has in that time been filled by four different persons, not one of whom remained in office two months together or had any opportunity to show either his industry or his fitness."

Writing again to the Colonial Minister, Señor Villa-amil exclaimed: "The original cause of the calamities which afflict this province can no longer be a mystery to any one. It is the vices of the Administration. They are the only enemies working to drive asunder the island and the motherland."

It must not be supposed that the home government was altogether oblivious to these dangers or to the representations of men like Concha or Villa-amil. Voluminous memorials, reports, ideas and projects of reform, (if there is anything a Spaniard likes it is an *idea* or *proyecto,*) attest the activity, not only of individual administrators, but of various boards and commissions. But the report and the project, when the exigencies had passed which gave them birth, were left to gather dust in the archives of the Colonial Office, until, at some new crisis, they would be dragged forth to become, in turn, the material for a new report and a new project.

Then, too, enlightened and conscientious governors, before Concha and after, endeavored to initiate reforms by their own authority. But these were of necessity personal and transitory.

Even radical changes in administrative method, such as the substitution of fixed salaries for judicial fees or the payment of salaries to the previously unpaid capitanes de partido, were stripped of their natural and expected effect. Because these latter places, for example,—as we learn twenty-odd years afterwards from Brigadier Acosta y Albear,—continued to be granted, for reasons of favor and patronage, to men without capacity or experience, who sought in the office not only a temporary livelihood, but an opportunity to accumulate, by fair means or foul, money enough to maintain them for the rest of their lives.

Any conscientious bureau chief who set about putting his own house in order would find, too, that before he could make any headway the employees who were, if only for the time being, giving better results, would be swept away by a new flood of office holders from Spain, for whom the necessities of politics had demanded posts of honor or profit.

All this was, in fact, treating the symptom and not the disease. If, in coming to the country of the Swag—where nobody came for his health—one left off one's shame at Cadiz (for so we may Anglicize some of the cant phrases of the official thieves' jargon), there must have been something on the Cadiz side which made the undressing business easy, if indeed it was necessary at all.

" When we consider," wrote Señor Villa-amil to the Minister of the Colonies on the 27th of May, 1873, " how political parties have been compelled, especially since 1840, to distribute political posts to their henchmen, regardless of character or intelligence, it will be easily understood how are formed these battalions of employees, without training, without capacity or morals, who paralyze instead of aiding the transaction of public business."

We discern a familiar political phenomenon : that revival

of office tenure by personal service which may be termed, not inaptly, the recrudescence of Feudalism. Political Feudalism—the very phrase is Villa-amil's. And for fear that I may be thought to read into it ideas drawn from our own vivid experience I shall leave him to explain its meaning in his own words.

" It is the ruthless and irresponsible power exercised by the influential multitude of the dominant party, who surround every politician, carry him into office and tear him down when he is no longer able to glut their insatiable appetite for spoils. . . . .

" This is the force which every year makes the national budget the objective of ardent aspirants, organized like an army corps, who, when victory has made it theirs, will divide it round as the spoil of war—or rather, looking on it as the legitimate profit of an enterprise more commercial than political, will issue it in shares like dividends of a joint-stock company.

" To nothing else is due the eager haste with which, at each change of government, the public offices are given over to pillage, that each applicant speaks of his ' right ' to such and such an office—a right founded on the friendship of the persons in power ; and that every aspirant bitterly denies that anybody else deserves the office he gets— in which point it is quite possible that most of them are right." . . . .

"As the supply of higher posts is not equal to the voracity of the ' persons of influence,' whose demands grow just as fast as the demoralization becomes evident, there arises the necessity of making a monopoly of the electoral districts. To accomplish this all places have to be conferred upon the persons designated by the representatives. As the ministers of the day almost always yield meekly to this exigency, the upshot of the business is that they simply hand over the administration entrusted to them to the tender mercies and kind offices of their ' influential ' friends."

In the midst of a political society infected with this deep organic disease, Spanish ministries went bravely on talking about reform for Cuba and tinkering at the machinery of her administration. The ten-years' insurrection had indeed been a sore trial; but its close was to be marked by a shower of golden decrees, ushering in a spring-time of reform. Everything was to move henceforth in harmony with what was known in Spanish statecraft as the " great principle of assimilation." This consisted in treating, or pretending to treat, Cuba and Porto Rico in all things, political and administrative as well as civil and social, just as if they were, in fact, integral parts of the Spanish peninsula. Apart from the consideration that much depends on what you are assimilated to, we may be permitted to doubt whether this great principle, however just and beneficent in the matter of civil rights and social advantages, for which it had, indeed, been originated—whether this great principle, I say, could ever have satisfied the natural desire of the Cubans to control the legislation and administration of their local concerns. What they wanted was not to share in the government of Spain, but to do a little governing on their own account. In obedience to this principle, however, the civil service of the Peninsula and that of the Colonies, hitherto distinct, were, by a decree of September 20th, 1878, consolidated into one service, the members of which were to be eligible indiscriminately for appointment at home or in the colonies. This act embraced the officers of the civil and economic administration, public instruction, and the ordinary courts of justice, every one, in fact, belonging to what are known as the civil careers. The most obvious result of this consolidation was that government being given a freer hand in the choice and transfer of preferred employees, all desirable places in the colonial service would continue to be filled from the Peninsula, in spite of the promised admission of Cubans and Porto Ricans to public employment. As an offset, to be sure, the Cubans might eventually have the satisfaction of seeing some stray Cuban mount to a solitary eminence in the service of the Peninsula. To add to the facility of transfer, it was further provided in the third clause of the act that employees serving in Spain should be eligible for appointment to the next higher grade in the colonies without having completed the term of service requisite for such promotion at home.

The burst of activity which produced this singular effort "to secure and strengthen the unity of the fatherland," and similar attempts at political re-organization which do not concern us here, was soon expended. Spanish colonial government relapsed into its traditional slumber; while the forces of insurrection, temporarily exhausted by the ten-years' struggle, again steadily gathered head.

At length, in May, 1890, a decree was passed reorganizing the Cuban civil service and regulating the method of appointment. The higher officers, heads of departments, bureaux and the like, and the judiciary were left to the appointment of the Minister for the Colonies. All employees in the five grades of the classified service receiving over 300 pesos per annum were to be appointed by the Governor-General of the island upon the proposal of the chief of the bureau in question; notice of the appointment, with evidence of the appointee's qualifications, to be sent to the Minister for the Colonies. For entrance to the fifth or lowest grade it was necessary, in addition to a two years' residence on the island and a minimum age of 18 years, that the candidate should (1) have filled an office of the same grade in the central or provincial administration; or (2) have held a clerkship with same qualifications and received for four years a salary of 300 pesos in Porto Rico or the Philippines or 600 in Cuba; or (3) have received the degree of A. B. or a professional diploma.

The provisions of this decree were confirmed in the belated autonomous constitution of February, 1897, as well as by the more extended one of the following November. It is, I believe, substantially the fundamental regulation of the civil service.

Of the political side, it worked a decided gain for the Cubans by increasing the appointment of residents and ex-residents. It is said that four-fifths of the offices, if we include all branches of the service, are held by Cubans. On the administrative side, although it restored in a measure the distinction between the peninsular and the colonial service, its effect was to make the fundamental regulations uniform in both and further to assimilate the service of the Island to the service of the Peninsula.

In this connection two things are particularly worthy of note, one relating to admission, the other to promotion, in the Spanish service. It will be observed at once that the only requirement for entrance to the Cuban service, except where the applicant has already served in the Peninsula or another colony, is that he shall have received the A. B. degree. In other words, it establishes a pass test. Now, it is needless to remind this audience that, if experience proves anything, it is that a pass test—particularly when the judgment of qualification rests with the appointing power—is wholly useless for the purposes of Civil Service Reform. It is wanting in the first element of reform, namely, that the method of appointment shall be, in a sense, automatic and thereby independent of personal considerations. It is wanting as well in the first element of a merit system, namely, that the candidate shall show his fitness in comparison with the fitness of others.

It was idle to talk of reform when the only limitation upon the discretion of the appointing power was that choice was restricted to that class of society which might be expected to have the greatest extent and variety of "pull."

The second point to be noted is a practice which is a cardinal rule in the Spanish civil service. It is the alternation, or turn of selection, in promotion, every other vacancy being filled not by seniority, but by discretionary choice, among all the employees of the same grade. This rule, the ostensible purpose of which is to temper routine with elasticity, innocent as it may look, is strongly recommended to all who may be engaged in the pleasing task of "taking the starch" out of a merit system. It must be obvious that, in a country where the political art enjoys a high degree of cultivation, the turn of selection becomes nothing less than the turn of pull. The charm of it is that the man of pull not only gets the benefit of each turn of seniority, but may be promoted over the heads of all the other men in his class at each turn of selection. A simple numerical illustration will show how the system can, with proper manipulation, be made to work. Let us suppose an office having ten clerks of each of the five grades into which the Spanish service is classified, and that one vacancy occurs every year, in the first place in the highest grade. Now let us imagine in the last place in the lowest grade— first, a man without, and secondly a man with a pull. The man without a pull being moved up only by seniority every second year, will take just nineteen years to reach the first place in the same grade; while the man with a pull, if he gets the possible extent of promotion at each turn of discretion, will in *nine* years be jumped through all five grades to the highest round of the administrative ladder. Increase the number of men in each class, and you only increase the number of those who may be jumped.

Simple devices like this help us to understand how young men of political connections, coming up to Madrid from the provinces, with a consuming ambition to dress in the Paris fashion, but without a penny in their pockets, may be seen, after a few years, clothed in frock coats and authority, their pockets stuffed with bank notes.

It would not be a difficult task to make a lurid sketch of the last stage of Spanish administration in Cuba. But it would be nothing to the purpose. It was, indeed, too much to ask: that Spain should give Cuba what she did not have herself—" a sound, upright and enlightened administration." A country whose political life is a desperate game for the distribution of the national revenues among the few hundred thousands who form its governing caste may no doubt give its colonies, as we have seen Spain give Cuba, eloquent decrees, exhaustive statutes, liberal constitutions, but it cannot give that which Concha hoped for—" administrative reform and the right choice of employees in every branch."

Just a year ago M. Benoist, a distinguished French publicist whose sympathies are altogether with Spain, and whose views were formed under the influence—if not the inspiration—of Cánovas del Castillo himself, admitting that Cuba has been detestably administered, had but this explanation to offer: " In Spain, as everywhere else, each politician drags at his heels, even in spite of himself, a gang of importunate office-seekers. And as ministries follow one another in rapid succession, it results . . . . . . " But we need not trouble M. Benoist to tell us what results.

Unless our survey of Spanish colonial administration has failed in its purpose, there can be no need to put its warning into words. But it may be well to indicate briefly certain applications of the leading principle to our present situation.

In undertaking the establishment of a colonial administration it is necessary above all to start right. Spain's unhappy experience shows how difficult it is to reform a system of corrupt influence when it is once firmly rooted. Not only do you have to overcome the resistance of all whose fortune, interest, importance and power are put at stake, bu you have to overcome as well the ingrained prejudice and fixed political habit of an entire people. In the present plastic state of society and institutions in our new possessions and dependencies we have an opportunity that will never come again. Our reform then should be early, first, that it may be effective, but chiefly, that it may leaven the political life of these peoples and have " a principle of growth."

It is a commonplace of Spanish politics that conditions in the Philippines are vastly different from conditions in Cuba and Porto Rico. The immense eastern archipelago, with its heterogeneous and primitive population, has no common basis of race or culture for an electorate, and no native institutions capable of becoming the organs of national life. It must remain for an indefinite period, if not forever, a sort of crown colony. That means, first, that it must have a strong government—a government whose "legislative body," as Fitz James Stephen said of India's, "is small enough and powerful enough to have a distinct collective will and to carry it out without being hampered by popular discussion." But it means also an expert government—a government whose officers know precisely what they are about and can be left to work out an effective system of administration face to face with the actual conditions of the country. Such a government is, in a sense, all administration, and its efficiency and success depend altogether on the character—the energy, ability, honor and training—of its administrators. For that reason we must follow our kinsmen, the English and the Dutch, and make our service in the Philippines a *corps d'élite*.

In Cuba and Porto Rico we have a somewhat different state of things. Not that intelligence, honesty and zeal are there of less importance, but that Cuba and Porto Rico, being autonomous states, with a self-sustaining social organization, must be left in a measure to their own devices They cannot be so plainly governed from above. But in laying the foundation for the administration in Porto Rico and in settling the organic law of its government our opportunity and our duty are equally clear. Having undertaken also to set up a stable government in Cuba, urgent reasons of polity impel us to insist upon the establishment there of a sound and permanent civil service, not only in the central, but in the local and municipal administrations. First among them is the need of assuring all peaceable and industrious people that the administration of their property and persons is not to be handed over to the late insurgents. Next is the consideration that through a skilled and honorable service we shall afford to the educated classes, whom an extensive franchise threatens to swamp, a share in government that will tend to preserve their just and necessary prestige. The last and most important reason is that in a government which does not promise to be the most stable in the world there may be at least one element of permanence, and that in a society long distracted by partisan strife the great fountain-head of spoils shall be forever dried up. Nothing, I imagine, will do more to give Cuba order and repose.

Coming next to the means necessary to these ends, the most obvious lesson from Spanish experience, it seems to me, is the need of a separate and independent board for the control of appointment and promotion. It is a great error to suppose that the Spanish civil service is not elaborately organized and regulated. Every place has a long schedule of qualifications which the appointee is supposed to possess. I do but follow a Royal Decree, however, when I say that papers containing evidence of these qualifications are not invariably to be found in the files. And such must be the case so long as the political officers of the administration are to be the judges of those qualifications. The only safeguard against the play of influence is a method of selection that is necessarily impersonal, that works automatically in obedience to definite rules of choice. Nothing less than an independent board or commission wholly disconnected from the political administration can afford such a method.

Impersonal appointment will, almost of itself, accomplish the great political end of Civil Service Reform; but administrative efficiency requires in addition two important incidents, pay and promotion. Not a little of the incompetence, corruption and oppression of Spanish colonial administration can be traced to the single cause of insufficient pay. In reports upon the Cuban service we frequently find complaint that honest and capable men throw up their posts because they cannot live on the pay, whilst others make the same posts sources of no little profit. " 'Tis a deadly system of administration," says one of these reports, " that bars out honest officials and, by inciting the others to peculate and plunder, makes the compensation of its servants the cause of the worst ills that afflict its subjects." So important is this consideration in colonial administration that the Dutch make it a rule in their East Indian service that the compensation of a colonial office should be three times as great as that of a similar position at home.

Not only must a colonial office carry compensation enough to attract men of ability and to preserve them from the temptation of corruption, but for the same reason it must offer them a future. The colonial administrator, even more than any other, must have the assurance of permanence and promotion as the recognition of faithful and efficient service. In a word, he must have a career.

With a colonial service chosen " with an eye single to the public interest," well paid and permanent, we shall have gone far towards meeting not the least of those responsibilities about which we now hear so much.

Nor is this all. The better government of the Philippines and the Antilles is a great thing, but for us there is even a greater. It is the better government of ourselves. At this critical moment of our history we cannot hazard the reaction upon our own political life of a fresh carnival of spoils. Shall we enlarge the dwindling patrimony of the spoilsman by the vast and rich estates of a colonial service ? Shall its numerous and succulent posts become, in the history of Civil-Service Reform, the great " South Sea " Exemption ?

A public man of distinction said not so long ago, " Empire can wait." But Empire has not waited. It has come to us unforeseen, borne by " the rough torrent of occasion." But in the use of our power we have still a free choice; and upon our choice depend the well-being of alien millions and our own happiness and security. We do not choose in the dark. The way is lighted with many lights, both of warning and encouragement. Then let us choose that it may not hereafter be said, in the superbly scornful words of Burke—" our dominion has been a vulgar thing."

Criminal Offences Among Federal Civil Servants in Maryland Under the Spoils and Under the Merit Systems.

BY JOHN C. ROSE.

It is of interest to inquire what effect the merit system has had upon the general morality of those parts of the public service to which it has been applied. There is no way of accurately testing the average comparative morality of different bodies of men. The subject, however, is important enough to make it worth while to collect and preserve available data upon it. I shall, therefore, lay before you very briefly, the results of an examination of the records of the United States District Court for the District of Maryland for the last twenty-eight years. I do not undertake to assert that the figures I am about to give, in themselves prove very much. They are as a rule too small to make generalizations from them safe or valuable. Such as they are, however, they may be worth the few minutes' time I shall ask you to give to them. In the twenty-eight years from 1870 to the present time, fifty-eight persons in Federal employ have been indicted in the United States Courts for this District. Of these, twenty eight were indicted in the thirteen years between 1870 and 1883, that is before the passage of the Pendleton act, and the remaining thirty in the fifteen years since it became a law. The average number of Federal employees in this State during the second period must have been very much greater than during the first, so that relatively there has been a large decrease in the number of government officers and employees against whom criminal proceedings have been instituted. In each period, the proportion of convictions to indictments has been about the same. In the earlier, nineteen were convicted or pleaded guilty, and in nine cases the prosecutions in one way or another, terminated in favor of the accused. During the latter period, twenty were found guilty upon their plea or by verdict; in nine cases the prosecution failed, and one is now in cusody awaiting trial. Of the thirty who have been indicted since the Civil Service Act went into effect, six were appointed as the result of successful competition, and twenty-four were not. Of these six, three have been convicted, two acquitted, and the case against one is now pending. Since 1883 the number of persons appointed as a result of their success in the examinations has been at least twelve hundred, so that the number indicted has been not more than one in two hundred, and those convicted not more than one in four hundred of the total number appointed. It is not possible, at least, without an amount of work utterly disproportioned to the value of the result to be attained, to ascertain accurately the number of persons appointed during these fifteen years to places outside the classified service. If common laborers be excluded, and they should be, because their official position gives them as a rule no special opportunities to commit offences against the Federal laws, the number of non-classified places must be less than four times the number of the classified. Consequently, prosecutions have been not only absolutely but relatively more frequent outside than in the classified service.

A study of the figures with reference to the different branches of the service tends to confirm this view. The Railway Mail Service was classified in May, 1889. In the nine and a half years since, one of its employees in Maryland has been indicted and he was acquitted.

In the preceding nineteen years, four were indicted, three of whom were convicted. In the fifteen years since the Custom House force here was classified, there has not been a single indictment found against any of its employees. In the preceding thirteen years there were two; both resulting in convictions. In the Post Office at Baltimore, there were in the thirteen years preceding the adoption of the law, eight indictments. Since the law has been in force the average number of employees has been nearly or quite doubled. The number of indictments during that period has been fourteen. Of these fourteen, however, nine were appointed otherwise than as the result of competitive examinations and only five were chosen by such examinations. Of these five, three have been convicted, one acquited, and one is now awaiting his trial. The proportion of classified places to non-classified was in 1897 as five hundred and fifty to one hundred and twenty-five. A similar proportion has been pretty steadily maintained since 1885; the extension of the classification within the Post Office itself being offset by the increase in the number of clerks in charge of postal sub-stations. Such clerks are usually druggists or other storekeepers, who receive a trifling salary, and are necessarily appointed without competition. Some of the indictments have been against persons who were in the federal service at the time the post office was classified, and who although then included in the classified service did not themselves obtain their positions by competitive examinations. The tenure of office of the last class of employees under the Civil Service Act, was, however, short. Postmasters Veazey and Brown dismissed practically all of them. Making proper allowance for the time during which they remained in the service, it is still true, that taking the whole period of fifteen years since 1883, into consideration, two-thirds of the entire force in the Baltimore Post Office has on the average been composed of men appointed in accordance with the methods of the merit system. It follows that there have been nearly twice as many prosecutions among the third of the force otherwise appointed as there have been in the two-thirds of the force so appointed. There is one allowance, however, that should be made in this connection. It should be borne in mind that the temptations in some of the excepted or non-classified places are much more insidious if not greater than is the case in most of the competitive places. The latter positions, as a rule, are those of clerks or carrier. Speaking generally, the only way in which people holding such positions have any special opportunity to steal either from the government or the public, is by rifling letters. There never can be any doubt in the mind of any man who takes and opens a letter, as to the character of his act. Many of the excepted or non-classified places on the other hand, are those of clerks in charge of sub-stations, doing a money order business. In spite of rigid regulations, it is probable that most of those who go wrong, begin by first making use of the government money for what they believe will be a temporary purpose, and they accordingly are able at first to persuade themselves that they are not doing anything very bad. In such places no matter how the incumbents are selected, there will always be a greater number of men who will get into trouble than will be the case where the first step in the downward path is absolutely unequivocal in its character.

At the present time the clerks in charge of these sub-stations are usually chosen neither by the merit or by the spoils system. There are as a rule tradesmen, who, at their own instance, at the request of their neighbors, or in some cases at the instance of the Post Office authorities, undertake for a trifling compensation to furnish the persons residing in their vicinity with the facilities of a postal sub-station.

In the five months in which I have been in office, three employees of the Baltimore Post Office have been indicted. Two of them were druggists in charge of these postal sub-stations appointed by the Postmasters without examination, and both were purely non-political appointments.

After making all proper allowance for the differing condition of employment and for the uncertainty as to the exact number of persons appointed to unclassified places, it remains true that in every department and branch of the service considered, the figures show, or at all events tend to show, that fewer appointees under the merit system have proven criminally false to their trust than was or is the case under the spoils system.

There is one large body of public servants as to whom the comparison can be made with what for practical purposes may be considered absolute precision. All letter carriers attached to the Baltimore Post Office appointed since July 1, 1883, have been chosen by competitive examination. Before that time none were so selected. On July 1st, 1870, the Baltimore Post Office had thirty-five carriers; on July 1, 1883, it had one hundred and five carriers. The average for the thirteen years may be taken with reasonable accuracy as seventy. The number of regular carriers is now three hundred and eight, so that the average number for the last fifteen and a half years during which the force has been classified, has been two hundred and six, or very nearly three times as many as during the preceding thirteen years.

Since 1870 eight carriers have been indicted and all of them have been convicted or have pleaded guilty. Of these eight, three were appointed as a result of their standing in open competitive examinations. Five were chosen for other reasons. The answer to a little problem in what at school used to be called the double rule of three, shows that the prosecutions against carriers appointed under the spoils system were relatively more than five times as numerous as they have been against those appointed under the merit system It is true as the opponents of civil service reform never weary of asserting, that moral worth cannot be tested by mental or physical examinations. But it is quite as true, however, that if a scoundrel when he takes a competitive examination is under no disadvantage by reason of his scoundrelism, he does not, on the other hand, find it of any advantage either. Can as much always be said when the competition is conducted in accordance with the accepted rules of the spoilsmen?

The Need and Best Means for Providing a Competent and Stable Civil Service for Our New Dependencies.

By Dorman B. Eaton.

These truths are equally fundamental and important : that a community cannot maintain its political morality, improve its government, or even prevent the decay of both, without habitually bringing into its official leadership true representatives of its best character and capacity. These great truths should be regarded as all the more admonishing, and they are all the more vital, when a government intervenes in the affairs of a foreign people while proclaiming its purpose of establishing its own dominion for their improvement.

The question, therefore, whether the United States can govern the Sandwich Islands, Porto Rico, Cuba, or the Phillipines —if the latter must come under our control—with honor to themselves or advantage to such dependencies is but another form of the question, whether we are capable of bringing, and are resolved to bring, worthy and competent men—fit representatives of the best character and capacity—into the official leadership of the people of those Islands.

When the National Civil Service Reform League requested a paper upon this subject, I am sure it felt that the subject was of vast and equal importance both to the United States and to the people of those dependencies.

I call them dependencies and not colonies—or territories— for neither of them was settled from the United States ; the people of neither are of our blood or language ; with some exceptions their religious institutions are very unlike our own ; they have lived under governments and laws radically different from those we intend to establish for them. Their experience, political methods and habits have not only very little fitted them for the reception of our institutions, but have developed prepossessions, theories and prejudices which will require very great wisdom and virtue in the governments we shall establish, to overcome.

Consequently, whatever kind feelings, sympathies or co-operation may arise between our people and theirs cannot spring from kindred blood, congenial habits, or common institutions, but must arise wholly from the blessings of justice and good administration, to be established by us.

We cannot, therefore, legitimately draw arguments, favorable to our success in governing these dependencies, from the experience of England in dealing with her many colonies—true colonies, founded by herself, peopled by her own children, and inheriting her sympathies, her political methods and her laws. Our task in these dependencies will be very different and far more difficult than hers in such colonies. We must establish governments so wise, so just and stable that they can be made effective over different races, over diverse civilizations and semi-barbarisms—despite the effect of laws, habits and political and ecclesiastical institutions which have prevailed for centuries, and which are very unlike those we should seek to establish. Our success will be a marvel, even if we shall use the very best means.

Yet, England has one dependency—British India—in no sense a colony—the problem of whose government has presented, on a vast scale, all the difficulties of race, religion, laws and habits, which the United States can encounter in their new dependencies. The manner in which England has surmounted these difficulties—and especially the means by which she rose above a selfish and partisan spirit, in the selection and government of the civil servants of India, is not only especially worthy of our study at this time, but it stands as the noblest, the most successful and beneficient example of the government of a political dependency, by a superior race and power, to be found in the history of ancient or modern times.

Let us first consider a few facts which we need to have in clear view in the outset, and then I shall ask your attention to the vital and admonishing lesson which the administration of British India has for us, at this time. In it, we shall largely see how and why the government of England has been able to greatly surpass every other in the conciliation and upbuilding of inferior races.

II.

The facts which should have our careful attention at this point, are these:

1. Our new dependencies will not be a part of any state, and consequently the legislative representation which our republican system provides, and the judicial protection which it guarantees, will be but imperfectly secured to them. Their people, will, therefore, be, far more than those of our states, dependent upon officers—both legislative and judicial—appointed to govern them—officers who will have to receive their appointments directly or indirectly from the President and Senate of the United States—thus greatly increasing the importance of a wise and non-partisan exercise of the appointing power, and causing the high character and capacity of the appointing officers to be, in a prëeminent degree, the fundamental conditions of good government.

It is by no means suggested that these appointed officers—this stable and competent civil service which they should constitute—will be the sole or supreme power for good government in these dependencies. Congress must devise a system of government for them, and enact general laws to be enforced. Our army and navy administrations will—for a time at least— t a great influence over their people.

These people—now largely incompetent for suffrage, and lamentably divided into antagonistic factions—if not into aed bands—must, as soon as practicable, be allowed a reasonable measure of suffrage and some proper means of legislative action. Yet, we must believe that a considerable time mnst elapse before controlling self-governments can exist— years during which the real character of the administration, and the question whether it will be a blessing to the people and honorable to the United States, will mainly depend upon the character of the appointed Civil Service.

The policy, as to these dependencies, will soon be devised and general laws for their government can be speedily enacted. All the rest—that which will decide whether the new governments are to be a blessing or a disgrace—will be administration —administration—honest and capable or dishonest, feeble and partisan. These are the great questions at this grave crisis.

3. I have no time for defining the fit limits of this Civil

Service administration, or the appropriate jurisdiction of its various classes of officers, which may need to be unlike in different dependencies. But it is plain that in the degree that suffrage and legislation must be limited—that the people cannot be trusted to elect their own officers—the number of appointed officers must be increased and their jurisdictions must be enlarged—or a hostile policy toward the United States may be enforced by the dominant local factions.

III.

Some parts of the administration, in which a non-partisan and stable civil service is indispensible, may be easily defined. Besides including a few executive and judicial officers of high and wide jurisdiction —which the President must appoint—it must extend to the customs, internal revenue, postal, life-saving and revenue marine administrations. Not only must the higher judicial officers be appointed, but it seems plain that, at present at least, in the many localities where general ignorance and violent passion prevail, it will be both unsafe and impracticable to select even the minor judicial officers through popular elections. Justices of the peace and the whole class of semi-judicial officials must be appointed. These appointments should be made by the judges, following the analogy of the appointment of United States Commissioners, who are really local justices of the peace—and who are chosen by the United States Circuit judges. By that means, the minor judicial administration may be most easily kept clear of partisan politics and factional violence and hate—which might be as disastrous to our dependencies as it would be disgraceful to the United States.

No part of the administration in Cuba or Porto Rico can be more essential to the safety of the people of the United States than that which relates to the preservation of the public health; nor can our safety, in that regard, be secured without competent and stable sanitary officers, at least in all the seaport cities—officers who will neither court party favor nor yield to selfish interests. All sanitary officials will greatly need stability of tenure, constant inspection by central authority, and long official experience.

I have no space for considering the great need of a high class of officers for attending to the many intricate and import-

ant questions which will grow out of disputed land titles and
the incompatibility of Spanish and American laws affecting
both property and personal rights.

IV.

It is plain that there can be no such civil service as is indispensible, unless these three conditions shall be complied
with : (1) the chief officers which shall be appointed by the
president and the senate must be competent administrators—
selected irrespective of party politics, and they must have an official tenure so stable that a change of administration in the
United States will not cause an administrative revolution for
party advantage in our dependencies. (2) The Civil Service
appointees, under these Chief officers, must be selected through
free and open competitions, regardless of their party or religious
opinions, and they must be retained in office so long as they
shall remain both faithful and efficient. (3) To make such selections and retensions possible, there must be a Civil Service
Commission for each of the dependencies—composed of men
of character and capacity—and not of superannuated officers
or mere politicians. They must be high-toned and effective
men, who shall have adequate powers, and a constant duty of
investigating and reporting as to the manner in which the
local civil service officers shall discharge their functions.
Nothing less than such safeguards can ensure fidelity and efficiency of administration in remote dependencies, and among
unassimilated and suspicious communities, where, for several
years at least, no just and enlightened public opinion will be
an adequate restraint.

V.

I cannot take time for explaining how greatly such an administrative system would aid in solving the many perplexing
questions which will arise as to how many Americans shall
hold office in these dependencies, or as to the race, religion
and politics of those to be given offices from the dependencies
themselves; nor can I more than glance at the very important fact that such free and open competitions would bring
into official control the most competent and worthy among
all those who shall seek office from among the native people

—thus placing before their eyes those superior officials whom they will be most likely to respect, and most readily obey—officers all of whom have won their places by merit and not gained them by favoritism or corruption.

VI.

There are two serious obstacles in the way of establishing the competent and stable Civil Service which we so much need:

(1) There is the old, hereditary Spanish spoils system—to say nothing of the little royal spoils system at the Sandwich Islands—extending alike to politics, society and religion, and everywhere corrupt, mercenary and despotic. It has continued its degrading influences through so many generations that the people under it have almost ceased to believe in the possibility of official virtue, and every officer is sure to be distrusted and maligned until he has actually demonstrated his worth and fidelity.

(2) There is that familiar American, party, spoils system in connection with appointments, with which we are all sadly familiar. Will it be safe to allow these new dependencies to add still more vicious and seductive elements to this system—especially to that part of it which is connected with nominations and the secret sessions of the Senate, where it is now most dangerous? The politicians and bosses of all parties will hustle and bribe to secure the offices and spoils of these dependencies—if we shall have no such safeguards as I have proposed. Such men and not a few members of Congress—from Oregon to Maine, from Florida to California, and all the states between—wrangling and clamoring over the appointments will insist that their state shall have its proportion of the offices and spoils. Every great boss and every little Blarneyville and Patronageville even will also demand a share of them. Unscrupulous corporations, and rich and able men now in these dependencies—or soon to go there to purchase plantations, to monopolize docks, to acquire mines, to make and manage railroads, to get control of the forests and fisheries, will hustle for patronage, and will soon become a mighty power in Congress and at the White House. They will bitterly oppose an honest, stable and competent Civil Service be-

cause it would interfere with their schemes and their illegitimate gains. They will have abundant nominees of their own for every office—nominees whom they will conspire with all corrupt politicians to press upon the Senate and the President. No thoughtful man can ponder these matters without a painful sense of the perils connected with the subject, and of the need of every instructive lesson of warning which history can supply.

VII.

No lesson is so instructive as that which British India can teach us, and therefore, again, I turn to it. ·England through brilliant deeds of war in the last century had won that vast dependency of more than 100,000,000 people of diverse civilizations, of many conflicting religions, of numerous languages and races. The early attempts to govern India resulted in such oppression, injustice, extortion and curruption as have been made familiar to the world through the trials of Clive and Hastings and the speeches of Sheridan and Burke.

The government of England, at that time, was strictly party government, with an aristocratic and royal accompaniment. Even administrative offices, until far into the 19th century, were gained both in England and India by party and official favor, by class influence and by the power of wealth and rank. A party, aristocratic and ecclesiastical spoils system prevailed.

More and more, after the great Indian wars were over, and government was reduced mainly to administration, it became apparent—soon after 1840—that the inferior partisan and unreliable officials which such a system put into the Indian Civil Service were incompetent for their duties and were also a source of grave peril. The people of India were not conciliated or elevated, but were exasperated and demoralized. The greatest difficulty of their government—the provision of a good Civil Service—yet confronted England. The mutterings of that fearful storm which burst over India in 1857, known as the Indian Mutiny—soon began to be heard. Anxiety for the future caused the trial of various remedial experiments—and among them pass examinations and a two-years' college course of study—for improving the class of persons appointed under this English Spoils System into the

Civil Service of India. These experiments were utterly inadequate. The alarming tendencies both in the army and in
the civil service increased. The foremost Englishmen in
public life became alarmed as to the fate of India.

Great statesmen and party leaders—Lord Aberdeen and
Lord Derby among them—had become convinced, in 1853,
that great and radical changes must be promptly made to
arrest the decay of India, or to long hold it as a British
dependency. Elaborate investigations were made, and the
result was that a very original and fundamental provision was
incorporated into the India act of 1853—one of the most enlightened, liberal, salutary and far-reaching provisions ever
incorporated into the administrative laws of any nation.

The whole system of party favor, spoils and influence for
making appointments for India, was rejected. In its place, it
was provided that any subject of Her Majesty might freely
compete—according to fixed regulations and regardless of
political or religious opinions—for appointments in the Indian
Civil Service, and that the most meritorious competitors
should be appointed and promoted.

Here was not merely a rejection of the old English Spoils
System, and of the theory of privilege and influence upon which
great parts of the English Constitution had rested, but there
was an adoption of the republican and democratic theory of
equal opportunties before the law and common justice which
are fundamental under our national constitution. It was a
grand triumph of English justice and statesmanship.

I cannot stop to explain to you the desperate efforts made
by the combined partisans, aristocrats and spoilsmen of
England for arresting this noble measure of democratic liberty
and justice—efforts much in the spirit of the attempt made during the present year to overturn our own Civil Service Reform
law of 1883, and to coerce the President. Many able men
had leading parts—Macaulay and Lord Ashburton among
them—in carrying the new system into effect. It was too
late to avert the Great Mutiny, but it was not too late to continually bring into the service of India those young men of
superior character and ability from all classes, races and
creeds of her people, which conciliated their favor, improved
their goverment, and elevated their moral tone—giving them
the best civil service any dependency of any nation, either

ancient or modern, has ever possessed. Indeed, I think it not too much to say that hardly any nation of the world has had in its administration, civil servants superior to the 60,000 or more which now conduct the administration of British India. The people of India have been made peaceful and contented; they have not only accepted the principles of justice and liberty, which prevail in England, but they have been made ready to fight under her flag wherever on the globe it may be unfurled. Perhaps, it may be said that there has been more bad administration, connected with our small Indian affairs in the last forty years, than there has been among the 200,000,000 of people of British India.

I have no time for explaining how the example in British India was soon copied in the British Colonies, or the extent to which it has contributed to that unapproached superiority of English Colonial administration which the whole world recognizes.

I cannot even show how the experiment in India before long resulted in the overthrow of the old spoils system in Great Britian itself, and to the substitution therefor of free, open, competitions of merit—both in the military and the civil administration—a revolution so great that now—though parties remain as vigorous as before—upon a change of administration in Great Britain there are not—disregarding a very few neglected petty places—a hundred changes of offices for party reasons in both the civil and military services combined —incredible as the fact may seem to us.

VIII.

I cannot think there can be a reasonable doubt as to whether the methods resorted to in British India would be efficacious if adopted for the Sandwich Islands, Porto Rico and Cuba— however we may distrust, even their saving efficiency,—or the Phillipines. The decisive, momentous question, however, is whether the majority of our party leaders and congressmen are sufficiently disinterested and patriotic to resort to them— to follow this noble precedent of the mother country—or whether the better public opinion of the American people is yet sufficiently enlightened to compel them to do so. I have an undoubting faith in the final and early triumph of that opinion, which is now greatly aroused.

But when we see the President, at so momentous a time as this, apparently yielding to partisan pressure in our own civil administration, we may well be anxious not only for the immediate future of these dependencies, but for the historic reputation of the government of the United States in one of the gravest crises of its history.

The Murrain of Spoils in the Indian Service.

BY HERBERT WELSH.

Murrain, as nearly everybody knows, is a terrible epidemic which sometimes attacks cattle,—wasting and destroying them sadly.

An old writer of the Thirteenth Century in England, during the time of Edward the First, states: "This plague of Murrain continued twenty-eight years ere it ended, and it was the first rot that ever appeared in England."

There is a disease in our American politics as virulent and as much to be dreaded as that of which this old worthy so bluntly and forcibly writes; it is the murrain of spoils. I wish to speak of what I have known of its ravages in the Indian service, of which I have been a practical observer since the year 1882,—a range of sixteen years. My position has been the gratuitous post of Secretary of the Indian Rights Association. In furthering the work of this organization I have been called upon to visit frequently the Sioux reservations in Dakota and Nebraska, and the Navajo, Moqui and Apache Reservations of New Mexico and Arizona. Other reprsentatives of the Association, trained and able men, have, in their investigations, covered almost the entire Indian field, and certainly all the more important Indian Reservations. Personally I have been brought in frequent contact with many army officers and civilians who have had wide experience with Indian affairs,—experience of the most practical and intimate nature. Such, stated in the briefest and most general terms, have been the means through which I have formed opinions on the Indian question, and have come' to a conclusion as to what are the main essentials for solving this difficult problem. I say this by way of preface to place the general listener or reader, as the case may be, in possession of my point of view.

THE INDIAN PROBLEM.

Whatever difference there may be as to details, there is a general concord of opinion among those who have studied the question as to the main outlines of a judicious policy for the United States to pursue toward the 250,000 red men who still remain as its dependent wards. Indeed, the Government itself has long since yielded to the current of popular opinion, so strong and united has it become. The old and fallacious idea which once attempted the formation of an Indian State west of the Mississippi, to be known as the Indian Territory, into which should be herded all the broken and scattered tribes of the country, with a view to their civilization as an independent Government, has long since broken down under the pressure of evident necessity. This idea of segregation has given way completely to that of absorption. The island reservation on which the waves of white civilization continually beat, fraying away yearly more and more of the receding shore, is soon to be absorbed in the element about it. The Indian must take his place with all possible speed in the common life of the American people. One alternative is presented to him,—and to us on his behalf; he must either take our education, religion, law, land,—in fact life, becoming one with us; or, when his reservation island has slipped from under his feet into the sea of advancing civilization, he must become a gypsy-like pauper and vagrant, stripped even of his savage virtues. Without hope, without self-respect or the respect of others, he must beg his bread, and eke out a miserable existence until he is utterly destroyed. Absorption or extermination are the only alternatives. But, while doomed as a race, there are evidences in abundance to be found in Indian schools and in Indian fields and workshops that it is possible to save him as an individual. To a solution of the problem along such lines the friends of the Indians, working in steady and permanent organization, have addressed themselves. They have demanded, in the name of civilization, justice for the Indian ; a reasonable continuous policy, with the end distinctly held in view of obtaining his education, training in civilized pursuits, protection in a secure holding of an individual tenure of land, so that he might have the settled means of self-support and a home that he could call his own. They have asked for him an abatement of that demoniacal race prejudice which makes our people so hard upon the weaker man, so willing, apparently, without a twinge of conscience, to plunder and destroy by every conceivable fraud, even to murder judicially or in-judicially, a member of the alien race. They have, during all these long years, asked the Government to adopt a policy, and to select machinery capable of carrying that policy out, so that the great and noble purpose to which the nation is committed, for which so many are unselfishly working, might not prove abortive.

Manifestly this was, from the beginning, a problem for experts. It was not a question into which the base and burning passions of party greed and contention should enter. It was a problem demanding wisdom, sympathy for a weak race, but a high order of statesmanlike prudence and business ability, both in dealing with its broad outlines and its minute details. Who will dispute that the man chosen to control the Indian Service at the top, the man responsible to the President and the Nation for the handling of his stewardship, should be selected on account of his knowledge of the Indians and their needs, and because he was imbued with the spirit fitted to carry a civilizing policy into effect?

I have known the Indian Service under five administrations—those of Presidents Arthur, Cleveland, Harrison, Cleveland in his second term, and McKinley. I have had opportunity to observe carefully, and I think dispassionately, the course pursued by the various Secretaries of the Interior and Indian Commissioners during that time. In none of these Presidential terms was a Secretary of the Interior chosen, I presume, with the slightest reference to the welfare of the Indians. Their protection and civilization was a consideration so trifling and incidental among many other serious burdens resting on the shoulders of that official, that I suppose it was hardly thought of as a matter of moment. Regarding Indian Commissioners during that period, I have known of a single case—that of Gen. T. J. Morgan, under President Harrison's administration, where choice was made, not primarily for partisan reason, but with an eye single to the welfare of the Indians. The circumstances leading to this choice need to be stated. Powerful pressure had been brought to bear to secure the retention of the former incumbent, a democrat; the President was not willing to depart so far from party custom, but yielded to the request of the Indian Rights Association, and appointed a man named by them as a desirable alternative to the retention of Mr. Oberly. To General Morgan is due the credit of having been very instrumental in effecting the extension of the Civil Service rules to about 700 places, principally in the Indian School service. This was accomplished during President Harrison's administration. To him also must be accorded the credit of great improvement in the Government School system. His energy and ability infused into this sphere of the Indian Service fresh life, and marked out the lines on which it was subsequently developed. The circumstances under which the Civil Service rules were extended to the Indian Service, are not only of general interest, but they show clearly the value of independent organized effort in promoting administrative reforms. The spoils system was responsible for the Sioux outbreak of 1890–91, as it has been for many a bloody Indian uprising. Under President Harrison's administration an unfortunate system of appointment of Indian Agents was adopted. It was called by an odd irony of expression the "Home Rule" system of appointment. Senators or other politicians from the various States in which the Indian reservations were located, were allowed to name the Incumbents for Agencies. This might be called "Home Rule" for the white man, while it was far from "Home Rule" for the Indian. The politicians chose the Agent from members of a community often bitterly hostile to the Indian, and usually from among his own political henchmen. Both lines of selections were bad, and the second very greatly restricted the good material that might have been had from the first. I present a striking illustration; after remarking that the Indian Rights Association earnestly protested at the outset against this policy, requesting Secretary Noble at the beginning of his administration, to avoid "the rock on which his predecessor had struck" by retaining good incumbents found in office and appointing, where changes were necessary, men especially fitted by character and training to serve the Indian. This suggestion was disregarded. Pine Ridge in South Dakota at this time became the seat of trouble. A weak Democratic Agent, named Gallagher, under Mr. Cleveland, had superseded the highly efficient Republican Agent, Dr. V. T. McGillycuddy, who was fully capable of dealing with the large and troublesome body of Indians at this place. Gallagher had allowed the efficient force of Indian police instituted by McGillycuddy. to run down. Royer, a wholly inefficient political henchman of Senator Pettigrew, who had been a failure in other pursuits, was appointed to supersede Gallagher. There was no intelligent action from Washington in making this appointment. It was simply the automatic working of "Home Rule" in South Dakota—a State Senator paying a political debt at the expense of the Indian and the country. Then came the religious fanaticism of the Messiah Craze, and the Ghost dance accompanied by turbulence and great excitement, which McGillycuddy and his police force could have controlled readily without military aid from outside, but which Royer, inexperienced and timid, was totally unable to cope with. Upon the trivial incident of failure to arrest an Indian who had killed another man's cow, he fled from his agency, leaving it without a head, and only returned when surrounded by 1000 United States troops. The Indians thinking the day of vengeance had come, fled to the bad lands where they fortified themselves, and the so-called Sioux outbreak was an accomplished fact. But, further even than this, did the spoils system contribute to the loss of approximately $1,000,000 in money and 200 lives of whites and Indians in this affair. The battle of Wounded Knee, where most of these lives were lost, was an encounter between the troops and Big Foot's band. Big Foot and his people belonged to the Cheyenne River Reservation, situated in the eastern part of the great reserve on the Missouri River. Here also had been an unfortunate change of Agents—Dr. McChesney—an able and trained man—had been removed for a political appointee, weak and inexperienced. The new agent had arrested Big Foot and had put him in the guard house, but weakly released him and allowed him to escape. A more perfect illustration, or one more tragic in its incidents, of the cost and suffering occasioned by the operations of the spoils system in the Indian service could scarcely be found. But out of this evil some good came—The Indian Rights Association called prompt attention to this illustrative case and secured petitions from various parts of the country asking President Harrison to extend the Civil Service Law to such positions in the Indian Service as were suitable to its operation. This petition was granted and in the spring of 1891, the 700 places referred to were included under the rules. This was virtually a significant declaration by the President that definite proof of fitness upon the part of applicants for positions should take the place of political influence. I will later refer to further extensions made by President Cleveland. It should be stated, in connection with the administration of President Harrison, that practically all Indian agents appointed by President Cleveland were removed. There was no attempt, in this sphere of the service, to adopt the principle that the position of agent, as well as minor posts, should be wholly separated from the baneful influence of partisan politics. Not until that principle is acted upon can satisfactory results be obtained, or the service be placed on a basis of dignity and efficiency. While criticising frankly what I believe to be this serious error of President Harrison's administration, I desire to give him full credit for the great good he did in appointing General Morgan Indian Commissioner, and for the extension of the Civil Service rules, and for being prompted by a sincere desire to do all for the Indian which the terrible exactions of party claims would permit. Progress will best be promoted in the Indian Administration by a fair statement of the debit and credit account of each succeeding President. It is fair to expect some forward step from each, notwithstanding failures or shortcomings. President Harrison must certainly be credited with a very important step in the development of the Indian school system, and in the extension of the Civil Service Rules.

I shall treat briefly and consecutively President Cleveland's two administrations. The first showed serious and disappointing faults. These were partly the result of inexperience, but more largely the grip of the partisan spoils system, which no President has the strength to resist, or, perhaps, we should say can, in the nature of things, wholly disregard. The appointments of Secretary of the Interior, Commissioner of Indian Affairs, and Assistant Commissioner, being what they were, a reign of spoils followed as a matter of course. Mr. Lamar, a courteous, honorable and able man, was from Mississippi. Messrs. Atkins and Upshaw from Tennessee. Changes were general in the service, and the jest ran through the Indian country that these two States must have been stripped of their inhabitants, since so many hailing from them were to be found on Indian reservations. Out of the sixty Indian agents all but two were ultimately changed. The general grade of efficiency was lower than that of Republican administrations, while some scandalous appointments were made. One man was sent as Agency physician to a reservation on the Pacific coast who was under sentence in his northern home to pay a fine of $3,000 for cheating the town. After a year's persistent exertions the Indian Rights' Association secured his removal. This was granted by the Secretary with the explanation that he presumed the man's friends had gained him this position "in order to give him a chance to retrieve his character." We need a higher view of the use of the public service than that it is an asylum for moral reformation. Such a conception does not promote the civilization of the Indian. Most of the spoilsmongering under Mr. Cleveland's first administration was done by Mr. Upshaw, the Assistant Commissioner.

When the President was at last convinced of the abuses which existed, the power of patronage was withdrawn from Upshaw. With this event his interest in the work of Indian civilization rapidly declined, and shortly after he retired. It must be said to President Cleveland's credit that his personal interest in the welfare of the Indians was more marked, and led to more good results than that of any President holding office during my acquaintance with the subject. He set himself earnestly to work to remedy abuses when he became acquainted with them, while he was courageous, determined, and active in correcting acts of injustice and wrong perpetrated upon Indians. The revocation of the order taking lands from the Crow Creek Indians in South Dakota, and the protection of the Indians in the Indian Territory against the depredations of cattle men, are illustrative cases.

He was remarkably accessible to the friends of the Indians, and showed himself most anxious to obtain from independent sources information fitted to guide his public acts. President Cleveland made large and good use of regular army officers, who were detailed to serve as Indian agents. This policy, which was adopted under an act of Congress that required such appointment, whenever in the opinion of the President the needs of the service required it, was directly in line with civil service reform. It not only usually gave the Indian an educated gentlemen,—secure of his position against political influence,—as a friend and administrator of his affairs, but it proved, so long as Mr. Cleveland was President, and until the policy was reversed under the subsequent administration of Mr. McKinley, a block to the efforts of spoilsmen to secure control of Indian agencies. As there seem to be serious dificulties in the way of bringing the post of Indian agent under the operation of civil service rules, owing to the fact that this is an appointment requiring confirmation by the Senate, it is to be hoped that, in the interest of Indian civilization, capable and experienced men may again be detailed from the army to serve as Indian agents. Equally good men might, it is true, be appointed from civil life were it the desire of the Secretary of the Interior and the Indian Commissioner to secure competent persons; but the principal fact remains that such men are not sought and consequently are not found because the "Home rule" plan of appointment has, under Mr. McKinley's administration, been revived, and Senators now dictate to the Indian office appointments to Indian agencies.

Mr. Hoke Smith, Secretary of the Interior under President Cleveland's second administration, deserves credit for distinct progress in the handling of the service. He showed a strong desire to understand the subject and was in many ways more accessible to the friends of Indian civilization than any Secretray with whom I have been brought in contact. He was not wholly free from political influences, but he showed a genuine desire to rise above them and to advance the merit principle in the conduct of Indian affairs. One of his notable acts was the appointment of Dr. William N. Hailmann, at that time the highly competent Superintendent of public schools at La Porte, Indiana, as Superintendent of Indian Schools. This was rearing a worthy superstructure on the sound foundations laid by Gen. Morgan. The appointment was purely non-political and was a fine example of the merit principle. Dr. Hailmann's name was suggested by Dr. Harris, the National Superintendent of Education, a high authority, and himself in politics a Republican. I do not to this day know Dr. Hailmann's politics, beyond the fact that he believes in honest and sensible administration, and despises "spoils." Dr. Hailmann's reputation in his profession is of the highest. This fact was brought out by inquiry on the part of the Indian Rights Association at the time when his appointment was pending. During the four years of his term of service he exerted himself bravely and continuously under grave difficulties, to purify the Indian Service, and to inspire it with his broad, hopeful and wise spirit. In a great measure he succeeded in spite of the fact that partisan politics, which were quite influential under the rule of the preceding administration, but which have become steadily more pronounced under this, sought to thwart his efforts at every turn. He has not been allowed to have School Inspectors of his own selection, who would have been men chosen wholly for educational reasons, but these officers were appointed by the Secretary of the Interior apparently solely to satisfy partisan considerations. In one instance in illustration of Secretary Hoke Smith's reform tendencies it may be noted that he re-appointed a republican Indian Agent (Major George G. Wright) at an important Agency, because of his ability and high character, and afterwards raised him to the post of Inspector. In this position Mr. Wright has been retained under the present Republican admistration. In another instance the Secretary re-appointed a former Republican Agent on the ground of merit to serve at the Blackfoot Agency.

We regret to say that the advance made under Mr. Cleveland's second term, which, with many distinct faults and shortcomings incident to spoils system pressure, has not been maintained under the present administration. This I think, one is forced by candor to say has been (if we view it broadly taking into consideration the action of the President, and the Secretary of the Interior) more distinctly partisan than any within the range of my experience of sixteen years. There has been no interest manifested by either words or specific acts on the part of the President, which places him individually as a benefactor of the service or the Indian race comparable to the notable acts of justice and progress for which both President Cleveland and President Harrison are greatfully remembered. On President Cleveland's credit sheet there is clearly written (a) Defence of the Indians at Crow Creek against administrative robbery, and of Cheyennes and Arapahoes against the impositions of Cattlemen—A general willingness to redress injustice when the facts were proven. (b) Final withdrawal of patronage from an assistant Indian Commissioner who abused the power. (c) Large use of Military Officers as Indian Agents with, in the main, excellent results. (d) In his second administration large extension of Civil Service rules. (e) Great advance secured in the Educational sphere of the Indian Service by the appointment of Dr. Hailmann. (f) Principle of merit appointments in Indian agencies, further emphasized by re-appointment of Majors Wright and Steele.

President Harrison's credit sheet showed (a) A distinctly reform appointment in the selection of Gen. Morgan as Indian Commissioner. (b) Support given to the Indian Commissioner when pressure of spoilsmen was brought to bear on him to prevent good school apppointments. (c) Recognition of the necessity for Civil Service Reform in the Indian Service by extension of the rules to 700 places.

So far in the present administration, to which I shall refer in its main features as I have done to others preceding it, the credit sheet remains virtually blank. No distinctively beneficial policy has been instituted, and no distinctly and conspicuously helpful act has been performed. The friends of the Indian openly rejoiced when the announcement of the appointment of the present Secretary of the Interior was made. We believed that this meant the maintenance and advance of Civil Service reform in the Indian Service, the application of expert knowledge to the solution of its difficult problems; the recognition of the entire question as one of philanthropy, education and business principles and ability, and from which, consequently, all partisanship should be excluded. On the contrary, so far as my knowledge of present conditions runs, precisely the reverse has been the case. I know of no case where spoils pressure has been resisted, and of a very large number of cases where it has been the controlling force. All the facts in the case with which I am cognizant, encourage the belief that "politics" and political considerations rule very largely. I have known no administration where the appeal of the disinterested friend of the Indian, based on facts and reason has so constantly gone unheeded, and where the voice of the politician, asking action for purely partisan or personal gratification, has so uniformly prevailed. The Secretary of the Interior is a generous and kind-hearted man, who has always treated me personally with the greatest civility—I have no personal complaint to make. Last winter he gave generously out of his own pocket to help provide

legal defense for a young Indian under sentence of death for
a crime which every one in his locality knew had been committed by another man. But the fact remains, and is generally recognized by the workers for Indian civilization, that
they are persona non grata with the administration while the
partisan has his will. Out of the 60 Indian agents a comparison of the list of 1896 with that of 1898 will show that 45
have already been changed. Of the number removed 11
were army officers, who have been replaced by civilians. It
may be urged that the war relieves the administration in the
replacement of army officers by civilians. Partly it does; but
not wholly. It certainly does not do so in the removal of
Capt. Stouch from the post of Agent of the Crow Reservation
in Montana. It was Senator Carter, not the Spanish war,
who is chargeable for this unfortunate change. Captain
Stouch was an ideal Indian Agent. He knew the Indians
and they knew and trusted him. He was ably assisted by
his excellent wife. He had done wonders for the Northern
Cheyennes, a fine tribe of brave Indians at Tongue River
Reservation, also in Montana.

His skill in dealing with these Indians undoubtedly prevented an outbreak, when the neighboring whites were
anxious to provoke one some two years ago, in order to effect
the removal of the Indians from the State. Captain Stouch
was unfortunately transferred from this Agency to that of the
Crows. His character, energy, and interest in the work of
civilizing these less hopeful Indians was producing marked effect upon them. He was assured that he would be retained
here by the office in Washington, but Senator Carter's influence prevailed. A local politician was appointed, wholly
unfit to continue the civilizing work begun by his predecessor.
An intemperate clerk, who had been removed, was brought
back to the agency and I am now able to say from the report
of a trusted representative of our Association, who recently
visited the reservation, that the drift will now be downward.
The same gentleman, Mr. S. M. Brosius, has travelled during
the past summer both in the southwest and the northwest and
has just returned within a fortnight from an investigation of
the condition of the Chippewa Indians in Minnesota. The
evidence obtained by him confirms the belief which I have already expressed, and the principles of Spoils is almost every-

where dominant. The recent outbreak among the Chippewa Indians, a people who have always been friendly to the whites, was the result of the most serious, long standing grievances. Enormous frauds which, however, are chargeable to past administrations rather than the present, have been perpetrated on those Indians in regard to the use of their valuable lumber supplies and through the appointment of Spoils system estimators, whose gross ignorance and subserviency to lumber ring interests, combined to rob year after year the helpless red men.

The Indian Rights Association asked of the present administration, the retention of Dr. William N. Hailmann, as superintendent of Indian Schools, unless something could be shown in connection with the performance of his duties which rendered him unfit to continue to hold that place. Some of the most influential names in the country were attached to this request. I submit here a number of them.

H. C. Potter, Bishop of New York.

W. S. Rainsford, Rector of St. George's Church, New York.

Joseph H. Choate, New York.

John Fiske, Cambridge, Mass.

James B. Thayer, Professor of law at Harvard University.

Agnes Irwin, Dean of Radcliff.

William H. Hare, Bishop of South Dakota.

Booker T. Washington, Principal of Tuskegee Normal and Industrial Institute, Tuskegee, Ala.

William Lawrence, Bishop of Massachusetts.

J. L. M. Curry, Trustee and General Manager of the Peabody and of the Slater Education Funds.

W. N. McVicker, Bishop of Rhode Island.

W. G. Sumner, Professor in Yale University.

G. W. Blatchford, Chicago.

John Graham Brooks, Cambridge, Mass.

William Crosswell Doane, Bishop of Albany.

W. E. Dodge, New York.

Charles Lanier, New York.

J. Pierpont Morgan, New York.

John Sloane, New York.

George Harris, Professor in Andover Seminary.

Parke Godwin, New York.

A. F. Schauffler, New York,
John S. Kennedy, New York.
Francis G. Peabody, Professor in Harvard University.
Charles Kendall Adams, President of University of Wisconsin.
Charles W. Eliot, President of Harvard University,
William Adam Brown, Professor in the Union Theological Seminary.
W. R. Huntington, Rector of Grace Church, New York.
Seth Low, President of Columbia College.
Daniel C. Gilman, President of the John Hopkins University.
Charles C. Harrison, Provost University of Pennsylvania.

It is clear that no school service and especially one of the range and importance of that which the government maintains for our Indians, can be properly conducted unless the element of politics is excluded from it, and capable and faithful officials are retained. It was on this ground that the President and Secretary of the Interior were asked to retain Dr. Hailmann. We were told that our plea was very irritating to the authorities,—but why should it have been so? It was a reasonable and right request, respectfully proffered. Why should it be irritating to the authorities when they are petitioned simply to do their duty? Dr. Hailmann was removed upon no charges or objections, certainly upon none which can stand the light, and thus the ablest and best equipped man who has ever held that position was lost to the Indian service. His successor was a young woman, unequipped, as I believe on excellent authority, for a place so responsible and difficult. Undoubtedly it was the pressure of the strong political backing which won for her the prize. I might multiply many illustrations to show the prevalence and the evil results of spoils system methods to-day in the Indian service. It is unnecessary to take up your time and to weary your patience by doing so. It must be apparent to every intelligent and impartial person who looks into the facts, that this method of managing a great responsibility thrown upon the government and people of the United States in the civilization of a helpless race, is worthy of the severest censure. It is wholly unnecessary that such a condition of affairs should exist. It is unworthy the conscience and intelligence of our people that it should be permitted longer to exist. How can we arouse our people to the point of action for securing an administration of Indian affairs in which trained and competent men and a continous policy shall rule? The moment is one, if ever such a moment is to be found, when we should demand of our government a reasonable, honorable, and business like administration of the Indian service, from which all idea of spoils should be excluded, and in which the merit idea and merit system should have full sway. We seem to be about to assume enormous responsibilities in the care of out-lying peoples, whose condition is in many respects similar to that of our Indians. If we cannot do well with that which is our own, how shall we care for that which is another's? Is it not apparent to every one that at such a time as this our people should demand of the government at Washington the adoption of the merit system in dealing with the Indians? It cannot be effected unless men are placed in control of the service who are chosen, not for political, but for higher reasons. The spoilsman must go, the trained expert, the unselfish and public spirited man must fill his place. Such men can be found and our government is perfectly capable of finding them, but it will not effect this reform unless there be such a demand from the people that it dare not disregard it. The greatest warrior of modern times is reported to have said that Providence was on the side of the heaviest artillery. Unless the demand of conscientious and patriotic people be heavier and more persistent than the scheming chicanery of the selfish wire puller, the Indian will continue to suffer and the possibilities of his civilization he held in doubt. So far, great good has been accomplished in many ways by the organized efforts of his self-appointed and,—financially considered,—his unrecompensed friends; but they have not yet conquered the murrain of spoils in the Indian service. My belief is that this moral pestilence effects not any one branch of the service alone, but others, and that when the popular force is aroused sufficient to stay the plague in others directions, it will be stayed here. The reform cannot come without long, and as a human affairs are arranged, bit controversy. As Secretary Stanton once said to bishop Whipple, " Congress "—and *we* might add the Executive— " redresses no wrong until the people demand it." To the people is our appeal. We trust in their virtue and intelligence, but are sometimes tempted to grow weary in waiting for the time when these high qualities will assert themselves and our victory shall be won. There is a simple secret by which it may be won,—when the man of average intelligence and average influence forgets his indifference and feels no longer his unimportance, but becomes charged with a strong sense of responsibility for using those talents which now he hides in a napkin and buries in the earth. When the average man will do his duty by public affairs, the cause of civil service reform, whether in the Indian service or elsewhere, will be victorious.

NOTE.—

To this address it seems desirable to add the following :

Indian Commissioner Jones was present at the annual meeting of the Indian Rights Association, which took place in Philadelphia shortly after the meeting of the League at Baltimore. The Commissioner, when the Chairman was informed of his presence, was asked to address the meeting. This he did with some reluctance, as the call was quite unexpected. The Commissioner spoke in excellent spirit and produced a good impression on the audience. Although the Commissioner based his remarks principally on the above address, which he had heard in Baltimore, he criticized this for alleged injustice to the present administration in giving it a "blank credit sheet." He justified the removal of a number of military men from the Indian Service on the ground of unfitness. Notwithstanding their strictness, the Commissioner made several very important admissions which reinforced some of the main contentions of the above paper. Mr. Jones stated that he regretted the removal of Dr. Hailman from the Superintendency of Indian Schools, and of Captain Stouch from the Crow Agencies. Both of these removals he had endeavored to prevent. He further stated that he was a warm advocate of Civil Service Reform in the Indian Service, and then added most significantly, that, in order to reach the best results, *the position of Indian Agent should be included* in the classified service. If President McKinley will assist Mr. Jones in carrying these views into practice the writer of this paper will gladly grant to him a credit sheet no longer blank, but with a substantial balance upon it. Since the above paper was made public the appointment of Mr. Ethan Allen Hitchcock as Secretary of the Interior, to succeed Mr. Bliss, gives rise to the hope that we are about to have an administration of Indian affairs more in accord with reform principles and the welfare of our wards.

Can We Trust Our Army To Spoilsmen?

BY CHARLES J. BONAPARTE.

The hardworking, clear-headed old man, homely and caustic of speech, perhaps mildly cynical, but withal kind and generous, who typifies in fable and caricature the American *demos*, has, in truth, little liking for the job of a conquering hero ; the tall, white hat he wears, may be neither elegant nor picturesque, but it constitutes a far more comfortable and healthful and a prodigiously less expensive form of headgear than a laurel crown, and he already shrewdly guesses, I fear he may soon know from experience, that there is more than a fair chance of finding among the spoils of victory a choice albino of the genus *elefas.* But Uncle Sam has also a terrible propensity for seeing things as they are ; for this, as a source both of strength and of weakness, have men of English speech been noted in all ages, in this have they differed most from Spaniards and Frenchmen and Germans, namely, that they live, not in memories or hopes, in ideas or theories, but in facts. It was emphatically a Yankee poet who said:

> " Trust no future, howe'er pleasant ; "
> " Let the dead past bury its dead ; "
> " Act, act in the living present,"
> " Heart within and God o'er head."

Now our good Uncle Sam sees in the world of the living present a world wherein

> " Strife comes with manhood as waking with day ; "

wherein the happiness, nay the continued life, of every man is the prize of an endless conflict, and wherein the weak go pitilessly to the wall ; wherein, among communties of men, the strong one armed holds what it hath secure, and the one not strong or not armed (for in modern times the terms tend daily to be more nearly equivalent in meaning) holds what it hath on sufferance until coveted by a stronger. He sees in the

world of Peace Societies and Arbitration Leagues the world of
a future, a future doubtless pleasant, but no more to be trusted
than is any of its kind. He sees this just as an Englishman
could see that Richard Plantagenet, Charles Stewart or George
of Hanover, by whatever name called, was yet only a man,
with no less than his share of human fraility and human passion, while to a Frenchman of the *ancien régime* it was well
nigh an article of faith to find in one annointed at Rheims a
Saint Louis, even when named Louis XV. He sees further
that in this world of the present, this world which, after all,
God o'er-head has made, not in a world of the future seen by
kindly men in day-dreams, he must live and do his appointed
work ; and, so seeing, if perchance some part of that work is
to be done in arms, he will do it, not, indeed, with a light
heart, but yet well, so well that there will be no need to do it
over again.

And he certainly does not believe a saying, now often quoted to various ends and in various senses, but true in none ;
the American people will not be readily convinced that " War
is Hell." I have said that, as a people, we do not live in
memories, but some memories do enter into our national life ;
it will be a changed nation which shall recognize in Washington a mortal Beelzebub, and in the men who left their homes
to fight at Bunker Hill, suffer at Valley Forge, conquer at
Saratoga or Yorktown, demons in training. In a great school
of self-sacrifice and obedience there is little to recall the eternal prison house of rebellious spirits, crushed for their disorderly ambition.

I have said so much to show my own standpoint and to
whom I would now speak ; I address, not those who think
the counsels of Washington " out of date " or " behind the
times," based upon principles of national policy which the
greater statesmen of our day have " outgrown ; " nor yet
those who think Washington's example one to be shunned and
Washington's profession one unworthy of a civilized or a
Christian man, but those of my fellow-countrymen (numbering
in my opinion certainly nine out of every ten of them) who
have no longing for wars or conquests and view with distrust
and misgiving our adoption of a meddlesome, visionary foreign
policy which leads to these, but who know that, while men
remain neither better nor worse than men, there will be times

when the sword must be drawn, and know, moreover, that often it can remain in the scabbard because, and only because, it is, and is known to be, sharp and ready to the hand which shall wield it. And, speaking to these, I propose to ask and answer two questions of profound interest to them as to me—Can the country's safety and honor be trusted in the care of our present public men? And, if these be unworthy of such trust, whence springs their unworthiness?

When Congress in April last demanded the immediate abandonment by the Spanish Crown of a territory which for four hundred years had formed part of its dominions, this action was, in at least one respect, absolutely without precedent in history; never before, so far as I know, had any government, intentionally and with knowledge, adopted a course which made war inevitable and the moment of its outbreak a question of hours, with nothing which could be called by the widest stretch of imagination or courtesy an army to sustain the issue thus raised. Yet this was then literally true of the United States; our regular army consisted of less than 27,000 troops, scattered over a territory as large as all Europe, and even these, as the event soon made painfully apparent, were wholly unprepared to take the field. As a so-called reserve, we had about 105,000 organized militia, on the whole a useful and meritorious force for its legitimate purposes (although its utility and merit varied greatly in different localities), but neither intended nor fit for active, and especially for foreign, service. Indeed, to call it a " reserve " at all, in any military sense, is hardly more appropriate than would be the same term applied to the police of our cities or the *posses* at the command of our sheriffs. As a body, it was not subject to the authority of the President or even of Congress, and, in fact, no company had a legal organization a foot beyond the borders of its own State. Moreover, it constituted at best, if not the literally raw, the less than half baked material of an army. The progress of civilization has not yet enabled us to dispense with mothers, so students of biology should be ready to admit that there may be in males of the species *homo sapiens* a latent hereditary passion for millinery and mantua making, for which, in civil life, they can usually find only the imperfect gratification derived from footing bills; nor is it surprising that this should render the young male of the same animal prone to perambulate in bright colored clothes and brass buttons, "toting" (as our Aunties would say) guns and swords and other shiny things "to dazzle and dismay." All this is doubtless magnificent, especially to the heroes' partners at the German, but it is not war; and if it be a school for war, it is hardly more than a kindergarten.

From what I have just said, it must not be supposed for a moment that I am inclined either to undervalue our National Guard or to sneer at those of its members who formed the nucleus of our improvised army last Spring. With the First Congress, I recognize "a well regulated militia" as "necessary to the security of a free State;" in the readiness wherewith so many thousands of our young men left their homes for a war, which, as I have reason to think, a large majority deemed unnecessary and unwise, in their cheerfulness and obedience under privations, all the harder to bear because plainly needless, and in the steadiness and gallantry displayed by substantially all of them who went into action, I see, perhaps, the most encouraging and healthful symptoms of our national life. It is, however, no less true that when Congress rushed into a war of aggression, this country, containing seventy millions of people, had not twenty thousand available soldiers.

A foreigner ignorant of the facts might conjecture from this astounding improvidence and levity that Congress did not expect the outbreak of hostilities or was ignorant of the country's plight or, perhaps, hesitated to sooner relieve this because unwilling to sustain the President in a warlike policy condemned by public opinion; in fact, Congress had been straining in the leash for months to make war inevitable despite the reluctance of both the President and the people, and one of the early measures introduced at its recent session was a bill to increase the regular army in time of war to a little over one hundred thousand men. For the consideration of this bill no time could be found during many weeks, while our Solons were relieving their pent-up bosoms of long diatribes against the Civil Service Law; at last it received attention only to be summarily rejected because some officers of the National Guard had (or were alleged to have) exhibited the almost incredible ignorance, presumption and vanity to claim that they could do all the fighting there might be to do. Another bill to authorize the trifling addition of some one thousand six hundred men to the artillery, although finally passed, was debated and opposed as though peace had been assured for a century.

A more plausible explanation, which will perhaps be one day added to the number of those lies made truth by History, is that Congress relied with confidence and reason on overwhelming naval superiority to give time for adequate military preparations after war had been declared. It is, in the first place, extremely doubtful whether more Senators or more Representatives than can be counted on one's ten fingers had formed, or were capable of forming, any intelligent opinion as to the relative strength of Spain's navy and of ours, or had ever given five minutes' thought to the subject. It is to be noted, secondly, that in fact no such disparity of force existed, or, at all events, was supposed by competent judges to exist, when the war commenced. On the Continent most European experts thought the navies were not unfairly matched; some thought the odds, on the whole, a little against us. An experienced and highly meritorious American officer, whose views I obtained, whilst predicting our victory, said the Spaniards had three really effective fighting ships to our one. Finally our politicians did not hesitate a few years since to offer grave provocations to Great Britain respecting a matter of no more moment than the Venezuelan boundary, with no thought of her immense naval strength, with no semblance of preparation for defence and with no controversy among themselves except as to which party was entitled to the greater credit for thus exposing the country to imminent risk of humiliating disaster.

It may be worth a moment's pause to fully realize the national danger involved in this incident, and which we escaped through no wisdom of our rulers, but solely through the wise forbearance of the government and people we so lightly challenged. Much is now said as to whether we should or should not persist in our "isolation" by those who forget that, in a military sense, this isolation is already, in great measure, a thing of the past. With our shores but six days' space from the harbors of the Old World, the transportation hither of 50,000 troops would be a less task for the navy and mercantile marine of England than was that of General Ross' brigade in 1814. Our present Secretary of War is said to have replied when asked, a year or more since, what we should do if at war with one of the great powers: "In thirty days the United States could place in the field millions of men and back them up with a wall of fire in the shape of veterans." Last summer, with this modest and judicious patriot in the War Department, not thirty, but sixty days after the war commenced, more time, be it remembered, than separated the declaration from Sedan, far more time than separated the declaration from Sadowa, we placed in the field, not "millions," but barely sixteen thousand men, and so neglected these that a well-informed, if somewhat unfriendly, foreign critic could say and say truthfully:

"Here, at the end of the nineteenth century, one of the richest nations on earth, one of the most intelligent and one which poses as being amongst the most civilized, sends out a small army to fight, but shows herself unable either to feed the soldiers that fight for her, tend the wounded that bleed for her, or bury the dead that die for her."

In the light of this experience, I do not know, nor am I much interested to know, what General Alger may think on the subject, but I ask any one of my present hearers, I ask any intelligent and fairly educated American, had we become involved in war, as we became involved in controversy, with a power having, not merely 50,000 troops ready to embark at a week's notice, but unquestioned command of the sea and almost unlimited resources in shipping, could any city of our seaboard have reasonably expected a better fate than befell Washington, could any have reasonably hoped to make so stout a defence as did Baltimore eighty-four years ago? As for the General's "wall of fire," it is formidable enough, no doubt, to the Pension Office; its "bricks" or "sparks" (whichever may be the proper metaphor) have levied huge contributions from our Treasury, but, like the Claudii, their

". . . . yoke has never lain on any neck but ours,"

and it is quite safe to assume that it never will.

The true explanation of this apparently inexplicable behavior of Congress is disgracefully simple; its members (with some honorable exceptions, which but prove the rule) are indifferent to the prosperity, the dignity, the security of the country they govern. Like Mr. Flannigan, of Texas, they might ask in astonishment, "What are we here for?" were it suggested that they give time or thought to questions of diplomacy or national defence, or anything except office-mongering and electioneering. Their hearts and lives are given to the task of quartering on the taxpayers for support as many as may be of their relatives and dependents and hangers-on of high and low degree, preferably such as are too lazy, stupid or vicious to support themselves; for anything else, unless it be the retention of their own places, they have but the leavings of their time and the dregs of their energy. This was curiously illustrated by their action respecting the additions to the clerical force of the War and Treasury Departments made necessary by the war. This increase was, of course, indispensable if the vastly augmented work of these departments was to be properly performed, but their efficiency did not really interest Congress; what the members had at heart was the following clause in the Urgent Deficiency Bill, adopted as an amendment by the House of Representatives on June 20th last:

" The temporary force authorized by this section of this act and the clerical force and other employees appropriated for in the act to provide ways and means to meet war expenditures, and for other purposes, approved June 13, 1898, and the act making appropriations to supply deficiencies in the appropriations for the payment of pensions and for other objects for the fiscal year 1898, and for other purposes, approved May 31. 1898, shall be appointed for a term not exceediug one year. as authorized, respectively, without compliance with the conditions prescribed by the act entitled "An act to regulate and improve the civil service," approved January 16, 1883.

In moving this amendment, Mr. Cannon, of Illinois, made the following statements:

" . . . . Your committee on investigation found that it was not practicable to call into motion the machinery of the Civil Service Commission for the purpose of making these appointments. It was necessary to have the force and to have it at once. Further than that, we were told, Mr. Chairman, that the machinery of the Civil Service Commission could not be invoked without damage to the Commission itself and damage to the so-called Civil Service Reform, because it is not adapted to the employment of emergency or temporary people. And when you undertake to make it grind out something that it is not adapted to and not intended for, and which does not come within the alleged evils for which the law was originally passed, you do not improve the character of the employees you acquire under it, and you only work injury to the reform itself. Therefore, from every standpoint, we found it much better, after the very fullest investigation we could give to the matter, to report this provision in the pending bill."

Every allegation of fact thus made was a falsehood. The Committee had not made "the very fullest investigation" on the subject; apparently it had made no investigation at all; certainly it had addressed no inquiry to the Civil Service Commission itself. It was perfectly "practicable to call into motion the machinery of the Civil Service Commission for the purpose of making these appointments;" indeed, they could have been thus made, not only far more satisfactorily, but also more rapidly than in any other way or than they were in fact. There were at the time thousands of eligibles on the registers of the Commission, and any desired number could have been certified for appointment within a few hours. It was absolutely false that "the machinery of the Civil Service Commission . . . . is not adapted to the employment of emergency or temporary people"; it has been used repeatedly for this purpose, and always with entirely satisfactory results; as instances, for several years the Railway Mail Service voluntarily selected its temporary weighers from the list of eligibles, and the temporary force of extra compositors employed in the Government printing office during the sessions of Congress are so chosen, more than a hundred being often appointed in a single day. Moreover, Mr. Cannon either knew what he said to be false or had made no attempt seriously and in good faith to learn the facts, whilst claiming to speak "after the very fullest investigation."

However, our statesmen got the places for their henchmen, and a precious lot of incapables they foisted on the Government! Some five hundred and sixty were appointed in the War Department alone. It is claimed on behalf of the Secretary of War that for the acknowledged incompetency of many among these five hundred and sixty he was not to blame; "he was obliged to rely upon the representations made to him by those who sought appointments. It was impossible for him to make adequate inquiry into their qualifications." Nevertheless, he could have filled their positions with men whose " qualifications " had been ascertained by " adequate inquiry "; the Civil Service Commission stood ready to furnish the names of thousands of men thus tested, and a resort to their registers, whilst not *required*, was yet not *forbidden* by the law, although it would have disappointed the selfish greed of those who framed this law.

His excuse bears a close resemblance to that offered by the Surgeon-General for that deficiency in the care of the army which has most keenly touched the people. The same foreigner whom I have already quoted says further:

"All through the fighting of the army in Cuba there was a scandalous want of medical attendance. For this there was absolutely no excuse. Hundreds of medical men throughout the States had volunteered their services for the war."

Indeed, in his memorandum to the Investigating Commission, General Sternberg says:

" The number of applications has been so great and the personal visits of applicants and their friends so numerous as to constitute a serious embarrassment in conducting the business of my office."

Yet, although he had to give up so much of his time to " personal visits of applicants and their friends " (were there, perchance, a few Senators and Representatives and other influential politicians among these " friends "?), he admits that:

" . . . . It has been impossible to make a careful selection, owing to the great pressure of business in the Surgeon-General's office, and the *urgency* has been so great that it has not been practicable to have examining boards to pass upon their qualifications."

Doubtless the " urgency " *was* great; the urgency, that is to say, of those men whose one thought in the nation's extremity was to find berths at its cost for themselves or others in their interest; and " urgent " people of this kind with a " pull " would object strongly to " examining boards to pass upon " the " qualifications " of their *proteges*. Doubtless they would deem such boards " un-American " and " Chinese." Examinations of any kind are very distasteful to our statesmen. But the fruits of such " urgency " on their part, and of such yielding to it on his part, were grim enough. In the words of my critic:

"There are times when blundering incompetence attains the dignity of crime. Those who were responsible for the management of the Army Medical Department have the blood of many of their fellow-countrymen to answer for. Sick men were hurried to their death by stupid mismanagement and the want of ordinary hospital care, while numbers of wounded men were practically murdered by neglect. No one who has not actually witnessed the scenes of this war can realize its tragedy."

As an instance of this "tragedy" he adds:

"Three days after the fight at San Juan the body of a man was found sitting up under a tree; his head had fallen on his right shoulder; his water bottle was at his side empty; in his right hand he held a photograph of a woman—evidently his wife, and in his left a photograph of a group of four children. He was shot through both knees, but had evidently been able to drag himself under the shade of the tree, and there waited for someone to stanch his wounds and attend to him; but, as was the case with so many others, nobody came."

General Sternberg says of cases such as this:

"It has not been the expectation of the medical department that every wounded man would receive immediately the attention of a surgeon."

Perhaps, then, three days is not an unreasonable time for him to wait, and, of course, it would be altogether captious to complain of the case reported by Captain Lee in *Scribner's* for October of a man shot through the stomach at eight in the morning, and left lying in a great pool of his own blood, with no care but that afforded by a badly wounded comrade, until one in the afternoon, and how much longer the narrator could not say—in all human probability until his death. It is noted by the writer whom I have so often quoted already:

"In General Shafter's official account there were eighty-one reported missing after the fighting in a few days about San Juan. General Shafter significantly remarks that most of those may be taken as having been killed."

He adds:

"I quite agree with him. They were killed—many of them were murdered by neglect."

I have said of this writer that his bias is decidedly unfriendly towards Americans; nevertheless, I think few fair-minded people will question the justice of his general conclusion thus expressed:

" Looking back at all the operations around Santiago, the Americans may feel proud of the bravery of their Regulars and some of the Volunteers, notably the Rough Riders. . . . The way in which men of all ranks, both Regulars and Volunteers, bore severe privations without murmuring is beyond all praise; but, having said that, I think there is nothing else connected with the American Army of which the people of the United States should not feel thoroughly ashamed."

He adds:

"When speaking about it to intelligent Americans I am always met with the same reply, ' that politics were at the bottom of it.' "

He had previously remarked the frequency with which he had heard it said of volunteer officers:

" So-and-so got that place because he was very useful during the late campaign."

Adding:

" For a few days I was rather under the impression that the campaign referred to was the last Civil War, but then discovered that it was the late election campaign that was meant. Men were placed in responsible positions, not so much upon their qualifications as on account of the services they had rendered to their party. The disastrous results of this system have been evident throughout the war. The political bosses had the appointment of men to the highest positions of the army and the army departments."

And what he and others saw at Santiago was the experience of competent observers elsewhere. Thus, in a very interesting unpublished narrative of personal experience at Chickamauga, prepared by an unusually well-informed and intelligent volunteer, which I had the opportunity to examine, the writer asks;

" . . . . why a whole army corps should have been placed under the medical care of a man whose only recent professional affiliations were those of a veterinary? Were no competent surgeons to be found whose interest in humanity was undivided? Or was this, after all, a case of pull ?"

Leaving this question to be answered by the Investigating Commission, he goes on to give many instances of obvious unfairness and favoritism. Thus he says:

" I have seen in one hospital a fourth year student in medicine kept twelve hours a day for several weeks merely emptying and cleaning bed pans, while men who knew absolutely nothing of medicine or drugs were nursing. Under such a *régime* as this, the worst kind of neglect could arise, and often did. It was common talk at one hospital how one poor fellow lay in his cot with parts of his body already covered with maggots before the merciful hand of the Angel of Death ended his suffering on his bed of filth. . . . . Another case of injustice was in placing the son of one of America's greatest surgeons, who had been his father's assistant, in charge of the ice-chest at a division hospital, where he handled milk and ice, while working in the typhoid wards were men who could not read a prescription, take a temperature or give a bath. Is it any wonder that under such conditions as these typhoid fever spread and increased? With this lack of sanitary precautions, and with men often totally devoid of medical attainments put over the sick, it is fortunate that things were not much worse even than they were."

His conclusions deserve our careful consideration:

" Much of our lack of preparation, in the medical department as well as in every other department, grew out of the long-cherished idea that our situation insured national safety. And we never seriously contemplated a campaign beyond our shore line until this emergency arose. This, however, does not wholly explain the disastrous results growing out of disease. It is notorious that appointments were made without proper consideration of the candidate or of the work he was expected to do. It is beyond doubt that some of the appointments were made solely because of the influence those appointed were able to bring to bear through political channels. The feeding and clothing of this army, which represented the very flower of our population, and the care of our sick was sometimes entrusted to men who were absolutely untried and who had never shown that they possessed the requisite executive ability or special training. Even when the deadly emergency was upon us, the best available material was often allowed to remain unutilized, because less competent persons stood in the way. Such a condition of affairs is an instance of the danger of the spoils system, and it is is also an arraignment of it."

Its "arraignment" is, however, yet more formidable when we consider the treatment of our army at the hands of the Commander-in-Chief, given the latter by the Constitution. The first duty to the army which Mr. McKinley was called upon to discharge was the choice of a fit man as Secretary of War; but how did he discharge that duty? In other words, what manner of man did he choose? And why did he choose him?

In the first place, he chose a man with a military record; this, be it remembered, he was under no obligation either of law, custom or public policy to do. The office is a civil, not a military one, and although in most European countries it is habitually filled by a soldier, the wisdom of this arrangement is by no means indisputable; the great "organizers of victory" have been civilians. But if the President saw fit to select as the administrative head of the army a man with a military record, he was under a manifest obligation to choose one with at least a clear record, that is to say, with such a record as his own; it was equally indecorous and impolitic to place in authority over soldiers a man whom most soldiers regarded with suspicion and contempt, and such a choice was the more unpardonable on the part of one who had been a soldier, and a good soldier, himself. Now, General Alger, as a soldier, comes before the public somewhat as Hood's Count came to marry Miss Kilmansegg, "not under a cloud, but in a fog;" he may have been treated with injustice, perhaps he was the victim of circumstances or else of prejudice or personal dislike, but I merely state notorious facts when I say that his service in the Civil War had been marked by unfortunate incidents, subjecting him to serious imputations, which may possibly have been unfounded, but none the less affected his standing with military men; and that he was further suspected, again perhaps unjustly, but on grounds, at least, plausible, of an attempt to misrepresent or conceal these incidents when an aspirant for the Presidency; and, finally, that, although he had some friends in the army, he did not enjoy its general respect and confidence. In studiously picking out a man of these antecedents for the place he thus filled Mr. McKinley showed, I will not say a defiance, but, at least, a disregard of professional opinion, differing widely in degree, but not in kind, from that exhibited by Charles X when he made the deserter of Waterloo his Minister of War.

The Secretary was, moreover, certainly past his prime and of uncertain health, and was not known to possess, or, at least, had never exhibited, any conspicuous administrative ability, or any conspicuous ability of any kind. His selection might well seem as incomprehensible to a foreigner as the failure of Congress to make any preparation for a war which it did everything to provoke, but the explanation is neither more obscure nor more creditable. General Alger will probably have the Michigan delegation to "deliver" in the Republican Convention of 1900, and he can do much to make the "Grand Army vote" serviceable both at primaries and at the polls; these reasons are no less sufficient to explain his retention; their weight is in no wise diminished by anything he has done or allowed to be done.

Of his official record I say little, not because there is little to say, but because there is little need to say anything. Two incidents, however, are sufficiently characteristic to deserve a word of notice. He received a confidential official letter from Col. Roosevelt, written with the approval of the latter's immediate superior, on a matter of grave public interest; this confidential official letter he published, together with a silly and disingenuous reply on his own part, because he foolishly imagined that its publication would injure the political prospects of its writer; would "lay-out Teddy," to use the words attributed to one of his confidants. This petty exhibition of senile spite did not "lay-out Teddy," doubtless to the great surprise of the mighty mind which devised it, but it served to lay out very thoroughly, if any such process were needed, the few fragments of its author's reputation as a man of honor. Together with the Adjutant-General of the Army he has been virtually accused by its ranking General of causing or permitting official communications to be garbled or suppressed in a published correspondence for the paltry and ridiculous purpose of misleading the public as to that officer's relation to the Santiago campaign; apparently because he also was supposed by one or both of them to have a political ambition, and to need "laying-out"; not only have the parties thus accused taken no steps to secure an official investigation of this charge, but the

President, seemingly in their interest, has carefully excluded it from the scope of the enquiry which he was at last goaded or shamed into ordering. Mention of the Adjutant-General here calls to mind a curious and significant episode. A special act to authorize his promotion was introduced in Congress, with, it was said, the cordial approval of the President. It may have been no more the fault of this officer that he was kept from the field than that he came from Ohio, but it seemed strange that a soldier who had never left Washington should be singled out for prompt and peculiar honor, especially when, to say the least, the administration of his office had not been either conspicuously successful or conspicuously popular. Here, again, however, the explanation is not difficult: like the Surgeon-General, he had been compelled to give up most of his time and strength, not to his legitimate duties, but to the solicitations of influential politicians for favors of all sorts, and so exhausting were his strenuous efforts to satisy their "urgency" that later in the summer he was said by the newspapers to be threatened with nervous prostration.

Many thoughtful and patriotic citizens view with anxiety, indeed with alarm, the new and grave responsibilities imposed upon the United States as fruits of the late war. A gentleman for whom I have great respect recently wrote me that he regarded Civil Service Reform as a matter of altogether subordinate importance compared with issues arising from these responsibilities. I could not agree with him; I regard the thorough and practical realization of that reform in all branches of our government as no less indispensable to the nation's safety and honor than to the nation's tranquility and morals. To have our army worthy of its duty and of its past, we must protect it, just as we must protect our judiciary and our schools and everything we prize, from the taint of "spoils" politics: on this condition only can the "respectable establishment" which Washington deemed essential to our national defense be "respectable" in any sense of the term. Some, and among them some to whom we rightly look for guidance, fear lest, as with other republics both of the past and of the present, we may sacrifice our liberty and prosperity to dreams of foreign conquest and military glory, lest the time come "when every American workman shall carry a soldier on his back." For me, that is not our peril; the honest American of every condition in life, in my eyes, is a Sinbad already, but his burden is a loathsome "spoils" politician, reeking with the contagion of moral vileness. We must free our country from this miserable bondage; if that can be done, her soldiers will be in the future, as, after all has been said, they have always been in the past, those among her children of whom she has least cause to be ashamed.

THE CENSUS BUREAU.

Your Special Investigating Committee, which examined among other things, the question of the desirability of classify ing the Census Bureau, begs leave to report : s follows:

On March 16th last, Senator Chandler introduced a bill for taking the twelfth and every subsequent census. Section 3 of the bill provided that the employees of the Census Bureau should be appointed according to the provisions of the Civil Service Act. The bill was referred to the Census Committee, and when it was reported Section 3 was stricken out, and a provision substituted that the employees should be appointed "according to the discretion of the Director of the Census, subject to such examination as said Director may with the approval of the Secretary of the Interior prescribe, and not otherwise."

The purpose of the Committee's substitute is to repeat the unfortunate experience of the last census in making the clerks and the employees of the office subject to political patronage. We desire to call attention to the evils which have resulted from this course, in

1st: The increased extravagance of the Bureau;
2d: The demoralization of the force employed;
3d: The worthlessness of a census so taken.
4th: The lack of public confidence in its accuracy and impartiality.

I.

The last census cost $10,620,000 (Cong. Record, December 16, 1897, page 214). The amount paid for salaries alone was $5,120,000. Mr. Carroll D. Wright, Chief of the Department of Labor, who had charge of the last Census Bureau for some years after the retirement of Mr. Robert P. Porter, as Superintendent, estimates that two million dollars and more than a year's time would have been saved if the Census force had been brought into the classified service. (Letter of Carroll D. Wright to Henry Cabot Lodge, Record of December 16, 1897, page 174.) Mr. Wright adds: "I do not hesitate to say that one-third of the amount expended under my own administration was absolutely wasted, and wasted principally on account of the fact that the office was not under Civil Service rules. . . . In October, 1893, when I took charge of the Census Office, there was an office force of 1,092. There had been a constant reduction for many months and this was kept up without cessation till the close of the census. There was never a month after October, 1893, that the clerical force reached the number then in office; nevertheless, while these general reductions were being made and in the absence of any necessity for the increase of the force, 389 new appointments were made."

That is, new appointments were made to a force where they were not needed, the new men replacing experienced clerks, and, in the words of Senator Lodge, "filling the office with beginners at the close of the work." This was manifestly done because these appointments were allowed to be political.

Mr. Porter disputes the estimate of Mr. Wright that the waste was as much as two million dollars from this cause alone. But whatever the precise amount, it was certainly very large; so large that it is the manifest duty of Congress to see that it does not occur again.

II.

In respect to the demoralization and inefficiency of a force selected upon the patronage plan, Mr. Porter himself now concedes the necessity of placing the Census Bureau in the classified service. For, in his article in the *North American Review* of December, 1897, he enumerates among the faults of the present system the following:

" Placing upon the shoulders of the Superintendent, whose mind should be fully occupied with his experts in planning the work, the responsibility of the appointment of an office force of several thousand clerks."

Mr. Porter suggests as a remedy:

" Making the Census a permanent office of the Government and applying to it precisely the same rules and regulations as to the employment of clerical help that are in vogue in the other Departments. If this were done," he says, " special Civil Service examinations might be held for the work prior to the time the clerk would be needed, and the Census Office would then have a sufficiently large eligible list to draw from. In 1890 I accepted Civil Service examinations of the higher grades, but that did not do away with the necessity of examining 2,700 clerks in the office, and this with the work of appointment, literally took up all the time of the Superintendent, whose mind should have been free for his purely statistical duties. . . . And then why transform the Census Office at its busiest season into an examination department for clerks, and the Director of a vast scientific investigation into a dispenser of political patronage. It is simply unjust to such an official. Having passed through the ordeal once, I am satisfied that the other way is more practical and in the end will be better for all concerned."

This declaration of Mr. Porter's experience is timely, if it will prevent the repetition of such a calamity.

Congressmen were advised systematically of the number of positions at their disposal. Mr. Porter kept regular books of account, charging each of the Congressmen with the number of appointments made at his request. Our Chairman has recently examined two of these books. In one of them, the appointments are classified according to States, and in another they are charged to the particular Congressman who solicited them. The latter book is a ledger of over four hundred pages. At the head of each page appears the name of the Congressman charged with the appointments. In the left hand column are the numbers of the files containing the recommendations and credentials. Then follow the names of the appointees, and then the grades and salaries. By means of this book the relative rights of members of Congress could be adjusted, and it could be seen at a glance whether any particular member had overdrawn his account. After a Congressman retired, the clerks appointed by him held their places by a precarious tenure, and frequently, perhaps generally, had to make way for persons appointed and protected by the influence of his successor, or some other Congressman, for in this ledger, following the accounts kept with existing Congressmen (a page to each) is the list of the appointees of ex-Congressmen all thrown together, as though to be the subjects of early decapitation. We are informed that there are other books of the same character as this ledger, in the Census Office, covering other periods of time.

It would be hard to find a better illustration of the working of the patronage system than is presented by this book, where appointees are classified as in a live-stock register as the property of particular Congressmen, but without reference to their records and individual qualifications. We frankly and gladly recognize the fact that there are members of Congress who did not approve this debasing system, and who will not now.

Patronage of this kind does not secure the political advantage which is supposed to be its object, for the most severe defeat ever sustained by the party then in power, occurred at the close of the very year that these appointments were parcelled out among the representatives of that party in Congress.

Mr. Porter testified that the appointees were, as a rule, recommended by Republicans. This rule, however, was not universal. There were Democrats who received a share of the appointments; perhaps where their votes in Congress were serviceable upon appropriation bills or otherwise. With this system of log-rolling in force it is not hard to understand how the enormous appropriations for taking the last census amounting to $10,620,000 were secured. Indeed, Mr. Porter stated some time since to our Chairman that if he had it to do again, he would select his clerks by Civil Service examinations, " even though the other plan *had* greatly smoothed the way to the passage of appropriations and other friendly legislation."

The plain English in regard to such transactions is that such legislation was bought with offices, and that the salaries of these offices were paid for out of the people's money. It was the people's money which paid for the keeping of the very books in which these transactions were recorded. Under such a system extravagance was a necessary result.

What was the character of the service under this patronage system ? Shortly before Mr. Wright took charge of the Bureau a large number of discharges of those then holding positions were made, on account of their lack, not only of ability, but of moral character. Doubtless there were many excellent persons who secured employment by patronage methods, but it was in spite of this system of barter and corruption, by which the places in this Bureau were filled. Under the competitive system it is at least impossible that applicants will get their places *because* of corruption or immorality. When appointed through favoritism this is not seldom *the very reason* for their appointment. Moreover, when a clerk or other employee owed his place to the favor of some Congressman, his loyalty was considered to be due, not so much to the Chief of the Bureau and to the public, as to the particular "influence" which secured the place. Removals from the Census Bureau even for just cause became difficult, therefore, and often impossible. Persons dismissed for inefficiency or misconduct, were actually reinstated against the will of the Chief of the Bureau himself, at the demand of some political friend, too powerful to be offended.

If the Census Bureau is not now put under a strict system of competitive examinations, the effect of the elections in 1900 must also be considered. Hardly will the Bureau have been put in running order before the campaign will have begun, and if the spoils system prevails the whole force will be affected by the political turmoil, connected first with the nominations for Congressmen and President, and then with the elections. Wherever the "influence" of the employee is defeated the employee himself will be discharged, while if a change of party ensures the whole Bureau will have to be reconstructed with untrained material at the most critical period of its work.

III.

The lamentable results of the patronage system are shown in the defective enumeration of inhabitants made in the last census. As a rule, the supervisors were chosen for political reasons, and the supervisors selected the enumerators. True, it was provided by law (Section 4, Act of March 6, '89) that the enumerators should be chosen for fitness and without reference to party affiliations, but this became impossible when the supervisors were chosen for political reasons. The enumeration was perverted in many places into an information bureau for party candidates.

The supervisor at Buffalo, New York, addressed the following circular letter to his enumerators:

"OCTOBER 28, 1890.

"As it is of the utmost importance that a Republican member of Congress be elected in this district, I shall feel personally obliged if on the day of election you will work especially for Benjamin H. Williams, the Republican candidate.

[Signed]   SILAS H. DOUGLAS."

In Geneva, New York, Congressman Raines secured the appointment of enumerators with the view of enhancing his political fortunes. He addressed to one of them, and probably to many others, the following letter:

"MY DEAR SIR :—As it is quite likely that you will in a few days be appointed enumerator for your district, I write you this in the strictest confidence. I would like very much that you should take the trouble, before you make your report to the Supervisor of the Census, and after you have taken all the names in your district, to copy in a small book *the name and post office address of every voter* on the list. After you have done so, I wish you to send the book to me at Canandaigua. I ask you to do this as a personal favor, and to make no mention of the matter to anyone. What I want is a *full list of all the voters* in your enumeration district. Will you please treat this matter as strictly confidential?

"Very truly yours,

[Signed]   J. RAINES."

Mr. Raines stated to our Chairman that he had sent this letter in ignorance of the law, which required enumerators to keep secret the results of the enumeration. In many other cases, for instance, at Bloomington, Indiana, enumerators were chosen on the recommendation of the chairman of the Republican County Committee, and made poll lists for the Republican party.

The evils of patronage were clearly apparent in New York city. Charles H. Murray was made Supervisor of the Census. He wrote the following circular letter which shows his manner of selecting enumerators.

"DEAR SIR :—You will please forward to this office a list of the applicants that the Republican organization of your district desires to have named as Census enumerators. The list must be sent here on or before April 1st."

General Walker who took the Ninth and Tenth Cens:
says: " If the selection of the enumerators was made upo:
any such basis as that, the census could not have been othe-
wise than bad." Many of the men thus appointed ver:
utterly unfit. The Police Inspector named one, a thief, wh:
had been three times an inmate of the State Prison, a ma:
whose name was known to all the city detectives, whose
picture was then in the Rogues' Gallery, and whose dealing
with the Census Bureau were under an alias; yet privat:
houses were opened to him under Government endorsemer:

New York was a Democratic city, and there was streng
reason for believing that the count had been defective. The
Police Department re-counted the city and found the population
two hundred thousand greater than that showed by the federal
census. The police count was sent to Washington where Mr.
Kenney, its custodian, offered it for comparison with the
census enumeration and a recount was asked, but refused.
Then a copy of the federal census for the Second Ward was
procured and compared with the police enumeration. The
federal list contained 826 names, and the police enumeration
1,340 names,—a difference of 45 per cent. Affidavits were
furnished showing the residence of 328 persons not enumerated in the federal census. Our Chairman inspected the
police enumeration, as well as the federal census, and a comparison of the two lists, followed by a personal investigation
in the ward, indicated that great numbers of the residents of
this ward were omitted in the census. There can be no doubt
but that many thousands of inhabitants of New York were
omitted from the census, and the patronage system was
directly responsible for these omissions.

One of those engaged in the taking of this census thus
describes some of the facts which came under his personal
observation :

" In a section consisting at one time of twenty-one people
who were engaged in the mailing department of the office,
addressing envelopes, mailing bulletins, and other duties incident to the mailing department, there were only four people,
other than the chief of the section, who were available for
any character of work whatsoever. Three clerks were absolutely demented; three were, by reason of being maimed
wholly unfit to be of any service; two, by reason of disease

(consumption), were valueless; two, being sons of chiefs of division in the office with a "pull," were immune; the other six were wholly worthless by reason of age or disinclination. It is but fair to say that this condition did not last throughout the period of the taking of the census. The larger number of these people, however, served more than two years, and several of them for a much longer period. It would seem that this particular section was the Botany Bay of the Eleventh Census, but the same state of affairs existed in a lesser degree throughout the office. It needs no argument to convince one that this state of affairs could not exist under the 'merit' system established under the civil service act and rules. Being appointed as skilled laborers, these people were not required to take an examination, although doing clerical work.

Another feature of the work of the Eleventh Census which makes clear to my mind that the next force should be selected from those who pass a competitive civil service examination was the exceedingly large percentage of errors made, particularly in the punching of cards. All of the data relating to the census were transferred from the original schedules to cards, each hole punched in a card representing some material fact, such as 'native born,' 'foreign parents,' 'white or colored,' etc., etc., in some cases as many as thirty or forty facts being indicated by punches on a single card. The symbol representing each condition or fact must be carried in mind, or else the progress of punching the cards would be so retarded as to make the electrical punching machines of little value. I think it will be readily conceded that a clerk doing this character of work should be a person of good mind as well as a skilled clerk.

There was at all times a 'Division of Revision and Results' in the office, consisting of a chief and from thirty to seventy of the best clerks obtainable. Notwithstanding this check upon error, it was found necessary to establish a section of about seventy people to look after the errors of punching cards alone. Here we find as many as one hundred and forty people whose time was wholly devoted to correcting faulty work. Errors, of course, would unavoidably creep into a work of the magnitude of the Eleventh Census, but I believe that a careful selection of the clerks under the rules of the Civil Service Commission would have tended to minimize their number. Notwithstanding the ' Revision ' division and the ' Error' section before spokenof, it was found at the very last moment before the publication of the final results that the work was so inaccurate that the portion of it relating to occupations (see report of Commissioner of Labor, in charge of Eleventh Census. June 30, 1895, pp. 4, 5) had to be subjected to still another revision, which delayed its publication for more than a year. The expense incident to this was great, owing to the fact that all other census work had been completed, and the office remained open only to complete that section of the report on ' Population, and Vital Statistics Relating to Occupation.'

Considerable stress is laid upon the fact that examinations were held in the office to test the fitness of clerks before they were employed. I beg to suggest that the highest number of clerks employed at any time numbered about 3,200. Of these, only about 1,700 were examined. The larger part of the working force of the office was, in point of fact, never subjected to an entrance examination. Only the high-grade clerks, namely, those from $900 per annum up, were required to pass the entrance examination. It can be readily shown, as I suggested above, that the greater part of the clerical work was performed by what were termed ' skilled laborers,' who received $600 per annum only, and were exempt from examination."

IV.

The census ought to be as free from partisan color as the Judiciary. Otherwise, no one can rely upon the accuracy of its conclusions. To gain the confidence of the people, it ought to be not merely fair and just, but free from even the appearance of corrupt or partisan influence.

If the government has a free choice between a non-political and a political agency for taking this enumeration. and chooses the latter, composed of officials of its own political faith, the presumption is against the fairness of a census so taken. And even if it were fair, many would not believe it to be fair. Suspicion is cast on such a census in advance of enumeration; and if, at the close of the work, inaccuracies are shown, resulting in some cases in advantage to the party by which it is taken, the work is sure to be discredited.

All of which is respectfully submitted with the recommendation that the efforts of the League be directed immediately toward gaining the support of the country and of Congress for the classification of the Census Bureau under the civil service rules.

(Signed)   WM. DUDLEY FOULKE,
                                              Chairman.

CHARLES J. BONAPARTE.
RICHARD H. DANA.
HERBERT WELSH.
GEORGE MCANENY.

BALTIMORE, DECEMBER 15, 1898.

CONSTITUTION

OF THE

National Civil-Service Reform League.

I.

The name of this organization shall be the National Civil-Service Reform League.

II.

The object of the National Civil Service Reform League shall be to promote the purposes and to facilitate the correspondence and the united action of the Civil Service Reform Associations.

III.

The League shall consist of all the Civil Service Reform Associations in the United States which signify their willingness to become members thereof. Any association hereafter expressing such willingness shall become a member of the League upon its being accepted as such by the League or the Executive Committee. Any member of any such association may be present at any meeting of the League and take part in the debates or discussions as the by-laws may provide.

IV.

At any meeting of the League, each association belonging to it shall be entitled to one vote upon every question coming before the League; such vote may be cast by a personal representative designated by each association, or by proxy, as the by-laws may provide. If no such designation be made the delegates from such association present at such meeting, or a majority of them, may cast the vote of such association.

V.

The officers of the League shall be a President, Secretary, Treasurer, and nine Vice-Presidents; and there shall be a General Committee and an Executive Committee. The officers and the committees shall hold office until their successors are appointed or elected.

VI.

The President and Vice-Presidents shall be elected by ballot at the annual meeting of the League.

The Secretary and Treasurer shall be chosen, and may be removed, by the General'Committee.

The General Committee shall be chosen annually, and shall consist of one delegate from each association belonging to the League; and one additional delegate for every two hundred members, or major fraction thereof, of such association as certified by its secretary. Each association shall elect its own delegates in such manner as it may determine.

The members of the Executive Committee shall be ex-officio members of the General Committee.

Any member of the General Committee may act by proxy.

The General Committee shall keep a record of its proceedings, and shall make a report to the League at the annual meeting. A vacancy in any office, except that of Vice-President, may be filled by the General Committee for the remainder of the term.

The General Committee may delegate to the Executive Committee any of its powers; provided, however, that it may at any time resume the powers so delegated.

The Executive Committee shall consist of twenty-one members to be elected annually by the General Committee and shall have power to fix its own quorum. And any member of the Executive Committee may act by proxy.

VII.

The General Committee may, subject to these articles, manage the affairs of the League, direct and dispose of the

funds, and may, from time to time, make and modify by-laws for the League and for its own action.

No debt shall be contracted, nor shall any appropriation of money be made, by the League or by the General Committee, beyond the amount in the hands of the Treasurer.

VIII.

There shall be an annual meeting of the League at such time in each year, and at such place as the General Committee may determine, at which officers shall be elected for the ensuing year, and other appropriate business may be transacted.

A meeting of the League may be called at the discretion of the General Committee whenever any association belonging to it notifies the Secretary of the League of its desire to have such a meeting, and the President may at any time call a meeting of the League.

IX.

Any provision of this Constitution may be suspended or amended by a vote of two-thirds of the members present at any meeting of the General Committee, due notice of such proposed suspension or amendment having been given at a previous meeting. Any association belonging to the League may, through its representatives, propose amendments to the Constitution which may be approved under the same conditions.

**The Beginning of the Spoils System in the National Govern-
ment, 1829-30.** (Reprinted, by permission, from Parton's "Life
of Andrew Jackson.") Per copy, 5 cts.

Term and Tenure of Office. By Dorman B. Eaton. Second edition,
abridged. Per copy, 15 cts.

Daniel Webster and the Spoils System. An extract from Senator
Bayard's oration at Dartmouth College, June, 1882.

A Primer of Civil-Service Reform, prepared by George William
Curtis. (English and German Editions.)

Address of Hon. Carl Schurz in opposition to the bill to amend the New
York Civil Service laws, commonly known as the "Black Act."
May 6, 1897.

Report on the Operation of the "Black Act." March 21, 1898.

**Annual Reports of the Civil Service Reform Association of New
York for the years 1883-1898 inclusive.** Per copy, 8 cts.

MISCELLANEOUS.

**United States Civil-Service Statutes and Revised Rules of May
6, 1896.**

**State Civil-Service Reform Acts of New York and Massachu-
setts.**

Decisions and Opinions in Construction of the Civil-Service Laws.
(1890) Per copy, 15 cts.

The Meaning of Civil-Service Reform. By E. O. Graves.

The Selection of Laborers. (In English and German Editions). By
James M. Bugbee late of the Massachusetts Civil-Service Commission.

Report of Select Committee on Reform in the Civil Service
(H. R.), regarding the registration of laborers in the United States
Service.

**Report of same Committee regarding selection of Fourth-Class
Postmasters.**

The Need of a Classified and Non-Partisan Census Bureau—
Report of a Special Committee of the National League. (1898)

George William Curtis. A commemorative address by Parke Godwin.
(Published by the Century Association). 10 cents per copy.

(A CHARGE IS MADE ONLY WHERE THE PRICE IS GIVEN.)

Orders for the publications will be filled by GEORGE MCANENY, Secretary, 54 William St., New York, or by G. P. PUTNAM'S SONS, 27 and 29 West
23d St., New York.

PROCEEDINGS

AT THE ANNUAL MEETING OF

THE NATIONAL CIVIL-SERVICE REFORM LEAGUE

HELD AT

INDIANAPOLIS, IND., DEC. 14 AND 15, 1899.

WITH THE ADDRESS OF THE PRESIDENT,

AND OTHER MATTERS.

———

NEW YORK:

PUBLISHED FOR THE

NATIONAL CIVIL-SERVICE REFORM LEAGUE.

1899.

Publications of the National Civil-Service Reform League

Proceedings at the Annual Meeting of the National Civil-Service Reform League, 1884, with address of the President, George William Curtis. Per copy, 8 cts.

The same, with address of the President, for '85, '86, '87, '91, '92, '93, '94 '95, '96, '97, '98 and '99. Per copy, 8 cts.

Civil-Service Reform under the present National Administration. By George William Curtis. (Address of 1885.)

The Situation. By George William Curtis. (Address of 1886.)

Party and Patronage. By George William Curtis. (Address of 1892.)

Civil-Service Reform and Democracy. By Carl Schurz. (Address of 1893.)

The Necessity and Progress of Civil-Service Reform. By Carl Schurz. (Address of 1894.)

Congress and the Spoils System. By Carl Schurz. (Address of 1895.)

Encouragements and Warnings. By Carl Schurz. (Address of 1896.)

The Democracy of the Merit System. By Carl Schurz. (Address of 1897.)

A Review of the Year. By Carl Schurz. (Address of 1898.)

Renewed Struggles. By Carl Schurz. (Address of 1899.)

Civil Service Reform as a Moral Question. By Charles J. Bonaparte. (1890.)

The Influence of the Spoils Idea upon the Government of American Cities. By Herbert Welsh. (1894.)

The Reform of the Consular Service. By Oscar S. Straus. (1894.)

The Appointment and Tenure of Postmasters. By R. H. Dana. (1895.)

Civil Service Reform and Municipal Government. Two papers, by Albert Shaw and Horace E. Deming. (1897.)

The Republican Party and Civil-Service Reform. By Henry Hitchcock. (1897.)

The Democratic Party and Civil-Service Reform. By Moorfield Storey. (1897.)

An open Letter to Hon. C. H. Grosvenor, in reply to recent attacks on the Civil Service Law and Rules. George McAneny. (1897.)

The Need and Best Means for Providing a Competent and Stable Civil Service for Our New Dependencies. By Dorman B. Eaton. (1898.)

Constitution of the National Civil-Service Reform League.

Good Government: Official Journal of the National Civil-Service Reform League. Published monthly at 54 William St., New York. One dollar per year. Ten cents per single copy.

PROCEEDINGS

AT THE ANNUAL MEETING OF

THE NATIONAL CIVIL-SERVICE REFORM LEAGUE

HELD AT

INDIANAPOLIS, IND., DEC. 14 AND 15, 1899.

WITH THE ADDRESS OF THE PRESIDENT,

AND OTHER MATTERS.

———

NEW YORK:
PUBLISHED FOR THE
NATIONAL CIVIL-SERVICE REFORM LEAGUE.
1899.

CONTENTS.

ANNUAL MEETING

OF THE

NATIONAL CIVIL SERVICE REFORM LEAGUE.

DECEMBER 14 AND 15, 1899.

PURSUANT to call, duly issued, the nineteenth annual meeting of the National Civil Service Reform League was held at Indianapolis, Ind., on the 14th and 15th of December, 1899. Among the delegates in attendance during the several sessions were the following:

BALTIMORE: Charles J. Bonaparte, A. Marshall Elliott, Thomas H. White, D. C. Wood.

BOSTON: Richard Henry Dana.

BUFFALO: Sherman S. Rogers, Henry A. Richmond, Henry W. Sprague.

CAMBRIDGE: W. W. Vaughan

CHICAGO: John W. Ela, Edwin Burritt Smith.

CINCINNATI: Charles B. Wilby, Max B. May, Joseph C. Butler, Nathaniel H. Davis, H. M. Levy, Howard C. Hollister, Lawrence Maxwell.

CONNECTICUT: W. A. Aiken, Norwich.

INDIANA: Lucius B. Swift, William Dudley Foulke, Jesse C. Reeves, Evans Woolen, W. P. Fishback.

NEW YORK: Carl Schurz, Silas W. Burt, George McAneny.

PHILADELPHIA: Herbert Welsh, R. Francis Wood.

ST. LOUIS: A. L. Berry.

In response to invitations issued by the League to Municipal Reform Associations and other bodies having the reform of the civil service among their objects, delegates were present from a number of such organizations, as follows;

CLEVELAND:—*Chamber of Commerce:* William E. Cushing.

BOSTON:—*Massachusetts Reform Club:* Charles Warren, Samuel Y. Nash.

The morning session of the 14th, commencing at 10.30 o'clock, was occupied by a joint meeting of the General and Executive Committees, held at the German House.

The annual address of the President, Hon. Carl Schurz, was delivered at Plymouth Church, at 8 o'clock on the evening of the 14th. It is as follows:

RENEWED STRUGGLES.

An Address delivered at the Annual Meeting of the National Civil Service Reform League, at Indianapolis, Ind., Thursday, December 14th, 1899.

By Hon. Carl Schurz.

THE centennial anniversary of the death of George Washington which we observe to-day, cannot but be full of solemn admonition to every American. It has always seemed to me that the greatest historic value of Washington's career to the American people consisted not so much in the battles he fought and in the fortitude with which he upheld the cause of his country during the darkest days of the revolutionary war, as in the fact that as the first President of the United States he set up at the very beginning of our republican government a standard of wisdom, public virtue, and patriotism which has been, and will always remain, to his successors in the presidency as well as to all men in public power the surest guide as to the principles to be followed, the motives to be obeyed, and the public ends to be pursued. His wisdom was so unfailing that during the past century of our history this republic achieved its best successes as it walked in the path of his precepts, and it suffered its failures as it strayed away from that path. His sense of public duty—the duty of serving the true interests of his country as he understood them—was so genuine, strong, and courageous, that no adverse current of opinion, no fear of personal unpopularity, could shake it. He was not without party feeling, but party was never anything more to him than a mere instrumentality for serving the public good. Nothing could have been farther from his purpose than to make the public service a pasture for personal favorites or an engine for party warfare. He was the very embodiment of the principle that public office is a public trust; and it is one of the greatest inspirations of our work that we are conscious of endeavoring to make the public service what he designed it to be. And from his lofty example we should learn that steadfastness of purpose which shrinks from no duty however arduous or unpleasing. Let us contemplate that which confronts us to-day.

The National Civil Service Reform League was founded to discuss the subject of civil service reform to the end of winning for it the support of public opinion; to promote the enactment of reform legislation by Congress, by the State Legislatures, and by Municipal governments, and finally to watch the enforcement of civil service laws and to keep the public truthfully informed thereon. For the performance of these duties it is essential that the League should be a non-partisan body; and I may truly affirm that it has faithfully and conscientiously maintained its non-partisan character. There have always been among its members Republicans, and Democrats, and Independents, differing in their views as to other matters of public interest, while agreeing as to the specific purposes of the League. Since the enactment of the National civil service law, the League has had to observe and criticise the conduct of five national administrations, three of which were Republican and two Democratic. However widely we may, during this period, have differed among ourselves as to the tariff, or imperialism, or the relative merits of parties or party leaders, we have always been of one mind as to the duty of praising in the conduct of each administration concerning the public service what was to be praised, or of criticising that which may have called for censure—praising or blaming in a spirit of perfect impartiality, and endeavoring to find and to tell the plain truth without the slightest bias of favor or of ill-will.

The faithful performance of the unpleasant part of this duty has occasionally drawn upon us, now from Democrats and then from Republicans, the charge that we were chronic fault-finders—never satisfied, always discontented, sometimes even with what was done by officials who had themselves been classed among the civil service reformers. Those who make this charge do not consider that it is the first duty of this League to hold up the true standard of civil service reform, and to be dissatisfied and to find fault with everything that does not come up to that standard. If it failed to do this, it would not be true to the reason of its being. It would be as flagrantly guilty of dereliction of duty as a policeman refusing to repress a breach of the peace that happened before his eyes, or to give warning to the occupant of a house the street door of which he found open during the night.

I find myself impelled to make these remarks by the unfortunate circumstance that we are now confronted by the duty of discussing the attitude of the present national administration with regard to civil service reform under especially critical circumstances. As to its relations with President McKinley, we all know that this League accepted his early promises with warm demonstrations of confidence, and greeted with expressions of grateful approval every one of his words or acts that looked like a fulfillment of those pledges. It was profuse in its commendation of his order of July 27, 1897, concerning removals, although that order contained also the exemption from the competitive system of a much larger number of positions than it added to the classified service; and for a long time the League carefully abstained from public utterance of its misgivings as to the tendency of certain acts of the administration in order to avoid every possible injustice to the President's intentions. It lost no opportunity for respectfully inviting the President's consideration to such violations of the law and the rules as came to our notice, appealing to him for such extensions of the merit system as the public interest seemed to demand, especially cautioning him against the issuing of the recent civil service order of May 29, 1899, while that order was only in contemplation, submitting to him urgent arguments against it and predicting what the inevitable consequences would be. Thus the League has done its full duty to the President. And I may add that if, upon mature reconsideration, the President should remedy the evils now to be complained of, the League would again be as happy to praise as it is now reluctant to blame.

In the meantime, however, we cannot shirk our duty of telling with entire candor the truth about this deplorable business, as we understand it. I frankly confess that on account of my position of antagonism to other policies of the administration, the performance of my part of that duty is an especially unwelcome task to me. I should gladly have left it to some one else, had that been possible. I can now only say that I shall conscientiously follow the rule of strictly impartial judgment as the League has so far always observed it; and if I err at all, it will be in the way of moderation of statement and charitableness of inference.

The most conspicuous and important event of the last year was the President's civil service order of May 29. There can be no doubt, for every observing man has witnessed the symptoms of it, that this order has given an unprecedented impulse of encouragement to the reactionary forces working against civil service reform. The spoils politicians and their following hailed it with a shout of triumph. Many of them expressed the confident hope that now the beginning of the end of civil service reform had come. The general expression of public opinion through the press, even through not a few papers otherwise strongly favorable to the administration, was a decided disapproval of the act.

This order, however, does not stand as an isolated fact. It appears rather as the outgrowth, perhaps as the culmination, of a general tendency that has in an alarming degree manifested itself under the present administration outside of the classified service as well as within it.

Ever since the introduction of the spoils element in the federal service members of Congress, Senators as well as Representatives, have sought to usurp the constitutional function of the Executive in the making of appointments to office, and this has been one of the principal sources of demoralization in our political life. Every administration, without distinction of party, has yielded more or less to that arrogation of members of Congress, thus fostering the dangerous abuse. But,—and here I am stating only a fact so notorious that nobody will dispute it—never has the President's constitutional power and responsibility in selecting persons for presidential appointments been so systematically surrendered to Senators and Congressional delegations as during the last years ; and never has that surrender so conspicuously served as an official recognition and as a practical support of boss rule in our politics.

As an illustrating instance we may regard the changes that have been made in consular positions. For a long time the commercial community has by all sorts of demonstrations and appeals endeavored to induce the government to take that branch of the service out of politics. The administrations preceding this have been sadly delinquent in satisfying this wise and patriotic demand—a fact which this League from time to time brought to the public notice by unsparing criticism. But a beginning of reform was at least made by the last administration, which might have been developed into something valuable. Not only has this beginning, instead of being so developed, been turned into a burlesque, but there have been, during the last three years, more changes of a political character in the consular service than during any corresponding period in the recent past.

There has always been since the enactment of the civil service law a certain disinclination on the part of some officers to comply with the law and the rules as well as with the executive orders issued under it, and in some instances distinct violations of the law and the rules, or acts of disobedience to executive orders have gone unpunished. But under former administrations some offenders at least were duly disciplined so as to let public servants know that they could not with the expectation of entire impunity treat the civil service law with contempt. Now page upon page of the reports of the Civil Service Commission has during this administration been filled with recitals of such contempt, some of a most defiant nature, and again and again has this League appealed to the President for the due correction of such lawless conduct, and yet in not a single instance has the offending officer been removed. On the contrary, a great many of such offences committed before the order of May 29th was issued, have been formally condoned by that order.

The platform of the party in power contained the solemn pledge that the civil service law should not only "be thoroughly and honestly enforced" but also "extended wherever practicable." Not a single new branch of the service has by this administration been brought under the merit system. On the contrary, a very large number of clerical appointments were under the war emergency acts made in Washington alone without examination, and in the face of the fact that the Civil Service Commission stood prepared to furnish from its eligible lists of examined candidates all of the extra force that might be needed,

The notorious wastefulness in the taking of the last census and the many imperfections of that work had, confessedly, in a large measure been owing to the organization of the census force on the political spoils plan. The enlightened public opinion of the country was therefore united in demanding that the taking of the census of 1900 should be organized on the basis of the merit system wherever practicable. But there are under the Census Director appointed by this administration, 2,500 clerks to be employed, and they, as well as the rest of the force, are to be appointed on the direct nomination by Congressmen. What kind of material is furnished by such nominations appears from a recent complaint of the Census Director reported in the press : "They cannot spell and they cannot do ordinary arithmetic. Fifty per cent. fail, and they fail because they cannot divide 100,000 by 4,038; that is they cannot get a correct result." And such men are urged for appointment by political influence. They would never have dared to apply under a competitive system. The pass examinations instituted by the Director will, as they always do, serve, not to secure the selection of the fittest persons, but only to eliminate the most incapable. This is common experience.

It is true, the war emergency appointments, as well as those in the Census Office, were excepted from the operation of the civil service rules by the legislative action of Congress. But it is also true that in neither case the Executive made the slightest attempt, either by official recommendation to Congress or otherwise, to bring about the "extension" of the civil service law over those employments, in accordance with the pledge of the Republican platform. On the contrary, whatever intervention there was by Administration officials, went distinctly in the opposite direction.

It was under such circumstances that the President issued his civil service order of May 29. That order withdrew from the civil service rules thousands of positions—a much larger number than preceding rumors had led us to apprehend. By extending the facilities of arbitrary transfer from lower to higher positions, by making possible, and thus encouraging, party reprisals on a great scale with each change of administration through ex-parte re-examinations of removals for cause without limit of time, by enlarging the power of making temporary employments permanent, and even by materially weakening the President's order of July 27, 1897, concerning removals, which at the time we praised so highly, it has opened new opportunities for circumventing the civil service law. I need not go into detail, for the matter has been well elucidated by the interesting public correspondence between the Secretary of the Treasury and Mr. McAneny, the Secretary of the League, which took place some time ago, as well as by various special reports submitted at this meeting of the League.

But the significance of the President's order is not determined by the number and individual importance of the places excluded from the competitive system. It consists still more in the circumstance that the solemn pledge of the party in power that "that the civil service law shall be thoroughly and honestly enforced and extended wherever practicable," and the President's own pledge never to take a "backward step upon this question," were distinctly broken. It consists in the fact, that while since the enactment of the civil service law, every President made valuable additions to the area of the merit syetem, now for the first time, by President McKinley's order of May 29th, the area of the merit system has been substantially curtailed. While the action of every other President was in the forward direction characteristic of an advancing movement, President McKinley's order was the first distinctly backward step indicative of a generally receding tendency.

I am aware the originators and the defenders of the order claim that it not only was not designed to be a backward step, but that it was only better to regulate the reformed service, and to insure the permanency of the progress hitherto made. I shall not question the sincerity of this claim, but only consider its justice and pertinence. To judge correctly the ultimate consequences which such an act will be apt to draw after it, the reasons given for it are of the greatest moment. For if those reasons were held to be good as to the cases now in question, they will also be held to be good in the future as to cases of a similar nature. In this respect nothing could be more instructive than the public defence made of the several provisions of the President's order by the Secretary of the Treasury, who stepped forward as the main champion of the act and may well be regarded as the administration spokesman.

Here is an illustration furnished by him. The President's order takes the "shipping commissioners" from under the competitive rule, and confides their appointment to the so-called discretion of the appointing power. I choose this example for first discussion because the exemption is in this case comparatively unimportant as to the number of positions concerned, and the reason given for it seems especially plausible. That reason, in the language of the administration spokesman, is that the duties of that office are "quasi-judicial in their character, and it is needless to point to the fact that an examination will not point out the presence of the judicial temperament." This has a fair sound. But is it a good reason for excepting positions of that kind from the competitive test? That an examination will not surely "point out the presence of the judicial temperament" may be admitted. But may not an examination demonstrate other capabilities required for the discharge of the duties in question, among them a knowledge of the things with which the judicial temperament will in that office have to deal? The administration spokesman was, perhaps, not aware that in the British India services those who wish to be judges in India and who need at least as much of the judicial temperament as our shipping commissioners, have to go through the examination mill, and that this is considered as one of the peculiar virtues of that system. He may also have forgotten that a shipping commissioner appointed upon competitive examination will, during his term of probation have an opportunity for showing whether he has or has not the necessary judicial temperament, that, if he has not, he may be dropped, and that, as to this matter, the shipping commissioners might, therefore, safely have remained in the classified service.

But let us go further. Since they have been taken out of the classified service for such a reason, who is there to test the "judicial temperament" of the candidates? The Secretary of the Treasury himself cannot do it, being occupied with too many other duties. Has he, then, any experts on "judicial temperament" at his elbow to do it for him? He himself would smile at the suggestion, for he knows as well as we all do, that as soon as such places are withdrawn from the protection of the merit system, spoils politics reach out for them, and they are, in nine cases of ten, demanded by—and I regret to say, yielded to—such eminent authorities on "judicial temperament" and on other qualifications for official usefulness as Boss Platt in New York, and Boss Quay in Pennsylvania. Nobody, however, believes, I think, that when such potentates make their selections, the "judicial temperament" or other qualifications of the candidates for the *public* service have nearly as much weight with them as a promise of efficient service to the party machine.

I shall not deny that in this way now and then a man may be put in such an office who has a "judicial temperament" as well as other virtues. But considering that he has really been selected for other reasons, this must be considered a happy accident, which surely should not be regarded as justifying the withdrawal of such offices from the merit system. Such a good officer has hardly got warm in his place when a change of administration occurs and another high authority on judicial temperament demands and gets that place for his man, and then, perhaps, a man that is only a good party worker but has no judicial temperament at all. The fact remains that, when persons are put into office for reasons other than their fitness for the duties to be performed, the aggregate result will inevitably be a demoralized, wasteful and inefficient service.

But this is not even the worst aspect of the matter. Here we have one of the cases in which the reasons given for an act are more injurious than the act itself. It may be that the President, exposed to a severe pressure from the spoils hunters in his own party, thought that he could appease their greed by giving them something and that then the pressure would stop. This will turn out to be a miscalculation. The giving of something to the spoils hunters has never satisfied, but always sharpened their appetite. They will be encouraged to demand more when those in power show a yielding disposition, and especially when reasons are pointed out to them why they may demand more.

Look from this point of view at the example under discussion. I repeat, the exemption of the shipping commissioners is, as to their small number, comparatively unimportant. But when the administration tells us that they had to be exempted because the required judicial temperament cannot be demonstrated by examination, the case becomes one of far reaching consequence. There is a very large number of positions now under the civil service rules, the duties of which are more or less quasi-judicial, such as the examiners in the patent office, and many division chiefs and high grade clerks in various departments who have to prepare the decision of cases. Now if the shipping commissioners must be exempted from the rules because their judicial temperament cannot be demonstrated by examination, although examination may demonstrate other required qualifications, why should not the other places I have named, be exempted for the same reason, thus to be placed within the reach of spoils politics?

But the question is a still larger one. Everybody knows that there is hardly an employment under the government for the perfect discharge of the duties of which this or that quality of character or mental habit is not desirable, that cannot be demonstrated by examination, while other and perhaps more important qualifications can be so demonstrated. Now, what would become of the whole merit system if we were to admit, as the administration virtually does, that because some qualfications cannot be demonstrated, the ascertainment by examination of other requirements must be abandoned, and the disposition of all those places must therefore be yielded to the party magnates as heretofore? The administration will, no doubt sincerely, say that they did not mean it so. But can they deny that by the futile reasons assigned for the exemption from the civil service rules of the places mentioned, they have given the spoils politicians a very strong encouragement to demand the exemption of a great many more—and an argument sure to turn up some day ?

Here is another example. In his first defence of the President's order the administration spokesman said, among other things: "The exceptions in the Alaskan service have been made necessary by the great distance from Washington and the time consumed in making certifications and appointments under civil service regulations." Again, the number of government places in Alaska is small, and in that respect the exception is unimportant. But if, as the Administration tells us, "the exemptions in the Alaskan service have been *made necessary* by the great distance from Washington," will not, according to the same authority, the exemption from the civil service rules of the colonial service in the Philippines, if we are to have that, on account of the greater distance be still more "necessary ? " Is not this extremely cold comfort to those of our fellow citizens who are in favor of a colonial policy, but who justly believe that such a policy will inevitably result in disaster and disgrace unless carried on under the strictest kind of a civil service system ? Has not thus the administration furnished a very specious argument to the politicians who will insist upon making the colonies, if there be such, pastures of spoils politics ? And did not the administration do this in the face of the fact that, in spite of much greater distance from the seat of imperial government, England is carrying on in India a most elaborate and exacting civil service system to which that part of the British Empire owes nearly all it has of good government ?

Still another example—the deputy internal revenue collectors, of whom there are a good many, and who are officers of great importance, as they have to collect more than half of the national revenue. They were put under the civil service rules by President Cleveland. The spokesman of the present administration has defended their exemption on various grounds—in the first place, because the law vests the appointment of these deputies in the collectors, and they were, therefore,

"according to the highest legal opinion the Treasury
Department could get, illegally classified." Let us examine this. Sec. 3148 of the U. S. Revised Statutes
provides: "Each collector shall be authorized to appoint
by an instrument in writing, under his hand, as many
deputies as he may think proper, to be compensated by
him for their services; to revoke any such appointment,
giving notice thereof as the Commissioner of Internal
Revenue shall prescribe; and to require and accept
bonds or other securities from such deputies, etc." The
question is whether this statute precludes the subjection
of the deputy internal revenue collectors to the civil service rules. The administration contends on the authority of "the highest legal opinion the Treasury Department could get," that it does. What was that "highest
legal opinion" attainable? I am informed that it was
not that of the Supreme Court, nor that of any U. S.
Court, nor even that of the Attorney-General, but simply the opinion of Mr. O'Connell, the Solicitor of the
Treasury, and that he gave that opinion not even in
writing, but orally in an off-hand way. If this information is correct, then the Administration must admit that
it is easily satisfied as to the legal merits of a very important matter; for on the other side, declaring that
those positions could be legally classified, there stood
President Cleveland, who made the order classifying
them, and who is far from being considered a mean lawyer, and also Mr. Conrad, a former Solicitor-General of
the United States, and Mr. Charles J. Bonaparte, a lawyer of high standing in Maryland, and Mr. Moorfield
Storey, a former president of the American Bar Association, whose opinions the Administration might have
read in the report of the Civil Service Commission for
1896–7. The Commission itself submitted a strong
argument sustaining the legality of the classification.

Now I ask in all candor, what will become of the merit
system in the public service if, when a Solicitor of some
department says that in his view the classification of a
certain numerous force of the service is illegal, that
declaration is at once accepted as "the highest legal

opinion the department can get," and the President thereupon actually exempts that branch of the service from the rules ?

If we take as valid such reasons for curtailing the classified service, how long shall we be able to resist the spoils-politicians showing us that there are other and far more numerous classes of places, the appointment to which is by statute vested in certain officers, and which, therefore, must be excluded from the merit system? They may even point out to us a. statute providing that "each head of a department is authorized to employ in his department such number of clerks of the several classes recognized by law, and such other employees, and at such rates of compensation respectively as may be appropriated for by Congress from year to year," and they may thereupon argue that, the law thus vesting the appointment of clerks and other employees in the heads of departments, no interference by civil service rules with the discretionary power of the heads of departments in making such appointments can be legal. And I should not at all wonder if one or more department solicitors could be found to deliver as their opinion that, although the language of one statute may be a little more elaborate or stronger than that of the other, their legal intent and effect is the same. Such a legal doctrine, applied to all departments, would, of course, sweep away at one swoop the whole merit system, root and branch; and the Secretary of the Treasury, as a friend of civil service reform, would have to find his consolation in thinking that this was "the highest legal opinion the department could get."

As another reason for exempting the deputy internal revenue collectors, the Administration tells us that the Civil Service Commission recommended it. So it did, after having long and strenuously argued that those officers should *not* be exempted. Why did the Commission at last recommend the exemption ? It gave its reason in a letter of May 8, 1899, addressed to the President, in these words: "The fact that the Internal Revenue Bureau continued to claim and exercise the right of Collectors to appoint deputies without compliance with the civil service act and rules, notwithstanding the arguments of the Commission to the contrary, was the principal reason for the Commission's recommendation to the President on June 1, 1898, that these positions be included in the list of positions excepted from the requirement of examination "

What a state of things this reveals! Here was the Civil Service Commission faithfully fighting for the enforcement of the law as it stood; on the other side a branch of the government persistently and defiantly violating that law, until the Commission, feeling itself utterly powerless against the government, at last threw up its hands in despair, saying: "Well, rather than have the law openly and continually violated under the eyes of the government, let the law be modified to suit the violators." And then that so-called "recommendation" of the Commission is paraded by the administration as justifying the President's order of May 29!

Consider what a precedent this will be! It teaches the spoilsmen in the public service that they need only find some pretext for rebelling against the civil service law, and that if they carry on that rebellion with sufficient boldness and persistency, they will have good ground for hoping that for the very reason of their bold and persistent lawlessness, the government will complacently revoke the part of the law or of the rules that displeases them. A precedent more demoralizing to the discipline of the service and subversive of the merit system can hardly be imagined.

I am not unmindful of what the administration spokesman has said about the peculiar fiduciary relations existing between the Collectors of Internal Revenue and their deputies, about the responsibility of the Collectors for the acts of their subordinates, about the personal confidence which should prevail between them, and so on. Now, that certain superior officers bear more or less responsibility for the conduct of their subordinates, that there are certain subordinate positions of a more confidential character than others, and that therefore the superior officers must in such cases have the discretionary power to select their subordinates without being troubled by any civil service rules, is one of the well worn stock arguments of the enemies of civil service reform. There are few positions above the lowest clerkships to which this argument may not be more or less applied, and to which the spoils politicians do not actually apply it.

Against this permit me a recital of personal experience. When, years ago, I became Secretary of the Interior, I thought it best not to take a single person with me into the Department, not even a private and confidential secretary. That private secretary I selected from among the force already in the department. I soon found a man of excellent capacity, entire trustworthiness and good manners, who at the same time had the important advantage of being already acquainted with departmental affairs. So much for that peculiarly "confidential" position. Now, when looking at the papers put before me for my signature—papers of importance which I could not possibly study in detail—I felt myself as to the discharge of very grave responsibilities—much graver than those of an Internal Revenue Collector—to an appalling extent at the mercy of my subordinates. At the same time I was set upon by Senators and Representatives and other political magnates, who urgently asked me to fill existing vacancies, or vacancies to be made by removals, with men whom they recommended to me for appointment. Most of them demanded places for their favorites for reasons which had nothing to do with the public interest. Some told me that in my responsible position I must have subordinates whom I could trust, and they were ready to furnish me just such men. I heard them all and concluded that the public interest would be best served if the vacant places in my department—fiduciary as well as others—were filled on the principles of the merit system, and I attempted the introduction of that system in the department—imperfectly of course, as I had no appropriation for the purpose, and only an improvised and constantly changing machinery, depending on clerks whose time was temporarily not fully employed, or who were willing to work after office hours. I carried this on for four years against the bitterest opposition of the patronage mongers high and low, and I learned thus from actual practice on that field of very complicated duties and heavy responsibilities quite thoroughly to appreciate the practical value of the merit system in the conduct of the service, and also the true nature of the difficulties standing in the way of a full development of that system.

Now, when in discussing this matter anybody indulges in solemn hints about mysterious things which the official mind has to deal with, but which the unofficial mind is unable to understand, he cannot make any impression upon me. I am familiar with the augur's wink and with the smiles that follow it. It is equally useless to talk to me about fiduciary or confidential positions which should be filled only at the free discretion of the appointing officer ; for I know from abundant experience that in an overwhelming majority of cases free discretion is a myth and that the fiduciary appointments are dictated by political influence ; and I know also that in a well-regulated civil service with merit appointment, merit promotion and merit tenure all those so-called extraordinary qualifications for certain positions can easily be secured without exposing any of the places to the chance of becoming the prey of spoils politics.

In fact, after four years' service, I left the Interior Department with the firm conviction that the positions in it, and no doubt in all the other departments, would, taking the general average, be vastly better filled and that the work would be much more efficiently and economically done—in one word, that the public interest would be much better served, if the whole force in and under those departments, without any exception worth mentioning, were subjected to the civil service rules, including even, if that were possible, the commissioners and assistant commissioners of the different bureaus, and in each department at least one permanent under-Secretary. And the same four years' official experience convinced me that there is only one real difficulty obstructing the full development of the merit system in our public service—and that is the pressure of political influence for patronage, and the lack of resisting power among appointing officers to stand firm against that pressure. Take away that one difficulty, and all your troubles about needed "extraordinary qualifications" that cannot be demonstrated by examination, and about "fiduciary positions," and about distances making the application of the merit system impracticable, and so on, will at once vanish into nothing. And it is the most baneful feature of the President's order of May 29 that it so seriously increases that difficulty by strengthening the belief of the spoils hunters and patronage mongers that neither the pledge of a great party to "enforce the civil service law honestly and thoroughly, and to extend it wherever practicable," nor a President's solemn promise that there shall be "no backward step" will hold out against the pressure of political influence if that pressure be only persevering and defiant.

You must pardon me for once more referring to my personal experience. Having served six years in the United States Senate, where, at the beginning at least— I was soon cured—I thought I had to do some patronage business myself, and where I learned pretty thoroughly how that business is usually done by members of Congress,—and having been four years at the head of a great government department where I learned still more, and having been for seventeen years a more or less active member of an association considering it its especial duty to study the means by which the merit system may be established, perfected, sustained and extended, and also the means by which its enemies seek to demoralize, to cripple, and finally to destroy it, I may, perhaps, without undue assumption pretend to some practical knowledge of the subject. And that knowledge fully warrants me in saying that if I were in a position of power and desired to undermine the merit system in the public service with a view to its final overthrow, but without proclaiming myself its enemy, the things contained in the President's order of May 29th, together with the reasons given to justify them, would suggest themselves to me as among the most effective shifts to bring about that end.

In saying this I candidly disclaim the intention of insinuating that such was the purpose of the President, or that of his official defender in this case, the Secretary of the Treasury. On the contrary, I honestly believe that they would gladly have carried out the pledge of the Republican platform "honestly and thoroughly to enforce the civil service law and to extend it wherever practicable," could they have done so without encountering the fierce antagonism of the so-called "practical politicians" within their own party. I further believe that in trying to appease that antagonism they would have liked to abstain from anything that might seriously injure the merit system, but that they relied upon subordinates to get up suitable amendments to the civil service rules and were misled by the advice of those subordinates farther than they had originally intended to go; and that finally when the thing was done, and met with very severe criticism, not only on the part of this League but of public sentiment generally, they tried to justify their step, as men who suddenly find themselves in a false position often do, by giving all sorts of reasons for their act — reasons probably also suggested by their ingenious subordinates—which made the effects of their act and their own situation even much worse than they otherwise would have been.

This is my candid belief; and that belief is not in the slightest degree shaken by the statement made by the Secretary of the Treasury in his public defense, that several of the exemptions were never demanded of him by any politicians. No wonder, for the politicians knew where they could put in their work much more effectively below. The real motive power was in any case the greed of politicians for patronage and their pressure upon the administration. Those who believe this as I do, can render the administration, as well as the cause of reform, no better service than by laying bare the true nature and tendency of what has been done, and by expressing at the same time the hope that after a sober and careful re-examination of the matter the President may see his way clear for retracing his step. After such a re-examination he will hardly fail to recognize the fact that his order of May 29, with the reasons given for it, has been the most hurtful blow civil service reform has ever received since the enactment of the law, as the reception that order has met with from friend and foe must have convinced him that the people generally regard it as such, and that subsequent excuses and explanations have not altered that judgment.

Neither can he close his eyes to the fact that encouraged by the general backsliding tendency under his administration that culminated in the order of May 29th, some of the most conspicuous abuses of the spoils system which under his immediate predecessors had become much restricted, are now developing new vitality. It is too notorious to be denied that persons in the Federal service have become much more forward again in what is called "pernicious partisan activity" than they were for many years. During several administrations, for instance, the business community of New York had been accustomed to see the great Custom House of that port "out of politics," the Collector of Customs devoting himself to his official duties without taking any active part in party movements. But now the Collector is a prominent figure again in party caucuses and other gatherings, and occasionally he finds it even proper to cheer his audiences with exhilarating remarks about the actual or prospective relaxation of the civil service rules by Executive action. Thus the great Custom House of New York is out of politics no longer ; and the same may be said of other large or small government establishments.

The contemptuously sportive view of the civil service law which at present is taken here and there has, of course, been very much encouraged by an opinion delivered by the Comptroller of the Treasury, Mr. R. J. Tracewell, as to whether persons shown to have been appointed in violation of the civil service rules should nevertheless be paid their salaries. The question having been referred to him by the Secretary of the Treasury, Comptroller Tracewell decided that inasmuch as the President has, under the law, made the civil service rules, if not directly then at least by his approval, he could also suspend them or sanction their suspension by his agents or subordinate officers; and that if the rules were thus suspended in individual cases by the appointment of persons in violation of them, the Comptroller has no choice but to accept the certificate of appointment as conclusive and to sanction the payment of the salaries of the persons so appointed. This decision looks like a huge jest at the expense of the civil service law; and we might conclude that it was intended as such when we read the following sentence which forms part of that important document: "If this ruling has a tendency to muddy the stream of civil service reform, which should always flow pure and clean from its fountain throughout its course, I can only answer that it would be as futile for me to attempt with my limited jurisdiction to purify this stream, as it would be to bail the ocean of its waters with a pint cup." Mr. R. J. Tracewell, who owes his appointment as Comptroller not to a civil service examination, but to the so-called free discretion of the President, has, it may be said by the way, furnished by this elegant sneer at civil service reform, in a judicial decision, a fine illustration of that "judicial temperament" which, according to the Secretary of the Treasury, every officer exercising quasi judicial functions must possess, and to secure which civil service examinations must be discarded and the appointing power must be left to make its choice with untramelled freedom. I have only to add that this decision has been accepted by the administration as final, that the persons appointed in proven violation of the civil service rules are regularly paid their salaries, that in this respect there is no trouble in the way of further illegal appointments, and that Mr. Tracewell has, after this performance, not been disturbed in his important position of Comptroller, where he continues to enjoy ample opportunity for giving his rare judicial temperament full play.

It is also a matter of notoriety that the levying of assessments upon persons in the Federal service has again assumed very formidable dimensions. This abuse, it is true, has to some extent existed all the while. But this year the public mind was rather seriously startled by the unusually defiant boldness with which the Republican State Committee of Ohio, the President's own state, put the Federal service all over the country under contribution to its party campaign fund, instructing, with rare cynicism, the public servants how the penal clauses of the law against assessments could be circumvented. This truly remarkable proceeding went on without the slightest mark of disapproval on the part of those charged with the execution of the law, until at last the Civil Service Commission remonstrated against it, the immediate result of which remonstrance was, according to the press reports, that the Republican State Committee of Ohio rushed out another call admonishing the Federal officeholders to be quick in paying up. In this way an unusually large amount of money was obtained from the public servants. This is not surprising, for, as everybody acquainted with placeholders knows, the member of the classified service feels himself no longer secure in his tenure if he merely does his duty faithfully and efficiently, but he is troubled again by a sense of danger unless he win the favor of the party potentates by rendering such political service as may be exacted of him. That this danger really exists I will not assert. But the feeling of apprehension, created by the things I have been describing, very extensively does exist, and it cannot fail to produce demoralizing effects most hurtful to the service.

An effort is being made to bring to justice those who have violated the law by the levying of assessments in the case mentioned as well as in another case, on the ground of an opinion recently rendered by ex-Senator Edmunds, who was the chairman of the Judiciary Committee of the Senate which reported the statute in question; and it is hoped that a salutary example will be made of the guilty persons. This, if successfully carried through, would indeed serve to prevent the repetition of such glaring excesses in the same line. But much more drastic measures on the part of the Administration, if it wishes to demonstrate its earnestness as to the maintenance of the merit system, will be required to cure that deterioration of the atmosphere in the public service which has been brought about by the multiplication of places filled by political influence as well as by the impunity with which in so many conspicuous cases the rules have been circumvented and the spirit of the law has been openly defied—an impunity which but too easily is taken for approval.

In this respect, I must confess, the paragraphs in the President's message referring to the civil service, fail to afford much comfort, for they may be summed up in the one sentence—that everything is now in satisfactory condition. We can only hope that the cheerful optimism betrayed by this utterance will not prevent the President from considering worthy of notice the investigations made by this League and the resulting reports upon the happenings in various branches of the service. Those reports, containing not mere theories or inferences, but facts, may serve to open his eyes to many things of which, it must be assumed, he was not aware or which, at least, he may not have seen in their true character, when he wrote his message, but a thorough appreciation of which may induce him to apply the appropriate remedies and to retrieve the grievous missteps we have now to deplore.

The picture of the retrograde tendencies in the Federal service which my duty to tell the plain truth has compelled me to draw, is relieved by some facts of a more encouraging nature. In the State of New York a distinct advance as to the maintenance as well as the further extension of the merit system has been achieved, with the valuable aid of Governor Roosevelt, by the enactment of a new civil service law. That law not only sweeps away the contrivances by which the late State administration sought to "take the starch out of civil service," but it places the merit system throughout on the firm basis of well-ordered regulations, securing to it a practicable machinery, and it provides for the extension of its operation over the counties, in which it had formerly not been in force. Even in the city of New York, where the sinister genius of Tammany Hall devotes itself with the accustomed zest and skill to the task of circumventing the civil service law, and where the local Civil Service Reform Association, co-operating with the State authorities, has to fight over every foot of ground, many valuable successes have been scored—at least in crossing iniquitous schemes and in making the ways of the transgressor duly hard. Also on the other side of the continent, in San Francisco, distinct progress has been recorded by the adoption of a city charter providing for the introduction of the merit system in the municipal service.

But the fact in which the friend of civil service reform may find the most cheering assurance of the triumph of his cause in the future, consists in the striking evidences of the growth of that cause in the favor of public opinion. The time is not far behind us when civil service reform was superciliously sniffed at as a whimsical notion of some dreamy theorists not to be taken seriously. Even when after the first attempt at the practical introduction of the merit system in the Federal service President Grant dropped it again in consequence of the refusal of Congress to make any appropriation for its support, the people generally accepted the event with cool indifference. There were indeed expressions of regret, but they came only from a comparatively small number of citizens who had become especially interested in the subject. But when six months ago President McKinley's order curtailing the area of the merit system appeared, the manifestations of popular disapproval were far more general and earnest than the originators of the measure had expected and than the friends of the merit systen had dared to hope. Not even party spirit, usually so potent in such cases, was proof against the popular feeling of disappointment, not a few journals otherwise staunch partisans of the Administration, giving voice to that feeling with remarkable emphasis.

The reason is simple. In President Grant's time civil service reform still appeared in this country as a new and strange scheme, running in the teeth of the political notions and habits of half a century, and clouded over by the uncertainties of a doubtful experiment. Now it is a stranger no longer. The people have made its acquaintance by actual observation. They know that it is not an idle fancy, but an eminently sober and practical conception; that its aim is to remedy real evils and to produce a real good, by delivering our political life of fatally demoralizing influences, and by giving the republic efficient, economical, and honest service. They know that it pursues this aim by methods which every intelligent business man standing at the head of a large establishment and exposed to constant and promiscuous pressure for employment would adopt for himself as eminently business-like. In one word, they know that civil service reform as embodied in the merit system is simply the application to the public service of the plainest principles of common sense and common honesty. Even its enemies are at heart recognizing its virtues.

This has become so widely understood by people of all classes in all parts of the country, that the propagation of correct knowledge of the objects and the means of civil service reform is becoming from day to day an easier task to the advocates of the merit system. Their foremost duty is now to baffle the efforts of the opposing forces, which, seeing the futility of attacking civil service reform on its general merits, strive to cripple or pervert it in the detail of its operation. Those forces consist of the small politicians who covet the offices for their personal advantage, the political leaders who seek to control the offices as party spoil in order to hold together and increase their following, and the unsteady statesmen in power who, while professing, often not without sincerity, to be "also" in favor of civil service reform, have indeed courage enough to assert their professed principles against their party enemies, but not firmness enough to maintain them against their party friends. The combination of these forces is an old one. It is expert in its business, and it will never do to underestimate its strength. How formidable it may become, we have in these days again had occasion for observing.

But, however powerful, it is far from being invincible. We cannot forget that against the same old combination the civil service reform movement has won all its successes, one after another, during periods of time when it was far less intelligently and vigorously supported by the public opinion of the country than it is to-day. While its friends have recently suffered a grievous disappointment, they have no reason for being discouraged. To retrieve the lost ground and to advance their cause further toward the final consummation, they have only to follow their old course with militant courage and constancy; to watch with keen vigilance the happenings in the public concerns; to gauge every measure taken by those in power by the true standard, recognizing gladly every step forward, and permitting nothing to pass that is not genuine; to aid the authorities whenever possible with information and candid counsel; to expose to the public eye the abuses they discover, the correction of which is refused;—in one word, to tell the people the truth without favor and without fear. A resolute and persevering appeal to public opinion, to the good sense and patriotism of such a people as ours, will not be in vain. So good a cause, supported by dauntless devotion, can never fail.

MEETING OF THE LEAGUE.

GERMAN HOUSE, December 14, 1899.

2 P. M.

The President took the chair.

The Secretary made an oral report reviewing certain matters pertaining to the work of his office during the year, and the relations of the League with Congress and Executive officers, in matters concerning the reform of the national civil service.

In the course of this report the Secretary stated that a letter had been addressed to President McKinley under date of March 30, last, adding a final protest against the reduction of the area of the competitive classified service, then proposed, and urging that the civil service law be maintained and extended in its operation—rather than restricted—wherever practicable. On May 29, however, an Executive order had been issued, removing approximately ten thousand offices and positions from the classified service, or from the competitive class within that service, and changing the rules in a manner calculated to increase materially the opportunities for appointments without examination, to positions remaining nominally competitive. This order had been reviewed in a public statement made on behalf of the League by the Executive Committee. The accuracy of certain of the Committee's allegations having been questioned by the Secretary of the Treasury, an open letter had been addressed to that officer by the Secretary, substantiating what had been said, and setting forth some of the effects of the order, and certain of the conditions existing at the time of its promulgation, in greater detail. Further public correspondence had followed, which would be submitted to the League, in full, at this meeting. During the six months since the date of the President's order, investigations had been made on behalf of the League, concerning the practical results of the operation of the altered rules, and concerning appointments made through methods other than those prescribed by the civil service act, in the war emergency forces of the War and Treasury departments, the Census Bureau, and other branches. The results of these inquiries would be made public in detail by the Special Investigating Committee.

In reply to a letter asking permission for an agent of the League to examine and copy the record of appointments in the Treasury Department under the war emergency acts, the Secretary of the Treasury had declined to permit such examination on the ground that it is the custom of the Department to furnish information concerning such appointments only to Congress or to a co-ordinate Executive Department, although lists of appointments in other branches of the Department had been furnished to the League on previous occasions, with the approval of the Appointment Division. The correspondence on this subject the Secretary read.

On motion the report of the Secretary was received.

Mr. Bonaparte, of Maryland, referring to that portion of the Secretary's report bearing upon the failure of the League to secure access to the record of "emergency" appointments under the war acts, moved the adoption of the following :

The League pronounces the action of the Treasury Department in refusing access to public records relating to matters of public concern, a violation of the undoubted right of citizens in a free country to learn, from official sources, how faithfully the public servants they pay administer the laws. The force of the reason assigned for this refusal is gravely impaired by the fact that similar information had been previously furnished to the League by the Department under the present Secretary of the Treasury. This refusal exposes to reasonable suspicion the good faith of the officials responsible for it, and suggests the existence of abuses which the records withheld from inspection might disclose, and we demand that this unworthy policy of concealment and secrecy be abandoned.

The President announced the business next in order to be the reception of reports from representatives of local Associations.

Reports were then received as follows :

For Connecticut, Gen. William A. Aiken :

"Owing to the absence in Europe of Prof. Henry W. Farnam, President of the New Haven Civil Service Commission, and to the non-reply to my requests for a report of progress from his acting successor, I am unable to present to the League anything more than impressions, derived from incidental sources of the progress which had been made, since the date of my report at our previous annual meeting, in the administration of the Civil Service Rules under the new charter of the city of New Haven.

"From the sources above referred to I gained the impression that the improvement noted all along the line in Prof. Farnam's letter of last year has continued, to the great betterment of the city administration, and, it is hoped, to the continued satisfaction of the heads of administrative departments.

"I regard the New Haven experiment as having an important bearing upon the smaller cities of the State in their pending and future charter amendments."

For New York State and City, the Secretary:

"We are able, the present year, to report some very satisfactory advances in New York State. At the time the League last met our civil service system was very much disordered. In the State service, applying to the various State departments and institutions, we had the very vicious law framed at the instance of Governor Black, and passed through his influence, which subsequently bore his name. The features of this reactionary piece of legislation have often been described, and I need not refer to them here.

"In the city of New York we had in operation a set of rules framed by the Tammany administration in pursuance of the civil service sections of the Greater New York Charter, which, our Courts had held, superseded the "Black Act" within the consolidated territory. In the smaller cities of the State we had the old system of 1888, revived by an act amending the "Black Act," passed in March of 1898. This situation led to much confusion, and to many contests in the Courts. It was claimed by the Association, in New York City, that the Tammany rules were invalid after March, 1898, not having received the approval of the State Commission as the act of that month required. Just as the Association had won a final victory in the Court of Appeals on this point the Legislature passed a new law in the framing of which the Association had been much concerned, which did away with all the previously existing statutes, setting in their place one comprehensive system of law, with uniform application, and embodying many improvements in detail suggested by the experience of the past decade. For the ultimate success of the movement for the passage of this bill we give full credit to Governor Roosevelt, who recommended legislation of the sort in his first annual message, and who did all in his power to secure its favorable consideration. The new act brings all classes of positions within the classified service, except those of the highest order. It requires competition for all classified places except where experience has shown that competition is not practicable, and for the Labor service it requires a very complete and satisfactory system of registration, the honest upholding of which will leave little or no room for the exercise of political or personal favor. In order to secure uniformity, city boards are required to submit their rules for approval to the State Commission, and where the Mayor of a city fails to act promptly, the State Board may appoint a Commission to frame proper rules.

"The inhibition upon payments of salary by fiscal officers to persons appointed without compliance with the law is greatly strengthened, and the rights of citizens to go to the Courts for proper enforcement are extended.

"The Municipal Commission in New York City, failing to frame rules that were acceptable to the State authorities, held a conference with the State Board, as the result of which some concessions were made on both sides, and a fairly acceptable set of rules put together. These Mayor Van Wyck in a fit of bad temper, declined to approve. The result was that under the authority given by the act, the State Board framed the rules independently, making them much stronger and better. These rules have been in full force since the 11th of July. The difference in the manner of administering the service is already most manifest. Throughout the State the smaller cities have also accepted many improvements suggested by the State Board, and although there is still some friction in putting the rules in force where previously they had been a dead letter, there is constant advancement.

"A feature of the new act is the extension of the system to the larger counties, and these, it is promised, will be brought in as soon as the State Commission is able to provide the machinery for carrying the rules as so extended into effect.

"We still expect to be obliged to bring occasional suits to secure proper constructions of disputed points. We have been aided by an excellent corps of volunteer lawyers, and so far they have met with the most gratifying degree of success in upholding our contentions."

For Buffalo, Henry A. Richmond:

"Our executive committee has held regular monthly meetings for the last nineteen years. The committee has twenty-one members, all of them enthusiastic workers. During the last year the special interest has been in relation to the White Civil Service Law, which took effect April 19. superseding the so-called 'Black Law.' The Buffalo Commission, of which Mr. D. V. Murphy is chairman, has, I think, the honor of being the first city board in the state to adopt rules in accordance with this law. Our committee did not need to interfere in the framing of these rules, and we are glad to say that they represent what seems to us the best developments in civil service reform. These rules, for the first time, include in the classified service the Chief of Police, the Chief of Departments, and other heads of departments. We could not ask for better or more stringent rules than the Buffalo Commission has prepared ; and it is pleasant to relate that public opinion in favor of the civil service law is now so strong in Buffalo that all six of our daily papers approve these rules. The Labor Unions in Buffalo are especially strong in their support of the civil service law and the President of the State Federation of Labor is a member of our Commission.

"Both the Buffalo Association and the Buffalo Commission have endeavored to expedite the classification of the county officers under the new law. Both have written frequently to the State Board to urge that Civil Service rules be applied as soon as possible to Erie County, and both have offered their services to the State Board in the classification of county offices.

"A valuable piece of work accomplished by our association was an investigation of the Water Department by a sub-committee, of which Mr. A. C. Richardson was chairman. This committee found upwards of thirty employees illegally on the roll, all of whom have since been dismissed. This condition of affairs arose largely from a confusion of legal opinion in regard to the force of the 'Black Law,' which for a time gave rise to many difficulties.

"We think it possible that the use of the voting machine in Buffalo at the last election was due in part to the strong recommendations in favor of a similar voting machine made by our Association three years ago."

For Pennsylvania, R. Francis Wood of Philadelphia :

"I regret to say that I can not offer a very encouraging report from Pennsylvania. In the Federal Service in Philadelphia, the heads of the two chief offices, the Post Office and the Custom House, are active partisans and leaders of opposing factions in the ward in which they both live. Several cases of violation of the law or rules in their respective offices have been brought to the notice of the Association, the most flagrant of which was that of the removal of five employees of the Appraiser's office, on charges which were so frivolous and so unsupported by evidence, that the men were reinstated, only, however, to be afterwards discharged without a hearing, their immediate superior admitting to them that the political pressure for their places was too great for him to resist.

"I submit a letter from the Civil Service Commission, enclosing its correspondence with the Secretary of the Treasury. in which the Commission declares its belief that there had been three distinct violations of the law in these discharges. The Secretary, however, in his letter, refuses to reopen the case.

"I have to report, further, that Philadelphia is also suffering in its Municipal Service, that the new Mayor has made several discharges of excellent officers without good reason, and that appointments have been made that are governed entirely by personal or partisan considerations and that have generally been from exceedingly poor material, The Pennsylvania Association intends to resume actively the distribution of literature, especially among young men, whose participation in its future work is peculiarly desirable."

At the suggestion of a member, the correspondence relative to the alleged violations of the Civil Service Rules in the customs service in Philadelphia, referred to in the report of Mr. Wood, was referred to the Special Investigating Committee. The order of reports for Associations was then resumed, as follows :

For Cincinnati, Charles B. Wilby :

"Cincinnati has seen recently an illustration of the truth that the spoils system will always react upon its friends. This is an old story, whtch has been heard again and again, but perhaps the recital here of the Cincinnati version may serve to emphasize the fact that no disease which is the result of poison can be cured until the patient is rid of the posion, and no municipal ailment which is the result of the spoils system, as all are more or less, but generally more, can be cured until that poison is thoroughly eliminated. Four years ago the citizens of Cincinnati broke out in one of those spasms of revolt which occasionally occur in boss ridden communities. There was a fusion between Democrats, Independent Republicans. disappointed office seekers, and all manners of discontent with the ' Boss.' We all helped, civil service reformers and disgruntled ward workers, all fighting together against the common enemy, and the result was that the machine was smashed and every office from the Mayor down, in that and the succeeding election, was turned over to the fusionists. Thereupon, instead of putting into practice their good words against the chief source of bossism, the victors immediately began to divide the spoils in the most approved spoilmen's fashion. With a few exceptions, whom some of the better element were able to save from the headsman, every appointee of the boss was thrown out, thereby depriving our community of the services of many servants whose experience had made them valuable, and whose only fault was that they were the offspring of an illegitimate system of appointment. Their places were forthwith filled with men in the main wholly inexperienced, whose selection was the result of the same methods which the so-called reformers had so vociferously denounced before the election. the only difference being that the power of appointment was now vested in a self constituted oligarchy of fusionists, instead of in its predecessor, the Boss. The natural result was a gradually growing discontent among the people, who began to suffer in some instances from even a poorer public service than the Boss had furnished. The glaring unfitness of certain appointments, and the palpable use of *pull* in securing them, disgusted the good citizen, and gradually he could be heard to say. ' If this is reform I want no more of it. We were better under the old Boss, who, at least, knew his business, etc,' and at the election two years ago the same old Boss and his old guard were successful and recaptured practically all of the offices then to be filled, and the net result of this campaign was that the word ' reform ' became a reproach and the Boss regained much of his former power. At the election this year, however, there were complications whieh prevented his success, and consequently we have what is on the whole an excellent delegation from Hamilton County to the Legislature, which may help us to pass a bill for the reformation of our civil service. We have heretofore introduced two different bills for this purpose, one of which was defeated four years ago, after it had passed the Senate, while the other was swamped in the storm over the election of United Satates Senator by the last Legislature, and hence was never voted on. At the last session, however, a commission was provided to revise, amend and modify the municipal laws of the State and, happily, the Governor appointed as members of this commission two learned gentlemen, who are thorough-going and sincere civil service reformers. In the draft charter bill included in their report, which will be presented to the coming session of the Legislature, they have embodied provisions for the establishment of the merit system in our municipalities in a very effective manner, and if these provisions are enacted into law we shall be able to report at the next meeting of the League that Ohio has at last come up out of the darkness and has joined those states which have laid, in the bedrock of the merit system, the only sure foundation for good government."

For Missouri, A. L. Berry, of St. Louis:

"Attached to the platform upon which our Honorable Mayor, as well as a majority of our present city officials, took office, I find these significant lines:

"'We further earnestly recommend to our city officials the merit system for all our city employees.'

"Somewhere in the progress to the City Hall, this good assurance must have been lost, for shortly after the election of the Mayor I called upon him to enlist his co-operation in having our Charter so amended as to embrace a provision known as the "Merit System Amendment," and I was told not only that he would have nothing to do with such a provision, but that "he would not touch it with a ten foot pole."

"Civil Service rules can be introduced under our city government, and their provisions made mandatory, only through an amendment to our Charter, submitted to the suffrage of the people through the Municipal Assembly, and it may be said, at least, that this issue will probably be the controlling one in our next municipal campaign.

"Our business men, our working classes, our citizens generally, all recognize the necessity and advantages of this reform. No matter how they may differ with reference to other public questions, they admit that they can rally with equal enthusiasm in favor of the "Merit System."

"Any one living near to the twentieth century, appreciates that the atmosphere is crisp with the keen air of rivalry, that every pursuit is geared to its highest point, and that efficiency, to-day, is the only assurance of permanent advantage in any commercial or economic field. Our municipal government cannot be left much longer to the spoilsman and political boss; our people may be depended on to demand that every department and every employee shall meet the test of proper qualification and wear the badge of fitness.

"The Merit System has very clearly caught the minds of our citizens and is recognized as the necessary foundation to any lasting improvement. Our city government is still greatly under the influence of partisan politics, but the constant, persistent, fearless discussion of municipal questions—among which this stands with us first—is having a most healthful effect.

" We may not correct our present evils with one great overthrow, but we are becoming fairly convinced of the hopelessness of any radical improvement under the spoils system, and no change in our Charter looking to the increase of taxation or to the strengthening of our revenues, will be accepted, unless the amendments provide as well for civil service reform ; and, once firmly established in the municipal government of St. Louis, the system will, we believe, soon prevail throughout the State.

" I am happy to assure this assemblage, and especially the officers of the National League, that the people of St. Louis, and throughout the State, are loyal to your cause.'

Brief reports were also made for Massachusetts, by Richard Henry Dana; for Cambridge, by W. W. Vaughan; for Maryland, by Charles J. Bonaparte, and for Indiana, by Lucius B. Swift.

The Secretary read letters from the Secretary of the Civil Service Reform Association of Denver, and from the President of the Merchants' Association of San Francisco with reference to recent movements in favor of the merit system by charter amendments in their respective cities, resulting, in the latter case, in the establishment of a complete and satisfactory system by popular vote.*

The following papers were then read :

"The Competitive Plan in the Filling of Offices of the Higher Grades." by Silas W. Burt, of New York; †

" Civil Service Reform as a Factor in Municipal Reform," by Clinton Rogers Woodruff, of Philadelphia; read by Mr. R. Francis Wood.

On motion the League then adjourned.

GERMAN HOUSE, December 15, 1899, 10 A. M.

The League reconvened at 10 o'clock.

The business in order being the annual election of officers. The President called Gen. Aiken to the chair.

Mr. Vaughan, of Massachusetts, for the Nominating Committee, reported the nomination of Hon. Carl Schurz as President for the ensuing year, and moved that the Secretary be instructed to cast the vote of the League for the re-election of

---

* Page 69. † Page 52.

Mr. Schurz. The motion was seconded by various members, and carried unanimously. The Secretary cast the ballot, and Mr. Schurz was declared elected. After a brief address, in which Mr. Schurz expressed the hope that the work of the League will prove as prosperous in the future as it has in the past, he resumed the chair.

On motion of Mr. Vaughan, the Secretary was instructed to cast one ballot for the re-election for one year of the present Vice-Presidents, as follows:

Charles Francis Adams, Boston; Augustus R. Mac-Donough, New York; Rt. Rev. Henry C. Potter, New York; J. Hall Pleasants, Baltimore; Henry Hitchcock, St. Louis; Henry Charles Lea, Philadelphia; Franklin McVeagh, Chicago; Most Rev. P. H. Ryan, Philadelphia; William Potts, New York.

The Secretary cast the ballot, and the gentlemen named were declared elected.

The President announced that Col. J. W. Ela, who had been absent during the order of reports for local associations, at the session of yesterday, would now submit the report for Chicago. Col. Ela reported as follows:

"There are encouraging features in the condition of civil service reform in Chicago this year, although these features relate rather to the recognition of the principle than to its practical operation.

"The Democratic party, which, last fall, lost the county election on a platform which—probably for the first time in the history of the reform—specifically demanded a repeal of the civil service law, was remarkably successful this spring in the city election on a platform which specifically endorsed the civil service law and declared it to be a necessity. This six months' conversion was probably too young to account for the entire increase in the Democratic vote, but many influential citizens, of both parties supported that ticket on account of its new attitude towards the reform, and with the expectation that its success would mean definite, aggressive action against the hungry crowd which hangs on the skirts of every local administration and tempts even the most conscientious official into an "easy" construction of the law.

"This administration has done much towards fulfilling the promise of the platform. The Mayor has surrounded himself with an excellent cabinet—composed of the heads of the principal departments. The Comptroller, Corporation Counsel and Commissioner of Public Works (the latter being the head of the largest and most difficult department) strongly favor the merit system and its effective execution. With such men as these in control of a large part of the city's work there ought to be no question about the faithful execution of this law.

" The Corporation Counsel supported the law and the Civil Service Commission, when he was alderman, and the several opinions relating to the law which have come from that office since his appointment have uniformly sustained it, and given a liberal construction to the sections submitted in time to secure their enforcement. It might seem as if there would be little room for a lawyer's personal prejudice in his consideration of a question of law ; but we are having an experience in Chicago of how the opinions of honest lawyers may differ according to the attitude in which they approach the question.

" It is only fair to say, however, that some of the friends of the city administration are not quite satisfied. They complain that there is not that vigorous execution of details which the promise of the platform led them to expect. But the administration is young. There is yet time.

"Complaints have been made to the Chicago Civil Service Reform Association, since the passage of the County Civil Service Act, regarding the execution of that act. The Association appointed a committee to investigate, and it appears from their report that the committee found that the enforcement of this county law, at certain times, has been far from satisfactory.

"This County law covers only a portion of the county service, including, however, the County Hospital. It was passed at the same session of the Legislature at which the city law was passed, and after the passage of the city law, and the provisions of the two laws are practically the same. The reason for not including the entire county service in this county law was, that under the State constitution a special act could be passed covering the institutions under the control of the Cook County Commissioners ; whereas in order to cover all the county institutions in that county it would have been necessary to pass a general act, including all the counties in the State, or all of a certain class, or all which should adopt the act ; and it was too late in the session to pass such an act, even if it could have been passed at all. As there was a bill pending, and at its second reading, regulating these special Cook county institutions, it was thought best to add the civil service provisions by way of amendment. In this manner an opportunity was furnished to test the application of the merit system to county institutions, with the hope that if successful a bill might be passed later applying it to all counties in the State.

"Cook County includes Chicago and several townships outside the city. The Republicans have had the county government ever since the passage of the civil service acts. The city government has been in the hands of the Democrats for something over two years. I know of no ethical standard by which to balance the blame between two parties, one of which talked loudly—in its platforms and otherwise—of its devotion to a law which—the Committee says—it was slack in enforcing, while the other demanded its repeal and—the first party says—was also slack in its enforcement. At all events there is nothing in such a situation to weaken the faith of the civil service reformers in that essential article of their creed—' Put not your trust in politicians.' "

At the invitation of the President, Mr. Charles B. Fowler,

of Albany, Chief Examiner of the New York State Civil Service Commission, addressed the League with reference to the present methods of conducting examinations in the New York service.

Mr. Welsh, of Philadelphia, for the Special Investigating Committee, read the draft of a proposed report on the condition of the Indian Service under the administration of President McKinley. Mr. Bonaparte moved that the report be accepted and referred back to the Investigating Committee with power to publish with such revision, if any, as they may deem necessary. The motion was carried.

Mr. Foulke, of Indiana, for the Committee on Resolutions, reported the general resolutions on the state of the reform, prepared in accordance with annual custom, for the League's consideration. General Aiken moved that the resolutions as read be considered *seriatim*, and the motion was carried. The resolutions were re-read, and, after slight amendment, adopted unanimously in the following form:

I. The League regards the order issued by the President on the 29th of May last, withdrawing several thousand places from the classified service and relaxing the rules intended to prevent evasions of the law, as the first unmistakable backward step taken by a Federal Administration since the Civil Service Law was passed. The injurious effects of this order have already been seen ; in the demoralization of many parts of the Federal service ; in the encouragement of the enemies of reform in their efforts to cripple the merit system and secure a further relaxation of the rules ; and in widespread distrust of the promises of the President and the party in power to enforce and extend the Civil Service Law.

Specific illustrations of these effects are set forth in the reports of our Special Committees.

II. The League believes that grave injury has also been done to the merit system by the unnecessary exemption of large classes of positions, under the War Emergency Acts, from the requirements of competitive examination.

III. We regret that the pledge of the party in power to extend the Civil Service Law wherever practicable, has not been observed in regard to the Census Bureau, either by the requirements of the law authorizing the census, or by executive action in the choice of a director willing to employ competitive methods in the appointment of his subordinates.

We believe that the retention of patronage in this Bureau will result as in the case of the last census ; in increased wastefulness and inefficiency ; in the demoralization of the force employed ; in the diminished value of the census so taken ; and in the lack of public confidence in its accuracy and impartiality.

IV. We also regret that the President has not yet fulfilled the assurances given by him to a Committee of the League of his intention to include in the classified service a much larger number of places than those withdrawn, but on the contrary has included none whatever. We venture to hope that such extensions may yet be made at no distant day.

V. The inefficiency and the recurrence of scandals in the Indian Service can be removed only by withdrawing the office of Indian Agent from the sphere of Congressional patronage. Although the appointment of such agents is subject to the confirmation by the Senate, the President has full power to devise for his own guidance a suitable system of competitive examinations and promotions for such places. The clerical force of the Indian Service itself would supply many excellent men for the higher post of Indian Agent, and from the ranks of agents the inspectorships might often be filled.

The restoration of all the places in that branch of the service accepted from classification by the recent order is especially necessary in the public interest. It cannot be too often repeated that the spoils system has proved the bane of the Indian service.

VI. Experience has emphasized the necessity for a reform thorough radical and complete in the Consular Service, and we ask of Congress such appropriate legislation and of the President (until this legislation be obtained) such reasonable rules for his own guidance in appointments as will secure us a service worthy of the country. and able to promote intelligently our vast and varied commercial interests.

VII. It is beyond the province of the League to pass upon the rightfulness or wisdom of territorial extension, but we demand that if any lands be brought under our dominion, public office therein be consistently treated as a trust to be administered for the sole benefit of their inhabitants. To abuse the public service of dependent provinces, in the interest of American parties or politicians, would constitute a crime against civilization and humanity, disgraceful to our Republic. As a safeguard against this shame and calamity. we urge that in the organization of any government, which may be established in such territory, adequate provision be made for a non-partisan service recruited through open competition and assured of promotion through merit and of continued employment during good behavior and efficiency. The President alone, without additional legislation. has the authority to make all reasonable regulations for executive appointments

VIII. We ask Congress to remove the legislative restriction upon the consolidation of post offices, to the end that the department may apply the merit system to minor offices, wherever practicable, by making them branches of larger offices, and filling them from the clerical force therein. The withdrawal of fourth class postmasterships from patronage would remove one of the most formidable remaining bulwarks of the spoils system.

IX. The League rejoices in the substantial progress made in civil service reform in the State of New York. by the passage of an effective reform law, and heartily commends Governor Roosevelt for his distinguished public service in aiding to restore the merit system which had been seriously impaired by his predecessor. The League expresses its satisfaction at the action of Governor Wolcott. of Massachusetts, in extending the classified service, and in resisting the insidious attempt made to cripple the merit system in that State.

We also rejoice in the renewed evidences of public interest in civil service reform. This interest is as clearly manifested by the general regret and dissatisfaction which has followed the President's order of May 29, as it was shown in the general approval which had greeted his previous order forbidding removals from the classified service except for stated cause.

We confidently rely upon public opinion to effect the ultimate extension of the merit system to all branches of our National, State and Municipal government.

Mr. Wilby, for the Auditing Committee, submitted the following report which, on motion, was received and ordered filed:

To the National Civil Service Reform League :

The undersigned, constituting the Auditing Committee, appointed by the Executive Committee, have examined and compared the accounts and vouchers of the Treasurer* and find them to be correct, and that the balance reported on hand on December 14. 1899, is $56.17.

Respectfully submitted,

CHAS. B. WILBY,
R. FRANCIS WOOD.

The Secretary, for the Special Committee on the organization of the Census Bureau, reported that copies of the report on the unfortunate results of the taking of the Eleventh Census by a force selected under the patronage system, and setting forth the arguments in favor of the adoption of the competitive merit plan in organizing the present force, had been sent to members of Congress and to the press, and that every effort had been made to secure favorable action in both the Senate and House of Representatives. The Census bill had been passed, however, after a deliberate rejection of the plan proposed, and provision had been made for the appointment of supervisors, statisticians and other clerical employees by the Director, after such examination only as he may prescribe. The President had appointed as Director, Ex-Governor Merriam, of

---

* Page 50.

Minnesota, a selection understood to have been made for political reasons. Ten thousand applications for clerkships had been received. The Civil Service Commission had offered the services of its Examining Boards for the holding of examinations for these but its offer had not been accepted. On the contrary, under the system adopted only those applicants endorsed by Members of Congress were admitted to examination, and such examinations as were held were of the non-competitive, or "pass" order merely. The Secretary read a letter from the Director of the Census, with reference to this practice, as follows:

CENSUS OFFICE, WASHINGTON, D. C., Oct. 19, 1899.

GEORGE MCANENY, ESQ.,
    Secretary National Civil Service Reform League.

MY DEAR SIR:
    Please pardon the delay in replying to your esteemed communication of October 7, regarding the question of the selection of a clerical force to carry on the work of this Bureau.
    I desire to state that, in accordance with the law, as understood by the writer, I was authorized to prescribe such methods of examination as would result in securing a proper force to perform all the duties connected with the census work. A system of examinations was devised, under the immediate charge of the Assistant Director, and in April regular examinations were commenced in this city, which were practically open to all who applied. It soon became evident, however, that it would be impracticable to make them competitive as it would be impossible to secure in the short time allowed for the selection of this force, a sufficient number of clerks to do the work, owing to the large number who would likely apply for the privilege of examination.*
    The law requires that the four general subjects mentioned in the Census Act shall be completed within two (2) years, and it would take nearly all that time to examine all who have applied for positions. The system was, therefore, adopted, of selecting persons for examination from the different states and territories, based on the apportionment plan now in use by the Civil Service Commission. Thus far, nearly two thousand people have been examined: of these about fifty per cent. have been successful in passing the examination. We now have an eligible list of about one thousand clerks. Examinations are being conducted in differ-

---

* The following is the form of letter addressed to applicants for examination under the plan adopted:

CENSUS OFFICE, Washington, D. C., Aug. 12, 1899.
DEAR SIR:
    In accordance with the instructions of the Director of the Census, I return herewith your application for a position in the Census Office.
    In selecting the force for this office, the Director has decided to

ent cities in the West and South, with a view to increasing the eligible list to about two thousand clerks.

In this connection, I may add that selection of persons to take the examination are made from the various political parties, namely, Republicans, Democrats and Populists.

The main question, after all, is the selection of a competent clerical force to carry on the prescribed work within the allotted time. Reports have been received from the Chief of Statistics and Division Chiefs that the clerks so far selected have proven to be thoroughly efficient. In view of the fact that the plan as outlined above has proceeded satisfactorily so far, it is not deemed advisable to make any change.

.Very respectfully,
W. R. MERRIAM, Director.

In conclusion, the Secretary reported for the Committee that, while it might undertake further correspondence with Director Merriam, it had no definite plan now in view beyond the publication of the facts.

The Secretary submitted copies of two open letters addressed by him to the Secretary of the Treasury in July last, with reference to the review of the President's order of May 29, published by the League, together with a letter of Secretary Gage replying to the first of these, addressed to the League, under date of July 14.

---

make an allotment to each State and Territory of an equitable proportion of the appointments, and then to make a subdivision among the Congressional Districts ; and as the Senators and Representatives of the various States and Districts are more familiar with the qualifications of persons residing therein than the Director of the Census, it has been decided to ask them to furnish the names only of such persons as they desire to be examined for positions in the Census Bureau ; who, should they pass successfully and are appointed, are to be accredited to the Senator or Representative so recommending them, and charged to his quota. It is for this reason that I return your application, with the information that it will not be received for filing unless accompanied by the request of a Senator or Representative in accordance with the foregoing statement. After such recommendations are received by this office the persons so recommended will be given a practical examination to determine their fitness for the work.

Examinations will be held in various parts of the country next fall for the purpose above indicated. You will please be kind enough to communicate with the Representative or one of the Senators from your State on the subject of your application.

Respectfully yours,
A. F. CHILDS,
Chief Clerk.

Mr. Bonaparte moved that this correspondence be referred to the Special Investigating Committee and that the Committee be authorized to make such further reply to the Secretary of the Treasury as they may deem necessary. The motion was carried.

Mr. Foulke moved that the League approve and adopt, as its own acts, the letters of the Secretary in the correspondence referred to, and the motion was carried.

On motion the session then adjourned.

GERMAN HOUSE, December 15, 2 P. M.

The League reconvened at two o'clock.

Mr. Bonaparte, of Maryland, read a paper entitled "The Spoils System in the Government of Dependencies."*

The Secretary, for the Special Investigating Committee, read the preliminary draft of a report on the Scope and Effect of the President's order of May 29, as evidenced by the operation of the civil service rules, as altered, since that date. Mr. Bonaparte moved that the report be referred back to the Investigating Committee with authority to publish after such revision as it may deem necessary, and the motion was carried.

Col. Ela called the attention of the League to the fact that the movement for reform in the Consular Service has been given a new impetus through the action of the Cleveland Chamber of Commerce, the National Business League, and other bodies of like character, in proposing legislation for adoption at the present session of Congress. He suggested that a special committee be appointed to represent the League in this matter. After some discussion, Mr. Wood, of Pennsylvania, moved that the President be authorized to appoint a committee, the number of which he shall determine, to take whatever action may be necessary, in co-operation with the business and commercial organizations at present moving for the reform of the Consular Service, and at such times and in such manner as may be desired by them. The motion was carried.

Mr. Dana, of Massachusetts, for the Special Committee on Superanuation in the Civil Service, made an informal report, stating that the Committee is directing its inquiries towards

* Page 60

discovering (1) whether it is not the fact that the evils resulting from superanuation, especially in the case of employees appointed under the civil service rules, have not been greatly exaggerated, and, (2) whether these evils, if they exist, do not belong less to the reformed civil service system than they do to the " spoils system " under which political influence has served to retain those unfit for efficient performance of duty. On motion the report was accepted.

Mr. Welsh, of Pennsylvania, moved that the report of a former committee on the violations of law in appointments and removals in the Philadelphia Post-office under the present administration be included among those published by the Investigating Committee, and the motion was carried.

Mr. Wilby, of Ohio, moved that the thanks of the League be extended to the ladies of the German Club for the generous hospitality extended by them to the members and visiting delegates, and the motion was carried unanimously.

General Aiken, of Connecticut, moved that the thanks of the League be extended also to the Indiana Civil Service Reform Association, the University Club, the German Club and the Trustees of Plymouth Church, for the entertainment and many courtesies received from these bodies, and from their members, during the course of the present meeting, and the motion wascarried unanimously.

The League then adjourned.

    Attest: GEORGE MCANENY,
                     Secretary.

On the evening of Thursday, the 14th, a reception to the members of the League and visiting delegates was given by the University Club of Indianapolis, the Honorable Benjamin Harrison, President of the club, receiving. On the afternoon of Friday the members were entertained at luncheon at the German House by the ladies of the German Club. On the evening of Friday a banquet was given at the Bates House, by the Civil Service Reform Association of Indiana, at which Lucius B. Swift, of Indianapolis, President of the Association, presided, and addresses were made by Carl Schurz, of New York, Charles J. Bonaparte, of Maryland, Sherman S. Rogers, of Buffalo, W. P. Fishback, of Indiana, and Herbert Welsh, of Pennsylvania.

ANNUAL REPORT OF THE TREASURER.

Balance on hand, Dec. 15, 1898, ... $62.57

RECEIPTS :

Subscriptions from New York Association...	$1,480.00	
" " Philadelphia " ...	540.00	
" " Massachusetts, Misc. ...	380.00	
" Cambridge Association...	200.00	
" Chicago " ...	125.00	
" Cincinnati " ...	100.00	
" Washington " ...	100.00	
" Baltimore " ...	75.00	
' Buffalo " ...	70.00	
" Pamphlets sold..........	1.84	3,071.84

$3,134.41

DISBURSEMENTS :

Salary of Secretary........................	$1,437.50	
Clerk hire.....	699.77	
Rent of office...........................	50.00	
Printing...............	556.95	
Postage and stamped envelopes............	124.75	
Traveling expenses......................	90.15	
Office expenses, miscellaneous.............	89.12	
Washington Agent......................	30.00	3,078.24

Balance on hand, December 14, 1899................... $ 56.17

E. & O. E.

(Signed) A. S. FRISSELL,

Treasurer.

The Competitive Plan in the Filling of Offices of the Higher Grades.

By Silas W. Burt.

IT has often been remarked that the question of civil service reform differs in one respect from the other political questions that have engaged the attention of our people—it neither touches closely their business interests, nor appeals to sentiment or passion. Its economical aspects, in the reduced expenses of government, and its moral significance, seem remote to the average citizen, whose practical contact with the civil service may be limited to the letter-carrier. It has, however, the great advantage of simplicity, and when it engages popular attention its reasonableness and conformity with the organic principles of our government invariably persuade and convert. Because it has seemed remote in importance, its growth has been slow, as compared with other policies more sensational or affecting material interests, but unexposed to the tempests of popular passion or selfishness, it has become so well rooted that even the spoilsmen confess, "that it has come to stay." I do not believe that any question of national policy is to-day so firmly established as this, and though in the violent contention as to other policies the merit system may have its vicissitudes, it cannot be overthrown and on it must finally rest our political administrative fabric, now existing or whenever to be constructed.

There remains one contention of the adherents of the patronage doctrine, shared, too, by some timid friends of the merit system—and that is that selection by open competition is applicable only to the lower grades, and must be a failure when extended to the higher ones. This means that merit and fitness for these superior positions cannot be ascertained by civil service examinations, and consequently must remain the prey of the spoilsmen. We do not believe this, for incontestible reasons, but, were it true, the value of our reform idea and methods would be comparatively inconsiderable. The successful development of the merit system has been an evolutionary process; a constant advance from simple and primitive types to more complex and higher ones—a process that by natural growth is healthy and ensures permanent results.

In the first application of the reform system to the United States service in 1871, the attempt was made to apply forthwith competitive methods to the whole subordinate civil service below the heads of departments and their chiefs of division. This was more than could be accomplished by the inadequate and untrained agencies at hand, and it was also far in advance of any sustaining public sentiment, as was soon revealed by experience, and a retreat from such an untenable position was in progress when the rules were suspended in 1875. Mr. Eaton, who at that time was Chairman of the Commission, fully recognized these restraining conditions, and the law of 1883, in the framing of which he took a leading part, provided that the initiatory application should be limited. The law of New York, enacted three months later, was constructed on the same general lines, but in neither law was there any prohibition of extension to the whole subordinate service, and such extension has been gradually progressive for a decade.

The positions which are here gathered under the general term "superior," differ in their requirements, which in the aggregate may be said to demand every kind of qualification.

These higher positions may be considered under several classes—the first of which comprehends those places found in all departments and offices where several or many persons are employed in identical or cognate and related duties, and which offices are generally organized in separate divisions under chief clerks, not only charged with the discipline of the force under them, but also with the decisions of questions arising in the work of that force, and in some cases with communication with that part of the public directly interested in it. Such positions demand all the qualifications for entrance to the lower grades and a knowledge of the laws, decisions and procedure governing the business, together with a certain executive ability. It is obvious that these positions can be best filled by promotion of those most fit in the lower grades in the office, and this rule applies to all the ascending positions below the head, in those great departments having a highly organized and complex structure. Often the requisite information and skill can be acquired only in the office itself, but if none of the subordinates have fitted themselves by such acquirement, the position can be filled by an open competition, with confidence that the higher dignity and compensation of the position will attract those capable of soon mastering the specific requirements. Such a necessity would be rare, since the rule of promotion by offering the opportunity for an honorable career to fit and meritorious persons, these would be induced to compete for entrance to the lower positions, and constitute a safe reserve from which to draw. In opening such positions to outside competition, the qualification questioned by cavillers would be that of executive ability, concerning which more will be said later.

The second class comprehends the positions demanding professional, scientific or expert attainments, and these are numerous in the ever increasing functions of government, and cover every branch of human knowledge. In the test of qualifications for these positions, the open competitive examinations have been invariably successful in obtaining eligible lists of qualified persons. The requisite knowledge and ability is so precisely defined, that its absolute and relative possession can be estimated with closer approximation to the truth than in any other class of positions. It has been said that men eminent in their profession or science would not enter a competition, but this has been proven not to be by any means an invariable rule, and furthermore it has been found that these highly qualified persons usually find no attraction in the meagre compensation paid by the government for abilities that command a high price in the business world. There might be cases where some person of recognized rare ability would be willing to serve the government, but not submit to examination—such as a renowned geologist or professor of international law. The New York civil service law provides that in such cases examination may be waived, but such exceptions must be reported to the Legislature at its next session, with reasons therefor. The number of such exceptions in the three years during which this rule has existed have been twelve.

The scope of these professional and expert positions in

the United States service has been broad, and at the risk of being tedious I will mention some for which successful competive examinations have been held for the New York State service within the last three years.

In the State hospitals, houses of refuge and all other charitable and corrective institutions:

> Superintendents.
> Physicians of all grades.
> Stewards.
> Apothecaries.

In the Pathological Institute:

> Associates severally in—
> Pathology,
> Anthropology,
> Psychology,
> Physiological Chemistry,
> Bacteriology,
> Biology,
> Comparative Neurology.

Assistants to the State Entomologist and the State Paleontologist:

In the Agricultural Departments:

> Assistant Commissioner,
> Bacteriologists,
> Station Editor and Librarian,
> Chemists,
> Milk, Butter, Cheese and Vinegar Experts,
> Inspectors of Veal and of Bees.

Under the Railroad Commission:

> Superintendent of Grade Crossings,
> Bridge Designer and Inspector,
> Electrical Expert.

Department of Public Works:

> Inspectors of Boilers, Bridges, Masonry,
> and other constructive work.

Every kind of Teachers, Inspectors of Teachers' Institutes and also of compulsory education. Examiners for Teachers' Licenses. Superintendents of Prison Industries, including Cabinet Making, Cloth Making, Knitting, Goodyear shoewares and School Furniture. Law Clerks in the various offices, including the important one of Statutory Revision Commissioners. Examiners of State Banks. Architects,

Civil, Electrical and Mechanical Engineers, and Interpreters of the score of European and Asiatic tongues spoken by immigrants into our country.

This by no means exhausts the variety of these high and special positions, but is fairly indicative of their range and character.

It may be noted here that entrance to examinations for all high grade positions is guarded by certain reasonable antecedent conditions; if the position is professional, the applicant must have been especially educated for such profession, and admitted to its practice in accordance with law, and in some cases have been a practioner for a certain period; if it is a position of scientific requirement much the same evidence must be produced—if it is a position requiring no such educational preparation the applicant must show such business training and experience as would fit him to discharge the duties of the position; in the latter case, however, these qualifications may be relatively estimated in the examination itself, and have due weight in its final results. Through this preliminary wicket only those presumptively fit can enter, with consequent economy in the cost of examination and in disappointment through failure.

We come now to the third class of positions concerning which the opponents of competitive examinations are most insistent as to their impracticability—in fact generally so insistent that they comprehend in it about every position not menial. Of course, I refer to the so-called confidential positions. Those who have had any part in the administration of civil service laws realize that the term " confidential " is the most elastic adjective in the vocabulary, and generally is intended to rival charity in covering a multitude of sins. The number of positions classed as confidential is being almost constantly diminished on the roster of the United States service, and the same may be said of that of New York. There is scarcely a trace of real confidential relations in the public service—it is *public* service in all senses, and only the highest executive officers and the judicial officers have any need of a confidential subordinate. The best test of the sincerity of these professions as to confidential relations is found in the occasional revelations as to the method of selecting those alleged to be charged with them when the positions are exempt from examinations. Not long ago, in a new classification of

subordinate, irascible or insolent, or who is uncleanly or a drunkard, or addicted to any phase of gross immorality.

I may appear to have wandered from the exact limits of my subject, but all the qualifications to be secured and the disqualifactions to be excluded that have been mentioned apply with larger force to the higher positions. So far as character and habits are concerned, the civil service method of securing what is desired and excluding what is unfit differs in no respect from what obtains in private concerns. It is the ascertainment of a man's reputation and traits as known by those acquainted with him—to use a somewhat perverted term in these days it is his "record" as verified by competent authority. The law of competitive examination is in some fields quite as potent as that of the survival of the fittest. We are all being estimated as to our moral qualities by those we are in contact with, and in the competition our average and relative standing on the eligible list—if one may talk "shop" here—is almost invaribly correct.

A perfectly unrestrained appointing officer desirious of getting a fit subordinate would verify, so far as he could, the reputation of the man to be selected, and this is the method of the merit system. One has no more advantage in this than the other, except that a formal certification by citizens, who know that their vouchers will remain permanently on file as a public record, carries an impressive significance of responsi-bility. In the New York State service, in cases of more than usual importance, these vouchers are supplemented by compre-hensive and searching inquiries addressed to all the parties to whom reference has been made in any connection by the applicant.

The supposititious independent official is confined to a nar-row range in his selection, and is apt to have a single aspirant in his eye, whose personality is agreeable to him, and whose qualifications he honestly believes are sufficient—in fact he very often builds up the necessary qualifications upon those he believes this aspirant to possess. The merit system opens the place to all citizens having the preliminary quaifications of citizenship, residence, age, etc., and bestows it upon one of these who has demonstrated in the highest degree his merit and fitness.

Now—no matter what may be the requirements of the position—I assert that their possessors can be obtained at least quite as readily by the latter method as by the former, and with due regard, furthermore, to the civic privileges of every citizen concerned, and if this be correct this assertion has redoubled force as regards the appointment by officials who in fact do not select, and this includes nearly all of them.

This assertion is fully borne out by the experience in New York State, where positions of a high grade, some of them mentioned before, have been filled by open competition, and all of the appointees have not only passed their probationary terms but have rendered such satisfactory service that not one has been dismissed. Among them have been superintendents of great hospitals for the insane, with inmates ranging in number from 500 to 7,000 each, and whose executive functions are of the highest importance and cover a great range of duties; bank examiners, who have the examination of all the assets, accounts, liabilities and records of the State banks, with aggregate liabilities of over $300,000,000, a function confidential in the very highest sense; stewards of institutions who purchase and dispense supplies of various kinds of millions in value annually; physicians, to whom are committed the decrepit, imbecile and insane wards of the State, inspectors of and teachers in every handicraft, engineers and architects, and scientists. Does not this experience prove that the higher grades of positions in the civil service can be filled successfully by open competition? Furthermore, does it not prove that equal success would attend the application of the same method to all the subordinate service, local, state and national—to the consular service and to such subordinate positions outside the United States as must be filled by its citizens?

I hope you will agree with me in an affirmative answer to these queries. But such a result cannot be attained at once. As heretofore, the development of the merit system must be slow and deliberate so as to make it sure. The varied requirements of the higher positions impose careful ascertainment of the proper prerequisite conditions and of the scope and methods of the competitive tests. Experience shows that a gradual and judicious extension will be sustained by an appreciative public sentiment so that competitive selection may safely occupy the indicated field, and our contention that admission to the subordinate civil service shall be governed by fixed rules, demanding the ascertainment of the highest fitness and merit attainable by tests open to every citizen, will be fully justified.

The Spoils System in the Government of Dependencies.

By Charles J. Bonaparte.

President Kruger is accredited with a prophecy that the price paid for his country's subjugation "will make humanity shudder." If he said this he doubtless should have known whereof he spoke, but I am happy to say I think him mistaken: what may be the destined end of the present struggle in South Africa no man may know; if it lead to an extension of British dominion, this will have certainly cost many lives and much blood, but, so far as there is any reason to believe, only the lives of fighting men and only the blood spilt in fair fight. To see soldiers slain by other soldiers in open strife is a grim reminder of this life's realities, but to my mind, no just cause for "shuddering." This war, like every other, will claim its meed of tears and heartaches, will add another to the unnumbered proofs in human experience

"That man was made to mourn,"

but again, like every other, its outcome, whatever this may be will also prove that he was not made only to mourn or to mourn forever. I am not among those who believe that to kill a man is always the least profitable use to which he can be put; many a life, neither useful nor edifying in itself, has so ended as to leave a well-spring of encouragement to all who would think the better of their kind, a heritage of just pride to all that bear the name of one who, indeed, lived as a fool and a prodigal, but died facing his country's foes.

"Know well, when, in some well fought fight
Stout warriors heed their fate's stern call,
They fall like shooting stars at night
That brighten as they fall."

But I see a grave danger least the Twentieth Century furnish to the World a spectacle whereat, in very truth, "humanity" may well shudder," the spectacle of the great American republic holding by the sword a vast vassal empire peopled by dumb, helpless millions of the East and placing over them as rulers those among its own citizens who are universally and unhesitatingly deemed and dealt with as the least worthy of respect or confidence in any of the relations of private life, in other words, the creatures of our "Bosses" and the satellites of our "Rings." Soon after the protocol which ended hostilities with Spain had been signed, I expressed to an enterprising representative of the Press who solicited my "views" on things in general and the results of the war in particular, my alarm and disgust at the prospect that poor, half-civilized Malays should be turned over to the tender mercies of such men as the members of our, then recently dethroned, "Ring" in Maryland or the worthies of the "Anti-Civil Service League," which, just at that time, was rather aggressively malodorous. To one of the most prominent newspapers in the country these sentiments seemed to imply a gross injustice to the American people, and I was asked, in substance, to say when we had failed to deal worthily with any burden imposed on us by Providence in the past, and why I entertained such calumnious fears for the future : it may be well for me now to answer these questions.

As a nation we have twice had committed to us duties which bear some measure of analogy to that apparently awaiting us to-day, although in neither case was the inherent difficulty of the task nearly so great. In 1865 we ruled as conquerors a large part of our own land, inhabited partly by white men of the same blood and speeeh as ourselves, partly by black men from whom we had just stricken the shackles of slavery. We had the strongest motives to wish well to both races, the most evident and cogent reasons, in our own interest no less than in theirs, to provide them, at a period so momentously critical for both, with the purest, most impartial and most provident government which the wit of man might devise. It were indeed a calumny to question our good will : the torrents of blood poured out on the battlefield in our Civil War were followed by no drop shed on the scaffold ; we had fought with our brethren only to compel them to remain our brothers ; for a brief season we ruled them by force only that, as soon as might be, they should again bear their share in ruling us. But, alas! to obtain these ends, we could do, or at least we did, no better than to turn them over to a Congress made up of our professional politicians, that these might turn them over to the carpet-baggers.

From the organization of our Federal Government the several Indian Tribes have been recognized as wards of the Nation: there can be no reasonable doubt that their welfare, civilization and conversion to Christianity have been always, and are now, sincerely and earnestly desired by the immense majority of the American people; and, whilst there has been often room for no little difference of opinion as to the wisdom of our Indian policy, in purpose, this has been consistently just and humane. Yet, with all these good intentions to pave our pathway to the goal, we have had "a Century of Dishonor", a long, dreary record of scandals and broken faith, of chronic injustice, oppression and perfidy in our public officers, of barbarous vengeance again and again wreaked on a devastated frontier, of all the bloodshed, suffering and outrages of periodic savage warfare. Why has all this been? Simply because for a century we entrusted the Western red man, as we entrusted the Southern white man and the Southern black man, when, for a brief season, these also were in our power, to those people who in our country make office hunting a profession, under the name of "politics", and they acted after their kind.

Is it then unreasonable for one who remembers the days of Reconstruction, who knows what manner of men have been chosen for Indian Agents or Inspectors of Agencies as well by a Democratic President in the past as by a Republican President of to-day, when the political patrons of such men, patrons who have risen to prominence and gained power through their unscrupulous service and need this none the less for the future, can reward them with opportunities to fatten leech-like upon hapless folk beyond the seas, is it, I say, unreasonable to fear that we may see again what we have too often seen already? Even if we had no special experience thus to mirror what may lie before us, would not a mere glance at our own *real* rulers, at Tammany and Tammany's pupils and rivals in our cities, at those dirty hands drawing the strings which move official puppets in our National and State governments, would not such a glance reveal to any thoughtful man the shadow of our impending disgrace and danger ? For, recollect well, the carpet-bagger pro-consul in our future subject provinces will find himself in a veritable land of promise for his ends. Major Chesney, after pointing out that, under the patronage system of appointment practised by the East India Company, an unfit official would occasionally, though rarely, obtain an important administrative or judicial position, says of the results :

"How mischievous might be a man in such a post will be understood when it is considered that a district officer was practically, in many cases, removed from all personal supervision ; that public opinion has no expression in these parts ; and that all that could be known of his proceedings was to be found in his own reports made to official superiors belonging to the same body with himself. In the case of a judge, indeed, the evil was experienced in greatest intensity only by the suitors at his Court ; but it would be difficult to measure the extent of the mischief which might be wrought, by placing an idle or incompetent magistrate in charge of an Indian district with its million or more of people." (Chesney's Indian Polity, page 223.)

This is said of a supposed " English gentleman," of one " in whom," to use the words of the author, " the power of indolence or deficiency of intelligence will be too strong to overcome," but whose integrity is not questioned, of one "idle or incompetent," but never dishonorable or selfseeking, and of one, be it remembered, assured of permanent employment on liberal pay and of a generous retiring pension. Put in the same position a choice specimen of the American blackguard, an outcast from some honorable profession or an adept in some shameful and noxious industry, as destitute of reputation as of conscience, with no certainty of tenure, owing his post to the favor of another of his class of greater influence but no greater worth than himself, expecting and expected to make out of the " pickings " of his office all it can possibly yield him in the very few years to elapse before he must give it up to a successor of the like kind, and suppose this to be, not, as in the India of fifty years ago, a rare and exceptional misfortune, but the normal condition of affairs throughout a wide dominion, possibly an immense empire; suppose all this, and, with the mind's eye, you will see that your children, possibly yourself, may yet see in fact, you will feel in thought the chill of conscience foreshadowing a shame and iniquity whereof their children may feel the judgment. For, believe me, no community of men has done or can do such wrong to their fellow-men, to their own better nature, to the Divine Law and the eternal principles of right and justice, with permanent impunity.

> "The gathered guilt of elder times
> Shall reproduce itself in crimes :
> There is a day of vengeance still,
> Linger it may. but come it will."

"Well! what are you going to do about it?" I think this is a fair question: I think it demands an answer, and an answer here and now. This is not, indeed, the place, nor is it my intention, to deal with one phase of the problem: I do not ask here if, in very truth, we must drain this chalice of Eastern sovereignty; for my present purposes, I *assume* that we must, or, at least, that we will; and, on this assumption, I avow my belief that, unless we first find and apply a remedy for the loathsome disease of our body politic wherewith we have so long paltered, we shall then drink a deadly poison. But I also believe no search needful to find this remedy: it lies open to our gaze, ready to our hand; have we the common sense and candor to own its need, the civic courage to use it? 'Therein lies the doubt.

The Century so soon to end has witnessed the profoundly interesting experiment of a vast Oriental empire governed by a free, Christian people of Western Europe, and, for any unbiased mind, the fruit of this experiment must be counted, beyond doubt or cavil, a prodigious advancement for humanity. It may be worth a moment's pause to point out what the British rule in India has meant for all the tribes and races of men inhabiting that land of well nigh continental bounds.

India is, roughly speaking, about as populous and about one-half as large as all Europe: from this huge territory and its teeming millions (nearly one-sixth of the inhabitants of the Earth) British dominion has banished war and famine, chronic misgovernment and oppression, perpetual, or perpetually recurring, pestilence, cruel and degrading superstitions bred of dense and universal ignorance. The increase in the country's wealth may be fairly called phenomenal: in 1834 the value of its sea borne trade was, in round numbers, seventy millions of dollars, in 1840 one hundred millions, in 1857 two hundred and seventy-five millions, in 1877 five hundred and seventy millions, in 1887 eight hundred and fifteen millions, in 1897 nine hundred and ninety four millions. Its material progress may be, in some sort, measured by the growth of its railway system, commenced only in 1853, embracing fourteen thousand miles in 1888 and extending to twenty-one thousand miles ten years later; or of its telegraph lines, first constructed in 1850, reaching eighty-two thousand miles in 1886, amounting to one hundred and forty-eight thousand miles in 1897, or by the expenditure of more than one hundred and fifty millions of dollars by the Government alone on productive works of irrigation within the past fifty years. The progress of the people in industry and education, in physical health and well being, in an enlightened morality and in consequent energy and happiness, are less readily shown by statistics, but no less indisputable and gratifying; to show this development in civilization, perhaps as fair and adequate a test as any readily available is the increase in the number of post offices from 753 in 1856 to 27,000 in 1898, and of the parcels carried by post from thirty-eight millions in the former to four hundred and fifty millions in the latter year.

Of this great work of beneficence and regeneration, at once the author and the instrument has been the Indian Civil Service; that body of trained public servants has made British India what it is to-day out of what it was a century since: the extraordinary prosperity of the country has been the legitimate fruit of their exceptional merit. In the words of the author I have already quoted:

" That, on the whole, the members of the civil administration of India, so far as their individual exertions are concerned, have been extraordinarily successful ; that they have been distinguished, not only for perfect integrity, but, with rare exceptions, for a high degree of zeal, industry, and public spirit ; that a large proportion of them have displayed conspicuous ability ; and that many great men have sprung from their ranks—this much, I believe, will·be admitted by all who have any practical acquaintance with the matter. The Indian Civil Service is the most able, as it is the most important, official service in the world." (Indian Polity, p. 216).

It is well known that in the selection and organization of this service there is to be now found the most thorough and practical application in the World of the principles of Civil Service Reform, but it has been sometimes erroneously asserted that it was at one time recruited and governed substantially on the American " Spoils " System ; this was never true.

"The Indian Civil Service took its rise from the establishment of merchants and agents employed in buying or selling the Company's wares. For many years after that occupation had ceased to be more than a subordinate part of the Company's business, they continued to be ranked in the grades, and styled by the titles, of senior and junior merchants, factors and writers. (Indian Polity, pp. 216, 217.)

This "establishment" resembled, in the main, that of a great corporation, say an important railroad company, of to-day. A large measure of personal favoritism undoubtedly entered into the original selection of its members, but fixity of tenure and promotion for merit were its rules from the very beginning. The facts that it was made up of nominees of the East India Directors whilst its official head was, or soon became, a Governor General, appointed by the Crown, exercised an early and profound influence on its character. It is said by Sir John Strachey :

"It was long ago laid down as a maxim, in regard to the employment of European officers in the more important branches of the service, that the first selection of young men shall not be made in India, but shall rest with the authorities in England, while after the first selection, those authorities shall exercise no interference. The distribution of offices, and all questions of appointment and promotion, are left absolutely to the Governments in India; 'it is a historical fact' (I am quoting from an official paper) ' that the observance of this wholesome rule has more than anything else conduced to the purity of Indian patronage, and to its general freedom from party and political bias.'" (Strachey's India, pp. 259, 260.)

In 1806 an important change was made in the method of its selection. A college was established at Haileybury at which candidates selected by the several Directors pursued studies calculated to fit them for the service : from that time until 1853 we may say that the Indian Civil Service was recruited by means of a civilian West Point. There was, however, a weak point in the system, a defect which, on the whole, cannot be charged against West Point. Major Chesney remarks of Haileybury :

"A highly competent staff of professors was appointed in every branch of study necessary for the education of. an Indian statesman or administrator. But this advantage was in a measure nullified, by fixing so low a standard for qualification, that study was virtually left optional with the students. The patronage of the first appointments to the Civil Service formed a highly valuable part of a seat in the Direction, affording an excellent provision for a director's family and relatives; and it was by no means in consonance with the views under which that seat was sought, that this advantage should be nullified by a scholastic test so severe as to exclude the Director's nominees from the service. The result was, that while the Haileybury course offered excellent means of instruction to those who chose to take advantage of it, it had no sufficient effect in eliminating incompetence ; and, with very rare exceptions, every young man who obtained a nomination to Haileybury was practically assured of obtaining an appointment to the Civil Service." (Indian Polity, pp. 220, 221.)

The same author adds :

"The defects of the nomination system need hardly be stated. Among every body of men chosen by chance—be the chance one of throwing dice, or of relationship to another set of men themselves in no way specially gifted—there must always be found some, in whom the power of indolence or deficiency of intelligence will be too strong to overcome. Had such men been always retained in subordinate posts, the evil would have been reduced to a minimum ; but, although promotion by seniority had long been abandoned, the traditions of the service still required that every man should be raised at least to the charge of a district, and eventually, to a judgeship. . . . .

If the Court of Directors had provided a sufficient remedy for these two weak points in the system—if they had required that every nominee should reach a reasonable minimum standard of qualification for admission to the service, and that no men should be advanced to posts of responsibility who had subsequently displayed marked incompetence—they might probably have retained the patronage of the service till the date of their extinction as a governing body. But such conditions would have pressed hardly, in some instances on family interests ; and when the enquiry of 1853 took place, public opinion pronounced that in these two points they had failed to administer their trust properly, and this valuable patronage was taken away. On the renewal of the Charter in that year, it was provided that appointments to the Civil Service should be thrown open to unrestricted open competition, an arrangement which has been maintained ever since." (Indian Polity, pp. 223, 224.)

By this change Civil Service Reform was finally and fully established in the Indian Service, and be it noted, it is almost precisely from this time, when public patronage was taken away, not, indeed, from politicians, for, in this case, these had never had it, but from private hands and given to the people, that the blessings of British rule upon the people of India began to be so direct, so evident and so overwhelming. Of these blessings one merits a moment's notice ere I close this prolonged trespass on your attention. It is thus described by Sir John Strachey :

"Out of the total number of civil employés in India, 90 per cent. are Natives, but, of course, the greater majority of these are in minor posts. Excluding the 765 offices held by covenanted officers, there are about 2,600 persons in the superior grades of the executive and judicial branches of service, and very nearly all of these are Natives. Thus, although the higher offices of control are held by Englishmen, the greater part of the actual administration is in Native hands. This is often ignored in discussing the question of the admission of Natives to a larger share of public employment. The organization of our great and highly efficient Native Civil Service is one of the most successful achievements of the British Government in India. Native officers manage most of the business connected with all branches of the revenue, and with the multifarious interests in land. Natives dispose of the greater part of the magisterial work. The duties of the Civil Courts, excepting the Courts of Appeal, are almost entirely entrusted to Native judges. A Native judge sits on the Bench in each of the High Courts. For many years past, Native judges have exercised jurisdiction in all classes of civil cases, over Natives and Europeans alike. I have already stated my belief that, as a rule, their work is quite as good as that of the English judges. Twenty years ago, the Native Civil Service was badly paid, comparatively inefficient, and not always trustworthy. In these respects there has been a great change. Nothing in the recent history of India has been more remarkable than the improvement that has taken place in the standard of morality among the higher classes of Native officials. Much of this has certainly been due to the fact that their positions and salaries are far better than they were, and that temptations to corruption have been removed, but I do not doubt that much has been due to their better education. Another powerful cause has been in silent and constant operation. The Native officials have had before them, through a long course of years, the example of the irreproachable integrity of the Englishmen employed in the higher ranks of the public service. Living in an atmosphere of official uprightness has made native judges and magistrates upright also." (India, pp. 260, 261, 262.)

Have we thus treated the unfortunate people in our midst whom we call by the same name as the natives of Hindostan? Have *our* Indians " had before them through a long course of years the example of the irreproachable integrity of the Americans employed in the public service? If we send to Manila, whenever civil may be there substituted for military government, such men as we choose to rule over our greatest cities, to speak in the Federal Senate for our greatest States, will," living in an atmosphere of official uprightness " make Filipino "judges and magistrates upright also?" To deal worthily with this momentous problem, to fulfil truly this portentous duty which awaits our country, these questions must be answered and answered truthfully: we must see, and own that we see, things as they are, without imposture or self-deception; if " it is better to be a patriot than a pessimist," which I have no mind to deny, it is better to be either than a liar.

The Merit System in San Francisco.

A OUTLINE OF ITS ORIGIN AND ADOPTION, SUBMITTED ON BEHALF
OF THE MERCHANTS' ASSOCIATION TO THE NATIONAL CIVIL
SERVICE REFORM LEAGUE.

IN many respects the past history of San Francisco presents a dismal aspect. Its efforts for public improvements have resulted generally in failure. The record of our municipal government heretofore has, in short, been generally marked by extravagance and inefficiency. The streets and sewers of the city have cost, for instance, over $34,000,000, a charge attributable most clearly to the continuous lack of method and discipline that has characterized our public work.

Various reasons are assigned as the cause of this apparent municipal failure. An impartial investigation will disclose as the primal cause the existence of the political "spoils" system. Aside from the management of the Free Public Library, civil service reform has been unknown in the administration of our city government. Nearly every other department has been made to subserve the purposes of party politics and patronage.

The principle of merit in the public service has been practically eliminated. Partisan politics has been the basis upon which have depended the appointment, promotion and removal of practically all our public officials and employees. Devotion to the city's welfare has rarely been considered in the selection of the servants of the people. Our predicaments, therefore, may truthfully be ascribed to the same general cause that James Bryce has cited as the reason that has made municipal government America's one conspicuous failure.

The Merchants' Association is largely responsible for the origin of the merit system in the future government of San Francisco. One of the first objects of this Association, as stated in its constitution, is "to devise and recommend such municipal measures as may seem wise and expedient." Pursuant thereto, the Merchants' Association advocated, as the cardinal principles of the new charter, "civil service reform, economical administration and home rule." It is gratifying to report that the charter as adopted by the people of San Francisco is in fact based upon these three fundamental doctrines.

On the first of the new year, the new charter will take effect. Its most significant feature is Article XIII, upon the Civil Service. This principle of the charter may really be considered as a pivot upon which the balance rests. In truth, we feel that the success or failure of the charter as a whole depends upon the faithful execution of its civil service provisions.

In a recent letter, Dr. Albert Shaw has declared to us that "The municipal service system of San Francisco must be regarded henceforth as one of the most advanced adopted anywhere." The civil service sections are clear, concise and simple. The language is plain and liable to no reasonable mis-interpretation. The various principles may be summarized in the declaration that appointment to office should be based upon merit, promotion for efficiency and removal for just cause only. Some other communities have by unfortunate errors discredited the merit system. We believe these mistakes have nearly all been avoided in our charter.

All rules and regulations governing the civil service should be clear and simple, and in this particular we feel that our system is not lacking. Clerks and other employees in the public service are required to pass examinations based upon the requirements of the positions sought. Laborers are selected by priority of registration. If properly fitted, those who first enroll for positions requiring unskilled labor will be the ones to be first selected. Examinations must be conduted in a public and impartial manner. Everything must be open and above board.

San Francisco may justly be congratulated upon having recently selected as Mayor, for the third term, a citizen who is sincerely committed to the principles of the merit system. His devotion to the cause of civil service reform has never been questioned. In accordance with the provisions of the new charter, Mayor Phelan will appoint the first three Civil

Service Commissioners, to hold office for one, two and three years. It is required in terms that they shall be "devoted to the principles of civil service reform." The regular term of the Commissioners will be for three years, one going out of office each year. This will preserve a continuity in the service, and prevent the appointment of an entirely new Commission by any later Mayor. It may truthfully be said that upon the judicious selection of the Civil Service Commissioners will rest the future welfare and prosperity of the government of San Francisco.

Though the achievement of securing and adoping a municipal charter with civil service reform as its first principle is indeed most encouraging, it is, nevertheless, only a step in the right direction. Excellent as are the provisions of our Civil Service Article, they will not execute themselves. Public opinion is an irresistible lever for good or evil municipal government. We shall not forget that our city is remote from the great centers of influence favorable to the merit system. Moreover, our state government is managed and conducted with little regard for civil service reform. California as yet has no state civil service law. The citizens of San Francisco, therefore, owe a solemn duty not only to themselves but to posterity, in taking care that the civil service provisions in the new charter are faithfully executed. The Merchants' Association may certainly be counted upon to put forth its best and strongest efforts to sustain the integrity of the system.

CONSTITUTION

OF THE

National Civil-Service Reform League.

I.

The name of this organization shall be the National Civil-Service Reform League.

II.

The object of the National Civil Service Reform League shall be to promote the purposes and to facilitate the correspondence and the united action of the Civil Service Reform Associations.

III.

The League shall consist of all the Civil Service Reform Associations in the United States which signify their willingness to become members thereof. Any association hereafter expressing such willingness shall become a member of the League upon its being accepted as such by the League or the Executive Committee. Any member of any such association may be present at any meeting of the League and take part in the debates or discussions as the by-laws may provide.

IV.

At any meeting of the League, each association belonging to it shall be entitled to one vote upon every question coming before the League; such vote may be cast by a personal representative designated by each association, or by proxy, as the by-laws may provide. If no such designation be made the delegates from such association present at such meeting, or a majority of them, may cast the vote of such association.

V.

The officers of the League shall be a President, Secretary, Treasurer, and nine Vice-Presidents; and there shall be a General Committee and an Executive Committee. The officers and the committees shall hold office until their successors are appointed or elected.

VI.

The President and Vice-Presidents shall be elected by ballot at the annual meeting of the League.

The Secretary and Treasurer shall be chosen, and may be removed, by the General Committee.

The General Committee shall be chosen annually, and shall consist of one delegate from each association belonging to the League; and one additional delegate for every two hundred members, or major fraction thereof, of such association as certified by its secretary. Each association shall elect its own delegates in such manner as it may determine.

The members of the Executive Committee shall be ex-officio members of the General Committee.

Any member of the General Committee may act by proxy.

The General Committee shall keep a record of its proceedings, and shall make a report to the League at the annual meeting. A vacancy in any office, except that of Vice-President, may be filled by the General Committee for the remainder of the term.

The General Committee may delegate to the Executive Committee any of its powers; provided, however, that it may at any time resume the powers so delegated.

The Executive Committee shall consist of twenty-one members to be elected annually by the General Committee and shall have power to fix its own quorum. And any member of the Executive Committee may act by proxy.

VII.

The General Committee may, subject to these articles, manage the affairs of the League, direct and dispose of the

funds, and may, from time to time, make and modify by-laws for the League and for its own action.

No debt shall be contracted, nor shall any appropriation of money be made, by the League or by the General Committee, beyond the amount in the hands of the Treasurer.

VIII.

There shall be an annual meeting of the League at such time in each year, and at such place as the General Committee may determine, at which officers shall be elected for the ensuing year, and other appropriate business may be transacted.

A meeting of the League may be called at the discretion of the General Committee whenever any association belonging to it notifies the Secretary of the League of its desire to have such a meeting, and the President may at any time call a meeting of the League.

IX.

Any provision of this Constitution may be suspended or amended by a vote of two-thirds of the members present at any meeting of the General Committee, due notice of such proposed suspension or amendment having been given at a previous meeting. Any association belonging to the League may, through its representatives, propose amendments to the Constitution which may be approved under the same conditions.

The Beginning of the Spoils System in the National Government, 1829-30. (Reprinted, by permission, from Parton's "Life of Andrew Jackson.") Per copy, 5 cts.

Term and Tenure of Office. By Dorman B. Eaton. Second edition, abridged. Per copy, 15 cts.

Daniel Webster and the Spoils System. An extract from Senator Bayard's oration at Dartmouth College, June, 1882.

Address of Hon. Carl Schurz in opposition to the bill to amend the New York Civil Service laws, commonly known as the "Black Act." May 6, 1897.

Report on the Operation of the "Black Act." March 21, 1898.

Annual Reports of the Civil Service Reform Association of New York for '83, '85, '86, '87, '88, '92, '93, '94, '95, '96, '97, '98 and '99. Per copy, 8 cts.

MISCELLANEOUS.

United States Civil-Service Statutes and Revised Rules of May 6, 1896.

Revised U. S. Civil Service Rules of May 29, 1899.

State Civil-Service Reform Acts of New York and Massachusetts.

Decisions and Opinions in Construction of the Civil-Service Laws. (1890) Per copy, 15 cts.

The Meaning of Civil-Service Reform. By E. O. Graves.

The Selection of Laborers. (In English and German Editions). By James M. Bugbee late of the Massachusetts Civil-Service Commission.

Report of Select Committee on Reform in the Civil Service (H. R.), regarding the registration of laborers in the United States Service.

Report of same Committee regarding selection of Fourth-Class Postmasters.

The Need of a Classified and Non-Partisan Census Bureau— Report of a Special Committee of the National League. (1898)

George William Curtis. A commemorative address by Parke Godwin. (Published by the Century Association). 10 cents per copy.

(A CHARGE IS MADE ONLY WHERE THE PRICE IS GIVEN.)

Orders for the publications will be filled by GEORGE MCANENY, Secretary, 54 William St., New York, or by G. P. PUTNAM'S SONS, 27 and 29 West 23d St., New York.

PROCEEDINGS

AT THE ANNUAL MEETING OF

THE NATIONAL CIVIL-SERVICE REFORM LEAGUE

HELD AT

NEW YORK CITY, DEC. 13 AND 14, 1900.

WITH THE REPORTS AND PAPERS READ,

AND OTHER MATTERS.

———

NEW YORK:
[PUBLISHED FOR THE
NATIONAL CIVIL-SERVICE REFORM LEAGUE.
1900.

Publications of the National Civil-Service Reform League

Proceedings at the Annual M_____ ___ National Civ 'e. vice Reform League, 1884 to 1900, inclusive, (excepting those of 1888, '89, '90 ; out of print).

Civil-Service Reform under the present National Administration. By George William Curtis. (Annual Address of the President, 1885.)

The Situation. By George William Curtis. (Address of 1886.)

Party and Patronage. By George William Curtis. (Address of 1892.)

Civil-Service Reform and Democracy. By Carl Schurz. (Annual Address of the President, 1893.)

The Necessity and Progress of Civil-Service Reform. By Carl Schurz. (Address of 1894.)

Congress and the Spoils System. By Carl Schurz. (Address of 1895.)

Encouragements and Warnings. By Carl Schurz. (Address of 1896.)

The Democracy of the Merit System. By Carl Schurz. (Address of 1897.)

A Review of the Year. By Carl Schurz. (Address of 1898.)

Renewed Struggles. By Carl Schurz. (Address of 1899.)

Civil Service Reform as a Moral Question. By Charles J. Bonaparte. (1889.)

The Influence of the Spoils Idea upon the Government of American Cities. By Herbert Welsh. (1894.)

The Reform of the Consular Service. By Oscar S. Straus. (1894.)

The Appointment and Tenure of Postmasters. By R. H. Dana. (1895.)

Civil Service Reform and Municipal Government. Two papers, by Albert Shaw and Horace E. Deming. (1897.)

The Republican Party and Civil-Service Reform. By Henry Hitchcock. (1897.)

The Democratic Party and Civil-Service Reform. By Moorfield Storey. (1897.)

An open Letter to Hon. C. H. Grosvenor, in reply to recent attacks on the Civil Service Law and Rules. George McAneny. (1897.)

The Need and Best Means for Providing a Competent and Stable Civil Service for Our New Dependencies. By Dorman B. Eaton. (1898.)

The Choice of Correct Methods in the Administration of American Dependencies. By Elliot H. Goodwin. (1900.)

Constitution of the National Civil-Service Reform League.

Good Government: Official Journal of the National Civil-Service Reform League. Published monthly at 54 William St., New York. One dollar per year. Ten cents per single copy.

PROCEEDINGS

AT THE ANNUAL MEETING OF

The National Civil-Service Reform League

HELD AT

NEW YORK CITY, DEC. 13 AND 14, 1900.

WITH THE REPORTS AND PAPERS READ,

AND OTHER MATTERS.

———

NEW YORK:

PUBLISHED FOR THE

NATIONAL CIVIL-SERVICE REFORM LEAGUE.

1900.

9384.40

(FEB 92 1901)

The League

PRESS OF GOOD GOVERNMENT.

CONTENTS.

CONTENTS

ANNUAL MEETING

OF THE

NATIONAL CIVIL SERVICE REFORM LEAGUE.

DECEMBER 13 AND 14, 1900.

PURSUANT to call, duly issued, the twentieth annual meeting of the National Civil Service Reform League was held at New York City, on the 13th and 14th of December, 1900. Among the delegates in attendance during the several sessions were the following:

BALTIMORE: Charles J. Bonaparte, George Frame, F. W. Shults, J. Crawford Lyon, Dr. H. O. Reik, W. Burns Trundle, William T. Brigham, William Keyser, Thomas Howard White, M. B. Billingslea, Phillip H. Tuck, Dr. Thomas Shearer, Theodore Marburg, Hiram Woods, D. C. Woods.

BOSTON: Richard Henry Dana, W. W. Vaughan, William V. Kellen, Charles S. Hamlin, N. E. Chamberlain, George T. Flynn, Grenville H. Norcross, Charles C. Soule.

BUFFALO: Henry A. Richmond, A. C. Richardson, Frederick Almy, Walter J. Shepard, Edward Hale Jennings.

CAMBRIDGE: Morrill Wyman, Jr., James G. Thorp, George F. Arnold, Archibald M. Howe, Arthur H. Brooks, Hugo R. Meyer, William H. Emerson.

CLEVELAND: Harry A. Garfield, William E. Cushing.

CONNECTICUT: W. A. Aiken, Adam Reid, J. Miller Wilson.

DENVER: Charles MacDowell, Irving Hale.

INDIANA: William Dudley Foulke, Henry J. Milligan.

NEW YORK: Carl Schurz, Jacob F. Miller, William G. Low, Everett P. Wheeler, Rt. Rev. Henry C. Potter, Charles Collins, Edward Cary, Horace White, Anson Phelps Stokes, Charles A. Schieren, Edward M. Shepard, Richard Watson

Gilder, George McAneny, Robert Shaw Minturn, Charles W. Watson, A. S. Frissell, Samuel H. Ordway, Seth Sprague Terry, Homer Folks, Charles C. Burlingham, George Haven Putnam, Elliot H. Goodwin, Samuel P. Avery, Jacob W. Mack, Robert Underwood Johnson, R. Fulton Cutting, R R. Bowker, William J. Schieffelin, Rev. Dr. C. B. Smith, Truman J. Backus, William Potts, Nelson S. Spencer, Henry De Forest Baldwin, F. G. Ireland, Rev. Thomas R. Slicer, Oscar S. Straus, George R. Bishop, Henry Winthrop Hardon, L. T. Chamberlain, George F. Carter, Silas W. Burt, Alford W. Cooley, S. William Briscoe, Roscoe C. E. Browne, James B. Ludlow, Horace E. Deming, Joseph K. Murray, Adolphe Openhym, Henry Loomis Nelson, Arthur C. Train, Edward Uhl, Charles H. Strong, Samuel Thorne, Jr., William Miller Collier, J. Warren Greene, Thomas A. Fulton, Frank J. Goodnow, John Brooks Leavitt, E. R. L. Gould, Charles MacVeagh, William A. Perrine, Rev. Dr. W. S. Rainsford, John A. O'Connor, Henry Sanger Snow.

PHILADELPHIA: Herbert Welsh, Wayne Mac Veagh, Stuart Wood, George Burnham, Jr., R. Francis Wood, Charles Richardson, C. R. Woodruff, Dr. Charles Cadwalader, John D. Avil, Walter Horstmann, H. M. Dyckman, James Macallister, Rev. L. Bradley, Rev. A. L. Elwyn, Edwin S. Sayres, Walter Wood, W. H. Pfahler, Albert W. Kelsey, Louis J. Lautenbach, Elliot Fields, John C. Donovan, Porter F. Cope, John J. Pinkerton, Edward Cole.

WASHINGTON: Frederick L. Siddons, George A. Warren.

ST. LOUIS: Francis R. Blair, John F. Lee.

In response to invitations issued by the League to Municipal Reform Associations and other bodies having the reform of the Civil Service among their objects, delegates were present from a number of such organizations, as follows:

MUNICIPAL LEAGUE OF PHILADELPHIA.—George Burnham, Jr., Robert C. Deardon, John Stokes Adams, William Kirkbridge, Hector MacIntosh, Houston Dunn, Samuel S. els, Charles Richardson, and Clinton Rogers WoodruffF

CITY CLUB OF NEW YORK:—J. Noble Hayes, James R. Burnet, C C. Nadal, James W. Pryor, and Charles H. Strong.

REFORM CLUB OF NEW YORK:—Everett P. Wheeler, John G. Agar, Seth Sprague Terry.

MASSACHUSETTS REFORM CLUB: — William Cushing Waite, and Samuel Y. Nash.

CLEVELAND CHAMBER OF COMMERCE:—Harry A. Garfield, and William E. Cushing.

LAW AND ORDER LEAGUE OF CONNECTICUT:—Walter F. Prince, of New Haven.

LAW ENFORCEMENT SOCIETY, BROOKLYN:—T. DeQuincy Tully.

CITIZEN'S LEAGUE OF HUNTINGTON, L I.:—E. D. Davidson, James M. Brush, Rev. J. C. York, William S. Funnell, William E. Jones.

THE CIVICS CLUB OF ORANGE, N. J.:—Winthrop Waite, Adolph Roeder, Nathan C. MacCrea, Richard K. Musley.

THE WOMEN'S AUXILIARY OF THE N. Y. CIVIL SERVICE REFORM ASSOCIATION:—Mrs. W. H. Schieffelin, Mrs. George William Curtis, Mrs. Charles Russell Lowell, Miss Lowell, Miss A. J. G. Perkins, Mrs. Henry N. Sanders, Mrs. Francis C. Barlow, Mrs. J. Kennedy Tod, Mrs. C. W. Watson, Miss Elisabeth Luther Cary, Mrs. S. B. Brownell, Miss Brownell, Miss Elizabeth M. Sharpe, Miss Helen C. Butler, Mrs. Charles A. Spofford, Miss Louise Lee Schuyler, Miss A. E. H. Meyer, and Mrs. Everett P. Wheeler.

THE CIVIC CLUB OF PHILADELPHIA:—Mrs. I. B. Oakley, Mrs. Charles Richardson, Miss Hallowell, Mrs. Frederic Merwin Ives, Mrs. George Burnham, and Mrs. Clinton Rogers Woodruff.

THE ARUNDEL GOOD GOVERNMENT CLUB, OF BALTIMORE.—Mrs. Charles J. Bonaparte, Miss Sarah G. Haydock, Mrs. George Huntington Williams.

MASSACHUSETTS WOMEN'S CLUBS:—Mrs. Robert M. Morse, and Miss Elizabeth Foster, of Boston.

CONNECTICUT FEDERATION OF WOMEN'S CLUBS:—Miss Mary M. Abbot, of Watertown.

MEETINGS OF THE LEAGUE.

THE morning session of the 13th, commencing at 9.30 o'clock, was occupied by a joint meeting of the General and Executive Committees, held at the City Club. At this, a revised Constitution was adopted, changing in various respects the form of organization of the League.* The proceedings at the several sessions of the League, the first of which was held on the afternoon of the 13th, were as follows :

FIRST SESSION.

THE CITY CLUB,
THURSDAY AFTERNOON, DECEMBER 13.

The League convened at 3 o'clock P. M., the President, Hon. Carl Schurz, in the Chair.

The minutes of the last preceding annual meeting having been printed and distributed, the reading of the same was, on motion, omitted.

The submission of the Report of the Nominating Committee, at the request of its Chairman, was deferred until a later session.

The Report of the Special Committee on the Civil Service in Dependencies was presented and read by the Chairman of the Committee, Mr. Bonaparte, of Maryland. On motion it was received and ordered to be filed and properly published.†

The Report of the Special Committee on Superannuation in the Civil Service was presented and read by the Chairman of that Committee, Mr. Dana, of Boston.‡ Mr. Bonaparte moved that this report be referred to the Council for such action as may hereafter be deemed necessary. Mr. Foulke,

---

* Printed in full at Page 49.
† Printed in full at Page 37.
‡ Printed in full at Page 41.

of Indiana, stated the substance of an interview he had had
with Representative Gillett, Chairman of the House Com-
mitte on Reform in the Civil Service, with reference to the
matters covered by the Committee's Report, in which Mr.
Gillett had stated his desire to introduce a bill for the retirement of superannuated employees founded on the system of
Victoria, as a substitute for certain pending measures. After
some further discussion, during the course of which it was
suggested that Mr. Gillett's proposition should also be considered by the Council, Mr. Bonaparte's motion was carried.

The Report of the Special Committee appointed to consider the action of a majority of the United States Civil Service Commission in revoking orders under which the League
had previously had access to such of the records and files of
the Commission as are not properly confidential was read by
its chairman, Mr. Bonaparte, and referred, on motion, to the
Council.*

Mr. Schurz at this point withdrew, and Mr. Bonaparte
took the chair.

The Secretary, for the Committee on Congressional action,
made a verbal report with reference to three bills of importance, now pending in Congress, the course of which the Committee had followed: (1) The bill providing for the reorganization of the Weather Bureau, and for the filling of positions
in that branch of the service through appointments made by
members of Congress, after non-competitive examination; (2)
that extending the preference now given to disabled veterans
over civilians in all competitive appointments to all persons
who have served either in the Civil War, or in the Spanish-
American War, or in the present war in the Philippines, and
providing also that such persons when appointed shall be preferred for promotions, and for retention in the service; and
(3) that providing for the reorganization of the Consular
Service.

The first of these measures, he stated, had been thoroughly
discussed during the last session, and opposed by a previous
Committee representing the League. Although favorably reported in the House, and within reach for final consideration

---

* Printed in full at Page 58.

at any time, the Committee had been assured that it would not be pressed further.

The Veteran bill had been reported favorably to the House, after a division in the Committee on Reform in the Civil Service, at the last session, and would be pressed to a vote at some time within the next few weeks. It had been passed by the Senate but recalled and re-submitted to the Committee on Civil Service and Retrenchment where it now remains. At a hearing before this Committee the bill had been opposed by representatives of the League and by the President of the United States Civil Service Commission, who had shown that its passage would create so large a preferred class that general competition would be discouraged—with the result that the government would be compelled to accept the services of inferior men—and, further, that the principle of discrimination on which the bill is based is distinctly un-American, if not unconstitutional. The danger of the early enactment of the bill was increased, however, by the fact that the President, in his letter accepting renomination, had approved the preference proposed and had recommended its further extension to the "widows and orphans" of those who had served in any war. The Committee purposed to continue the campaign against the measure vigorously.

The Consular Reorganization bill, which, when introduced had the approval of the Cleveland Chamber of Commerce and of other similar bodies that had taken an active interest in the subject, had been reported in the Senate in a radically modified form, without adequate provision for appointments after competitive examination or for the establishment of a properly constituted examining board. Doubt had arisen as to whether it would be better to support the bill as amended or to advise its abandonment until a more satisfactory start might be made, but, in pursuance of the League's previous policy, the Committee had concluded that the judgment of the commercial organizations in this respect should govern the League's own action. On motion the report was received and referred to the Council.

At the invitation of the Chairman, Mr. Garfield of Ohio, Chairman of the Special Committee of the Cleveland Chamber of Commerce, addressed the meeting with reference to the Consular bill. Mr. Garfield stated that the bill as reported in the Senate is objectionable to the commercial organizations, also, and that the question as to the expediency of supporting it has arisen among them, as well. It was intended, however, that the movement for this reform should be carried on aggressively, until a satisfactory bill had been secured as a basis for legislation, and the continued co-operation of the League, he added, would be welcomed.

The Chairman announced the final order of the session to be the reception of reports from representatives of local Associations. Reports were made by Messrs. Clinton Rogers Woodruff, for Pennsylvania; W. B. Trundle, for Maryland; A. C. Richardson, for Buffalo; H. J. Milligan, for Indiana; and Col. J. W. Ela, through the Secretary, for Chicago. The session then adjourned.

SECOND SESSION.

THE CARNEGIE LYCEUM
THURSDAY EVENING, DECEMBER 13.

The evening meeting convened at half-past eight o'clock, when addresses were made on the general subject of Civil Service Reform by Charles J. Bonaparte of Maryland, William Dudley Foulke of Indiana, and Rev. William S. Rainsford, D. D., of New York. Hon. Carl Schurz presided and made the following introductory remarks:

"As the president of the Civil Service Reform Association of New York, I bid you, the members of the National League and the friends of our cause here assembled, a most hearty welcome and thank you for the favor of your presence.

"For various reasons the old custom of presenting in a president's address at the annual meeting of the League a comprehensive review of the actual status of the civil service reform cause, has been abandoned—at least for this occasion—and a public meeting has been substituted to be addressed by several eminent advocates of the reform, while the critical review will appear in the shape of reports of Committees.

"As the ex-officio chairman of this meeting I conceive it to be my first duty—a duty prescribed by a primary rule of courtesy—not to anticipate by an elaborate speech on my part what the orators of the evening, to whom your attention belongs, may have to say. I shall therefore confine myself to a very few remarks, the pertinency and appropriateness of which I trust, will not be questioned, considering the experience I have gathered during my long service in this cause.

"The office to be performed by this League and the local associations is two-fold: first the missionary work which consists in enlightening and stimulating public opinion as to the objects to be accomplished by civil service reform and as to means to be used for the attainment of those objects; and, secondly, the promotion of proper, and the prevention of improper legislation concerning the public service; a watchful surveillance over the enforcement of civil service laws and rules by those in power; and the conveying to the public of truthful information as to the effect or tendency of what is being done.

"To secure a successful performance of this office it is essentially required that this League, as well as the local associations, should be absolutely non-partisan in their character—that is to say, while their members, as individual citizens, may attach themselves to this or that political party, or, if they prefer, remain unattached, the League and the local Associations, should in their action as to legislation or executive measures to be obtained or prevented, and in their pronouncements of praise or censure as to the conduct of those in power. be absolutely free of partizan bias—in other words, that they should justly stand in public opinion above the suspicion of political or personal partiality.

"That they have so far in this respect fully deserved public confidence, may safely be affirmed. We may to-day assuredly repeat what our departed leader, George William Curtis, whose memory, teachings, and example we cannot too highly revere, said in his annual address of 1886: 'I challenge any man to show that it—this League—has in any degree, or at any time, betrayed the trust voluntarily assumed by it, of honestly and adequately representing this sentiment in its criticisms and demands upon political parties and public men. The League has pandered to no personal ambition, to no party purpose. It has been no man's instrument, nor has it been the organ of any faction.'

"No doubt it is the unanimous wish and the determined resolve of all true friends of civil service reform that it shall remain so. Indeed, if it did not, if this League and the local associations ever failed to merit and possess the confidence of the public in this respect, their usefulness would be fatally impaired. No effort, no sacrifice should therefore be spared to maintain their character for strictest impartiality. and to avoid anything apt, even in appearance, to cloud their title to the popular belief, that they will tell the truth and pronounce just judgment according to the true standard of civil service reform under all circumstances, without fear or favor.

"This is not always an easy and agreeable task. Those who undertake it must not only cast aside all partizan predilections and personal likes or dislikes that might stand in the way of honest impartiality, but they must also be willing to expose themselves to the imputation of belonging to that odious class of people called 'chronic faultfinders,' who will never be satisfied. For it is their business not to be satisfied so long as the true standard of civil service reform is not practically reached.

"We have had to do with various Republican and various Democratic administrations, National, State and Municipal, some of which were honestly solicitous to advance the cause of civil service reform, so that we found in their conduct much to praise; which we did most gladly and heartily. But even these sometimes considered us quite unreasonable and disagreeable when to the praise of their good acts we joined, never without regret, our criticism of their occasional slips and shortcomings, our plain duty not allowing us to accept as a full justification their plea that in the face of the difficulties they had to contend with, they had done the best they could. On the contrary it was our evident duty to judge, not whether what was done was difficult or politic or not, but whether it was genuine civil service reform or not. Of course, those who have always been loudest in charging us with captious unfairness were the men who instead of trying to do the best they could, did only the worst they dared.

"To be sure there is, morally, a very great difference between these two classes. But in one respect the Civil Service Reform League, in its official capacity, has to treat them alike. It will certainly with gladness welcome and encourage every honest effort in the right direction, be it ever so slight. It will gratefully recognize every effective step in advance be it ever so short. But as to being satisfied—it has no right to be, or to confess itself satisfied, until the reform is, in design, and execution, complete and perfect.

"It must never permit any one entrusted with power to think that a faithful observance of correct principle in one case can serve as an excuse for a violation of it in another. It must never tolerate tricks of spoils politics under the guise of the forms of the merit system to be passed off as the genuine article. For it must never forget that more harm is done to the cause of civil service reform by false pretences of it, by the use of its name to cover up vicious dealings, than by open attack on it under the undisguised spoils flag.

"In one word, it must incessantly preach its principles, diligently study and strive to perfect laws, and rules, and methods, vigilantly watch their enforcement, stoutly defend what is honest and right, boldly and belligerently denounce what is wrong or false, with fearless justice tell the truth and spare not, no matter whom it may please or displease, and thus with inflexible firmness uphold the true standard.

"The League cannot overestimate its duty and responsibility in this respect. For, I ask you, if an organization founded for that very object, and composed of men unselfishly devoted to the cause, and as such entitled to the public confidence, did not bear up that true standard, full high, who would? To whom could the public look for safe counsel and guidance in a work of such vital interest to the republic? Fortunately, there is no reason for doubting that this League will always fully recognize its duty and courageously do it."

THIRD SESSION.

THE CITY CLUB,
FRIDAY MORNING, DECEMBER 14.

The League convened at 10.30 A. M., the President in the chair.

Mr. Bonaparte, as Chairman, read the report of the Executive Committee. Mr. Wheeler, of New York, moved that the report be accepted, and that it be printed with the Proceedings of the meeting, and the motion was carried.*

---

* Printed in full at Page 25.

Mr. Wood, for the Auditing Committee, submitted the following report, which, on motion was received and ordered filed:

New York, December 14, 1900.

To the National Civil Service Reform League:

The undersigned, constituting the Auditing Committee appointed at the joint session of the General and Executive Committees, respectfully report that they have examined the accounts and vouchers of the Treasurer, and find them correct; that the balance on hand December 14, 1899, was $56.17; the receipts from all sources during the year $4,841.87; the disbursements for all purposes $4,852.49; and that the balance on hand at the end of the fiscal year on November 30, 1900, was $45.55.

Very respectfully,
R. Francis Wood,
W. W. Vaughan,
Committee.

The Secretary presented and read the Report of the Investigating Committee, on the general state of the federal civil service and the operation of the reform law under the present Administration.*

Mr. Richmond, of Buffalo, referring to the passage in the report regarding the refusal of the Comptroller of the Treasury to withhold payments of salary from persons appointed to positions in violation of the Civil Service law, moved that the question of testing the validity of this action in the Courts, or of taking such other steps as may be practicable to secure its reversal, be referred to a Special Committee to consist of five lawyers, who are members of the League, and the motion was carried.

Mr. Bonaparte moved that the report of the Investigating Committee be immediately published, with such verbal changes as the Secretary may deem necessary and as he may be able to make.

Mr. Foulke moved, as an amendment, that before publication the report be submitted to the President of the United States for his consideration.

Mr. Dana moved as a substitute for the amendment, (1) That a copy of the report be sent to the President by the Secretary of this League at the time of its publication; and

---

* Abstract printed on page 28,

(2) that the Investigating Committee be instructed to prepare an abstract of the full report to be furnished in advance to the press for publication on a date not later than Wednesday next, the 19th inst. With the consent of the mover these propositions were considered separately. On the first there were 20 ayes and 36 noes, so that that part of the motion was lost. The second was accepted as a substitute by both Mr. Bonaparte and Mr. Foulke, and was carried.

The Secretary than read the preliminary draft of a second report of the Investigating Committee, treating in detail the scope and effect of the President's order of May 29, 1899, changing the federal civil service rules. On motion this report was referred back to the Committee with power to publish later, in their discretion.

The session then adjourned.

FOURTH SESSION.

THE CARNEGIE LYCEUM.
FRIDAY AFTERNOON, DECEMBER 14.

The League convened at three o'clock, P. M., Mr. Schurz in the chair.

Mr. Dana, of Boston, presented and read the following report of the Committee on Nominations:

To the National Civil Service Reform League :

At the joint meeting of the General and Executive Committees of the National Civil Service Reform League, held October 20, 1900, it was

"*Resolved*, that in the judgment of the General and Executive Committees, and in accordance with the uniform practice of the League. the independent political action of any member of a Civil Service Reform Association should not affect his standing as an officer of the League, composed as it is of citizens of the most diverse opinions on public questions not connected with civil service reform ; and that, therefore, the reasons given by the President of the League, in his letter of September 22, last, for the tender of his resignation. are, in the judgment of these Committees, insufficient to justify its acceptance.

"*Resolved*, therefore, that the President is very respectfully requested to withdraw his said resignation."

On December 1, the Hon. Carl Schurz wrote the following letter to the Secretary:

GEORGE MCANENY, ESQ.,

SECRETARY, NATIONAL CIVIL SERVICE REFORM LEAGUE.

DEAR SIR:

The resolutions passed by the Executive Committee of the National Civil Service Reform League, by which they have done me the honor of requesting me to withdraw my resignation as their president, have had my most careful and deferential consideration. I admit that the principle upon which the two Committees have based their action, is essentially correct. But at the same time I continue to believe that the position I have taken with regard to other policies of the national administration might create practical inconveniences to the League, if I remained its president; and to such inconveniences I should be loth to expose an organization the aims of which I have so much at heart. . . . . As the officers of the National League are to be newly elected at the coming annual meeting, you will oblige me by asking, in my name, the Committee on Nominations of that body to select some other member for the position hitherto held by me,   Very truly yours,

C. SCHURZ.

The Committee therefore, understanding that Mr. Schurz is firm in his opinion, have suggested the name of Mr. Daniel C. Gilman, President of the Johns-Hopkins University, who is about to retire from that position, as President of this League. In his letter, allowing his name to be used, Mr. Gilman says:

"It is a pity that Mr. Schurz cannot be pursuaded to serve us in the future as he has in the past."

The Committee in view of the change in the Constitution, has proposed only the name of the President, and the following lists of Vice-Presidents. Their action on these names are unanimous.

Charles Francis Adams, ...	Boston.
Joseph H. Choate, ...	New York.
Grover Cleveland, ...	Princeton.
Henry W. Farnam, ...	New Haven.
Henry Hitchcock, ...	St. Louis,
Henry Charles Lea, ...	Philadelphia.
Seth Low, ...	New York.
Franklin MacVeagh, ...	Chicago.
Henry C. Potter, D.D., . . .	New York.
P. J. Ryan, D.D., ...	Philadelphia.

All of which the Committee herewith respectfully submits,

RICHARD HENRY DANA,
Chairman.

On Mr. Dana's motion the gentlemen named for President and Vice-Presidents respectively, were unanimously elected.

Mr. Foulke, of Indiana, for the Committee on Nominations, presented and read the following resolution relative to the retirement of Mr. Schurz from the office of President:

The National Civil Service Reform League deeply regrets the determination of the Honorable Carl Schurz to retire from its presidency. Nearly eight years ago he assumed the office, after the death of the first president of the League, George William Curtis. Mr. Schurz, his successor, has served the League and its cause with the same noble and practical wisdom which belonged to that great American, now held in precious and abiding memory by those who believe that the American democracy should administer its government in honor and with equal privileges to its citizens. The progress of the merit system has, no doubt, often seemed precarious and disappointing; but in the retrospect of eighteen years since the passage of the first directly effective legislation in our country against the spoils system, it is clear beyond any doubt that the progress,—in spite of enormous difficulties in the way,—has been great,—very great,—and that the reform has secured a deep hold upon the intelligence and conscience of the people, and has effected a practical and lasting change in public administration. This beneficent change,—already one of the large achievements of our generation, has been due to no influence more than to the zeal, persistence, courage, eloquence, statesmanlike skill and wide influence of Carl Schurz. To all these qualities were added his practical knowledge gained during his long and distinguished service in official and political life. He has truly and precisely appreciated the relation of the spoils system to administrative procedure and detail no less than its more corrupting effect upon political morality throughout the Nation. The substitution in its place of the merit system has been a cause lacking the obvious and personal interest which sustains many public causes and that brings the exhilaration of immediate honor to those who promote them. With other really abiding benefactions to humanity this cause has required the faculty of patient self-sacrifice. And this, Carl Schurz has given in an unstinted measure. The fruits of his work will surely be gathered more and more. They will bring to him more and more the gratitude and homage of his countrymen at large as they now do of this League and of all in sympathy with the reform for which it stands. The League gives him its best greeting, and ventures to hope that, although he will not be its president, he will nevertheless give it his powerful and faithful aid.

On motion of Mr. McAneny, seconded by a number of members, the resolution was adopted unanimously. Mr. Schurz, in a brief response, expressed his appreciation of the action taken by the League, and called Mr. Miller of New York to the Chair.

Mr. Woodruff, of Pennsylvania, for the Committée appointed to report nominations for members of the Council, presented the names of the following :

Moorfield Storey, . . .	Boston.
W. W. Vaughan, . . .	"
Richard Henry Dana, . .	Cambridge.
Morrill Wyman, Jr., . .	"
William A. Aiken, . . .	Norwich, Ct.
Silas W. Burt, . . .	New York City.
Charles Collins, . . .	" " "
Richard Watson Gilder, . .	" " "
Samuel H. Ordway, . .	
William Potts, ...	
Carl Schurz, ...	
Everett P. Wheeler, . . .	" "
Edward Cary, ...	Brooklyn.
William G. Low, . . .	"
Edward M. Shepard, . .	"
Henry A. Richmond, . .	Buffalo.
Charles Richardson, . . .	Philadelphia.
Herbert Welsh, . . .	"
B. Francis Wood . . .	"
Clinton Rogers Woodruff, .	"
Charles J. Bonaparte, . .	Baltimore.
George A. Pope, . . .	"
Dr. H. O. Reik, . . .	"
John Joy Edson, . . .	Washington.
F. L. Siddons, . . .	"
Charles B. Wilby, . . .	Cincinnati.
Lucius B. Swift. . . .	Indianapolis.
William Dudley Foulke, . .	Richmond, Ind.
John W. Ela, ...	Chicago.
Henry Hitchcock, . . .	St. Louis.
Henry Van Kleeck, . . .	Denver.

On motion, the gentlemen nominated were elected unanimously as members of the Council for the ensuing year.

The following papers were then read :

The Purpose of Civil Service Reformers—By Henry Loomis Nelson, of New Rochelle : *

---

* Published in the Forum, for January, 1901.

The Results of Civil Service Reform in Australia—By
Hugo R. Meyer, of Harvard University: *

A Report on the Movement in the Women's Clubs in aid
of Civil Service Reform: by Miss Elizabeth Foster,
of Boston; read by the Secretary; † and

The Choice of Correct Methods in the Administration of
the Civil Service of American Dependencies—by Elliott H. Goodwin, of New York. ‡

After the reading of papers Mr. Bonaparte, on behalf of
the Committee on Resolutions, read the resolutions prepared
by the Committee, and moved their adoption as follows :

The National Civil Service Reform League, assembled in its sixteenth annual meeting, was compelled to notice the fact that during the
year 1896, for the first time since its organization, its principles had
been openly repudiated and a revival of discarded abuses threatened in
a platform put forth by a National Convention, and in the public declarations of a candidate for the Presidency. These features of that
platform were again approved and enunciated by the same National
party and by the same candidate during the current year. We can, at
least, say that this avowal of hostility to the merit system does not seem
to have brought additional support to the party whose leaders were responsible for it.

At its last Annual Meeting the League protested against the President's order of the 29th of May, 1899, exempting thousands of places from
the competitive classified service and relaxing the safeguards of the service, not only because the order was wrong in principle as taking the
first backward step, as encouraging the enemies of the Merit System in
their attacks, and as creating distrust of the President's faithfulness to
his reform pledges, but also because it was certain to prove injurious to
the service in its results. The year has shown that the step remains as
unjustified in principle as ever, and that it has produced, in practical
results, just the injuries to the service that were feared, as the reports
of our Committee on various branches of the service have proved. The
League therefore asserts without hesitancy, that the restoration of very
nearly all the places in every branch of the service excepted from classification by this deplorable order is demanded by the public interest
and that the order itself should be substantially revoked.

At its last Annual Meeting the League further demanded that, if
any alien lands should be brought under our national dominion, public
office therein should be consistently treated as a trust to be administered

---

* Printed in full at page 79.
† Printed in full at page 86.
‡ Printed in full at page 70.

for the sole benefit of their inhabitants, and declared that to abuse the public service of dependent provinces in the interest of American parties or politicians would constitute a crime against civilization and humanity, disgraceful to our Republic. As a safeguard against this shame and calamity it urged that, in the organization of any governments which might be established for such territories, adequate provision should be made for a non-partisan service, recruited through open competition and assured of promotion through merit, and of continued employment during good behavior and efficiency; and recorded its belief that the President alone, without additional legislation, had authority to make all reasonable regulations for executive appointments. The League now renews these declarations and demands. It has seen with great gratification the recent action of the Philippine Commission appointed by the President, which provides for the establishment of such a service in the Philippine Islands, as an important step in the right direction.

The League pronounces the action of a majority of the Civil Service Commission in refusing access to public records relating to matters of public concern, and in no wise confidential in their character, a violation of the right of citizens in a free country to learn from official sources how faithfully the public servants they pay administer the laws. The force of the reasons assigned for this refusal is gravely impaired by the fact that such access has been for years permitted to the League by the Commission without objection or inconvenience of any kind. This refusal exposes to suspicion the good faith of the officials responsible for it, and suggests the existence of abuses which the records withheld from inspection might disclose. The League demands that this unworthy policy of concealment and secrecy be forthwith abandoned as un-Republican, un-Democratic and un-American.

It cannot be too clearly and generally understood that the principles of Civil Service Reform in no wise countenance any tenure of office other than during the continuance of merit and fitness. The League again expressly disclaims any advocacy of Civil Service pensions as a part of the Merit System, which contemplates such pensions no more than did the system of appointment and removal by favor prevailing before the Merit System was introduced. On the contrary, the protection which an assured tenure during efficiency affords to public servants should enable them, by the exercise of frugality and forethought displayed by all prudent persons, to provide out of their current earnings for the ordinary contingencies of age and infirmity, and the League would see with pleasure the adoption of reasonable rules for the ascertainment from time to time of continued efficiency on the part of public officers through fair and practical tests applied impartially and in good faith.

As it is the evident duty of the President to remove unfaithful or inefficient public servants and bring to justice offenders against the laws of the United States, the League demands the dismissal of every Federal officer who has failed to obey in letter and in spirit the Civil Service law, and also demands the effective prosecution of all who have violated its penal provisions. The League congratulates the country on the comparative infrequency and secrecy at present of attempts on the part of political managers to plunder public servants through virtually compulsory contributions for partisan purposes, and it regrets that during the last campaign the Chairman of the Republican National Committee failed to aid it, when requested, in discouraging such abuses and crimes.

The League protests against the mischievous practice of distribution among administration Senators the presentation to federal offices in their respective States. This is in violation of the Constitution which gives to the President the power of appointment. The requirement that such appointments be made by and with the advice and consent of the Senate has been perverted so as to give to Senators the appointments, reserving to the President alone the power to consent or decline. Such gross abuse of Senatorial power by Senators sworn to support the Constitution should receive the condemnation of all good citizens.

The League again urges the importance of a sufficient and practical test of character and fitness, to control the selection of Indian Agents, so that the grave abuses and serious evils which at present afflict the Indian Service from the treatment of these positions as political spoils may be abated and partisanship strictly excluded from the entire force.

The League is opposed to the passage of the veteran preference bill now pending before Congress, as calculated to overthrow the Merit System, and as creating a privileged class contrary to the provisions of the Constitution and the principles of Republican government.

The League notes with great satisfaction an extraordinary increase in the number and activity of agencies working for better government throughout the country; it calls attention to the significant fact that such agencies invariably recognize the principles of Civil Service Reform as fundamental in all well considered movements for improvement in the public service and the purification of our political life; it rejoices in the renewed evidence of public interest in Civil Service Reform, which recent events have provoked, and it confidently relies upon an enlightened public opinion to effect the final extension of the Merit System to all branches of our National, State and Municipal governments.

The resolutions as submitted were adopted by unanimous vote.

Mr. Bonaparte moved that the Secretary be authorized to incorporate in the Proceedings the report of the Committee on Political Assessments, which had not been completed in time for formal presentation, and the motion was carried.*

General Aiken, of Connecticut, moved that the thanks of the League be extended to the Civil Service Reform Association of New York, to Mr. and Mrs. William Jay Schieffelin,

---

* Printed in full at page 54.

and to the City Club, for the courteous and generous hospitality extended to the visiting delegates throughout the course of 'this meeting. The motion was carried unanimously, and the League then adjourned.

Attest: GEORGE McANENY,

_____   *Secretary,*

At one o'clock on the afternoon of Friday the 14th, the members of the League were entertained at a reception and luncheon given by Mr. and Mrs. Schieffelin at No. 5 East Sixty-sixth Street.

On the evening of Friday a banquet was tendered the visiting delegates by the Civil Service Reform Association of New York, at the Hotel Savoy, which was attended by two hundred and twenty-five, including forty members of the Auxiliary of the New York Association and other affiliated women's organizations. The Right Rev. Henry C. Potter, Bishop of New York, presided, and addresses were made by Hon. Theodore Roosevelt, Governor of New York, Hon. Wayne MacVeagh, Charles J. Bonaparte, Esq., Hon. Oscar S. Straus, Minister of the United States to Turkey, Herbert Welsh, Esq., and Hon. William Dudley Foulke.

ANNUAL REPORT OF THE TREASURER.

NOVEMBER 30, 1900.

Balance on hand, Dec. 14, 1899, ... $56.17

RECEIPTS :

Subscriptions from New York Association...	$1,625.00	
" " Chicago "	...	319.00
" " Washington "	...	300.00
" Boston "	...	195.00
" Philadelphia "	...	330.00
" Baltimore "	...	515.00
" Norwich "	...	100.00
" Buffalo "	...	100.00
" Massachusetts Reform		
Club................	250.00
" Andrew Carnegie........	500.00
" Augustus Hemenway....	500.00
" " Miscellaneous..........	105.00
Pamphlets sold........................	2.87	4,841.87

$4,898.04

DISBURSEMENTS :

Proportion of Salary of Secretary............	$1,500.00	
" " " " Assistant-Secretary..	1,100.00
Clerical services.........................	860.70
Rent of office...........................	200.00
Traveling expenses......................	249.71
Office expenses.....	191.28
Printing...............	216.15
Postage................................	41.00
Washington Agent......................	111.50
Paid to F. E. Leupp, balance due on account of expenses of publication of "Good Government".........................	382.15	4,852.49

Balance on hand....... .. .. $ 45.55

E. & O. E.

A. S. FRISSELL,
Treasurer.

REPORT OF THE EXECUTIVE COMMITTEE.

To the National Civil Service Reform League :

THE task of reformers in a free country is to make the people think and feel as they think and feel; when the people shall wish what they wish, and shall wish this in earnest, too much in earnest to brook any resistance or any evasion, then, but not until then, will their reform be an established and permanent fact in the national life. When, therefore, we members of the League, look around us, as we do to-day, that we may see what we have done and what we have yet to do, the vital questions which confront us are: "What do the American people think of civil service reform? How far have we awakened the Nation to the iniquities and dangers of the 'spoils' system of politics? What prejudices, what sophistries, what falsehoods yet cloud the judgment, yet drug the conscience, of the people?" For light on these questions, we look first to the meaning of the people's verdict at the late election.

In 1896 there could be no doubt or dispute as to this: then the Republican party received a mandate to carry out the promises it had made. Doubtless this mandate endorsed much more than the promise to take no backward step in civil service reform, to honestly and thoroughly enforce the existing Federal law and to extend its scope wherever practicable, but it endorsed nothing more unequivocally or more emphatically. This year the platform of the same party substituted silence for its pledge of four years since; it had taken a backward step, and a long one; it had failed to enforce the existing law either thoroughly or honestly; it had failed to extend that law's scope where such extension was practicable and even easy.

On the other hand, the Democratic platform reaffirmed its frankly hostile utterances of 1896, and its principal candidate expressed again, in substance, the same sentiments

against which the Executive Committee, with the subsequent
sanction of the League, had protested four years before;
moreover the choice of its candidate for the Vice Presidency,
when contrasted with that of its rival, gave significance to the
contest. A friend of the reform could not fail to see that the
past of Adlai Stevenson illustrated one set of ideas and principles and the past of Theodore Roosevelt illustrated another.

There are, however, two facts which recent history has
proved anew for any who still needed the proof: one must
indeed be blind and deaf to now doubt that our typical professional politicians, those men among us who are in politics
for what they can make out of politics, whatever the party to
which they have fastened themselves, whatever the shibboleth
they repeat or the opinions they profess to hold, are all alike
enemies to civil service reform. They may wrangle among
themselves over the offices, but one and all recognize in us,
who would take the offices away from parties and factions
and bosses and rings, and give them back to the people, all
recognize in us their natural enemies. And it is no less evident for those who can and will see the plain truth that avowed
hostility to civil service reform strengthens no party at the
polls. It was well for the Republicans that they were silent
when the Democrats assailed it openly; it would have been
better had they stood forth its defenders, as in 1896. The
periodical outburst of vituperation against the law and the
Commission, which had become a matter of course in Congress until at this session the country was happily spared it,
may have helped the second and third class politicians who
figured in it to curry favor with their dependents useful at primaries and conventions; but it has never gained votes for
their respective parties, never raised themselves in the esteem
of honest men.

In every part of the Union the past ten years have seen
associations formed among the most reputable and most enlightened members of the community, each having for at least
one of its objects to promote good government in one or more
of our cities or states. Nearly five hundred such societies
were invited to take part in the recent conference called by
the National Municipal League in Milwaukee and almost
every day we hear of a new one. This widespread agitation
shows that the people feel daily more and more keenly, see

daily more and more clearly that the abuses of our government, the corruption of our politics, the degradation of our public men, constitute a burden, a peril and a disgrace for the nation; but if we scan it more closely, it shows us more. Of these societies all the more recent and more prominent recognize the establishment of the merit system as a feature, and a feature of growing importance, in their programme. Twenty years ago many worthy citizens *really* doubted whether civil service reform was practicable or suited to our institutions; to-day one who *says* he doubts this, makes more than doubtful his claim to political intelligence.

The people already see that the principles of this League are the principles of honest government and pure politics; they may see this yet but as in a glass darkly, but the day will come, it is rapidly coming, when they will see this clearly, and when they thus see it the League's work will be done.

For the Committee,

CHARLES J. BONAPARTE,
Chairman.

Abstract of the Report of the Investigating Committee: On the Condition of the Civil Service under the present National Administration.

IN enacting the Civil Service Law, in 1883, the Committee shows, Congress intended that the system should ultimately embrace the entire subordinate Executive service, or, as the Senate Committee declared in reporting the bill, " all that vast number of appointed officials who carry into effect the orders of the President . . . whose duties do not change with a change of Administration, and who have nothing to do with framing the political policies of the Government." Section six of the act made provision, in very clear terms, for a gradual extension of the system, through the action of the President and heads of departments, until this end might be effected.

From the date of the passage of the act, until May 29, 1899, this extension continued almost without interruption, each President making important additions to the classified list and each strengthening the rules to guard against evasions. The latest of these additions had been in effect for about a year when the present Admininistration came into power—but by far the greater part of the work necessary to the completion of the reform remained to be done. With this fact no doubt in view, the Republican party, at its Convention in 1896, had "renewed its repeated declarations not only that the law should be thoroughly and honestly enforced, but that it should be extended wherever practicable."

The Committee reports, however, that, while in many of the branches that have been longest classified, the system has been unimpaired and has continued to produce excellent results, it cannot be said that the law has been " thoroughly and honestly enforced," while—with the exception of the start made in the establishment of rules for the Philippine service, covered in a separate report to the League—conspicuous and unusual opportunities for its extension where clearly "practicable," have deliberately been set aside.

The progress of the reform, in its application to the Federal service, has, in brief, been seriously checked. That this is at variance with the declared purposes of President McKinley, and with his professed wishes for the welfare of the service while under his control, is recognized, and the Committee earnestly recommends that the facts it submits be presented for the President's consideration.

HOW FAR THE LAW IS ACTUALLY APPLIED.

On March 3, 1897, approximately 86,000 positions were in the classified service while 92,000, including 5,000 Presidential officers, several thousand laborers, and other miscellaneous classes, and the great army of fourth-class postmasters, remained unclassified.

It might naturally have been expected that proper compliance with the law and recognition of its principles, on the part of both Congress and the heads of departments, would, at this stage, have secured the appointment through competition of almost all the great number required for service in offices and positions of the sort that are classified. The Committee, however, from the data it has at hand, reports surprisingly different results. During the first year following the order of May 29, 1899, that ended on June 1 last, the appointments made within this area were as follows:

THROUGH COMPETITIVE TESTS.

Appointments from competitive eligible lists...................*4,640

WITHOUT COMPETITIVE TESTS.

Appointments to excepted positions, not subject to examination..   254
Appointments to excepted positions, subject to "non competitive" examination......................................   800
Appointments under "temporary" certificates.................*2,242
"Temporary" appointments made permanent without examination   973
Reinstatements without examination......................... 1,170
Transfers of unexamined persons within the service...........   107
Unexamined persons having "special qualifications"...........   7
Appointments to clerical positions in the departments under the War Appropriation Acts.............. 1,200
Appointments to clerical positions in the Census Office......... 2,400

Total... 9,153

* Full returns for last month of 1899 lacking.

These figures show that the "exceptions" from the requirements of the civil-service law, whether brought about through Executive or Legislative action, have been, during the year they cover, almost twice as numerous as appointments made in the manner the law intended. A certain proportion of the appointments so made were, no doubt, unavoidable, but these cases are exceptional, and cannot materially affect the totals given.

The Committee gives the following summary of the general course of the Administration and of the present Congress in relation to the civil service; incidentally, showing more clearly the significance of the above figures:

PRESIDENTIAL APPOINTMENTS.

I. So far as the Committee has been able to learn, appointments of local Federal officers of the Presidential class have been controlled almost exclusively by Senators and Representatives, or unofficial political leaders, whose selections the President has ratified. While good men are sometimes secured through this system, in the majority of cases those appointed are active local politicians, whose disposition to provide places for their adherents furnishes a serious obstacle to the satisfactory administration of the civil-service rules at the outset. Among Presidential officers in the general branches—including business officers strictly, and not those that are properly political—the changes have been almost universal. In the Consular Service, for instance, more than 90 per cent. of the salaried offices were refilled during the first year of the Administration, and in the Indian service, during the same period, 62 per cent. of the agents.

CHANGES IN "EXCEPTED" POSITIONS.

II. Positions in the classified service excepted from competitive examinations are virtually unclassified, for removals may be made from them without restraint, and appointments are absolutely at the will of the appointing officer. The number of these positions has been greatly increased. On March 3, 1897, at the close of the preceding Administration. there were, all told, only 866, of which number 570 were of assistant postmasters. On July 27, 1897, President McKinley added 533, deputies and others in the Customs and Internal-

Revenue services, previously subject to competitive examination, and on May 29, 1899, approximately 4,000 more, in addition to the number removed absolutely from the classified service at that time.

III. As the classified service has grown, it has been observed that violations of the civil-service law, both now and heretofore, have occurred most frequently in the branches most recently included. After the change of March 3, 1897, there were many irregular appointments in the classes brought under the rules a year, or three years before, and not a few in branches longer established, coupled very frequently with irregular removals. These were mainly in the Internal Revenue Service, the Land Office service, the Government Printing Office, the branches of the Department of Justice outside Washington, and the Pension Bureau, and in certain of the custom-houses and post offices—notably at the post-office in Philadelphia. The Civil-Service Commission addressed repeated protests to the departments concerned in these violations, but in very few cases with satisfactory results. The records of their investigations, which the committee has examined carefully, cover 127 pages of their fourteenth annual report, 114 of the fifteenth, and 67 of the sixteenth.

On September 17, 1897, the League addressed a letter directly to the President, inviting attention to the growing number of offences, and asking that measures be taken to stop them. Where the rules had been most flagrantly disregarded, the dismissal of the guilty officer was urged, and the very satisfactory results of the examples of this sort made by President Cleveland were cited. On March 12, 1898, the League submitted a report showing the results of its investigations in the Philadelphia Post-office, where, it was shown, the Postmaster, Mr. Hicks, had removed many subordinates of known efficiency from positions of the higher order because of their political or factional affiliations. On March 15, 1898, it presented to the President a general report on violations throughout the service, with exhibits, and again asked that the offending officers be dismissed. In these cases also, however, there was no correction—except in so far as irregular appointments were nominally validated by the order of May 29, 1899.

It is also true that no single officer has been removed for violation of the rules, although the rules themselves, in clearest terms, provide this penalty. The nearest approach to discipline of this sort was in the case of Chenowith, Collector of Customs at Nogales, Ariz., who was caught in the theft of question papers in advance of an examination, as well as in other acts of dishonesty, showing his unfitness for any trust. Chenowith was ordered to be removed by Secretary Gage. Through the apparent intervention of powerful influence, however, this order was withdrawn and a resignation accepted. The man is now serving, presumably not far from the American border at Nogales, as a " special agent of the Treasury Department, for confidential duty in a foreign country," at $4 per day. This assignment is in itself a violation of the rules, against which the Commission has protested, as yet without avail.

Although the President's order of July 27, 1897, seemed to furnish the first substantial check upon removals to be embodied in either the Civil-Service Law or rules—an advance for which Mr. McKinley was most heartily commended at the time by the League—it was feared that through imperfect enforcement the value of this rule, also, would be seriously impaired, and experience has since shown that it has been.

EVASION OF THE RULES.

IV. While direct violations of the rules have been more or less common, indirect evasions have been more so. " Temporary appointments" are an instance in point. Under the rules, persons may be appointed without examination for ninety days' temporary service, in the absence of an eligible list, for emergency work. It is required that this shall be permitted only when the Civil-Service Commission has given its certificate that there is no adequate list. In practice the great majority of these appointments have been made at pleasure and without inquiry as to the state of the lists, continue! indefinitely, and reported as long afterwards as the appointing officer chose. This practice, moreover, has grown alarmingly During the thirteen months following the amended rules of May 6, 1896, 729 temporary appointments were authorized, and during the eleven months from June 1, 1897, to May 31, 1898, 2,365, of which not more than 80 were authorized by the Commission in any manner. These figures do not include War Department appointments in either case.

In many instances appointing officers failed to assist the Civil Service Commission when called on in preparing examinations to secure permanent appointees, and in others, when lists were actually prepared, they have refused to appoint from them.

Another common method of evasion is the appointment of persons as "laborers"—in which class examination is not required—and their assignment immediately to duties of a higher class. The growth of this practice the Commission frankly discusses in its Fifteenth Report. "Excepted" places are also used to bring persons surreptitiously into the competitive service, as in the San Francisco Custom-house, where the principal deputy was made Chief Clerk, and the son of the Collector appointed, without examination, to the vacancy, only to change places with the deputy when it came to the assignment of duties.

The Post-office Department has adopted a device for evasion that the Committee deems peculiarly reprehensible. When a small post-office is about to be given free delivery (which of itself brings the office force into the classified service), persons have been brought from other cities and even from other States, to take positions in such offices just before they enter the free-delivery class, to be transferred immediately afterward to the office for which they are really destined, thus escaping examination altogether. More than a hundred appointments of this sort have already occurred, despite the earnest protest of the Civil Service Commission. Twelve of those so appointed (presumably without the least experience) have been transferred to the important and high-salaried office of Post-Office Inspector, a proceeding which has been made easily possible by the change in the transfer rule contained in the President's order of May, 1899.

RESTRAINT ON IRREGULAR APPOINTMENTS DELIBERATELY WITHHELD.

V. One of the most serious features of the situation is that, no matter how plainly or how frequently appointments may be made in violation of the law, the Civil Service Commission is powerless to prevent them. The Commission may protest to the department involved, or it may appeal from the Department's decision to that of the President; but, failing to secure relief from either of these authorities, it is obliged to permit abuses to go unchecked. In the cities of New York and Chicago, and in almost every other place where a civil service system has been established, fiscal officers are forbidden to pay salaries to persons whose appointment is not made in the manner the law prescribes. The Federal Commission assumed that the same rule applied, of necessity, at Washington, and three years ago asked the Secretary of the Treasury to aid it in establishing a proper system of audit. Failing to secure the cooperation of that officer, lists of the names of persons known to be illegally in office were sent to the Comptroller, Mr. Tracewell, with the request that their claims for salary be not recognized. The Comptroller declined to interfere, although the Commission, under date of December 12, 1898, again wrote to him : "A state of anarchy in these appointments obtains at the present time, involving the honor of the administration of the Civil Service Act. With the information given you by the Commission, which is capable of easy verification in case of the slightest doubt concerning the facts, can you not take official cognizance of the matter ?" This communication Mr. Tracewell did not answer, but on April 1 following, he gave out a very remarkable opinion, addressed to a United States marshal, to the effect that, even though the Civil Service Act declares that " no officer or clerk shall be appointed " to a classified position except in conformity with its terms, an appointment otherwise made is *not* illegal; that the civil service rules have no force except such as the executive or head of department chooses to give them ; and that all persons whose names are on pay-rolls presented to him will be assumed to be regularly appointed, the Civil Service Commission's denial notwithstanding. The decision, although directly opposed to rulings of the Supreme Court, is, nevertheless, binding, so long as Mr. Tracewell himself remains undisturbed. Its effect is disastrous, for although, of course, many appointments continue to be made in compliance with the law, the full number that are not so made, and that may never be reported, remains quite unknown and undeterminable.

The two following ready instances show what can be done : In the report of appointments in the Post-office Department for June, 1899, there appeared the names of twenty-four persons under the head of "temporary clerks appointed under the act of Congress, approved February, 1899." The act in question merely gave the right to appoint, and did not exempt from civil service examination. This was promptly explained by the Commission to Assistant Postmaster-General Heath, but the letter remains unanswered, while the clerks are retained.

Again, in the Treasury Department, noncompetitive examinations are required, under the President's late order, for certain positions in the Customs and Internal Revenue services. Few of these have been held, but in cases where they have, and where the candidates have failed absolutely to secure the minimum of 70 per cent., qualifying them for appointment, they are still retained, their rejection by the Commission notwithstanding.

THE "WAR EMERGENCY" APPOINTMENTS.

VI. On the plea that the Civil Service Commission had no means of meeting the emergencies growing out of the war with Spain, about 1,200 further appointments without examination were made in different departments under special provisions in the war-appropriation acts. There is no means of securing exact figures, since these appointments have not been reported to the Commission, and the League's request for access to the proper records in the Treasury Department has been denied. On August 1, 1899, however, the number was known to be at least 1,042. At the time of these appointments there were on the Commission's lists of eligible clerks 6,180 names, so that practically the entire force required might have been selected therefrom in less time than it took to get them through the means actually adopted. In the subsequent appropriation bills, where provision has been made for additions to this force, the exemption from examination has been invariably repeated, although the adequacy of the Commission's machinery has been repeatedly explained by its President to the appropriate Congressional committees. Any clerk may now be appointed without examination if it is declared that the necessity for his employment "arises out of the war with Spain."

THE CENSUS FORCE.

VII. Although Mr. Carroll D. Wright, *ad-interim* Director of the Census, informed Congress that more than $3,000,000 had been added to the cost of the Tenth Census by reason of the failure to select the working force through the merit system, this system was again deliberately set aside in the taking of the present census, and—though the heads of bureaus have been efficient and well-trained men—otherwise, the methods adopted in the former census, which proved such a costly failure, were followed almost exactly. The tests required, which were of the " pass " description, no doubt debarred the absolutely unfit, but the benefit of open competition was lost, and, as the process of selecting clerks and other subordinates continued, only persons endorsed by a Senator or Representative were considered at all.

THE ORDER OF MAY 29, 1899.

VIII. It was while the state of the service was as low as the Committee declares, that the President's order of May 29, 1899, was issued. That order and its effects the Committee will review in a separate report. It may be stated in connection with the present report, however, (1) that it removed from the competitive to the " excepted " list about 4,000 places, and from the classified to the unclassified service about 6,000 more, the latter being mainly in the field branches of the War Department, subject at the time to a competitive registration system—which, owing to the failure of the Department to make other provision, is still voluntarily employed by some individual appointing officers; (2) that it validated, nominally, many appointments previously made in violation of the law; (3) that it weakened the rules governing transfers, reinstatements and removals, so as to permit new and most serious abuses; and, finally, that it marked the first great reduction in the actual area of the merit system since the act of 1883 was passed.

The Committee presents this review of what it considers a very unfortunate situation, not only that the action of the President may be asked where he has the power to correct, but that every other necessary step may be taken to regain the ground that has been lost, and again to turn the direction of the reform towards the ends the framers and advocates of the Civil Service Law had in view. It will shortly submit a number of specific recommendations for action on the part of the League.

Report of the Committee on the Civil Service in Dependencies.

To the National Civil Service Reform League:

A T the Nineteenth Annual Meeting of the League, held at Indianapolis, in December, 1899, the following resolution was adopted:

" It is beyond the province of the League to pass upon the rightfulness or wisdom of territorial extension, but we demand that if any lands be brought under our dominion, public office therein be consistently treated as a trust to be administered for the sole benefit of their inhabitants. To abuse the public service of dependent provinces, in the interest of American parties or politicians would constitute a crime against civilization and humanity, disgraceful to our Republic. As a safeguard against this shame and calamity we urge that in the organization of any government which may be established in such territory adequate provisions be made for a non-partisan service recruited through open competition and assured of promotion through merit and continued employment during good behavior and efficiency. The President alone without additional legislation has the authority to make all reasonable regulations for executive appointments."

At a subsequent meeting of the Executive Committee the undersigned were appointed a special committee to consider and report upon public measures relating to the subject matter of the foregoing resolution. The situation of the various territories brought under the control of the government as a result of the late war with Spain is in some respects very anomalous, has already given rise to grave problems in national policy and constitutional law, and may yet be productive of results which no one can now forecast with any confidence. But there are, however, certain general principles of government whose recognition is essential to the success of any scheme of administration in these lands; if those principles be disregarded our rule can be neither beneficial nor creditable to us and must be a source of misery to their inhabitants. These principles are succinctly stated in the resolution of the League already quoted. If we forget that public office in those countries is a trust for the sole benefit of their inhabitants, if we make their civil service a place of refuge for needy American politicians with damaged reputations—or current coin to pay partisian service, and further support for the dependents and satellites of our public men—if, in short, we repeat the errors of our Reconstruction Period without the excuse of inexperience which may be pleaded for those errors, and place the government of the land we have conquered in the hands of " carpet-baggers," sure to be neither more competent nor more scrupulous than those of the decade after the Civil War, such conduct were mildly criticised if called " a crime against civilization and humanity disgraceful to our Republic."

It is, therefore, with much gratification that the Committee is able to report an apparent recognition of these truths by the National Administration, and a desire to organize the Civil Service of our dependencies upon the basis of appointment for merit, and tenure during good conduct and efficiency. This has been manifested in the first place by the character of those appointed to high office in the countries we thus hold, which, with a few very unfortunate exceptions, has been uniformly good, and, in several instances exceptionally fortunate.

We have further to note with satisfaction the course of the Philippine Commission, by which, if it be persevered in, the Merit System will be established in the islands of that archipelago at least as thoroughly and consistently as in any department of government, Federal, State or Municipal, in the Union. This must be, in any case, regarded as a gratifying recognition of sound principles of administration on the part of the Commission, and justifies the hope that, within the limits of their jurisdiction at least, no repetition of the scandals of *post-bellum* days will be tolerated.

The ruling of the several Departments that the provisions of the Civil Service Law and Rules, being applicable *proprio vigore* to Federal offices established in the Dependencies which would be classified if within the United States, is also a matter to be noted with satisfaction by the friends of good government. In this connection a serious and delicate question has arisen respecting the status of natives of Porto Rico under the rule restricting admission to the competitive examinations to " citizens of the United States." By the terms of the bill establishing a civil government in Porto Rico, they are recognized as "Citizens of *Porto Rico* and as such entitled to the protection of the United States." This designation which, *mutatis mutandis,* would be perfectly applicable to an inhabitant of the District of Columbia, and in itself certainly in no wise excludes American citizenship, has, nevertheless, been held by certain officials to shut them out from the competitive examinations under the Civil Service Law. It would seem that a precedent of great force for the determination of this question could be found in the practice of the Commission admitting to examination Tribal Indians, who, it is well established, are not "citizens of the United States." (Elk v. Wilkins, 113 U. S. 94.)

Indeed, the relations to the Federal Government of the various Indian Tribes, as established by the decisions of the Supreme Court, would seem to bear a very close resemblance to those of Porto Rico and the Philippines under existing conditions. (U. S. vs. Kagama, 118 U. S., 379,—Cherokee Nation vs. Kansas Railway Company, 135 U. S., 641.) And if Indians, who can be "citizens" only in the broad sense which extends citizenship to all persons (whatever their political rights) who are at once entitled to protection from the government and owe it allegiance in return for such protection, can be admitted to the examinations, it would seem that no good reason exists for denying this privilege to inhabitants of Porto Rico. This, it should be noted, is a well recognized definition of the word "citizen" which is thus defined in the Century Dictionary:

"A member of the State or Nation, one bound to the State by the reciprocal obligation of allegiance on the one hand and protection on the other."

Since, however, the right of the Commission to admit natives of Forto Rico to its examinations has been questioned, the Committee suggests the advisability of an amendment to the Rules which will in terms permit this, at least in the case of offices to be exercised within the Island. That its inhabitants should be debarred from competition for such places, they regard as wholly inconsistent with justice and sound policy.

In conclusion, the Committee respectfully recommend that the subject matter entrusted to them continue to engage the vigilant attention of the League. We must recognize that a wide difference of opinion exists among patriotic, intelligent and well informed citizens as to the expediency of our recent territorial acquisitions; but, whatever his opinion as to this question, no American, truly solicitous for the honor and welfare of his country, can fail to be profoundly interested in their good government.

Very respectfully submitted,

CHARLES J. BONAPARTE,
RICHARD HENRY DANA,
WM. DUDLEY FOULKE.

Report of the Committee on Superannuation in the Civil Service.

To the National Civil Service Reform League :

THOSE now in the classified civil service of the United States who have become superannuated, have not entered through the civil service examinations. As pointed out in the last annual report of the U. S. Civil Service Commission, the average age of entrance has been only 28, while the law has been in operation only seventeen years, so that the average age of those who entered in the beginning can be only 45. Neither the law nor the rules require permanency of tenure. Any one can be dismissed for incapacity or inefficiency, as well as for misconduct. In order to secure justice, the appointing officer must give his reasons, and the employee concerned must be given a chance to reply, or to explain, before the final act of dismissal.

If the temptation to make dismissals for political purposes has been removed so that old men are no longer put out simply to make room for political favorites, on the other hand, under the old system there were often political reasons for keeping incompetent old men in office, and stillmore frequently were original appointments made of men who had already passed the age of usefulness just to please influential politicians who wished to foist on the government incapable men who would otherwise be on their own hands or on the hands of influential supporters. Indeed, numerous appointing officers of large experience under the " spoils system" have testified without contradiction that the *needs* of the applicant were most frequently and urgently set forth ; his fitness hardly ever.

It is very difficult for public officials, unless compelled by some stringent regulations, to discharge subordinates who have become incapable from old age when these subordinates have been faithful in the past and are absolutely dependent on their salaries for support. The extent of this evil it is hard to ascertain, some experienced officials considering it greater than others. It is true that mere age tables do not tell the whole story. Some men at seventy-five have more vigor than others at fifty. Yet as an average, seventy may be taken as the general age of the end of activity. In the United States Army sixty-four is the age of retiring. In the civil service the requirements are not so exacting on the physical forces as in the army, with the exception of a few small departments like the Railway Mail Service. It is to be remembered in this connection that experience and knowledge of the history of a department make a man, too old to enter new employment, yet invaluable in that in which he has long served. Every man of business is familiar with such cases. If we assume then that about as many over seventy are thoroughly useful as under it are incapable from old age, we may use seventy as a fair basis for obtaining an approximate estimate of the situation. In the eight departments at Washington in 1893 there were 228 persons of seventy years of age and over out of 11,657, or almost exactly 2 per cent. In 1900, the only other year for which the data are accessible, we find there are 262 of seventy years of age and over out of 10,967, or a little over 2 per cent., making an increase in seven years in the ratio of 6 2/7 in 10,000, while the number of persons of eighty years and over has actually decreased in those seven years. In the New York Post Office in 1900 there were only 21 of seventy years of age and over out of 3,561 employees, or less than 6/10 of 1 per cent.

The best answer to the claim that the new system will "fill the public service with old men" is found in the experience of the State Service of Massaehusetts. There are 800 positions in that service strictly under competitive examinations. The civil service law has been applied to them for 16 years, and for 24 years before, the appointing power in the state had always been under the control of one party only, the heads of the departments had been retained for long periods without change, and there were no clean sweeps. While vacancies were filled for political reasons, practically no removals were made during all this time except for cause. Therefore this service represents the most stable service for 40 or 42 years, that is known in the United States, quite as stable as the present classified service of the United States. There is no system of pensions or fixed retirement or fixed terms of office, or age limit or recurring examinations, and yet the Secretary of the Massachusetts Civil Service Commission informs us that only 3 out of the 800 or 3/8 of one per cent. are of 70 years of age or over.

As to the remedies, the more radical ones now generally proposed for superannuation are the following :

I. A civil pension list.

II. A retirement fund to be made up by deductions from salaries.

III. A provision requiring endowment or deferred annuity insurance from all seeking admission to the Civil Service.

IV. Provision for the forced retirement of a certain percentage of employees each year.

V. Recurring examinations for promotion, reductions and dismissals.

VI. A daily record of efficiency for the same purpose.

VII. Fixed terms of office.

VIII. Forced retirement at a certain age.

And also certain combinations of these.

The three first plans provide for old age support while the last five provide for compelling retirement with no other means of support than what the incumbent may voluntarily have provided for himself. Under provision for old age support a more stable and experienced service is secured. Under the present system in the United States there is great complaint that the more active and efficient public servants who have entered through competitive examinations too frequently retire from the service just as they have gained experience and have reached their most useful period, in order to take positions in private life where promotion and provision for old age can better be secured. Of course, no forced retirement system would lessen this tendency. On the other hand, old age provisions tend to make employees stay on after the age of maximum usefulness till they have reached the age for retiring on a pension, and the number of old employees to be dealt with is larger than in a system where no such provision is made; that is, the supply of old age support increases the demand for it.

I.

The civil pension system has led to great abuses in the past in England. It is extremely unpopular in America. There is danger of a civil service lobby in Congress should the system be adopted. The retired list for the United States Army officers was established in 1861. The officers receive 75 per cent. of their active service pay, and the retiring age is sixty-four, and below that age in case of permanent disability. In the army this system has worked to great advantage and has led to no important abuses and no one thinks of abolishing it. In England the age of retirement in the civil service is sixty, and separation from the service at that age is compulsory with some rare exceptions, while pensions on retirement before sixty are granted in most cases of permanent incapacity. No persons are granted a pension who have not been at least ten years in the service, and then the payment is calculated on one-sixtieth of the salary on retiring for each year of service with 40/60ths as a maximum. The pensions paid in the British service amount to 16 per cent. of the salaries paid for active work. The British pension list is, however, unduly enlarged. For example, many gratuities on retirement are granted where regular pensions are not allowed, and in some cases the pensions are made equal to the full salary. If we should take the retiring age for the United States civil service, as has been before suggested, at 70, instead of 60, as in the English service, the pension list would cost eventually, it is estimated, from 4.3 to 7.2 per cent. of the salaries paid for active service, in order to give pensions of 60 per cent. of the average salary during employment, the average age at entrance being 28. The per cent. varies according to circumstances. It depends upon whether only strong and healthy employees are allowed to enter the civil service or persons of average health. The above per cents. are calculated on the basis of no resignations. With a reasonable number of resignations before 70 the per cent. would be still lower. That the highest rate suggested, namely, 7 2/10 per cent., is amply high is proved from the experience of the British retired civil list where the actual per centage of those retired to those in the service is far below the theoretical maximum that the application of the same mortuary tables, without allowing for resignations, (viz. 21 per cent.) would show, taking the average age of entrance into the British service and the British age of forced retirement.

It is fairer to base a provision for old age on the average salary during employment rather than on the salary at retirement, as the salary at retirement is usually the highest received by the employee, and as otherwise there would be the temptation to secure an increase of salary just before retirement in order to increase the pension.

II.

A retirement fund made up of deductions from salaries might be in two forms, (a) a deduction from all salaries for the immediate support of a retired list and (b) annual deductions from the salaries of those hereafter to enter the service, which should be allowed to accumulate at compound interest to form a fund for annuities payable only to those who have thus contributed.

(a) At present it would take only about 2 per cent. of the average salaries of those in the departments at Washington to pay the full average salaries of those of seventy years of age and over, and only 1.2 per cent. to pay pensions at 60 per cent. of the average salary, and if a further deduction were made from the pensions of those who had been in the service for less than forty years, on the English system, it would require still less. But those now in the service include only those who are able to do some work, while the retired list would also include the absolutely helpless. Besides this a pension at the end of the service tends to increase the number of persons who will stay on for the sake of pension; so that in the future we should have to allow for deductions 4.3 per cent., and possibly even more. Besides other objections this system is extremely unfair to those coming into the service young and staying on for many years. They would have had deducted from their salaries very much more than would have insured them the same annuity at the same age in any insurance company, and those older and nearer the age of retiring would have paid far less than their share.

(b) The plan of beginning with those now entering the service would be more fair. In England this system was begun in 1829. The deductions were 2.5 per cent. on all salaries not exceeding $500 (100 pounds), and 5 per cent. on all others. This deduction, considering the high rates of interest on safe investments at that time, and considering the early age of entering the service, might have sufficed but for the large number of persons under 60 years of age who became entitled to share in the fund, and but for the basing of the pensions on the maximum or retiring salaries and some unexpected charges on this fund. In 1857 the fund had amounted, after all payments out of it to over $5,000,000, but the chief charges on the fund had not then fully matured and it became evident that with the greatly swelled pension list this fund was inadequate, so it was turned into the general exchequer and regular pensions at the same rates were assumed by the government. A royal commission in 1888 reported in favor of returning to the plan of forming a superannuation fund by annual deductions from salaries under proper conditions, but this recommendation has never been followed.

The average age of entering our classified service is 28 years. Starting with that, it would require annual payments of $27 a year on male lives to pay an annuity of $600 to those who should attain 70 years of age for every year for the rest of their lives. That would be 2.7 per cent. on a salary of $1,000. This cost is based upon information furnished by one of the largest life insurance companies in the United States to cover the special case. They actually issue such policies now, under the name of " deferred annuities." On the basis of paying the same annuity at the age of 65 and over, instead of 70. it would cost $55.20 a year or a little over twice as much as if payable at 70 years of age and over. This difference is caused by deducting five years of payments and five years of accumulatious at compound interest and adding five years of annuities to be paid. This difference suggests how much is added to the cost of pensions in Great Britain by making the age of retirement sixty, instead of 65 or 70.

The cost of these deferred annuities includes, of course, expenses and profits of the insurance company. Theoretically the government could insure at less cost, but on the other hand, it must be assumed that the government would be limited to investments in United States bonds with very low rates of interest, while insurance companies can secure 4.5 per cent. It should be borne in mind that the rate of interest is a very important factor in calculating the accumulations for long periods. Accumulations at 4 per cent. compound interest are far more than twice as great as those at 2 per cent. compound, because compound interest accumulations are on a basis of geometric progression. So that after all, the cost of insurance by the government would be greater than in first class companies.

The government might make deductions on the basis of the cost of company insurance, use the fund for its own purposes and pay the annuities on the same basis as the companies, but this would be making up the difference out of the pockets of the people, and when once the annuities, at least for any considerable length of time, are not strictly confined to a self-sustaining fund, there comes in the old danger of a lobby and claims for special privileges, as in the case of direct pensions. The Brosius bill introduced December 4, 1899, provides a deduction of 2 per cent. for a civil service retirement fund to be invested in United States bonds. The retiring annuities are to equal 75 per cent. of the highest pay received. All persons 70 years of age who have been in the service 35 years are to be compulsorily retired. Persons 60 years old who have been 30 years in the service may be voluntarily retired and so may all disabled persons who have been in the service twenty years. The Civil Service Commission is to decide all questions of retirement and establish regulations. Annuities are to be paid from the retirement fund and not otherwise, and if demands exceed the fund, they fail. Employees who are discharged or die before retirement are to be refunded the amount of pay withheld. It seems quite evident that the 2 per cent. withheld under such conditions will not suffice to pay these annuities.

III.

The advisability of requiring insurance in the way of deferred annuities from all those who enter the service is largely a matter of the cost of this insurance. A deferred annuity payable, for example, at $600 a year every year of life over 70 on male lives beginning at 28, (the average age of entrance into the classified service), would require payments of $27 a year, or 2.7 per cent. on an average salary of $1,000. On a larger average salary the proportion would be the same. For example, 60 per cent. of an average salary of $2,000 would be 1,200, and an annuity of $1,200 at 70 and over would cost $54 a year beginning at 28 or just 2.7 per cent. of $2,000. Those entering under 28 would pay less, and over 28 correspondingly more. While this remedy applies only to those entering the service it could be extended by correspondingly larger payments, according to increase of age, so as to apply to all who have been in the service for some reasonable number of years. At the age of 38 for example, which is 10 years over the average of entering the classified service, an annuity of $600 a year at 70 years of age and over would require annual payments of $52.20. For those somewhat longer in the service and older, and to whom the increased deductions would come hard, a smaller annuity might be required. To those who are still nearer the age of 70, however, the cost of such a deferred annuity would entail too large a deduction from the salary to be reasonable. For example, it would take a payment of about $3,600 from one at the age of 69 to procure an annuity of $500 a year for the rest of his life beginning at 70. As all those now in the service nearing 70 years of age came in before the civil service law was enacted, that law could not be blamed, if the United States government were asked to deal liberally with these cases. Their number is very limited. A considerable part of the cost could be deducted from their salaries, and in a few years the extra expense from this source would cease entirely.

The insurance companies would, we feel sure, after inquiry, be willing to make deposits of good securities in the United States treasury to assure the payment of these deferred annuities. They already make such deposits with various state treasuries as security. The insurance should be limited to all such companies as would consent to this plan and perhaps to such as would also submit to and pass national inspection. There will be no objection to this latter. It would be a good advertisement, and if it would lead to substituting a national examination for the frequent and often useless re-examinations by numerous state authorities, it would be of great advantage to the life insurance system of the country.

To the pure deferred annuities could be added a life insurance payable in case of death under 70 years of age, or various other forms of life insurance at the option of the employees

by paying additional rates so that in case of a death before
70 the estate of the deceased might receive back the face value
of the deductions made from the salary. The cost of this added
life insurance would be about $20 a year, beginning at 28 years
of age, for one thousand dollars, payable only in case of death
before 70 years of age, so that, beginning at 28, an annuity
could be secured of $600 a year if he survived the age of 70,
and a cash payment of $1,000 on death if he should die be-
fore 70, on an annual payment of $47.00, or 4.7 per cent. of
the salary of $1,000. The amount of added insurance is
taken at $1,000, as that represents roughly a little above the
average amount deducted from the salaries of those who would
die between 28 and 70.

The plan above suggested in its general features has
already been adopted in Victoria by the Act of 1890, which requires that such insurance shall be effected during the term of
probation as a prerequisite for final appointment. The policies are made non-assignable, and in this country it might be
well also to have them deposited with the government.

One of the objections to this plan is that it does not provide for those who become prematurely old before the age of
70 or allow those over 70 who are still useful to stay on.
Perhaps a good modification of the plan would be for the Government to allow as many of its employees over the age of 70
as are really useful, to stay on on regular salary, on condition
that the annuities falling due on their lives would be used, as
long as they remained in the service, as a fund from which to
pay annuities to those who had become superannuated under
70 years of age, so that the government could be supporting as
many of the superannuate under 70, as there were employees
staying on in the service of 70 years of age and over. This
more elastic arrangement would cost the government nothing.
It would be fair to all, as all on entering would have an equal
chance of receiving the annuity before 70 if incapacitated, or
of being employed at a salary larger than the annuity when
over 70. Some age limits and minimum length of service
should be fixed for those receiving annuities under 70. On
separation from the service (such as resignation) for other
reasons than would entitle one to an annuity, the policy could
be assigned to the employee going out, and he could keep it
up for his own benefit by continuing the annual payments, or

turn it into other forms of insurance on equitable arrangements with the insurance companies.

In addition to this plan it might be well to provide for honorable transfers in some cases with diminished salaries. Some positions require unusual activity and energy. An incumbent may be unable to do the work of such a position as well as when at the prime of life, and yet be not generally incapacitated, and indeed might be extremely valuable to the government in some other position for which his energies are amply sufficient and where his experience and knowledge would tell. To allow such transfers would give the government the benefit of younger men in the more active offices and yet not lose the experience of the older.

The average age of retirement and the amount and kind of insurance might well be very different from what is suggested here. The suggestions have been made with an idea of presenting some conception of the cost and advantages of such a system.

IV.

Forced retirement of a certain percentage of employees each year has some precedent in the navy of the United States, where it was recently adopted and did good at the time. As a permanent policy it is subject to the objection that it will retire too many at one time, and in one department, and too few at another time, and in another department, and if no provision were made for old age support of some kind, it would be very hard on those who have been long in the service, and have become old, but, not having had previous notice of any such regulation, have made no provision of their own for support after retirement.

V.

Recurring examinations for promotions, reductions and dismissals without provision for the support of those dismissed, are open to the objection last stated; so are also the plans of daily records of efficiency for the same purpose, or fixed terms of office, or retirement at a certain age if taken alone.

Without going too much into detail, it seems that the system of recurring examinations combined with personal inspection and report by a government physician and with the following plan of daily records of efficiency, would be a good method of ascertaining the period when retirement should come to each individual. If it were combined with the more flexible plan of annuities above suggested it would serve as a basis for determining those who could still be retained to advantage though over 70, and those who should be retired under that age.

VI.

As to the plan of daily records of efficiency for promotions, reductions and dismissals whether alone or in combination with recurring examinations and physician's inspection, it certainly seems to have many advantages. The appointing officers can tell better than any one else the real merits of the employees where they are directly under them and where the office is too large for that, the head of the division can do the same, and if a record of daily efficiency is kept, based on a good system of ascertaining the amount and quality of the work done, it would certainly aid very much in securing fairness of treatment and in weeding out the inefficient. Such a system was adopted in the Navy Department under Secretary Long, in 1897, for preliminary tests for promotion, and has been recommended by the Civil Service Commission in its 16th report as very valuable. As to political motives influencing the action of the heads of divisions it may be stated that most of such heads of divisions are now within the classified service, and receive their places by promotion from those who have entered under civil service examinations. As to the best plan to be adopted, however, although the views of experienced appointing officers at present differ a good deal, it seems that in the end they will work out a better plan than this committee can do. But it may be prophesied that any such plan would combine many of the features of both the last two remedies.

VII.

As to fixed terms of office the remedy does not seem advisable. The plan for fixed terms of offices may have two interpretations. It may allow for reappointment at the end of the term, or, dismissal may be final and absolute when the term is completed. If reappointments are allowed it is but a haphazard remedy at best and pretty sure to be ineffectual. It is haphazard, as many may need to be dismissed before the term expires and it will be ineffectual because the same reasons that prevent removal for old age and incapacity will induce reappointment. Under the four year term law, if there is no political motive for removal, there is never any pretense even of an examination of the record of efficiency, and reappointment becomes a perfunctory affair, and many illustrations can be given of reappointment of persons who have passed the age of usefulness, on grounds of pity, even apart from any political influence. For example in the service of the State House at Massachusetts the only old man kept in an important position of late years after his usefulness had passed, held one of the few offices that was subject to a four year term. What little political influence there may have been was rather in favor of creating a vacancy, but it seemed so hard to refuse reappointment when he was too feeble to find employment elsewhere, and as his subordinates could do the work, he was continued on and recently died in office. If the dismissals, on the other hand, are made final and absolute it would work great injury to the service by depriving it of the experience gained in office and of some of the material needed for promotions to higher positions. For example, if the ten year limit, which is often suggested, were applied, the very time that an employee has shown his ability for promotion by the best possible test, that of experience in office, he is forever put out of the service.

VIII.

The system of forced retirement at a fixed age has the double disadvantage that some men are dismissed whose services are still of the greatest value and that others who have not reached the specified age are, and perhaps long have been incapacitated are retained. The British system and the United States Army system provide for retirement at a fixed age, but they also provide for putting on the retired list, under suitable conditions, those who have become unfit for service before reaching that age. So those systems are open to only one of the two objections.

RECOMMENDATIONS.

Your committee unanimously recommend as the best rem edy for superannuation a system requiring life insurance on the deferred annuity plan by all employees during probation, as a prerequisite to final appointment, the policies to be non-assignable and in government control; and to be secured by deposits from the insuring companies in government control; those employees still capable and useful at the fixed age to be allowed to stay in the service at regular salary, on condition that their annuities go to a surplus fund with which to pay annuities to those under that fixed age who have become incapable from age and through no fault of their own, and a system of daily records of efficiency, combined perhaps with recurring inspection by a government physician and in some cases, with examinations, to determine who can stay in over the fixed age and who below it are to share in the surplus annuities. The exact age at which the annuities would normally be payable, varying perhaps for different kinds of service, the amount of annuity to be paid for in the various grades, the age and conditions under which the surplus annuities would be paid to those superannuated below the normal age, and all other details necessary to carry out the plan as more fully outlined heretofore, should be fixed by regulations to be drawn by some special commission, composed perhaps of the Civil Service Commission and some experienced officials of the departments appointed by the President. It might be well to apply this system to a portion only of the classified civil service, say to the departments at Washington, and the larger post-offices and custom-houses, just as was done when the civil service law was first put in operation, and then extend the system as fast as the commission, with the approval of the President, may deem expedient.

Respectfully submitted:

RICHARD HENRY DANA,
WM. DUDLEY FOULKE,
SILAS W. BURT.

Report of the Special Committee on Political Assessments.

To the National Civil Service Reform League:

A T a joint meeting of the General and Executive Committees of the League, held at the Sagamore Hotel, Lake George, on July 28th last, the following resolution was adopted:

That a joint letter be addressed on behalf of the League, by a Committee of three, to be appointed for the purpose, to the Chairman of the respective National Committees, citing the provisions of law respecting the solicitation or receipt of assessments, subscriptions or contributions from government employees, for political purposes, and calling attention to the fact that even in the absence of law this practice is condemned by enlightened public opinion; and, further, that the Secretary be instructed to furnish copies of this letter to the press.

The undersigned were appointed the Special Committee therein mentioned. On August 21st, following, they addressed the following letter to Hon. M. A. Hanna, Chairman of the Republican National Committee:

NEW YORK, AUGUST 21, 1900.

HON. MARCUS A. HANNA,

CHAIRMAN, REPUBLICAN NATIONAL COMMITTEE,

SIR:

On behalf of the National Civil Service Reform League, we ask your aid to prevent the levying of assessments for political purposes upon public servants during the present campaign. The prevalence of this abuse had awakened such general indignation that Congress, in enacting the Civil Service Law, inserted special safeguards against its recurrence in the Federal service. Sections XI, XII and XIV of that law are as follows:

"Sec. XI. No Senator, or Representative, or Territorial Delegate of the Congress, or Senator, Representative, or Delegate elect, or any officer or employee of either of the said Houses, and no executive, judicial, military or naval officer of the United States, and no clerk, or employee of any department, branch, or bureau of the executive, judicial or military or naval service of the United States, shall, directly or indirectly, solicit or receive or be in any manner concerned in soliciting or receiving, any assessment, subscription or contribution for any political purpose whatever from any officer, clerk or employee of the United States, or any department, branch, or bureau thereof, or from any person receiving any salary or compensation from moneys derived from the Treasury of the United States.

"Sec. XII. No person shall, in any room or building occupied in the discharge of official duties by any officer or employee of the United States mentioned in this act, or in any navy yard, fort or arsenal, solicit in any manner whatever, or receive any contribution of money or any other thing of value for any political purpose whatever."

"Sec. XIV. That no officer, clerk or other person in the service of the United States shall, directly or indirectly, give or hand over to any other officer, clerk or person in the service of the United States, or to any Senator or Member of the House of Representatives, or Territorial Delegate, any money or valuable thing on account of or to be applied to the promotion of any political object whatever."

These provisions of law testify to the solicitude wherewith it was then sought to protect all those in the service of the United States from the injustice and oppression involved in such assessments, and there is the more reason to note in this connection the terms of Section XI because, like the Chairman of the National Democratic Committee, you are a Senator of the United States, so that any solicitation or even any receipt of contributions from Federal public servants, by either Committee, no matter whether "directly" or "indirectly," that is to say, through the agency of any sub-committee or representative, would constitute a plain violation of law. In fact any officer or employee of the United States asked to give an assessment or contribution for political purposes "directly or indirectly" to a committee of which a Senator of the United States is chairman, is solicited to commit a crime.

We cannot question the desire of both Senator Jones and yourself to secure obedience to this law on the part of all who are required to respect and enforce it; but it is, nevertheless, true that in previous campaigns attempts have been repeatedly made to evade its salutary provisions; indeed alleged offences of this nature are even now the subject of offical inquiry by the law officers of the government. It is in no wise our purpose, however, to confine what we now say to assessments on Federal office-holders or to acts made unlawful by particular statutes. We believe that, in a free country, the collection of such enforced contributions from public servants of any grade or kind, whether Federal, State or Municipal, who may make them through fear lest refusal be followed by injurious consequences to themselves and their families, is a grave scandal; we have no doubt that such is the belief of honorable and patriotic men, whatever their politics or party, throughout the Union, and we request you, as a good citizen, to join with us in a protest against these wrongs.

We ask from you, therefore, a public declaration that you recognise the right of every man, whether in public or private employ, to the wages of his labor without such molestation and that, so far as may be in your power, you will see that no one suffers because of refusal to comply with any demand for contributions made professedly on behalf of your Committee or of the great party which you represent.

We remain. Sir, Yours very respectfully,

CHARLES J. BONAPARTE, WM. DUDLEY FOULKE, HENRY A. RICHMOND,
Special Committee.

At the same time a precisely similar letter was addressed to Hon. James K. Jones, Chairman of the Democratic National Committee. To the latter communication we received the following reply:

THE DEMOCRATIC NATIONAL COMMITTEE.

CHICAGO, ILL., Sept. 1, 1900.

Messrs. CHARLES J. BONAPARTE,
 W. D. FOULKE, and
 H. A. RICHMOND, *Sub-Committee,*
54 William Street, New York City.

GENTLEMEN:

Your favor is received, and I hasten to say in reply that I have observed, and shall continue to do so, the entire civil service law in all respects. Evasions of the law are equivalent to violations, and it is the duty of every American citizen, and especially of every officer, to live up to the law strictly.

I agree with you fully that "in a free country, the collection of enforced contributions from public servants of any kind, whether federal, state or municipal, who might make them through fear that refusal might be followed by injurious consequences to themselves and families," is a grave scandal and I sincerely hope that a healthy public sentiment may very soon render such things absolutely impossible.

I am sure that all of those with whom I am associated politically will continue to observe the law, and that if our party should be successful in the approaching campaign that there will be at no time, during its administration of the affairs of the government, any just ground for complaint that any statute has been evaded or violated in letter or in spirit.   Very respectfully,

JAMES K. JONES.

Senator Hanna returned no acknowledgment of the letter sent to him. The letters of the Committee and of Senator Jones were furnished by the Secretary of the League to the press, and obtained considerable publicity.

The action taken by the League at its present meeting has relieved the Committee from the necessity of comment on

Senator Hanna's failure to comply with their request or even to acknowledge their letter. They heartily endorse the League's congratulations to the country on the undoubted fact that the evils mentioned in their letters to the Chairmen, although still scandalously flagrant and tolerated by prominent politicians, are yet, on the whole, far less frequent, far less open and far less profitable than these have been in the past.

Very respectfully submitted.

CHARLES J. BONAPARTE
WM DUDLEY FOULKE,
HENRY A. RICHMOND,

Special Committee.

Report of the Committee on Access to the Records of the Civil Service Commission.

To the National Civil Service Reform League:

SOME two weeks after the President's order of May 29th, 1899, the United States Civil Service Commission, for the first time in its history, refused, by a vote of two to one (its President, Mr. Procter, dissenting and stating his reasons for dissent in a carefully prepared and out-spoken minute) to permit access to its records to a representative of the League, for the rather vague reasons that to grant this " would be against public policy and not in the interests of the public service." The League, represented in this instance by the Secretary of the Civil Service Reform Association of the District of Columbia, had asked for data with reference to reported violation of the rules in the Appraiser's Department at New York, to removals at certain of the larger Post Offices and Custom Houses, and to the nominations made by the Secretary of the Treasury for non-competitive examinations under the amended rules of July 27, 1897.

Why a disclosure of these matters should have been regarded as peculiarly impolitic at that particular time can be matter of conjecture only, but after some four months of intermittent correspondence, and a hearing given the Secretary of the League in the latter part of October, 1899, access was again granted to all such records as the League had ever desired to inspect. The decision of the Commission was set forth in the following letter:

UNITED STATES CIVIL SERVICE COMMISSION.

WASHINGTON, November 2, 1899.

MR. GEORGE MCANENY,
    SECRETARY NATIONAL CIVIL SERVICE REFORM LEAGUE.
SIR:
    In response to your communications of October 7 and 30, you are informed that the Commission will allow an agent of your League access to the records of the Commission as requested by you, as follows:

1. Figures and statistics relative to the operation of the civil service act and rules as derived from the periodical reports of appointing officers.

2. The names of persons appointed, promoted or transferred to, or reinstated in, or removed or resigned from positions in the classified service.

3. Files relating to investigations that have been completed or closed touching on the operation of the civil service act and rules,—with the modification that the request shall specify the particular file desired, and that such file shall be submitted to the Commissioners for their approval before access is permitted. This restriction is made for protection of employees and others who may have written to the Commission in confidence.

4. The minutes of the Commission kept in pursuance of section 2 of the civil service act.

Very respectfully,

JOHN R. PROCTER, *President.*

Thereupon the League continued its investigations for about a month, and, in the Spring of the present year, resumed them, until it had ascertained and tabulated facts which sufficiently showed, *inter alia*, the practical results of the President's order of May 29th, 1899, from its date to January 1st, 1900. For reasons set forth in our second letter hereinafter contained, it was subsequently determined to bring the tabulation of these results down to May 29th, 1900; so as to portray the working of the order in practice during a full year; but, shortly after this purpose on the League's part became apparent, the denial of access was repeated. On July 14 a new minute was adopted closing *all* records to any except the Commission's own employees, Mr. Procter again dissenting, and the League's investigations were necessarily suspended. To test the scope and meaning of this minute the League on July 23 made a written request for permission to examine certain records clearly covered by the terms of the letter of November 2nd. This was refused after a long delay and several inconclusive replies on the part of the Commission. The undersigned had been meantime appointed a Special Committee to take such further action on behalf of the League as might seem appropriate in the premises; as soon as informed of the Commission's definitive refusal, we addressed it the following letter:

NEW YORK, September 12, 1900.

TO THE UNITED STATES CIVIL SERVICE COMMISSION,

GENTLEMEN :

On July 23rd last, the Secretary of the National Civil Service Reform League, Mr, George McAneny, requested permission for a representative of the League to examine such records of the Commission as would show :

"(1) The number of persons appointed from eligible lists to competitive positions in the several Executive Departments and offices during the period from May 29, 1899, to December 31, 1899.

"(2) The number of persons appointed under temporary certicates to competitive positions during the same period.

"(3) The number of persons appointed to excepted positions not subject to non-competitive examination during the same period.

"(4) The names of persons holding positions in the Internal Revenue and Custom services (excepting storekeepers and gaugers) who have been appointed since May 29, 1899, or who were appointed prior to that date and examined after it, showing in each case, (a) the date of appointment or nomination, (b) the date (where entered) of the request of the Department for examination, (c) the date of examination and (d) the rating received in percentage."

At the same time Mr. McAneny further requested on behalf of the League that its representative might be permitted to ascertain whether six specified persons were "still in the Customs Service ; if not, at what dates they were separated therefrom."

On November 2, preceding this request, you had informed the League that its agents would be allowed access to your records, including such as would show, *inter alia :*

"1. Figures and statistics relative to the operation of the civil service act and rules as derived from the periodical reports of appointing officers.

"2. The names of persons appointed, promoted or transferred to, or reinstated in, or removed or resigned from positions in the classified service."

Prior to the incident leading to the correspondence, of which your letter of November 2 formed part, the Commission had acted consistently upon a principle thus stated by your President in an official minute :

"Nothing so much fosters the spoils system as secrecy in the administration of patronage. . . . . People have a right to know what their officials are doing, and if the records are closed to their inspection they will imagine evils which do not exist."

In the language of its Eighth Report, published during the administration of President Harrison by Messrs. Charles D. Lyman (now Appointment Clerk of the Treasury Department), Theodore Roosevelt (now

Governor of New York and candidate for the Vice-Presidency) and Hugh S. Thompson :

"One of the chief aims of the Commission is to keep the public thoroughly informed of the workings of the law, ... to keep the public confident of the honesty with which the law is administered." . . . .

"The books and records of the Commission and of all the local Boards are open to any responsible person. . . . . No fraud can be committed without leaving a record by which it can be found out."

Investigations made by the League into the immediate effects of the President's order of May 29, 1899, which was the first act of any President since the enactment of the Civil Service Law whereby the application of the Merit System to the Federal Service was sensibly curtailed, led on June 13, 1899, to the discovery that a majority of the present Commission appeared to dissent from the views thus expressed by Messrs. Lyman, Roosevelt and Thompson, and that the Commission, as well as the President, had seemingly adopted a new policy.

Whatever may have been the League's regret at this change in the Commission's course, it adapted its action to the views expressed in the Commission's letter of November 2, above quoted. The information for which it subsequently asked, from time to time, was precisely such as the Commission had then announced itself ready to afford; moreover, in obtaining this information, it was careful to guard against imposing any expense on the Government or interfering in any wise with the current work of the office. On July 23, it requested leave to ascertain, at its own cost, from the very records mentioned in the Commission's letter of November 2, certain facts which were evidently calculated to shed light upon the operation of "the Civil Service Act and Rules" since the President's order of May 29, 1899. But this request, after a long delay, has been finally refused, and, consequently, at a joint meeting of the General and Executive Committees of the League we were directed to lay before you and the public, appropriate representations respecting this refusal.

We submit that officers of the United States, whatever their rank or duties, are servants of the American people ; that they receive the people's pay and spend the people's money ; that their business is to give effect to the people's will and protect the people's interest ; and that from their masters they have no proper secrets; what they do or leave undone, in the work they are employed or paid to do, cocerns all Americans and can rightfully be hidden from none. To this elementary principle of free government there are, indeed, certain recognized qualifications, justified by the exigency of war or diplomacy, or the avoidance of needless publicity for scandalous or confidential matters. With these, however, we have no concern, for, in the present case, no such considerations apply ; the information asked relates to no secret of State, to no question of individual morals or private live. The League wishes to discover, and, if need be, to publish, results of certain action on the part of the President. action taken in the discharge of his official duty ; these are facts which in the public interest ought to be made known just as soon as they can be stated with certainty. We submit that your refusal to permit the League's representative to examine public records, creates a gratuitous hinderance to the people's knowing the truth as to the conduct of their own officer.

In view of these very serious considerations, we hope that you will rescind your recent action on this subject, and remain,

Yours very respectfully,

CHARLES J. BONAPARTE, EDWARD CARY, FREDERICK L. SIDDONS.
Special Committee, National Civil Service Reform League.

This letter led to further correspondence as follows:

UNITED STATES CIVIL SERVICE COMMISSION.

WASHINGTON, D. C., September 28, 1900.

Messrs. CHARLES J. BONAPARTE, EDWARD CARY, and
FREDERICK L. SIDDONS,
Special Committee, National Civil Service Reform League,

GENTLEMEN :

This Commission is in receipt of your communication of September 12, transmitted by the Secretary of the National Civil Service Reform League, submitting certain statements concerning the furnishing of information to your League by the Commission. Reply to your letter has been delayed in order to enable the Commission to determine to what extent information had been furnished on request of the Secretary of your League in the past.

Apparently your communication is the result of entire misapprehension, as this Commission is, and always has been, in full harmony and accord with what is said and quoted in your letter respecting the desirability of the widest possible publicity concerning the operation of the civil service law and rules and the results of the work of the Commission ; and the Commission knows of no action on its part which, expressly or by any implication, could be regarded as contrary to these views, and is not aware of any change of policy whatever in this respect ; on the contrary, the present Commission has gone further in the direction of publicity than any previous Commission, notably in the opening to persons in interest of registers which had previously been kept secret, so that every appointment thereafter might be thoroughly scrutinized in order to determine whether the law and rules in this respect were honestly and fairly administered, and a much wider diversity and amount of information has been published in the annual reports of this Commission than heretofore. Moreover, the records of the Commission show that all of the great amount of information requested by the Secretary of your League since June 13, 1899, the date you allege as the beginning of a change of policy, has been furnished as promptly as the condition of the Commission's business and the status of the matters involved would permit, with the single exception of the last request made at the end of his letter under date of July 23, 1900, for information concerning the continuance of six persons in the customs service, which request was evidently overlooked because not enumerated with the requests contained in the body of his letter, As soon, however, as this item was brought to the attention of the Commission, steps were taken to furnish the information.

On July 14, 1900, the Commission adopted the following minute :

"Ordered, That hereafter whenever a request is received for information concerning the Commission's work, before the data for such information has been prepared for the annual report or for other public use, if the information desired be such as to justify it, the Commission will furnish such official information and facts as may be in its posession, as well as copies of its files and records, to such outside parties or organizations as request the same, so far as the good of the public service and the limited force of employees of the Commission will warrant.

"It is further ordered, That hereafter no person who is not a member of the Commission's force shall have access to its files and records for the purpose of preparing information for any unofficial purpose."

It will be seen that this minute again emphasizes the purpose of the Commission to continue to furnish all possible information to the public. so far as the good of the service and its limited force of employees will warrant. At the same time, because of the embarrassment the Commission has suffered through the action of persons not responsible to it who have from time to time obtained almost unrestricted access to its files and records, including some which at the time were of a nature which the public interest demanded should not then be made generally known, and because of the failure of the precautions which the Commission had taken to prevent improper use of the privileges granted such persons, and also the undue interference with the transaction of its current business, it was ordered that no persons not members of the Commission's force should have access to its files and records in order to prepare information for unofficial purposes. This latter provision does not in any way curtail or abridge the opportunity to secure all proper information concerning the operation of the civil service law and rules, and it is believed that through it the Commission will be relieved from the embarrassment and interference with its work heretofore referred to, as well as the further liability of wide misconception and misrepresentation in regard to its work occasioned by the many errors which have been made heretofore by persons engaged in compiling information who had little or no knowledge of the Commission's work and consequently were prone to fall into egregious errors concerning it, thus prejudicing and rendering practically valueless their results.

Notwithstanding the statements made by the Secretary of your League, the Commission's files and records show that substantially all of the information proper to be furnished to the public which was requested in his letter of July 15, had already been furnished to him, and therefore he was advised, under date of September 8, that because this information had been furnished and because of the urgency of the public business, the transaction of which had been and would again be interfered with by the presence of your agent, "The Commission must therefore at present decline to permit your representative to consult the records as requested in your letter of July 23." Inasmuch as your Secretary again requested, under date of September 12, that the League's representative be given access to the files and records in order to again compile the information, he was informed under date of September 20, in pursuance of the minute of July 14 above quoted, how the information desired might be secured without causing the public interest to suffer and at the same time furnishing information entitled to all the credit given to that officially promulgated by the Commission, as it would be prepared by the persons most competent and best qualified to accurately and correctly compile it.

In conclusion, this Commission desires it to be distinctly understood that the files and records showing the operation of the civil service law and rules and of the results of the Commission's work continue to be open to the public in the same manner and to the same degree as formerly, and that any person desiring information on any specific point, not incompatible with the public interest, will be promptly furnished therewith, and will be shown the file and record in relation thereto if desired; but, in the discretion vested in the Commission as the responsible custodian of its files and records, it has determined, for the reasons herein stated, that it is clearly in the public interest that this publicity be given in the manner herein described, and that it clearly is not in the public interest to allow unrestricted and indiscriminate access to its files and records.

By direction of the Commission.

Very respectfully,

JOHN B. HARLOW,
Acting President.

NEW YORK, October 18, 1900.

TO THE UNITED STATES CIVIL SERVICE COMMISSION,
WASHINGTON, D. C.

GENTLEMEN:

Your letter of September 28, in reply to ours of the 12th, with reference to the right of access to the Commission's records, informs us that:

"The Commission is and always has been in full harmony and accord with what is said in the Committee's letter . . . . and knows of no action on its part which expressly or by implication could be regarded as contrary to these views, or of any change of policy whatever in this respect."

This information is very gratifying, but we must add that it is no less surprising. The policy of the Commission before the President's Order of May 29, 1899, was described by Messrs. Lyman, Thompson and Roosevelt, as follows:

"The books and records of the Commission and of all the local Boards are open to any responsible person. No fraud can be committed without leaving a record by which it can be found out."

In the minute of July 14, 1900, to which you refer, the Commission declared its purpose to deny thereafter access to *any* of its records *to all* persons "not members of the Commission's force" and added:

"All orders or minutes heretofore made by the Commission in conflict with the provisions of this order, are hereby revoked."

This latter part of the minute you did not quote.

Until enlightened by your letter, we certainly regarded this action as indicating a definitive abandonment of the policy of Messrs. Lyman, Thompson and Roosevelt; and no less certainly we were not alone in that opinion, for, on June 13, 1899, when, for the first time in its history, the Commission denied to the National Civil Service Reform League access to its files, the President of the Commission (Mr. Proctor) said in a dissenting minute:

"The vote of the Commission to keep its records secret is an absolute reversal, for the first time in the history of the Commission, of a policy which has been universally commended as wise."

"It has been the constant public boast of the Commission that its records are subject to inspection and that the inspection is invited. I can conceive of nothing which is calculated to do more damage to the work of the Commission, and its power for good, than the refusal to permit access to files of cases in which action has been completed."

Since, however, you say that "misapprehension" exists as to the consistency of the present with the past practice of the Commission in this respect, we respectfully suggest that you can readily remove this "misapprehension:" your predecessors, Messrs. Lyman, Thompson and Roosevelt, told the public: "The books and records of the Commission . . . . are open to any responsible person;" you have only to tell the public that this is still true.

You further tell us that:

"Notwithstanding the statements made by the Secretary of your League, the Commission's files and records show that substantially all the information proper to be furnished to the public, which was requested in his letter of July 23, had already been furnished to him."

This passage in your letter has caused the delay in its acknowledgment by leading the Secretary of the League to request that we further examine his somewhat voluminous correspondence with the Commission before replying.

While we do not understand that the question as to what had or had not been secured by the League at the time of previous examinations of the records has any pertinence to the question really at issue, we feel that the facts in this regard may be briefly stated: Having obtained limited access to the files of the Commission in November, 1899, after a tedious delay of five months, the League ascertained and tabulated facts which showed, with certain omissions, the practical working of the President's order of May 29, 1899, from its date to January 1, 1900. It was subsequently decided to extend this investigation until the results of a year's application of the order could be shown, and, at the same time, both to complete and verify the work already done, and to take up certain additional subjects. Before the new work was finished however, the Commission's minute of July 14 was adopted. It was this that led to the Secretary's letter of July 23, asking directly for access to records clearly covered by the Commission's concession of November, 1899.

The particular omissions to be covered in completing tables were not specified for the reason that this, very naturally, was not understood to be necessary. The letter was met with a repetition of the denial of access contained in the minute of July 14. Aside from the question of pertinency, we do not see why the Commission should cite the incident of July 23 as a reason for its action taken nine days previously; nor can we agree with the Commission if it holds either that "substantially all the information" to be gained by *twelve* months' experience is afforded by the first *seven*, or that such information can be "proper to be furnished to the public" when it relates to the year 1899, and improper when it relates to the year 1900.

It so happens that the additional enquiry referred to was undertaken by reason of a conversation of our Secretary with the President himself. The results of the League's investigation, although incomplete, were so startling that Mr. McAneny, by direction of the Executive Committee, obtained an audience of the President, and asked if he would give consideration to a memorial, pointing out in detail the deplorable consequences of his Order, and praying for its revocation. The President replied courteously that he would *consider* anything the League submitted, but that he regarded any criticism of the Order's working as premature until it had been given a fair trial. The League then determined to await the expiration of the full year from May 29, 1899, before preparing its intended memorial, and circumstances caused some further delay.

Whilst the Commission has never said that the agents employed by the League in its investigations are not "responsible persons," or that in any specified instance the work of the Commission has been impeded by their presence, the language it has used might well give this impression to a careless reader. We deem it proper, therefore, to mention in this letter that the two gentlemen, Mr. F. B. Tracy and Mr. George A. Warren, successively employed by the League for these purposes, are, as you well know, men, not only of high standing and excellent reputation, but also exceptionally competent for this particular work, and that tables originally prepared by them for the League are published, with certain additions, among the appendices to your Sixteenth Annual Report. The League has been glad to furnish copies of such tables to the Secretary of the Commission, in reciprocation of his personal courtesies, whenever they have been desired, and has been gratified to learn that they have proved practically useful.

In conclusion, permit us to say that the Commission's professed readiness to furnish such measure of information as "it is clearly within the public interest to give" and "so far as the good of the public service and its limited force of employees will warrant" is, again, quite beside the question at issue. Everyone knows that you have confidential records touching the character and antecedents of applicants for public office ; to these the League has never asked or desired access. Your remaining records, in the words of Messrs. Lyman, Thompson and Roosevelt, of right "are open to any responsible person", and for this freedom of access no substitute will, we venture to say, be accepted as sufficient by public opinion. We therefore respectfully renew the request of our previous letter, that we may among other things, complete, in accordance with the suggestion of the President, an accurate and adequate statement of the operation and consequences of his order of May 29, 1899, after it had been given a fair trial.

We remain, Gentlemen, Yours very truly,

CHARLES J. BONAPARTE, EDWARD CARY, FREDERICK L. SIDDONS.
Special Committee, National Civil Service Reform League.

UNITED STATES CIVIL SERVICE COMMISSION,

WASHINGTON, D. C., Oct. 25, 1900.

Messrs. CHARLES J. BONAPARTE, EDWARD CARY and
FREDERICK L. SIDDONS,
Special Committee, National Civil Service Reform League.

GENTLEMEN :

This Commission is in receipt of your communication under date of October 18, 1900, in reply to the Commission's communication under date of September 28, 1900, and respectfully advises you that, after a careful reading, your communication does not seem to contain or advance any matters upon which the views of the Commission are not already expressed in its communication under date of September 28, 1900.

As to your request contained in your communication of October 18, that you "may, among other things, complete, in accordance with the suggestion of the President, an accurate and adequate statement of the operation and consequences of his order of May 29, 1899, after it had been given a fair trial," your attention is again respectfully invited to the Commission's communication of September 28 and to the Commission's communication to your Secretary under date of September 20, 1900, wherein it is pointed out in detail how all proper information which is obtainable from the Commission's records, and which you may desire in the compiling of any statements which you may be preparing or for use in connection with any investigations which you may be prosecuting, may, in the opinion of the Commission be best and most satisfactorily obtained, and wherein it is stated that, in accordance with the method pointed out, the Commission will always be glad to consider requests from your Secretary for such information as the League may desire.

Therefore, if you, your Secretary, or any other member of your League, will kindly indicate just what information is desired at this time, the Commission will be pleased to have the same furnished in accordance with its communications of September 20 and September 27.

By direction of the Commission :

Very respectfully,
JOHN B. HARLOW,
Acting President.

We deem no further comment necessary on the Commission's attitude than is implied in plainly stating it. The Commission offers to let its own employees obtain information for the League from its files; it refuses to let the employees of the League, to whose character and fitness for such work it has no objection to offer, obtain this information at the League's expense, under whatever reasonable regulations may be needful to prevent interference with the work of the office, no complaint of such interference having ever been made in the past or being made now. The Commission professes its willingness to furnish information 'if the information desired be such as to justify it' and '*so far as* the good of the public service . . . . will warrant,' but its decision on these questions must be made when each application is received and is not to be governed by any such general rules as were set forth in its letter of November 2nd, 1899; so that precisely the same data may be furnished at one time and denied at another, or granted to one applicant and refused to the next. Moreover, the information furnished on any subject will be, not necessarily *the whole* truth, as shown by the Commission's records, but the truth thus shown *so far as* in the judgment of the Commission, 'the good of the public service will warrant' its disclosure.

We have said that in our judgment this attitude, when clearly defined, needs no comment, but one word may be fitly said of it in conclusion; this was not the attitude of the Commission when the present Vice-President elect was one of its members. Then, in the words of the Eighth Report, 'the books and records of the Commission' were 'open to any responsible person'; now, under the minute of July 14, 'no person who is not a member of the Commission's force shall have access to its files and records'; then, Mr. Roosevelt and his colleagues said: 'No fraud can be committed without leaving a record by which it can be found out'; now, such a record may perhaps be left, but whether its exists or not, no one but 'a member of the Commission's force' can know, and whether the fraud shall be found out by the public depends on the Commission's judgment as to *how far* 'the good of the public service will warrant' letting in the light of day. In their Eighth Report, above quoted, the Commissioners then in office spoke like men conscious that they were doing their duty and having the courage born of such consciousness; on the language of the majority of the present Commission we have already declared comment needless.

Very respectfully submitted,

CHARLES J. BONAPARTE,
EDWARD CARY,
FREDERICK L. SIDDONS,
Special Committee.

The Choice of Correct Methods in the Administration of American Dependencies.

BY ELLIOT H. GOODWIN.

TWO years ago, at the annual meeting of the National Civil Service Reform League in Baltimore, Mr. Dorman B. Eaton spoke on the need and best means for providing a competent and stable civil service for our new dependencies. His thorough study of civil service reform in Great Britain, his experience in the institution and practice of civil service reform in this country, add weight to the words in which he approached the new problem:

" These truths are equally fundamental and important : that a community cannot maintain its political morality, improve its government, or even prevent the decay of both, without habitually bringing into its official leadership true representatives of its best character and capacity. These great truths should be regarded as all the more admonishing, and they are all the more vital, when a government intervenes in the affairs of a foreign people while proclaiming its purpose of establishing its own dominion for their improvement."

The results of the recent election have made it patent to all that—if not permanently—at least for a considerable time to come we must face the problem of governing dependent peoples, in race, language and custom widely differing from us. Few, even among the bitterest opponents of the policy of the administration regarding Porto Rico and the Philippines, wish to see them eventually separated from this country as a result of maladministration. Yet our success in our new calling depends upon the readiness with which we meet our new responsibilities; and among these none is more important—as Mr. Eaton has pointed out—than the establishment of an honest and efficient corps of officials. In an earnest search for the best method for recruiting such a corps, we are met at the outset by the fact that the application of the civil service reform system [in the only form in which it is known to us in this country, may well serve as a means for selecting men to fill the subordinate positions; but it is, to say the least, doubtful whether it will suffice as a method of procuring officials to occupy the posts of trust and responsibility in the administrative service.

Briefly stated, the merit system as applied in America contemplates the existence in the community of men whose training and experience have fitted them to fill the positions for which the government requires them. For all kinds of clerical positions, and even for those demanding technical knowledge, there are plenty to choose from. The examinations are in no sense academic; they aim to test the applicant's knowledge of the duties of the position and great weight is allowed in marking for actual experience in a similar position. But there is no class in the community which has had experience in the government of eastern races, or anything similar to it. No examination based on the recognized duties of these administrative officials can adequately test the capacity of the candidates to cope with new and unforseen problems, or their tact in dealing with the natives. These results can only be obtained by a course of training in the country itself, and the problem narrows to the question of the method of selecting the men best fitted to undergo this training.

It is precisely this question of the best methods of selection and training which can be introduced in this country, which, within the limited time allotted to me for so large a subject, I propose to discuss.

England has already solved the problem to her own satisfaction. From her experience in India we have the most to learn, both because it is a large dependency, not suited to western colonization, and because, in the course of a long history, England has made trial of three distinct methods of recruiting the administrative service. At first a system of open patronage prevailed. This was followed by the foundation of Haileybury College in 1806 as a training school for future administrators. Admission was obtained only on nomination by the Directors of the East India Company, but the College made use of the same means for weeding out the poor material that are employed in West Point and Annapolis. The third stage resulted from the report of the Macaulay Commission in 1853. Haileybury was abolished, and since that time appointments to the administrative and judicial service of India has been made from the candidates standing highest in an open competitive examination, conducted annually by the Civil Service Commissioners in London.

Throughout this varied course, England has clung to one principle, to which may be largely attributed her success, that the training received in India is of prime importance to the aspirant for a high administrative position, and for this training no substitute is sufficient. Whether under a patronage or a merit system, it has been her consistent policy to send out men young enough to assimilate themselves easily to new duties and new conditions. The report of the commission of 1853, drafted by Lord Macaulay, marks a complete departure from the idea of training young men before going out with special reference to the conditions which they would encounter and the duties they would have to perform. Yet as this plan has proved itself the most successful of any that has been tried, it will bear closer analysis.

The report contemplates the establishment of an examination open to all subjects of Great Britain between the ages of eighteen and twenty-three. The Commision believed it desirable that university men who had received a degree should be attracted, and to this end the subjects of examination were arranged in accordance with the courses of studies which prevailed at the leading universities. The pursuit of studies which would be of little or no value in case the applicant was unsuccessful at the examination was discouraged. None of the subjects were to deal specifically with India or the duties to be performed. To quote the words of the report :

" We believe that men who have been engaged, up to one or two and twenty, in studies which have no immediate connection with the business of any profession, and of which the effect is to open, to invigorate, and to enrich the mind, will generally be found in the business of every profession, superior to men who have at eighteen or nineteen devoted themselves to the special studies of their calling."

The Commission anticipated about forty vacancies each year. The high salaries, liberal pensions and security of tenure attaching to these positions would, it was thought, secure sharp competition. There was no provision for a choice among successful candidates; on the contrary the forty—or such number as might be required—who stood highest in the examination were to become of right probationers. With the examination the successful candidates were to be regarded as having completed their general education and were to devote a period of probation of not less than one nor more than two years to preparation for their future duties.

It was recognized that the greater part of this special knowledge could be acquired much more readily in India; and the Commission recommended that the probationer should devote his final year in England to the study of Indian history, the science of jurisprudence, commercial and financial science, and to mastering the rudiments of the Indian languages. At the end of the period of probation a second examination was to be held; competitive only in so far as it should allow the candidates, in the order of their standing, to select the place to which they wished to go.

This system, but slightly modified in detail, has now successfully stood the test of forty years' experience. Examinations are held each year in London, during the month of August, open to all natural born British subjects between the ages of twenty-one and twenty-three, not physically unfit, of good moral character, who pay the entrance fee of six pounds. The list of subjects, from which the candidate is allowed entire freedom to select those in which he wishes to be examined, includes English, Sanscrit and Arabic, Latin and Greek, modern languages, mathematics, natural science, ancient and modern history, philosophy, political economy and law. To each subject is attached a number denoting the greatest number of marks that can be obtained in it. The candidates receiving the greatest aggregate number of marks are selected for service. They are encouraged to spend their probationary year at a university. At the end of probation comes the second examination, based on the lines laid down by the Macaulay Commission. They must undergo further a physical examination and a test of their proficiency in riding.

The system of training here briefly outlined is to supply the vacancies in the administrative and judicial service only. The subordinate officials are recruited in India. It has never been the practice of England to appoint the Governor-General from the administrative service, but to select a man of large experience and proved ability in other walks of life.

Such a method of selecting colonial officials strikes one at once as peculiarly foreign to American tradition and practice; so much so, in fact, as to present an almost insurmountable barrier to its introduction here. But it should be taken into account that in going beyond our natural boundaries to annex distant territories, populated by an Eastern race, we have already made a departure from American tradition and practice, and it cannot surprise any one if for their successful government we must make an equal departure from our accustomed methods of administration.

Indeed, it is hard to see where to turn if not to English experience. The French have tried various methods of training their officials for colonial service, but, following a national trait, they have never remained consistently by one system for a long enough time for it to show its merits. Holland has made the serious blunder of training her officials exclusively with reference to their future positions and duties. A recent report of a commission appointed to inquire into the methods of training condemns this system, and recommends a free choice from among the holders of a Doctor's degree. This throws us back on the great principles underlying the English system as the only sound basis on which a colonial service can be founded.

The essential qualifications of the candidates for administrative positions in an Eastern dependency are, youth, health, and a liberal education. Equally important for a successful administration as correct method of choice are high salaries, security of tenure, and a thorough course of training in the country itself before entering upon administrative duties.

In attempting to apply these principles to America we are brought face to face with many practical difficulties. Foremost among them is the prevalence of the spoils system; but I need not stop to explain to *this* audience that to allow it to gain a foothold in our dependencies would mean failure from the start. Secondly, I would mention the deep-rooted prejudice against highly educated, especially college-educated, men. Thirdly, the jealousy with which high salaries and long tenure are regarded. To overcome these difficulties is essential to success, but the existence of these prejudices must be taken into account in attempting to devise a method of selection that shall be not merely ideal but capable of introduction.

At first sight the field does not seem to be clear for the introduction of a new system. The President has shown that he realized the difficulty of the situation by the excellent appointments he has made to the Philippine Commission. Among its first acts was a Philippine Civil Service Bill intended to cover the whole service. It follows closely the model of our national and state laws, but is more stringent than any in its classification of high positions. An excellent feature is the preference for appointment given to natives who pass the examination. Its worst provision grants a second preference to all honorably discharged soldiers of the United States without regard to the length or severity of their service. The system of employing laborers in the order in which they register may be worthy of trial, although the restraints it imposes will only be necessary in case the natives,—of whom this force should be composed—should develop an aptitude for machine politics.

If the Filipinos are capable of organizing honest and efficient local governments at once, the method of selection by means of practical examinations will suffice for filling the subordinate positions in the service of the Federal departments whose functions are extended to the islands. But if these people prove to be incapable of self-government—the contention upon which the policy of the administration rests—then there will be necessary a class of administrative officials for whose training the Philippine Civil Service Bill makes no adequate provision.

Whether they shall be actual administrators or,—in order to carry out the President's policy of granting the largest measure of self-government possible—a system of residents, with power to advise and report only, shall be established does not affect the importance of introducing an adequate system of selection and training. These positions will first be naturally and best filled by military officers; but they should be succeeded by carefully trained civilians. The Philippine bill makes no provision for their training. In ignoring entirely the necessity for a different method of selection than in the case of subordinate officers the Commissioners have failed to profit by English experience, and have left the question of how these administrative posts may best be filled still to be solved.

The introduction of the English system as it stands would necessitate the holding of yearly examinations open to all subjects of the United States between the ages of 21 and 23. As there would be but few vacancies, the examination would have to be of a very high grade, more searching than that prescribed for graduation at our universities. The age limit is set high enough to allow graduates of our colleges to compete, and this would result in their being the only ones to obtain the places. A system which would confine these desirable appointments to college graduates is out of the question in this country. Nevertheless, experience has shown that precisely this university training is the best. The obvious thing to do is to lower the standard of examination, select the candidates when younger, and provide them with the college education—or one as equally as good—afterwards.

The university training is a feature upon which great stress is laid in England and the next question that arises is whether it must be abandoned here on account of existing prejudices. If this training were not made requisite to a choice, but was entered upon by the candidates after the selection was made, it might be possible to meet these prejudices. The plan would then be for a competitive examination conducted each year by the civil service commissioners, open to all persons between the ages of 18 and 21. A few more than the number of vacancies anticipated should be selected in the order of their standing to undergo a four years' training at a university or college. They should receive a yearly allowance of about six hundred dollars contingent upon their passing the yearly examinations. They should have the right to choose which college they would attend among those that met the requirements laid down by the Civil Service Commission. These requirements should be very stringent. In order to accomplish the desired result no university or college should be admitted to the list which did not have at least one thousand students, and the commissioners should pass on the question whether the general curriculum and the opportunities for special study were sufficient. Finally, it might be necessary to apportion the selected colleges to the different sections of the country—say, three to the East, three to the middle West, two to the far West, one to the South.

Not more than a fourth of the student's time should be devoted to the special studies in line with his future duties. The rest should be spent in acquiring a high general education. At the end of four years they should undergo another examination by the commissioners, compulsory in the special studies, elective in the general, and, in the order of their standing, should have a right to choose among existing vacancies. They should then be sent out at once for that most important feature, the long training preparatory to assuming administrative duties, in the country which they have chosen for a life career.

Another plan has been suggested by Professor A. Lawrence Lowell, in his book on Colonial Civil Service, on which I have drawn almost exclusively for my facts. In setting forth, just at this time, within the limit of two hundred and fifty pages, a history of the experience of England, France and Holland in training colonial officials, Professor Lowell has done a great service, which is not made less by the fact that we are little likely to profit by the experience of others. He recommends the establishment of a government college, to do for the colonial service that which West Point does for the army and Annapolis for the navy. Such a college could provide the young men selected with a high general education and maintain peculiar facilities for the special training. The course of study would be practically that outlined above; three years devoted to general education, and not more than one year spent on those special subjects a knowledge of which would be of little or no value to the student if he stayed at home.

In the matter of admission to the college, Professor Lowell thinks it wise to make a concession to the politicians, and allow the apportionment of places among senators and representatives as is done in the case of West Point and Annapolis. While not the ideal system, he points out that the high standard maintained in these two schools eliminates at an early stage the poor material and prevents it from working extensive detriment to the service. But this same high standard has made the patronage of comparative little value, and, in view of this fact, it should not be difficult to introduce in connection with a new college the far more democratic system of open, competitive examination for admission. The prizes to be gained in the colonial service will be more valuable than in the army and navy, and this will mean greater interference in the organization and working of such a college if any loophole is left for patronage.

This plan of a government college sacrifices an important element in the English system,—the broadening influence of a university training among a large body of young men with widely varying interests. The *esprit du corps* and the knowledge of one another's capabilities which would be gained by uniting all the candidates together in one school, would go far toward making up the deficiency. A government college would undoubtedly encounter less of popular prejudice as less of an innovation than a plan involving a university education.

Professor Lowell sees an obstacle to the government college in the small number of students. He estimates the number of vacancies, after the system is well established, as probably not more than twenty each year. This would mean about one hundred in the school, entirely too small a number to accomplish the desired results.

Might not his suggestion that to this number should be added the candidates for eastern consulships, be enlarged by including the candidates for the entire consular service? To that service as it now exists, the main objections are the lack of general education and culture as well as ignorance of a consul's duties. A college course of three years devoted to general education and one year to special studies would go far to remedy this. The question of establishing a consular school has often been agitated in this country and doubtless, in good time, such a school will be introduced.

In order, then, to meet the future demands of the administrative service in the dependencies, I have ventured to suggest the introduction of a system by which the candidates shall be selected by competitive examination, open to all between the ages of eighteen and twenty-one; those selected to undergo a four years' training, three-fourths of which is to be devoted to general education, either at a university, or at a government college founded especially for the purpose of educating and training our future consuls and colonial officials.

The Results of Civil Service Reform in Australia.

BY HUGO R. MEYER.

THE history of the civil service in Australia interests us because it is the history of the civil service in an English-speaking community that is making the experiment of the state ownership and state management of the railways. Again, the problem of the civil service in Australia can be studied only as a part of the larger problem of the extension of the activity of the state to the inclusion of various industrial and commercial activities, such as the management of the railways, the construction of irrigation works, the lending of money to farmers, the management of state banks, and the insurance of life. The Australian civil service problem is to make the state employees submissive to the discipline and the high standards of efficiency exacted in private employment; and to keep within reasonable limits the wages and salaries paid to this body of men, who number from 10 per cent. to 12 per cent. of the adult male population in a community in which from 25 per cent. to 35 per cent. of the voters regularly fail to vote.

For reasons which I cannot take time to recount, the power of dismissal never has been seriously abused in Australia. Suffice it to say, that the expansion of the various state enterprises under the growth of population constantly called for new appointments, so that it was possible to combine the exercise of political patronage with the system of permanent tenure of office. The serious abuse of political patronage has thus been limited to the practice of obtaining for friends and supporters appointment, promotion, increase of pay, and the remission of fines and penalties imposed for breaches of discipline.

The first efforts to abolish political patronage consisted in legislation of the familiar kind which classified the public service, fixed minimum and maximum salaries, provided for entrance into the state's service by way of examinations, and also for promotion. Such legislation also provided for emergencies and any unusual rush of business by authorizing the appointment of "temporary" employees who needed not to comply with the conditions of entrance to the service, but were not to be employed for a longer period than two years. But legislation of this kind usually remained a dead letter in consequence of the tremendous pressure brought to bear upon the Governments of the day. Victoria, for example, enacted a Civil Service Act in 1862, yet in 1883, not less than 77 per cent. of the civil servants were "temporary" employees with permanent tenure of office. These men, who had come in "over the wall," as a body, had used political influence to get their appointments, subsequent promotions, and increase of pay. They looked to their representatives in Parliament for immunity from punishment, and, in a measure, deemed themselves independent of their superior officers. Ministers not infrequently found it inexpedient to protect their officers against attacks in Parliament made by representatives acting under pressure from civil servants who had been disciplined or had been denied a favor. This so intimidated the leading officers of the Ministers, that even flagrant breaches of duty were likely not to be reported. In all these respects the experience of Victoria was typical of the experience of the Australian colonies generally.

In 1883, Victoria, confronted with an alarming increase of railway accidents, put the management of the railways into the hands of three commissioners, who were appointed for seven years and were removable only upon an address from both Houses of Parliament. At the same time, Victoria put the administration of the rest of the civil service into the hands of three other commissioners, the Public Service Board. The theory of this departure was that Parliament for the future should limit itself to indicating the general policy under which the railways were to be conducted and the civil service was to be managed. The execution of that policy was to be left to the Railway Commissioners and the Public Service Board respectively. And the duty of seeing to it that the policy indicated by Parliament was properly executed was to be left to the Government of the day. In other words, Parliament was to abandon its past practice of encroaching on the work of the Executive by interfering—either as a body or through its individual members—in the details of the management of the railways and the administration of the civil service. New South Wales followed suit by putting the civil service "in commission" in 1884; and the railways in 1888. South Australia, Queensland, and New Zealand put the railways "in commission" in 1887 and 1888. South Australia abandoned the commission system in 1895, because the machine politicians feared that they were losing their grip on politics. In New Zealand, the trade-unions in 1893 overthrew the commissioner systems because the Railway Commissioners had frustrated the attempt to tie up the railways in the great strike of 1890. In Victoria and New South Wales, Parliament continued its interference in the details of management to such an extent as to embarrass seriously the Railway Commissioners. In Victoria, the Government instructed the Commissioners that they must not attempt to secure the efficiency or the discipline exacted in private employment; and Parliament gave them to understand that they must retain the staff as they found it, though it was excessive and contained many men who were incompetent and not submissive to discipline. The New South Wales Commissioners assumed their duties in October, 1888. To officers whom they dismissed they paid twelve months and eighteen months salary as a gratuity; and still they had to proceed so slowly that in December, 1890, there still were superior officers who were trying to block the traffic with the object of discrediting the commissoner system. In this course the officers in question had the support of certain members of Parliament. As late as 1892, the service had not yet been cleared of all incompetent men. Both in New South Wales and in Victoria, Parliament forced the Commissioners to pay the rank and file, as well as the intermediate officers, wages and salaries largely in excess of the wages and salaries paid for corresponding services in private employment. On the other hand, Parliament refused to allow the Commissioners to pay men occupying positions which called for ability of a high order such salaries as the men in question could have obtained in private employment. The labor members in Parliament are opposed on principle to the payment of high salaries, and the opponents of the commissioner system join hands with them from a desire to embarrass the Commissioners.

The following incidents will indicate the extent to which Parliament interferes with the efficient and economical administration of the railways. In August, 1899, Sir George Turner, Premier and Treasurer of Victoria, informed Parliament that in the year just closed the railways had failed by £427,000 to earn the interest on the bonds outstanding against them—£39,000,000. But he added that private parties were ready to purchase the railways at any time for £48,800,000. A few weeks afterward, Mr. Outtrim, Minister of Railways, reminded Parliament that the increases in wages and other concessions granted to the railway staff since 1895–96 aggregated £212,000 a year. Yet in 1896, wages and salaries had been almost as high as in 1890, when they were appreciably above the rates ruling in private employment. On the other hand, the wages of skilled and unskilled labor outside of government employment had fallen from 25 per cent. to 40 per cent. since 1890, and employment was exceedingly precarious even at those reduced rates of remuneration. In October, 1889, Mr. McMillan, Treasurer and Minister of Railways in New South Wales, said in Parliament: "I will stake my reputation as a public man and shall be backed up by the leader of the Opposition, that we can sell the railways within twenty-fours hours in London for £50,000,000." The railway deficit at the time was £206,000 a year on a supposed capitalization of £30,000,000.

The Public Service Boards established in Victoria in 1883 and in New South Wales in 1884 have both turned out failures. In Victoria certain heads of departments openly joined certain members of Parliament in fighting the Board; and ultimately Parliament passed an act which phrased in general terms, but was designed to force the resignation of the one member of the Board who made a determined effort to manage the affairs of the state in the same energetic fashion in which he managed his own affairs. In New South Wales the Public Service Board was rendered ineffective through the administrative rulings made by the different Governments of the day, under pressure brought to bear by the civil servants and the machine politicians.

In 1895, Mr. Reid, Premier of New South Wales, established a new Public Service Board, which, in two years, cut down the cost of the civil service (exclusive of the railway department) by £350,000 a year—in a community of 1,200,000 people. To all men who were dismissed for incompetence, the Board paid by way of gratuity a sum equivalent to one fortnight's salary for every year of service; and to competent men, who were dismissed because there was no work for them, the Board paid one month's salary for every year of service. The Board also kept the salaries of the lowest grades of employees approximately 25 per cent. above the rate prevailing in private employment, and the salaries of superior clerks and special clerks it fixed respectively at 17½ per cent. and 12 per cent. above the rates prevailing in commercial and banking houses. And yet, in the general elections of July, 1898, Mr. Barton, the foremost man in the Australian Federation movement, denounced the Public Service Board as inhuman in its harshness, and promised the civil servants that he would undo much of Mr. Reid's work of retrenchment, if he should be made Premier. And when Mr. Barton's party came into power, in September, 1899, the Attorney-General, Mr. Wise, a graduate of Oxford University, England, and a "scholar in politics," straightway proceeded to keep the promises made by Mr. Barton and himself.

The great body of the civil servants of Australia, acting through their powerful public service associations, and aided by the labor party and the machine politicians, thus far have succeeded in maintaining themselves in a degree of comfort not attainable by men of the same ability who are not fortunate enough to be in the employ of the state. But while the state service is a haven of refuge for men of average ability and ambition, it affords no career for men of high capacity and exceptional energy. In the first place, such men are woefully underpaid. For example, a Chairman Commissioner in charge of some three thousand miles of railway, in Australia, receives from £2,500 to £3,500 a year, whereas the manager of the Melbourne Tramway Co. receives £4,000, and the managers of the large Australian banks receive from £3,000 to £5,000. Then, again, an Australian civil servant who offends either his subordinates or the politicians is liable to have Parliament reduce his salary, and is liable also to be attacked in Parliament and the newspaper press and condemned on an *ex parte* statement. Libelous and slanderous statements made in Parliament are of course made under the cloak of parliamentary privilege; and as to attacks made in the newspaper press, the Supreme Court of Victoria recently has laid down the doctrine: "what as a fact is untrue may be fair comment as an opinion." There would be no virtue in the plea of "fair comment," and no protection for the citizen who criticised the conduct of a public officer, if, by "fair comment" the law were to understand "right comment" or "intelligent comment" or "well informed comment."

The essential failure of the attempt made in Australia to take the civil service out of politics, was summed up as follows in 1893 by Mr. James Service, who, in 1883, as the Premier of Victoria, had introduced the system of management by commission. Said Mr. Service: "However much Parliament may endeavor by legislation to create commissions and boards that shall be independent of Parliament, such boards will be prevented often from doing the duty expected of them, and properly expected of them. They will be prevented from doing their duty, either by the intention, or by the negligence and indifference of the Parliament, or the Ministry of the day." But, if any one should incline to forget the nature of "practical politics," and should incline to be unduly severe in his judgment of the politicians, let him be reminded of the words once uttered by the late Chief Justice Higinbotham, one of the most disinterested men who ever served the people of Victoria. "Parliament has no faults and no shortcomings which are not also political faults and shortcomings of all the adult men in this community. Parliament is just what the people of Victoria have made it; and although it may not be better, it is assuredly not worse than the source from which it sprung."

It would be unfair to the civil servants not to add that in the matter of public spirit, or the lack thereof, the civil servants do not differ from the rest of the community. Organized labor, for example, constantly forces Governments to loan money for expenditure upon public works with the object of making work for skilled and unskilled labor. Again, in 1883, Sir George Dibbs, the Treasurer of New South Wales, floated a loan of £3,000,000 in London, largely for the purpose of affording relief to the Sydney money market, which was tight, in consequence of over-speculations in grazing lands. And the politics of Victoria from 1890 to 1892 can be understood only when interpreted as an effort on the part of the Munro Government and the Shiels Government to use the state's credit for the purpose of warding off an impending financial crisis, the result of mad speculations in country and urban property.

The population of Australia consists almost entirely of emigrants from Great Britain and their descendants. And yet, Parliamentary government in Australia works as in France, rather than as in England. Party ties are loose, and Parliament tends to split up into numerous groups, formed for the purpose of securing what members of Parliament are pleased to term justice for the interests which they represent. Sir Henry Wrixon, late Attorney-General of Victoria, and one of the most judicial men in public life in Australia, has well expressed the situation in the following words: "The many functions undertaken by our Australian Governments, . . . enfeeble the position of the representative, and impair the public spirit of the constituencies. Each locality [and each class interest] naturally seeks to get as much as it can, and for that purpose wants rather an agent to look after its interests than a statesman to take care of those of the country at large. The forbearance of many constituencies toward a member whom they respect upon public grounds, and the sense of duty to the state of members of Parliament, have so far done something to mitigate the worst results of this principle. But the representative is harrassed by a divided duty. That I take to be the greatest impediment to statesmanship in our ranks; and the more socialistic Governments become, the greater is the danger that Burke's prophetic fear may be realized, and 'national representation degraded into a confused and scuffling bustle of local agency.'"

A Report on the Movement in the Women's Clubs in Aid of Civil Service Reform.

BY ELIZABETH FOSTER.

THE Woman's Federated Club Movement in aid of Civil Service Reform began in Concord, Massachusetts, a town which, in its day, has initiated more than one successful protest against powerful evils.

Last January Miss Perkins of Concord, became convinced of the latent possibilities of the nine thousand Woman's Clubs of the United States if their force could be concentrated on the cause of the merit system. She began by interesting the Concord Woman's Club, which agreed to hold a series of public meetings addressed by civil service reformers. Her next step was the publication of a circular called " A Plea for the Study of Civil Service Reform by the Woman's Clubs of America." This was widely circulated among the clubs in every section of the country and aroused great interest. The various Civil Service Reform Associations were consulted, and gave their hearty support. Individual clubs all over the United States endorsed the movement, and the Massachusetts Federation took immediate action by appointing a Civil Service Reform Committee of which Miss Perkins was made chairman.

The next attempt was to obtain a hearing for the subject at the biennial meeting of the General Federation of Woman's Clubs in Milwaukee last June. Mrs. Lowe, President of the Federation, was consulted and referred the proposition with her approval to the Programme Committee, which agreed to allot five minutes to the subject.

Correspondence was then started with the Presidents of the various State Federations to prepare the ground before the subject of Civil Service Reform should be presented in pursuance of this plan, at the General meeting. Many were interested and wrote approving warmly of the scheme.

After the Milwaukee meeting, the address then read before the assembled clubs was published and was even more widely circulated than Miss Perkins' first paper. In every State in the Union the daily and weekly press reprinted it in full or in part and heartily welcomed the project of uniting the organized women of the country on so broad and patriotic a movement.

The Presidents or other officials of the Federations of California, Colorado, Connecticut, Delaware, Georgia, Illinois, Indiana, Kansas, Kentucky, Maine, Maryland, Minnesota, Michigan, Missouri, Nebraska, North Dakota, Ohio, Pennsylvania, Rhode Island, Texas, Washington and Wisconsin, have since approved of Miss Perkins' plan and have assisted by bringing it before their respective clubs and by recommending and distributing civil service reform pamphlets. In eight States the question was considered by the clubs at their autumn Federation meetings.

In New York, the subject was ably presented to the Federation by Mrs. Schieffelin and Mrs. McAneny, whose admirable papers resulted in an unanimous resolution in favor of a committee to study the subject of the reform of the civil service, municipal, state and federal, and to report in what way individual clubs could best further the reform.

In Illinois, an Auxiliary Civil Service Reform Committee was appointed, which is to begin immediately to strengthen the movement to place the State charitable institutions upon a merit basis.

In Connecticut, the President, Mrs. Noble, appealed to the clubs to support the cause, and distribute literature. Although no action was taken by the Federation, at the next Board meeting the incoming President, Miss Abbott, and Mrs. Noble, who as Honorary President has a seat upon the Executive Board, intend to present the subject and will make every effort to have a Civil Service Reform Committee appointed.

In Minnesota, although the subject was included in the programme by the President, at the last moment an unexpected State matter of great importance caused the arrangements to be altered, and the question of the Merit System was crowded out. Next year, however, the President hopes to secure some civil service reformer of national reputation who will address the Federation on the subject.

In Pennsylvania, the President writes that "many were interested, and asked for and received literature." The Honorary President of the New Hampshire Federation promises that the question of civil service reform shall be introduced at the annual meeting in May and brought before the Executive Board at an early date. From Maryland we are assured of the support of the President, who offers to distribute literature, to present the subject before the Board of Directors immediately, and before the Federation at its annual meeting in March.

The President of the District of Columbia Federation called attention to the subject in her annual address. In Georgia, the President volunteers to see that, from time to time, information is published in the Club paper, which will bring the merits of civil service reform before the women of the State.

The President of the Federation of Kentucky is one of our warmest advocates, and has given wise and able assistance. The President of the Kansas Federation has done much active work both in the clubs and through the newspapers.

In Colorado, we have many friends and co-workers. Indeed the clubs there were first in the field and have always worked zealously for the reform. The Civil Service Reform Association of that State, on whose board women as well as men are represented was not formed until two years after the reform department of the Denver Club began agitation.

The Massachusetts Federation has invited the clubs of the six New England States to attend a conference in Boston in April next, and has arranged for an evening meeting on civil service reform at which the delegates and their guests shall be addressed by eminent civil service reformers. Through the generosity of a public-spirited citizen of Boston who wishes that his name shall be withheld, the new Symphony Hall has been secured for this meeting. Mr. Charles J. Bonaparte of Baltimore has kindly consented to make an address. The Massachusetts Federation believes that in no other way could the interests of the New England clubs be so thoroughly aroused and their active co-operation be secured.

It would be impossible to enumerate the individual clubs

all over the country which have endorsed the Civil Service Reform movement, and are now taking steps towards studying its history, and planning public lectures to be delivered by prominent men on its aims. A Boston club, after hearing such an address, took a step which seems to us a model action for others to follow. It appointed a committee to keep its members informed on civil service reform matters, and directed this committee to communicate with the Civil Service Reform Association, in offering the co-operation of the club, whenever desired, in any practical action.

A plan is now under discussion for the creation of a Massachusetts Auxiliary to the Civil Service Reform Association, which will unite the women outside of the clubs, as well as the club women themselves in this movement.

We often hear it asked, What practical steps can women take to aid in the reform of the Civil Service? It seems to us that there are many ways in which active and useful work can be done, but, necessarily, these must differ in the various sections of the country. In Massachusetts several plans have been proposed which may serve as an indication of the kind of work that may easily be undertaken. In two manufacturing towns public meetings are planned under the auspices of the clubs, to which the Mayor and chief officials, the principal clergymen of all denominations, prominent citizens and the graduating class of the High School will be invited to hear addresses on civil service reform. In other places it is proposed to interest boy's clubs and to distribute suitable literature, such as the " Citizen's Manual," and other simple pamphlets. The same course will be pursued in Working Girl's Clubs. In one normal school the Amherst report of the Woman's movement will be distributed among the pupils. .

Last summer sixty public libraries permitted the publications of the United States Civil Service Commission to lie on their tables for months; if appealed to by women many other libraries would undoubtedly follow this course.

The prize competition offered by the New York Auxiliary to members of woman's clubs for the best essay on civil service reform, has stimulated interest in the subject, while the admirable Bibliography, published by this Auxiliary may well serve as the best guide to the serious study of a question so vital to the higher interests of the nation.

To clubs inquiring for a scheme of work, a course of six elementary papers is suggested, each of which could easily be prepared through study of the books recommended to the Bibliography. Such a course should pursue some such outline as the following :

(1) The Aim of the Civil Service Reform Movement.
(2) The History of the Reform in England.
(3) The History of the Reform in America.
(4) Present State of the Reform in America with local illustrations.
(5) The Colonial Civil Services of England, France and Holland.
(6) The Needs and Prospects of the Civil Service in the Dependencies of the United States.

This plan might be amplified and extended according to the time and interest of the clubs undertaking such study, and should always, when possible, be illustrated and made vivid by the consideration of local conditions.

Many a woman who is bored and indifferent when general causes and principles are set before her, is aroused to instant interest and action when she learns of some abuse of the appointing power affecting shool, charitable institution or prison in her own town or village.

In interesting individual clubs and Federations it is necessary to emphasize one fact in particular—that from the beginning of this movement we have been fortunate enough to receive the cordial support of the Civil Service Commission in Washington, the National Civil Service Reform League and the state associations. These organizations have helped us in every possible way. This has been of the utmost assistance to those who have attempted to do pioneer work, and it is, we believe, the best guarantee of the future success of the movement that this same corporation should be continued. To this end it has been everywhere suggested that no important step should be taken without consultation with one or other of these organizations. It may be said, generally, that in arousing the woman's clubs to the support and extension of the merit system, advantage is taken of an organized body of women trained to work together, and fully conscious of the importance of subordinating the individual to the organization. During the years that the clubs have worked and studied together, trivial as many of their objects have doubtless been, they have yet enforced upon the minds of club-women the value of system and cohesion. In club-life the first step has usually been purely social, the next self-culture; but out of that has come the attempt to better social conditions in town and village, and to enter more intelligently into municipal questions. From "Village Improvement Societies," "Vacation Schools," "Manual Training Classes," "Social Settlements," "Consumer's Leagues," and "Arts and Crafts" Committees, they have acquired practical knowledge of the necessity of organization and concentration. Slowly but steadily they have learned the duties and privileges of the higher citizenship. They have joined the ranks of those who as Dante says: "*Discernesse della vera cittade almen la torre*,"—who recognize afar off the heights to which the true city some day must rise.

We believe that this body of women so trained and so informed is now ready for a national movement. We find a vast federated system with ramifications throughout the country trained to co-operation, with earnest convictions and ideals. If this force can be induced to concentrate its energies on civil service reform it is easy to see how far reaching its influence may be and how great its educational possibilities. Can it be so utilized? That is the question.

There has never been a time in our history when in every section of the country women have been more earnestly considering the moral responsibilities of the nation. Everywhere interest in political conditions has been stimulated by the colonial problems of the United States. Women are asking themselves what will be the future of the differing nationalities whose guidance we have so lightly undertaken; what will safeguard their liberties; what will guarantee their protection and development?

These questions are leading women to study for themselves the history of the great colonizing nations. They are forming their own opinions as to the theories of Government which underlie and determine the prosperity of English colonies and the inevitable decadence of those founded by France. They see plainly how large a factor in these results is the superior quality of the English colonial civil service, where merit is the sole criterion and character and intelligence the only passports to promotion. They recognize of what paramount importance the selection of the Philippine civil service is considered by the wisest of those who advocate the retention of the Islands.

Earnest women throughout the country are considering these matters. They are turning them over in their minds; and when they read the comprehensive laws prepared by the Philippine Commission to regulate the Philippine civil service, they ask themselves what guarantee is there that these carefully prepared laws will ever be enforced.

Seeking the reason of this doubt, which pervades so many minds, they discover that the root of the evil lies not in the Government, not even in the politicians, but in the general indifference of the public. Are we not all responsible to a greater or less degree? Surely it is our sloth and indifference which alone permits the politicians to betray us and to follow out their selfish ends; our apathy which allows them to evade existing laws and prevent the enactment of better ones. What is it but our lack of cohesion which enables them to band together in an almost irresistable force? Certainly it is our stupidity which allows rival bosses to play into each others hands, and to cheat the nation, the state, the city and the citizen of that intelligence and fitting service for which we are taxed and which it is our duty to require.

We all know the remedy for these evils—and the only remedy—an educated public opinion and an aroused national conscience. Can women do nothing to further this? We believe that there is no work for which they are better fitted. The organized system of woman's clubs is a perfect instrument to further such ends. The preliminary step must be, however, a campaign of education in the clubs themselves; this is being rigorously carried on. Women must be convinced that it is their privilege as well as their duty to enter more seriously into the national life. They must learn how poor and shallow are the excuses of those who stand aside from a moral question, because it is connected with politics, and therefore against their principles; or of those who refuse to aid such a cause because, believing in woman's suffrage, they despise all means of influence except the ballot box.

The merit system is not in any true sense a question of partisan politics; it goes far deeper and concerns the moral ife of the nation. It should unite all those of every political creed who love their country, and desire to see her standing among the nations as she should stand, the exponent of the ideal. A country founded upon an ideal, risking her future on the fight for an ideal, should no longer bear the yoke of the spoils system within her borders. When we ask women to support the cause of civil service reform, we ask them to support the cause of honesty, efficiency, economy and national dignity, and to aid in the struggle against the forces of selfishness, greed, ignorance and waste. Surely women ought not to hesitate on which side to throw their influence.

CONSTITUTION

OF THE

National Civil-Service Reform League.

[REVISED DECEMBER 13, 1900.]

ARTICLE I.

The name of this organization shall be the National Civil Service Reform League.

ARTICLE II.

The object of the Civil Service Reform League shall be to promote the purposes and to facilitate the correspondence and united action of the Civil Service Reform Associations, and generally to advance the cause of Civil Service Reform in the United States.

ARTICLE III.

The League shall consist of all the Civil Service Reform Associations in the United States which signify their willingness to become members thereof. Any such association hereafter expressing such willingness shall become a member of the League upon its being accepted as such by the League or the Council. Any member of any such association, and any individual specially invited by the Council, may be present at any meeting of the League and take part in the debates or discussions subject to such restrictions, if any, as the By-Laws may prescribe. The Council may in its discretion invite representatives of any other Society or organization to take part in any designated meeting of the League.

With the approval of the Council the Secretary may organize Correspondence Committees, of not less than three members, for the promotion of the work of the League in localities where there is no Civil Service Reform Association; the members of such Committees shall have the same status at the meetings of the League as the members of a Civil Service Reform Association.

ARTICLE IV.

At any meeting of the League all questions shall be decided by a majority vote of the individuals present and entitled to take part in the proceedings, unless a majority of the representatives of any association shall demand a vote by associations, in which case each association represented shall be entitled to one vote, which vote shall be cast by the delegates from such association present at such meeting or by a majority of them.

ARTICLE V.

The officers of the League shall be a President, a Secretary, and an Assistant-Secretary, and a Treasurer, who shall discharge the usual duties of such officers, and not less than ten Vice-Presidents; and there shall be a Council, to be constituted as hereinafter provided. The said officers and Council shall hold office until their respective successors are chosen.

ARTICLE VI.

The President and Vice-Presidents shall be elected by ballot at the Annual Meeting of the League.

The Secretary, Assistant-Secretary and Treasurer shall be chosen, and may be removed by the Council.

The Council shall be elected by the League at the annual meeting, and shall consist of at least thirty members, of whom there shall be at least one member from each Association belonging to the League. Ten members of the Council shall be a quorum.

The officers of the League, except the Vice-Presidents, shall be *ex-officio* members of the Council, and either the League or the Council itself may from time to time elect additional members to hold office until the annual meeting next following. Any member of the Council may act by proxy.

The Council shall elect its own chairman. It shall keep a record of its own proceedings and shall make a report to the League at the annual meeting. A vacancy in any office except that of Vice-President may be filled by the Council until the annual meeting next following.

ARTICLE VII.

The Council may, subject to these articles, manage the affairs of the League, direct and dispose of the funds and, from time to time, make and modify By-Laws for the League and for its own action.

No debt shall be contracted by the League or by the Council beyond the amount in the hands of the Treasurer.

ARTICLE VIII.

There shall be an Annual Meeting of the League at such time in each year, and at such place as the council may determine, at which officers shall be elected for the ensuing year, and other appropriate business may be transacted.

A special meeting of the League may be called at the discretion of the Council, or of the President, at any time, upon at least ten days' notice to be given by the Secretary.

ARTICLE IX.

Any provision of this Constitution may be suspended or amended by a vote of two-thirds of the members, or of the Associations, if a vote by Associations be demanded, present at a meeting of the League, due notice of such proposed suspension or amendment having been given at a previous meeting of the League, or of the Council.

The Beginning of the Spoils System in the National Government, 1829-30. (Reprinted, by permission, from Parton's "Life of Andrew Jackson.") Per copy, 5 cents.

Term and Tenure of Office. By Dorman B. Eaton. Second edition, abridged. Per copy, 15 cents.

Daniel Webster and the Spoils System. An extract from Senator Bayard's oration at Dartmouth College, June, 1882.

Address of Hon. Carl Schurz in opposition to the bill to amend the New York Civil Service laws, commonly known as the "Black Act." May 6, 1897.

Report on the Operation of the "Black Act." March 21, 1898.

Annual Reports of the Civil Service Reform Association of New York for '83, '85, '86, '87, '88, '92, '93, '94, '95, '96, '97, '98, '99 and 1900. Per copy, 8 cents.

MISCELLANEOUS.

United States Civil-Service Statutes and Revised Rules of May 6, 1896.

Revised U. S. Civil Service Rules of May 29, 1899.

State Civil-Service Reform Acts of New York and Massachusetts.

Decisions and Opinions in Construction of the Civil-Service Laws. (1890) Per copy, 15 cts.

The Meaning of Civil-Service Reform. By E. O. Graves.

The Selection of Laborers. (In English and German Editions). By James M. Bugbee late of the Massachusetts Civil-Service Commission.

Report of Select Committee on Reform in the Civil Service (H. R.), regarding the registration of laborers in the United States Service.

Report of same Committee regarding selection of Fourth-Class Postmasters.

The Need of a Classified and Non-Partisan Census Bureau— Report of a Special Committee of the National League. (1898.)

Superannuation in the Civil Service. Report of a Special Committee. (1900.)

George William Curtis. A commemorative address by Parke Godwin. (Published by the Century Association). Per copy, 10 cents.

Bibliography of Civil Service Reform. Published by The Women's Auxiliary to the C. S. R. Ass'n. (1900.) Per copy, 10 cents.

(A CHARGE IS MADE ONLY WHERE THE PRICE IS STATED.)
